MAX-PLANCK-INSTITUT
FÜR AUSLÄNDISCHES ÖFFENTLICHES RECHT
UND VÖLKERRECHT

Beiträge zum ausländischen öffentlichen Recht und Völkerrecht

Begründet von Viktor Bruns

Herausgegeben von
Armin von Bogdandy • Anne Peters

Volume 298

Armin von Bogdandy • Piotr Bogdanowicz •
Iris Canor • Christoph Grabenwarter •
Maciej Taborowski • Matthias Schmidt
Editors

Defending Checks and Balances in EU Member States

Taking Stock of Europe's Actions

Springer

ISSN 0172-4770 ISSN 2197-7135 (electronic)
Beiträge zum ausländischen öffentlichen Recht und Völkerrecht
ISBN 978-3-662-62316-9 ISBN 978-3-662-62317-6 (eBook)
https://doi.org/10.1007/978-3-662-62317-6

This Springer imprint is published by the registered company Springer-Verlag GmbH, DE, part of Springer Nature.
The registered company address is: Heidelberger Platz 3, 14197 Berlin, Germany

Preface

For much time, the general impression has been that Europe is doing little to nothing in responding to developments that threaten checks and balances in the European legal space. Today that is not true anymore, so the discussion should move on. This book brings together insight from two conferences on this topic. One conference was held at the University of Warsaw in September 2017, the topic being "Protecting European Union Values: Breaches of Article 2 TUE and their Consequences." The other conference, held in Berlin at the Wissenschaftskolleg in January 2019, focused under the title of "Constitutional Courts and Political Change" on the role of domestic constitutional courts in this respect. The common thread is to better understand how checks and balances are threatened in some Member States and to assess what Europe is doing about it.

At the time when the first conference took place, few could expect that the whole situation develops so dynamically. A few months later, in December 2017, the European Commission triggered Article 7 (1) TEU for the first time in relation to Polish judicial reforms. There have been three infringement proceedings started against Poland by the Commission under Article 258 of the Treaty on the functioning of the European Union (TFEU). One of them concerning the regime of disciplinary liability of Polish judges is still pending (C-791/19). Two of them concerning aspects of judicial independence of Polish Common Courts (C-192/18) and the Polish Supreme Court (C-619/18) have been already brought to the end.

Worth mentioning is especially the latter case, which in fact saved the substance and independence of the Polish Supreme Court. The Court of Justice imposed on Poland a groundbreaking interim order (C-619/18 R), consisting not only of the suspension of the application of the regulations lowering the retirement age but also in reinstating the judges of the Supreme Court dismissed. The Court pointed out that ordering interim measures has the effect of directly and immediately suspending the application of the challenged national regulations, including those that led to repealing or replacement of the regulations formerly fixing the retirement age of Supreme Court judges, in view of which those former regulations shall apply until delivery of final judgment in the case. Consequently, the Court "brought back to life" the former law that had been repealed by the national legislature.

In the final judgment, the Court held in strong words that doubts may be raised as to whether the reform of the retirement age was made by the Polish government in pursuance of standardizing the retirement age of judges and all other employees and not "with the aim of side-lining a certain group of Supreme Court judges." By the same, it rejected Poland's explanation that the introduced changes had an important, justified purpose and were proportionate.

It should also be stated that since 2018, Polish courts, including but not limited to the Supreme Court and the Supreme Administrative Court, referred to the Court of Justice for numerous preliminary references concerning the independence of judiciary treating EU law as a shield against governmental measures undermining the judiciary. A variety of these references are still pending before the Court of Justice.

One of the last notable events in Poland was the judgment issued by the Court of Justice on 19 November 2019 in Joined Cases *A.K. v. Krajowa Rada Sądownictwa* (C-585/18) and *CP* (C-624/18), *DO* (C-625/18) *v. Sąd Najwyższy*. This judgment made it clear that judicial independence must be guaranteed also in the context of procedures of appointing judges which must exclude any reasonable doubt as to the court's independence of any external factors as well as its neutrality with respect to the overlapping interests on which it rules. It opened the door to questioning panels in courts that include individuals appointed with the recommendation of the Polish National Council of Judiciary and judgments issued by them.

Following the Court's Judgment, the Chamber of Labour and Social Security of the SC issued three rulings in which it has been stated that the Disciplinary Chamber of the SC is not a court within the meaning of EU law due to its lack of independence according to the criteria established by the ECJ. Worth mentioning is also the resolution adopted by three "old" chambers of the Polish Supreme Court on 23 January 2020, which adopts binding criteria of the Court's November ruling to Polish judicial procedures and national courts. That resolution states i.a. that two "new" chambers of the Polish Supreme Court (Chamber for Disciplinary matters and the Chamber of Extraordinary Control and Public Affairs), appointed by the current governmental majority, are not independent Courts in the meaning of EU Law and according to the Polish legal system.

As courts across Poland started to apply those criteria, the ruling majority started a counter-attack: massive disciplinary proceedings against judges (even with criminal charges) are being initiated under the supervision of the Prosecutor General who is at the same time the Minister of Justice. The government and the "new" part of the Supreme Court simply ignore the binding resolution of the "old" Supreme Court. A special "muzzle" law has been prepared in order to silence those judges who try to apply the ECJ's judgment. According to that law actions challenging the existence of a service relationship of a judge, the effectiveness of a judge's appointment or the legitimacy of a constitutional authority of the Republic of Poland constitutes a disciplinary offense for which the judge may be punished with dismissal from office.

In January 2020, few days before we finished this foreword, the Polish Constitutional Tribunal, which has already been subordinated to the will of the executive power and does not guarantee impartial and effective constitutional control, issued an interim measure suspending the judgment of the Supreme Court which followed the aforementioned ruling of the Court of Justice. That suspension is without precedent and according to the majority of constitutional scholars also without any legal grounds. One of the contributions in this book emphasizes the importance of the "red lines". Is it a moment in which these lines are just crossed?

Finally, one should not lose sight of numerous proceedings which are still pending before Polish courts, aimed at the verification of legislative solutions adopted by the ruling majority in Poland from the perspective of judicial independence. Those cases include preliminary referrals i.a. on suspending a national law on the basis of the principle of effective judicial protection (C-522/18), on the scope of application of Art. 19 (1) TEU in judicial proceedings that have no EU element at all (C-558/18 and C-563/18), on whether two chambers of the SC are "established by law" due to a flagrant infringement of national law during the appointing process of judges sitting on those benches (C-508/19 and C-487/19), or on the right to judicial control of the appointment process of judges to the SC from the perspective of candidates for judicial positions (C-824/18). There is no doubt that after those questions have been answered by the Court, a huge step in developing the standard of judicial independence in EU law will be made.

We wish to thank the Leibniz Program of the Deutsche Forschungsgemeinschaft for generous support as well as the rector of the Wissenschaftskolleg, Barbara Stollberg-Rilinger, for her generous welcome, as well as Giacomo Rugge, Dimitri Spieker, and the MPIL's Editorial Department for bringing the volume to publication.

Heidelberg, Germany — Armin von Bogdandy
Warsaw, Poland — Piotr Bogdanowicz
Tel Aviv, Israel — Iris Canor
Vienna, Austria — Christoph Grabenwarter
Warsaw, Poland — Maciej Taborowski
Heidelberg, Germany — Matthias Schmidt
February 2020

Contents

Part I
Understanding the Development in EU Member States

Not on Bread Alone Doth Man Liveth (Deut. 8:3; Mat 4:4): Some Iconoclastic Views on Populism, Democracy, the Rule of Law and the Polish Circumstance

Joseph H. H. Weiler

Contents

Abstract Polarization in today's politics, pre- and post COVID, transcends nations, states regions and continents. It's a feature of politics which, in and on itself, when played to extremes by demonizing one's opponents, it threatens democracy itself—since it frays the demos some cohesion of which is necessary for the legitimacy of majoritarianism, one of the pillars of national democracies. Its lexical manifestation is to be found with expressions such as 'traitors' or 'not real' Americans, Italians, Israelis—take your pick and fill in the gap.

It has, lamentably in my view, a spillover effect also into the academic world of scholarship. A word of criticism of, say, the European Court of Justice instantly brands you a 'Eurosceptic' and one of 'them'. To speak of Universal Values, casts you as an enemy of this or that national cause. This is not to say, not at all, that one cannot bring to one's scholarship a fully engaged normative and ethical commitment, especially in the field of law which has, or should have, at its roots a commitment to justice. But it militates against careful listening, complex reasoning and understanding and more fine grained normative judgments. Justice is oftentimes not black and white.

It is particularly so when it comes to dealing with the phenomenon of Populism which has moved from the fringe to the center of politics. Trying to understand Populism is not akin to justifying it.

J. H. H. Weiler (✉)
New York University, New York, NY, USA
e-mail: weilersoffice@nyu.edu

A. von Bogdandy et al. (eds.), *Defending Checks and Balances in EU Member States*, Beiträge zum ausländischen öffentlichen Recht und Völkerrecht 298,
https://doi.org/10.1007/978-3-662-62317-6_1

1 Populism

I despise the word Populism. When you like them, (Tzipras in Greece or Podemos in Spain perhaps?) they are Popular. When you dislike them, they are Populist. But this is just the beginning. In a political circumstance which requires discernment and careful judgment in arriving at moral and political conclusions, 'Populism' is a broad and lazy paintbrush which colors everyone with the same damning color and allows one to feel virtuous, basking in one's own self-righteousness. Salvini, Hungary, Marine Le Pen, Poland, Brexiteers, AfD etc? They are all the same, are they not? Well, they are not, far from it. It is as wrong as it is unhelpful.

'Populism' is a proxy for two judgmental sentiments: 'They' are either fascists, or at best crypto-fascists, whom you can thus just write off and consign to the beyond-the-pale waste bin, (which is appropriate for those who are truly so!) And/or, they are (resorting to that odious Marxist trope of False Consciousness) simply dumb. 'They' do not get it, if only they understood. . .Yes, there are among them quite a few which are both, but I refuse to accept that millions of Europeans, in Member States from East to West, from North to South, are either dumb or have become in short order fascists.

Be that as it may, there is a deep self-exculpatory streak in the simplistic narrative concerning those 'awful populists'. It exculpates us, the *bien pensants* of the Post WWII political and moral comfort zone which extends between Christian Democracy and Social Democracy and an ironclad commitment to European integration. It obviates the necessity of some serious soul searching of what in the established political order has led to this major, non-peripheral rupture in the European consensus and to examine, what if anything is our responsibility for such.

The two principal sins of the 'populists' is a growing Euroskepticism and a disillusionment with the fundamentals of the liberal democratic order.

I hope my credentials are such that my lifelong commitment to the European construct will not be called into question nor, my old fashioned liberal commitment. When it comes to Europe, this enduring commitment is rooted not only or even principally in the material and utilitarian benefits of such, but in the deep moral and even spiritual dimensions of the construct—aimed at forging a different kind of human relations among peoples divided by borders: *Nous ne coalisons pas des Etats nous unissons des hommes*. And the commitment to liberal democracy (which in Europe can cover the gamut from Socialism, through social democracy, through liberalism, Christian Democracy including democratic social conservatives) is to be considered as the oxygen of our shared political life.

But we cannot turn a blind eye to some major fault lines in the construct which contradict its most cherished values. Despite the full empowerment of the European Parliament European democracy remains deeply flawed. The two most primitive features of democracy, which cut across the rich variety of specific arrangements in our Member States, are the ability of the electorate, through parliamentary elections (in this case elections to the European Parliament) to determine, or have a decisive weight in deciding, by whom we will be governed, and, at least in a broad way, what will be the ideological and policy direction by which we will be governed. It is not comfortable to admit, but European democracy fails on both grounds. The first point was painfully visible in relation to electing the current incumbent heading the Commission (like her predecessor I think she is an impressive incumbent, but this is beside the point); and over the years we have come to realize that voter preference in the outcome of such elections has had a tenuous connection to the policies of the Union. Our system does not allow European citizens to feel, even in relation to these two primitive parameters, that they have any appreciable impact on the governance of the polity.

It should surprise no one that the slogan, iterated in different forms by Eurosceptics, Taking back Control, had and has so much resonance. The resulting alienation is not simply understandable but in no small measure justified.

These defects of the *political* process give added weight to the importance of the European Court of Justice and the European legal order. It is not perfect, far from it; I have published from time to time trenchant critiques of some of its judgments and certain aspects of its modus operandi.[1] But it is fiercely independent in its spirit and self-understanding, does not kowtow to Member State government interests and has placed the individual and his or her rights squarely in the center of its juridical sensibilities. It is not only the *de facto* constitutional court of the Union, but more than Brussels, Luxembourg epitomizes the meaning that may be given to European citizenship. The Court might infuriate us from time to time. If the motto of the EU is United in Diversity, in its jurisprudence it might have, in the eyes of some, given more weight to United than to Diversity. One could argue that it would be well advised to foster a veritably more dialogical process with its Statal judicial interlocutors. But the way to change, if change is needed, is through constitutional channels. If the authority of and the loyalty to the European Court of Justice were to be seriously undermined, it would not only be a blow to the rule of law in the transnational arena for which Europe is the world leader, the very European construct as a space of justice would be threatened.

2 What of the Disillusionment with Liberal Democracy?

The 'Holy Trinity' of the liberal order are Democracy (free elections and majoritarian rule), Human Rights and the Rule of Law. I use the term 'Holy Trinity' only with limited irony. Since, like the real Holy Trinity, the three are one: Majority governance without the constraints of human rights and the rule of law is but a tyranny of the majority. Human rights without effective rule of law are but slogans. The rule of law, outside a democracy is simply the most effective instrument of authoritarianism and worse. That is why so called 'illiberal democracy' is an oxymoron. It is no democracy at all.

[1] See for example https://www.ejiltalk.org/je-suis-achbita/.

There is a second sense in which I use the metaphor of 'Holy Trinity'. These three values represent the bedrock of our civil faith, the reason we fought to overturn both fascism and Communism in the twentieth Century.

But whence, then, the disillusionment with these noble values?

It is oft forgotten that these are peculiar values in the sense that they are mostly but conditions for the Good Life (in the ancient Greek and Biblical sense). Democracy is a 'technology' of governance, flawed but the best we have. But it gives no instruction as to the content that has to be put in place in the act of governance. A democracy of evil people will be an evil democracy even if enjoying majoritarian support, does not violate human rights and respects the rule of law. Human Rights guarantee our liberties but give no instruction as to how one should exercise such liberties. One can use freedom of expression, for example, to be vile. One can be mean spirited, egoistic, hard hearted and lacking in charity and mercy and yet not violate anyone's human rights. And provided our laws do not violate fundamental human rights, they too, can be uncaring, socially unjust, draconian and yet the rule of law would still be observed.

In this sense, then, the 'Holy Trinity' are but a framework to be filled. They are like the oxygen of physical life. You need it to live, but it does not determine how your life will be lived.

What has been, generally speaking, the governance policy content that has been put into this framework in the Post WWII decades by the European political consensus, and what has been left out?

It has been primarily material: Prosperity. The Treaty of Rome expresses this enduring concern very well: The [European] Community shall have as its task, by establishing a common market and progressively approximating the economic policies of Member States, to promote throughout the Community a harmonious development of economic activities, a continuous and balanced expansion, an increase in stability, an accelerated raising of the standard of living and closer relations between the States belonging to it.

The Treaty of Nice further elaborated this concern by stating: The Community shall have as its task, by establishing a common market and an economic and monetary union and by implementing common policies or activities referred to in Articles 3 and 4, to promote throughout the Community a harmonious, balanced and sustainable development of economic activities, a high level of employment and of social protection, equality between men and women, sustainable and non-inflationary growth, a high degree of competitiveness and convergence of economic performance, a high level of protection and improvement of the quality of the environment, the raising of the standard of living and quality of life, and economic and social cohesion and solidarity among Member States.[2]

---

[2]Treaty establishing the European Community (Nice consolidated version), Article 2, *Official Journal C 325, 24/12/2002 P. 0033—0184, Official Journal C 340, 10/11/1997 P. 0173—Consolidated version.*

The magic square of development of economic activities, expansion (growth), increased stability (low inflation) and raising standard of living—the Canon of Ordo-Liberalism—has been the bedrock of European politics for decades. This is mainly what the main parties argue about—the best way to achieve such: Fiscal austerity or otherwise and how much? And what policies of redistribution are the best to ensure prosperity with social justice. There are some notable theorists of democracy who claim that the essence of democratic governance is but the issue of redistributive politics. Christian democracy and social democracy, until recently occupying the central space of European politics shared this same bed.

Our record in this sphere is both spectacular and dismal. These politics, the different political divisions between the center left and center right notwithstanding, has resulted in remarkable *overall* growth in prosperity and the European construct has played a critical role in such. But these politics, the different political divisions between the center left and center right notwithstanding, has also seen a remarkable growth in the uneven distribution of the deserts of this political project and of, more recently economic globalization. It is a common place that as a result of this gap, a growing segment of the population has felt left out of this success story.

A blind spot of Ordo-liberalism which under different guises and labels has so dominated our political landscape is that it regards the human person, in as much as politics is concerned, as Homo Economicus. But Not on Bread Alone doth Man Liveth. When one, explicitly and implicitly, places Prosperity at the center of your politics, one is transmitting a value, a measurement of 'worth' and of Respect. Just think of the respect that is accorded those States that 'make it' in these terms: The Germanys and Americas and Switzerlands of this world. And the same becomes true at the social and individual human level. The gap thus produces not only a resentment at the material unequal distribution of prosperity, but a deep sense of 'not making it' in a society which values 'making it' above all, an attendant sense of disrespect.

One cannot overstate the centrality of respect (and the lack of it) to human wellbeing. If we consider how, in Europe, in our various constitutions and charters of rights we have placed the inviolability of dignity as our primary human right, one can understand how potent will this disrespect be, real and perceived, in the political arena. The sense of material inequality pales in comparison to the sense of dignitarian inequality and deprivation. It is no answer to say that personally one does not disrespect persons because of their economic condition, if the system, as a whole, privileges so much material well-being and prosperity.

Our centrist politics are characterized not only by what has been placed at the center but by what has been removed.

In the critique of liberalism by such as Michael Sandel and Michael Walzer to name but two, a central argument concerns the very focus of liberalism on the individual and his or her liberties. Yet, the human person is always 'situated', sociality is integral to the sense of self. And I would add I would postulate—that as part of the very human condition there is a quest to give 'meaning' to one's life in the sense that the sum of one's existence not be limited to self-betterment—the engine of the free market—but will have some meaning that transcends such. And indeed it is the social condition that often provides this because it is only in sociality that altruism may be practiced and experienced. Moreover, the social situates the individual within a collective identity; it is commonplace that it is the collective identity which contributes to the sense of meaning that goes beyond the self.

In the pre-War era the two institutions which were most prevalent in this respect were national patriotism and religious faith. People found deep meaning in both. It is important to state, immediately, that the understanding of both is not exhausted, not even remotely so, by the meaning that was given to them in that era.

For reasons that are quite understandable, the very word 'patriotism' became 'unprintable' after the War notably in Western Europe. Fascist regimes (among others), by abusing the word and the concept, had 'burned' it from our collective consciousness. And in many ways this has been a positive thing. But we also pay a high price for having banished this word—and the sentiment it expresses—from our psycho-political vocabulary. Since patriotism also has a noble side: the discipline of love, the duty to take care of one's homeland and people, of one's neighbour; of accepting our civic responsibility toward the community in which we live. In reality, true patriotism is the opposite of Fascism: 'We do not belong to the State as fascism claims; it's the State that belongs to us' and we are responsible for it and what happens to it which is the essence of democratic republicanism.

But the baby—a liberal and enlightened sense of national belongingness and pride—was thrown out with the bathwater of pre-War odious atavistic nationalism.

For reasons which I will not elaborate here, Europe, with probably the exception of Poland and a handful of others, underwent in the post war politics a rapid process of secularization. Not only did Laicite become prevalent and normative, but with time it has, as I argue in my book A Christian Europe,[3] been accompanied by distinct Christophobic manifestations.

This is obviously not a call for evangelization. I never judge a person by their faith or lack of it. I know religious persons who are awful human beings and atheists who are noble. But as a society we have paid two heavy prices for this process. First, we have lost a voice which was at one time universal and ubiquitous. A voice in which the emphasis was on duty and responsibility and not only rights, on personal responsibility in the face of what happens to us, our neighbours and our society. It has been replaced by an instinctive appeal to public institutions as both the source of all ills and as the remedy. In Church you do not hear about your entitlements from the State and others but on your duty towards society and others. No politician today in Europe could or would repeat the famous Kennedy Inauguration speech of 1960—Don't ask what your country can do for you but what you can do .... Etc. The Citizenship chapter of the European Treaties are a poignant example. They speak of rights and duties which the citizen enjoys and owes—but then no duties are ever mentioned.

Duty and responsibility—towards others and not only ourselves and our families—are empowering as citizens and human beings. They, like identity, are meaning

---

[3]Weiler (2004).

giving. And, of course, with a laique culture which consigns religions to the private sphere at best, and disdains it at worst, those to whom religion is an important point of reference feel marginalized, at times disrespected and under (non physical) threat.

Our commitment to rights, as has been pointed out by many is not, too, without ambiguities. We've accepted, both at the national and international levels, a serious and irreversible obligation rooted in our Constitutions to protect the fundamental rights of individuals, even against the political tyranny of the majority. At a more general level, our political-juridical vocabulary has become a discussion of legal rights. The rights of, say, a German citizen are protected by our Courts, and, above all, by the Constitutional Court. But also by the Court of Justice of the EU in Luxembourg, and—again—by the European Court of Human Rights in Strasbourg. It's enough to make your head spin. And this is true for the other Member States.

Just think about how common it has become, in the political discourse of today, to speak more and more about 'rights.' To try and turn any political action into a legal action about rights, and entitlements. And using the courts, again and again, to achieve our political objectives. It's enormously important. I would never want to live in a country in which fundamental rights are not effectively defended. But here too—as with the banishment of patriotism—we pay a dear price. Actually, we pay two prices.

First and foremost, the noble culture of rights does put the individual at the center, but little by little, almost without realizing it, it turns him or her into a self-centered individual. It not only atomizes the individual since most fundamental right battles poses an individual and his or her liberties against the collective good but it also 'objectifies' him or her—as an object of someone else's power. The (justified) concern with human rights at the European level gives some cover to the loss of power resulting from our flawed democratic process.

And the second effect of this 'culture of rights'—which is a framework all Europeans have in common—is a kind of flattening of political and cultural specificity, of one's own unique national identity.

For the most part 'Identity' politics are considered an evil. And when identitarianism turns into atavism and worse, it is an evil. But Identity, individual and collective, like patriotism, have, too, a noble dimension. The notion of human dignity—(in the secular version it is part of human ontology; in the religion version it flows from the fact that we have been created in the image of God) contains, at one and the same time, two facets. On the one hand, it means that we are all equal in our fundamental human dignity: rich and poor, Italians and Germans, men and women, Gentile and Jew. To assign more worth to the life of one individual over another, is an assault on our dignity. On the other hand, recognizing human dignity means accepting that each of us is an entire universe, distinct and different from any other person. To treat any of us as fungible with others is an equal assault. And the same is true for each of our societies. To deracinate the cultural specificity of each of our nations and societies is, in this sense, to compromise an essential element of our dignity. When this element of diversity is diminished or derided, we rebel.

And since with only small differences of nuance our supreme value as Europeans are our belief in the Holy Trinity of Rights, Democracy and Rule of Law (and thankfully this is the case) the specificities of our identities are seen to be devalued.

The 'Holy Trinity' remain indispensable, a 'sacred' dimension of our civil life. But I have argued that they are accompanied by a vacuum as regards the politics of meaning which I had ostulated as indispensable to the human condition.

The vacuum thus created has not been filled by mainstream politics, and the 'populist' turn at least in some appreciable measure has been a response to such. Of course it is tragic if the vacuum is filled by a return to pre-War versions of atavistic identity but the pretense that all is well if only the material needs of the human person are satisfied—as in Clinton's famous adage 'It's the Economy, Stupid' is terribly reductionist and as wrong in America as it has proven to be in Europe.

Mussolini understood this perfectly and his Family, Church, Nation slogan had immense mobilizing power for just this reason—it catered to the politics of meaning. But it has to be emphasized again and again—different imaginaries exist. There can be, if we are to fasten on those three social institutions—and they are not the only ones—a concept of Patria and patriotism which is neither fascist nor atavistic but inclusive and celebrating diversity richness; there can be family which is not patriarchal but progressive and egalitarian and there are forms of our classical religions which are non-hierarchical but communitarian. This is not the place to elaborate on these but simply to remind us that a politics which and a social telos which reduces men and women to homo economicus are bound to produce the backlash we are experiencing today.

3 Poland

I turn now to Poland. The Polish narrative leaves few indifferent. Decades of oppression by both fascism and then Communism followed by liberation and impressive rejuvenation is a success story widely shared. Poland enjoys both high prestige and affection. It was Poland and the Polish who rocked the foundations of the Soviet empire and toppled the first domino which ended with the fall of the Berlin Wall. Who cannot feel deep solidarity, admiration and, yes, gratitude for Solidarnosc, for Tischner, for Wałęsa, for father Jerzy Popiełuszko and all the rest?

And the story of Poland in WWII—the heroism of Warsaw 44 is unique among those countries occupied by Germany. It was neither Paris or Rome or Amsterdam which rose in quite the same way and with quite the same cost.

And in more recent times, once liberated, who cannot but exclaim at the creativity and industriousness resulting in such rapid economic and political transformation, second to none?

I am not ignorant or oblivious to the shadows—we do not live in a society of saints and Poland is no exception; I am aware of the current critique of Polish democracy, both from within and without, some fully justified, some exaggerated, some outright fanciful. But Polish democracy endures. No one can fault the integrity of Polish elections themselves; the 2019 elections with power in the Senate changing hands is just one testimony to such. No one is afraid of a knock on the door in the middle of the night. There are no political prisoners languishing in camps or prisons. There is still a robust free media, traditional and social, as some counterweight to a government dominated public media, and the pro- and anti-government demonstrations are proof of an engaged citizenship, the life of a vibrant democracy. Yes, I detest the use of criminal sanctions in cases of alleged or real defamation, especially in the political arena. But I detest it as much in France as I do in Poland.

Can Polish democracy be better? Of course it can. Are there dangers and threats? There are. Should one be vigilant and engaged? One should. But this should not cloud one's overall judgment—which is far from black and white.

Do I agree with the policies of the current government? With some I do. I have, for example, sympathy for their concern for those segments of the population which suffered the unequal distribution of the deserts of the 'Polish economic miracle.' I also have sympathy for the legitimate concern to cherish that which is unique and special in Polish identity, including its Catholic heritage (though naturally I recoil when for some this legitimate and even essential value provides cover for vulgar expressions of xenophobia, homophobia and anti-Semitism). I do think the World needs educating on the suffering and heroism of Poland in WWII. The outrageous comments of Mr. Putin are particularly revolting in this context.

With other policies I do not. For example, government use of public media in the political arena is, against the American and British practice to which I am accustomed, alien to me and mars Polish democracy.

But I am always mindful that it is the democratically elected government of Poland, and it is well to remember that the discipline of democracy is such that one has to accept the discipline of democracy.

In my view the gravest threat to democracy in Poland and some other Western countries (the USA, Italy, Spain, Israel and others) is, as noted above, a polarization of society which goes beyond the normal divisions between strongly held views of, say, Left and Right. A polarization which entirely delegitimizes one's political adversaries, considers them as betraying the patria and worse. This not only stifles civic discourse it also fractures the demos; a sense of shared destiny, beyond political divisions is essential to democracy. The word Demos in democracy is not a lexical artifact. It is an ontological necessity for a functioning democracy. This imposes a duty, easier to preach than to practice, to moderate the tones of contentious political discourse for both sides and to realize that once a certain line has been crossed it is extremely difficult to pull back. Lack of restraint on one side feeds the same on the other and the vicious spiral just deepens.

But when it comes to the Rule of Law one cannot but lament some of the measures recently introduced. One should not get the impression that the functioning of the Polish judicial system pre 2015 was a bed of roses. Voices both of the left and right of the political spectrum identified serious flaws which called for reform. But the manner in which this reform has been taken has been, in my view, impatient, short sighted and damaging in the long term to one of the foundations of democracy.

There is no need to list these measures, the principal ones of which have been the subject of litigation and already condemnation by the European Court of Justice.

I say this for several reasons.

Politics have some role in the appointment of the judiciary, and different countries manage such in different ways. In the United States some State judges are selected by a popular vote on election day. A terrible system. And appointments to the Supreme Court have become a highly charged political battle, an example for no one. One better look to, say, Italy or Germany for more thoughtful and politically balanced systems. Be that as it may, once appointed, the independence of the judiciary becomes, for obvious reasons, the bedrock of the Rule of Law. Judicial misconduct such as bribe taking has of course to be dealt with, including eventually by criminal sanctions. But objectionable judicial decision making is to be dealt with through the judicial appeal process. Disciplinary proceedings affect directly the kind of judicial independence in deciding a case essential to the judicial function. A threat is no different from a bribe. I think this point has been made sufficiently and I do not need to add. But there is one dimension which troubles me beyond the intrinsic point. Poland is a democracy which means that sooner or later, as in all our European democracies, a new party and a new government will come into power. It would be a disaster, if the practice were established, that each new government would feel it had a license to reshape the judiciary to fit its own sensibility. The damage, thus, is not simply to the immediate independence of the judiciary but to the long term culture of judicial independence. Democrats in the USA might be furious with judicial appointments made during a Republican administration and no less so with decisions of judges so appointed. And vice versa, of course. But both sides would consider it anathema to seek to touch those sitting judges precisely for realizing that the principle of judicial independence in the political culture of the nation is in the long term more important than a short terms gain in, say, the manner of appointing or disciplining judges. Self restraint and patience are the only viable approach to this dilemma if the essential balance between democracy, human rights and the rule of law is compromised. The rule of law and the independence of the judiciary is what stands between democracy and the tyranny of the majority.

There has also been enough discussion on the ill will towards Poland which the various judicial reform plans have generated, even among firm friends of Poland. Seen from the outside, Poland is paying an increasingly heavy reputational price for a project which is intrinsically flawed.

But here, too, I want to add, with humility, a point which has received somewhat less attention. I have already expressed, in word and deed, my sympathy for a country such as Poland which wants to hold on to its Christian identity respecting at the same time, in the European tradition, full freedom of religion and freedom from religion. In some ways it is one of the few remaining countries in Europe which is serious about such and certainly the most important. It is the embodiment of JPIIs encyclical Centesimus Annus, a foundational document of the twentieth Century, which argued persuasively the manner in which Christianity and democracy are not antagonists. This is not only important for Poland but for Europe as a whole. This places a special responsibility on the State. There are certain lines which Poland crosses not only compromise the reputation of Poland but the perception of the viability of the Centesimus Annus proposition to the detriment of European civilization.

Reference

Weiler JHH (2004) Ein christliches Europa: Erkundungsgänge. Verlag Anton Pustet, Salzburg

Joseph H. H. Weiler is serving as European Union Jean Monnet Chair at New York University Law School and Senior Fellow of the Minda de Gunzburg Center for European Studies, Harvard.

Constitutional Crisis in Poland 2015–2016 in the Light of the Rule of Law Principle

Marcin Wiącek

Contents

Abstract This chapter concerns the constitutional crisis in Poland that began in 2015. It was triggered by appointing judges of the Constitutional Tribunal, by the outgoing Parliament, and then by re-appointing new judges for the same vacancies. Thus, the status of three judges elected by the previous Parliament and three judges elected by the current Parliament remains disputable.

One of the crucial elements of the rule of law is the principle of legality. There are two aspects of this principle: the presumption of legality that covers all acts of state bodies; the revoking of this presumption may be performed only within procedures prescribed by the law. The law should indicate a state body competent to revoke the presumption of legality and define the legal effects of such revoking. If the law is incomplete, incoherent or imprecise in that scope—that may lead to legal and political crisis. Polish legislation and Constitution fail to comply with the said standard. This is one of the causes of the constitutional crisis in Poland.

In a state governed by the rule of law state bodies should mutually respect their acts. State bodies should not treat acts or decisions issued by other state bodies as invalid or non-existent, unless it is declared within a procedure prescribed by the law. Otherwise, a legal chaos may occur. Courts are not empowered to evaluate the

M. Wiącek (✉)
Faculty of Law and Administration, University of Warsaw, Warszawa, Poland

A. von Bogdandy et al. (eds.), *Defending Checks and Balances in EU Member States*, Beiträge zum ausländischen öffentlichen Recht und Völkerrecht 298,
https://doi.org/10.1007/978-3-662-62317-6_2

lawfulness of the Tribunal's judgments. One of the crucial elements of the rule of law principle is the certainty of law.

1 Introduction

This contribution concerns the crisis that was caused by the election of five judges of the Polish Constitutional Tribunal (CT) in October and December 2015. The events that took place at that time led to the greatest constitutional dispute in the modern history of Poland and to the so-called 'rule of law crisis' in Poland that was subject to numerous procedures, in particular, before the organs of the European Union and the Council of Europe.[1] The principal aim of this contribution is to explain and evaluate *sine studio et ira* the sequence of actions that led to the crisis and to identify its root causes from the perspective of the rule of law principle.

It should be emphasised that the precise analysis of the aforementioned question is crucial, since the whole rule of law crisis in Poland began with the Constitutional Tribunal-related problem.[2]

2 Facts and Law

The constitutional crisis in Poland began in October 2015. It was triggered by appointing, by the outgoing Parliament (elected for the 2011–2015 term of office), five new judges of the CT. Subsequently, in December 2015, after parliamentary elections, the newly-elected Sejm re-appointed constitutional judges for the same vacancies.[3]

According to Art. 194 para. 1 of the Polish Constitution:[4] 'The Constitutional Tribunal shall be composed of 15 judges chosen individually by the Sejm for a term

[1]See, in particular, Opinion no. 833/2015 of the Venice Commission on Amendments to the Act of 25 June 2015 on the Constitutional Tribunal of Poland; Opinion no. 860/2016 of the Venice Commission on the Act on the Constitutional Tribunal; Commission Recommendation (EU) 2016/1374 of 27 July 2016 regarding the rule of law in Poland; Commission Recommendation (EU) 2017/146 of 21 December 2016 regarding the rule of law in Poland complementary to Commission Recommendation (EU) 2016/1374.

[2]Cf. Sadurski (2019), pp. 15–16.

[3]Detailed information, concerning subsequent stages of the constitutional crisis in Poland 2015–2016, is presented, in particular, in the following publications: Kustra (2016), Szuleka et al. (2016), Krzywoń (2018) and Sadurski (2019).

[4]Constitution of the Republic of Poland, adopted by the National Assembly on 2 April 1997 (English translation: www.sejm.gov.pl/prawo/konst/angielski/kon1.htm [accessed 19 August 2019]).

of office of 9 years from amongst persons distinguished by their knowledge of the law. No person may be chosen for more than one term of office.'[5] On the basis of this constitutional provision, in 2006, five constitutional judges were appointed. Their terms of office began on 6 November (three judges), on 2 December (one judge) and on 8 December 2006 (one judge). Thus, five vacancies opened 9 years later, accordingly, on 7 November, on 3 December and on 9 December 2015.

On 25 June 2015, a few months prior to parliamentary elections, the Parliament adopted the new CT Act (2015 Act) which repealed the hitherto binding CT Act 1997.[6] The principal aim of the new Act was to simplify the procedure for the constitutional review, to accelerate this procedure and to explain certain procedural doubts that had arisen in the past.

The Sejm decided, however, that the 2015 Act should comprise also some transitional provisions which would concern the election procedure for the vacancies that would open on November and December 2015. According to Art. 137 of the 2015 Act: 'With regard to judges of the Tribunal whose terms of office end in 2015, the time-limit for submitting the proposal referred to in Art. 19 para. 2 shall be 30 days from the date of entry into force of the Act.'[7]

On 21 July 2015, the then Polish President signed the new CT Act. On 30 July 2015 it was published in the Journal of Laws and it entered into force after the expiry of a 1-month *vacatio legis* period.[8] In the meantime, i.e. on 17 July 2015, the President summoned the parliamentary elections. The day of elections was set for 25 October 2015.

During the last session of the outgoing Sejm, the Deputies decided to elect five new constitutional judges. Five Sejm's resolutions on appointing judges were adopted on 8 October 2015, i.e. 17 days before the parliamentary elections. Each resolution indicated the exact date when the term of office of a newly-elected judge would commence. Three of them indicated 7 November (R. Hauser, A. Jakubecki, K. Ślebzak), one—3 December (B. Sitek) and one—9 December 2015 (A. Sokala).

According to Art. 21 para. 1 of the 2015 Act, a person elected by the Sejm to assume the office of a constitutional judge was subsequently obliged to take the oath of office in the presence of the Polish President.[9] As regards persons elected on 8 October 2015, the President did not, however, organize the swearing-in ceremony.

---

[5]Sejm is the first chamber of the Polish Parliament.

[6]English translations of the 1997 Act and the 2015 Act: www.trybunal.gov.pl/en/about-the-tribunal/legal-basis/the-constitutional-tribunal-act/archive/ (accessed 19 August 2019).

[7]Art. 19 para. 2 of the 2015 Act: 'A proposal of a candidate for the judgeship at the Tribunal shall be lodged with the Marshal of the Sejm no later than 3 months prior to the end of the term of office of a judge of the Tribunal.'

[8]See Art. 139 of the 2015 Act.

[9]According to Art. 21 para. 2 of the 2015 Act: 'Refusal to take the oath of office shall be tantamount to resignation from the office of a judge of the Tribunal.'

Parliamentary elections were held on 25 October 2015. The term of office of the newly-elected Sejm began on 12 November 2015, according to the order of the Polish President, issued on 5 November 2015.[10]

Immediately after the inauguration of the new Sejm's term of office, on 17 November 2015, a group of Sejm Deputies lodged with the CT a motion to review the constitutionality of Art. 137 and some other provisions of the 2015 Act, in particular provisions concerning the swearing-in stage of a constitutional judge nomination procedure. Two days after having received the motion, the CT announced that the hearing of the case would be carried out 2 weeks later, i.e. on 3 December 2015.

A few days before the hearing, on 25 November 2015, the Sejm adopted five resolutions declaring that the elections of constitutional judges, performed by the previous Sejm on 8 October 2015, had been null and void due to procedural irregularities. In the reasoning for these resolutions their authors (a group of Sejm Deputies) acknowledged that the Sejm was not empowered to dismiss a constitutional judge from office, once he/she had been lawfully elected. The Sejm was, however, authorized to proclaim—merely in the form of a declaration, as opposed to a law-making decision—that a resolution on appointing a constitutional judge had been adopted in breach of law and thus it had been invalid from the very beginning. The authors of the November 2015 resolutions argued that, notwithstanding the transitional provisions of the 2015 Act, the resolutions of 8 October 2015 had contravened the Sejm's Rules of Procedure (Standing Orders).[11] For that reason, the majority of the Deputies expressed the opinion that the said resolutions had not brought about any legal effects and, consequently, there were still five judicial vacancies opened at the CT.

Three days before hearing the case, on 30 November 2015, the CT issued a decision on temporary (interim) injunction. The Tribunal called upon the Sejm not to appoint new judges until pronouncing a judgment on constitutionality of the 2015 Act (i.e. until 3 December 2015). It should be pointed out that the temporary injunction was not directly based on the 2015 Act, since this Act did not explicitly empower the Tribunal to issue such injunctions, unless the procedure was initiated by an individual's constitutional complaint (referred to in Art. 79 of the Constitution). The Tribunal explained, however, that legal bases for the injunction have been

[10]According to Art. 98 para. 1 of the Constitution: 'The Sejm and the Senate shall be chosen each for a 4-year term of office. The term of office of the Sejm and Senate shall begin on the day on which the Sejm assembles for its first sitting and shall continue until the day preceding the assembly of the Sejm of the succeeding term of office.' According to Art. 109 para. 2 of the Constitution: 'The first sitting of the Sejm and Senate shall be summoned by the President of the Republic to be held on a day within 30 days following the day of the elections (...).'

[11]The Deputies argued that, on the day of the elections of constitutional judges by the previous Sejm, Art. 137 of the 2015 Act had been contrary to Art. 30 para. 3(1) of the Sejm's Rules of Procedure according to which a candidature for the office of a constitutional judge shall be presented to the Marshall of the Sejm 30 days before the expiry of a constitutional judge mandate. That lack of coherence between Art. 137 of the 2015 Act and Art. 30 para. 3 subpara. 1 of the Sejm's Rules of Procedure led to the invalidity of the resolutions of 8 October 2015.

found in the Civil Procedure Code 1964 which was applicable, *mutatis mutandis*, to the procedure before the Tribunal in matters not regulated within the 2015 Act.[12]

The Sejm decided not to follow the temporary injunction. On 2 December 2015 (a day before the CT judgment) the Sejm elected five persons for the offices of constitutional judges (H. Cioch, L. Morawski, M. Muszyński, J. Przyłębska, P. Pszczółkowski). They have been forthwith sworn by the Polish President.[13]

Next day, on 3 December 2015, the Tribunal issued the judgment (ref. no. K 34/15).[14] In the operative part of the judgment the Tribunal ruled, *inter alia*, that Art. 137 of the 2015 Act, insofar as it concerned three judges whose terms of office ended on 6 November 2015, was consistent with the Constitution and, insofar as it concerned two judges whose terms of office either ended on 2 December 2015 or would end on 8 December 2015, violated the Constitution. Furthermore, the Tribunal ruled that the Polish President was, in general, devoid of the power to deny giving the oath of office to a person elected by the Sejm for the office of a constitutional judge. In the reasoning part of its judgment, the CT expressed the viewpoint that three judges had been lawfully elected by the previous Sejm and, therefore, the President was still under obligation to give them the oath of office. The Tribunal was of the opinion that the appointment of two other judges lay within the scope of competence of the newly-elected Sejm and, therefore, the previous Sejm had not been constitutionally empowered to fill in these two vacancies 'in advance.'[15]

One day after the Tribunal had delivered the aforementioned judgment, a group of Sejm Deputies lodged with the Tribunal a motion to review five Sejm's resolutions of 25 November 2015 (declaring that the appointments performed by the previous Sejm had been invalid) and five resolutions of 2 December 2015 (on appointing new constitutional judges). These motions were not, however, adjudicated to their merits. On 7 January 2016, the CT discontinued proceedings (ref. no. U 8/15), since according to the majority of judges the Tribunal was not constitutionally authorized to review the aforementioned resolutions.

Subsequently, the then CT President A. Rzepliński expressed an opinion that, as a result of the K 34/15 judgment, three judges elected by the previous Sejm for the

[12]See Art. 74 of the 2015 Act. In its hitherto jurisprudence the CT had always rejected motions to issue temporary injunctions in proceedings initiated by a group of Sejm Deputies, due to the lack of legal basis to issue such injunctions (see e.g. the decision of 11 May 2004, ref. no. K 15/04; English summary: www.trybunal.gov.pl/fileadmin/content/omowienia/K_15_04_pp_GB.pdf [accessed 19 August 2019]).

[13]Four judges were sworn on 3 December 2015, prior to the opening of the hearing before the CT. Judge J. Przyłębska was sworn on 9 December 2015, since she had been appointed for the term of office which would inaugurate on this day.

[14]English translation: www.trybunal.gov.pl/en/hearings/judgments/art/8748-ustawa-o-trybunale-konstytucyjnym (accessed 19 August 2019).

[15]See also the similar judgment of 9 December 2015, ref. no. K 35/15 (English translation: www.trybunal.gov.pl/en/hearings/judgments/art/8792-nowelizacja-ustawy-o-trybunale-konstytucyjnym [accessed 19 August 2019]).

terms of office beginning on 7 November 2015 (R. Hauser, A. Jakubecki, K. Ślebzak) were still expecting to be sworn by the Polish President. In consequence, the CT President allowed only two judges, from amongst five persons elected by the new Sejm and sworn by the Polish President, to perform their judicial duties, i.e. judges elected for the terms of office beginning on 3 December and 9 December 2015 (P. Pszczółkowski, J. Przyłębska). The CT President denied assigning cases to three other judges elected by the new Sejm (H. Cioch, L. Morawski, M. Muszyński). The CT President did, however, make it possible for these persons to work at the Tribunal, as its employees. They obtained their own office rooms and their judicial salary has been paid every month.

As a result of the aforementioned facts, the CT was composed of 12 judges allowed by the CT President to perform their judicial duties. Three remaining judgeships have become disputable, since, on one hand, the Polish President did not give the oath of office to three persons elected by the previous Sejm and, on the other hand, the CT President did not allow three persons elected by the new Sejm to perform their judicial duties.

In the meantime, on 22 December 2015, the Parliament adopted the Amendment Act, modifying the 2015 Act (Amendment Act). It envisaged, *inter alia*, that the CT should have adjudicated most of the cases sitting in a plenary session composed of at least 13 judges. It also imposed upon the CT the obligation to adjudicate cases in accordance with the order in which the motions were received by the Tribunal. Furthermore, the Tribunal's judgments, issued by the full bench, were to be adopted by the qualified majority of 2/3 votes. The Amendment Act entered into force upon the day of its publication (on 28 November 2015), without any *vacatio legis* period.

After its entry into force, the Amendment Act was immediately challenged before the Tribunal by two groups of Sejm Deputies, the First President of the Supreme Court, the National Council of the Judiciary and by the Ombudsman. The Tribunal decided to bypass some of the Amendment Act's provisions and to rule upon its conformity with the Constitution sitting in a panel composed of 12 judges, i.e. ten judges appointed prior to parliamentary elections and two judges appointed by the new Sejm, who had been allowed to perform their judicial duties by the CT President. The judgment was issued on 9 March 2016 (ref. no. K 47/15).[16] The Tribunal ruled that the whole Amendment Act was unconstitutional and the Act failed to bring about any legal consequences, in particular it did not effectively modify the original version of the 2015 Act. The majority of judges decided to proceed the case directly on the basis of the Constitution. These judges were of the opinion that Art. 8 para. 2 and Art. 195 para. 1 of the Constitution[17] empowered the Tribunal to deny applying provisions of the Act of Parliament. Hence, the CT

[16]English translation: www.konstytucja.wpia.uw.edu.pl/wp-content/uploads/2017/05/Judgment-of-the-Polish-Constitutional-Tribunal_ref.-no.-K_47_15_en.pdf (accessed 19 August 2019).

[17]Art. 8 para. 2 of the Constitution: 'The provisions of the Constitution shall apply directly, unless the Constitution provides otherwise.' Art. 195 para. 1 of the Constitution: 'Judges of the Constitutional Tribunal, in the exercise of their office, shall be independent and subject only to the Constitution.'

disregarded, *inter alia*, the provision pursuant to which the full bench of the CT should have been composed of at least 13 judges.

On 9 March 2016, the K 47/15 judgment was verbally announced in the courtroom and, subsequently, its operative part, signed by 12 judges,[18] was delivered to the Chancellery of the Prime Minister for official publication in the Journal of Laws. It should be pointed out that according to Art. 190 para. 2 of the Constitution: 'Judgments of the Constitutional Tribunal (...) shall be required to be immediately published in the official publication in which the original normative act was promulgated (...).' Art. 190 para. 3 of the Constitution stipulates that 'A judgment of the Constitutional Tribunal shall take effect from the day of its publication (...).' The duty to publish the Journal of Laws is vested in the Chancellery of the Prime Minister.

The Prime Minister's Chancellery expressed the opinion that the K 47/15 judgment was null and void, since it had been delivered by the 12-judge panel, as opposed to the panel composed of at least 13 judges, as it had been required by the Amendment Act which, during the Tribunal's session, had been in force and had enjoyed the presumption of constitutionality. Therefore, the judgment was not perceived by the Prime Minister as a CT's decision, but rather as a non-binding opinion of the majority of constitutional judges. For this reason, the Prime Minister's Chancellery denied publishing the judgment. However, according to the majority of the constitutional judges, the act delivered on 9 March 2016 was indeed the CT's judgment, its verbal announcement resulted in the revoking of the Amendment Act's presumption of constitutionality and, therefore, this Act may not be applied in the future.

From that moment, the Tribunal continued its routine adjudicating work, but the Prime Minister's Chancellery refused to publish its judgments in the Journal of Laws. It stemmed from the fact that the Tribunal respected the K 47/15 judgment and went on proceeding on the basis of the 2015 Act in its original wording. The Prime Minister's Chancellery was of the opinion that the K 47/15 judgment had not brought about any legal effects. Therefore, in the Chancellery's opinion, the Amendment Act was still in force and decisions issued in breach thereof may not be treated as CT's judgments.

On 22 July 2016, the Parliament adopted the new CT Act, repealing the 2015 Act. The new Act obliged the Prime Minister to publish all CT's judgments issued 'in breach of the 2015 Act,' except for the K 47/15 judgment. The situation became more complex after the Tribunal, several days before the Act of 22 July 2016 entered into force, had ruled that some of this Act's provisions had been unconstitutional (judgment of 11 August 2016, ref. no. K 39/16). That judgment has not been published either, since the procedure within which it was issued ignored the

[18]Two newly-elected judges (J. Przyłębska, P. Pszczółkowski) presented dissenting opinions. They expressed the viewpoint that the CT was not empowered to bypass the Amendment Act, even when reviewing its conformity with the Constitution, and that three remaining persons, who had been elected to be the CT judges in December 2015 (H. Cioch, L. Morawski, M. Muszyński), should have been allowed by the CT President to participate in the adjudication of the K 47/15 case.

Amendment Act of 22 December 2015. Therefore, not only the K 39/16 judgment, but also other CT's decisions pronounced after that judgment were denied being published.[19]

On 30 November and 13 December 2016, three new Acts concerning the CT, the status of its judges and transitional provisions were issued by the Parliament, signed by the President and entered into force.[20] On 19 December 2016, the term of office of the hitherto CT President expired. Two days later the Polish President nominated a new CT President (judge J. Przyłębska).[21]

The newly-appointed CT President allowed the three judges elected on 2 December 2015, who had not been hitherto assigned cases by the previous Tribunal's President (H. Cioch, L. Morawski, M. Muszyński), to perform their judicial duties. Furthermore, the CT President ordered the publication of the hitherto unpublished judgments (except for the K 47/15, K 39/16 and K 44/16 judgments).[22] These CT President's orders were based on transitional provisions contained within the Act of 13 December 2016.[23] The aforementioned three judgments were also removed from the official collection of the CT's rulings.[24] Eventually, the aforementioned three judgments were officially published in 2018.[25]

---

[19]For more details, see Sadurski (2019), pp. 75 et seq.

[20]English translations: www.trybunal.gov.pl/en/about-the-tribunal/legal-basis/the-constitutional-tribunal-act (accessed 1 March 2018).

[21]According to Art. 194 para. 2 of the Constitution: 'The President and Vice-President of the Constitutional Tribunal shall be appointed by the President of the Republic from amongst candidates proposed by the General Assembly of the Judges of the Constitutional Tribunal.' The procedure of proposing candidates for the position of new CT President provoked certain legal doubts as to whether the General Assembly lawfully presented candidatures to the President. These doubts stemmed from the fact that, on 20 December 2016, during the sitting of the General Assembly, only six judges did cast their votes, eight judges denied voting and one judge was on leave. The procedure was based on a special transitional provision (Art. 21 of the Act of 13 December 2016). On one hand, this provision envisaged that candidatures should have been presented 'by resolution' of the General Assembly. On the other hand, it did not require any particular quorum that should have been reached in order to adopt resolutions. That problem has been presented before the Supreme Court by the Warsaw Court of Appeal's referral. The Supreme Court, however, refused to rule the case to its merits (decision of 12 September 2017, ref. no. III SZP 2/17).

[22]The judgment K 44/16, issued on 7 November 2016, concerned the procedure for electing candidates for the positions of the President and the Vice-President of the Tribunal.

[23]According to Art. 18 para. 2 of the Act of 13 December 2016 (containing the transitional provisions), a person performing the duties of the CT President 'shall (...) assign cases to the judges of the Tribunal who have taken the oath of office before the President of the Republic of Poland and create conditions that make it possible for the judges of the Tribunal to perform their judicial duties.' The special basis for publishing judgments which had been issued 'in breach of' CT Acts of 2015 or 2016 had been created in Art. 19 of the said Act.

[24]It is published in the electronic form by the CT (see Art. 115 of the Act of 30 November 2016 on the Organization of the CT and the Mode of Proceedings before the CT).

[25]The specific legal basis for these publications was created by the Amendment Act of 12 April 2018. For more details, see Sadurski (2019), p. 78.

3 Controversies Concerning Three Constitutional Judges

From the moment when the new CT President assumed her office, the Tribunal started to continue its routine adjudicating work being composed of 15 judges. However, some constitutional judges, participants to procedures, scholars and publicists express the opinion that the Tribunal's composition is contrary to law, since three mandates at the Tribunal are not exercised by legally-appointed persons. Judges holding these mandates are sometimes even called 'anti-judges' or 'body doubles'.

Some argue that judgments issued with the participation of at least one of the aforementioned three persons are illegal and invalid. For instance, in his dissenting opinion attached to the CT judgment of 4 April 2017 (ref. no. P 56/14), judge S. Rymar stated that one of judges of the adjudicating panel (H. Cioch) was not a constitutional judge, since he had been elected by the Sejm for the judgeship that had been already occupied by a person appointed by the previous Sejm. Therefore, in judge Rymar's opinion, the P 56/14 judgment has been invalid, since it was delivered with the participation of a person who was not legally capable to perform his judicial duties.[26]

On the other hand, arguments are being raised that, currently, the Tribunal is lawfully-composed, since due to the law violations committed by the previous Parliament, the new Sejm was empowered to fill in all five vacancies at the Tribunal. For instance, in the reasoning for one of its latest decisions, i.e. the judgment of 24 October 2017, ref. no. K 10/17, the CT, sitting as a 5-judge panel, expressed the opinion that it was a misunderstanding to argue that the legal status of three constitutional judges had been determined by hitherto-delivered CT's judgments. In particular, the K 34/15 judgment concerned merely the constitutionality of Art. 137 of the 2015 Act which regulated nothing more than time-limits for submitting candidatures for the offices of a constitutional judge. As regards the Sejm's resolutions on appointing constitutional judges, the Tribunal declared, in the U 8/15 decision, that it was not constitutionally authorized to perform the review of such acts. In conclusion of the K 10/17 judgment, the Tribunal stated that the K 34/15 judgment's entry into force did not affect the legality of any of five appointments performed by the new Sejm on 2 December 2015.[27] The detailed analysis of this complicated constitutional problem will be performed hereinafter (in point 6 below).

---

[26]See also dissenting opinions attached to the following CT's decisions: judgment of 16 March 2017, ref. no. Kp 1/17 (judges L. Kieres, M. Pyziak-Szafnicka, S. Wronkowska-Jaśkiewicz); procedural decisions of 20 April 2017, ref. no. K 23/15, of 16 May 2017, ref. no. P 115/15, and of 11 October 2017, ref. no. K 14/16 (judge P. Tuleja); judgment of 24 October 2017, ref. no. K 1/17 (judge L. Kieres).

[27]See also: CT's procedural decisions of 15 February 2017, ref. no. K 2/15, and of 19 April 2017, ref. no. K 10/15; Muszyński (2017), pp. 127 et seq.

4 The Rule of Law and the Principle of Legality

The rule of law principle, enshrined in Art. 2 of the Constitution and in Art. 2 of the Treaty on the European Union, is a very broad concept and the source of several detailed principles.[28] One of the crucial elements of the rule of law is the principle of legality which, in general, means that all state bodies should act on the basis and within the limits of the law (see also Art. 7 of the Constitution). The discussion on the constitutional crisis in Poland should take into account the fact that there are two specific aspects of the principle of legality:

Firstly, it is the presumption of legality that covers all acts of public power, namely Acts of Parliament, courts judgments, administrative decisions, acts of the President etc. In general, all acts of public powers should be presumed legal and valid.[29]

Secondly, the presumption of legality may be challenged and then revoked. It is obvious that, on one hand, the violation of law by state bodies, or the abuse of powers, should not take place, but, on the other hand, it is not *per se* anything unusual in a state governed by the rule of law that such situations may occur. In the light of the rule of law principle, the revoking of the presumption of legality may, however, be performed only within procedures prescribed by the law. The law should, in particular, precisely indicate a state body competent to revoke the presumption of legality and define the legal effects of such revoking. Should the law be incomplete, incoherent or imprecise in that scope—that may lead to legal and political crisis.

Against that background, I express an opinion that Polish legislation and Constitution fail to comply with the aforementioned standard. The legality of state bodies' activity, which is the element of the rule of law principle, is not sufficiently safeguarded by appropriate procedural provisions of Polish law. That is one of the root causes of the crisis concerning the Polish CT. The Constitution and legislation fail to provide for exhaustive and sufficiently precise procedures within which certain essential legal disputes might be resolved. Therefore, as regards certain legal acts (e.g. constitutional judges' appointments, judgments of the CT), there is no procedural way to finally revoke or confirm their presumption of legality in case of a dispute.

---

[28] See, on the conceptual vagueness of the rule of law principle, e.g. Bárd (2016), pp. 190 et seq. See also Taborowski (2019), pp. 59 et seq.

[29] The concept of the presumption of legality may be found, in particular, in the ECJ case-law, cf. ECJ, Case 101/78 ECR 1979, 38 paras. 4–5; see also General Court Case T 471/11 ECLI EU T 2014, 739 para 117.

5 Constitutional Tribunal's Scope of Competence

The main source of the constitutional crisis were controversies concerning the legality of the Sejm's resolutions, issued on 8 October 2015, on electing new constitutional judges. They have not been sworn by the President, and, after the parliamentary elections, the Sejm declared aforementioned resolutions to be legally-ineffective (resolutions of 25 November 2015) and, consequently, appointed five new constitutional judges (resolutions of 2 December 2015).

One may pose a question whether there is an independent state body which would be legally capable to review the legality and constitutionality of the aforementioned Sejm's resolutions. The answer is 'no', since the Polish Constitution empowers neither the CT, nor any other judicial body, with the competence to examine the legality of the Sejm's individual resolutions, i.e. resolutions on personal nominations. In general, the CT may examine only statutes (Acts of Parliament), international agreements and legal provisions issued by central state bodies.[30] In consequence, certain Sejm's resolutions are reviewable in the proceedings before the Tribunal, but that refers only to so-called 'normative' resolutions, i.e. resolutions that are the source of general and abstract legal norms.[31] For that reason, in the aforementioned procedural decision of 7 January 2016 (ref. no. U 8/15), the Tribunal ruled that it was deprived of the power to review the Sejm's resolutions on appointing constitutional judges.

The Polish Constitution failed to introduce any systemic mechanism enabling constitutional review of state bodies' acts of applying the law, in particular acts issued by the Parliamentary Chambers.[32] Perhaps the situation would be different, should the Polish Constitution expressly empower the Tribunal to review all acts enacted by the Parliament, notwithstanding their contents, like it is, for instance, in Lithuania.[33] In particular, in 2005 the Lithuanian Constitutional Court ruled that the parliamentary resolution on the appointment of a constitutional judge was consistent with the Constitution.[34] Another good example is Spain. The Spanish Constitutional Court is explicitly authorized to control the appointments of constitutional judges.[35] Possibly, should the Polish CT have a similar scope of competence, the

[30]See Art. 188 para. 1–3 of the Constitution.

[31]E.g. the CT found itself to be authorized to examine some provisions of the Sejm's resolution on appointing an investigative committee (see the judgment of 22 September 2006, ref. no. U 4/06; English translation: www.trybunal.gov.pl/en/case-list/judicial-decisions/art/5888-zakres-dzialania-tzw-bankowej-komisji-sledczej [accessed 19 August 2019]; see also Wiącek (2007), pp. 193 et seq.

[32]Cf. Brzozowski (2017), p. 20.

[33]See Art. 102 of the Lithuanian Constitution 1992.

[34]Judgment of 2 June 2005, ref. no. 10/05 (English translation: www.lrkt.lt/en/court-acts/search/170/ta924/content [accessed 19 August 2019]).

[35]See Art. 2 para. 1 lit. (g) of the Organic Law 2/1979 on the Constitutional Court of 3 October 1979 (English translation: www.tribunalconstitucional.es/es/tribunal/normativa/Normativa/LOTC-en.pdf [accessed 19 August 2019]).

constitutional crisis could have been avoided or, at least, it would not have so escalated as it proved to be.

6 Legal Effects of the K 34/15 Judgment

During the debate on the constitutional crisis in Poland the argument was frequently raised that, as a result of the CT judgment of 3 December 2015 (ref. no. K 34/15), the Polish President became obliged to give the oath of office to three judges appointed by the previous Sejm. This judgment was also referred to as the justification of the CT President's refusal to assign cases to three judges elected by the new Parliament. In general, the aforementioned judgment is often understood as declaring the lawfulness of elections of three judges appointed by the previous Sejm.[36] Some important questions should be, however, explained in a more detailed manner.

First of all, it should be explained that the K 34/15 judgment was announced already after the new Sejm had appointed five constitutional judges and the President had sworn four of them. Furthermore, the judgment concerned merely some legal provisions of the CT Act 2015. The Tribunal did not directly examine the Sejm's resolutions adopted within the constitutional judges' appointment procedure, since (as it was explained herein before) it was not constitutionally authorized to review such resolutions. Nonetheless, in the reasoning of the K 34/15 judgment, the Tribunal expressed a viewpoint that the previous Sejm had been empowered to elect, and actually had effectively elected, three judges who should have been sworn by the President, despite the fact that, a few hours before, the President had sworn judges elected by the new Parliament.[37]

It is undisputable that, under the rule of law principle, all state bodies should respect and implement the CT's judgments. Simultaneously, there are many doubts concerning the legal effects of these judgments. Pursuant to the Constitution, the CT's judgments are, in general, prospective and they do not automatically exert influence upon acts or decisions issued before a judgment's entry into force.[38] For

[36]Cf., *inter alia*, the Venice Commission's Opinion no. 833/2015 (referred to in footnote 1), margin numbers 26, 124; the Commission Recommendation (EU) 2016/1374 (referred to in footnote 1), 8.

[37]In the Tribunal's opinion: 'In the case of the two judges of the Tribunal whose terms of office either ended on 2.12 or will end on 8.12.2015, the legal basis of the significant stage of the judicial election process was challenged by the Tribunal as unconstitutional. (. . .) the derogation of the relevant scope of Art. 137 of the CT Act should result in the discontinuance and closure of the procedure (. . .). The completion of the aforementioned procedure is inadmissible (. . .). (. . .) what does not raise constitutional doubts is the legal basis of the election of the three judges of the Tribunal who were to take office after the judges whose terms of office had ended on 6.11.2015. The derogation of Art. 137 of the CT Act within the indicated scope does not affect the election of those judges. (. . .) the judicial election carried out on that basis was valid and there are no obstacles to complete the procedure by the oath of office taken, before the President of Poland, by the persons elected to the judicial offices in the Tribunal.'

[38]See Art. 190 para. 2–4 of the Constitution.

that reason, it is debatable whether, and in what manner, the K 34/15 judgment affected the Sejm's resolutions of 8 October and 2 December 2015 on electing constitutional judges. It would be an oversimplification to argue that the said judgment nullified three out of five resolutions of the new Sejm (adopted on 2 December 2015) and definitively confirmed the legality of three out of five resolutions of the previous Sejm (adopted on 8 October 2015). The constitutional judges have been appointed directly on the basis of Art. 194 para. 1 of the Constitution, as opposed to the 2015 Act which only provided for certain procedural components of the appointment process.

According to the legal doctrine and courts' jurisprudence, including the jurisprudence of the CT, only the operative part of a CT judgment is legally binding within the meaning of Art. 190 para. 1 of the Constitution.[39] Arguments or opinions expressed by the CT in the reasoning parts of its judgments are, on one hand, frequently respected and applied by courts and other state bodies but, on the other hand, they are not universally binding since the Constitution did not introduce such an obligation. Consequently, state bodies are not legally compelled to obey such directives in their activity.[40] It is not unusual that a state body, e.g. a court, refuses to follow the CT's instructions contained within the reasoning part of a CT's judgment, in particular the instructions concerning the legal effects produced by the judgment. Therefore, ignoring certain considerations contained in the reasoning of a CT's judgment, including considerations concerning the legal effects of a judgment, may not be, in general, tantamount to the law violation.

It should also be noted that, as regards the participation of the Polish President in the appointment procedure (the swearing-in stage), the Tribunal issued a so-called interpretative judgment.[41] Yet, the Tribunal's power to issue such judgments remains disputable and, for many years, it has been questioned in some courts' jurisprudence. In particular, in 2009, the Polish Supreme Court adopted a resolution in which it expressed an opinion that the Tribunal was not constitutionally empowered to declare, in a universally binding manner, which interpretation of a legal provision is constitutional and which violates the Constitution.[42]

The legal problem concerning the swearing-in stage is pivotal, since the Constitution fails to envisage any form of the Polish President's participation in the procedure of appointing constitutional judges. One may, therefore, pose a question why the Tribunal decided to resolve the aforementioned problem in the controversial form of an interpretative judgment. Should the Tribunal have quashed the whole

---

[39] 'Judgments of the Constitutional Tribunal shall be of universally binding application and shall be final.'

[40] See, in particular, the resolution of the Supreme Administrative Court of 10 January 2011, ref. no. I OPS 3/10.

[41] See point 5 of the K 34/15 judgment's operative part: 'Art. 21 para. 1 of the Act (...), interpreted other than that the President of the Republic of Poland is obliged to give the oath of office forthwith to a judge of the CT who has been elected by the Sejm, is inconsistent with Art. 194 para. 1 of the Constitution.'

[42] See the resolution of the Supreme Court of 17 December 2009, ref. no. III PZP 2/09.

provision concerning the swearing-in procedure, the legal effects of its judgment would have been, to that extent, less ambiguous.[43]

In consequence, the legal effects of the K 34/15 judgment remain vague. Perhaps the situation would have been different, should the law have expressly empowered the Tribunal to define the legal effects produced by its judgments and the way they should be implemented, like it is, for instance, in Germany.[44] Maybe it would be also worthy of searching for some ideas in the Amendment of the Spanish Constitutional Court Act, concerning the enforcement of the Court's judgments.[45]

7 May the Constitutional Tribunal Bypass an Act of Parliament?

One of the most important stages of the constitutional crisis occurred when, on 9 March 2016, the majority of the Tribunal's judges decided to bypass some provisions of the Amendment Act of 22 December 2015, which entered into force on the day of its official publication, and to declare this Act's unconstitutionality (the K 47/15 judgment). As it was explained herein before, the judgment was passed by the 12-judge panel, despite the fact that, according to the Amendment Act which had already been in force, the plenary session of the Tribunal should have been composed of at least 13 judges. For that reason, the Prime Minister's Chancellery denied the official publishing of the judgment.

Some arguments that justified the constitutional judges' decision to bypass certain provisions of the binding Act of Parliament might have been found in Art. 195 para. 1 of the Constitution, according to which constitutional judges are subject only to the Constitution.[46] A similar provision is contained in Article 178 para. 1 of the Constitution which stipulates that 'regular' judges (in particular, judges of common and administrative courts) are subject only to the Constitution and statutes (Acts of Parliament). The aforementioned provision is commonly understood in Polish legal doctrine and jurisprudence as empowering judges to bypass sub-statutory acts (*inter alia*, governmental regulations, referred to in Article 92 of the Constitution) which are, in a court's opinion, inconsistent with an Act of Parliament or with the Constitution. Accordingly, Article 195 para. 1 of the Constitution may be interpreted as granting judges of the CT the power to deny applying a sub-constitutional act, in

[43]See Wiącek (2016), pp. 125 et seq.

[44]See Art. 35 of the Act on the Federal Constitutional Court 1951.

[45]See Organic Law 15/2015 of 16 October 2015 on the reform of Organic Law 2/1979 of the Constitutional Court concerning the execution of decisions of the Constitutional Court as a guarantee of the rule of law (English translation: www.venice.coe.int/webforms/documents/default.aspx?pdffile=CDL-REF(2016)035-e [accessed 19 August 2019]).

[46]Cf. Radziewicz (2017), pp. 23 et seq.; Safjan (2016), pp. 35 et seq.

particular an Act of Parliament, in the situation where according to the CT an act in question is unconstitutional.

There are, however, scholars and constitutional judges who express the opinion that the Tribunal should obey even constitutionally questionable procedural norms, since—until ruling upon their inconformity with the Constitution—these norms enjoy the presumption of constitutionality. Furthermore, on one hand, pursuant to Article 195 para. 1 of the Constitution, constitutional judges are bound only by the Constitution but, on the other hand, the Constitution itself, in Art. 197, stipulates that the mode of proceedings before the Tribunal shall be regulated by the Act of Parliament.[47]

Perhaps the situation would be different, if acts concerning the mode of proceedings before the Tribunal were under obligatory constitutional review prior to their entry into force, like it is, for instance, in France.[48] Such a provision would make it possible to avoid the paradox situation where the Tribunal would be obliged to proceed on the basis of an Act which already came into force and, at the same time, is under constitutional review.

Furthermore, the constitutional crisis in Poland could have proved to be less escalated, if the law explicitly stated that the Tribunal may refuse to apply provisions that it deems unconstitutional, like it is in Lithuania. Art. 17 sentence 2 of the Lithuanian Constitutional Court Act 1993 stipulates that the Constitutional Court shall obey the Constitution and only such laws that are not inconsistent with the Constitution.

8 Presumption of Legality of Acts Issued by State Bodies

In the debate concerning the constitutional crisis in Poland, another fundamental question arose, namely whether a Tribunal's judgment may be found, by another organ of public power—e.g. by the Prime Minister (whose duty is to officially publish the Tribunal's judgments) or by a court (whose duty is to apply the Tribunal's judgments in individual cases)—illegal and non-existent due to controversies concerning the composition of a Tribunal's panel that adjudicated a particular case.

In my opinion, the answer to that question is 'no'. Neither the Constitution nor the legislation vest any state body with the power to evaluate the lawfulness of the Tribunal's judgments—in particular, with the power to declare that a judgment was delivered by the unlawfully-composed panel and thus was illegal or non-existent. From the moment when a judgment is ordered to be published by the CT President and referred to the Prime Minister's Chancellery, it should be presumed legal, then

[47]See, in particular, the dissenting opinions of judges J. Przyłębska and P. Pszczółkowski attached to the K 47/15 judgment (referred to in footnote 18). Cf. Zubik (2011), p. 116.

[48]It stems from Art. 61, read in conjunction with Art. 63, of the French Constitution 1958.

officially published and respected by individuals and all state bodies, in particular courts. It is the CT President's legal responsibility that an act sent for publication is indeed a legally-delivered Tribunal's judgment. That act enjoys the presumption of legality.

Nonetheless, I am of the opinion that the Parliament would be empowered to introduce a procedure under which, in certain exceptional circumstances, the Tribunal's judgments might be challenged. In particular, the current Polish legislation makes it possible to nullify a final court judgment issued by the wrongfully-composed judicial panel.[49] There are no constitutional obstacles against introducing such an extraordinary procedure when it comes to the Tribunal's judgments. Not only a final court decision but also a judgment delivered by the CT may be, hypothetically, burdened with such procedural defects that may justify the nullification of a judgment and re-considering a particular case.[50] It should be emphasized that there are some states in Europe where the proceedings before constitutional courts may be, in certain circumstances, re-opened what, in consequence, may lead to the re-examination of a case which was already settled by a final judgment.[51]

9 Closing Remarks. The Crisis of Procedures

The constitutional crisis in Poland is, to some extent, the crisis of procedures. There are some crucial constitutional issues which are not reviewable and, therefore, some pivotal constitutional disputes may remain unsettled by the judiciary. In particular, the authors of the Constitution failed to anticipate that the appointment of a constitutional judge may be subject to legal controversies and they failed to provide for procedures that could lead to the definite resolving of such controversies by an impartial organ of the judiciary. A constitution of a state governed by the rule of law should provide for, one may call it, 'fail-safe procedures', guaranteeing the respect for the principle of legality. The constitutional crisis proved that the Polish Constitution is not sufficiently consistent with this standard. As it turned out, the political will of the majority of Parliament was capable to break the hitherto established

[49]See, in particular, Art. 401 para. 1 of the Civil Procedure Code 1964; Art. 542 para. 3, read in conjunction with Art. 439 para. 1 subpara. 1–2, of the Criminal Procedure Code 1997; Art. 271 para. 1 of the Act on the Proceedings before Administrative Courts 2002.

[50]For instance, one of the judges sitting in the Tribunal's panel which pronounced the judgment of 2 April 2003 (ref. no. K 13/02) had been previously a Senator and had voted on the provision that was under review in this case. The Tribunal, however, decided that there was no basis for the re-opening of procedure (see the decision of 17 July 2003, ref. no. K 13/02, English summary: www.trybunal.gov.pl/fileadmin/content/omowienia/K_13_02_GB.pdf [accessed 19 August 2019]; see also Tuleja (2014), pp. 62 et seq.

[51]See, in particular, Art. 119–119b of the Czech Republic Constitutional Court Act 1993; Art. 75–75b of the Slovakian Constitutional Court Act 1993; Art. 62 of the Lithuanian Constitutional Court Act 1993.

practice in electing the CT judges and there was no legal remedy to be filed directly against these decisions.

In particular, the question of legality of electing three judges by the previous Sejm remains controversial and debatable, since no organ of judicial power is vested with the power to finally adjudicate upon that question in a binding manner. As it was explained herein before, the legal effects of the K 34/15 judgment are unclear. Simultaneously, the Sejm's resolutions on electing judges may not be reviewed by the Tribunal, what was confirmed by the Tribunal in the U 8/15 decision. Hence, on one hand, one may raise arguments, based on the CT's stance, expressed in the reasoning parts of judgments delivered in 2015 and 2016, that the previous Sejm was empowered to appoint three constitutional judges who, subsequently, should have been sworn by the Polish President. On the other hand, it should be noticed that the thesis that the previous Sejm was authorized to elect three judges is founded on the assumption that three vacancies at the CT undoubtedly opened in the course of the previous Sejm's term of office (i.e. on 7 November 2015). Such an assumption has basis in facts, the calendar of these facts was, however, unknown on the day when the previous Sejm appointed judges. In other words, on 8 October 2015 it was uncertain whether the previous Sejm's term of office would encompass the day when three vacancies at the Tribunal would open.[52] A question whether this argument, overlooked in the CT's judgments, influenced—in the light of the *tempus regit actum* principle—upon the legality of elections, performed by the previous Sejm, remains open.

Under the rule of law principle, all state bodies should mutually respect their acts and decisions. It means that, except for certain extraordinary and evident situations, a state body should not treat acts or decisions issued by another state body as invalid or non-existent, unless it is declared within a procedure prescribed by the law. Otherwise, a legal chaos may occur, what would be *per se* contrary to the rule of law principle. In particular, in the current system of law the Prime Minister's Chancellery is not vested with the power to deny publishing a CT's judgment in the situation where it was properly sent for publication on the basis of the CT President's order. For the same reasons, Polish courts are not empowered to evaluate the lawfulness of CT's judgments, including the situation where a court raises doubts as regards the composition of a particular Tribunal's adjudicating panel. Such a conclusion flows from the fact that one of the crucial elements of the rule of law principle is the certainty of law. Notwithstanding the legal controversies concerning the current composition of the Tribunal, its judgments should be published, respected and

---

[52]In the light of Art. 98 para. 1 and Art. 109 para. 2 of the Constitution (see footnote 10) the Sejm's term of office is, to some extent, flexible. The exact date of the inauguration of new Sejm's term of office had been unknown until 5 November 2015, when the President summoned the first sitting of the new Sejm and set its date for 12 November 2015. Theoretically, the new Sejm could have inaugurated its term of office even one day after parliamentary elections, on 26 October 2015. It was, therefore, conditional upon the decision of the Polish President. Cf. Brzozowski (2016), p. 149.

applied by courts and other state bodies. The protection of the principle of legality may not lead to the negation of the principle of law certainty.

References

Bárd P (2016) Scrutiny over the rule of law in the European Union. Polish Yearb Int Law 36:187–208

Brzozowski W (2016) Niezależność konstytucyjnego organu państwa i jej ochrona [Independence of a constitutional state body and its protection]. Wydawnictwo Sejmowe, Warsaw

Brzozowski W (2017) O potrzebie reformy konstytucyjnej [On the need for a constitutional reform]. Państwo i Prawo 12:3–22

Krzywoń A (2018) La crisis constitucional en Polonia (2015–2017): cómo cuestionar el sistema del equilibrio constitucional en dos años. Teoría y Realidad Constitucional 41:359–379

Kustra A (2016) Poland's constitutional crisis. From court-packing agenda to denial of Constitutional Court's judgments. Toruńskie Studia Polsko-Włoskie – Studi Polacco-Italiani di Toruń XII:343–366

Muszyński M (2017) Legal analysis of the election process of the judges of the Polish Constitutional Tribunal in the autumn of 2015. Iustum Aequum Salutare XIII(1):127–143

Radziewicz P (2017) Refusal of the Polish Constitutional tribunal to apply the act stipulating the constitutional review procedure. Rev Comp Law 1(28):23–40

Sadurski W (2019) Poland's constitutional breakdown. Oxford University Press, Oxford

Safjan M (2016) Politics and the constitutional tribunal. The constitution – the last instrument of defence against politics. Ruch Prawniczy, Ekonomiczny i Socjologiczny 1(78):35–42

Szuleka M, Wolny M, Szwed M (2016) The constitutional crisis in Poland 2015–2016. https://www.hfhr.pl/wp-content/uploads/2016/09/HFHR_The-constitutional-crisis-in-Poland-2015-2016.pdf. Accessed 19 Aug 2019

Taborowski M (2019) Mechanizmy ochrony praworządności państw członkowskich w prawie Unii Europejskiej. Studium przebudzenia systemu ponadnarodowego [The European Union law's mechanisms for protecting the rule of law in the Member States: a study on the awakening of the supranational systemta]. Wolters Kluwer, Warsaw

Tuleja P (2014) Proceedings before the Constitutional Court in relation to the Hierarchical Review of Norms. Sejm Rev:47–64. Fifth Special Edition

Wiącek M (2007) A review of the principal reasons for selected judicial decisions issued by the Constitutional Tribunal in the years 1997–2006. Sejm Rev:165–199. Third Special Edition

Wiącek M (2016) Commentary to the judgment of the Constitutional Tribunal of 3.12.2015 (ref. no. K 34/15). Przegląd Sejmowy 2(133):124–132

Zubik M (2011) Status prawny sędziego Trybunału Konstytucyjnego [The legal status of the judge of the constitutional tribunal]. Wydawnictwo Sejmowe, Warsaw

Marcin Wiącek is a professor of the Faculty of Law and Administration at the University of Warsaw; the Head of the Human Rights Division.

Hungary's Latest Experiences with Article 2 TEU: The Need for 'Informed' EU Sanctions

Beáta Bakó

Contents

B. Bakó (✉)
Department of Law, European University Institute, Florence, Italy

A. von Bogdandy et al. (eds.), *Defending Checks and Balances in EU Member States*, Beiträge zum ausländischen öffentlichen Recht und Völkerrecht 298,
https://doi.org/10.1007/978-3-662-62317-6_3

Abstract This contribution will concentrate on the Hungarian situation by analysing the generalised practice of targeted legislation and the different causes for legal uncertainty on the constitutional level. The European Parliament initiated an Article 7 TEU sanctioning procedure against Hungary in September 2018 and several infringement proceedings have been launched by the Commission. Unfortunately, these EU responses were not able to grasp the gist of the Hungarian developments. Even the so called Sargentini report of the European Parliament—intended to be a comprehensive analysis of the rule of law deficiencies in Hungary—could not identify the most significant patterns of the Hungarian rule of law decline. This reveals a central shortcoming of EU sanctioning mechanisms employed against 'backsliding' Member States: the need for 'informed' sanctions. Some recent legislative proposals for measuring the rule of law illustrate, that the need for such informed sanctions has been realised by EU institutions. However, the question of 'how' is still unanswered. Taking the case of Hungary as an example, I will finally recommend some aspects to be considered in order to grasp the patterns of 'systemic' rule of law decline.

Polak, Węgier, dwa bratanki / I do szabli, i do szklanki
Lengyel, magyar, két jó barát / együtt harcol, s issza borát[1]

1 Introduction

Today, this proverb of Polish-Hungarian friendship has developed a new meaning, as Hungary and Poland 'fight together' against the EU and its founding values as listed (but not defined) in Article 2 TEU. Both countries are shifting towards an extreme version of what Richard Bellamy termed 'political constitutionalism'.[2] Against 'legal constitutionalism' and judicial review as one of its key features, Richard Bellamy argues that the democratic mechanisms and decision-making by majority rule offer superior and sufficient methods for upholding rights and the rule of law. The absence of popular accountability renders judicial review a form of arbitrary rule which lacks the incentive structure democracy provides to ensure rulers treat the ruled with equal concern and respect. According to Bellamy, one of the key legal constitutionalist methods is establishing boundaries for the political sphere by 'designating certain values . . . as beyond the realm of politics.'[3]

Applying Bellamy's words to the current debates revolving around the 'Copenhagen dilemma', it is hard to decide whether the current events should be framed in political or legal terms. Indeed, it seems that Article 2 TEU is at the interface of the

[1]'Polish and Hungarian are two *brothers* [Polish]/two *good friends* [Hungarian]; they fight and drink together.'

[2]About constitutionalism as understood in the EU legal order see e.g. Glencross (2014), pp. 1165–1167; Walker (2007), pp. 254–267.

[3]Bellamy (2007), p. 147.

political and legal realm. While the EU's founding values are clearly beyond the realm of day-to-day politics, the contours of their exact meaning and their enforcement could hardly be more politicised: Article 7 TEU is commonly labelled as a 'nuclear option'.[4] Just like nuclear weapons, pressing the button is exclusively up to politicians. In this light, the defence of the Union's common values faces a twofold risk: first, the risk of becoming a highly politicised question, and second, the risk of losing the bigger picture in narrow and particularized judicial proceedings.

On one hand, politicians usually do not decide in line with constitutional concepts and ideas but rather in line with their *interests*. An important interest that concerns all EU Member States is to maintain peaceful relations and not to give reason for any kind of 'revenge' or 'retaliation'. The recent procedures against Poland and Hungary are testimony to this: After Poland,[5] a second Article 7 TEU procedure was launched against Hungary.[6] Yet, nothing moved forward in the Council. Indeed, the risk of 'mutual indulgence'[7] has increased especially after the Polish and the Hungarian governments enormously contributed to the nomination of the surprise candidate for the presidency of the Commission.

On the other hand, the infringement procedures brought by the Commission were unable to sufficiently address the gist of the illiberal developments in the respective Member States. They were instead, focused on particularized, individual details while leaving the systemic patterns aside.

The Hungarian example perfectly illustrates these shortcomings. Taking Hungary as a case study, this paper will reveal that systemic patterns might be complex and not always visible in the Member States. First, this contribution systematizes the developments in Hungary and reveals two crucial threats to the rule of law: on one hand, the Hungarian government established a skilfully designed, complex and nuanced system of legislation targeting specifically its 'enemies' and 'friends'. On the other hand, there are serious malfunctions on the constitutional level like the questionable use of constitutional amendments as an instrument of every-day politics and the declining role of the Constitutional Court (see Sect. 2). This analysis demonstrates how difficult it is for EU institutions to grasp these developments—especially in a highly politicised (Art. 7 TEU) or particularized legal procedure (Art. 258 TFEU). Seen in this light, it becomes clear that the developments in Hungary were only partially addressed by the Commission's infringement procedures (see Sect. 3) and the Article 7 TEU procedure initiated by the European Parliament (see Sect. 4). These procedures concentrate on specific laws without having the bigger picture in mind. What could be responses to these shortcomings? I argue that there

[4]Critically on the 'nuclear myth', see Kochenov (2017).

[5]Proposal for a Council decision on the determination of a clear risk of a serious breach by the Republic of Poland of the rule of law (2017/0360(APP), 20. December 2017.

[6]European Parliament resolution of 12 September 2018 on a proposal calling on the Council to determine, pursuant to Article 7(1) of the Treaty on European Union, the existence of a clear risk of a serious breach by Hungary of the values on which the Union is founded (2017/2131(INL)), P8_TA(2018)0340.

[7]von Bogdandy et al. (2012), p. 497.

should be no procedures against 'backsliding' Member States without a profound legal assessment involving independent experts beforehand—in a nutshell: there is a need for more 'informed' EU sanctions. Some recent legislative proposals reflect the need for 'measuring' the rule of law. However, it is important that any system of indicators should follow a comprehensive approach (see Sect. 5).

2 The Big Picture: Targeted Legislation and Constitutional Malfunctions

2.1 Lex Friends and Lex Enemies

Targeted legislation can take different forms and shapes. In the first years after setting up the new constitutional system in January 2012, several independent state institutions were affected by organisational changes and this was a proper occasion to dispense with independent officials, like the data protection ombudsman (see Sect. 2.1.1), the president of the Supreme Court and 'communist judges' in general (see Sect. 2.1.2). As the years passed and the new constitutional system was consolidated, targeted legislation has diverged from constitutional institutions to everyday subjects: some of them were also useful in the political communication of the governing parties (see Sects. 2.1.3–6).

2.1.1 Turning the Data Protection Ombudsman into an Authority Influenced by the Government

As the new Hungarian Fundamental Law entered into force in January 2012, the office, and together with that, the term of the former data protection ombudsman was terminated and a new Data Protection Authority was established.[8] Contrary to the ombudsman who had been elected by the parliament, the president of the National Data Protection and Freedom of Information Authority (NAIH) is nominated by the President of the Republic on the proposal of the Prime Minister. He may be reappointed for a second term which only strengthens his political dependency.[9]

---

[8] § 38 of Act CXII. of 2011 on the Right to Informational Self-determination and Freedom of Information.

[9] In details see also Polyák and Szőke (2011), pp. 164–165.

2.1.2 Sending Judges into Retirement

Similar reorganisational measures have been adopted in the judiciary: new administrative organs have been established[10] and the Supreme Court has been renamed 'Curia'.[11] At the same time, the president of the Supreme Court was released and the Curia started its work with a new president.[12] The new constitution further prescribed that 'with the exception of the President of the Curia, no judge may serve who is older than the general retirement age.'[13]

The law on the status of judges prescribed that judges had to retire at the age of 62 instead of the former 70. The new rule affected about 10% of the judges.[14] Prosecutors and notaries had to meet the same age-requirements too. The law would have entered into force with a tight *vacatio legis*: half a year before the affected judges would have had to retire.

2.1.3 Labelling Foreign Funded NGOs

Unlike in 2012 and 2013, when the institutional reforms concerned state institutions, the Hungarian government found quite different targets by 2017. These were nongovernmental institutions: civil society organisations on one hand, and a university, on the other—moreover, only a few particular players within these specific categories were affected.

After the government started to systematically undermine the rule of law, to limit the powers of the Hungarian Constitutional Court (HCC) and to amend the constitution routinely in line with its political interests, it had received harsh criticism from civil society, particularly from different NGOs like the Hungarian Civil Liberties

---

[10]The National Judicial Office (NJO) has been established by the new Fundamental Law. It is led by its president who is elected by the parliament: accidentally, she is the wife of a Fidesz-politician and an old friend of the Prime Minister. Her most criticised competence was the transfer of cases between different courts but later this was abrogated by the fifth amendment of the constitution in autumn 2013. For details about the judiciary reform see e.g. Sonnevend et al. (2015), pp. 102–103. Since the beginning of 2017, a conflict has developed between the NJO and the self-administration body of the judiciary, the National Judiciary Council (NJC). Namely, the president of the NJO often declared applications to judicial positions as void in order to avoid the control of the NJC. The controversies in details are discussed by Vadász (2018).

[11]Originally: Art. 25 (1) of the Fundamental Law, due to amendments now Art. 25 (2).

[12]The former Supreme Court president, András Baka made a complaint before the European Court of Human Rights on the issue. The Strasbourg court dismissed Hungary on the grounds of the right to access to court and the freedom of expression. Concerning the latter, the Court found that the reason of 'the early termination of his mandate as President of the Supreme Court was not the result of a justified restructuring of the supreme judicial authority in Hungary, but in fact was set up on account of the views and criticisms that he had publicly expressed in his professional capacity on the legislative reforms concerned'. (ECHR decision no. 20261/12, Baka v. Hungary, paras. 75, 96.).

[13]Art. 26 (2) of the Fundamental Law.

[14]Szente (2017), p. 466.

Union (TASZ), the Hungarian Helsinki Committee, or, the Hungarian division of Amnesty International.

Their activity must have been a thorn in the government's eye for a couple of years but the first concrete legislative step against them was linked to the migration crisis—at least on the rhetorical level. According to the government's narrative, the Hungarian-American billionaire George Soros planned to smuggle millions of migrants into Europe and is financing NGOs to fulfil this plan.[15]

The new law on the transparency of foreign funded NGOs was adopted in June 2017. According to the new rules, NGOs receiving more than 7.2 million HUF (approximately 24,000 Euros) from abroad per year must register themselves as 'organisations supported from abroad'. This label must be used on their website and on their materials. They were also obliged to provide detailed information to the authorities about the funding they receive.[16]

Some affected NGOs declared civil disobedience and refused to register themselves as being financed from abroad, emphasizing at the same time, that their financial background was already transparent.[17] Several NGOs made constitutional complaints before the Constitutional Court based on personality and privacy rights and the freedom of expression.[18] Additionally, opposition MPs issued a norm control procedure before the Constitutional Court, arguing that the law violated the principles of legal certainty and the rule of law and threatened the freedom of association.[19] For now, all cases are pending before the Court.

2.1.4 Targeting the 'Soros University'

The other problematic law applies to an even narrower circle of addressees and has an important overlap with the NGO law: George Soros. The amendment of the Higher Education Law adopted in April 2017 clearly targets the Central European University (CEU) founded by the Hungarian-American billionaire. The amendment has set up new requirements for universities operating from a third country (non-EEA) to continue their activities in Hungary.

The most significant change is that an international agreement between Hungary and the third state is needed. If this is a federal state, a prior agreement with the

[15]The story contains truth in small and fragmented pieces in so far as the abovementioned NGOs get funding from the Soros founded Open Society Foundations and some of them offer legal aid to asylum seekers. However, it is not the only and main focus of their activity and the financing sources (including the OSF) had been published in their financial reports at their website already earlier.

[16]Act LXXVI of 2017 on the transparency of civil organisations financed from abroad.

[17]The boycott declared by HCLU/TASZ, Amnesty International and Hungarian Helsinki Committee was joined later by four further NGOs. By doing so, they are risking a fine between 10,000 and 900,000 HUF (30-3,000 Euros). For now, they have not announced being fined because of that.

[18]AB cases no. IV/01830/2017, IV/01685/2017 and IV/01857/2017.

[19]AB case no. II/01460/2017.

federal government is required. The amendment further prescribes that the affected foreign universities must perform educational activity in their country of origin too.[20] There are 27 third country universities operating in Hungary but most of them have only a few study programs together with other Hungarian universities. Conversely, the entirety of CEU's educational program has been threatened by this law. Further, this is the only university among the addressees having no campus and educational activity in its country of origin (the U.S.) at all. The sum of these special requirements has made one thing clear: the exclusive target was the 'Soros University', the CEU.

The amendment has set a tight *vacatio legis*: originally, the deadline for compliance with the new rules was the 1st of January 2018. However, in October 2017—after an infringement procedure and several constitutional reviews had been initiated[21]—the government suddenly realised that this was not realistic and extended the deadline for one more year.[22] In December 2018 the CEU announced it would move to Vienna because the Hungarian government rejected to sign or ratify the required international agreement.[23]

The decision on the constitutionality of the law still has not been made by the Constitutional Court. The Constitutional Court suspended the procedures of the lex CEU and the NGO law in June 2018 with a very strange reasoning. Namely, referring to the European constitutional dialogue and the obligation of cooperation within the European Union, the Court found it necessary to wait for the closing of the parallel cases pending before the European Court of Justice.[24] The decision illustrates that the HCC did not (want to) acknowledge that the CJEU will decide on grounds of EU law, which is a totally different yardstick than the Hungarian constitution.[25]

---

[20] § 2 of Act XXV of 2017 on the amendment of Act CCIV of 2011 on the national higher education.

[21] The university issued a constitutional complaint and opposition politicians initiated norm control before the Constitutional Court. Both cases are still pending under case numbers II/01036/2017 and IV/01810/2017. Details about the infringement procedures in Sect. 3 below.

[22] Act CXXVII on the amendment of Act CCIV of 2011 on the national higher education and of Act XXV of 2017 *supra* note 20.

[23] The development that started with the lex CEU, continued in the Summer of 2019 the law on the Hungarian Academy of Sciences was amended. The most important point of the amendment is that the Academy would be deprived of its research network (Act. LXVIII of 2019). Opposition MPs initiated a norm control before the Constitutional Court (pending case no. II/01214/2019). The president of the Academy also announced to file a constitutional complaint in the matter. Since the Academy is a public institution and a part of the central budget, the reform itself does not necessarily mean that it was a *lex enemy*. However, such motivations cannot be excluded either, especially taking into account that the government has no visible and constructive plans for a reasonable restructuration of the Academy.

[24] AB orders no. 3198/2018 (VI. 21), 3200/2018 (VI. 21) and 3199/2018 (VI. 21) (ABH 2018, 1050, 1057, 1064, respectively).

[25] This point is however addressed in some parallel reasonings and dissenting opinions. See e.g. the dissenting opinion of István Stumpf and the parallel reasoning of Balázs Schanda and Ildikó Hörcherné Marosi to AB order no. 3200/2018, *supra* note 24.

2.1.5 'Stopping Soros' (and Migration)

The latest package amending several laws related to immigration has been named 'Stop Soros'[26] by the government in order to link the fight against immigration and Soros stronger in their political rhetoric. However, contrary to the name, this is not a typical piece of targeted legislation (unlike the 'lex CEU' that was officially labelled the amendment of the Higher Education Law).

The package was adopted in Summer 2018, after Fidesz won a third two thirds majority in the parliament in the aftermath of the elections held in Spring 2018. The most striking point of the law is the introduction of a new criminal offense called 'facilitating illegal migration.' The offence refers to any 'organisational activity' aimed at enabling a person to file an asylum application in the event that the latter is ineligible for asylum.[27] The police is also empowered to issue injunctions against persons suspected (not even accused or condemned) to facilitate illegal migration or other immigration-related offences from approaching the border closer than 8 km.[28] Therefore, it seems that the ultimate objective is not to condemn but rather to keep away any *persona non grata* from the border.

2.1.6 The System of *Lex Friends* and *Lex Enemies*: The Fundamental Challenge to the Rule of Law in Hungary

The above listed pieces of targeted legislation are by far not unique examples, but they are the ones that have been noticed in Brussels. However, many other targeted legislations have not triggered the EU's attention yet. One of the most striking examples of *lex enemies* is strongly related to the EU-values, especially to the principle of democracy. It is most commonly known as the 'billboard law' and was adopted with a procedural trick. In the summer of 2017—ahead of the 2018 elections—the parliamentary majority adopted an amendment of Act LXXIV of 2016 on the protection of the landscape.[29] On its face, the law has nothing to do with political campaigns. Yet its new § 11/G prohibits parties ('organisations supported from the central budget') to advertise under a certain listed price beyond the period of election campaigns.

The new provisions clearly target opposition parties, especially Jobbik, which was supported at the 2018 elections by an investor owning several billboards. The

---

[26]Officially: Act VI. of 2018 on the amendment of certain law related to the measures against illegal immigration.

[27]§ 353/A of Act C of 2012 on the Criminal Code. It must be noted that according to the general rules of Hungarian criminal law, intentional crimes can only be committed deliberately: See Blaskó (2016). Therefore, it is not that easy to condemn someone according to this provision: it has to be proven before the court that the accused person exactly knew that the migrant he helped was safe in his home country or during his journey.

[28]New § 46/F of Act XXXIV of 1994 on the police.

[29]Act CIV of 2017.

governing Fidesz, however, can easily avoid the scope of this law by labelling its advertising as 'government information' instead of party campaigning.[30] The reason why this provision had to be implemented through the law on landscape protection was the fact that at that time Fidesz did not have the two-thirds majority in parliament. Both the election procedure—including the rules of campaigning—and party financing must be regulated through cardinal laws that require the support of the two-thirds majority of attending MPs.[31] So Fidesz bypassed its 'own' Basic Law by hiding the rules in a piece of ordinary legislation that could be adopted with simple majority.

Besides these examples, several laws have been made to favour 'friends', to make them eligible to certain positions[32] or to benefit them otherwise. The content of such *lex friends* may change according to who the friend is, and which position he holds. For example, the company called MAHIR was owned by an oligarch who had been an old friend of the Prime Minister: MAHIR owned several billboards in the country. A concurrent company, the ESMA owned smaller advertisements on electricity poles along the roads. In order to influence the competition between both companies, the government amended the law on road traffic and prohibited advertising on electricity poles and similar objects.[33] However, the Prime Minister broke with said friend and competition was immediately restored. After another government-friendly oligarch purchased the ESMA, the law was changed again allowing to advertise on objects along the roads with permission.[34] Further, a lex friend has been introduced, that may be applied flexibly to any friendly businesses if needed. A specific exception was added to the law on the prohibition of unfair commercial practices and of restriction of competition in 2013. The general rule prescribed that corporate mergers concerning companies whose annual turnover exceeded 15 billion HUF (47–48 million EUR) in total, were bound to take permission from the Competition Authority. The new exception rule made it possible for the government

[30]See e.g. decision no. 647/2018 of the National Election Office. The Office argued that basically, the 'information campaign of the government' should not be able to be confused with the campaign of the ruling party. However, in the concrete case, the massive anti-immigration 'government information' was not found to be such intervention to the election campaign—even if it happened only 8 days before the day of the election. The law was challenged before the Constitutional Court by opposition parties but the Court found no violation of the constitution. The Constitutional Court argued that the law in question did not regulate a cardinal subject because in fact, it did not change the normative content of the law on the functioning and management of parties. That law (Act XXXIII of 1989) is also cardinal and it sets up the elements of the asset of a party (§ 4). See AB decision no. 3001/2019. (I. 7.), ABH 2019, 35, especially para. 68 et seq.

[31]Art. VIII of the Basic Law, § 354 of Act XXXVI of 2014 on the election procedure.

[32]The news portal Index collected many of them: https://index.hu/belfold/2012/06/04/lexek/. Beyond these examples, the so called 'lex Mocsai' is worth to be added. Namely Act XXXVI. of 2014 on the amendment of certain education laws prescribed (in its § 39) that Olympic medals count to be equal to an academic PhD in the higher education of sport: a month later, ex-trainer of the national water polo team, Lajos Mocsai became the rector of the University of Physical Education.

[33]§ 7 (3b) of Act CXIX of 2012 on amending certain laws related to the traffic.

[34]§ 1 of LXXXVII of 2015 on amending certain laws related to the traffic.

to qualify certain mergers to be of strategical importance: such mergers do not have to be reviewed by the Competition Authority.[35] Since then, this exception has been used several times: for the first time, in the same year, through a two-step privatisation of the biggest savings bank Takarékbank.[36]

In light of these examples, one thing becomes clear: these laws are targeted. Some have a wider, some have a narrower scope but the intention behind them is always the same: to punish the enemies or favour the friends of the government. Legislation designed to target individuals is not a new feature in the Hungarian legal system.[37] A good example for this is the CEU itself which was recognised by a distinct law in 2004 by the then socialist government.[38]

Yet, individually designed legislation is always problematic because the rule of law requires laws to be general, applying to subjects in an undifferentiated manner.[39] Therefore, it is questionable whether laws that genuinely apply only to a distinct scope of individuals, institutions or companies fulfil these essential requirements. Even more dangerous are laws, which pretend to have general effect but are designed in a way that they *de facto* apply only to a circumscribed circle of people. This is the common feature of the recent *lex friends* and *lex enemies* which became everyday practice of Hungarian politics. They became the 'silver bullets' for resolving almost any problem. This is one of the most important systemic rule of law problems in Hungary now—even if it has not been acknowledged by the EU institutions as a general pattern.

2.2 *Unrestrained Constitutional Amendments*

Even more alarming, however, are the developments at the constitutional level. The amendment of the constitution is relatively easy in the Hungarian unicameral parliamentary system: it simply requires the two-thirds majority of all MPs.[40] With regard to the Hungarian mixed election system,[41] however, it was not expected that one single party could obtain such an overwhelming majority. In this sense, the two thirds majority requirement seemed to be a proper guarantee for political

[35] § 24/A of Act LVII of 1996 on the prohibition of unfair commercial practices and of restriction of competition.

[36] The case was especially delicate because smaller savings banks were forced by law (Act no. CXXXV of 2013) to integrate into that Takarékbank, but their constitutional complaint against that law remained unsuccessful for the most part: see AB decision no. 20/2014 (VII. 3).

[37] In details Erdős (2013), pp. 47–56.

[38] Act LXI. of 2004 on the recognition of the Central European University.

[39] Similarly Erdős (2013), p. 55.

[40] Art. S of the Fundamental Law. The majority requirement has not changed with the new constitution, see § 24 (3) of Act XX of 1949 on the constitution of the Republic of Hungary (in effect until 31. December 2011).

[41] About the half of MPs are elected in constituencies, and the other half from party lists.

compromises. The situation changed in 2010 when—due to the scandalous governance of the socialists—the right-conservative Fidesz gained a two-thirds majority alone. After this victory, the Fidesz party did not feel obliged to prescribe stricter rules for amendments of the constitution.

To the contrary: the governing party used its overwhelming power for amending the constitution with controversial provisions several times. Some of these new provisions had even been annulled by the Constitutional Court previously.[42] The probably most notorious of these amendments, was the Fourth Amendment to the Fundamental Law in April 2013. As a result of this amendment, the government implemented significant parts of the so called 'transitional provisions' to the Fundamental Law. These provisions had formerly been annulled by the Constitutional Court because they would have introduced some 'actually not transitional' provisions into the constitution. The Court had also pointed out that the 'transitional provisions' were neither parts of the constitution nor constitutional amendments: they were in the 'no men's land of public law'.[43]

Further, the Fourth Amendment concerned topics like the possibility of levying taxes to finance obligations stemming from judgments of the Constitutional Court or of international courts, the National Judicial Office's president's right to reallocate cases,[44] the introduction of the concept of 'dignity of communities' as a special limit to the freedom of speech,[45] and the possibility of local governments to penalize homeless people if they live on the streets.[46] Some of these laws had earlier—as ordinary legislation—been declared void by the Constitutional Court[47] or were pending before the Court at that time.[48] Further, point 5 of the closing provisions to the Fourth Amendment states: 'the decisions of the Constitutional Court taken prior to the entry into force of the Fundamental Law are repealed'. The reason for

[42]The first over constitutionalisation of the Fidesz government happened under the old constitution yet. After the Constitutional Court annulled the introduced 98% special tax on redundancy payments in the public sector, the Fidesz-majority amended the old constitution and explicitly allowed that and also limited the competences of the Constitutional Court in financial matters. See AB decision no 184/2010 (X. 28) (ABH 2010, 1161) and §§ 1-2 of Act CXIX of 2010 on the amendment of Act XX of 1949 on the Constitution of the Republic of Hungary. The rate of the tax was decreased to 75% at the end of 2013, and after the third election victory resulting in two third majority, the Fidesz-majority of the parliament silently terminated this extra tax (§§ 41-42 of Act XLI of 2018 on the amendment of certain laws about taxation and on the immigration tax).

[43]AB decision no. 45/2012 (XII. 29.), (Magyar Közlöny [Official Journal] 184/2012, p. 38979).

[44]These two provisions have been later abolished by the Fifth Amendment of the Fundamental Law in September 2013.

[45]Art. IX (5) of the Fundamental Law. Since then, the seventh amendment codified an explicit prohibition.

[46]Art. XXII (3) of the Fundamental Law.

[47]See e.g. AB decision no. 38/2012 (XI. 14.) (ABH 2012, 185) on the unconstitutionality of criminalising homelessness, AB decision no. 6/2013 (III. 1.) (ABH 2013, 194) on the unconstitutionality of the regulation of churches.

[48]See e.g. AB decision no. 36/2013 (XII. 5.) (ABH, 2013, 1045) on the 'case transfer' within the judiciary.

this provision was that the Court often followed its former case law even after the Fundamental Law entered into force, at least in cases when the affected provision of the Fundamental Law and of the old constitution were the same or very similar.[49] However the Court interpreted the newly amended closing provisions very creatively: it pointed out that point 5 of the closing provisions only gave the Court the *opportunity*, not to refer to its former decisions even if the affected rules and the context are the same.[50]

In order to overcome any restrictions and constitutional checks placed upon the government by the Constitutional Court, the Fidesz government established a strategy of 'over-constitutionalisation'. Namely, after the Court declared ordinary laws to be unconstitutional, the two-thirds majority simply 'solved the problem' by amending the respective provision of the constitution. Since the Constitutional Court cannot review the substance of constitutional amendments,[51] constitutional checks and balances are in fact disabled. Further these constitutional amendments concern topics, which would normally be considered to be a matter of ordinary law. As such they lead to an inflated, trivialized constitutional law—to an 'over-constitutionalisation'. The consequences of this development for the Hungarian constitutional architecture are difficult to foresee.

Recently, this practice can be further illustrated with the seventh constitutional amendment. The Hungarian government has been a strict opponent of the EU migration policy and especially of the Council decision no. 2015/1601 on the relocation of 120,000 asylum applicants. While the government challenged this decision before the CJEU, the Hungarian Commissioner for Fundamental Rights initiated proceedings before the Hungarian Constitutional Court, practically requesting an ultra vires- and fundamental rights review. The motion was pending before the HCC when the Hungarian government decided to hold a referendum on the 'EU migrant quota system' (without an explicit legal basis).[52] Since the turnout remained under 50%, the referendum was legally invalid.[53] In order to make it 'valid', the prime minister initiated a constitutional amendment in the autumn of 2016. Alongside the prohibition of settling 'foreign population' in Hungary, the amendment would have introduced an obligation for all state bodies to respect the constitutional identity of Hungary—without, however, defining this concept. This explicit reference to constitutional identity was obviously aimed at challenging the authority of EU law. Further, the constitution's EU-clause was intended to be

[49]See primarily AB decision no. 22/2012 (V. 11) (Magyar Közlöny [Official Journal, 52/2012, p. 9737), para. 40.

[50]AB decision no. 13/2013 (VI. 17) (Magyar Közlöny [Official Journal], 98/2013, p. 54958), para. 31.

[51]See on this under Sect. 2.3.2.

[52]It makes no sense to hold a national referendum on an issue ruled by EU law: neither it is foreseen by the Hungarian constitution as it allows referendums only in questions which belong to the competence of the Hungarian National Assembly. See Art. 8 of the Hungarian Fundamental Law.

[53]According to Art. 8 (4) of the Fundamental Law, a referendum is valid if the number of valid votes exceed 50% of all citizens eligible to vote.

amended so as to make the 'joint exercise of competences' subject to the fundamental rights and freedoms guaranteed by the Hungarian Fundamental Law and without limiting Hungary's sovereign right to command its population, territory and state order.[54] Yet, this amendment failed because by that time the governing party did not hold the needed two-thirds majority anymore. After Fidesz regained a two-thirds majority in spring 2018, the seventh constitutional amendment[55] was placed on the agenda again—this time with success. The amendment did not only provide for the constitutionality of the aforementioned 'Stop Soros' package on facilitating 'illegal migration'.[56] It further concerned the law on the administrative courts,[57] the new law on the freedom of assembly[58] and the criminalisation of homelessness. Concerning the latter it not only established the possibility to ban habitual residence at public spaces by local governments' decrees[59] but generally prohibits it at the constitutional level.[60] In addition, the rules on the EU-clause and the reference to the obligation of all state bodies to respect constitutional identity have been codified at the

[54]Draft legislation no. T/12458. The text is available in Hungarian at the website of the National Assembly: www.parlament.hu/irom40/12458/12458.pdf.

[55]The consolidated version of the Fundamental Law after the seventh amendment is available in official English translation at: www.njt.hu/translated/doc/TheFundamentalLawofHungary_20181015_FIN.pdf.

[56]The new Art. XIV of the Fundamental Law now stipulates that foreign population cannot be settled in Hungary and the basic rules of granting asylum and asylum procedure must be defined by cardinal law. That means that an eventual future easing on the asylum rules will require a two thirds majority in the parliament. Further, it has been codified on the constitutional level that those who arrived through a safe third country, are not eligible to get asylum (this last point is codified also in the German Basic Law anyway: see Article 16a (2) GG). The 'Stop Soros' anti migration package was published in the official journal on the same day than the seventh constitutional amendment. See Act VI. of 2018 on the amendment of certain laws related to measures against illegal immigration.

[57]The constitutional amendment established the constitutional basis of a distinct system of administrative courts with the Administrative High Court on the top of it (new Article 25 of the Fundamental Law). See also Act CXXX of 2018 on the administrative courts. After the European elections of 2019, the government decided to delay the entering into force of this law for an indefinite period. The reason behind is most probably political: Fidesz still wants to stay in the European People's Party—where its membership has been suspended because of concerns over the rule-of-law-conformity of their governance—and therefore they made a gesture to show some willingness for a compromise.

[58]Art. VI of the Fundamental Law has been amended with a sentence with regard to the collision of privacy rights and of the freedom of expression and assembly. Namely, 'exercising the right to freedom of expression and assembly shall not impair the private and family life and home of others.' less than a month later, on the 20th of July 2018, the parliament adopted the new law on the freedom of assembly. The new law makes it possible to ban an assembly if it is likely to violate others' right to privacy and family, or to human dignity. (§ 13 (4) of Act LV of 2018 on the freedom of assembly.).

[59]As it had been the case since the fourth amendment which overruled AB decision no. 38/2012 (XI. 14.) (MK 2012/25417).

[60]Art. XXII (3) of the Fundamental Law as amended through the seventh amendment. In effect since 15. October 2018.

constitutional level.[61] This latter part of the amendment is especially interesting because it perfectly illustrates how the role and significance of the Constitutional Court has changed. Namely, through implementing these provisions into the constitution, an earlier decision of the Constitutional Court has not been overruled, but on the contrary, confirmed.

2.3 The Constitutional Court: Still a Counterbalance or, Already an Ally of the Government?

The significant event between the first attempt for the seventh constitutional amendment and its adoption in its final form was a judgment of the Constitutional Court. A few weeks after the planned constitutional amendment introducing the notion of constitutional identity in the constitution failed in autumn 2016, the Constitutional Court delivered a decision on the aforementioned motion of the Commissioner for Fundamental Rights concerning the Council decision on refugee-quotas.[62] In that judgment, the Court established the possibility of an identity review of EU law (without being asked on such a review competence). Until then, the concept of constitutional identity had no significance in the case law of the Constitutional Court.[63] The Court recycled the German case law on the matter, however in a rather selective way without clearly defining the content of this constitutional identity.[64]

The decision perfectly shows how the attitude of the Constitutional Court towards the government has changed in the last couple of years. Indeed, the case illustrates how the initial relationship between the Court and the government has been reversed: initially, the government tried to circumvent decisions of the court striking down ordinary laws through constitutional amendments. After the governing party lost its constitution-amending majority in the parliament, the Court presented itself as an institution compensating the government's lack of majority by constitutional interpretation. The Court substituted the requirement of two thirds majority through constitutional interpretation.

[61] New Art. E and the Preamble of the Fundamental Law as amended.

[62] AB decision no. 22/2016 (XII. 5.) (ABH 2016, 1418).

[63] The concept occurred only once, in the parallel reasoning of (then constitutional judge, now justice minister) László Trócsányi to the Lisbon-decision (AB decision no. 143/2010 (VII. 14.), (ABH 2010, 872). Since then, the concept has only been referred by Fidesz-appointed constitutional judges at the Fide Congress in the spring of 2016—when the motion of the ombudsman was already pending before the Court. See the speeches of András Zs. Varga and Tamás Sulyok at the XXVII. FIDE Congress. See Varga Zs (2016), pp. 9–10; Sulyok (2016), p. 40.

[64] There is only an illustrative list of the elements of constitutional identity in the decision with e.g. rights and freedoms, separation of powers, republican state form, parliamentarism, equality, protection of ethnic minorities. The rule of law is lacking from the list. AB decision no. 22/2016 *supra* note 62, para. 65. For a detailed critical analysis of the judgment see Bakó (2018), pp. 863–902.

The push for the seventh amendment of the Fundamental Law shows, however, that the government still does not regard the Court as a 'trustworthy' ally. A portion of the seventh amendment secured the constitutionality of some reforms in the event that the Court's helpful attitude should change. On the other hand, the amendment, concerning the EU clause and the question of constitutional identity, illustrates the misgivings that the government still harbours regarding the Constitutional Court. Safe is only what is codified in the constitution—that is the general strategy of the Fidesz-government.

The changed relationship between the parliamentary majority and the Constitutional Court is easier to understand by analysing the changed composition and competences of the Court and the new strategies applied by the Court in its everyday practice.

2.3.1 Filling the Court with Fidesz-Loyalist Judges

Constitutional judges are elected with two thirds majority of the parliament. This has not changed since 1990. However, prior to 2010, candidates used to be proposed by a parity-based committee comprising of all parliamentary groups. Therefore, even if a government had a supermajority in the parliament, a compromise with the opposition would have been required concerning the candidates.

In July 2010, Fidesz with their supermajority amended the old constitution to ensure that the composition of the committee represents the power relations in the parliament.[65] Since then, no compromise has been needed—at least as long as the governing parties had a supermajority. In September 2011, the number of the constitutional judges was raised from eleven to fifteen and their mandate was extended from 9 to 12 years.[66] Between 2010 and 2013, eight constitutional judges had been appointed exclusively with the votes of the Fidesz. By spring 2013, Fidesz-appointed judges had a majority in the Court. In autumn 2014, three further judges were elected by the Fidesz-MPs.[67] While Fidesz temporarily lost its two-third majority in February 2015, the term of some judges expired. In order to not jeopardize the Court's pro-Fidesz attitude by electing judges of a different political orientation, the Court was left to operate with 11 judges instead of 15 for months and the election of new constitutional judges was not even put on the agenda of parliament for some time. Finally, in autumn 2016, the parliament elected four

[65] § 32/A (5) of the old constitution as amended on the 5th of July 2010.

[66] Act LXI of 2011 on the amendment to the (old) constitution, § 3; Act LXII. of 2011 on the amendment to the (old) Act on the Constitutional Court (Act XXXII. of 1989), § 1 (2). New Fundamental Law Art. 24 (8) and the new Act on the Constitutional Court (Act CLI of 2011), § 6 (3)—both have been in force since 1. January 2012.

[67] In his empirical analysis focusing on the period between 2010 and 2014, Zoltán Szente pointed out that the level of political adaptation of the majority of the constitutional judges was surprisingly high. In details see Szente (2016), p. 66.

new judges with the support of the green party. However, this could not significantly change the balance and the attitude of the Court.

2.3.2 Limiting Constitutional Review in Important Cases

Concerning the powers of the Court, two problematic points must be emphasized. First, substantive review of constitutional amendments has been explicitly excluded.[68] Neither the old constitution nor the original version of the new Fundamental Law contained any reference to the substantive review of constitutional amendments. Yet the Constitutional Court generally considered itself not competent for such a review.[69] From 2011 on, it has happened several times that constitutional amendments have been introduced to incorporate provisions that had been formerly invalidated by the Constitutional Court. As described above,[70] the government acting through parliamentary supermajority amended the constitution incorporating several provisions that were previously declared invalid. While the Constitutional Court theoretically had the chance to take an activist step by changing its former case law and review constitutional amendments on their substance, the Fourth Amendment erased the Court's discretion in this regard. The Fourth Amendment of the Fundamental Law explicitly prohibits the Constitutional Court to substantially review constitutional amendments by limiting judicial review of constitutional amendments to *procedural* aspects alone.[71] Absent any other constitutional guarantees limiting the amending power of the parliament, these constraints placed on the Constitutional Court raise substantial concerns. Since constitutional amendments are also excluded subjects for referendums,[72] neither the Constitutional Court nor the people have any direct control over how the two thirds majority in parliament amends the constitution.

Second the new Fundamental Law restricted the competence of the Constitutional Court regarding the review of acts concerning public revenue and expenditure. Until the state debt exceeds 50% of the GDP, the Constitutional Court may review the Act

[68]Art. 24 (5) of the constitution stipulates: 'The Constitutional Court may review the Fundamental Law or the amendment of the Fundamental Law *only* in relation to the procedural requirements laid down in the Fundamental Law for making and promulgating it.' (My italics).

[69]For details see e.g. Jakab and Szente (2009), para 117; Bakó (2017), pp. 105–108.

[70]See Sect. 2.2.

[71]See the present Art. 24 (5) of the Fundamental Law. The Commissioner for Fundamental Rights made a motion against the Fourth Amendment, arguing that the amendment caused inner contradictions within the constitution. However, the Court declared its lacking competence for the review of the constitutional amendment, referring to the terms of the constitution as amended through the amendment subject to that review, see AB decision no. 12/2013 (V. 24.) (ABH 2013, 390).

[72]Holding a referendum about constitutional questions is now explicitly excluded by Art. 8 of the Fundamental Law: under the old constitution, it was an unwritten taboo, established and consequently reaffirmed by the Constitutional Court. See primarily AB decisions no. 2/1993 (I. 22.) and 25/1999 (VII. 7.).

on State Budget and other acts related to public finances only if they violate human dignity or other enumerated fundamental rights.[73] Some authors consider this rule to be a 'dishearteningly materialistic reading of constitutionalism' as it practically means the suspension of the rule of law until a certain debt is reached[74] implying that the constitution is not necessarily the highest law anymore.[75] On a theoretical level, such criticism is right and well founded, especially taking into account the circumstances. The taboo of reviewing financial laws has been a part of the strategy of 'over-constitutionalisation', described above. After the Constitutional Court struck down a law that levied a 98% tax on certain severance payments in the public service,[76] the old constitution was amended in order to allow levying special taxes on remunerations 'received against the good morals' *retroactively.*[77] Further, the aforementioned limitation of the Constitutional Court's competences concerning laws related to the central budget, was introduced.[78] Following this new restriction, constitutional complaints in financial and economic matters have mostly been rejected in their entirety or to a large extent.[79] However, these complaints were not necessarily rejected on the grounds of lack of jurisdiction but because the respective limitations of fundamental rights were not unnecessary and disproportional.[80]

2.3.3 New Strategies of the Constitutional Court: Shifting Away from the Control of the Legislative

In light of the changes to the competences and composition of the Court, a crucial question relates to if and how the attitude of the institution has evolved. Although

---

[73]Art. 37 (4) of the Fundamental Law. The state debt was 77.6% of the GDP at the beginning of 2012—as the Fundamental law entered into force. According to the last data of the Hungarian Central Statistical Office, the debt was 73.3% in 2017 (http://www.ksh.hu/docs/hun/xftp/stattukor/edp/edp181024.pdf). So, this restriction probably will remain in place for a while.

[74]Vincze and Varju (2012), p. 451.

[75]Halmai (2012), p. 1082.

[76]AB decision no. 184/2010. (X. 28), ABH 2010, 1161.

[77]§ 70/I (2) of the old constitution as amended. At the same time it must be seen, especially in the EU-context, that national constitutional courts and the effectiveness of national constitutional principles are often limited by EU-law and by measures of EU institutions in the field of financial legislation. See the *OMT* case (BVerfG, 2 BvR 2728/13, *OMT* and CJEU, Case C-62/14 *Gauweiler*, ECLI:EU:C:2015:400) and the PSPP case (BVerfG, 2 BvR 859/15, *PSPP* and CJEU, Case C-493/17 *Weiss*, ECLI:EU:C:2018:1000).

[78]In details see e.g. Sonnevend et al. (2015), pp. 94–95.

[79]Gárdos-Orosz (2016), p. 444.

[80]See e.g. AB decision no. 20/2014 (VII. 3.) (MK 91/2014, 10918) regarding the integration of cooperative banks and AB decision no. 3194/2014 (VII. 15.) (ABH 20/2014, 991) regarding the commerce of tobacco products. For an overview of the Constitutional Court's case law on budgetary matters see Tilk (2014).

there are some positive examples in the Court's latest case law related to fundamental rights[81] and the rule of law,[82] two relevant tendencies can be identified.

First, the Court has distanced itself from politically relevant questions. As the abstract norm control has been subsequently displaced by concrete forms of judicial review, primarily by the newly established constitutional complaint, the focus has shifted from the constitutional review of *legislation* towards the constitutional review of the *application* of the law.[83] Thus, the role of the Constitutional Court in the system of checks and balances has changed profoundly.[84] The Court is no real counterweight to the parliament anymore. A recent example is the judgment on the penalisation of homelessness, established by the seventh amendment to the constitution. Finding first that the newly introduced offence was constitutionally valid, the Court established a constitutional requirement for the practical application of the relevant paragraph. In order to comply with the aim of this constitutional prohibition, respectively the integration of homeless people into the social care system, § 178/B of the Act on Offences may only be applied if the affected person can be provided with accommodation at the time the offence was committed.[85] However, the Court did not even discuss the question of whether the penalisation itself was a proportional tool for the implementation of the constitutional prohibition. The Court decided to avoid any conflict with parliament by annulling the law. Instead, it left the law in force and only modified its interpretation in light of constitutional requirements.

Second, even when the Court adjudicates on the validly of a piece of legislation and finds it to be contrary to the constitution, it has been cautious to strike it down and applied a more lenient approach.[86] Instead of annulling a law, it often prescribes constitutional requirements for the law's interpretation by ordinary courts. This happens even in politically significant matters or cases concerning fundamental rights.[87] Further, the timing of the decisions (in relation to politically important events, like referendums or elections) might also have significant impact (see e.g. the constitutional identity decision discussed above).

---

[81] In December 2017, the Court ruled that it is an obligation for the parliament to decide on the status on churches within a reasonable time and ordered the legislator to establish proper guarantees in order to keep the 60 days deadline. See decision no 36/2017. (XII. 29.), ABH 2018, 2. Another recent case concerned media freedom: a CC judgment delivered at the end of 2017 made clear that a medium is not liable for the violation of personality rights if it was covering a press conference. AB decision no. 34/2017. (XII. 11.), ABH 2017, 2058.

[82] The Constitutional Court annulled some parts of an order of the president of the National Judicial Office because it foresaw unconstitutional sanctions against judges, moreover, without the right of appeal. AB decision no. 33/2017. (XII. 6.), ABH 2017, 2031.

[83] For empirical data see Gárdos-Orosz (2016), pp. 448–452.

[84] Orbán (2016), pp. 7–9.

[85] AB decision no. 19/2019 (VI. 18.), ABH 2019, 1052, paras. 105–110.

[86] Gárdos-Orosz (2016), p. 449.

[87] Id. See also Halmai (2015), p. 146.

Finally, many sensitive cases are still pending before the Court—like the NGO law and the 'lex CEU', which are both subject to an infringement procedure and therefore (questionably) suspended by the Constitutional Court with the probable motivation of avoiding any conflict with the government.[88]

3 Why Infringement Procedures Are Ineffective in the Case of Hungary

Currently, the only judicial tool of enforcing EU values compliance is the infringement action. However, this procedure is intended to enforce compliance with EU law concerning rather specific matters, instead of addressing systemic rule of law deficiencies. This problem is also illustrated by the infringement actions launched against Hungary in the past few years related to EU values. Although Hungary did *de facto* not comply with the CJEU's decisions in some of the cases, the respective issues were regarded as solved. In this section, I will briefly discuss the infringement proceedings regarding some of the above-mentioned targeted laws. It is important to recall that 'rule of law' deficiencies in Hungary arise from the whole gamut of constitutional malfunctions on one hand and the system of targeted legislation on the other. Therefore, individual infringement procedures against some selected pieces of targeted legislation cannot solve the problem, even if the Hungarian government fully complies with the decisions of the CJEU.

3.1 CJEU Judgments Being Fully or Partly Ignored

In the case concerning the premature termination of the data protection ombudsman's term of office, the European Commission initiated an infringement procedure based on a violation of the Data Protection Directive (95/46/EC). The Hungarian government argued that the directive required independence in an operational sense[89] which had not been violated by the personal and institutional changes.

The CJEU delivered its decision in April 2014 dismissing Hungary's plea. According to the Court, the threat of a premature termination of the term of office 'could lead it to enter into a form of prior compliance with the political authority, which is incompatible with the requirement of independence'.[90] It stated that merely preserving the operational independence of the president of the new Data Protection

---

[88]See Sect. 2.1.4 above.

[89]95/46/EC directive, Art. 28 (1).

[90]CJEU, Case C-288/12 *Commission v. Hungary*, ECLI:EU:C:2014:237, para. 54.

Authority was not enough[91] and the reorganisation of the institutional framework was not sufficient ground for the termination of the ombudsman's term without applying proper transitional measures.[92] The status of the Data Protection Authority has not been changed since the judgment.

Regarding the new retirement rules applying to judges, the government has shown some readiness for compromise and recommended raising the retirement age to 65 from the originally intended 62. The Commission did not accept that and initiated an accelerated infringement procedure.

Simultaneously, the Hungarian Constitutional Court also examined the question and ruled in July 2012 that the regulation was violative of judicial independence and thus unconstitutional. The Hungarian Constitutional Court knew that a parallel infringement procedure was in progress. As such, the Constitutional Court could challenge the government without taking any risk[93] and voided the law retroactively.[94]

The decision of the CJEU in the infringement procedure, delivered 4 months later examined the case as pertaining to a question of discrimination under Directive 2000/78. The CJEU ruled that the Hungarian regulation violated the directive[95] without, however, basing its decision on the requirement of judicial independence.[96]

Following these rulings, the laws on the status of judges (and of prosecutors and notaries too) have been amended: affected judges had to choose whether they wanted to retire or continue assuming their office. Such decisions were also motivated by a legal amendment according to which those judges who do not want to return to service were eligible to compensation in the amount of 12 months remuneration.[97]

[91]Id., para. 51.

[92]Id., para. 61.

[93]For a comparative analysis of the judgments of the CJEU and of the Hungarian Constitutional Court, see Vincze (2013), pp. 330–333. Of course, normally, a constitutional court would not have to take any risk in cases like that but in Hungary, the government's recent practice shows that it is likely to amend the constitution with the content of laws which has been just annulled by the Constitutional Court.

[94]AB decision no. 33/2012. (VII. 17) (MK [official journal] 2012, 13918). The meanwhile retired judges did not get back to office automatically, but they had to claim an action before the Labour Court—many of them decided rather not to do that.

[95]CJEU, Case C-286/12 *Commission v. Hungary*, ECLI:EU:C:2012:687. The Court did not take into account that the Hungarian Constitutional Court meanwhile annulled the provisions in question because that happened after the start of the infringement procedure.

[96]Interestingly, the case law of the CJEU had changed significantly within a couple of years. In the very similar case of sending Polish Supreme Court judges into retirement, the CJEU's dismissing judgment, delivered in June 2019, was primarily based on the principle of judicial independence and to Art. 19 (1) TEU. CJEU, C-619/18 *Commission v. Poland*, ECLI:EU:C:2019:531, paras. 96, 124.

[97]§ 323/I (6) of Act XX of 2013 on certain legal amendments related to the age limit in certain positions in the justice system.

Thus, many judges were not reinstated into their former, leading positions.[98] Further, they must still retire by reaching the general retirement age of 65 years.[99] To sum up, the initial situation has not fully been restored. Further, other threats to judicial independence, like the controversial appointment practice of the president of the National Judicial Office,[100] have not even been addressed by infringement procedures.[101]

3.2 *Infringement Cases Regarding the NGO Law and the Lex CEU*

In parallel to the procedure before the Hungarian Constitutional Court, the European Commission launched an infringement procedure concerning the NGO law. The ECJ ruled in June 2020 that the law represented unjustified restrictions to the free movement of capital and to the right to privacy, data protection and the freedom of association as guaranteed by the EU Charter of Fundamental Rights.[102]

Further, the 'Stop Soros package' has been subject to an infringement procedure since July 2018. The procedure is based on a twofold argument. First, the Commission criticises the non-compliance with the Asylum Procedures Directive, the Asylum Qualifications Directive and the Reception Conditions Directive by criminalising the support for asylum applications and by introducing a new non-admissibility ground.[103] Second, the Commission challenges the injunction to stay away from the border, arguing that the respective legal provision is contrary to the TFEU, the Charter and the Free Movement Directive because it 'unduly restricts the exercise of free movement rights of EU citizens without due regard for procedural guarantees.' In September 2018, the Hungarian government refused to make any changes to the package.[104]

---

[98]This was also the subject of a complaint of more than 150 judges before the ECtHR. The Strasbourg Court finally dismissed the complaints. In the appendix of the judgment it is apparent that the majority of the applicants accepted the lump-sum compensation for not being reinstated. See *J. B. and others v. Hungary*, ECtHR case no. 45434/12.

[99]See the new § 91 of Act CLXII of 2011 on the Legal Status and Remuneration of Judges (following Act XX of 2013 on amendments regarding the retirement age in certain jurisdictional position).

[100]See Vadász (2018). Meanwhile, the practice of the NJO president has been subject to a preliminary reference, see CJEU, Case C-564/19, *IS*.

[101]The problem, that systemic deficiencies of the independence of the judiciary, are not holistically handled by the CJEU, occurred more clearly in the case of Poland. See e.g. opinion of AG Tanchev in Joined Cases C-585/18, C-624/18 and C-625/18, *A.K.*, para. 147.

[102]Judgment in case no. C-78/18, para 143. ECLI:EU:C:2020:476

[103]See press release no. IP/18/4522.

[104]A kormány válasza az Európai Bizottságnak: marad a Stop Soros [The government's answer to the European Commission: Stop Soros remains] http://www.kormany.hu/hu/igazsagugyi-

Concurrently, affected NGOs launched constitutional complaints before the Hungarian Constitutional Court arguing that the introduction of the new offence of 'facilitating illegal migration' unconstitutionally restricted the freedom of association and the freedom of expression. One of these complaints has already been rejected. Nevertheless, the Court seemed to have a rather open attitude towards the case. First, the complaint was not submitted by an affected person (but by an organisation with a more abstract relationship to the contested provision) and without exhausting the ordinary remedies beforehand.[105] Instead of dismissing the case as inadmissible, however, the Court referred to an exceptional rule of the Act on the Constitutional Court[106] and to the HCC's function as a protector of fundamental rights[107] and examined (and eventually rejected the case) on the merits.

Finally, the 'lex CEU' is by far the most problematic case. Generally, education is a Member States' competence. The Commission based its charges on the freedom of establishment and the freedom to provide services with reference to universities from third countries. The applicability of EU law, however, is highly questionable in this case considering that only universities with links to *third countries* are affected.[108] Due to the lack of any *intra-EU* cross-border element, this argument presupposes an extensive interpretation of the freedom of establishment clause: an understanding similar to that adopted in *Ruiz Zambrano*.[109] However, unlike the applicants in the *Zambrano* case, the CEU is a *legal* person and thus could not rely on the 'substance' of Union citizenship under Article 20 TEU. Therefore, the Commission's reference to academic freedom, freedom of education and freedom to conduct a business as guaranteed by the EU Charter of Fundamental Rights raises the question: how can the scope of EU law in the sense of Article 51 (1) of the Charter be triggered? A way to circumvent these problems happened to be WTO law. The CJEU, contrary to its former case law, applied WTO law directly in the case and ruled that Hungary failed to comply with its commitments under the GATS convention and this equals to the failing to fulfil its obligations under EU law. The fact that this convention was an integral part of EU law was found to be enough reason also for the application of the Charter.[110]

---

miniszterium/parlamenti-allamtitkarsag/hirek/a-kormany-valasza-az-europai-bizottsagnak-marad-a-stop-soros.

[105] See §§ 26-27 of Act CLI of 2011 on the Constitutional Court about the requirements of submitting a constitutional complaint.

[106] § 26 (2) of Act CLI of 2011 on the Constitutional Court regulates the exceptional requirements when constitutional complaints are acceptable also beyond the general conditions. These include cases when the threat of fundamental rights violation is direct and does not require a judicial decision and cases when no remedies are provided. In the case of the amendment of the Criminal Code, neither requirement is fulfilled, so by accepting the complaint, the Constitutional Court obviously made an activist step in the field of individual fundamental rights protection.

[107] AB decision no. 3/2019 (III. 7.), Magyar Közlöny [official journal] 2019, 912, paras. 32–42.

[108] See press release no. IP/17/1952 and MEMO/17/3494.

[109] See e.g. the Zambrano judgment: C-34/09, ECLI:EU:C:2011:124.

[110] Judgment in case no. C-66/18, especially paras 86–93. and 212–215. ECLI:EU:C:2020:792.

The amendment of the Higher Education Law—or, the 'lex CEU' as it is often referred to—is much easier to be challenged under Hungarian constitutional law than under EU law. Unlike the Charter provisions, the academic freedom and freedom of education as guaranteed by the Hungarian constitution undoubtedly apply to the act in question. Further, the legislation arguably violates the principle of the rule of law as guaranteed in Article B) (1) of the Fundamental Law: not only through the tight—although later extended—*vacatio legis*, but also by posing a threat to legal certainty and legitimate expectations. Further, by requiring prior consent of the federal government for agreements with federal states, the law demands the legally impossible.[111] Additionally, if an international agreement is a prerequisite for the further functioning of an accredited university, it practically means that the exercise of academic freedom 'depends on the political discretion of two sovereigns'.[112] This is very problematic regarding both fundamental rights and the rule of law.

Yet the Hungarian Constitutional Court suspended the review of the lex CEU with reference to the pending cases before the CJEU. The strategy of the HCC was probably the following: waiting for the decision of the CJEU and hoping that the lex CEU will get the green light under EU law. That would have been a win-win situation for the HCC: it would have been able to reaffirm the constitutionality of the law and avoid any conflict with the CJEU or the government. The strategy did not work, the CJEU dismissed Hungary. The aforementioned infringement proceedings were directed against specific pieces of targeted legislation, without embedding them in the broader context and evaluating the general practice of personalised legislation. The fact, that 'ordinary' infringement procedures are not suitable to address systemic patterns, has been pointed out by legal scholarship long ago.[113] Yet, the respective proposals have not been implemented in EU legislation or practice.

[111]In detail see the amicus curiae brief of András Jakab, Miklós Lévay, László Sólyom and Zoltán Szente to the Constitutional Court (case no. II/01036/2017). It has to be added that this impossible requirement has already been ignored by the Hungarian Government itself by closing such an agreement with the state of Maryland. See the Agreement between the government of Hungary and the state of Maryland and on cooperation in the field of higher education as promulgated by Act CXIV. of 2017. The agreement provides the further functioning of the McDaniel College in Budapest under the new legal framework. In the agreement, there is no reference to any prior consent of the US federal government.

[112]Uitz (2017).

[113]Scheppele (2013a) and Bárd and Śledzińska-Simon (2019).

4 Making a Try with Article 7: The Sargentini Report on Hungary

As seen above, the infringement procedure as currently operated by the Commission is insufficient for addressing the systemic key issues in Hungary. The following section will analyse whether procedures in the political realm are more apt to challenge the Hungarian rule of law deficiencies.

The first comprehensive political document on the new Hungarian constitutional system and its compatibility with EU values was adopted as early as June 2013: this was the non-binding EP resolution named after its rapporteur Tavares.[114] The report criticised the media situation,[115] the legislation concerning the judiciary and the Constitutional Court,[116] some fundamental rights issues, especially the rules of the recognition of churches,[117] the reform of the election system[118] and not least, the practice of amending the Fundamental Law systematically along political interests, with special regard to its Fourth Amendment.[119] As a reaction to the Tavares report, the Fundamental Law has been amended for the fifth time in September 2013. Some points of criticism have been slightly modified or suspended (like the case transfer within the judiciary or, the possibility of levying special taxes to finance obligations stemming from decisions of the HCC or of international courts). Yet, the main

[114]EP report no. P7_TA(2013)0315.

[115]The most criticised point was the independence of the Media Authority. However, it has been proven in the last years that the media problem is not of an institutional kind. It is rather about the fact that government friendly investors purchase even more formerly independent media platforms and turn them to be loyal to the government or even propagandistic (or they just simply close them, as it happened to the biggest daily newspaper called Népszabadság in October 2016). In detail, see e.g. Bátorfy (2017), pp. 12–13.

[116]See Sects. 2.1.2 and 2.3.2 above on these matters.

[117]The Constitutional Court annulled some earlier versions of the law on churches: AB decisions no 164/2011 (XII. 20) (ABH 2011, 1263) and 6/2013 (II. 26.) (ABH 2013, 334). In its later decisions, it called the government more times for amending the relevant laws, see AB decisions no. 23/2015 (VII. 7.) (ABH 2015, 1043), 36/2017 (XII. 29) (ABH 2018, 2). The ECtHR also dismissed Hungary upon the issue (*Magyar Keresztény Mennonita Egyház and others v. Hungary*, Application Nos. 70945/11 23611/12, 26998/12 et al.). The rules have been changed quite often meanwhile, most recently in November 2018. The basic idea is however the same: there are different categories of churches, and they are recognised by the parliament. Pursuant to the latest amendment, the recognition by the parliament only applies to 'settled churches' while other religious communities will be registered by courts (see Act CXXXII of 2018 on the amendment of Act CCVI of 2011 on the freedom of religion and on the status of churches and other religious communities, especially the new §§ 9/A-9/G).

[118]The new election law (Act CCIII of 2011 on the election of the members of parliament) basically upholds the former mixed system but it has been complemented with a tricky gerrymandering and some unfair rules for the campaign (Section VIII of Act. XXXVI. of 2013 on the election procedure).

[119]More details in Sect. 2.2 above.

problematic points remained in place and the rule of law in Hungary has not improved through this amendment.[120]

4.1 Getting Lost in Details, Missing the Bigger Picture

Unfortunately, very little of the deficiencies discussed above were addressed by the Sargentini report adopted in September 2018. This second comprehensive EP resolution on the situation in Hungary triggered an Article 7 TEU procedure[121] and concentrated on 12 issues related mainly to fundamental rights protection[122] and the rule of law.[123] Although the report mentions many relevant deficiencies, it gets lost in irrelevant details and misses the bigger picture.

To name just but a few examples: concerning the Constitutional Court, the Data Protection Authority and judicial independence, mostly the findings of the Tavares report remain repetitive without analysing the recent developments in these fields (points 8–9, 12–18). Related to fundamental rights, the report echoes some partly unfounded criticism concerning the alleged oppression of Roma, Jewish minorities or women (points 59-61, 46).[124] Further issues included in the report relate to media freedom (points 27-30), the secret surveillance for national security purposes without sufficient legal guarantees (points 25–26), the penalization of homelessness (point 73), and violations of the academic freedom, the freedom of assembly and the freedom of expression (points 33–36, 41–45). Furthermore, a new topic took centre stage: corruption. On the one hand, the report correctly mentions cases where OLAF found serious irregularities and possible fraudulent activities related to the spending of EU funds, some of them share links to the family of the prime minister (point 23).[125] On the other hand, the report also discusses irrelevant technical details like MPs asset declarations or the system of campaign financing (points 20–21).

[120] Similarly, Szente (2017), p. 470.

[121] European Parliament resolution of 12 September 2018 on a proposal calling on the Council to determine, pursuant to Article 7(1) of the Treaty on European Union, the existence of a clear risk of a serious breach by Hungary of the values on which the Union is founded (2017/2131(INL)).

[122] Freedom of expression, freedom of association, academic freedom, freedom of religion, privacy and data protection, the right to equal treatment, social rights, rights of asylum seekers.

[123] Functioning of the constitutional system, the independence of the judiciary, corruption.

[124] The most striking false statement is that the Criminal Code does not fully protect women who have been victims of domestic violence (point 46). Actually, a new offense has been introduced already during the governance of the Fidesz, exactly in order to address this problem. See 212/A. § of Act C of 2012 on the Criminal Code.

[125] The company of the son-in-law of the prime minister won public procurement procedures in several towns and villages for the modernisation of street lightings. Many of the procurement tenders were directly designed exactly and exclusively for his company. The Hungarian authorities started an investigation but it was finally cancelled in November 2018. (Hungarian investigative portal Átlátszó wrote about the story in details: https://atlatszo.hu/category/cikkek/eliosaktak/.) It is

Eventually, the report does the Hungarian government a huge favour when dealing exhaustively with Fidesz's old-time campaign topic—migration. Yet even here the report misses the crucial point: the introduction and emphasis by the government on the 'crisis situation caused by mass migration'. This new state of emergency enables the government to apply less guarantees during the asylum application procedures in order to significantly accelerate them.[126] The crisis situation has constantly been prolonged since 2015, even if the legal requirements are clearly not fulfilled.[127] Instead of identifying this obvious and systemic rule of law deficiency, the report rather concentrates on recording statistical data on the detention circumstances and the frequent refusal of appeals (points 62–72). Moreover, by criticising a judgment in a specific criminal case, the report makes the impression of intervening into that case,[128] which is highly questionable with regard to the rule of law itself.

In sum, proper grounds could be found for launching an Article 7 procedure against Hungary, but only a few of them have been identified. And even those elements that have been identified, are not convincingly placed within the system of constitutional malfunctions. The report failed to realise the patterns: neither the tendency of targeted legislation, nor the logic of "over-constitutionalisation" behind some constitutional amendments were identified. Further, relevant arguments are diluted with rather strange and minor, sometimes unfounded allegations:[129] this feeds such counterarguments that portray the report as a purely politically motivated attack. Based on such an ill-founded report, Article 7 will surely remain a tool of political cherry picking, failing to play a serious role in safeguarding the rule of law.

4.2 Limited Political Relevance

Despite several shortcomings of the Sargentini report, the Hungarian government decided not to go into a substantial debate on the rule of law or fundamental rights. Instead, the government challenged the report on formal grounds arguing that the

---

worth to recall at this point that the Prosecutor General was elected by the two thirds majority of the parliament and actually, he is an ex-Fidesz member and an old friend of the Prime Minister.

[126]§§ 80/I-J-K of Act LXXX of 2007 on asylum.

[127]Such crisis situation may be announced basically if more than 500 applicants arrive daily in the average of at least a month. This is not the case for a long time according to the statistics, but there is a more flexible rule too- namely, the threatening of the public order in any Hungarian municipality (not necessarily closed to the border). The interpretation and application of this flexible provision belongs to the discretion of the government. See 80/A § of Act LXXX of 2007 on asylum.

[128]That is the case Ahmed H, who has been condemned for 5 years imprisonment because of an 'act of terror' by the Hungarian courts following a riot at the boarder to Serbia. See Article 67 of the report. In January, 2019 he was ordered to be expelled from Hungary.

[129]For example the oppression of LGBT, Jewish or Roma minorities and the lacking protection of women from domestic violence etc.

two thirds majority requirement for the EP voting was not fulfilled because abstentions were not counted as votes cast.[130] After referring to these procedural defects and declaring the Sargentini report as void, there seems to be no place for stepping back and finding compromises. As such, the Sargentini report was an ideal target for the Hungarian government in the campaign before the EP-election of 2019. Fidesz called the Hungarian voters to resist pro-migration EU bureaucrats 'punishing their own border guards': 52.56% of them did so by voting for the Fidesz.

More than two years have passed since the EP adopted the Sargentini report, but the Council still has not made any decision. Only some hearings took place over 2019. This is not a surprise as a similar inertia can be observed with regard to Poland. Nevertheless, rapporteur Sargentini has been eager to keep the issue of Hungary on the agenda of the LIBE committee and to pressure the Romanian Council presidency to table the case during the first half of 2019. In light of the fact that serious concerns have been raised concerning the rule of law in Romania,[131] it is no surprise that the Romanian Council presidency did not hurry up with the Article 7 processes either against Hungary or Poland. It is worth recalling that the Hungarian and Polish governments promised to veto any steps against each-other in the Article 7 procedure.

5 How to Take 'Informed' Measures in Defence of the Union's Values?

Until here, I have tried to illustrate the complexity of the Hungarian developments and also show how insufficient the different processes launched by EU institutions have been. If values are codified normatively—as they are in Article 2 TEU—and rule of law is to be taken seriously, there should be an objective and transparent tool to "measure the unmeasurable".[132] As such, it comes as no surprise that the idea of measuring the rule of law is a matter of increasing importance within the EU institutions nowadays. In this last section, I will briefly outline some recent proposals and point out the difficulties of using indicators to detect systemic rule of law problems.

[130] CJEU, Case C-650/18, *Hungary v. Parliament* (pending). The legal situation is not obvious at this point. The Rules of Procedure reads that 'in calculating whether a text has been adopted or rejected, account shall be taken only of votes cast for and against, except in those cases for which the Treaties lay down a specific majority' (Rule 178 (3) RoP). So the question is whether the two thirds majority required by Article 354 (4) TFEU counts as a 'specific majority'.

[131] See EP resolution no. P8_TA(2018)0446.

[132] Cf. Schmitt (1996), p. 3.

5.1 Measuring, Buying or Monitoring the Rule of Law?

In October 2016 the European Parliament made a proposal to the Commission[133] to introduce an Interinstitutional Agreement—the European Union Pact on Democracy, the Rule of Law, and Fundamental Rights (DRF Pact). It seemed to be inspired by an earlier academic debate on the 'Copenhagen dilemma' and especially by Jan-Werner Müller's idea of a 'Copenhagen Commission'.[134] The proposal concentrated primarily on two shortcomings of the present system: first, the EP intended to define the Article 2 TEU values by setting up a framework of indicators. Second, it would have provided for the Member States to be assessed regularly by an expert group according to a 'DRF Scoreboard'. A 'DRF policy cycle' was also foreseen to assess the EU institutions.

The draft of the DRF Scoreboard outlined some rather general indicators to measure democracy, rule of law and fundamental rights in the Member States, involving existing expert bodies, civil organisations, EU institutions and not least, national parliaments (Articles 6–8). Depending on the scores of the Member States, the draft proposed initiating different proceedings under the Rule of Law Framework, Article 7 (1) or even 7 (2) TEU. Further, the EP suggested that the Commission launch systemic infringement procedures by bundling several infringement cases together.[135]

Of course there are difficulties: In light of the considerable differences between the systems of the Member States with regard to democracy and rule of law, a comprehensive and detailed list of indicators, which claims validity for *all* Member States, would have been difficult to establish.[136] Further, the proposal mentioned the Charter as the only indicator for fundamental rights: however, that would have meant an extension of the Charter's scope beyond the limits of Article 51 (1).

Yet the proposal had some obvious advantages. Monitoring all Member States (and the EU institutions as well) would certainly be more just and balanced than criticising only some selected 'suspicious' Member States. The DRF proposal would not have changed the current system of EU values enforcement fundamentally in so far as Article 7 TEU would have remained the main and final tool of sanctioning non-compliance with EU values. However, the political process would have been *preceded* by an exhaustive legal analysis: this way, expertise and political considerations could have been better balanced. Unfortunately, the Commission has opted for the usual course and refused to initiate any legislative proposal following the

[133]European Parliament resolution of 25 October 2016 with recommendations to the Commission on the establishment of an EU mechanism on democracy, the rule of law and fundamental rights (2015/2254(INL)), 8_TA(2016)0409.[DRF Proposal].

[134]Müller (2016), pp. 206–224.

[135]The systemic infringement action was first advised by Scheppele (2013a).

[136]For details about the methodological questions see e.g. Jakab and Lőrincz (2017).

EP's DRF-proposal.[137] The Commission argued that it had 'serious doubts about the need and feasibility' of setting up such annual reports. Further, the involvement of an expert panel raised 'serious questions of legality, institutional legitimacy and accountability,' and rather, 'best possible use should be made of existing instruments while avoiding duplication', the Commission argued.[138]

These arguments are hypocritical for several reasons. First, the Commission presumes that its own Rule of Law Framework does not pose legality and legitimacy concerns.[139] Second, the Commission is clearly aware of the fact that the existing instruments are not very effective to solve the EU's value crisis, as illustrated by the case of Poland[140] and Hungary.[141] The legality and legitimacy concerns could be allayed exactly if Article 7 would result in *informed* sanctions: and the best way to inform politicians about the legal system of other Member States is a thorough and holistic legal assessment. Further, the judicial dialogue through preliminary proceedings also raised great hopes. Yet, after the LM judgment,[142] it seems that simply triggering an Article 7 procedure against the affected Member State is not enough to generally overcome the present 'horizontal Solange' model[143] operating with exceptions from the mutual trust.

By rejecting the DRF proposal, it seemed that the Commission waived the legal assessment in order to keep inappropriate tools of political threat. This raised the question of whether the Commission's position corresponds to its function as guardian of the Treaties.[144] The proposals on the protection of EU values developed since then, still reflect the need for a thorough legal assessment.

An example for that is the Commission's proposal from 2018 for a regulation to protect 'the Union's budget in case of generalised deficiencies as regards the rule of law in the Member States'.[145] The proposal aims to withhold payments from EU sources in the case of generalised rule of law deficiencies, trying to find the balance

---

[137]Follow up to the European Parliament resolution on with recommendations to the Commission on the establishment of an EU mechanism on democracy, the rule of law and fundamental rights, adopted by the Commission on 17 January 2017, Ref. no. A8-0283/2016/P8_TA-PROV(2016) 0409.

[138]See the follow up document no. A8-0283/2016, point 6.

[139]See e.g. Skouris (2015), p. 14.

[140]In its third Rule of Law recommendation, the Commission admitted that the situation of a systemic threat to the rule of law in Poland has 'seriously deteriorated' since the start of the process. (Commission recommendation no. C(2017) 5320, point 45). This impression definitely was strengthened after triggering Article 7 TEU against Poland—following that efforts made in the frames of the Rule of Law Framework were useless. (Proposal for a Council decision on the determination of a clear risk of a serious breach by the Republic of Poland of the rule of law (2017/ 0360(APP, especially para. 175).

[141]See Sect. 3.1 above.

[142]Case no. C-216/18 PPU (ECLI:EU:C:2018:586).

[143]Canor (2013), pp. 383–421.

[144]Petra Bárd and Sergio Carrera answer this question obviously for the disadvantage of the Commission. See Bárd and Carrera (2017), pp. 9–10.

[145]A8-0469/2018, procedure no. 2018/0136 (COD).

between the general and systemic rule of law violations and the concrete individual cases of fraud or corruption regarding EU sources. In fact, the proposal of the Commission basically foresees a somewhat similar but much simpler political process than that of the Article 7, to be applied to a narrower circle of problems. The main practical differences are that this process has only one stage, the European Council would not be involved and the required majority in the Council would be much lower. In the first reading of the legislative procedure, the European Parliament suggested that both the consent of the Parliament and of the Council should be needed to approve a transfer proposal for a budgetary reserve.[146]

The problem is that the proposal of the Commission explains only very briefly, what is meant under the 'rule of law' or 'generalised deficiency' of the rule of law, which gives ground to restrict the use of EU funds by the affected Member State. Different aspects of the proper functioning of the judiciary system are set out in the proposal: judicial independence, legal remedies, effective investigation and the implementation of judgments, legal certainty, pluralistic and transparent legislative process, lack of arbitrariness and so on. The proposal defines not only legal acts and measures but also 'widespread and recurrent practices and omissions' as possible sources of a generalised rule of law deficiency (Article 2 b).

However, it was not clear from the original proposal, how the Commission and the Council would find out whether such a practice takes places in a Member State. The European Parliament made an important amendment at this point and suggested setting up an advisory panel composed of independent experts in constitutional law and financial and budgetary matters, appointed by each of the national parliaments and by the European Parliament (new Article 3 a as proposed). The suggestion clearly reflects the idea of the failed DRF proposal[147] but applied only to a narrower field, related to rule of law deficiencies affecting the financial interests of the EU.

Regardless of this ongoing legislative process, the Commission seems to realise that it was a mistake to dismiss the Parliament's DRF Scoreboard. It is hard to find any other reason, why the Commission returned to the basic idea of that scoreboard. Namely, in July 2019, the Commission announced the introduction of a 'Rule of Law Review Cycle' and the publication of an 'Annual rule of law report' in order to prevent 'negative developments' regarding the rule of law in the Member States.[148] Similar to the DRF Scoreboard, all Member States will be subject to this monitoring mechanism, but unlike that scoreboard without a distinct expert panel. Further, the Commission aims at collecting data from existing bodies, also beyond the EU, like the OSCE, the Council of Europe or the EU Fundamental Rights Agency. The reason for that are the Commission's legitimacy and accountability concerns again. In its communication, however, the Commission made clear that 'external expertise cannot take the place of an assessment made by the Commission itself,

[146] New Art. 5, paras. 6a-6c as proposed and Art. 5 paras. 7–8 as proposed to be deleted.

[147] See Sect. 5.1 above.

[148] COM(2019) 343 final.

particularly when the Commission's conclusions could be the basis for acts that come with legal and financial consequences'.

The question occurs, why extra-EU expert bodies count automatically as accountable and legitimate in the matter of EU values, and how is it guaranteed that the Commission will make an informed assessment concerning the rule of law in the Member States. The first annual rule of law reports, published in September 2020, unfortunately verified these concerns. In the country report on Hungary, the Commission correctly raised criticism concerning a number of issues, but it failed to point out to the big picture: how the criticised elements will affect the constitutional reality in context.

5.2 *How to Indicate Overlapping Systemic Rule of Law Deficiencies?*

To 'measure' the rule of law, it is clearly not enough to 'simply take the Copenhagen criteria off the legal shelf'.[149] Simple governance checklists do not work either.[150] However, that is not a reason for giving up any attempts to 'measure' the rule of law. Yet, complex indicators should be used instead of checklists. Aggregating the presence or absence of certain institutional structures does not make much sense without taking into account the wider context and the interrelatedness of different aspects within (and beyond) the rule of law.[151]

Several international rule of law indicators exist, which are based on different factors of the rule of law: still, their results usually are almost identical.[152] If the EU wants to set up a rule of law indicator, that will be a ground for sanctions, this must be more than a mere *checklist*. Such a rule of law indicator could only work if it follows a truly holistic approach. The Hungarian example illustrates very well, how many levels of rule of law problems could occur. Particular rule of law problems may affect each other in a way that is extremely difficult to translate into scores and numbers if we work with strictly distinct factors of the rule of law.

For example, targeted legislation seems to be a problem that is relatively easy to detect by assessing to whom a certain law actually applies. Still, the issue becomes more difficult, once the options for constitutional remedies are taken into account. The constitutionality of that targeted law will be reviewed by a Constitutional Court that is composed of judges loyal to the government. Moreover, if the law regulates a financial subject or is part of an 'over-constitutionalisation', it might not be constitutionally reviewed at all. Of course, a weakened Constitutional Court will get lower scores in any system of indicators—but it is questionable whether this lower score

---

[149]Müller (2017), p. 241.

[150]Scheppele (2013b), p. 562 et seq.

[151]Similarly, Ginsburg (2011), p. 272.

[152]See the empirical analysis of Versteeg and Ginsburg (2017), p. 102 et seq.

properly describes its actual effects on the legal system. Such complex outcomes can hardly be expressed in a score-system based on separate factors.

But there is another side of the coin too: if once a constitutional court gets a lower score because of its restricted competences, to what extent does it make sense to complain further about the method of selecting judges? Namely: if the Court could not decide about anything important, why does it matter that it is composed of government-friendly judges? Of course, the question is simplified in so far that *some* important decisions could surely be made by any constitutional court. Still, if the factors of competence and composition are put in proportion, the final score of a constitutional court will be better balanced.

The correlation and interrelatedness of different factors should not only be measured within the elements of the rule of law (e.g. generality of laws, independence of judges, constitutionalism), but also in the broader context of the state order. For example, it might sound good that two thirds parliamentary majority is needed for appointments for the most important positions and for the amendment of the constitution. But it should also be measured, how easy or how difficult it is to win such a majority in the given election system. By asking this question, we are already beyond the realm of the rule of law, and within the principle of democracy, which is another founding value of the EU. A founding value that seems to be overlooked in the current rule of law debates. And that is a pity for an important reason.

The above-analysed legislative changes are protected by the government always with the same argumentation: they are legitimised by the people to make such reforms and this legitimation does not only establish an opportunity for them, but also an obligation. They must fulfil the people's will by implementing these legislative changes, and anyone who doubts that these reforms comply with the rule of law, actually questions the democratically expressed will of the Hungarian people. As such, they are echoing the idea of 'political constitutionalism' under the slogan of 'illiberal democracy'. However, not only the rule of law, but also the functioning of democracy could convincingly be criticised in Hungary.[153] The difference between the paradigms of legal and political constitutionalism, between the ideas of 'liberal' and 'majoritarian' democracy was perfectly illustrated through the debates on the Hungarian rule of law. EU institutions could be much more successful in these debates if they distanced themselves from the idea of legal constitutionalism and tried to set a trap for Orbán in his own territory by pointing out to some problems of democratic legitimacy beyond (but related to) the strictly understood rule of law concerns.

Such arguments are more effective if they are not echoed (only) by politicians, but they have a solid background. A background that is more than a report made by a MEP who was bound to party bargains, and more than a mere checklist based on scores of *separate* factors. A complex EU-indicator of the rule of law (or more

[153] E.g. the rules of the election procedure and campaigning (see Sect. 2.1.6 and *supra* note 113), restrictions regarding direct democracy (*supra* note 78) and the media situation (*supra* note 110).

broadly, of EU values) can only be set out if it is sensitive to correlations and it is based on legal reality instead of abstract legal possibilities.

Of course, such an indicator will not be a solution for every problem either. It would also be necessary that the Commission repeatedly launches infringement actions if judgments of the CJEU in rule of law related matters are not respected, and it would further be useful if the CJEU would be more eager to systemically scrutinise the rule of law breaches in those processes.[154]

6 Conclusion

As seen above, the Hungarian government works primarily with the instrument of personalised, targeted legislation—this tendency has not been acknowledged in Brussels as one of the main pillars of Hungary's rule of law-deficit. Only some individual pieces of the targeted legal regime reach the thresholds of EU criticism from time to time. The reason for limiting the powers of the Hungarian Constitutional Court was mainly to ensure that the Court does not prevent the introduction of some targeted and politically important laws and constitutional amendments. Ultimately, Hungary has been made subject to an Article 7 procedure. Yet from the Sargentini report it is clear that the rule of law problems of Hungary are only partly captured by the EP: the 'lex CEU' and the 'lex NGO' were the obvious red lines in the eyes of many politicians but they are by far not the most problematic points in the whole constitutional pattern. That pattern could have been identified if EU values would be considered at least worth to be defined—at best, along factors of a scoreboard that takes systemic correlations into account. For Hungary and Poland the purely political Article 7 procedure still awaits—without a minimum of legal certainty provided by clear concepts but with guaranteed political motivations behind the decision. If a final decision comes at all...

References

Bakó B (2017) Láthatatlan után inkoherens alkotmány. A korlátlan alkotmánymódosító hatalomról [First invisible, then incoherent constitution. On the unlimited constitution-amending power]. Magyar Jog 2017:2

Bakó B (2018) The Zauberlehrling unchained? The recycling of the German Federal Constitutional Court's case law on identity-, ultra vires- and fundamental rights review in Hungary. ZaöRV 78 (4):863–902

Bárd P, Carrera S (2017) The Commission's decision on 'Less EU' in safeguarding the rule of law: a play in four acts. CEPS Policy Insights 1:8

[154] AG Tanchev already criticised the CJEU's approach followed in the infringement case regarding the Polish Supreme Court. See the opinion of AG Tanchev in Joined Cases C-585/18, C-624/18 and C-625/18, *A.K.*, para 147.

Bárd P, Śledzińska-Simon A (2019) Rule of law infringement procedures A proposal to extend the EU's rule of law toolbox. CEPS Papers in Liberty and Security in Europe, 2019-09
Bátorfy A (2017) Az állam foglyul ejtésétől a piac fogvatartásáig. Orbán Viktor és a kormány médiamodellje 2014 után [From state capture to market capture. The media model of Viktor Orbán and the government]. Médiakutató 2017:1–2
Bellamy R (2007) Political Constitutionalism. A Republican defence of the constitutionality of democracy. Cambridge University Press, Cambridge
Blaskó B (2016) Commentary to § 7 to the Hungarian Criminal Code. In: Polt P (ed) A Büntető Törvénykönyvről szóló 2012. évi C. törvény nagykommentárja [Great Commentary to Act c. of 2012 on the Criminal Code]. Opten, Budapest
Canor I (2013) My brother's keeper? Horizontal Solange: "An ever closer distrust among the peoples of Europe". Common Market Law Rev 50:383. 2
Erdős C (2013) Visszaélés a jogalkotással – avagy egyedi rendelkezések jogszabályba foglalásának alkotmányossági megítélése [Misuse of legislation – assessing the constitutionality of including individual provisions into law]. Diskurzus 2
Gárdos-Orosz F (2016) Alkotmánybíróság 2010-2015 [Constitutional Court 2010-2015]. In: Jakab A, Gajduschek G (eds) A magyar jogrendszer állapota [The state of the Hungarian legal system]. MTA TK, Budapest, p 2016
Ginsburg T (2011) Pitfalls of measuring the rule of law. Hague J Rule Law 3(2):269–280
Glencross A (2014) The absence of political constitutionalism in the EU: three models for enhancing constitutional agency. J Eur Public Policy 21(8):1163–1180
Halmai G (2012) From 'Rule of Law Revolution' to an illiberal democracy in Hungary. In: Sachs M, Siekmann H (eds) Festschrift für Klaus Stern zum. 80. Geburtstag. Duncker & Humblot, Berlin
Halmai G (2015) Pártos alkotmánybíráskodás 2010–2014 [Partisan constitutional jurisdiction 2010–2014]. In: Gárdos-Orosz F, Szente Z (eds) Jog és politika határán. Alkotmánybíráskodás Magyarországon 2010 után [At the border of law and politics. Constitutional jurisdiction in Hungary after 2010]. hvg orac, Budapest
Jakab A, Szente Z (2009) Commentary to paragraph 19 § of the constitution. In: Jakab A (ed) Az Alkotmány kommentárja [Commentary of the Constitution], vol 1. Századvég, Budapest
Jakab A, Lőrincz OV (2017) International indices as models for the rule of law scoreboard of the European Union: methodological issues. Max Planck Institute for Comparative Public Law & International Law (MPIL) Research Paper 21/2017
Kochenov D (2017) Busting the myths nuclear: a commentary on Article 7 TEU. EUI Working Paper Law, 2017/10
Müller J-W (2016) Protecting the rule of law (and Democracy!) in the EU. The idea of a Copenhagen Commission. In: Closa C, Kochenov D (eds) Reinforcing rule of law oversight in the European Union. Cambridge University Press, Cambridge
Müller J-W (2017) A democracy commission of one's own, or what it would take for the EU to safeguard liberal democracy in its member states. In: Jakab A, Kochenov D (eds) The enforcement of EU law and values ensuring member states' compliance. Oxford University Press, Oxford
Orbán E (2016) A bírói döntések ellen benyújtott alkotmányjogi panaszok tapasztalatai [Experiences of constitutional complaints directed against judicial decisions]. Pázmány Law Working Papers, 2016/20
Polyák G, Szőke GL (2011) Elszalasztott lehetőség? Az új adatvédelmi törvény főbb rendelkezései [A missed opportunity? The main provisions of the new data protection law]. In: Drinóczi T (ed) Magyarország új alkotmányossága [The new constitutionality of Hungary]. Pécsi Tudományegyetem Állam- és Jogtudományi Kar, Pécs
Scheppele KL (2013a) What can the European Commission do when member states violate basic principles of the European Union? The case for systemic infringement actions (her proposal is available at the website of the Commission: http://ec.europa.eu/justice/events/assises-justice-2013/files/contributions/45.princetonuniversityscheppelesystemicinfringementaction brusselsversion_en.pdf)

Scheppele KL (2013b) The rule of law and the frankenstate: why governance checklists do not work. Governance 26(4):559–562
Schmitt C (1996) The Tyranny of values. Plutarch Press, Washington DC
Skouris V (2015) Die Rechtsstaatlichkeit in der Europäischen Union [The rule of law in the European Union]. Europarecht Beiheft 2
Sonnevend P, Jakab A, Csink L (2015) The constitution as an instrument of everyday party politics: the basic law of Hungary. In: von Bogdandy A, Sonnevend P (eds) Constitutional crisis in the European constitutional area. Theory, law and politics in Hungary and Romania. Hart Publishing, Oxford
Sulyok T (2016) Erga omnes Effect of Member States' Constitutions and Composite Constitutionality. Fontes Iuris 2016, Special Edition on the FIDE Congress
Szente Z (2016) Die politische Orientierung der Mitglieder des ungarischen Verfassungsgerichts zwischen 2010 und 2014. Jahrbuch für Ostrecht 18(1):45–67
Szente Z (2017) Challenging the basic values – problems in the rule of law in Hungary and the failure of the EU to tackle them. In: Jakab A, Kochenov D (eds) The enforcement of EU law and values. Ensuring member states' compliance. Oxford University Press, Oxford
Tilk P (2014) Az Alkotmánybíróság és a pénzügyi tárgyú törvények vizsgálati lehetősége [The Constitutional Court and its possibility to review financial acts]. Fundamentum 2014:1–2
Uitz R (2017) Academic freedom in an illiberal democracy: From rule of law through rule by law to rule by men in Hungary. Verfassungsblog, 13. October, 2017
Vadász V (2018) Krízis a bírósági igazgatásban? [Crisis in the judiciary administration?]. MTA Law Working Papers 2018/13
Varga Zs A (2016) Final conferral of sovereignty or limited power-transfer?. Fontes Iuris 2016, Special Edition on the FIDE Congress
Versteeg M, Ginsburg T (2017) Measuring the rule of law: a comparison of indicators. Law Soc Inq 42(1):100–137
Vincze A (2013) Der EuGH als Hüter der ungarischen Verfassung – Anmerkung zum Urteil des EuGH 6. 11. 2012, Rs. C-286/12 (Kommission/Ungarn) [The ECJ as the guardian of the Hungarian constitution – A remark to the ruling of the ECJ in case C-276/12 from the 6th of November 2012]. Europarecht 3
Vincze A, Varju M (2012) Hungary: the new fundamental law. Eur Public Law 18:437. 3
von Bogdandy A et al (2012) Reverse Solange – protecting the essence of fundamental rights against EU member states. Common Market Law Rev 49:489. 2
Walker N (2007) Constituent constitutionalism? The case of the European Union. In: Loughlin M, Walker N (eds) The paradox of constitutionalism. Constituent power and constitutional form. Oxford University Press, Oxford

Beáta Bakó is a Max Weber Fellow at the Law Department of the European University Institute, Florence. She is the co-editor-in chief of the Hungarian online newspaper Azonnali.hu.

Part II
European Action

Towards a Tyranny of Values?

Principles on Defending Checks and Balances in EU Member States

Armin von Bogdandy

Contents

Abstract This contribution develops the framework of European reactions to the undermining of checks and balances in EU Member States. It surveys the normative setting with its various institutional options and contrasting constitutional principles and then applies these principles to the panoply of relevant instruments. The building blocks of this framework are *competence*, *procedure*, *standards,* and *control.* This should help Europe to speak with a principled voice. The contribution shows how

---

A slightly different and longer version has been published in the *Common Market Law Review* 57 (2020).

A. von Bogdandy (✉)
Max Planck Institute for Comparative Public Law and International Law, Heidelberg, Germany
e-mail: sekreavb@mpil.de

A. von Bogdandy et al. (eds.), *Defending Checks and Balances in EU Member States*, Beiträge zum ausländischen öffentlichen Recht und Völkerrecht 298,
https://doi.org/10.1007/978-3-662-62317-6_4

red lines can be drawn that respect constitutional pluralism, and how any action's legitimacy is enhanced if many institutions undertake it jointly.

1 What Is at Stake

In some EU Member States, governing majorities are modifying controlling institutions. These attempts go far beyond the traditional three branches and affect political parties, ombudspersons, the media, NGOs and academia. As such, they critically weaken the domestic checks and balances in a larger sense.[1] Most consider the value of the rule of law to be endangered, but the values of democracy and of respect for human dignity are no less at stake.[2] Indeed, political science sees such measures as symptomatic for illiberal democracies, i.e. for authoritarian tendencies.[3]

This book has been triggered by the remodelling of the Polish Judiciary since 2015.[4] However, the Polish developments are not isolated. Similar tendencies manifest in a series of EU Member States, especially in Hungary.[5] European constitutionalism is perhaps facing a 'constitutional moment':[6] the decision whether it *comprises* illiberal democracies or whether it *fights* them. The first case would herald the end of the European Union's current self-understanding, as 'illiberal democracies' would co-inform the common values of Article 2 TEU in the future. The alternative path requires the Union to counter threats to domestic checks and balances. To achieve this, European constitutionalism must draw and defend 'red lines', which would also imply a considerable constitutional development: European

[1]See Ackerman et al. (2011), p. 264.

[2]On the interrelatedness of these values, see already Habermas (1992), p. 109 et seq.; similarly, Möllers and Schneider (2018), p. 97 et seq. Similarly Commission Proposal for a Regulation of the European Parliament and of the Council on the protection of the Union's budget in case of generalised deficiencies as regards the rule of law in the Member States (COM(2018) 324 final), recital (3).

[3]Lauth and Sehring (2009), p. 165; Kailitz and Köllner (2012), p. 11; Merkel (2013), p. 223 et seq.

[4]For an enumeration of particularly problematic measures, see Proposal for a Council Decision on the determination of a clear risk of a serious breach by the Republic of Poland of the rule of law (COM(2017) 835 final), para. 6 et seq.; on the context, Bachmann (2018), p. 9 et seq.; Sadurski (2019).

[5]Halmai (2018a), p. 85; European Parliament resolution of 12 September 2018 on a proposal calling on the Council to determine, pursuant to Article 7(1) of the Treaty on European Union, the existence of a clear risk of a serious breach by Hungary of the values on which the Union is founded (2017/2131(INL)). On Romania, see Venice Commission, Romania—Opinion on draft amendments to Law No. 303/2004 on the Statute of Judges and Prosecutors, Law No. 304/2004 on Judicial Organisation, and Law No. 317/2004 on the Superior Council for Magistracy (Oct. 22, 2018), CDL-AD(2018)017; European Parliament resolution of 13 November 2018 on the rule of law in Romania (2018/2844(RSP)).

[6]The concept was coined by Ackerman (1991), p. 6, though with a different thrust.

constitutionalism would gain in profile and develop elements of a militant democracy.

This chapter explores the latter path, which leads into unchartered waters. The legality and the legitimacy of the European actions are disputed. Even the Council of the European Union considers one of the European Commission's instruments inadmissible.[7] Some voices, not least the European Parliament, regard European actions as too one-sided.[8] Others accuse the Union of double standards, as it allegedly fails the same values which it demands its Members to respect.[9] Some hold the European Commission as generally 'unsuited' as a guardian of liberal democracy.[10]

Some even detect in these unchartered waters what Carl Schmitt branded as the 'tyranny of values': a defence of values that destroys the very values it aims to protect.[11] In April 2017, the Polish ambassador in Berlin announced that Poland respects all European values and that there merely was 'a problem of interpretation. Brussels is far too strongly informed by liberal left-wing ideology.'[12] In similar terms, Viktor Orbán explained his rejection of Frans Timmermans' nomination as President of the Commission by calling him 'an ideological warrior who accepts no diversity, who tolerates no views which diverge from his own and from liberal democracy, and who wants to force his own conception on all EU Member States'.[13] Such positioning is symptomatic. As Uwe Volkmann observes, in today's European society there are 'different worlds of values which only rotate around themselves and hardly ever intersect'.[14] The predominance of one of these worlds is then quickly considered tyranny by the other.

In the first step, I will explore the constitutional horizon of the question of whether one should intervene in a case such as the Polish one (2). Factors militating against such action are national democracy, the risk of failure, but also the possibility of an unwanted European state (Sect. 2.1), while considerations of the current constitutional self-understanding, Union citizenship and mutual trust speak in favour of such action (Sect. 2.2). The second step develops a legal frame for pertinent instruments of European law, Member States' law and international law (Sect. 3.1),

---

[7]Council Legal Service, Commission's Communication on a new EU Framework to strengthen the rule of law: – compatibility with the Treaties (10296/14).

[8]Mendelski (2016), p. 390; Franzius (2018), p. 382 and 386; Resolution on the need for a comprehensive EU mechanism for the protection of democracy, the rule of law and fundamental rights (2018/2886(RSP)), recital (K).

[9]Weiler (2016), p. 326.

[10]Schorkopf (2016), p. 159; Janse (2019), p. 43.

[11]Schmitt (2011), p. 48 et seq. The expression 'tyranny of values' was first used by Hartmann (1926), p. 524 et seq.

[12]Quoted after Voßkuhle (2018), p. 17.

[13]Press Release, 'They want to make Soros's man the President of the Commission' (2 July 2019), www.kormany.hu/en/the-prime-minister/news/they-want-to-make-soros-s-man-the-president-of-the-commission.

[14]Volkmann (2018), p. 14.

consisting of the building blocks *legal basis* (Sect. 3.2), *procedure* (Sect. 3.3), *standards* (Sect. 3.4), and *control* (Sect. 3.5).

2 The Principles in Abstract

2.1 Options

The European legal space requires that all institutions exercising public authority within its scope respect its fundamental values. Its legal orders have mutually committed themselves to a constitutional core.[15] This is expressed most clearly in Articles 2, 7, and 49 TEU, but national constitutional law sets out similar requirements.[16] These requirements are complemented by international law, especially Article 3 Statute of the Council of Europe as well as the ECHR.[17] These requirements may not be identical, given European constitutional pluralism, but they certainly rest on largely overlapping core values.[18]

At the same time, it is not clear whether and how public institutions are to defend these fundamental values. Article 7 TEU, which stipulates specific mechanisms, provides much discretion: The Union 'may', but is not bound to defend the European values against its Member States.[19] All the other instruments, too, leave ample scope.[20] There is legal room for considering various options.

From the perspective of Union law, a first option is to avoid any conflict, to do nothing, and—with liberal optimism—to trust into the self-healing powers of liberal constitutionalism. A second option would be to primarily address authoritarian tendencies in the Council of Europe, thus acknowledging the Council's special role regarding questions of Member State constitutional law.[21] This would relieve cooperation within the Union from this conflict. A third option for the Union is to adhere to the established scope of Union law und thus avoid the highly conflictual discussion about values. The Commission acted against Hungary in this sense: it brought the disempowerment of the judiciary to the CJEU as an inadmissible

[15]For an overview see von Bogdandy (2014), p. 980.

[16]BVerfGE 140, 317 – *Identitätskontrolle*; *The Minister for Justice and Equality v. Celmer*, [2018] IEHC 119 (2018).

[17]In detail Uerpmann-Wittzack (2009), p. 131.

[18]Opinion of AG Cruz Villalón in CJEU, Case C-62/14 *Gauweiler and Others*, ECLI:EU:C:2015:7, para. 61.

[19]Communication from the Commission to the Council and the European Parliament on Article 7 of the Treaty on European Union. Respect for and promotion of the values on which the EU is based (COM(2003) 606 final) p. 6; Ruffert (2016), para. 8.

[20]However, there may also be constellations in which there is a duty to take action, Huber (2017), p. 389.

[21]Tuori (2016), p. 237. On the procedure under Art. 20 (c) Statute of the European Council, see Wittinger (2005), p. 130 et seq.

discrimination of elderly judges under the Anti-Discrimination Directive 2000/78.[22] As a fourth option, the Union could leave the issue to its Member States. The Member States in turn could act collectively, as in case of the sanctions against Austria,[23] or individually, e.g., by denying the Member State in question judicial cooperation or by utilising Article 259 TFEU.[24]

Exercising such discretion must be based on valid grounds. The structuring of such grounds is a task of legal doctrine. While such a doctrine cannot recommend any specific outcome, it can rationalise matters. As is the case with most difficult decisions, there are valid reasons both for and against defending the Union's values.

2.2 *Grounds Against Defending the Union's Values*

Powerful arguments suggest caution. One of these, much deployed by the Polish government, refers to the pair of democracy and national identity. Article 2 TEU states democracy as a fundamental value; Article 4 (2) TEU protects the Member States' 'national identities, inherent in their fundamental structures, political and constitutional'. If a democratically elected governing majority modifies these fundamental political and constitutional structures—this most 'sacred' area of national sovereignty—there is strong reason to assume that neither the Union nor other Member States should intervene. From a comparative view, the situation in Poland or in Hungary is far less critical than the one in Russia or Turkey.[25] Furthermore, understanding the Union's values in an exacting manner would create the need to intervene in many Member States. This can hardly be the intention of the TEU.

Another valid argument is the consideration not to damage the Union. Articles 1 and 3 TEU task the Union to develop policies for the good of its citizens. Any attempt to force an elected government under a common constitution can easily result in explosive conflicts. They may even endanger the constitution itself.[26] One need only think of the escalation caused by the actions of the Spanish central state against the governing majority of Catalonia.[27] And European actions against the current governing majority in Poland lack important resources which supported the Spanish central state against the Catalonian government: a clear democratic mandate, a developed national consciousness, and the hard instrument of federal execution. Polish representatives have already declared that they consider European

[22] CJEU, Case C-286/12 *Commission v. Hungary*, ECLI:EU:C:2012:687, para. 24 et seq.; critically Halmai (2017), p. 471.

[23] On this Ahtisaari et al. (2000), para. 116; Schorkopf (2002), Lachmayer (2017).

[24] BVerfGE 140, 317 – *Identitätskontrolle*; Hirsch Ballin (2016), p. 133; Kochenov (2015), p. 153.

[25] Weiler (2016), p. 314.

[26] Dyzenhaus (2012); comparative Federalism is instructive in this respect, Möllers and Schneider (2018), p. 5 et seq.

[27] García Morales (2018), p. 791 et seq.

actions against their remodelling of the judiciary as illegitimate.[28] It appears possible that a European defence of values may fail, which might inflict lasting damage on the Union's authority and demonstrate the frailty of the foundations of the common European house. The Union is not built for such conflict: since its 'constitutional moment' of overcoming the French 'empty seat', the search for consensus is key to its operation.[29]

But success, too, might plunge the Union into serious trouble. If the Union prevails over the combative Polish government, this would imply an enormous proof of power. The Union would significantly gain in stature vis-à-vis its Member States should it succeed in transforming its instruments, so far widely considered as rather ineffective, into a kind of effective federal execution.[30] This could be regarded as a huge step towards the EU's becoming a federal state, since what the Union primarily lacks in this regard is precisely such power. Such a prospect of *Staatswerdung* could cause a backlash from many Member States, which might equally endanger the Union. For all these reasons, the Union's hesitations should not be misconceived as mere opportunism.[31]

2.3 *Grounds in Favour of Defending the Union's Values*

At the same time, there are substantial legal grounds for the Union to defend European values. Three of them appear particularly pertinent: the European self-understanding as a community of values, Union citizenship and the principle of mutual trust.[32]

A first reason for the Union to defend its values results from its self-understanding, stipulated in the Treaties, as a liberal-democratic peace project. According to Article 2 TEU, the Union has been 'founded' on the respect for these values. This applies not only to the Union's supranational institutions, but also to its Member States. Article 2 TEU expresses standards for *any* public action in the European legal space.[33] Respecting and promoting these values is the key requirement for membership, as stipulated in Article 49 TEU. The term 'value' underlines the character of these principles as 'supreme and final normative

[28]See the statement by Polish Prime Minister Mateusz Morawiecki, quoted after Steinbeis (2018); the Vice President of the Polish Constitutional Court has announced that he would consider any judgment of the Court of Justice of the European Union against Poland as illegitimate, see Muszyński (2018).

[29]van Middelaar (2016), pp. 107 et seq., 120.

[30]The Polish compliance with the interim measures ordered by the CJEU in Case C-619/18, *Commission v. Poland*, with regard to the Supreme Court might be an indication.

[31]Cf., e.g., Kochenov and Pech (2016), p. 1062.

[32]On the legal grounds for intervention Closa et al. (2014), pp. 5–7; Hillion (2016), pp. 60–64.

[33]In detail von Bogdandy (2010), p. 13 et seq.

grounds'.[34] In Article 2 TEU, all Member States declare who they are and what they stand for; they articulate the deep logic of their institutional practice and the moral convictions of their citizens. In short: Article 2 TEU positivises the Union's self-understanding as a community of values.

In the light of substantiated evidence that Polish measures violate European values, a European silence would speak volumes. It would question this very community: the common axiological basis would appear either as an unfounded illusion or as a foundation that includes developments such as the Polish ones. In both cases, the self-understanding cultivated so far would hardly prove sustainable. The distance to Trump's USA would diminish. The Union would face a severe identity crisis.

Another legal ground results from the Union's mandate to protect all individuals in the European legal space, which includes protecting Polish citizens against their own government.[35] The CJEU says that 'Article 20 TFEU precludes national measures which have the effect of depriving citizens of the Union of the genuine enjoyment of the substance of the rights conferred by virtue of their status as citizens of the Union'.[36] This includes the 'essence' of EU fundamental rights, which is protected by Article 2 TEU. In *L.M. (Deficiencies in the system of justice)*, which deals precisely with the Polish measures, the CJEU emphasized this link between the essence of a Charter right (the right to a fair trial and an impartial court in Article 47 (2) CFR) and Article 2 TEU and allowed a Polish national to invoke this essence against the internal developments in his home state.[37] With this logic, presumably *any* violation of a value can somehow be tried in court.[38] This is a kind of 'reverse' *Solange* doctrine: outside the scope of application of the Charter of Fundamental Rights, Member States remain autonomous with respect to fundamental rights, *as long as* they guarantee the standard of Article 2 TEU.[39] If this standard is undercut, all public institutions in the European legal space must enforce the essence of the Union's fundamental rights against any measures of the Member State concerned.[40]

The Union's steps against Poland are important not only on a normative, but also on a cognitive level.[41] Such steps disprove the assumption that all Polish citizens stand with the governing majority. Indeed, many Polish citizens fight for liberal

---

[34]Luhmann (1993), p. 19; cf. also Habermas (1992), p. 311 et seq.

[35]Franzius (2018), p. 384.

[36]CJEU, Case C-34/09 *Ruiz Zambrano*, ECLI:EU:C:2011:124, para. 42.

[37]CJEU, Case C-216/18 PPU *Minister for Justice and Equality*, ECLI:EU:C:2018:586. The term 'deficiency' can be found in the case's denomination by the Advocate General as well as in the press release, CJEU, Press Release No. 113/18. In detail von Bogdandy and Spieker (2019).

[38]Spieker (2019), Schmidt and Bogdanowicz (2018), p. 1090.

[39]In detail von Bogdandy et al. (2012), p. 489; von Bogdandy et al. (2015), p. 235; von Bogdandy and Spieker (2019).

[40]Cf. the contributions in Steinbeis et al. (2015), Croon-Gestefeld (2017), p. 371; Blauberger (2016), p. 280; Russo (2014), Kochenov (2013), p. 145.

[41]Mälksoo (2009), p. 653.

democracy in their country.[42] In doing so, they refer to their status as citizens of the Union, as is shown by the European flag accompanying government-critical demonstrations. For Union citizenship, this might be a historic moment: it gains genuine political weight.

A third reason for the Union to defend its values is the principle of mutual trust. In the *L.M. (Deficiencies in the system of justice)* judgment, the Court made a clear point: measures like the Polish ones endanger the fundamental structure of the Union because they undermine mutual trust, without which vital areas of European cooperation cease to function.[43] The principle of mutual trust states: all Member States *must trust* that all Member States respect Union law and its fundamental rights in particular.[44] The status quo of integration can hardly be maintained without mutual trust.[45] But such trust requires defending the values on which it stands.[46]

3 The Principles Applied

3.1 The Toolbox

Many instruments might be used to defend European values. They are of diverse legal nature (political, administrative and judicial, binding and non-binding), they pertain to different legal orders and they are applied by different, sometimes even competing institutions, such as a constitutional court and the CJEU. That calls for a coordinating legal doctrine comprehending several legal orders.

Such a doctrine should not force the different instruments into a Procrustean bed. Instead, it should elaborate their diversity while indicating how to connect them as part of a functional tool box. Coordinated actions are more promising, whereas uncoordinated ones might be counterproductive. In more general terms: a clear and univocal reaction of the many European voices is essential for the protection of the Union's values.

Instruments of Union law are at the centre of attention.[47] This is justified insofar as action by the Union reduces the pressure on Member States to take steps on an individual level: the latter, e.g., a reprisal, can be even more explosive than pressure

[42]The current governing majority only received 37.58% of all votes cast, with a voter turnout of 50.92%.

[43]CJEU, *Minister for Justice and Equality*, *supra* note 37, para. 35. In detail, Regan (2018), p. 231.

[44]CJEU, Opinion 2/13 *Adhésion de l'Union à la CEDH*, ECLI:EU:C:2014:2454, para. 191; Lenaerts (2017), p. 805.

[45]CJEU, Case C-411/10 *N.S. and Others*, ECLI:EU:C:2011:865, para. 83; in detail von Bogdandy (2018), p. 487.

[46]CJEU, Case C-578/16 PPU *C.K. and Others*, ECLI:EU:C:2017:127, para. 95.

[47]For an overview see Closa et al. (2014) as well as the accounts given in Closa and Kochenov (2016) and Jakab and Kochenov (2017).

by the Union.[48] Among the instruments of the political institutions, measures taken under Article 7 TEU, the Commission's Rule of Law Framework and the rule of law dialogue of the Council are at the forefront.[49] The Commission's Justice Scoreboard 2018 has become a supervisory instrument, too,[50] as has the Commission's Country Report on Poland within the framework of the European Semester.[51] Regarding some Member States, the Union disposes of additional instruments. The Cooperation and Verification Mechanism in the Treaties of Accession with Bulgaria and Romania is meant to 'see the two countries develop the effective administrative and judicial systems needed'.[52] The Treaty of Accession with Croatia contains a similar instrument.[53] Further instruments are being planned: the Commission wants to make funding subject to respecting EU values[54] and to launch an 'EU Justice, Rights and Values Fund' with an overall budget allocation of 947 million EUR.[55]

In the framework of the European Parliament, there are the plenary debate, the law on sanctioning radical political parties,[56] as well as disciplining instruments within Europe's political alliances.[57]

---

[48]Müller (2015), p. 145.

[49]Conclusions of the Council of the EU and the Member States meeting within the Council on ensuring respect for the rule of law (16134/14).

[50]Cf. Communication from the Commission to the European Parliament, the Council, the European Central Bank, the European Economic and Social Committee and the Committee of the Regions. The 2018 EU Justice Scoreboard (COM(2018) 364 final), p. 4 et seq. On the Justice Scoreboard, Dori (2015), Jakab and Lorincz (2017).

[51]Country Report Poland 2018 accompanying the document Communication from the Commission to the European Parliament, the Council, the European Central Bank and the Eurogroup: 2018 European Semester: Assessment of progress on structural reforms, prevention and correction of macroeconomic imbalances, and results of in-depth reviews under Regulation (EU) No 1176/2011 (SWD(2018) 219 final), pp. 3, 29.

[52]Cf. the corresponding reports by the Commission, most recently Report from the Commission to the European Parliament and the Council, On Progress in Bulgaria under the Cooperation and Verification (COM(2018) 850 final); Vachudova (2016), p. 270; Carp (2014), p. 1.

[53]Act concerning the conditions of accession of the Republic of Croatia and the adjustments to the Treaty on European Union, the Treaty on the Functioning of the European Union and the Treaty establishing the European Atomic Energy Community (2012) OJ L112/21, Art. 36. In detail, Łazowski (2012), pp. 33–36.

[54]Commission Proposal for a Regulation of the European Parliament and of the Council on the protection of the Union's budget in case of generalised deficiencies as regards the rule of law in the Member States (COM(2018) 324 final), Art. 2; see also Halmai (2018b).

[55]Annex to the Communication from the Commission to the European Parliament, the European Council, the Council, the European Economic and Social Committee and the Committee of the Regions, A modern budget for a Union that protects, empowers and defends: The multiannual financial framework for 2021–2027 (COM(2018) 321 final), p. 48.

[56]Regulation (EU, Euratom) 1141/2014 on the statute and funding of European political parties and European political foundations (2014) OJ L317/1, art. 3 and art. 6.

[57]Art. 9 of the European People's Party Statutes, for example, permits the exclusion of both individual and Member State political parties, but does not define a reason for exclusion. Similar provisions are contained in Art. 16 Statutes of the Alliance of Liberals and Democrats for Europe Party.

Then there are the courts.[58] Unlike political bodies, they cannot avoid making decisions. The CJEU can be called upon to decide via the infringement and the preliminary ruling procedures; both can lead to severe financial sanctions. Furthermore, the CJEU can support actions of political institutions: an important example for this is the role it attributes to the qualifications made in the Commission's proposal to institute a procedure under Article 7 TEU.[59] Accordingly, such a proposal is sensible even when the Council and the European Council are unlikely to act.

The Union's institutions apart, those of the Member States can also defend European values. In this context, the tool box of international law is to be considered, from retaliatory measures to the mechanisms of the Vienna Convention on the Law of Treaties[60] to the extreme and contested option of an eventual humanitarian intervention in case a state turns to state terrorism.[61] The governments of the Member States can coordinate such international instruments, as was the case against Austria in 2000.[62] They could also consider, and threaten, to advance integration among themselves, excluding the countries that do not conform with the values.[63]

Member State courts, too, dispose of relevant instruments. They can defend European values against their own state in the light of a 'reverse Solange' doctrine[64] or against another Member State in the light of a 'horizontal Solange' doctrine.[65] The CJEU can support them in this via preliminary rulings. An important question is to what extent national courts can proceed independently from Union law on such matters.[66]

Other pertinent measures are those of the Council of Europe, especially recommendations issued by its political institutions or by the Commission for Democracy through Law (Venice Commission), as well as decisions of the ECtHR.[67] While the Council of Europe far exceeds the EU-centred European legal space, its relevance inside the European legal space flows from Article 6 (3) TEU, Article 52 (3) and Article 53 of the CFR. On an operative level, there is a close institutional connection.[68]

---

[58] On this, see in particular Huber (2017), p. 409 et seq.

[59] CJEU, *Minister for Justice and Equality*, *supra* note 37, paras. 69 et seq.

[60] In detail, see Binder (2013).

[61] Crawford (2013), p. 931; International Law Association (2018), p. 20 et seq.

[62] In detail, see Schorkopf (2002), p. 77.

[63] Franzius (2018), p. 388.

[64] On this, see above, Sect. 2.3. See also the presently pending references on a preliminary ruling in the cases *Miasto Łowicz v Skarb Państwa – Wojewoda Łódzki* (C-558/18); *Prokuratura Okręgowa w Płocku v VX, WW, XV* (C-563/18); *Prokuratura Rejonowa w Słubicach* (C-623/18).

[65] See in particular Canor (2013); a first case of application is the judgment of the Irish High Court in the *Celmer* case, *supra* note 16.

[66] As indicated in BVerfGE 140, 317 – *Identitätskontrolle*.

[67] Cf. on the Venice Commission, Nergelius (2015), p. 291; Grabenwarter (2018), p. 21.

[68] von Bogdandy (2008), p. 69 et seq.

Given that this legal framework comprises instruments of Union law, international law and the law of the Member States, it pertains to European law and not simply to Union law, international or domestic law alone.[69] In the tradition of public law thinking, such a doctrinal framework is to contribute to legal instruments promoting their legitimacy as well as their efficacy. Its most important building blocks are legal basis (Sect. 3.2), procedure (Sect. 3.3), the material standards (Sect. 3.4), and control (Sect. 3.5).

3.2 Questions of Competence

Any action to protect European values is prone to escalation. Therefore, it should be in the hands of institutions that can shoulder such a responsibility and manage conflicts. The first aspect responding to this concern is the requirement of a legal basis, in many cases even the need of a specific competence.[70] Thus, the first question is to verify whether its adoption and use are supported by a legal basis.

3.2.1 Article 7 TEU in the Order of Competences

Article 7 TEU plays a key role in this respect, as it might bar other reactions to systemic deficiencies under Article 2 TEU. In this case, the defence of the values would be completely under the control of the governments of the Member States, united in the Union's institutions. Responsibility, therefore, would be crystal clear. The drawback is that the extremely high requirements of Article 7 TEU might leave EU values without defence. Besides this consequentialist consideration, doctrinal arguments likewise militate against interpreting Article 7 TEU as an exclusive mechanism.

A first issue is whether Article 7 TEU prohibits pertinent measures by Member States. Article 3 TFEU does not list Article 7 TEU. Article 4 TFEU, which enumerates the main areas of shared responsibilities, does not feature Article 7 TEU either. However, it lists the space of freedom, security and law. Hence, there could be an argument to assume precedence of measures of Union law vis-à-vis a defence by Member States. Then there is Article 344 TFEU.[71]

The CJEU's case-law seemed to point towards pre-emption, especially in cases like *Melloni*, which excluded the unilateral enforcement of one Member State's

[69] On this understanding of European law, see in detail already Mosler (1968), p. 481 et seq.; von Bogdandy (2016), p. 589.

[70] Bast (2006), p. 30 et seq.; Bast (2018), para. 13 et seq.

[71] On the expansive interpretation of this clause, see CJEU, Case C-459/03 *Commission v. Ireland (Mox Plant)*, ECLI:EU:C:2006:345, paras. 123 et seq.

constitutional principles against another.[72] After the German Federal Constitutional Court emphasized its competence to protect the constitutional identity of the German Basic Law against measures taken by other Member States, too,[73] the CJEU has acknowledged that European law leaves room for the national defence of fundamental principles.[74] Since the European values of Article 2 TEU and the identity-informing fundamental principles of the Member State constitutions widely overlap,[75] neither the competences of Article 7 TEU nor other instruments of Union law block Member State institutions from defending European values, according to this case-law. This corresponds to the logic of the European legal space not to monopolise a central question such as value defence in one institution. The considerable need for coordination must be met with other means.[76]

The second issue is whether Article 7 TEU bars actions *taken by other Union institutions*. Article 7 TEU does not contain an explicit statement as to whether other Union institutions may defend European values using other instruments. The general rules apply. It is well established that a specific procedure designed to deal with a certain problem does not exclude developing other instruments,[77] a core statement since the *Van Gend en Loos* judgment.[78] Accordingly, it is, in principle, admissible to develop new instruments,[79] such as the Commission's Rule of Law Framework, or the Justice Score Board.

Nevertheless, Article 7 TEU plays a role. Its wording, the inclusion of the European Council and the extremely laborious procedure in Article 7 TEU indicate that it stipulates the most *intensive* form of defence of values. Therefore, the Union lacks any competence for developing stronger instruments. Hence, the expulsion of a Member State[80] or the dismissal of its government, an instrument the Spanish government used against the Catalan government, are off limits.[81] All instruments complementing those of Article 7 TEU in defending the values of Article 2 TEU must be less severe.[82]

---

[72] CJEU, Case C-399/11 *Melloni*, ECLI:EU:C:2013:107.

[73] BVerfGE 140, 317 – *Identitätskontrolle*.

[74] At least within the scope of fundamental rights, CJEU, Joined Cases C-404 and C-659/15 PPU *Aranyosi and Căldăraru*, ECLI:EU:C:2016:198.

[75] Cf. Opinion of Advocate General Cruz Villalón in CJEU, *Gauweiler and Others*, *supra* note 18.

[76] On this Sects. 3.3 and 3.4.

[77] Bast (2006), pp. 60–63.

[78] CJEU, Case C-26/62 *Van Gend en Loos v. Administratie der Belastingen*, ECLI:EU:C:1963:1, p. 11.

[79] Bast (2006), pp. 42–67. Cf. also Brauneck (2019), pp. 37 and 59.

[80] On this, see the proposal by Stein (1998), p. 890; Blagoev (2011), p. 191.

[81] Recently in Spain under Article 155 Spanish Constitution. On this, García Morales (2018).

[82] In this sense also CJEU, *Minister for Justice and Equality*, *supra* note 37; see also below, Sect. 3.4.

3.2.2 Instruments of Secondary Law

So far, action under Article 7 TEU is paralyzed by the Council and the European Council. Can other institutions defend the values through other instruments? As has been shown, Article 7 TEU does not prohibit other instruments. But any new instrument needs an appropriate legal basis. This requirement results from the necessity to legitimise any action of public authorities, including 'soft' measures.[83] A new instrument might even need a specific competence.[84]

With a view to the European Parliament, its general tasks allow it to discuss any systemic deficiencies in the Member States,[85] and it has done so for a long time. Its resolutions have gained public attention. However, they have not had much impact yet.

Measures taken by the other institutions could yield more powerful results, which is why the law is more demanding than with respect to the European Parliament, as has been shown by developments in other fields. The CJEU has declared Commission Communications invalid due to lack of competence (!).[86] The Court's requirement of a legal basis is particularly striking in the OMT procedure, whose subject was the mere announcement of a new instrument for purchasing bonds by ECB president Mario Draghi.[87]

The legal service of the Council has disputed the power of the Commission to establish the rule of law mechanism;[88] here, the general problem comes to the fore. However, the admissibility of this mechanism flows from the Commission's right to make requests under Article 7 TEU as well as its general role of a guardian of the Treaties according to Article 17 (1) TEU. On that basis, the Commission can also examine whether the Member States respect the values of Article 2 TEU. The competence to issue corresponding recommendations follows from Article 292 4th sentence TFEU.[89] These considerations also support the Justice Score Board.

Similar questions have emerged in the Council of Europe. One need only think of the sanctions imposed by its Parliamentary Assembly against Russian

[83]See Nettesheim (2018), para. 200; Senden (2004), p. 478 et seq. On the legal boundaries, von Bogdandy et al. (2015), pp. 273–275.

[84]In detail Bast (2006), para. 23 et seq.

[85]Bast (2006), para. 28.

[86]CJEU, Case C-57/95 *France v. Commission*, ECLI:EU:C:1997:164; CJEU, Case C-233/02 *France v. Commission*, ECLI:EU:C:2004:173, para. 40; Opinion of Advocate General Michal Bobek in CJEU, Case C-16/16 P *Commission v. Belgium*, ECLI:EU:C:2017:959.

[87]Opinion of Advocate General Cruz Villalón in CJEU, *Gauweiler and Others*, *supra* note 18.

[88]Commission's Communication on a new EU Framework to strengthen the rule of law: – compatibility with the Treaties (10296/14).

[89]Giegerich (2015), pp. 535–536; Toggenburg (2013).

parliamentarians since the annexation of the Crimea.[90] Another example are the opinions from the Venice Commission issued without a request from the Convention state concerned.[91] All these measures constitute reactions to systemic problems and can be treated analogously to the considerations on the instrument tool box of Union law.

3.2.3 The Justiciability of the Values

The defence of values by political institutions has not been very effective so far. As so often in the history of integration, the question arises whether the judiciary can compensate for this. For the CJEU, this is a question of its powers within the procedures of the Articles 257, 258 and 267 TFEU. Article 7 TEU does not block these procedures; Article 269 TFEU only determines that the Court cannot review the material prerequisites of Article 7 TEU. Given the lack of any explicit ban and the CJEU's general role in the *union of law,* there is good reason to assume that values can play a role in procedures under the Articles 257, 258 and 267 TFEU.[92]

The actual crux is the justiciability of the values of Article 2 TEU. The term *value* can be interpreted as the Treaty makers' attributing a vagueness to Article 2 TEU that excludes judicial application.[93] Arguments relating to the separation of powers might support this conclusion. The judicial application of values would immensely extend the courts' sphere of power to highly political conflicts.[94] All of this can be avoided by considering the values not to be justiciable.

However, following the established path of European Union law, the Commission and the CJEU have legally and credibly condensed the values of Article 2 TEU so that they have become accessible to judicial decision making, the value of the rule of law being at the centre. The most important path to condensing the values lies in connecting these values to fundamental rights and the well-established principles of the common constitutional traditions.[95] The effort has proven successful: even from the Polish 'White paper on the reform of the Polish judiciary'—which presents the highly controversial changes in the Polish judiciary as conforming to the values—

---

[90]Reconsideration on substantive grounds of the previously ratified credentials of the Russian delegation (Resolution 1990 (2014) Final version) as well as the extension through: Challenge, on substantive grounds, of the still unratified credentials of the delegation of the Russian Federation (Resolution 2034 (2015) Final version); Steininger (2018), Henderson (2018), p. 393.

[91]von Bogdandy and Sonnevend (2015).

[92]In detail, Spieker (2019), Schmidt and Bogdanowicz (2018), pp. 1069–1073; Hilf and Schorkopf (2017), para. 46; Hillion (2016), p. 59; Franzius (2018), p. 381 (386); a different attitude is expressed by Levits (2018), p. 239 (262); Nicolisi (2015), p. 613 (643); Martenczuk (2018), p. 41 (46).

[93]Kochenov and Pech (2018), p. 512 (520); Nicolisi (2015), p. 643.

[94]On the German discussion, Schmitt (2011), Böckenförde (1990), p. 25.

[95]CJEU, *Minister for Justice and Equality*, *supra* note 37. On the common constitutional traditions, see Cassese (2017), p. 939 et seq.; Graziadei and de Caria (2017), p. 949 et seq.

one can gather that European values have come to permit concrete legal assessment.[96] Two Commission communications in 2019 bring these developments together.[97]

Two judgments by the CJEU from 2018 are leading the way for the judicial operationalisation of the value of the rule of law. In the case *Associação Sindical dos Juízes Portugueses* (*ASJP*), the Court has operationalized the value of the rule of law by applying it together with another, specific and directly applicable Treaty provision. In the crucial passage, the Court states that 'Article 19 TEU [. . .] gives concrete expression to the value of the rule of law stated in Article 2'.[98] In the *L.M.* (*Deficiencies in the system of justice*) case, it enabled individuals to defend European values.[99] The case dealt with the protection of the separation of powers via an independent judiciary, and it accomplished this via the fundamental right to an impartial court and to a fair trial. The Court's approach is reminiscent of the German Federal Constitutional Court's Maastricht decision, which also made a fundamental principle (democracy) justiciable via an individual right (right to vote, Article 38 (1) of German Basic Law).[100] Since the *L.M.* case, the 'vigilance of individuals concerned to protect their rights' might also protect European values.[101]

Accordingly, the courts, including Member State courts, can decide on the values of Article 2 TEU.[102] The values have become judicially applicable though the doctrinal paths may vary.[103] This expansion of judicial competence mirrors the importance of the values and the judiciary's general role in the European legal space. By now, there is a judicial line of defence beyond the political rationality of Article 7 TEU.

The judicial applicability of European values means that constitutional courts, too, can defend them. However, in many Member States, Union law does not provide a *standard* of constitutional review, according to most constitutional courts concerned.[104] Some reasons for this reticence are of a rather more legal nature, especially the fact that Union law lacks constitutional rank in the domestic sphere. Other considerations are of a more political nature, in particular the consideration

---

[96]Chancellery of the Prime Minister of Poland (2018), para. 166.

[97]Communication from the Commission to the European Parliament, the European Council, the Council, the European Economic and Social Committee and thee Committee of the Regions, Strengthening the rule of law within the Union. A blueprint for action, COM/2019/343 final.

[98]CJEU, Case C-64/16 *Associação Sindical dos Juízes Portugueses*, ECLI:EU:C:2018:117.

[99]CJEU, *Minister for Justice and Equality*, *supra* note 37, para. 47 et seq.

[100]BVerfGE, 123, 267 – *Lissabon*; BVerfGE, 89, 155 – *Maastricht*; see, critically, Nettesheim (2009), p. 2869.

[101]CJEU, *Van Gend en Loos v. Administratie der Belastingen*, *supra* note 78.

[102]See, especially, CJEU, *Associação Sindical dos Juízes Portugueses*, *supra* note 98; CJEU, *Minister for Justice and Equality*, *supra* note 37; now also CJEU, Case C-619/18 *Commission/Poland*, ECLI:EU:C:2019:531, para. 47; AG Tanchev, Opinion in Case C-192/18 – *Commission/Poland*, para. 71; AG Tanchev, Opinion in Joined Cases C-585, C-624 and C-625/18 – *A.K.* (*Indépendance de la chambre disciplinaire de la Cour suprême*), para. 77.

[103]von Bogdandy and Spieker (2019).

[104]In detail, Paris (2017), p. 798 et seq.; Mengozzi (2015), p. 707; Lacchi (2015), p. 1663.

that the constitutional courts' abstention from applying Union law facilitates a division of tasks that reduces conflicts between the CJEU and the constitutional courts.[105]

These considerations meet with objections. There is enough interpretive scope to include Union law into the purview of constitutional courts,[106] as just decided by the so far reticent German Federal Constitutional Court.[107] Substantively, such a step would result in a more effective implementation of Union law. Moreover, it would strengthen the constitutional courts themselves: they could take a more active role in interpreting Union law and shaping the European legal space.[108]

3.3 Procedure

The pivotal point of the CJEU's *L.M.* (*Deficiencies in the system of justice*) judgment is the fundamental right to a fair trial, Article 47 (2) CFR. It expresses a general legal principle which, in the European legal space, protects not only individuals, but also public authorities.[109] Moreover, it applies not only in judicial procedures, but whenever a legal subject is faced with the exercise of public authority,[110] especially when substantial interests are at stake.[111] This is the case with conflicts concerning systemic deficiencies: the interests in question here are the national reputation, the interest of prosecution, the effective functioning of the national judiciary, financial interests as well as the participation in institutions of the Union. A fair procedure is important not only for the legitimacy of any specific decision, but also for general cohesion in Europe.[112]

Of the many procedural questions, only two will be addressed here. The first one concerns political and administrative procedures. A point of criticism regarding the measures taken by the Commission and the European Parliament is that their motivation is not the defence of Union values, but the sanctioning of an EU-critical stance. To prove this point, it is said that measures comparable to the Polish ones, when taken by EU-friendly governments, do not elicit any reaction.[113]

---

[105]See Paris (2017), p. 814.

[106]In detail Paris (2017), p. 809 et seq.; Griebel (2014), p. 204; Bäcker (2015), p. 411.

[107]BVerfG, Order of 6 November 2019, 1 BvR 16/13 – *Recht auf Vergessen II.*

[108]On this discussion, Voßkuhle (2018), pp. 175 and 197; Komárek (2015), p. 75; Thym (2015), p. 56.

[109]Jarass (2016), para. 12.

[110]In this respect, Art. 47 of the Charter transcends Art. 6 ECHR; see also Alber (2016), para. 10. On the validity of art. 47 para. 2 CFR also from an administrative procedural level, Nowak (2011), para. 44.

[111]On the spill-over effects over administrative procedure, cf. Jarass (2016).

[112]Luhmann (1975), pp. 34 et seq., 48 et seq., 116–120; this was also an insight from the Eurozone crisis, Farahat and Krenn (2018), p. 384.

[113]Mendelski (2016).

Hence, the two institutions are accused of misusing their powers for partisan purposes.

As described above (Sect. 2.1), there is room for discretion when deciding whether to initiate a procedure. The accusation is thus to be dealt with under the doctrine on discretion. This doctrine does, however, not limit parliamentary debate: indeed, it is a general principle that parliaments enjoy full freedom of what to debate.[114] By contrast, the European Commission faces limits.[115] If it uses an instrument of supervision to sanction an integration-critical general attitude, this would amount to an illegal use of discretion. But to identify such improper use, hard evidence is needed. To date, the Commission's actions seem justified by the extraordinary severity of the situations at hand.[116]

With regard to judicial procedures, the core question is as to whether Member State courts have to refer a case to the CJEU if its subject is a possible systemic deficiency in another Member State. A national court can treat such a deficiency both in the light of the European values, as did the Irish High Court in the *Celmer* case,[117] and in the light of the fundamental principles of the national constitution, as in the case 'Identitätskontrolle' of the German Federal Constitutional Court.[118] The German Court has been much criticised for not having made a preliminary reference.[119]

The general question of a constitutional court's obligation to make such a reference has extensively been discussed.[120] When it comes to defending values, such a referral to the CJEU is of particular importance for hedging the relationship between the Member States in question. Only a procedure before the CJEU allows for defending European values in a process which respects the very rule of law because it requires a fair procedure. The Member State concerned must be involved. A national court can hardly provide the government of another state with adequate participation. A procedure before the CJEU appears to provide the only orderly way of deciding critical questions in another legal order. There is, moreover, the consideration that 'Europe should speak with one voice'. Even if national courts refer to *principles of national identity* instead of *European values*, such national principles can be defended better in the framework of European values.[121]

---

[114]CJEU, Case C–230/81 *Luxemburg v. Parliament*, ECLI:EU:C:1983:32, para. 39; Bast (2006), para. 28.

[115]Bleckmann (1997), p. 59 et seq.

[116]In detail, Hoffmeister (2015), p. 195 et seq.

[117]IEHC, *supra* note 16.

[118]BVerfGE 140, 317 – *Identitätskontrolle*.

[119]On the criticism, Burchardt (2016), p. 527 et seq.; Schönberger (2016), p. 422; Nettesheim (2016), p. 424; Sauer (2016), p. 1134; Classen (2016), p. 304; Nowag (2016), p. 1450 et seq.; Rugge (2016), p. 789.

[120]On this, see Paris (2017).

[121]In detail, Spieker (2020).

3.4 Material Standards

All *systemic deficiency* instruments contain elements describing a particularly problematic situation. Therefore, similar questions of interpretation and application arise. Three questions will be discussed: the interpretive condensing of the requirements (Sect. 3.4.1), the importance of a comprehensive and moreover collective assessment (Sect. 3.4.2) as well as the question of how concrete a violation must be (Sect. 3.4.3).

3.4.1 Red Lines

As doctrinal treaties, handbooks and commentaries on the German Basic Law show, many important features of a constitution, even of an entire legal order, can be inferred from principles such as human dignity, rule of law and democracy. To this end, German doctrine considers these principles as 'laws of construction'[122] and even 'optimization requirements',[123] thereby justifying a scholarship that has something to say on almost any important issue as well as a judiciary that is confident in its sweeping law-making role. There are hints that the Commission is moving towards a similar expansive understanding of EU values, in particular of the rule of law value.[124] Indeed, the Venice Commission's Rule of Law Checklist with its 53 pages, to which the European Commission refers, almost looks like a detailed manual that provides practitioners with guidance on almost any relevant question.[125]

This cannot be a model for dealing with the values of Article 2 TEU, particularly insofar as they apply to the Member States' legal orders. By using the term *value* in Article 2 TEU, the Treaty makers imply that its provisions are to be understood as vague and, thus, open.[126] And this openness is not an authorisation for the Union's institutions to gradually outline an ever more detailed common constitutional law. While Article 2 TEU has become judicially applicable (see above Sect. 3.2), this does not change the fact that it should not develop into a homogeneity clause similar to Article 28 German Basic Law or Article IV Sec. 4 and Articles XIII to XV of the US Constitution.[127] That would force the constitutional autonomy of the Member

---

[122]Dreier (2015), paras. 5, 8 et seq.; Reimer (2001), p. 26 et seq.

[123]Schulze-Fielitz (2015), para. 44.

[124]Communication from the Commission to the European Parliament, the European Council and the Council, Further strengthening the Rule of Law within the Union State of play and possible next steps, COM(2019) 163 final, p. 1.

[125]European Commission for Democracy Through Law, Rule of Law Checklist, CDL-AD(2016) 007 with its 53 pages just on the rule of law. The European Commission refers to this document as authoritative, see Communication from the Commission, COM(2019) 163 final, p. 8.

[126]Openness is a pivotal point of Schmitt's criticism, Schmitt (2011), pp. 23, 53 et seq.

[127]On this, see Giegerich (2015), p. 499 et seq. For a comparative view, Palermo and Kösserl (2017), p. 321 et seq.

States into a far too narrow corridor, going against European constitutional pluralism.

The 'thickening' of the Article 2 values might endanger European constitutional pluralism. The diversity of Member State constitutions, which is protected by Union law, is enormous. It comprises states with strong, weak or no constitutional courts, markedly different ways of organizing judicial independence, and considerably divergent protections of fundamental rights; it allows for republics and monarchies, parliamentary and semi-presidential systems, strong and weak parliaments, Westminster democracies and consociational democracies, and democracies with strong or weak party structures; and it respects strong or weak societal institutions, unitarian or federal orders as well as anarcho-syndicalist, Catholic, civic, laic, Ottoman, postcolonial, Protestant, socialist and statist constitutional traditions. All these elements play into the various systems of checks and balances, which is why European diversity is particularly pronounced when it comes to this basic feature of any constitutional order. It would be incompatible with this diversity to interpret and apply the values of Article 2 TEU in concrete cases in order to develop them into a kind of DNA of how to set up checks and balances on public authority in the European legal space.

Against this understanding one might argue that the EU Commission has made very detailed requirements on candidate countries,[128] including, for example, extraditing a former Croat general to the ICTY.[129] These detailed requirements, never challenged in Court, might be applicable to Member States after accession as well.[130] Technically, however, these requirements are not linked to Article 2 TEU but to the political Copenhagen criteria. Moreover, candidate countries and Member States have a fundamentally different status, and the accession criteria, finally, are subject to severe criticism themselves.[131]

The constitutional considerations (2) resulted in the conclusion that the instruments for fighting systemic deficiencies serve the cause of ensuring essentials of the European union (*Verbund*), in particular its self-understanding as a community of values, the core of fundamental rights, and the principle of mutual trust, but nothing more. This explains the values' vagueness as well as the extremely high hurdles in Article 7 TEU. The logic of restraint extends to the entire tool box. Consequently, the values are to be interpreted such as to only prohibit particularly problematic measures, without indicating a 'right way', let alone stipulating the basic organisation of Member State institutions. In this sense, they do not constitute 'laws of construction', but rather 'red lines'.[132]

---

[128]See, e.g., European Commission, Communication: Agenda 2000. Vol. I: For a stronger and wider Union, COM(2000) 97 final, p. 42.

[129]For a detailed analysis, see Rötting (2009), pp. 117 et seq.

[130]On the Copenhagen criteria as guidelines for the application of Article 2 TEU, see Hillion (2016), p. 66.

[131]Kochenov (2008), p. 311; Kosar et al. (2019), 443 et seq.

[132]In detail, von Bogdandy et al. (2018), p. 963.

The CJEU's decisions can be understood in this light. The logic of red lines explains a reasoning which may appear rather 'thin' and therefore little convincing at first sight. In most cases, the pertinent value is illustrated only in a general manner, with reference to principles;[133] but there is only little interpretive development in view of the matter concerned. The central aspect is *what cannot be tolerated*. While the lack of interpretive development limits the persuasive power of the judgment, it is by this abstaining that interpretative standards which could considerably limit the Member States' constitutional autonomy can be avoided.[134]

In the seminal *Aranyosi e Căldăraru* judgment, the Court refers only to absolute rights, especially to the prohibition of inhuman treatment,[135] i.e. to norms which are part of the core of European self-understanding.[136] This likewise holds true for the essence of non-absolute rights: In the *L.M. (Deficiencies in the system of justice)* judgment, the CJEU states that the newly established disciplinary chamber is problematic, given its appearance as an instrument to cow judges.[137] The judgment outlines further 'red lines' by referring to the qualifications on Poland made in the Commission proposal under Article 7 TEU. Of course, the Court does not treat the proposal as a source of law. Nevertheless, the 'information (...) is particularly relevant' and thus serves to assess the Polish measures.[138] This Commission proposal concretely articulates which measures are incompatible with the values and must therefore be revoked for crossing 'red lines'.

This logic of 'red lines' provides indications on how to rebut the presumption, founded in Article 49 TEU, that a Member State complies with European values. Such a doctrine, however, is fundamentally different from a conventional constitutional doctrine of principles that aims at developing from principles an 'overall structure' for the entire legal order.[139] It would rather have to follow the logic of 'negative dialectics', which is characterised by the very fact of not specifying what the ideal situation should look like, but rather what must not be.

---

[133]Cf., in particular, Proposal for a Council Decision on the determination of a clear risk of a serious breach by the Republic of Poland of the rule of law (COM(2017) 835 final), para. 6 et seq., and CJEU, *Minister for Justice and Equality*, *supra* note 37, paras. 62–67. At the same time, it should be underlined that the *L.M.* judgment provides much more justification than the similarly seminal CJEU, *Ruiz Zambrano*, *supra* note 36.

[134]On this way of forming standards, Lepsius (2011), p. 182 et seq.; von Bogdandy and Venzke (2014), p. 254 et seq.

[135]CJEU, *Aranyosi and Căldăraru*, *supra* note 74.

[136]Grabenwarter (2017), p. 3052.

[137]CJEU, *Minister for Justice and Equality*, *supra* note 37, para. 67.

[138]*Id.*, para. 61.

[139]Schuppert and Bumke (2000), pp. 28, 39; on 'guiding principles', Volkmann (2008), p. 67 et seq.

3.4.2 The Comprehensive and Collective Assessment

Most institutions base the determination that a value has been violated on a *comprehensive assessment*. The analysis of the Commission's and the CJEU's pertinent decisions shows that they consider a series of facts to this end, often described in detail, in the light of principles that remain abstract.[140] Such an application, which essentially consists in a comprehensive assessment of developments, events, measures and political statements, is an exercise in discretion and hence inevitably evaluative, and in that sense political. This easily gives rise to the accusation that the decisions are biased or motivated by illicit considerations.[141]

Yet, this practice of assessing is justified by three aspects. Firstly, it is the inevitable consequence of the restrained interpretation, which in turn is justified by the constitutional considerations described in the preceding passage. Secondly, the practice responds to the specific problems of legally capturing authoritarian tendencies. Thirdly, it must be taken into account that the comprehensive assessment is often based on similar perceptions of other institutions and thus takes place collectively (*Einschätzungsverbund*).

The central role of a comprehensive assessment is justified by the very nature of *systemic deficiencies*. Usually, the law is applied to a single action or measure. This mode fails with regard to authoritarian developments, as in most cases only a series of actions and measures *in their entirety* will reach the critical threshold. The actions and measures, taken individually, can often be plausibly justified.[142] The Polish government defends its judicial reforms by means of a legal comparison with 'unsuspicious' countries.[143] In order to establish a 'clear risk of a serious breach' of Article 2 TEU, a comprehensive view of all measures taken by the Polish government with regard to the judiciary is needed, with due consideration of the general political and social conditions of the country. One needs to assess the actions against the judiciary in the context of the actions against other controlling institutions, mainly the parliamentary opposition, the media, science, and NGOs.[144] This contextual approach has been confirmed by the Court of Justice stated in *A.K.*, which

[140]Proposal for a Council decision on the determination of a clear risk of a serious breach by the Republic of Poland of the rule of law (COM(2017) 835 final), paras. 109, 173; CJEU, *Minister for Justice and Equality*, *supra* note 37, para. 68; CJEU, Joined Cases C-585/18, C-624/18 and C-625/18 *A.K. (Indépendance de la chambre disciplinaire de la Cour supreme)*, ECLI:EU:C:2019:982, para. 127, 134, 152.

[141]See above, Sect. 3.3.

[142]Scheppele (2016), p. 105. Nevertheless, some Polish measures against the country's own constitutional court appear as rather clear cases, cf. Iustitia (2018), Gersdorf (2018); Venice Commission, Opinion on Amendments to the Act of 25 June 2015 on the Constitutional Tribunal of Poland, Opinion no. 833/2015, CDL-AD(2016)001, paras. 126, 137, 138.

[143]Chancellery of the Prime Minister of Poland (2018).

[144]This logic of the comprehensive assessment is by no means restricted to the values. The process of establishing a systemic deficiency in the banking sector is similar, cf. Regulation (EU) on European Union macro-prudential oversight of the financial system and establishing a European Systemic Risk Board (2010) OJ L331/1.

dealt with the independence of the Polish Supreme Court's Disciplinary Chamber.[145]

A third aspect contributing to the legitimacy of a comprehensive assessment lies in basing it on concurrent evaluations of other independent institutions, institutions with a recognized authority in questions of values. The regular application takes place in an *Einschätzungsverbund,* i.e., the comprehensive assessment of all circumstances must be widely shared. The more institutions perceive a substantial problem, the stronger the evidence for a systemic deficiency.

It is noteworthy that when it comes to systemic deficiencies, interpretation and application are not presented as being autonomous, but as part of a collective assessment involving many institutions of various legal orders. The Commission and the CJEU, but also many other institutions, recur to other authoritative sources when dealing with such questions, in particular to judgments of the ECtHR and opinions of the Venice Commission.[146] Evaluations of international bodies as well as civic organisations are also significant.[147] In the light of the cherished autonomy of Union law, it appears especially noteworthy that the Commission and the Court give much weight to evaluations under the national legal order concerned; such evaluations even enjoy particular relevance. In the Polish case, an important point is that authoritative Polish voices consider the governing majority's reforms as deeply unconstitutional.[148] Thus, a situation or measure is more likely to qualify as *systemically deficient* the more institutions of the various legal orders share this qualification.

Such a comprehensive assessment is also important in other respects. One need only think of the accusation that the Union itself does not meet the requirements that it demands Poland to fulfil.[149] Certainly, the possibility of the CJEU's judges to be re-elected does not meet the highest standards of judicial independence. However, in pertinent research, it is undisputed that the CJEU is an independent court.[150]

3.4.3 On the Concreteness of the Risk

The political institutions usually assess a general situation and decide whether there is a general risk for the values, for example by the Polish remodelling of its judiciary

[145] CJEU, *A.K. (Indépendance de la chambre disciplinaire de la Cour supreme)*, ECLI:EU:C:2019:982, paras. 142, 152.

[146] Cf. Proposal for a Council decision on the determination of a clear risk of a serious breach by the Republic of Poland of the rule of law (COM(2017) 835 final), paras. 18, 32, 95, 116 et seq.; CJEU, Case C-404/15 *Aranyosi and Căldăraru*, *supra* note 74, para. 90; Opinion of AG Tanchev in CJEU, *Minister for Justice and Equality*, *supra* note 37, para. 10.

[147] Proposal for a Council decision on the determination of a clear risk of a serious breach by the Republic of Poland of the rule of law (COM(2017) 835 final), paras. 33, 63, 76, 80, 82.

[148] *Id.*, paras. 19, 21, 29, 81, 83, 86; cf. in particular Iustitia (2018), Gersdorf (2018).

[149] Cf. Weiler (2016).

[150] Krenn (2018), p. 2024.

since 2015. For the courts, the question arises whether such abstract risk is enough for a judicial decision, or whether a risk would have to materialise concretely in the case at hand in order to be relevant. The *L.M.* case concerned the question of whether an Irish court must surrender an individual to Poland under a European arrest warrant notwithstanding the general remodelling of the Polish judiciary. The CJEU answered that the national court must verify in a two-step procedure (1) whether there is a systemic deficiency in Poland and (2) if there are 'substantial grounds for believing that the individual concerned will run a real risk of breach of his fundamental right to an independent tribunal and, therefore, of the essence of his fundamental right to a fair trial'.[151]

This two-step review helps to distinguish the legal procedure from the political one under Article 7 TEU. It thus contributes to justifying the CJEU's decision.[152] However, it meets with considerable doubts. Since the measures of the Polish government undermine the independence of the entire Polish judiciary, any case runs the risk of being decided by a compromised judge at some point. Moreover, the CJEU's stipulation that Member State judges must review the independence of their Polish colleagues[153] appears hardly feasible.[154] At least there is a reversal of the burden of proof: in case of a (general) systemic deficiency, it is the Member State in question to give evidence that there is no concrete risk for the individual concerned.[155]

3.5 Control

The last building block is the issue of legal protection. It deals with the question of whether and how the instruments' lawfulness as well as the lawfulness of their use can be judicially reviewed. Such review is a core aspect of the European rule of law: the control of public authority by independent and impartial courts is sometimes even considered the crowning element of the rule of law.[156] Article 269 TFEU therefore describes an exception that is to be interpreted narrowly.

Self-evident as this principle might appear, its application is problematic with regard to instruments that do not yield a legal consequence; the protection by the CJEU has long been fragmentary and uncertain in this respect. It appears anything but certain that a Member State can take legal action against a recommendation of the Commission in the framework of the rule of law procedure or against a

---

[151]CJEU, *Minister for Justice and Equality*, *supra* note 37, para. 75. On this, von Bogdandy et al. (2018), p. 983.

[152]Cf. above, Sect. 3.2.

[153]CJEU, *Minister for Justice and Equality*, *supra* note 37, para. 77 et seq.

[154]Wendel (2019), p. 111; Krajewski (2018), p. 792; Bárd and van Ballegooij (2018), p. 353.

[155]CJEU, *Minister for Justice and Equality*, *supra* note 37, para. 78.

[156]Cf. CJEU, Case C-294/83 *Les Verts v. Parliament*, ECLI:EU:C:1986:166.

classification in the Justice Score Board that damages its reputation. Yet, the more recent case-law of the CJEU is expanding judicial control with regard to such measures.[157] This should make control possible at least when a recommendation of the Commission results in indirect legal consequences, e.g., when it provides a basis for assuming a systemic deficiency.[158] However, there is need for more legal protection, e.g., against recommendations damaging a Member State's reputation.

Another challenge is how to coordinate judicial control between the various legal orders of the European legal space. This leads again to Article 267 TFEU. There is an urgent need for such coordination when defending European values or their equivalents in the national constitutions. The coordination and control of national courts is primarily a task of the CJEU. Yet this does not imply that the CJEU itself is beyond control: it remains subject to the general mechanisms, which assume particular importance with regard to this explosive question. In this respect, the multilevel cooperation of the European courts might find here its finest hour.[159]

4 Towards a Tyranny of Values?

To many people, the European institutions appear distant and foreign. If they urge or even try to force democratically elected governments to revise important political projects, invoking European values, they run the risk of being rejected as self-important, arbitrary and illegitimate actors. Just thumping on the lawfulness of such actions is hardly an appropriate response to accusations of moving towards a tyranny of values. 'Being right' is not sufficient. In order to credibly defend European values, one must make use of fair procedures to convincingly show a broad European public what the values require, why they have been violated and what needs to be done. Defending European values in such a way will not appear as potentially tyrannical, but rather what most European citizens expect the Union to do.[160]

Acknowledgments Translated from German by Annika Müller. I would like to thank the *Dienstagsrunde*, in particular Dr. Laura Hering, Giacomo Rugge, Matthias Schmidt, and Dimitri Spieker, for their valuable critique and support. Unless stated otherwise, all quotes translated from German were translated by the author.

---

[157]CJEU, Case C-16/16 P *Belgium v. Commission*, ECLI:EU:C:2018:79, para. 44; Case C-258/14 *Florescu and Others*, ECLI:EU:C:2017:448, para. 30; Case C-207/01 *Altair Chimica*, ECLI:EU:C:2003:451, para. 41; Opinion of Advocate General Cruz Villalón in CJEU, *Gauweiler and Others*, *supra* note 18, para. 27 et seq.; Gundel (2018), p. 593; Schmidt-Aßmann (2013), p. 103.

[158]In detail, see above, Sect. 3.4.1.

[159]Voßkuhle (2018), Huber (2017), p. 389.

[160]Special Eurobarometer 489 rule of law, <data.europa.eu/euodp/en/data/dataset/S2235_91_3_489_ENG>.

References

Ackerman B (1991) We the people, Volume 1: foundations. Belknap Press of Harvard University Press, Cambridge

Ackerman R, Desierto D, Volosin N (2011) Hyper-Presidentialism: separation of powers without checks and balances in Argentina and Philippines. Berkeley J Int Law 20:246–271

Ahtisaari M, Frowein J, Oreja M (2000) Report on the commitment of the Austrian Government to the common European values, adopted in Paris on 8 September 2000

Alber S (2016) Art. 47. In: Stern K, Sachs M (eds) Europäische Grundrechte-Charta. C.H. Beck, München, pp 699–730

Bachmann K (2018) Zur Entwicklung der polnischen Demokratie. Aus Politik und Zeitgeschichte 10–11:9–14

Bäcker M (2015) Das Grundgesetz als Implementationsgarant der Unionsgrundrechte. EuR 50:389–414

Bárd P, van Ballegooij W (2018) Judicial independence as a precondition for mutual trust? The CJEU in Minister for Justice and Equality v. LM. New J Eur Crim Law 9

Bast J (2006) Grundbegriffe der Handlungsformen der EU. Springer, Berlin

Bast J (2018) Art. 5 EUV. In: Grabitz E, Hilf M, Nettesheim M (eds) Das Recht der Europäischen Union. C.H. Beck, München

Binder C (2013) Die Grenzen der Vertragstreue im Völkerrecht. Springer, Berlin

Blagoev B (2011) Expulsion of a Member State from the EU after Lisbon: political threat or legal reality? Tilburg Law Rev 16:191–237

Blauberger M (2016) Europäischer Schutz gegen nationale Demokratiedefizite? Leviathan 44:280–302

Bleckmann A (1997) Ermessensfehlerlehre: Völker- und Europarecht, vergleichendes Verwaltungsrecht. Heymanns, Köln

Böckenförde EW (1990) Grundrechte als Grundsatznormen: Zur gegenwärtigen Lage der Grundrechtsdogmatik. Der Staat 29:1–31

Brauneck J (2019) Gefährdung des EU-Haushalts durch rechtsstaatliche Mängel in den Mitgliedstaaten? EuR 54:37–61

Burchardt D (2016) Die Ausübung der Identitätskontrolle durch das Bundesverfassungsgericht. ZaöRV 76:527–551

Canor I (2013) *My brother's keeper*? Horizontal *solange*: "An ever closer *distrust* among the peoples of Europe". Common Mark Law Rev 50:383–422

Carp R (2014) The struggle for the rule of law in Romania as an EU Member State: the role of the cooperation and verification mechanism. Utrecht Law Rev 10(1):16

Cassese S (2017) The 'constitutional traditions common to the Member States' of the European Union. Rivista Trimestrale di Diritto Pubblico:939–948

Chancellery of the Prime Minister of Poland (2018) White Paper on the Reform of the Polish Judiciary. https://www.premier.gov.pl/files/files/white_paper_en_full.pdf

Classen CD (2016) Zu wenig, zu fundamentalistisch – zur grundrechtlichen Kontrolle "unionsrechtlich determinierter" nationaler Hoheitsakte. EuR 51:304–312

Closa C, Kochenov D (eds) (2016) Reinforcing the rule of law oversight in the European Union. Cambridge University Press, Cambridge

Closa C, Kochenov D, Weiler JHH (2014) Reinforcing rule of law oversight in the European Union. EUI Working Paper RSCAS 2014/25

Crawford JR (2013) Overview of part three of the articles on state responsibility. In: Crawford JR, Pellet A, Olleson S (eds) The law of international state responsibility. Oxford University Press, Oxford, pp 931–940

Croon-Gestefeld J (2017) Reverse Solange – Union Citizenship as a Detour on the Route to European Rights Protection Against National Infringements. In: Kochenov D (ed) EU citizenship and federalism: the role of rights. Cambridge University Press, Cambridge, pp 665–683

Dori A (2015) The EU Justice Scoreboard – Judicial Evaluation as a new Governance Tool. MPILux Working Paper 2. http://www.mpi.lu/fileadmin/mpi/medien/persons/Dori_Adriani/The_EU_Justice_Scoreboard_-_Judicial_Evaluation_as_a_New_Governance_Tool.pdf
Dreier H (2015) Art. 20 (Einführung). In: Dreier H (ed) Grundgesetz-Kommentar, 3rd edn. Mohr Siebeck, Tübingen, pp 1–10
Dyzenhaus D (2012) State of emergency. In: Rosenfeld M, Sajó A (eds) The Oxford handbook of comparative constitutional law. Oxford University Press, Oxford, pp 442–460
Farahat A, Krenn C (2018) Der Europäische Gerichtshof in der Eurokrise: eine konflikttheoretische Perspektive. Der Staat 57:357–385
Franzius C (2018) Der Kampf um Demokratie in Polen und Ungarn. DÖV 71:381–388
García Morales MJ (2018) Federal execution, Article 155 of the Spanish Constitution and the crisis in Catalonia. ZöR 73:791–830
Gersdorf M (2018) Opinion on the White Paper on the Reform of the Polish judiciary. http://www.sn.pl/aktualnosci/SiteAssets/Lists/Wydarzenia/EditForm/Supreme%20Court%20-%20Opinion%20on%20the%20white%20paper%20on%20the%20Reform%20of%20the%20Polish%20Judiciary.pdf
Giegerich T (2015) Verfassungshomogenität, Verfassungsautonomie und Verfassungsaufsicht in der EU: Zum 'neuen Rechtsstaatsmechanismus' der Europäischen Kommission. In: Calliess C (ed) Herausforderungen an Staat und Verfassung: Liber Amicorum für Torsten Stein zum 70. Geburtstag, Nomos, Baden-Baden, pp 499–542
Grabenwarter C (2017) Konventionswidrigkeit der Auslieferung bei drohender Todesstrafe – Fall Soering. NJW 70:3052
Grabenwarter C (2018) Die Herausbildung europäischer Verfassungsstandards in der Venedig-Kommission. JöR 66:21–41
Graziadei M, de Caria R (2017) The "Constitutional Traditions Common to the Member States" in the case-law of the European Court of Justice. Judicial Dialogue at its Finest. Rivista Trimestrale di Diritto Pubblico:949–971
Griebel J (2014) Europäische Grundrechte als Prüfungsmaßstab der Verfassungsbeschwerde. DVBl 2014:204–211
Gundel J (2018) Rechtsschutz gegen Empfehlungen der EU-Kommission? Anmerkung zum Urteil des EuGH (GK) v. 20.2.2018, Rs. C-16/16 P (Belgien/Kommission). EuR 53:593–605
Habermas J (1992) Faktizität und Geltung. Suhrkamp, Berlin
Halmai G (2017) The early retirement age of the Hungarian Judges. In: Nicola F, Davies B (eds) EU law stories. Cambridge University Press, Cambridge, pp 471–488
Halmai G (2018a) Illiberal constitutionalism? The Hungarian Constitution in a European perspective. In: Kadelbach S (ed) Verfassungskrisen in der Europäischen Union. Nomos, Baden-Baden, pp 85–104
Halmai G (2018b) The possibility and desirability of rule of law conditionality. Hague J Rule Law 11:171–188
Hartmann N (1926) Ethik. De Gruyter, Berlin
Henderson J (2018) Russia's recent dealings with the Council of Europe and European Court of Human Rights. Eur Public Law 24:393–402
Hilf M, Schorkopf F (2017) Art. 2 EUV. In: Grabitz E, Hilf M, Nettesheim M (eds) Das Recht der Europäischen Union. C.H. Beck, München
Hillion C (2016) Overseeing the rule of law in the EU: legal mandate and means. In: Closa C, Kochenov D (eds) Reinforcing the rule of law oversight in the European Union. Cambridge University Press, Cambridge, pp 59–81
Hirsch Ballin E (2016) Mutual trust: the virtue of reciprocity – strengthening the acceptance of the rule of law through peer review. In: Closa C, Kochenov D (eds) Reinforcing the rule of law oversight in the European Union. Cambridge University Press, Cambridge, pp 133–146
Hoffmeister F (2015) Enforcing the EU Charter of Fundamental Rights in Member States: how far are Rome, Budapest and Bucharest from Brussels. In: von Bogdandy A, Sonnevend P (eds)

Constitutional crisis in the European constitutional area. C.H. Beck/Hart/Nomos, Baden-Baden, pp 195–233
Huber PM (2017) Europäische Verfassungs- und Rechtsstaatlichkeit in Bedrängnis. Der Staat 56:389–414
International Law Association (2018) Final Report on Aggression and the Use of Force, Sydney. http://www.ila-hq.org/images/ILA/DraftReports/DraftReport_UseOfForce.pdf
Iustitia (2018) Response to the White Paper Compendium on the reforms of the Polish justice system. Presented by the Government of the Republic of Poland to the European Commission. http://www.statewatch.org/news/2018/mar/pl-judges-association-response-judiciary-reform-3-18.pdf
Jakab A, Kochenov D (eds) (2017) Protecting European values. Oxford University Press, Oxford
Jakab A, Lorincz VO (2017) International Indices as Models for the Rule of Law Scoreboard of the European Union: Methodological Issues. MPIL Research Paper No. 2017-21. https://papers.ssrn.com/sol3/papers.cfm?abstract_id=3032501
Janse R (2019) Is the European Commission a credible guardian of the values?: A revisionist account of the Copenhagen political criteria during the Big Bang enlargement. Int J Const Law 17:43–65
Jarass H (2016) Art. 47 GRCh. In: Jarass H (ed) Charta der Grundrechte der EU, 3rd edn. C.H. Beck, München, pp 405–427
Kailitz S, Köllner P (2012) Zur Autokratieforschung der Gegenwart: Klassifikatorische Vorschläge, theoretische Ansätze und analytische Dimensionen. Politische Vierteljahresschrift 47:9–41
Kochenov D (2008) EU enlargement and the failure of conditionality: pre-accession conditionality in the fields of democracy and the rule of law. Wolters-Kluwer, Austin
Kochenov D (2013) On policing Article 2 TEU compliance – Reverse Solange and systemic infringements analyzed. Polish Yearb Int Law 33:145–170
Kochenov D (2015) Biting intergouvernmentalism: the case for the reinvention of Article 259 TFEU to make it a viable rule of law enforcement tool. Hague J Rule Law 7:153–174
Kochenov D, Pech L (2016) Better late than never? On the European Commission's rule of law framework and its first activation. J Common Mark Stud 54:1062–1074
Kochenov D, Pech L (2018) Monitoring and enforcement of the rule of law in the EU: rhetoric and reality. EuConst 11:512–540
Komárek J (2015) Why National Constitutional Courts should not embrace EU fundamental rights. In: de Vries S, Bernitz U, Weatherill S (eds) The EU Charter of fundamental rights as binding instruments. Hart, Oxford, pp 75–92
Kosar D, Baros J, Dufek P (2019) The twin challenges to separation of powers in Central Europe: technocratic governance and populism. EuConst 15:427–461
Krajewski M (2018) Who is afraid of the European Council? The Court of Justice's cautious approach to independence of domestic judges. EuConst 14:792–813
Krenn C (2018) Self-Government at the Court of Justice of the European Union: a bedrock for institutional success. Germ Law J 19:2007–2030
Lacchi C (2015) Review by constitutional courts of the obligation of National Courts of last instance to refer a preliminary question to the Court of Justice of the EU. Germ Law J 16:1663–1700
Lachmayer K (2017) Questioning the basic values – Austria and Jörg Haider. In: Jakab A, Kochenov D (eds) The enforcement of EU law and values. Oxford University Press, Oxford
Lauth H, Sehring J (2009) Putting Deficient Rechtsstaat on the Research Agenda: reflections on diminished subtypes. Comp Sociol 8:165–201
Łazowski A (2012) European Union do not worry, Croatia is behind you: a commentary on the Seventh Accession Treaty. Croatian Yearb Eur Law Policy 8:1–39
Lenaerts K (2017) La vie après l'avis: exploring the principle of mutual (yet not blind) trust. Common Mark Law Rev 54:805–840
Lepsius O (2011) Die maßstabsetzende Gewalt. In: Jestaedt M, Lepsius O, Möllers C, Schönberger C (eds) Das entgrenzte Gericht. Suhrkamp, Berlin, pp 159–280

Levits E (2018) Die Europäische Union als Wertegemeinschaft. In: Jaeger T (ed) Europa 4.0. Jan Sramek Verlag KG, Wien, pp 239–270
Luhmann N (1975) Legitimation durch Verfahren, 2nd edn. Suhrkamp, Berlin
Luhmann N (1993) Gibt es in unserer Gesellschaft noch unverzichtbare Normen? C.F. Müller, Heidelberg
Mälksoo M (2009) The memory politics of becoming European: the East European subalterns and the collective memory of Europe. Eur J Int Relat 15:653–680
Martenczuk B (2018) Art. 7 EUV und der Rechtsstaatsrahmen als Instrument der Wahrung der Grundwerte der Union. In: Kadelbach S (ed) Verfassungskrisen in der Europäischen Union. Nomos, Baden-Baden
Mendelski M (2016) Das europäische Evaluierungsdefizit der Rechtsstaatlichkeit. Leviathan 44:366–398
Mengozzi P (2015) A European Partnership of Courts. Judicial Dialogue between the EU Court of Justice and National Constitutional Courts. Il Diritto dell'Unione Europea 701–720
Merkel W (2013) Vergleich politischer Systeme: Demokratien und Autokratien. In: Schmidt MG, Wolf F, Wurster S (eds) Studienbuch Politikwissenschaft. Springer, Berlin, pp 207–236
Möllers C, Schneider L (2018) Demokratiesicherung in der Europäischen Union. Mohr Siebeck, Tübingen
Mosler H (1968) Begriff und Gegenstand des Europarechts. ZaöRV 28:481–502
Müller JW (2015) Should the EU protect democracy and the rule of law inside Member States? Eur Law J 21:141–160
Muszyński M (2018) Polski Trybunał w unijnej rzeczywistości. Rzeczpospolita. https://www.rp.pl/Opinie/303229983-Polski-Trybunal-w-unijnej-rzeczywistosci%2D%2D-Mariusz-Muszynski-o-mocy-wyrokow-TSUE-w-Polsce.html
Nergelius J (2015) The role of the Venice Commission in maintaining the rule of law in Hungary and in Romania. In: von Bogdandy A, Sonnevend P (eds) Constitutional crisis in the European constitutional area. C.H. Beck/Hart/Nomos, Baden-Baden, pp 291–308
Nettesheim M (2009) Ein Individualrecht auf Staatlichkeit? Die Lissabon-Entscheidung des BVerfG. NJW 62:2867–2869
Nettesheim M (2016) Anmerkung. JZ 71:424–428
Nettesheim M (2018) Art. 288 AEUV. In: Grabitz E, Hilf M, Nettesheim M (eds) Das Recht der Europäischen Union. C.H. Beck, München
Nicolisi S (2015) The Contribution of the Court of Justice to the codification of the founding values of the European Union. Revista de Derecho Comunitario Europeo 51:613–643
Nowag J (2016) EU law, constitutional identity, and human dignity: A toxic mix? Bundesverfassungsgericht: Mr R. Common Mark Law Rev 53:1441–1453
Nowak C (2011) Europäisches Verwaltungsrecht und Grundrechte. In: Terhechte JP (ed) Verwaltungsrecht der Europäischen Union. Nomos, Baden-Baden, pp 519–584
Palermo F, Kösserl K (2017) Comparative Federalism. Hart, Oxford
Paris D (2017) Constitutional courts as European Union courts: the current and potential use of EU law as a yardstick for constitutional review. Maastricht J Eur Comp Law 24:792–821
Regan E (2018) The role of the principles of mutual trust and mutual recognition in EU law. Il Diritto dell'Unione Europea 231–248
Reimer F (2001) Verfassungsprinzipien. Duncker & Humblot, Berlin
Rötting M (2009) Das verfassungsrechtliche Beitrittsverfahren zur Europäischen Union. Springer, Berlin
Ruffert M (2016) Art. 7 EUV. In: Calliess C, Ruffert M (eds) EUV/AEUV, 5th edn, pp 166–174
Rugge G (2016) Bundesverfassungsgericht e Corte di Giustizia dell'UE: quale futuro per il dialogo sul rispetto dell'identità nazionale?. Il Diritto dell'Unione Europea pp 789–812
Russo AM (2014) La cittadinanza 'sostanziale' dell'UE alla luce della proposta del gruppo di Heidelberg: verso una 'reverse Solange'?. federalismi.it
Sadurski W (2019) Poland's constitutional breakdown. Oxford University Press, Oxford

Sauer H (2016) "Solange" geht in Altersteilzeit – Der unbedingte Vorrang der Menschenwürde vor dem Unionsrecht. NJW 69:1134–1138
Scheppele K (2016) Enforcing the basic principles of EU law through systemic infringement actions. In: Closa C, Kochenov D (eds) Reinforcing the rule of law oversight in the European Union. Cambridge University Press, Cambridge, pp 105–132
Schmidt M, Bogdanowicz P (2018) The infringement procedure in the rule of law crisis: how to make effective use of Article 258 TFEU. Common Mark Law Rev 55:1061–1100
Schmidt-Aßmann E (2013) Verwaltungsrechtliche Dogmatik. Mohr Siebeck, Tübingen
Schmitt C (2011) Die Tyrannei der Werte. 3rd corrected edn, with an afterword by Christoph Schönberger. Duncker & Humblot, Berlin
Schönberger C (2016) Anmerkung. JZ 71:422–424
Schorkopf F (2002) Die Maßnahmen der XIV EU-Mitgliedstaaten gegen Österreich. Springer, Berlin
Schorkopf F (2016) Wertesicherung in der Europäischen Union. Prävention, Quarantäne und Aufsicht als Bausteine eines Rechts der Verfassungskrise? EuR 51:147–163
Schulze-Fielitz H (2015) Art. 20 Abs. 2 Satz 2 und Abs. 3 (Rechtsstaat). In: Dreier H (ed) Grundgesetz-Kommentar, Band 2, 3rd edn 2015. Mohr Siebeck, Tübingen, pp 186–291
Schuppert GF, Bumke C (2000) Die Konstitutionalisierung der Rechtsordnung. Nomos, Baden-Baden
Senden L (2004) Soft law in European community law. Hart, Oxford
Spieker LD (2019) Breathing life into the Union's common values: on the Judicial Application of Article 2 TEU in the EU value crisis. Germ Law J 20:1182–1213
Spieker LD (2020) Framing and managing constitutional identity conflicts: how to stabilize the modus vivendi between the Court of Justice and national constitutional courts. Common Mark Law Rev 20:361–398
Stein T (1998) Die rechtlichen Reaktionsmöglichkeiten der Europäischen Union bei schwerwiegender und anhaltender Verletzung der demokratischen und rechtsstaatlichen Grundsätze in einem Mitgliedstaat. In: Götz V, Selmer P, Wolfrum R (eds) Liber amicorum Günther Jaenicke. Springer, Berlin, pp 871–898
Steinbeis M (2018) The Deed, not the Doer. Verfassungsblog. https://verfassungsblog.de/the-deed-not-the-doer/
Steinbeis M, Kemmerer A, Möllers C (eds) (2015) Gebändigte Macht: Verfassung im europäischen Nationalstaat. Nomos, Baden-Baden
Steininger S (2018) Managing the Backlash? The PACE and the Question of Participation Rights for Russia. Verfassungsblog. https://verfassungsblog.de/managing-the-backlash-the-pace-and-the-question-of-participation-rights-for-russia/
Thym D (2015) Vereinigt die Grundrechte! JZ 70:53–63
Toggenburg GN (2013) Was soll die EU können dürfen, um die EU-Verfassungswerte und die Rechtsstaatlichkeit der Mitgliedstaaten zu schützen? Ausblick auf eine neue Europäische Rechtsstaatshygiene. ÖGfE Policy Brief. https://oegfe.at/wordpress/wp-content/uploads/2015/07/OEGfE_Policy_Brief-2013.10.pdf
Tuori K (2016) From Copenhagen to Venice. In: Closa C, Kochenov D (eds) Reinforcing the rule of law oversight in the European Union. Cambridge University Press, Cambridge, pp 225–246
Uerpmann-Wittzack R (2009) The constitutional role of international law. In: von Bogdandy A, Bast J (eds) Principles of European constitutional law, 2nd rev. edn. Hart/C.H. Beck/Nomos, Oxford/München, pp 131–167
Vachudova MA (2016) Why improve EU oversight of rule of law. In: Closa C, Kochenov D (eds) Reinforcing the rule of law oversight in the European Union. Cambridge University Press, Cambridge, pp 270–289
van Middelaar L (2016) Vom Kontinent zur Union. Gegenwart und Geschichte des vereinten Europa. Suhrkamp, Berlin
Volkmann U (2008) Verfassungsrecht zwischen normativem Anspruch und politischer Wirklichkeit. VVDStRL 67:57–93

Volkmann U (2018) Wertedämmerung. Merkur 72:5–17
von Bogdandy A (2008) The European Union as situation, executive, and promoter of the international law of cultural diversity – elements of a beautiful friendship. Eur J Int Law 19 (2):241–275
von Bogdandy A (2010) Constitutional principles. In: von Bogdandy A, Bast J (eds) Principles of European constitutional law. Modern studies in European law. Hart, Oxford, pp 11–52
von Bogdandy A (2014) Common principles for a plurality of orders: a study on public authority in the European legal area. I•CON 12:980–1007
von Bogdandy A (2016) European law beyond 'Ever Closer Union' repositioning the concept, its thrust and the EJC's comparative methodology. Eur Law J 22(4):519–538
von Bogdandy A (2018) Ways to frame the European rule of law: Rechtsgemeinschaft, trust, revolution, and Kantian Peace. EuConst 14:657–699
von Bogdandy A, Sonnevend P (eds) (2015) Constitutional crisis in the European constitutional area. C.H. Beck/Hart/Nomos, Oxford/Portland
von Bogdandy A, Spieker D (2019) Countering the Judicial Silencing of critics: Article 2 TEU values, reverse Solange, and the responsibilities of National Judges. EuConst 15:391–426
von Bogdandy A, Venzke I (2014) In wessen Namen? Internationale Gerichte in Zeiten globalen Regierens. Suhrkamp, Berlin
von Bogdandy A, Kottmann M, Antpöhler C, Dickschen J, Hentrei S, Smrkol M (2012) Reverse Solange – protecting the essence of fundamental rights against EU Member States. Common Mark Law Rev 49:489–519
von Bogdandy A, Kottmann M, Antpöhler C, Dickschen J, Hentrei S, Smrkol M (2015) A European response to domestic constitutional crisis: advancing the Reverse-Solange Doctrine. In: von Bogdandy A, Sonnevend P (eds) Constitutional crisis in the European constitutional area. Theory law and politics in Hungary and Romania. C.H. Beck/Hart/Nomos, Oxford/ Portland, pp 248–267
von Bogdandy A, Bogdanovic P, Canor I, Schmidt M, Taborowski M (2018) Guest editorial: a potential constitutional moment for the European rule of law – the importance of red lines. Common Mark Law Rev 55:983–995
Voßkuhle A (2018) Die Idee der Europäischen Wertegemeinschaft. Verlag der Buchhandlung Klaus Bittner, Köln
Weiler JHH (2016) Epilogue: living in a glass house: Europe, democracy and the rule of law. In: Closa C, Kochenov D (eds) Reinforcing the rule of law oversight in the European Union. Cambridge University Press, Cambridge, pp 313–326
Wendel M (2019) Rechtsstaatlichkeitsaufsicht und gegenseitiges Vertrauen. EuR 54:111–132
Wittinger M (2005) Der Europarat: Die Entwicklung seines Rechts und der "europäischen Verfassungswerte". Nomos, Baden-Baden

Armin von Bogdandy is Director at the Max Planck Institute for Comparative Public Law and International Law, Heidelberg.

The Rule of Law As a Value in the Sense of Article 2 TEU: What Does It Mean and Imply?

Werner Schroeder

Contents

Abstract The rule of law is a value on which the European Union is founded, and which shall be respected and observed by its Member States. This value is not merely an ethical standard but a binding legal principle that is applicable to legal disputes under Union law. The treaties, however, do not provide a definition of this principle. From a Union law perspective, it is therefore indispensable to determine the rule of law more precisely; not only is it referred to in treaty law (Article 2 TEU), but understood by Union courts as a constitutional meta-principle that informs other constitutional norms and may justify review proceedings and sanctions against Member States. The Commission Framework to strengthen the Rule of Law of 2014 does not suffice to shape a 'Union rule of law'. It relies primarily on the case

W. Schroeder (✉)
Department of European Law and Public International Law, University of Innsbruck, Innsbruck, Austria
e-mail: werner.schroeder@uibk.ac.at

A. von Bogdandy et al. (eds.), *Defending Checks and Balances in EU Member States*, Beiträge zum ausländischen öffentlichen Recht und Völkerrecht 298,
https://doi.org/10.1007/978-3-662-62317-6_5

law of the Court of Justice of the European Union. Yet, this judicial concept of the rule of law is somehow restricted as it focuses almost exclusively on the role of the judicial branch in the Union's constitutional system. Common European constitutional traditions, however, show that the core concern of the rule of law is the containment of public authority by institutional arrangements. In view of these traditions and the practice of the Union institutions, including the CJEU, consensus at the Union level might be achieved on the fact that the rule of law comprises not only strictly formal standards, but also material criteria of justice related to the juridical shaping of decision-making processes. These elements of the rule of law are intrinsically linked to fundamental rights and shall ensure that within the scope of Union law any public power is exercised in a non-arbitrary and legitimate way. To this end, the Union rule of law may not only be understood as a formal set of objective norms, but as ensuring the protection of individual rights as well.

1 Dangers for the Rule of Law in the Union

According to the first sentence of Article 2 of the Treaty on European Union (TEU), the European Union is founded on values among which figure the respect for human dignity, freedom, democracy, equality, the rule of law and the respect for human rights, including the rights of persons belonging to minorities. The second sentence of this provision assumes that the Member States respect and observe these values. In the last years, however, the political situation in some Member States has made manifest that these values are in part jeopardised to a considerable degree; this notably holds true for the principle of the rule of law[1] which, as a common principle of the EU Member States, restricts the majority rule in the State through institutions such as separation of powers, independence of the courts and which guarantees the liberty of individuals.[2] Since the Union draws a great part of its legitimacy from the fact that its organs and Member States respect the rule of law, the indicated dangers for the rule have meanwhile grown into a significant problem for European integration.[3]

It is problematic, however, to operationalise the rule of law in the Union's constitutional system and, in particular, to use it as an argument for sanctioning certain Member States without having clarified its normative character, its meaning and scope. In this contribution the issue of 'content' shall be addressed: What does the principle of the rule of law, as mentioned in Article 2 TEU, actually mean and imply?

[1]Scheppele (2015), p. 112.

[2]For the genesis of Art 2 TEU, see Mangiameli (2013), para. 2 note 6.

[3]Kochenov (2013); von Bogdandy and Ioannidis (2014), p. 60; Hillion (2016), pp. 59 et seq.; von Bogdandy et al. (2018), pp. 983 et seq.

2 Origins As a Principle of Union Constitutional Law

Already at the beginning of the 1960s, Walter Hallstein coined, in regard to the then European Economic Community (EEC), the concept of a 'community based on law'.[4] This term has made a remarkable career since then and represents an essential element of Union law doctrine nowadays.[5] Interestingly, however, Hallstein's remark did not refer to the Member States of the then Community as all being States governed by the rule of law. He did not primarily seek to illustrate that the Community has institutions such as fundamental rights, separation of powers, legal protection and so on, and is therefore endowed with all insignia of a State based on the rule of law. He rather aimed at emphasising that the Community 'solely' disposed of legal power, not of means of coercion. Hence, the Union's power is exclusively based on the respect for the law.[6] The Union's legal concept for the handling of borderline situations[7] that involve a threat of the rule of law in and by Member States does not provide for the use of force, but—as it is common in other modern federal systems—relies on cooperation[8] and consideration. The sanctioning procedure for massive violations of rule of law principles, as enshrined in Article 7 TEU, does little to change this, precisely because it does not allow for the use of force against a Member State.

As is commonly known, the Court of Justice endorsed the notion of a 'community based on law' in its famous *Les Verts v. Parliament*-Ruling in 1986, linking it to the constitutional character of the Treaties. According to the Court, the then EEC is 'a Community based on the rule of law, inasmuch as neither its Member States nor its institutions can avoid a review of the question whether the measures adopted by them are in conformity with the basic constitutional charter, the Treaty'.[9] Methodologically, this jurisprudence draws on the fact that the rule of law stems from a common European heritage. It can be conceived of as an element of the common constitutional traditions of the Member States and as an element of the European Convention for the Protection of Human Rights and, therefore, as a general principle of Union Constitutional law.[10] The Court of Justice made the *topos* of the rule of law

---

[4]Hallstein (1979), p. 109. See also Fuß (1968), pp. 16 et seq.

[5]Critically von Bogdandy (2017), p. 487.

[6]Hallstein (1969), p. 33.

[7]For the state of emergency as a test case of jurisdiction, see Schmitt (1985), p. 11. Critically with regard to the application of Schmitt's theory to the Union system, see Pernice (1995), pp. 109 et seq.; Schroeder (2002), p. 220.

[8]Scharpf (1985), pp. 323 et seq.

[9]CJEU, Case C-294/83 *Les Verts v. Parliament*, ECLI:EU:C:1986:166, para. 23; Joined Cases C-402/05 P and C-415/05 P *Kadi and Al Barakaat International Foundation v. Council and Commission*, ECLI:EU:C:2008:461, para. 281. But see CJEU, Case C-362/14 *Schrems v. Data Protection Commissioner*, ECLI:EU:C:2015:650, para. 60: the European Union is a 'union based on the rule of law'.

[10]von Bogdandy (2009), pp. 23, 28 et seq.; Pech (2010), pp. 361 et seq., 367. On the general principle see Tridimas (2013).

part and parcel of its own constitutionalisation strategy.[11] It perfectly lends itself to support the proposition that the Union is not an intergovernmental organisation as the others, but a public authority *sui generis* endowed with a supranational constitution.[12] The Court of Justice also applies such 'constitutional' and 'rule of law' terminology to the effect of securing the substantial legitimacy of the law of the Union, particularly by underscoring that the rule of law constitutes an element of the Union's particular identity on the international plane.[13]

It has, however, taken several decades for the rule of law to acquire the status of and establish itself as a principle pertaining to the constitutional law profile of the Union (Article 2, second sentence and Article 7 TEU), i.e. to be understood as a 'constitutional principle'.[14] This is understandable, given the fact that the objectives and means of operation originally agreed upon by the Member States of the Community were primarily of an economic and social-policy character, with the 'Common Market' and 'market freedoms' forming the heart of this economic order. Therefore, the Treaties of Rome did not contain, with the exception of legal protection, any elements testifying an explicit rule of law terminology.[15]

With the advent of the interpretation of the Treaties as a constitution which organises and legitimises supranational public authority not only in economic, but also in highly political fields, the Member States became increasingly interested in giving an explicit status to 'constitutional principles' governing the Union's public authority. The rule of law principle, as one of these constitutional principles, is first mentioned in a Union law context in the Conclusions of the European Council of Copenhagen in 1993 committing the candidate countries for EU membership to 'stability of institutions guaranteeing democracy, the rule of law, human rights, respect for and protection of minorities'.[16] The Amsterdam Treaty of 1997 adopts this approach inasmuch as in Article 6 paragraph 1 TEU it states that the Union is founded on the principles of liberty, democracy, the respect for human rights and fundamental freedoms; these principles are common to all Member States. In Article I-2 of the 2004 Treaty establishing a Constitution for Europe which has not entered into force, these principles were re-baptised as 'values'. This very term, by the way, is also used by the identical provision of Article 2 TEU.

---

[11]See Weiler (1981), p. 274; Mancini (1989), pp. 595 et seq.; Lenaerts (1990), pp. 205 et seq. See also Fuß (1968), pp. 16 et seq.; Hallstein (1969), pp. 41, 48 et seq.

[12]CJEU, Opinion 1/91 *EEA I*, ECLI:EU:C:1991:490, para. 108; Opinion 2/13 *Accession of the EU to the ECHR II*, ECLI:EU:C:2014:2454, paras. 156 et seq., 163 et seq.

[13]In contrast to the UN system, see CJEU, *Kadi*, *supra* note 9, paras. 281 et seq. See further Hilf and Schorkopf (2015), paras. 12–54.

[14]See von Bogdandy (2009), pp. 13, 22.

[15]Calliess (2011), para. 1. On the impact of the deepening of European integration for the meaning of the rule of law see Lenaerts (2017a), p. 640.

[16](1993) 26 (6) EC Bull, para. I.13.

3 No Homogeneity as Regards the Rule of Law in the Union

Article 2 TEU is sometimes referred to as a 'homogeneity clause'. It is derived from Article 2, first and second sentence TEU as well as from Article 7 TEU that a similar rule of law standard applies both vertically between the Union level and the Member States' level and horizontally among the Member States themselves. Every exercise of public authority, irrespective of whether it has its origin on the Union or national level, is subject to a set of legal limitations and shall be assessed according to this standard.[17]

Such claims for congruence of constitutional principles in federal systems are often based on federal ideas or models.[18] When applied to the law of the Union, they imply the existence of a supremacy of the Union vis-à-vis its Member States and suggest supervisory powers in the relationship between the both. But can a claim for constitutional homogeneity and for similar rule of law standards on Union and national level be sustained under these conditions in the first place? Such a claim is in need of critical reflection. First of all, it is problematic to reconstruct the Union's constitution in the light of federal state models since the institutional situation of the Union follows its own rules.[19] Even though the Union exercises and organises public authority,[20] only limited conclusions for the understanding of the Union's constitution can be drawn from theories that take national federal systems as their point of reference. In view of the different nature of the Union as a community of integration, its constitutional structures and principles differ from those of the Member States.[21] The claim for constitutional homogeneity between Union and Member States must thus be rejected.[22]

Furthermore, it is difficult to assume that there exists a form of rule of law homogeneity in the relationship among the Member States (horizontally). No Union law fiction is available in this regard since, concerning essential constitutional

---

[17]Hilf and Schorkopf (2015), paras. 9 et seq.; Pech (2010), p. 364; Mangiameli (2013), paras. 42 et seq.; von Bogdandy et al. (2012), pp. 509 et seq.

[18]For a homogeneity requirement with respect to federalism and the principle of democracy, Schmitt (2008), p. 388. With respect to positive constitutional law see Art. 28 para. 1 German Basic Law, which is calling for constitutional homogeneity between the German Basic Law and the federal states. The German Constitutional Court handles the claim strictly, see BVerfG, 1 BvL 30/88, *Rundfunkentscheidung*, Judgment of 22 February 1994, paras. 84–88. See also Art. 99 para. 1 B-VG, which states that the state constitutions in Austria may not contradict the federal constitution. This does also apply for the principle of the rule of law.

[19]See CJEU, Case C-359/92 *Germany v. Council*, ECLI:EU:C:1994:306, para. 38. Against constitutional analogies, see also ECtHR [GC], *Matthews v. United Kingdom*, Judgment of 18 February 1999, Application No. 24833/94, para. 48.

[20]CJEU, Opinion 1/78 *International Agreement on Natural Rubber*, ECLI:EU:C:1979:224, para. 7.

[21]BVerfG, Judgment of 31 May 1995, 2 BvR 635/95. See previously BVerfG, 1 BvR 1474/92, *Maastricht*, Judgment of 17 August 993, para. 182; BVerfG, 2 BvE 2/08, *Lissabon*, Judgment of 30 June 2009, para. 370.

[22]But see von Bogdandy et al. (2012), p. 489.

principles such as the content of human dignity, there is no respective 'common conception' of the Member States, as the CJEU has acknowledged.[23] Also with respect to the other elements of the rule of law such as legal protection, separation of powers and so on, as regards the details a common conception of the Member States cannot be found.[24]

The claim for the rule of law should therefore not be understood as a claim for homogeneity. This would do justice neither to the European constitutional reality nor to the Treaties. Article 4 paragraph 2 TEU acknowledges that the 'national identity' of the Member States, which the Union shall respect, is based on their 'fundamental structures, political and constitutional'. Thus, it is the law of the Union itself recognising that, in spite of the common constitutional values of Article 2 TEU, there exist differences between the Union's constitution and the constitutions of the Member States. Individual national approaches as to the legal classification of the rule of law confirm such an understanding.[25] In areas where Union law may not ensure a uniform level of legal protection, it leaves room for 'rule of law diversity', provided that the 'primacy, unity and effectiveness of EU law are not thereby compromised'.[26] The idea that Article 2 TEU orders and supervises a federal state-type constitutional homogeneity—vertically as well as horizontally—is not compatible with such a model of constitutional pluralism[27] as it is after all laid down explicitly in the Treaty.

The claim for the rule of law of the Union and the Member States does therefore not seek the existence of uniform principles and rules, but solely the observance of a European minimum standard in terms of the rule of law.[28] To define this minimum standard, however, is not an easy task (see Sect. 5 below).

4 Normative Character of the Union Rule of Law

4.1 Rule of Law As Value and Principle

It has already been mentioned that the rule of law was first referred to as a 'principle' in the Amsterdam Treaty and has only been modified into a 'value' with the Lisbon

---

[23]CJEU, Case C-36/02 *Omega*, ECLI:EU:C:2004:614, para. 37.

[24]Regarding the difference of the rule of law in common law and continental legal systems, see Dicey (1961), pp. 189 et seq., 267 et seq.; Konstantinides (2017), pp. 30 et seq., 39; Krygier (2012), p. 233; Classen (2013), pp. 56 et seq.

[25]On the constitutional identity control, see BVerfG, *Lissabon*, *supra* note 21, para. 343, according to which the 'inviolable core content of the constitutional identity of the Basic Law' has to be respected within the framework of the Union.

[26]CJEU, Case C-399/11 *Melloni*, EU:C:2013:107, para. 60.

[27]On constitutional pluralism in the EU, see MacCormick (1995), p. 259; Baquero Cruz (2008), p. 389.

[28]Lenaerts (2017a), p. 640.

Treaty. Although terminology issues should not be overrated in Union law, the question arises what normative consequences this renaming may have. Most scholars take the position that nothing has changed from a legal point of view. They continue to use the term 'principles' as it represents a common category of legal hermeneutics.[29] They interpret the 'linguistic turn' as merely indicating the theoretical uncertainties of the law of the Union in the dealing with constitutional principles. In addition, they refer to the case law of the CJEU, Article 21 TEU and the Preamble of the FRC which, in the context of the rule of law and fundamental rights, continue speaking of 'constitutional principles'[30] and 'principles'.[31]

It is indeed problematic to use the term 'values' in Article 2 TEU because it is a meta-legal term. Values shall, beyond the realm of legal norms, guide the individual in decision-making situations to ethically 'right' conduct. They articulate general considerations on the basis of which one state of affairs is declared preferable in relation to another state of affairs.[32] As moral strategies, values only function on the basis of a consensus on their respective set and content which cannot, however, be assumed and realised at any given time.

However, the distinction between principles and values can be normatively reconstructed on the basis of Union law itself. First of all, values, insofar as they are laid down in black-letter legal texts, such as Article 2 TEU, refer to doctrinal principles which shall guide decision-makers in the Union in their structuring of the legal order. In this context, principles are understood in a pragmatic manner.[33] They are understood as legal norms which do not state specific rights or duties, but which are of a general nature and are in need of being concretised by the legislative, the executive and the judiciary. They can be made operable in the Union legal system by means of adopting more specific legal rules, in particular, by the courts that—by drawing on principles, values, interests and goods which, thus, become an element of a balancing decision—identify them as legally relevant. In so doing, the CJEU has, for instance, derived the principle of legal certainty from the rule of law principle.[34] In such a case, a principle can even turn into a self-standing standard of legality.

Secondly, in the Union legal system, values as being ethical, supra-positive norms have an orientation and ordering function. They are therefore of an identity-building and legitimacy-creating character.[35] This is also the function of the rule of

---

[29] See von Bogdandy (2009), pp. 22 et seq.; Pech (2010), pp. 366 et seq.; Hilf and Schorkopf (2015), para. 21.

[30] CJEU, *Kadi, supra* note 9, paras. 281, 285; Case C-355/04 *Segi*, ECLI:EU:C:2007:116, para. 51.

[31] CJEU, *Accession of the EU to the ECHR II, supra* note 12, para. 167.

[32] Luhmann (1987), p. 433.

[33] On different interpretations of the function of principles in the law of the Union, see von Bogdandy (2009), p. 20; Bengoetxea (1993), pp. 183 et seq.; Schroeder (2002), pp. 262 et seq.

[34] See CJEU, Case C-234/04 *Kapferer v. Schlank & Schick GmbH*, ECLI:EU:C:2006:178, paras. 20 et seq.

[35] Calliess (2004), p. 1034.

law and of the other values mentioned in Article 2 TEU which shall endow the Union with a particular identity,[36] especially on the international level (see Article 3 paragraphs 1 and 5 TEU, Article 8 TEU in Article 21 paragraph 2, Article 32 and Article 42 paragraph 5 TEU), but also vis-à-vis the Union citizens inasmuch as they can form the basis of a common political conscience.[37] The value of the rule of law, in particular, is that of a reference standard for the common self-assurance of the Union and its Member States.[38]

In view of the foregoing, the third point is that values have therefore a legal and ethical double-nature. Legal norms concretise values and transform them from the societal system into the legal system. This double-nature of the rule of law as a value of the Union and a principle of Union law also becomes manifest in the structure of Article 2 TEU. In Article 2, second sentence TEU values such as pluralism, tolerance, solidarity are characterised as contents of the European societal model that have no legal character. The Union is not 'founded' on these values but presupposes them as societal values. This distinction is taken further in the provision on the sanctioning procedure in Article 7 paragraph 1 TEU which solely refers to the 'legally relevant values' in the meaning of Article 2 paragraph 1 TEU. It has also left terminological traces in the CJEU's case law. In the context of human dignity, the Court of Justice, on the one hand, speaks of it as a 'fundamental value' laid down in the national constitutions, but on the other hand also as a 'general principle of [Union] law'.[39] And in its opinion on the accession of the Union to the ECHR, the Court of Justice declares that the legal structure of the Union is based on the fundamental premise that each Member State shares with all the other Member States [...] a set of common values on which the EU is founded, as stated in Article 2 TEU.[40]

4.2 *Binding Legal Norm*

If a norm is referred to as a value, this means to shift it to a political or ethical level. In terms of legal doctrine, this creates problems. It notably gives rise to the question of how the values which are laid down in the Union's constitution should be interpreted and applied. Are they subject to judicial control or a standard for such a control?

[36]See Commission 'Communication on Article 7 of the Treaty on European Union: Respect for and promotion of the values on which the Union is based' COM (2003) 606 final, 3.

[37]von Bogdandy (2009), p. 14.

[38]Lenaerts (2017a), p. 640.

[39]CJEU, *Omega*, *supra* note 23, paras. 23, 32, 34.

[40]CJEU, *Accession of the EU to the ECHR II*, *supra* note 12, para. 168.

First of all, one must refer to the fact that the rule of law is enshrined in Article 2 TEU, i.e. in a legal text, and has therefore normative character.[41] This proposition is emphasised by the wording and system of the Treaty, namely by pointing out that the rule of law is 'common' to the Member States and that the Union is 'founded' on it, amongst others (Article 2 TEU). The normative character of the rule of law also becomes manifest in Article 3 paragraph 1 TEU which makes it the Union's primary goal to promote its values, as well as in Article 13 paragraph 1 TEU which makes the promotion of values the reference point of the 'institutional framework' of the Union. Both the Union's institutions and the Member States are legally bound by the treaty objectives of the Union, as also follows from Article 4 paragraph 3 TEU. The normative character of the rule of law is further confirmed by the references in the sanctioning procedure pursuant to Article 7 TEU[42] and the accession procedure pursuant to Article 49 TEU.[43] In these cases, specific legal consequences are tied to the respect for and the promotion of the rule of law. This presupposes that the rule of law itself is of legally binding nature.

Moreover, Article 2 TEU only constitutes the black-letter law manifestation of principles which have already been developed by the CJEU in the 1980s as unwritten general principles of law.[44] Against this background, the reference in Article 2 TEU to such principles and their denomination as values is of solely declaratory nature. They do not change their already existing normative character. Their codification is above all relevant as a reference point for the sanctioning procedure against the Member States pursuant to Article 7 TEU as well as for reasons of legal certainty.

In addition, the rule of law has, together with the other values referred to in Article 2 TEU, a programmatic function. Their respect by the Member States is evoked in Article 2, second sentence TEU, and for the Union itself this provision serves as characterisation of the classical structural features of the liberal constitutional model.[45] Due to the systematic position at the beginning of the Treaties, its profound character, its open wording as well as its significance similar to goal and value clauses in the constitutions of some Member States, Article 2 TEU constitutes the fundament of a membership in the Union.[46] Besides, the promotion of the rule of law is, according to Article 3 paragraph 1 TEU, one of the overarching objectives of the Union and its institutional framework (Article 13 paragraph 1 TEU). The realisation of the principle of the rule of law, therefore, pertains to the decision-making programme for the Union's institutions which determines the handling of their

[41]This can be illustrated in the light of the CJEU's case law on Articles 2 and 3 EEC Treaty, which were regarded as legally binding norms, see CJEU, Case C-126/86 *Giménez Zaera*, ECLI:EU:C:1987:395, para. 14; Case C-339/89 *Alsthom Atlantique*, ECLI:EU:C:1991:28, paras. 8 et seq.

[42]See Commission 'Reasoned proposal under Article 7 para. 1 TEU regarding the rule of law in Poland' COM (2017) 835 final, para. 1.

[43]Ohler (2015), para. 15; Cremona (2005), p. 3.

[44]CJEU, Case C-138/79 *Roquette Frères*, ECLI:EU:C:1980:249, para. 33; *Les Verts*, *supra* note 9, paras. 23 et seq. See also Lenaerts (2017a), p. 640.

[45]Hilf and Schorkopf (2015), para. 9; von Bogdandy (2009), p. 22.

[46]Pech (2010), pp. 361 et seq.; Calliess (2004), p. 1036.

discretionary powers[47] and constitutes a guideline for the interpretation of Union law provisions.[48] By virtue of Article 4 paragraph 3 TEU, this objective entails legal effect vis-à-vis the Member States which must refrain from any measures that could jeopardise the attainment of the Union's objectives and shall, *vice versa*, do everything to facilitate the achievement of the Union's tasks.[49]

4.3 Operational Legal Norm

Although it is now undisputed that the rule of law is a legally binding norm, the question arises whether it is also applicable in a legal dispute. The vagueness of the concept of the rule of law—more on this later—raises the question of whether this norm has any self-standing value in legal procedures.[50]

In fact, the Court of Justice has emphasized the normative character of the rule of law principle very early by deriving concrete legal rules from this principle, for example, the duty of the Union to provide legal protection mechanisms.[51] Later, the Court has operationalised the rule of law. Specifically, by referring to the rule of law it called on the Member States to ensure judicial independence and the full judicial protection of the rights of individuals.[52] By now, the rule of law is well established as an operational principle and as a basis for legally assessing the Member States.[53]

The premise that each Member State respects the rule of law, as stated in Article 2 TEU, also entails legal consequences as far as it forms the basis of the principle of mutual recognition. The legal concept of mutual recognition, which is based upon mutual trust among the Member States that Union law will be respected,[54] draws on the idea that in areas which have not been fully harmonised by the Union, the authorities of a Member State have to accept the legal acts of another Member State in regard to certain factual circumstances as binding, thus treating them as if they had been decided upon by the Member State's own legal order.[55] Important fields of application of this principle are the Union citizenship, where the Member States must recognise the grant of citizenship by another Member State,[56] or legal acts in

---

[47]CJEU, Case C-14/68 *Wilhelm and Others v. Bundeskartellamt*, ECLI:EU:C:1969:4, para. 5.

[48]See Case C-6/72 *Europemballage Corporation and Continental Can Company v. Commission*, ECLI:EU:C:1973:22, para 24; *EEA I*, *supra* note 12, para. 18.

[49]CJEU, *Wilhelm and Others v. Bundeskartellamt*, *supra* note 47, paras. 6 et seq.

[50]Kochenov (2015), p. 88.

[51]CJEU, *Les Verts*, *supra* note 9, para. 23.

[52]CJEU, Case C-619/18, *Commission v. Poland*, ECLI:EU:C:2018:910, para. 21; Case C-216/18 PPU, *Minister for Justice and Equality (LM)*, ECLI:EU:C:2018:586, paras. 48 et seq.

[53]von Bogdandy et al. (2018), p. 986.

[54]CJEU, *EEA I*, *supra* note 12, para. 168.

[55]Möstl (2010), p. 405.

[56]CJEU, Case C-200/02 *Zhu and Chen*, ECLI:EU:C:2004:639, para. 37.

the Area of Freedom, Security and Justice (AFSJ) such as the European Arrest Warrant on the basis of Framework Decision 2002/584/JHA.[57]

It becomes clearer and clearer, however, that in some Member States the legislative, administrative and judicial procedures do not satisfy the rule of law minimum standards which are presupposed by the principle of mutual recognition. In such a case, there is no basis in Union law for the recognition of such procedures and decisions by other Member States[58] since 'mutual recognition' must be performed in conformity with primary law, i.e. in conformity with Article 2 TEU. Hence, the CJEU has expressly obliged the Member States, in particular, national courts and administrative bodies to suspend their legal cooperation with such Member States that massively violated rule of law minimum standards.[59] More recent legal acts demonstrate that the Union legislator has become aware of this problem, too. For instance, according to Article 11 paragraph 1 lit f) of the Directive 2014/41/EU regarding the European Investigation Order in criminal matters[60] the recognition or execution of a European Investigation Order on gathering evidence for criminal proceedings issued by the authorities of one Member State may be rejected by the authorities of other Member States where there are substantial grounds to believe this could be incompatible with Article 6 TEU and the FRC. Besides, Article 3 paragraph 2 sub-paragraph 2 of the Regulation (EU) 604/2013[61] (Dublin III Regulation) obliges the Member States, when determining which Member State is responsible for the examining of an application for international protection, to also check whether 'there are substantial grounds for believing that there are systemic flaws in the asylum procedure and in the reception conditions for applicants in [another] Member State, resulting in a risk of inhuman or degrading treatment'. In such case, the determining Member State must not transfer the applicants in that other Member State.[62]

---

[57]See CJEU, Case C-303/05 *Advocaten voor de Wereld*, ECLI:EU:C:2007:261, paras. 28 et seq.

[58]See CJEU, Case C-135/08 *Rottmann*, ECLI:EU:C:2010:104, paras. 48 et seq. for the limits of recognition of granting citizenship by a Member State by the others in arbitrary decisions.

[59]See CJEU, Joined Cases C-411/10 and C-493/10 *N.S. and Others*, ECLI:EU:C:2011:865, para. 86, regarding Council Regulation (EC) 343/2003 establishing criteria and mechanisms for determining the Member State responsible for examining an asylum application lodged in one of the Member States by a third-country nation (Dublin II Regulation) (2003) OJ L 50/1. With regard to the European Arrest Warrant, see CJEU, Joined Cases C-404/15 and C-659/15 PPU *Aranyosi and Căldăraru*, ECLI: EU:C:2016:198, paras. 77 et seq.; Case C-452/16 PPU *Poltorak*, ECLI:EU: C:2016:858, paras. 44 et seq.; *LM*, *supra* note 52, para. 59. See further Lenaerts (2017b), pp. 810 et seq.

[60](2014) OJ L130/1.

[61]Regulation (EU) 604/2013 of the European Parliament and of the Council establishing the criteria and mechanisms for determining the Member State responsible for examining an application for international protection lodged in one of the Member States by a third-country national or a stateless person (Dublin III Regulation) (2013) OJ L 180/31.

[62]See CJEU, Case C-578/16 PPU *C.K.*, ECLI:EU:C:2017:127, paras. 92 et seq.

These examples demonstrate that the systematic disregard by a Member State of rule of law minimum standards in the scope of application of EU law also can have directs effects on the legal cooperation with other Member States.[63]

5 The Rule of Law As a Legal Concept

It is problematic, however, to operationalise the rule of law without having clarified its content before.

5.1 Determining the Content of the Rule of Law

In fact, it is often questioned whether the rule of law, despite its importance being undisputed, is able to perform a valuable function for the Union's legal order as it is too vague and undetermined.[64] Ambiguities as to the content of the Union rule of law can be explained, first of all, by the fact that the Treaties do not contain explicit statements on rule of law issues. To be sure, Articles 7 and 49 TEU refer to the rule of law via Article 2 TEU. Yet, the Treaties do not define what is to be understood by this concept.

The Commission and the courts when enforcing the rule of law vis-à-vis a certain Member State, however, cannot simply refer to Article 2 TEU and content themselves to an 'I know it when I see it'-approach.[65] A concretisation of the rule of law beyond the mere reference in Article 2 TEU is, however, needed from the point of view of the rule of law itself. The principle of legal determinateness requires that legal provisions which impose a certain code of conduct on legal subjects are sufficiently specific, so that the persons affected by them can align their conduct with these provisions.[66] In addition, the policies adopted by some Member States have shown that a lack of consensus on the content of the Union rule of law might be understood as an invitation to test the limits of Article 2 and 7 TEU.

---

[63]von Bogdandy et al. (2018), pp. 992 et seq.

[64]Kochenov (2015), p. 79; Claes and Bonelli (2016), pp. 267 et seq.; Barnett (2018), p. 24.

[65]This famous phrase on the difficulties of legal decision-making appears in U.S. Supreme Court, *Jacobellis v. Ohio*, 378 U.S. 184 (1964) p. 197 (Stewart, J, concurring).

[66]CJEU, Joined cases 212 to 217/80 *Amministrazione delle finanze dello Stato v. Meridionale Industria Salumi and Others*, ECLI:EU:C:1981:270, para. 10; Barnett (2018), p. 26.

5.2 The European Tradition of the Rule of Law

There might be a number of reasons why the conceptions as to the content and significance of the rule of law in Europe are unclear, even though the preamble of the TEU refers to the rule of law as a 'universal value'.[67] One of these reasons is certainly that the concept of the rule of law has a more limited European tradition than, for example, the concept of democracy which is meanwhile extensively described in Articles 9 et seq. TEU.

To be sure, the concept of rule of law can be long traced back, at least in the English history of law. The concepts of rule of law in the UK, of 'Rechtsstaatlichkeit' in Germany and of 'État de droit' in France have, however, developed a particular impact only after the nineteenth century and flourished in the era of European constitutionalism.[68] Even more, most EU Member States' constitutions are familiar with the concept of the rule of law only since the 1970s. Ultimately, there is a considerable range of legal concepts in Europe which are gathered under the notion of the rule of law.

5.3 Formal and Material Aspects of the Rule of Law

Regardless of different approaches and rule of law traditions most would agree that a basic meaning of the rule of law comes down to the idea that all public power must act within certain constraints by law, i.e. that it is bound by legal norms which are outside of its control.[69] The rule of law is a legal principle organising the relationship between a community and its governing institutions, reducing the discretion of public power by subjecting it to means of effective legal and judicial control.[70]

Sometimes doubts are expressed concerning the usefulness of this broad definition.[71] It reveals that the rule of law does not constitute a straightforward concept, but rather an aggregate notion for a set of subprinciples which are themselves in need of concretisation depending on the respective context.[72] It is correct that constitutional law problems are primarily to be solved on the basis of constitutional subprinciples that form part of the meta-concept of the rule of law but are closer to the problem, for example, principles such as legal certainty or separation of powers; the concept of rule of law should be drawn upon only subsidiarily. At the same time,

[67] Cruz Villalón (2007), para. 60.

[68] For a comparative analysis, see Loughlin (2010), pp. 312 et seq., especially 314 et seq.; Heuschling (2002), pp. 384 et seq.; Holterhus (2017), pp. 453 et seq.

[69] Kochenov (2015), p. 81; Crabit and Bael (2016), p. 198.

[70] Holterhus (2017), p. 432; Konstantinides (2017), pp. 29 et seq.; Sobotta (1997), pp. 21 et seq.

[71] See Kunig (1986), pp. 89 et seq., 457 et seq.

[72] Waldron (2008), p. 3; Holterhus (2017), p. 432. See the case law of the German Constitutional Court, e.g. BVerfG, 2 BvL 25/81, Judgment of 22 November 1983 (BVerfGE 65, 283, 290).

the rule of law is far from being a mere ideological formula without any normative self-reliance. It has an autonomous role where the challenge is to link these various elements in systematic fashion in order to thereby obtain functional insights.[73]

Against this background, it may not come as a surprise that there is a discourse in Europe on which subprinciples may be attributed to the rule of law and form part of it. At the heart of the struggle for conceptualising the rule of law lies the choice between a formal ('thin') or on a material ('thick') concept.[74] Behind this discourse lies the question of whether the rule of law principle is identical to claims regarding 'process and form' or whether it also contains demands concerning the content of legal norms in terms of fairness. Formal interpretations of the rule of law as mere obligation to respect the law were for a long time not only common in the UK.[75] The principle of legality and other aspects associated with formal rule of law qualities like the hierarchy of norms also constitute the core elements of the formal 'Rechtsstaatlichkeit' in Germany, Austria and France.[76] In fact, representatives of a 'negative' or 'thin' concept of the rule of law caution even today against overburdening the concept with diverse social objectives, so that it does not become devoid of content and practically irrelevant. They assert that the core of the rule of law rather consists of a set of requirements such as that the legal norms of a given legal order should be general, public, prospective and certain.[77]

There is some truth to this warning, but it is also true that according to most constitutional provisions in Europe, legal norms must satisfy elementary requirements of justice in regard to an obligation of fairness and prohibition of arbitrariness. This claim for a just creation, application and interpretation of legal norms is secured by virtue of binding the legislator to the constitution and material constitutional principles such as fairness, equality and certainty of law.[78] This conception of the rule of law which is based on a combination of both formal and material aspects has become the most accepted one in many Member States.[79] This approach has also found favour on the Union level as will be shown below.

[73]Schmidt-Aßmann (2004), § 26 paras. 8 et seq. See also BVerfG, 2 BvR 215/81, Judgment of 26 March 1981 (BVerfGE 57, 250, 276) where the principle of the rule of law 'selbst' (itself) is used as a systematically relevant anchor for requirements of procedures.

[74]Magen (2016), p. 1052; Wennerström (2007), pp. 76 et seq.

[75]See especially Dicey (1961), p. 188. Critically, Craig (1997), pp. 470 et seq.; Krygier (2012), pp. 236 et seq.

[76]Classen (2013), pp. 63 et seq.; Loughlin (2010), pp. 315 et seq.

[77]See e.g. Raz (1977), pp. 210 et seq.

[78]See e.g. Dworkin (1985), pp. 335 et seq. Regarding Germany, see von Simson (1982), p. 109.

[79]Bingham (2010), p. 37.

6 The Rule of Law in the Union's Practice

6.1 Rule of Law As Described in the Commission Framework

The Commission has sought such clarification in its Communication of 11 March 2014 on a 'New framework to strengthen the rule of law'.[80] The text represents some principles meant to be common to the constitutional traditions in Europe. It relies, however, on the case law of the CJEU when identifying the elements of the rule of law.[81] The CJEU judgments cited in the Communication refer to the principles of legality, legal certainty, effective legal protection as well as prohibition of arbitrariness, but only in regard to the conduct of the Union's institutions and mostly in the field of European competition law. These judgements of the Court of Justice do, however, not deal with the legal situation in the Member States, i.e. whether the conduct of the national powers meets the rule of law standard of the Union.

This does not suffice to give shape to a Union rule of law in the meaning of Article 2 TEU. The reference of the framework to the CJEU's jurisprudence may serve as an indicator when determining the rule of law, but it should be taken into account that the exercise of public authority by Union institutions and national authorities cannot be equally treated in legal terms[82] and that the national constitutional traditions regarding the rule of law in Europe may differ from the concept pursued by the CJEU. Moreover, the framework itself has the character of a checklist that has been created in an inductive way. Like other rule of law checklists, it does not claim to be exhaustive nor of absolute character.[83]

The added value of the new rule of law framework of the Commission particularly lies in the fact that on the basis of a dialogue between the Commission and Member States, the Member States' obligations deriving from the rule of law can be specified. Accordingly, the biggest shortcoming of the Union rule of law, i.e. the indeterminacy as regards its content, can be overcome. The Commission has sought to strengthen the normative relevance of its rule of law definition by reiterating the framework in legal documents relating to the rule of law situation in certain Member States.[84] In addition, it has relied on the framework's rule of law interpretation in its proposal for a regulation on the protection of the Union's budget in case of generalised deficiencies as regards the rule of law in the Member States. However,

---

[80]Commission 'Communication from the Commission to the European Parliament and the Council: a new EU Framework to strengthen the Rule of Law' COM (2014)158 final, 4 and Annex 1; see Crabit and Bael (2016), p. 197; von Bogdandy et al. (2018), pp. 985 et seq.

[81]See Lenaerts (2017a), p. 641.

[82]See CJEU, *Germany v. Council*, *supra* note 19, para 38. Against constitutional analogies also ECtHR, *Matthews v. United Kingdom*, *supra* note 19, para. 48.

[83]See Fuchs (2018), pp. 239, 243 with regard to the 'Rule of Law Checklist' of the Venice Commission for Democracy through Law (Study No. 711/2013, CDL-AD(2016)007 Strasbourg 18 March 2016).

[84]See COM (2017) 835 final, *supra* note 42, para. 1 and other documents relating to the situation in Poland (SWD/2018/219 final).

these measures have contributed little to the establishment of a specific Union rule of law definition because the Commission's definition merely consists of a list of legal subprinciples.[85]

6.2 Rule of Law in the Case Law of the CJEU

It has already been outlined that the Court of Justice uses a rule of law terminology reminiscent of national constitutional law and has located the source of the rule of law in the general legal principles of Union law. However, questions arise as to which substantive changes are associated with the conceptual extension and application of the rule of law to the Union level. What are the attributes of a 'Union based on the rule of law'?[86]

The case law of the Court of Justice is based on a twofold concept reflecting formal as well as substantive aspects of the rule of law. The formal binding of the public authority to the law and the requirement that any intervention by public authorities in the sphere of private activities of any person must have a legal basis is—in line with prominent constitutional traditions of the Member States—the nucleus of the rule of law of the Union.[87] Another typical formal aspect of the rule of law, which can also be found in Union law, is the principle on the hierarchical relationship of norms[88] which helps the structuring of the legal order.

Article 19 paragraph 1, second sentence TEU manifests, however, that the Union law contains also material aspects of the rule of law. The Union's public authority must be exercised by respecting supra-positive elements of justice ('the law').[89] This notion of the 'law' itself as mentioned in Article 19 paragraph 1, second sentence TEU served in the jurisprudence as the starting point for the developing of the Union rule of law as a general principle of law. Yet, this judicial concept of the rule of law is somehow restricted. It refers, due to the systematic place of Article 19 TEU within the Treaty, mainly to the role of the judicial branch in the constitutional system of the

[85]See Article 2 lit a) of the proposed regulation of the European Parliament and of the Council on the protection of the Union's budget in case of generalised deficiencies as regards the rule of law in the Member States, COM (2018) 324 final defining the rule of law as 'the Union value enshrined in Article 2 of the Treaty on European Union which includes the principles of legality, implying a transparent, accountable, democratic and pluralistic process for enacting laws; legal certainty; prohibition of arbitrariness of the executive powers; effective judicial protection by independent courts, including of fundamental rights; separation of powers and equality before the law'.

[86]See CJEU, *Schrems*, *supra* note 9, para. 60.

[87]CJEU, Case C-496/99 P *Commission v. CAS Succhi di Frutta*, ECLI:EU:C:2004:236, para. 63. See also CJEU, Joined Cases C-46/87 and 227/88 *Hoechst v. Commission*, ECLI:EU:C:1989:337, para. 19. But see Kochenov (2015), pp. 81 et seq.

[88]See CFI, Case T-51/89 *Tetra Pak v. Commission*, ECLI:EU:T:1990:41, para. 25. See Merli (2016), p. 37.

[89]See Rodríguez Iglesias (1996), pp. 125, 128.

Union.[90] This becomes particularly clear when the Court emphasises the relevance of judicial independence to the Union rule of law.[91]

First of all, the Community of law defines itself in view of the obligation of comprehensive and effective legal protection.[92] The CJEU's major reference point for the development of the rule of law was therefore for a long time Article 6 ECHR. Further elements of the rule of law, as emphasised by the Court, such as the right to a fair trial and independent courts, which ensure the respect for rules and rights established by Union law,[93] and even the principle of separation of powers[94] are also interpreted to serve legal protection before the European Courts.

To be sure, one can derive from the case law further propositions on legal principles such as fundamental rights which are inseparably linked to a material perception of the rule of law.[95] Without doubt, also the principles of legal certainty and the protection of legitimate expectations[96] as well as the principle of proportionality pertain to the material concept of 'law', as enshrined in Article 19 TEU, which guarantees 'protection against arbitrary and disproportionate intervention'.[97] The Court of Justice has, however, always placed these material principles in the context of the legal protection in the Union. It regards the respect for these principles as a requirement for the legality of acts 'which it is for the Court to review in the framework of the complete system of legal remedies established by the Treaty'.[98] The Court has repeatedly pointed out that the material elements of the rule of law must integrate themselves into the system of legal protection in the Union.[99]

---

[90]E.g. CFI, Case T-411/06 *Sogelma v. AER*, ECLI:EU:T:2008:419, para. 37. See also Rodríguez Iglesias (1996), p. 125; Lenaerts (2007), p. 1625.

[91]See CJEU, Case C-619/18 *Commission v. Poland*, ECLI:EU:C:2018:1021, paras. 41 et seq.; *Commission v. Poland, supra* note 52, paras. 21 et seq. See von Danwitz (2016), p. 155.

[92]This principle is specified in: CJEU, *Les Verts, supra* note 9, para. 23. With respect to Community actions and Member States, see respectively CJEU, Case C-222/84 *Johnston v. Chief Constable of the Royal Ulster Constabulary*, ECLI:EU:C:1986:206, paras. 18 et seq.; *Kadi, supra* note 9, paras. 281, 316. See von Bogdandy (2017), p. 497 who perceives judicial control as the core of the 'Rechtsidee' (i.e. legal idea) of the Union.

[93]CJEU, Joined Cases C-174/98 P and C-189/98 P *Netherlands and Van der Wal v. Commission*, ECLI:EU:C:2000:1, para. 17. See Badó and Bóka (2016), p. 46.

[94]CJEU, *Poltorak, supra* note 59, paras. 44–45; Case C-477/16 *Kovalkovas*, ECLI:EU:C:2016:861, paras. 43–44.

[95]CJEU, *Kadi, supra* note 9, para. 285.

[96]CJEU, Case C-10/69 *Portelange v. Smith Corona Marchant International*, ECLI:EU:C:1969:36, para. 15/16; Joined Cases 205 to 215/82 *Deutsche Milchkontor GmbH v. Germany*, ECLI:EU:C:1983:233, paras. 27 et seq. See Gamper (2016), p. 80.

[97]This norm is understood to be a general principle of (EU) law, see CJEU, Case C-4/73 *Nold KG v. Commission*, ECLI:EU:C:1974:51, para. 13; *Hoechst v. Commission, supra* note 87, para. 19. See Huber (2016), p. 98.

[98]CJEU, *Kadi, supra* note 9, para. 285.

[99]CJEU, *Accession of the EU to the ECHR II, supra* note 12, para. 177. See Jaeger (2018), pp. 626 et seq.

The motive of the Court's quest for legal protection is not only a demand for the safeguarding of individual rights, but also a demand for the full and effective application of Union law in the Member States. The legal requirement that all courts and tribunals in the Union have 'to ensure the full application of EU law in all Member States and judicial protection of the rights of individuals under that law', is, in the words of the CJEU, an 'expression (of) the value of the rule of law affirmed in Article 2 TEU'.[100] By this token, the rule of law may be regarded also as an instrument safeguarding the autonomy of the Union legal order and to protect it against internal and external challenges.[101]

7 Essence of the Union Rule of Law

What remains is the insight that the rule of law constitutes a 'conceptual puzzle' in the Union legal order since there exist different conceptions of its significance and its content beyond its basic meaning that any form of public power must be subordinated to some kind of primary, unchangeable norms. This principle cannot be defined conclusively and it may evolve over time.

At the same time, from the point of view of Union law, it is indispensable to determine the rule of law more precisely; not only is it referred to in black-letter treaty law (Article 2 TEU), but understood by Union courts as a constitutional meta-principle that provides a justification for review proceedings and informs other constitutional norms.[102] Moreover, its respect, or not, entails legal consequences. Inasmuch as the rule of law constitutes a general principle of law, it is necessary to draw on both the pertinent case law of the European courts as well as the common constitutional traditions of the Member States (Article 6 paragraph 3 TEU).

Due to the above-explained common European constitutional tradition it is well established that the European rule of law does not only have a formal, but also a material side and includes substantive claims for justice and the prohibition of arbitrariness. At the same time, the vehement warning that the rule of law might be overstretched shows that the containment of public authority by institutional arrangements is still one of the core concerns of the rule of law. This also corresponds to the jurisprudence of the European courts which underscores the procedural safeguarding of justice. Among these principles figure the principle of hierarchy of norms and of legality, i.e. the binding of the legislator to the constitution and of the administrative and judicial powers to the law, the transparency and perceptibility of

[100]CJEU, *LM*, *supra* note 52, para. 50. Similar CJEU, Case C-64/16 *Associação Sindical dos Juízes Portugueses v. Tribunal de Contas*, ECLI:EU:C:2018:117, para. 32; Case C-284/16 *Achmea*, ECLI:EU:C:2018:158, para. 36.

[101]This does, however, not imply that in the case law of the CJEU the rule of law is 'pre-empted' by considerations of Union autonomy as Kochenov (2015), pp. 78, 93 et seq. suggests.

[102]Pech (2010), pp. 376 et seq.; Holterhus (2017), p. 460; Barnett (2018), p. 34.

norms. In addition, also the principles of separation of powers and of effective legal protection by independent courts are counted among the formal institutional guarantees of the rule of law. As far as the implementation and understanding of these principles in a more detailed fashion are concerned, there exist significant differences among the Member States' constitutions.

In view of the strong tradition of a formal approach to the rule of law in Europe, consensus at the Union level might be achieved on the fact that the rule of law comprises not only strictly formal standards but also material criteria of justice that are related to the juridical shaping of decision-making processes. Characteristic examples are principles such as legal certainty, protection of legitimate expectations and proportionality.

All these subprinciples of the rule of law shall ensure that any public power is exercised in a non-arbitrary and legitimate way. To this end, they may not only be understood as objective norms but also ensure the protection of individual rights. As Article 52 paragraph 1 of the FRC makes clear in relation to the principle of proportionality, these material standards are intrinsically linked to fundamental rights.[103] To the extent that a restriction of fundamental rights is effected without a legal basis within the meaning of Article 52 paragraph 1, first sentence FRC,[104] that this restriction is disproportionate given certain common interests, that it does not satisfy the claims of legal certainty or that it does not provide for an appropriate legal protection mechanism, one may not only assume that human rights have been violated but also that a violation of the rule of law has occurred, which may be challenged by any individual before a Union court of law.[105]

Fundamental rights and rule of law principles are, in the Union constitutional system, mutually dependent and reinforce each other.[106] The Union rule of law aims at protecting individual fundamental rights and, conversely, fundamental rights are a material prerequisite of such a rule of law. At most, one can say that the guarantee of the institution of fundamental rights is an essential component of a Union under the rule of law. Individual fundamental rights are, however, not necessarily part of the rule of law,[107] as is also made clear by Article 2 TEU which conceives the rule of law and fundamental rights as different principles. Moreover, there is no constitutional law surplus value in qualifying single human rights additionally as an element of the rule of law as they are sufficiently assured by the Article 6 TEU and the European Charter of Fundamental Rights which is legally binding.

---

[103]Venice Commission for Democracy through Law, Study No. 711/2013, *supra* note 83, para. 31.

[104]CJEU, *Hoechst v. Commission*, *supra* note 87, para. 19.

[105]CJEU, *Kadi*, *supra* note 9, para. 316; *Commission v. Poland*, *supra* note 52, para. 21; *LM*, *supra* note 52, para. 48 et seq.

[106]This applies in particular to the principle of effective judicial protection which forms part of the rule of law but finds also expression in Article 47 FRC, see Konstantinides (2017), p. 83.

[107]Lenaerts (2017a), p. 641.

References

Badó A, Bóka J (2016) Access to justice and judicial independence. In: Schroeder W (ed) Strengthening the rule of law in Europe. Hart, Oxford, pp 46–60

Baquero Cruz J (2008) The legacy of the Maastricht-Urteil and the pluralist movement. Eur Law J 14:389–422

Barnett G (2018) Reflections on what the rule of law means and its significance at EU level. In: Hatje A, Tichý L (eds) Liability of member states for the violation of fundamental values of the European Union. Nomos Verlagsgesellschaft mbH & Co. KG, Baden-Baden, pp 23–38. EuR Beiheft 1

Bengoetxea J (1993) The legal reasoning of the European court of justice: towards a European jurisprudence. Clarendon Press, Oxford

Bingham T (2010) The rule of law. Allen Lane, London

Calliess C (2004) Europa als Wertegemeinschaft – Integration und Identität durch europäisches Verfassungsrecht? Juristenzeitung 59:1033–1084

Calliess C (2011) EUV Art 2. In: Calliess C, Ruffert M (eds) EUV/AEUV: Kommentar, 4th edn. CH Beck, Munich

Claes M, Bonelli M (2016) The rule of law and the constitutionalisation of the European Union. In: Schroeder W (ed) Strengthening the rule of law in Europe. Hart, Oxford, pp 265–289

Classen CD (2013) Nationales Verfassungsrecht in der Europäischen Union: eine integrierte Darstellung der 27 Verfassungsordnungen. Nomos, Baden-Baden

Crabit E, Bael N (2016) The EU rule of law framework. In: Schroeder W (ed) Strengthening the rule of law in Europe. Hart, Oxford, pp 197–206

Craig PP (1997) Formal and substantive conceptions of the rule of law: an analytical framework. Public Law 467:1–15

Cremona M (2005) EU enlargement: solidarity and conditionality. Eur Law Rev 30:3–22

Cruz Villalón P (2007) Vergleich. In: von Bogdandy A, Huber PM, Cruz Villalón P (eds) Handbuch Ius Publicum Europaeum, Band I: Grundlagen und Grundzüge staatlichen Verfassungsrechts. CF Müller, Heidelberg, pp 729–778, § 13

Dicey AV (1961) Introduction to the study of the law of the constitution, 10th edn. Palgrave Macmillan, London

Dworkin R (1985) A matter of principle. Oxford University Press, Oxford

Fuchs M (2018) Die Vermessung der Rechtsstaatlichkeit – Die 'Rule of Law Checklist' der Venedig-Kommission des Europarates. EuGRZ 45:237–243

Fuß EW (1968) Die Europäischen Gemeinschaften und der Rechtsstaatsgedanke. UGA, Heule

Gamper A (2016) Legal certainty. In: Schroeder W (ed) Strengthening the rule of law in Europe. Hart, Oxford, pp 80–97

Hallstein W (1969) Der unvollendete Bundesstaat: europäische Erfahrungen und Erkenntnisse. Econ-Verlag, Düsseldorf

Hallstein W (1979) Die EWG als Schritt zur Europäischen Einheit. In: Oppermann T (ed) Walter Hallstein — Europäische Reden. Deutsche Verlags-Anstalt, Stuttgart, pp 103–112

Heuschling L (2002) État de Droit: Rechtsstaat: rule of law. Dalloz, Paris

Hilf M, Schorkopf F (2015) EUV Art 2. In: Grabitz E, Hilf M, Nettesheim M (eds) Das Recht der Europäischen Union: EUV/AEUV, 57th edn. CH Beck, Munich

Hillion C (2016) Overseeing the rule of law in the EU: legal mandate and means. In: Closa C, Kochenev D (eds) Reinforcing rule of law oversight in the EU. Cambridge University Press, Cambridge, pp 59–81

Holterhus T (2017) The history of the rule of law. Max Planck Yearb United Nations Law 21:430–466

Huber PM (2016) The principle of proportionality. In: Schroeder W (ed) Strengthening the rule of law in Europe. Hart, Oxford, pp 98–112

Jaeger T (2018) Gerichtsorganisation und EU-Recht: Eine Standortbestimmung. Europarecht 53:611–652

Kochenov D (2013) The EU in its most serious crisis ever (and that's not the Euro crisis). http://verfassungsblog.de/en/the-eu-in-its-most-serious-crisis-ever-and-thats-not-the-euro-crisis-2. Accessed 15 Mar 2019
Kochenov D (2015) EU law without the rule of law: is the veneration of autonomy worth it? Yearb Eur Law 34:74–96
Konstantinides T (2017) The rule of law in the European Union – the internal dimension. Hart, Oxford
Krygier M (2012) Rule of law. In: Rosenfeld M, Sajó A (eds) The Oxford handbook of comparative constitutional law. Oxford University Press, Oxford, pp 233–249
Kunig P (1986) Das Rechtsstaatsprinzip: Überlegungen zu seiner Bedeutung für das Verfassungsrecht der Bundesrepublik Deutschland. Mohr Siebeck, Tübingen
Lenaerts K (1990) Constitutionalism and many faces of federalism. Am J Comp Law 38:205–263
Lenaerts K (2007) The rule of law and the coherence of the judicial system of the European Union. Common Market Law Rev 44:1625–1659
Lenaerts K (2017a) Die Werte der Europäischen Union in der Rechtsprechung des Gerichtshofs der Europäischen Union: eine Annäherung. EuGRZ 21:639–642
Lenaerts K (2017b) La vie après l'avis: exploring the principle of mutual (yet not blind) trust. Common Market Law Rev 54:805–840
Loughlin M (2010) Foundations of public law. Oxford University Press, Oxford
Luhmann N (1987) Soziale Systeme: Grundriß einer allgemeinen Theorie. Suhrkamp, Frankfurt am Main
MacCormick N (1995) The Maastricht-Urteil: sovereignity now. Eur Law J 1:259–266
Magen A (2016) Cracks in the foundation: understanding the great rule of law debate in the EU. J Common Market Stud 54:1050–1061
Mancini GF (1989) The making of a constitution for Europe. Common Market Law Rev 26:595–614
Mangiameli S (2013) Article 2: the homogeneity clause. In: Blanke H-J, Mangiameli S (eds) The treaty on European Union (TEU). A commentary. Springer, Heidelberg, pp 109–155
Merli F (2016) Principle of legality and the hierarchy of norms. In: Schroeder W (ed) Strengthening the rule of law in Europe. Hart, Oxford, pp 37–45
Möstl M (2010) Preconditions and limits of mutual recognition. Common Market Law Rev 47:405–436
Ohler C (2015) EUV Art 49. In: Grabitz E, Hilf M, Nettesheim M (eds) Das Recht der Europäischen Union: EUV/AEUV, 57th edn. CH Beck, Munich
Pech L (2010) 'A union founded on the rule of law': meaning and reality of the rule of law as a constitutional principle of EU law. Eur Const Law Rev 6:359–396
Pernice I (1995) Carl Schmitt, Rudolf Smend und die europäische Integration. Archiv des öffentlichen Rechts 120:100–120
Raz J (1977) The rule of law and its virtue. Law Q Rev 93:195–211
Rodríguez Iglesias GC (1996) Zur 'Verfassung' der Europäischen Gemeinschaft. EuGRZ 23:125–131
Scharpf FW (1985) Die Politikverflechtungsfalle: Europäische Integration und deutscher Föderalismus im Vergleich. Politische Vierteljahresschrift 26:323–356
Scheppele KL (2015) Understanding Hungary's constitutional revolution. In: von Bogdandy A, Sonnevend P (eds) Constitutional crisis in the European constitutional area: theory, law and politics in Hungary and Romania. Hart, Oxford, pp 111–124
Schmidt-Aßmann E (2004) Der Rechtsstaat. In: Isensee J, Kirchhof P (eds) Handbuch des Staatsrechts der Republik Deutschland, Band II: Verfassungsstaat. C.F. Müller, Heidelberg, pp 541–612, § 26
Schmitt C (1985) Politische Theologie - Vier Kapitel zur Lehre von der Souveränität, 4th edn. Duncker & Humblot, reprint, Berlin
Schmitt C (2008) Constitutional theory. Duke University Press, Durham

Schroeder W (2002) Das Gemeinschaftsrechtssystem: eine Untersuchung zu den rechtsdogmatischen, rechtstheoretischen und verfassungsrechtlichen Grundlagen des Systemdenkens im Europäischen Gemeinschaftsrecht. Mohr Siebeck, Tübingen
Sobotta K (1997) Das Prinzip Rechtsstaat: Verfassungs- und verwaltungsrechtliche Aspekte. Mohr Siebeck, Tübingen
Tridimas T (2013) The general principles of EU law, 3rd edn. Oxford University Press, Oxford
von Bogdandy A (2009) Founding principles. In: von Bogdandy A, Bast J (eds) Principles of European constitutional law, 2nd edn. Hart, Portland, pp 11–54
von Bogdandy A (2017) Jenseits der Rechtsgemeinschaft – Begriffsarbeit in der europäischen Sinn- und Rechtsstaatlichkeitskrise. EuR 52:487–511
von Bogdandy A, Ioannidis M (2014) Systemic deficiency in the rule of law: what it is, what has been done, what can be done. Common Market Law Rev 51:59–96
von Bogdandy A et al (2012) Reverse Solange – protecting the essence of fundamental rights against member states. Common Market Law Rev 49:489–520
von Bogdandy A et al (2018) A potential constitutional moment for the European rule of law – the importance of red lines. Common Market Law Rev 55:983–996
von Danwitz T (2016) The rule of law in the recent jurisprudence of the ECJ. In: Schroeder W (ed) Strengthening the rule of law in Europe. Hart, Oxford, pp 155–169
von Simson W (1982) Die Deutschen und ihr Rechtsstaat. Der Staat 21:97–112
Waldron J (2008) The concept and the rule of law. Georgia Law Rev 43:1–61
Weiler JHH (1981) The community system: the dual character of supranationalism. Yearb Eur Law 1:267–306
Wennerström EO (2007) The rule of law and the European Union. Lustu Forlag, Uppsala

Werner Schroeder is Full Professor at the Department of European Law and Public International Law, University of Innsbruck, Austria.

Article 7: A Commentary on a Much Talked-About 'Dead' Provision

Dimitry Kochenov

Contents

Abstract The goal of this chapter is to contribute to the growing Article 7 TEU literature by showcasing the strong and weak points of this provision in the context of the on-going rule of law backsliding in Hungary and Poland threatening the very fabric of EU constitutionalism. This is done by presenting the general context of the institutional reactions to the so-called 'reforms' in Poland and Hungary aimed to hijack the state machinery by the political parties in charge; introducing the background of Article 7 TEU and the hopes of the drafters the provision was endowed with; to move on to the analysis of its scope and all the procedures made available through this instrument as well as the key procedural rules in place. The conclusion restates the necessity of putting our hopes in alternative instruments of combatting

This Chapter has been previously published in *Polish Yearbook of Inernational Law* XXXVIII (2018), 165.

D. Kochenov (✉)
University of Groningen, Groningen, The Netherlands
e-mail: D.Kochenov@rug.nl

A. von Bogdandy et al. (eds.), *Defending Checks and Balances in EU Member States*, Beiträge zum ausländischen öffentlichen Recht und Völkerrecht 298,
https://doi.org/10.1007/978-3-662-62317-6_6

rule of law backsliding, outlining three possible scenarios of this, which are not (necessarily) connected to Article 7 as such.

'Article 7 is dead. The European Commission lost.'
Polish Minister of Foreign Affairs on the National TV in December 2018.[1]

1 Introduction

What is the situation with the rule of law in the European Union (EU) today? Is the Minister responsible for undermining Polish constitutionalism right? Looking at the most dramatic examples, Poland[2] has now joined Hungary,[3] and following the apt description of what is going on provided by Pech and Scheppele, it is possible to characterise the on-going troubles in the EU as 'rule of law backsliding', which is deemed to be a 'process through which elected public authorities deliberately implement governmental blueprints which aim to systematically weaken, annihilate or capture internal checks on power with the view of dismantling the liberal democratic state and entrenching the long-term rule of the dominant party.'[4] Considering that more states could follow this approach, the EU's position is, apparently, very weak: new soft law of questionable quality has been produced by each of its institutions.[5]

---

[1]PolsatNews (2018).

[2]European Commission, *Reasoned Proposal in Accordance with Article 7(1) of the Treaty on European Union Regarding the Rule of Law in Poland – Proposal for a Council Decision on the Determination of a Clear Risk of a Serious Breach by the Republic of Poland of the Rule of Law* [2017] (COM(2017) 835 final). Cf., most importantly: Sadurski (2018), Bodnar (2018), Koncewicz (2018), Pech and Platon (2017), Koncewicz (2016). See also The Venice Commission for Democracy through Law, *Opinion on amendments to the Act of 25 June 2015 on the Constitutional Tribunal of Poland*, CDL-AD(2016)001, (Venice, 11 March 2016), http://www.venice.coe.int/webforms/documents/?pdf=CDL-AD%282016%29001-e.

[3]European Parliament, *Resolution of 12 September 2018 on a proposal calling on the Council to determine, pursuant to Article 7(1) of the Treaty on European Union, the existence of a clear risk of a serious breach by Hungary of the values on which the Union is founded* (2017/2131(INL)). Cf., most importantly, Szente (2017), Varju and Papp (2016), Scheppele (2015), Sólyom (2015), Collot (2013), Bánkuti et al. (2012).

[4]Pech and Scheppele (2017), p. 8; Bugarič (2019). Aspects of this phenomenon have equally been branded as 'systemic deficiencies' and 'statutory anti-constitutionalism': von Bogdandy (2019), Bernatt and Ziółkowski (2019). For an overarching analysis, see, Bignami (2019).

[5]Council of the EU Press Release no. 16936/14, *3362nd Council meeting, General Affairs*, (2014), pp. 20–21; European Commission, *A New EU Framework to Strengthen the Rule of Law* (2014) (COM(2014)158); European Parliament, *Report with Recommendations to the Commission on the Establishment of an EU Mechanism on Democracy, the Rule of Law and Fundamental Rights* (2016) (2015/2254(INL)). For a comparison of all these instruments, see Kochenov et al. (2016), Kochenov and Pech (2016), Oliver and Stefanelli (2016); but see Hirsch Ballin (2016), Kochenov et al. (2015), Kochenov and Pech (2015a); See also Kochenov (2019c).

The Treaties contain a special provision to deal specifically with situations of rule of law backsliding: Art. 7 of the Treaty on European Union (TEU), which however has not emerged as a particularly effective instrument to solve the outstanding problems the Union is facing. Thus the picture is grim, notwithstanding even the belated activation of the Art. 7(1) TEU mechanism against both countries in question.[6] This activation *per se* is obviously somewhat misplaced, as we will see, since Art. 7(1) TEU is about 'threats' to values, and the assault on the values in Poland and Hungary are way beyond the 'threat' point, thus begging the question of how appropriate the legal basis chosen actually is.[7] Indeed, the situation would seem to be evolving extremely fast and mainly—almost uniquely—in the direction of the deterioration of the rule of law and abuses by the executive of independent national institutions. The EU's ability to effectively intervene and bring about significant change, although discussed quite extensively in the literature, has failed to materialise on the ground.[8] Most worryingly, it seems that there is total disagreement among essentially all the actors involved concerning what should be done, and the political will to sort out the current impasse is lacking at the level of the Member States too.

The goal of this contribution is to contribute to the growing Art. 7 TEU literature[9] by showcasing the strong and weak points of this provision in the context of the on-going rule of law backsliding in Hungary and Poland, which is threatening the very fabric of EU constitutionalism. This is done by presenting the general context of the institutional reactions to the so-called 'reforms' in Poland and Hungary aimed at hijacking the state machinery by the political parties in charge; introducing the background of Art. 7 TEU and the hopes of the drafters the provision was endowed with; then moving on to an analysis of its scope and all the procedures made available through this instrument as well as the key procedural rules in place. The conclusion restates the necessity of putting our hopes in alternative instruments for combatting rule of law backsliding, outlining three possible scenarios of this, which are not (necessarily) connected to Art. 7 as such.

[6]European Parliament, 2017/2131(INL), *supra* note 3; European Commission, COM(2017) 835 final, *supra* note 2. Pech and Scheppele (2017), Blay-Grabarczyk (2019).

[7]Kochenov (2019a).

[8]Safjan (2018), Waelbroek and Oliver (2017), Jakab and Kochenov (2017a), Pech and Scheppele (2017), von Bogdandy and Sonnevend (2015), Closa and Kochenov (2016), Mori (2016), p. 204; Sedelmeier (2014), Müller (2014).

[9]On Article 7 TEU see, most importantly, Besselink (2017), Wilms (2017), Waelbroek and Oliver (2017), pp. 313–319; Bugarič (2016), Hillion (2016), Bieber and Maiani (2014), Sadurski (2010), Schmidt von Sydow (2001).

2 A Brief Context of Coping with Rule of Law Backsliding

Art. 7 TEU, whatever sanctions it contains, cannot be a panacea. Blokker has been absolutely correct in constantly reminding us of the need to deal with the deeper roots of soft totalitarianism and populist turns.[10] At issue is the phenomenon characterised by Scheppele as 'autocratic legalism', which has deep implications for the very fabric of the societies in question, potentially making the return to liberal democracy difficult.[11] Moreover, the problem of 'democratic decay', 'backsliding' and populism seems to be a global one,[12] rather than confined to some EU Member States *per se*. In the EU, just as elsewhere in the world—from Venezuela to Turkey—'sociological legitimacy'[13] is crucially important and cannot be ignored. The core issue is how to ensure that the EU's own rule of law is meticulously and consistently upheld, while enjoying, crucially, solid legitimacy? The issue of societal internalisation of the core principles of Art. 2 TEU in the face of a populist wave is fundamental here. Framed in this way, the problem clearly emerges as too ambitious for the EU institutions to digest.

The Council is the most guilty of all the institutions in terms of downplaying the importance of the rule of law backsliding and even presenting key moves by other institutions to tackle it as potentially illegal. The Council legal service has been negative—with no solid arguments for its position[14]—about the Commission's 'pre-Article 7 proposal'.[15] It similarly dismissed the attempts to cut the EU funding of the backsliding states.[16] Topping the list, however, is the position of the Council Legal Service on the proposal to invite MEP Judith Sargentini to present in Council her report that triggered the request from the Parliament to start Art. 7(1) procedure against Hungary: the Council does not want to listen to Miss Sargentini in person. Its position is based on legal advice which has been given 'orally', with the arguments not disclosed, which however does not shield the Council's position from criticism. A more absurd move could only be to support Hungary in front of the Court, where it has argued—not convincingly—that the Parliament managed to violate its own rules of procedure in adopting the Sargentini Report under Art. 7(1) TEU.[17]

The explanation behind the Council's unwillingness to act could be an obvious one: since the Internal Market is an emanation of deep economic interpenetration, aimed at making outright hostilities between the Member States impossible—

[10]Blokker (2016, 2018).

[11]Scheppele (2018).

[12]Daly (2019) and Anselmi (2018).

[13]Blokker (2019).

[14]Kochenov and Pech (2015b).

[15]Council of the European Union, *Opinion of the Legal Service 10296/14*, 14 May 2014, especially para. 28.

[16]Kelemen et al. (2018).

[17]CJEU, Case C-650/18 *Hungary v. European Parliament* (pending at time of writing). Cf. Kochenov (2019b).

precisely the reason behind picking economic tools to achieve the goal of peace[18]—it has shaped the day-to-day reality of European integration, leaving no room for Art. 7 TEU. The very logic of the provision, which is both deeply politicised and deeply confrontational, contradicts the logic of the Internal Market and the rich Member States potentially stand to lose a lot as a result of taking a principled value-laden position on rule of law backsliding. This is why expecting too much of the Council—and, by extension, of Art. 7 TEU—would be naïve. Unless something truly terrible happens in a backsliding Member State,[19] the Internal Market, after all, functions as designed.[20]

When the Council is naturally ill-inclined and other EU institutions are profoundly ineffective, the CJEU, like in Andersen's tale, *de facto* plays the role of the last soldier standing. It 'stands' by gradually learning from own mistakes and from the significant missteps of the Commission—especially in the 'age-discrimination' cases, where the hijacking of the Hungarian judiciary went unnoticed[21]—bringing about a radically more robust result in *Commission v. Poland* on virtually identical facts in the context of an attempted assault on the Supreme Court (more on this in the last section).[22]

Undoubtedly however, the Court cannot solve the outstanding problems alone, even when helped by the national judiciaries. A much more concerted effort is required of all the actors involved in order to get the EU out of the current impasse. In the meantime, the supranational political party groups, instead of helping, seem to aggravate the situation.[23] This inaction—or even attempts to hinder positive change—on the part of the political institutions helps the powers of the backsliding Member States consolidate their assault upon EU values even further, undermining the truly heroic efforts of the Court of Justice and the national courts in Poland,[24] Ireland,[25] and elsewhere in the Union. The 'stone-by-stone' approach of the CJEU,[26] although unable to solve the outstanding problems by itself, nevertheless gives reason for optimism and could amount to one of the key legacies of the Lenaerts court.

---

[18]This is exactly why the objective of peace has proven to be unexportable: Williams (2009). Cf. Kochenov and Basheska (2016).

[19]But see Hirsch Ballin (2016).

[20]For a number of divergent perspectives, see Amtenbrink et al. (2019).

[21]CJEU, Case C–286/12 *Commission v. Hungary* (compulsory retirement of judges), ECLI:EU:C:2012:687; cf. Belavusau (2013).

[22]CJEU, Case C–619/18 R *Commission v. Poland,* ECLI:EU:C:2018:852 and EU:C:2018:1021, Order ex parte of 19 October 2018 and Order of 17 December 2018; cf. Editorial comment (2019). Cf. Kochenov and Bárd (2019).

[23]Kelemen (2017).

[24]Biernat and Kawczyńska (2018).

[25]See the whole saga surrounding CJEU, Case C-216/18 PPU *Minister for Justice and Equality (LM),* EU:C:2018:586.

[26]As explained by President Lenaerts in the context of the EU citizenship law field: Lenaerts (2015), p. 1.

The inventiveness of the autocrats, populist voting, and the weakness of the EU's track record and current position on values are no doubt among the large variety of factors that have produced a previously unimaginable situation; whereby the EU harbours Member States which, besides obviously not qualifying for Union membership if they were to apply today (even the EU's usual 'window dressing' of rule of law conditionality notwithstanding)[27] are working hard to undermine key principles the EU was created to safeguard and promote: democracy, the rule of law, and the protection of fundamental rights.[28] The underlying issue is the creation of a *modus vivendi* where the EU's own instrumentalist understanding of the rule of law, including principles such as mutual trust or the autonomy of EU law, reinforces rather than jeopardises the respect for values enshrined in Art. 2 TEU.[29]

The claims that little to nothing can be done under the current legal framework—which are heard with remarkable regularity—are entirely baseless, as Hillion, Besselink and other scholars have consistently pointed out.[30] In making such claims the Commission and other institutions point to the fact that the powerlessness is not caused by an absolute lack of Treaty instruments that would warrant intervention. Rather, the instruments that are available are, apparently, *too strong*, or to put it differently, *too toxic* to be used. The EU has a 'nuclear' option, we are told: Art. 7 TEU, which should not be used too easily. Indeed, the institutions observed the deterioration of the Rule of Law in Hungary and Poland while embroiled in a clearly useless commotion of constantly inventing new rules instead of using the tools at hand. Art. 7 TEU was only activated at the end of 2018, offering too little too late.[31]

The talk of the legal difficulties surrounding the provision seems to be triggered by two considerations. Firstly, the Member States and the institutions alike apparently lack a strong and unreserved political commitment to throw their full weight behind the defence of the Rule of Law. Secondly—and most importantly—Art. 7 TEU does not *per se* guarantee any successes in the fight. Its effectiveness is highly doubtful. Such doubts stem from two considerations. The first, as already mentioned, is the very logic of the internal market—created to socialise and intertwine the Member States' economies to ensure a lasting peace and common prosperity, the internal market logic is poorly equipped to deal with the backsliding states due to the overwhelming economic costs any serious intervention is prone to generate. These costs will be, to a large extent, external to the backsliding Member State. For example, in order to initiate regime change in Poland one needs to come up with really stinging measures, which however will unquestionably hamper the success of German, Dutch and British businesses in Warsaw, Cracow and other places. The second consideration relates to the EU's very nature: as it stands it is not necessarily

[27] De Ridder and Kochenov (2011).

[28] As well as other values expressed in Art. 2 TEU; Rideau (2012), Pech (2010), Kochenov (2017a). Cf. Carpano (2005).

[29] Klamert and Kochenov (2019).

[30] Hillion (2016), Besselink (2017) and Scheppele (2016).

[31] Kochenov et al. (2017).

well positioned to lecture the Member States on democracy and the Rule of Law—an argument we have to take into account notwithstanding how urgent and pressing we think the need for action might be.[32] These two elements explaining why Art. 7 TEU was only activated so late are unquestionably related. If one is asked to trigger a legal mechanism which does offer any guarantees of success of the intervention—knowing that the activation will harm businesses across Europe and is bound to bring about new scrutiny of the EU's own track-record—the doubts appear not so irrational anymore.

3 Background of Art. 7 TEU

The initial versions of the Treaties relied on the presumption of compliance by the Member States with the—then non-codified—values of the Communities, expressed in the Schuman Declaration[33] and the unwritten founding values of the Union,[34] which gradually crystallised in the context of its enlargements.[35] The enforcement of compliance was strictly confined to the scope of the *acquis*, via what are now Arts. 258 and 259 of the Treaty on the functioning of the European Union (TFEU) (later reinforced by Art. 260 TFEU).[36] This initial design created an unbalanced picture, where compliance with the rules of EU law was strictly enforced while the enforcement of the core principles on which all the law in question rested remained seemingly out of reach for the supranational institutions in a situation where, ironically, the legal nature of the core principles of EU law in terms of their enforceability and contents remained and remains largely unclear.[37] What this configuration made obvious, however, was that the *acquis* did not necessarily include the key values. So Poland, the crucial example of the aberration of constitutionalism in Europe, is also the only 'Developed Market'[38] in Central and Eastern Europe, while Hungary, the second key example of aberration of constitutionalism, is the only 'Partly Free'[39] regime in the history of the EU. Thus, respecting the *acquis* and Art. 2 TEU values do not seem to correlate. As a consequence, once one turns to the issue of enforcement, the enforcement of the *acquis* and the enforcement of values cannot be regarded as one and the same thing.[40]

[32] Weiler (2016) and Kochenov (2015).

[33] Weiler (2012).

[34] Perju (2018).

[35] Kochenov (2005).

[36] Gormley (2017), Wennerås (2017). Bárd and Śledzińska-Simon (2019).

[37] Kochenov (2017b).

[38] Day (2018).

[39] Simon (2019).

[40] Kochenov (2017a).

Given the importance of the duties of loyalty and mutual trust, which lie at the foundation of EU law, the articulation of supranational policing of compliance with the values was only a matter of time.[41] This was particularly so because the diversity of the Member States has been increasing with the numerous successive rounds of enlargement, incorporating a large number of newly-democratised and post-totalitarian states seeking democracy, the rule of law, and political stability in the Union.[42] From the incorporation of Greece, Spain and Portugal on to the former republics and satellite states of the USSR, the issue of enforcing the values of the EU in cases of eventual breaches was becoming more and more acute: the tradition of a democratic rule of law-based state in these new Member States, so engrained as the basis of EU law, was largely lacking. Art. 7 TEU now attempts to bridge the gap between the presumptions of the founding fathers that all the Member States are good enough to achieve the baseline values and the need to enforce the values of the Union should this presumption turn out to be untenable. The scope of this provision, which is, like Arts. 2 and 49 TEU, necessarily broader than what has been conferred on the EU under Art. 5(1) TEU, is key to the understanding of the instruments Art. 7 contains, as will be discussed below under 'scope'.

The acuteness of the potential problems arising from the discrepancy between the crucial importance of the presumption of compliance of the Member States with the values of the Union and the Union's inability to check whether this indeed is the case—let alone intervene—was quite apparent from early on. Already in 1978 the Commission contemplated a proposal for a sanctions mechanism against the back-drop of Greek accession and the obvious threat of backsliding from democracy and the rule of law in that economically weak, newly-democratised state, fresh from the experience of the colonels' junta rule.[43] It is thus not surprising that the draft EU Treaty prepared by the European Parliament (EP) in 1984 contained such a mechanism.[44]

Since 1991, the EU has included 'human rights clauses' in all association and cooperation ('Europe-') agreements and incorporated these into the fabric of the pre-accession political conditionality in the areas of democracy, the rule of law, and human rights—which are now at the core of Art. 2 TEU.[45] Deployed in the pre-accession context via the Copenhagen Criteria,[46] the sanctions for non-compliance with the values and the core principles of the Union had only limited implications for the Member States once full membership had been secured, creating the so-called 'Copenhagen dilemma'. Beyond the so-called Cooperation

[41]Closa (2016).

[42]Sadurski (2012).

[43]Tsoukalis (1981).

[44]Article 44, Draft Treaty Establishing the European Union (1984) (never entered into force). The Court of Justice was supposed to play the key role in finding a breach. Cf. Mastroianni (2017a), pp. 611–612.

[45]Kochenov (2007) and Inglis (2000).

[46]Hillion (2004) and Janse (2019).

and Verification Mechanism, which was only applicable post-accession to Bulgaria and Romania, the new Member States were out of reach of values enforcement, if not for Art. 7 TEU.[47]

The current instrument goes back to the Treaty of Amsterdam—i.e. was adopted in direct anticipation of the 'big-bang' Eastern enlargement of the EU—and was explicitly linked to ex Art. 6 TEC, which listed the then 'principles' on which the Union is built, which now regrettably came to be recodified as 'values' in Art. 2 TEU.[48]

From the very beginning Art. 7 TEU followed the principle of equal treatment of the Member States. Although clearly designed with the new Member States in mind, the instrument was framed from its very inception to apply to all the Members, unlike, for instance, the Cooperation and Verification Mechanism.

The initial version of the provision contained only a sanctioning mechanism for a 'serious and persistent breach' of values, which made the provision unusable in the event a swift reaction to a breach was necessary, which was exactly the situation in Austria in 2000 as perceived by the majority of the European capitals following the securing of the participation of the extreme-right FPÖ in government in Austria. The reaction to this electoral result came in a series of illegal ad hoc 'bilateral sanctions' imposed on Austria by the 14 other Member States and orchestrated by the EU institutions, which in addition to not relying on Art. 7 TEU were entirely placed outside of the framework of EU law.[49] Austria has never been accused by the Commission or any other EU institution of violating any of the EU's values and principles. Moreover, the assessment by the 'three wise men' of the situation on the ground concluded that *ad hoc* sanctions were introduced for no good reason at all.[50] It is thus beyond any doubt that Austria was mistreated in breach of EU law.[51] The 'FPÖ crisis' teaches us, ironically, that the EU *does not need any law* or a formal legal basis if the political will is in place to act—so much for the supranational rule of law, an issue we return to *infra*. The current Hungarian and Polish situations cannot be compared to the former Austrian one, since the Hungarian and Polish situations are long in the state of 'constitutional capture', which is well documented both by European institutions and in the academic literature.

The Austrian story had two direct and important consequences. Firstly, it led to a chilling effect, preventing the effective deployment of Art. 7 TEU when problems with values are strongly observable on the ground: Austria was constantly and erroneously cited by the EU institutions as a tale of caution about the momentous

---

47 Vachudova and Spendzharova (2012).

48 Pech (2010); cf. Levrat (2018), p. 157.

49 The EU Council Presidency of 31 January 2010 formally launched the sanctions against Austria on behalf of all the other Member States.

50 Ahtisaari et al. (2001).

51 Lachmayer (2017), Besselink (2017), von Toggenburg (2001), Merlingen et al. (2001), Bribosia et al. (2000).

implications of the use of Art. 7, even though the provision had not been used then.[52] Secondly, it led to the upgrade of Art. 7 by the Treaty of Nice. The preventive mechanism in Art. 7(1) to deal with serious and persistent threats of a breach of values goes back to the Treaty of Nice. Art. 7(5) was changed with the Treaty of Lisbon.

As the provision stands today, it thus incorporates three different procedures which can be deployed to safeguard the values of Art. 2 TEU:

(1) a procedure to declare the existence of a 'clear risk of a serious breach' of the values referred to in Art. 2 TEU and the adoption of recommendations how to remedy the situation addressed to the Member State in breach (Art. 7(1) TEU);
(2) a procedure to state the existence of a serious and persistent breach of values (Art. 7(2) TEU);
(3) and a sanctioning mechanism following a finding of a serious and persistent breach (Art. 7(3) TEU).

The above procedures should not be regarded as small steps in a grand chronological order of things. In fact, Art. 7 does not exclude the possibility of starting the procedure laid down in Art. 7(2) TEU directly, i.e. all the three paragraphs of it are not part of one procedure with three steps. This fact is constantly forgotten in the political speeches by the key actors responsible for the operation of Art. 7 TEU.[53] The most popular presentation of Art. 7 TEU today—a consequence of the post-Austria chilling effect—is to refer to it as the 'nuclear option'.[54] This is based on the assumption that invoking the provision is extremely difficult and the results of its application are too devastating to make it practicable.[55] This view clearly ignores the differences between the three procedures of Art. 7 TEU and is not justifiable from the legal point of view.[56] Moreover, given the overwhelming costs of regime change and our general knowledge—based on countless historical examples—that sanctions are not the most effective way to bring about compliance, the potential effectiveness of Art. 7 TEU is clearly questionable, even if not impossible to attain.

The concerns of the drafters who included Art. 7 TEU into the Treaties have recently been proven entirely justified, as outstanding problems persist in the field of adherence to values. Following the 'reforms' of the Fidesz party in Hungary starting with the second Orbán government, which used its constitutional supermajority to provide an overwhelming overhaul of the totality of the legal-political system in the country with a view to building an 'illiberal democracy' à la Putin, it is clear that the problems Art. 7 was designed to tackle are not at all theoretical.[57] Adding to the situation in Hungary, where according to the Venice Commission the Constitution

[52] E.g. Timmermans (2015).
[53] Besselink (2017) and Wilms (2017).
[54] E.g. Barroso (2012).
[55] For strong arguments against this view, see Besselink (2017).
[56] Kochenov and Pech (2016), Oliver and Stefanelli (2016).
[57] Scheppele (2017), Szente (2017), p. 456; Tóth (2017).

ended up being turned into a political tool of one-party rule, Poland followed suit after the election of *Prawo i Sprawedliwość* (PiS) in 2015.[58] Lacking a super-majority to change the Constitution, the Polish government has simply ignored it, systematically failing to comply with its laws: a situation amply documented by scholars and analysed in detail by the Venice Commission.[59] Democratic- and rule of law-backsliding is thus on the rise in the EU and there is no guarantee that Poland and Hungary will not be joined by more Member States which fail to adhere to the values of Art. 2 TEU.

What Art. 7 has to say about the involvement and jurisdiction of the Court begs the question of whether the provision is largely political in nature. As per Arts. 19 TEU and 269 TFEU, the CJEU only has jurisdiction over procedural issues.[60] The observance of the voting arrangements applying to the EP, the European Council and the Council, as laid down in Art. 354 TFEU, could thus be policed by the Court. Importantly however there is no express exclusion of Art. 7 from the CJEU's jurisdiction, which means that the Court could be called upon to check how the institutions involved used their discretion in a concrete case, broadening judicial involvement somewhat compared with the silence of the provision itself about the Court. Given the limited involvement of the judicial power, as well as the fact that the Commission does not have an exclusive right of initiative, Art. 7 TEU remains a blend of law and politics.[61] It is a fundamental fact, however, that both these components unquestionably play an important role in the functioning of this provision.

4 The Scope of Application of Art. 7 TEU

The scope of application of Art. 7 TEU is necessarily broader than what is implied by the principle of conferral: it is not confined to the scope of the *acquis*. As explained by the Commission, Art. 7 'seeks to secure respect for the conditions of Union membership. There would be something paradoxical about confining the Union's possibilities of action to the areas covered by Union law and asking it to ignore serious breaches in areas of national jurisdiction. If a Member State breaches the fundamental values in a manner sufficiently serious to be caught by Article 7, this is likely to undermine the very foundations of the Union and the trust between its members, whatever the field in which the breach occurs.'[62] This position of the

[58]Cf. Bugarič (2015).

[59]Sadurski (2018).

[60]Cf. CF, Case T-337/03 *Luis Bertelli Gálvez v Commission,* ECLI:EU:T:2004:106; Case T-280/09 *Morte Navarro v. Parliament,* EU:T:2010:28; Besselink (2017), p. 133.

[61]Williams (2006).

[62]European Commission, Article 7 of the Treaty on European Union – Respect for and promotion of the values on which the Union is based (COM(2003) 606 final), 5.

Commission finds overwhelming support in the literature. Only a very broad view of the scope of Art. 7 TEU can make this provision an effective tool for safeguarding the EU's values.

All in all, as a *lex specialis* with a remarkably broad scope of application, Article 7 clearly does not preclude the application of Arts. 258, 259 and 260 TFEU in the area of the defence of EU values. While some value violations can clearly fall within or are paralleled by a breach of the *acquis*, a series of systemic *acquis* violations could also amount to a serious breach of values.[63] This is why the Commission insists in its 'Rule of Law Mechanism' on approaching Art. 7 and standard infringement proceedings as deployable side by side.[64]

4.1 Clear Risk of a Serious Breach (Procedure No. 1)

Out of the three procedures contained in Art. 7 TEU, initiating 7(1) in order to state a clear risk of a serious breach of values of Art. 2 TEU and address recommendations on how to remedy the situation to the relevant Member State can be done by the broadest array of actors: 1/3 of the Member States, the EP, or the European Commission. Compare this with 1/3 of the Member States and the Commission for the initiation of 7(2), and only the Council for the initiation of the actual sanctioning procedure in Art. 7(3) TEU. All the three procedures are in clear deviation from the main principle that the Commission holds the exclusive right of initiative in EU law.

The aim of opening up the procedure to so many possible initiators clearly seems to have been to make it easier to use, compared with other elements of Art. 7. It is undoubtedly true that both under-enforcement and over-enforcement of Art. 2 TEU values could create problems.[65] Yet, given that the 7(1) procedure cannot possibly lead to sanctions, as for the initiation of 7(3) by the Council the statement of a breach under 7(2) is required, the essence of 7(1) seems to lie in pushing the Member States where the breach could occur to engage in dialogue with the EU institutions in order to prevent a possible breach. This is confirmed by the provision's authorization, addressed to the Council, to issue recommendations to the Member State concerned in order to prevent a breach of values from occurring. The same procedure—a 4/5 majority in the members of the Council with the consent of the EP, is used both for the statement finding the existence of a serious risk of breach and for the adoption of the recommendations to be addressed to the Member State on the brink of breaching the values. Moreover, basic requirements of the rule of law have to be observed throughout, i.e. the Member State subjected to the procedure has to be heard. The

[63] Scheppele (2016).

[64] European Commission, *supra* note 5; European Parliament, *supra* note 5.

[65] Wilms (2017).

institutions also have to react to the changes on the ground by regularly verifying whether the grounds behind triggering Art. 7(1) TEU still persist.

With the Commission, the EP, and 1/3 of the Member States able to initiate the procedure, it is obvious that the prevailing opinion of Art. 7's 'nuclear' nature is exceedingly exaggerated. Moreover, the 4/5 majority of the members of the Council is not so difficult to reach, given that the Member State subjected to the procedure will necessarily not be allowed to cast a vote. This threshold, however high it seems to be, is clearly far below the unanimity in the European Council required for a statement of an actual breach under Art. 7(2) TEU. It is notable in this regard that Art. 7, which requires the opinion behind the initiation of 7(1) to be 'reasoned', also requires the initiating actors to do their 'homework' and prepare the case by collecting and systematising the necessary information and evidence. Such preparatory work is clearly implied in the text of the provision.

Given that the Art. 7(1) procedure is relatively easy to trigger, the arguments to the contrary underlying the Commission's 'Rule of Law Mechanism'—a non-binding explanation on how the Commission will prepare its own activation of Art. 7(1) or 7(2) TEU[66]—are hardly convincing. In introducing the mechanism, the Commission aimed at introducing some informal dialogue with the problematic Member State before Art. 7—the misnamed 'nuclear option'—is triggered. The Commission would thus address recommendations to that Member State and receive replies: a procedure criticised by the Council Legal Service; but for very bad reasons, given that as one of the initiators of the 7(1) (and also 7(2)) procedures the Commission clearly has to have internal rules for judging the situation on the ground and the collection of evidence to prepare its Reasoned Opinion.[67] However, the Rule of Law mechanism as introduced looks suspiciously like a double of Art. 7 (1) TEU—only with no involvement of other institutions.[68]

The only effect of the mechanism's deployment can be a delay in the triggering of Art. 7—even though other institutions having the power to trigger Art. 7 clearly are not obliged to wait for the Commission to finish with the non-Treaty mechanism of its own creation. In practice the delay is the least of the evils created by the Commission in order to ultimately *not* trigger Art. 7. When such triggering was needed, it showed three things.[69] Firstly, it showed that the Commission is incapable of being coherent and consistent in managing its own newly-created procedure. The Mechanism has never been triggered against Hungary, even though the situation there was as bad—if not worse—than in Poland, against which the Mechanism was triggered. Secondly, it demonstrated that the Commission is incapable of sticking to the steps of its own procedure: following Poland's de facto refusal to cooperate and following the Commission's recommendation under the Mechanism, the Commission, instead of triggering Art. 7(1) TEU as its own Mechanism required, came up

[66]European Commission, *supra* note 5; Kochenov and Pech (2015b).

[67]Council of the European Union, *supra* note 15; Kochenov and Pech (2015b).

[68]Kochenov and Pech (2016).

[69]*Id.*

with a new, supposedly ad hoc recommendation instead, while the situation with the Rule of Law and democracy in Poland continued to deteriorate at an increasing pace. Thirdly, it demonstrated that triggering Art. 7 and its related mechanisms should be done without committing grave tactical mistakes: having moved against one out of the two current backsliding Member States, the Commission handed the veto power over any serious move under Art. 7(2) TEU against Poland to Hungary, making the deployment of the Treaty provision de facto impossible as a result of its own inventiveness and masking profound indecision. In the event the Rule of Law Mechanism is now regarded as a semi-official step preceding the deployment of Art. 7 TEU—which could be a possibility in practice—the undermining of the *effet utile* of this provision by the Commission would extend even further, creating an unwelcome and dangerous precedent.

The main question that the Rule of Law Mechanism supposedly had to answer is how to decipher a threat of a serious breach of Art. 2 values. In this sense the mechanism is useful in that it builds on the Venice Commission practice (see the discussion of Art. 2 TEU) in defining the elements of the rule of law, which could be useful to the institutions in finding a risk of breach under Art. 7(1) TEU. Moreover, the Commission relies on the Venice Commission's opinions in its Rule of Law recommendations.

It is fundamental to keep in mind that a statement finding the existence of a serious risk of breach under Art. 7(1) TEU is not necessary to activate Art. 7(2) TEU. The same applies, of course, to the Commission's Rule of Law Mechanism which, as the Commission itself stated, is not obligatory and not legally binding.[70] Although activated at the time of this writing against both Poland and Hungary, Art. 7(1) TEU is too little too late: both countries are at such a stage of backsliding that only pro-government trolls could benevolently characterise it as a 'threat': the capture of the state is a done deal in both countries—and this is absolutely not what Art. 7 (1) TEU could in any way remedy. By saying that the provision is 'dead', the Polish minister could not be more right, in part: it is both dead *and misused*.

4.2 Stating the Existence of a Serious Breach (Procedure No. 2)

There is a huge difference between a mere 'serious threat' of a breach of values and a serious breach of values actually observable in a Member State of the Union. This difference explains the existence of a separate procedure in Art. 7 TEU for finding such a breach, as well as the definitively higher thresholds required by this procedure: unanimity in the European Council and consent of the EP. Unlike Art. 7(1), Art. 7(2) cannot be initiated by the European Parliament, even though the EP can, under its own Rules of Procedure, call on others to act in the context of both

[70] European Commission, *supra* note 5.

paragraphs in question.[71] Even taking into account the fact that unanimity does not imply that each member of the European Council—not counting the representative of the Member State potentially subjected to 7(2), which will not, logically, take part in the vote—has to vote in favour of triggering the procedure,[72] this makes finding the existence of a serious breach procedurally very difficult.

This difficulty is not illogical, since a simple breach of Art. 2 TEU is not enough to activate Art. 7(2) TEU. What is required—and what is meant by 'serious'—is presumably the systemic nature of the breach, which means that the institutions of the Member State concerned cannot, on their own, successfully resolve the problem of failing to adhere to EU values.[73] In this context it is only logical to have a procedure in place that makes it extremely difficult to over-police Art. 2 TEU, which is the objective behind the high thresholds contained in Art. 7(2) TEU. The emphasis on 'systemic' helps understand why the question of Art. 7(2) has never been raised with regard to some Member States which have manifestly underperformed under Art. 2—like Berlusconi's Italy with its terrible track-record on media pluralism;[74] or Sarkozy's France deporting EU citizens of Roma origin in violation of EU law.[75] If there is a certain 'spectrum of defiance', Art. 7(2) TEU only covers the absolute extremes of such defiance.[76] What is required is the constitutional capture of the Member State's institutions, resulting in the paralysis of the liberal democracy and rendering making it impossible for the State's institutions to make auto-corrections (as were made in Italy and France).[77] Hungary and Poland are cases in point, as they represent an example of ideological defiance: a choice made by the government to reform the Member State institutions (in the case of Poland in direct violation of the Constitution and the decisions of the Constitutional Court[78]) in such a way as to make wholehearted adherence to the values of Art. 2 TEU impossible.

While naming and shaming could be a potent tool for change, in order to be effective the shaming of those Member States which have chosen a path of systemic non-compliance needs to be backed by possible sanctions, as in and of itself it may have little effect on the ground. This is why, while the main outcome of a successful deployment of Art. 7(2) TEU is a statement finding a serious breach by the Member State concerned of the values of Art. 2 TEU, the core significance of the 7

[71]European Parliament, Rule 83, 'Rule of Procedure' (2014) (10296/14).

[72]Art. 7 TEU does not limit its activation to one Member State at a time, so in a situation where more than one Member State is suspected of a breach of Art. 2 values, the activation of Art. 7 against both states is indispensable to avoid the blockage of the Art. 7 procedures by the backsliding Member States supporting each other.

[73]von Bogdandy and Ioannidis (2014).

[74]CJEU, Case C-380/05 *Centro Europa 7 S.r.l.*, ECLI:EU:C:2008:59. Cf. Mastroianni (2017b).

[75]Carrera and Faure Atger (2010).

[76]Jakab and Kochenov (2017b), p. 3.

[77]Müller (2015).

[78]Koncewicz (2018).

(2) procedure seems to lie in the fact that it opens the way to the triggering of the Art. 7(3) procedure by the Council, thus making real sanctions a possibility—unlike in the case of the 7(1) procedure.

4.3 Suspension of Rights and Revocation of Sanctions (Procedure No. 3)

The third procedure is contained in Art. 7(3) TEU, which goes beyond the 'shaming' resulting from the deployment of the 7(1) and 7(2) procedures and implies actual sanctioning of a Member State. This procedure is initiated by the Council and requires a reinforced qualified majority voting (QMV), since Art. 354 TFEU makes a reference to the requirements of Art. 238(3)(b) in this respect, implying the support of at least 72% of participating Council Members comprising 65% of the Union population (again with the representative of the Member State subjected to the procedure not taking part in the vote or affecting any counts towards the vote as per Art. 354 TFEU). Yet the procedural threshold is very high, since Art. 7(3) TEU cannot be initiated without a successful deployment of Art. 7(2) TFEU.

The 7(3) procedure is suitably vague so as to allow the Council to adapt the exact scope of the sanctions as it sees fit with a view of maximizing the likelihood of compliance in the Member State concerned. While the provision speaks of the suspension of 'certain rights deriving from the application of the Treaty', it is clear that the sanctions meant to be invoked can be either economic and non-economic in nature. Both access to EU funds and the voting of the Member State in breach in the Council—just to give two examples—can be affected. While the academic literature is sceptical about the effect of the sanctions, in those cases when a Member State is heavily reliant on EU funds and concerned about its prestige in EU institutions these could probably bring about the desired effect, although there is no successful example to cite here since Art. 7(3) TEU has never been invoked.

What is absolutely clear, vagueness notwithstanding, is that Art. 7(3) does not authorise the exclusion of the Member State from the Union: the very issue of membership of the Union cannot be put in question.[79] Only Art. 50 TEU provides guidelines for leaving the Union.[80]

Under Art. 7(4) TEU, lifting the sanctions is very straightforward: again, a simple QMV in the Council without the participation of the violator state is required. Importantly, the same procedure applies to altering the substance of the sanctions in place, giving the Council sufficient flexibility to react to the changes on the ground in the Member State concerned.

[79]Besselink (2017), p. 130.
[80]Blagoev (2011).

4.4 Procedural Requirements Specific to Article 7 TEU

Now let us look in some more detail at Art. 354 TFEU, which lays down the rules of the procedural aspects of Art. 7 TEU. There are several significant points of difference compared with the familiar procedures used by the institutions involved, which can be found elsewhere in the Treaties. Firstly—and most importantly—although Art. 354 TFEU refers to a concrete Member State which is to be excluded from voting in such cases, the wording clearly implies that in the cases where several Member States are suspected of failing to adhere to EU values all such Member States should not be given a chance to derail the application of Art. 7 TEU. Should the contrary be the case, all the procedural requirements of Art. 7 TEU, especially those requiring unanimity, would end up being deprived of their intended *effet utile*, given that the backsliding Member States would most likely obstruct the application of sanctions to each other's cases. Excluding several Member States from voting can thus be deemed as implicitly authorised by Art. 354 TFEU in the context of Art. 7, especially in the context of the Art. 7(2) TEU procedure. It will be up to the Court, when approached by one such Member State under Art. 269 TFEU, to clarify the exact extent of such an exclusion. Options potentially range from requiring the simultaneous consideration of the application of Art. 7(2) TEU to several backsliding Member States already subject to Art. 7(1) TEU procedure, to the default exclusion from the vote in the context of Art. 7 TEU of any state subjected to Art. 7(1) TEU in the context of any proceedings arising under Art. 7 TEU, without necessarily taking into simultaneous consideration the situation regarding the infringement of values in the several Member States.

The QMV required under Art. 354(2) TFEU is of the strictest nature, since the support of at least 72% of participating Council Members comprising 65% of the Union population is required as per direct reference to Art. 238(3)(b). As already mentioned, the Member State subjected to the procedure does not participate. The QMV could be even stricter in practice than its strictest emanation in the Treaties, since while Art. 354 TFEU speaks of excluding the Member State subjected to the procedure from the procedural thresholds concerning the numbers of Member States required to reach Art. 7 TEU decisions by the text of that provision, nothing in Art. 354 TFEU refers to the population threshold counts, which are part of the QMV. This leaves open two possible interpretations of QMV under Art. 354 TFEU: one including and one excluding the population of the Member State subjected to Art. 7 TEU procedure in the 65% of the Union population required. Given that no express reference is made to such an exclusion in Art. 354 TFEU, a strong argument can be made to include the population while excluding the Member State, while the contrary reading (exclusion of both the Member State and its population from the count) is more consistent with the *raison d'être* of the special procedure in question. The obvious lack of absolute clarity on this issue allows for the likelihood that the exact count of QMV thresholds will be the subject of a case in front of the CJEU under Art. 269 TFEU once an Art. 7 TEU procedure is activated. Art. 354 TFEU thus potentially requires the strictest QMV threshold available in the Treaties.

Also, the EP's decision-making procedure deployed in Art. 7 TEU, as specified in Art. 354(4) TFEU, is exceptionally strict. A two-thirds majority of the votes cast representing the majority of component MEPs amounts to a much higher procedural threshold than a similar majority of the EP members present and voting. The votes cast in favour should thus come from at least the majority of the component members of the House, while also not falling below two-thirds of those present on the day of voting. How to count abstentions is not entirely clear based on the wording of Art. 354(4) TFEU, which posed a problem during the EP vote to activate Art. 7 TEU against Hungary in September 2018. Following the advice of the Directorate of Legislative Acts (the EP service responsible for the procedures), abstentions were not deemed to be 'votes cast', which affected the majority required. This reading is consistent with the interpretation of 'votes cast' in the context of Art. 231 TFEU and is supported by Rule 178(3) of the EP Rules of Procedure. Thus by analogy the two-thirds majority of 'votes cast' required in the context of Art. 354(4) TFEU is counted disregarding the abstentions.[81] All in all the procedure thus contains two thresholds to be met by the EP, both of which are exceptionally high, especially in the context of the relatively low quorum rules in the EP.

5 (Utopian) Scenarios for the Future: No Room for Art. 7

Art. 7 TEU is unique in that it establishes the procedures for finding the threat of a breach of EU values by a Member State; the existence of such breach; as well as a possible sanctioning mechanism to bring the recalcitrant Member State(s) back into compliance, while not being confined by the general EU competence limitations. This commentary has briefly discussed all the sub-instruments and stages of deployment of the provisions in question and has demonstrated Art. 7's eminent usability, despite the claims by the institutions to the contrary, which are as baseless as they are persistent. The 'nuclear' myth, proclaiming Art. 7 TEU to be 'unusable' clearly lacks any connection with the observable legal reality. It is deployed by those in search of a valid pretext—however feeble—to exclude EU law from resolving a rule of law crisis of the European Union, which is a most problematic way of interpreting and employing EU law. In activating the 'naming and shaming' part of Art. 7 TEU, as we have seen with regard to Hungary and Poland, the EU does not and cannot solve any of the outstanding problems: this provision has not been designed to ensure regime change.

Crucially, Art. 7—and especially 7(2) TEU, which would be most appropriate in the current context—is atypical and difficult to use since it both contradicts the logic of the internal market and makes clear the Union's own vulnerabilities in the field of

[81] This did not prevent the Hungarian government from attempting to challenge the outcome of the vote in front of the CJEU, Case C-650/18 *Hungary v. European Parliament* (pending at the time of writing).

the Rule of Law and democracy. It is a confrontational provision with a broad mandate for sanctions, which ensures economic losses throughout the internal market at the moment when its sanctions kick in, which is a direct spillover of the logic of economic integration into the sphere of protection of democracy and the rule of law. As a consequence, gathering the necessary political will to activate Art. 7 TEU is both immensely difficult and—ultimately—most likely a pointless exercise: Art. 7 TEU, no matter which procedural aspect of it we are talking about, does not bring with it any guarantee of regime change of the backsliding Member State. Consequently, it is not at all surprising that the only activations of Art. 7 TEU known to us happened only when the Member States in question *de facto* left the ambit of the rule of law world, as Sadurski,[82] Scheppele, Sólyom[83] and other scholars have clearly demonstrated. It seems that such activations, being ultimately entirely inconsequential—while offering one argument in a world of mutual recognition of disputes could potentially harm the EU more than the powers that be in Hungary and Poland.

Indeed, it is unfortunately beyond any doubt that the Commission's move to activate 7(1) TEU against Poland in 2018 will *not result in any positive change on the ground in Poland*. The Hungarian case is in no way different. Abundant time has passed to see that PiS and Fidesz do not inhabit a dialogue-friendly universe. The result of the Art. 7(1) procedure is thus most likely a new flow of insults from Warsaw, which does not help European values and is probably counter-productive in the eyes of ordinary Poles. The Commission and EP's actions are thus unlikely to bring about any positive change, and should be viewed as what they are—symbolic signals. Let us be frank here: the Treaties have failed to avert backsliding disasters in the Member States.

Three scenarios of possible action emerge in this context, *all of them unrelated to Art. 7 TEU.*

5.1 Thinking Short-Term: Scenario No. 1: Cutting the Funds

The preferred outcome of this realistic scenario would be a shake-up of the Polish and Hungarian political life to an extent likely to bring about speedy change—the populist government running out of cash will have to change its course. Unfortunately the amounts flowing into these backsliding states, however significant, are probably not suffient to bring about the expected result, so they should be scrutinised both with caution and skepticism.

[82]Sadurski (2018).

[83]Scheppele (2015), Sólyom (2015).

5.2 *Thinking Mid-Term: Scenario No. 2: Overwhelming* Ad Hoc *Political Pressure*

Leaving aside its timidity with respect to the use of Art. 7, the Haider affair of 2000 has taught the Union a great lesson about how powerful political pressure outside the context of the Treaty framework can be. This aggressive tool, even if lying outside the realm of EU law *sensu stricto*, is sure to topple the PiS or Fidesz governments, triggering speedy change. The questions that arise in this regard are related to the sociological legitimacy of such actions and the powers to replace the autocrats. Blokker urges a lot of caution on this count, and he is most likely right.

5.3 *Thinking Long-Term: Scenario No. 3: A Multi-Speed Union*

This instrument would require strict political conditionality with respect to any move towards the core. A conditionality-based multi-speed Europe is unavoidable and the incorporation of conditionality techniques into policing each of the integration's concentric circles will be a necessary element of the edifice. As the speed and vectors of integration evolve, Poland and the likes of Poland could find themselves outside the scope of meaningful activity, i.e. behind the door of the integration kitchen. With the growing pressure on the Union's values from a number of countries, this seems like the most realistic way to preserve the EU as a union of values over the long term, while also being sufficiently open towards those states hijacked by Belarus-inspired plutocrats. Before blessing any moves between the concentric circles, a strict quarantine should be applied to the poisonous regimes outside the ambit of the values contained in Art. 2. However here too a voice of caution is in order: since the Commission has failed the conditionality exercise once, there is no guarantee it would succeed the second time round.

6 A Realistic Scenario for the Future: No Room for Art. 7

Gradual adaptation of the infringement proceedings to the needs of the current context is the final scenario proposed here for consideration. This scenario gets no number, since it is merely a description of the on-going developments. The Commission, together with the Court of Justice, is gradually pushing for the increasing the effectiveness of Arts. 258, 259, 260 and 279 TFEU as well as the Charter by using the principle of the independence of the judiciary and the EU-level function of the local judicial institutions in the backsliding Member States as the key trigger of jurisdiction.[84] This approach is starting to yield results and is much less utopian that the other three outlined above. In being less utopian, it is also the most incremental and the least political, which endows it with additional legitimacy.

The crises have allowed the judiciaries of the EU to shine, bringing inter-court dialogue to a vital new level and upgrading its substance.[85] At the core of this dialogue are also the fundamental principles of EU law, even those not confined in their entirety to the EU's scope of powers.[86] In particular this includes the independence of the judiciary—interpreted by the CJEU as an EU-law principle and a vital element of the Rule of Law,[87] as opposed to merely issues of validity and the interpretation of EU law *per se*, however broadly conceived.[88] Such an interpretation—a spectacular innovation reshaping the constitutional system of the Union as we speak—has given voice to vertical concerns related to the independence of the judiciary,[89] as well as horizontal rule of law concerns, leading to a significant refinement of the principle of mutual recognition.[90] This has allowed the Court to learn from its past mistakes in dealing with assaults on the rule of law.[91] The presumption that the strict enforcement of the *acquis* is sufficient to guarantee adherence to the EU's values is clearly not valid any more.[92] Together with the endowment of Art. 19(1) TEU with a new significance, the on-going crisis of the rule of law has helped open a new chapter of European constitutionalism. The very fact that the current concerns arose, rather than being strictly confined to the national legal orders, demonstrates the actual maturity of the level of supranational law and integration, or at least of its aspirations.[93]

A key element in the ongoing fight for the rule of law is, at the EU-level, the principle of the independence of the judiciary. This is derived from Art. 19(1) TEU

---

[84]Safjan and Düsterhaus (2014).

[85]Editorial comment (2019), p. 3; Dawson (2013), p. 371.

[86]For more on the shift of Art. 2 TEU principles from 'principles' to 'values' without undermining the essence of the former, see Pech (2010).

[87]CJEU, Case C–64/16 *Associação sindical dos juízes portugueses,* ECLI:EU:C:2018:117; Krajewski (2018), Pech and Platon (2018), Ciampi (2018).

[88]For a criticism of the classical inter-court dialogue before the most recent case-law, see e.g. Kochenov and van Wolferen (2018).

[89]This allowed the national courts under threat to deploy the preliminary ruling procedure in an innovative way in order to guarantee the preservation of their own independence: Biernat and Kawczyńska (2018); cf. Broberg (2017).

[90]E.g. CJEU, *LM*, Case C-216/18 PPU, *supra* note 25; Rizcallah (2018). Cf. Lenaerts (2017).

[91]Compare CJEU, *Commission v. Hungary*, Case C–286/12, *supra* note 21, with *Commission v. Poland*, Case C–619/18, *supra* note 22, Order ex parte of 19 October 2018 and Order of 17 December 2018.

[92]For more on this difference, see Kochenov (2017a).

[93]Even though numerous international organizations around the world facing similar crises are trying to resolve these with varyings degree of success: Closa (2017).

and regarded as a vital part of the value of the rule of law.[94] Judicial independence has thus emerged as a crucial nexus between EU law and the enforcement of Art. 2 TEU values outside of the scope of the *acquis sensu stricto*,[95] which explains the relative silence over the Charter of Fundamental Rights (CFR) among those who are busy trying to deal hands-on with the ongoing rule of law concerns:[96] Art. 51 CFR still stands, despite all the literature on the need to move on from this competence block.[97] After all, we are learning that 19(1) TEU is good enough.[98] A range of tools from pecuniary[99] to interim measures having retroactive force[100] can now be deployed to freeze at least some attempts on the part of the backsliding governments to undermine the independence of the judiciary even further. This new, more thoughtful approach could definitely have a significant impact of other areas of EU law too. It is marked however by one fundamental aspect: there is no place in it for Art. 7 TEU.

Acknowledgements I am grateful to Petra Bárd, Barabara Grabowska-Moroz, Marcus Klamert, Laurent Pech and Kim Lane Scheppele for their comments and reactions to earlier drafts. The research assistance of Chiraz Belhajali, Anna Gnap, Flips Schøyen and Jacquelyn Veraldi is gratefully acknowledged. This work has been conducted under the auspices of the EU's Horizon 2020 research and innovation programme as part of the RECONNECT project under Grant Agreement no. 770142. The chapter is a slightly rereferenced version of the contribution published by the *Polish Yearbook of International Law* in 2018.

References

Ahtisaari M, Frowein J, Oreja M (2001) Report on the Austrian Government's Commitment to the Common European Values, in particular concerning the rights of minorities, refugees and immigrants, and the evolution of the political nature of the FPÖ (The 'Wise Men Report'). Int Legal Mater 40:102–123

Amtenbrink F et al (2019) The internal market and the future of European integration. Cambridge University Press, Cambridge

Anselmi M (2018) Populism: an introduction (trans: Fano Morrisey L). Routledge, Oxon

Bánkuti M, Halmai G, Scheppele KL (2012) Hungary's illiberal turn: disabling the constitution. J Democr 23:138–146

[94] CJEU, *Associação sindical dos juízes portugueses,* Case C–64/16, *supra* note 87, paras. 36, 37 and 41.

[95] Christophe Hillion predicted this development: Hillion (2016).

[96] Pech and Platon (2018), pp. 1833–1836.

[97] Jakab (2016, 2017). Cf. von Bogdandy et al. (2017).

[98] The connection with the Charter is however obvious: CJEU, *Commission v. Poland*, Case C–619/18, *supra* note 22, Order ex parte of 19 October 2018 and Order of 17 December 2018.

[99] Especially when the backsliding Member States attempt to openly defy the Court, CJEU, Case C–441/17 *Commission v. Poland,* ECLI:EU:C:2018:255.

[100] CJEU, *Commission v. Poland*, Case C–619/18, *supra* note 22, Order ex parte of 19 October 2018 and Order of 17 December 2018.

Bárd P, Śledzińska-Simon S (2019) Rule of Law Infringement Procedures: A Proposal to Extend the EU's Rule of Law Toolbox. CEPS Paper, 2019-09
Barroso JM (2012) State of the Union Address (Speech/12/596). European Parliament, Strasbourg, 12 September 2012. http://europa.eu/rapid/press-release_SPEECH-12-596_en.htm (last accessed 12 Sept 2019)
Belavusau U (2013) Case C-286/12 Commission v Hungary. Common Mark Law Rev 50:1145–1160
Bernatt M, Ziółkowski M (2019) Statutory anti-constitutionalism. Wash Int Law J 28:487–526
Besselink LFM (2017) The bite, the bark and the howl: Article 7 TEU and the rule of law initiatives. In: Jakab A, Kochenov D (eds) The enforcement of EU law and values. Oxford University Press, Oxford, pp 128–144
Bieber R, Maiani F (2014) Enhancing centralized enforcement of EU law: Pandora's toolbox? Common Mark Law Rev 51:1057–1092
Biernat S, Kawczyńska M (2018) Why the Polish Supreme Court's Reference on Judicial Independence to the ECJ is Admissible after All. Verfassungsblog, https://bit.ly/2IQxBvc (last accessed 12 Sept 2019)
Bignami F (ed) (2019) EU law in populist times. Cambridge University Press, Cambridge
Blagoev B (2011) Expulsion of a Member State from the EU after Lisbon: political threat or legal reality. Tilburg Law J 16:191–237
Blay-Grabarczyk K (2019) Les mécanismes de suivi à l'épreuve de la pratique: L'exemple de la Pologne. Revue Trimestrielle de Droit Européen 2019(2):321–335
Blokker P (2016) EU democratic oversight and domestic deviation from the rule of law: sociological reflections. In: Closa C, Kochenov D (eds) Reinforcing rule of law oversight in the European Union. Cambridge University Press, Cambridge, pp 249–269
Blokker P (2018) Populist Constitutionalism and Meaningful Popular Engagement. The Foundation for Law, Justice and Society Policy Brief
Blokker P (2019) Response to 'Public Law and Populism'. Germ Law J 20:284–290
Bodnar A (2018) Protection of human rights after the constitutional crisis in Poland. Jahrbuch des Öffentlichen Rechts der Gegenwart 66:639–663
Bribosia E, De Schutter O, Ronse T, Weyembergh A (2000) Le contrôle par l'Union européenne du respect de la démocratie et des droits de l'homme par ces États membres: à propos de l'Autriche. J Talent Dev Excell 67:61–64
Broberg M (2017) Preliminary references as a means of enforcement of EU law. In: Jakab A, Kochenov D (eds) The enforcement of EU law and values. Oxford University Press, Oxford, pp 99–111
Bugarič B (2015) A crisis of constitutional democracy in Central and Eastern Europe: 'lands in-between' democracy and autoritarianism. Int J Const Law 13:219–245
Bugarič B (2016) Protecting democracy inside the EU: on Article 7 TEU and the Hungarian turn to authoritarianism. In: Closa C, Kochenov D (eds) Reinforcing rule of law oversight in the European Union. Cambridge University Press, Cambridge, pp 82–102
Bugarič B (2019) Central Europe's descent into autocracy: a constitutional analysis of authoritarian populism. Int J Const Law 17:597–616
Carpano E (2005) État de droit et droits européens – l'évolution du modèle de l'État de droit dans le cadre de l'européanisation des systèmes juridiques. L'Harmattan, Paris
Carrera S, Faure Atger A (2010) L'affaire des Roms: A Challenge to the EU's Area of Freedom, Security and Justice. CEPS Liberty and Security in Europe Policy Paper, September 2010
Ciampi A (2018) Can the EU ensure respect for the rule of law by its Member States? The Case of Poland. Osservatorio sulle fonti 3:1–14
Closa C (2016) Reinforcing the rule of law: normative arguments, institutional proposals and procedural limitations. In: Closa C, Kochenov D (eds) Reinforcing rule of law oversight in the European Union. Cambridge University Press, Cambridge, pp 15–35

Closa C (2017) Securing compliance with democracy in regional organizations. In: Jakab A, Kochenov D (eds) The enforcement of EU law and values. Oxford University Press, Oxford, pp 379–402

Closa C, Kochenov D (eds) (2016) Reinforcing rule of law oversight in the European Union. Cambridge University Press, Cambridge

Collot PA (2013) Difficulté contre-majoritaire et usage impérieux du pouvoir constituent dérivé au regard de la quatrième revision de la loi fondamentale de Hongrie. Revue française de droit constitutionel 14:789–812

Daly T (2019) Democratic decay: conceptualizing the emerging research field. Hague J Rule Law 11:9–36

Dawson M (2013) Constitutional dialogue between courts and legislatures in the European Union. Eur Public Law 19:369–396

Day (2018) Poland Becomes the First Country from Former Soviet Bloc to Be Ranked a 'Developed Market'. The Telegraph 24/09/2018. https://www.telegraph.co.uk/business/2018/09/24/poland-becomes-first-country-former-soviet-bloc-ranked-developed/ (last accessed 12 Sept 2019)

De Ridder E, Kochenov D (2011) Democratic conditionality in Eastern enlargement: ambitious window dressing. Eur Foreign Affairs Rev 16:589–605

Editorial Comment (2019) 2019 Shaping up as a challenging year for the Union, not least as a community of values. Common Mark Law Rev 56:3–22

Gormley LW (2017) Infringement proceedings. In: Jakab A, Kochenov D (eds) The enforcement of EU law and values. Oxford University Press, Oxford, pp 65–78

Hillion C (2004) The Copenhagen criteria and their progeny. In: Hillion C (ed) EU enlargement: a legal approach. Hart, Oxford, pp 1–22

Hillion C (2016) Overseeing the rule of law in the EU: legal mandate and means. In: Closa C, Kochenov D (eds) Reinforcing rule of law oversight in the European Union. Cambridge University Press, Cambridge, pp 59–81

Hirsch Ballin E (2016) Mutual trust: the virtue of reciprocity – strengthening the acceptance of the rule of law through peer review. In: Closa C, Kochenov D (eds) Reinforcing rule of law oversight in the European Union. Cambridge University Press, Cambridge, pp 133–146

Inglis K (2000) The Europe agreements compared in the light of their pre-accession reorientation. Common Mark Law Rev 37:1173–1210

Jakab A (2016) The EU Charter of fundamental rights as the most promising way of enforcing the rule of law against EU Member States. In: Closa C, Kochenov D (eds) Reinforcing rule of law oversight in the European Union. Cambridge University Press, Cambridge, pp 187–205

Jakab A (2017) The application of the EU Charter in National Courts in purely domestic cases. In: Jakab A, Kochenov D (eds) The enforcement of EU law and values. Oxford University Press, Oxford, pp 252–264

Jakab A, Kochenov D (eds) (2017a) The enforcement of EU law and values. Oxford University Press, Oxford

Jakab A, Kochenov D (2017b) Introductory remarks. In: Jakab A, Kochenov D (eds) The enforcement of EU law and values. Oxford University Press, Oxford, pp 1–8

Janse R (2019) Is the European Commission a credible guardian of the values? A revisionist account of the copenhagen political criteria during the big bang enlargement. Int J Const Law 17:43–65

Kelemen RD (2017) Europe's other democratic deficit: national authoritarianism in Europe's Democratic Union. Gov Oppos 52:211–238

Kelemen RD, Pech L, Scheppele KL (2018) Never Missing an Opportunity to Miss an Opportunity: The Council Legal Service Opinion on the Commission's EU Budget-Related Rule of Law Mechanism. Verfassungsblog, https://bit.ly/2PwVEy6 (last accessed 12 Sept 2019)

Klamert M, Kochenov D (2019) Article 2. In: Kellerbauer M, Klamert M, Tomkin J (eds) The treaties and the Charter of fundamental rights – a commentary. Oxford University Press, Oxford, pp 22–30

Kochenov D (2005) EU enlargement law: history and recent developments – treaty-custom concubinage? Eur Integr Online Papers 9(6)

Kochenov D (2007) EU enlargement and the failure of conditionality. Kluwer Law International, New York

Kochenov D (2015) EU law without the rule of law: is the veneration of autonomy worth it? Yearb Eur Law 34:74–96

Kochenov D (2017a) The *Acquis* and its principles: the enforcement of the 'law' versus the enforcement of 'values' in the EU. In: Jakab A, Kochenov D (eds) The enforcement of EU law and values. Oxford University Press, Oxford, pp 9–27

Kochenov D (2017b) The EU and the Rule of Law – Naïveté or a Grand Design? In: Adams M, Meuwese A, Hirsch Ballin E (eds) Constitutionalism and the rule of law: bridging idealism and realism. Cambridge University Press, Cambridge

Kochenov D (2019a) Article 7 TEU. In: Kellerbauer M, Klamert M, Tomkin J (eds) The treaties and the Charter of fundamental rights – a commentary. Oxford University Press, Oxford, pp 88–102

Kochenov D (2019b) Article 354 TFEU. In: Kellerbauer M, Klamert M, Tomkin J (eds) The treaties and the Charter of fundamental rights – a commentary. Oxford University Press, Oxford, pp 2081–2091

Kochenov D (2019c) Elephants in the room: the European Commission's 2019 communication on the rule of law. Hague J Rule Law 11:423–438

Kochenov D, Bárd P (2019) The last soldier standing? Courts vs politicians and the rule of law crisis in the New Member States of the EU. Eur Yearb Const Law 1:243–287

Kochenov D, Basheska E (2016) ENP's values conditionality from enlargements to post-crimea. In: Poli S (ed) The EU and its values in the neighbourhood. Routledge, Oxon, pp 145–166

Kochenov D, Pech L (2015a) Renforcer le respect de l'État de droit dans l'UE: Regards critiques sur les noubeaux mécanismes proposes par la Commission et le Conseil. Fondation Robert Schuman Policy Paper no. 356/2015

Kochenov D, Pech L (2015b) Monitoring and enforcement of the rule of law in the European Union: rhetoric and reality. Eur Const Law Rev 11:512–540

Kochenov D, Pech L (2016) Better late than never? On the commission's rule of law framework and its first activation. J Common Mark Stud 24:1062–1074

Kochenov D, van Wolferen M (2018) The Dialogical Rule of Law and the Breakdown of Dialogue in the EU. EUI Working Paper, LAW 2018/01

Kochenov D, Pech L, Platon S (2015) Ni panacée, ni gadget: le 'nouveau cadre de l'Union européenne pour renforcer l'État de droit. Revue trimestrielle de droit européen 2015 (4):689–714

Kochenov D, Magen A, Pech L (eds) (2016) The great rule of law debate in the European Union. Symposium, J Common Mark Stud 54

Kochenov D, Pech L, Scheppele KL (2017) The European Commission's Activation of Article 7 TEU. Verfassungsblog. https://verfassungsblog.de/the-european-commissions-activation-of-article-7-better-late-than-never/ (last accessed 12 Sept 2019)

Koncewicz TT (2016) Of institutions, democracy, constitutional self-defence. Common Mark Law Rev 53:1753–1792

Koncewicz TT (2018) The capture of the polish constitutional tribunal and beyond: of institution(s), fidelities and the rule of law in flux. Rev Central East Eur Law 43:116–173

Krajewski M (2018) *Associação sindical dos juízes portugueses*: The Court of Justice and Athena's Dilemma. Eur Pap 3:395–407

Lachmayer K (2017) Questioning the basic values – Austria and Jörg Haider. In: Jakab A, Kochenov D (eds) The enforcement of EU law and values. Oxford University Press, Oxford, pp 436–455

Lenaerts K (2015) EU citizenship and the European Court of Justice's 'Stone-by-Stone' approach. Int Comp Jurisprud 1:1–10

Lenaerts K (2017) La vie après l'avis: exploring the principle of mutual (yet not blind) trust. Common Mark Law Rev 54:805–840
Levrat N (2018) L'État de droit est-il une valuer européenne dont l'UE assure la promotion? In: Sidjanski D, Saint-Ouen F, Stephanou C (eds) Union des valuers? La mise en œuvre des valuers et des principes fondamentaux de l'Union Européenne. Global Studies Institute de l'Université de Genève, Geneva
Mastroianni R (2017a) Stato di diritto o ragion di stato? La difficcile rotta verso un controllo europeo del rispetto dei valori dell'unione negli stati memberi. In: Triggiani E et al (eds) Dialoghi con Ugo Villani. Cacucci, Bari, pp 605–617
Mastroianni R (2017b) Media Pluralism in Centro Europa 7 Srl, or when your competitor sets the rules. In: Nicola F, Davies B (eds) EU law stories: contextual and critical histories of European Jurisprudence. Cambridge University Press, Cambridge, pp 245–258
Merlingen M, Mudde C, Sedelmeier U (2001) The right and the righteous? European norms, domestic politics, and the sanctions against Austria. J Common Mark Stud 39:59–77
Mori P (2016) Strumenti giuridici e strumenti politici di controlle del rispetto dei diritti fondamentali da parte degli Stati membri dell'Unione europea. In: Tizzano A (ed) Verso 60 anni dai Trattati di Roma: stato e prospettive dell'Unione europea. Giappichelli, Torino, pp 199–209
Müller JW (2014) The EU as a Militant Democracy, or: are there limits to constitutional mutations within the Member States. Revista de Estudios Políticos 165:141–162
Müller JW (2015) Should the EU protect democracy and the rule of law inside Member States? Eur Law J 21:141–160
Oliver P, Stefanelli J (2016) Strengthening the rule of law in the EU: the council's inaction. J Common Mark Stud 24:1075–1084
Pech L (2010) 'A Union founded on the rule of law': meaning and reality of the rule of law as a constitutional principle of EU law. EU Const Law Rev 6:359–396
Pech L, Platon S (2017) Menace systémique envers l'État de droit en Pologne: entre action et proctastination. Fondation Robert Schuman Policy Paper no. 451, 13 Nov. 2017
Pech L, Platon S (2018) Judicial independence under threat: the Court of Justice to the rescue in the AJSP Case. Common Mark Law Rev 55:1827–1854
Pech L, Scheppele KL (2017) Illiberalism within: rule of law backsliding in the EU. Cambridge Yearb Eur Legal Stud 19:3–47, 8
Perju V (2018) On uses and misuses of human rights in European constitutionalism. In: Vöneky S, Neuman GL (eds) Human rights, democracy, and legitimacy in a world in disorder. Cambridge University Press, Cambridge
PolsatNews (2018) Artykuł 7 jest martwy; Komisja Europejska przegrała [Article 7 is dead; the European Commission has lost]. https://bit.ly/2IHo3Cy (last accessed on 13 Sept 2019)
Rideau J (2012) Les valeurs de l'Union européenne. Revue des affaires européennes 2012 (2):329–349
Rizcallah C (2018) Arrêt 'LM': un risqué de violation du droit fundamental à un tribunal indépendant s'oppose-t-il à l'exécution d'un mandate d'arrêt européen? Journal de droit européen 9:348–350
Sadurski W (2010) Adding bite to a bark: the story of Article 7, EU Enlargement, and Jörg Haider. Columbia J Eur Law 16:385–426
Sadurski W (2012) Constitutionalism and enlargement of Europe. Oxford University Press, Oxford
Sadurski W (2018) How Democracy Dies (in Poland): A Case Study of Anti-Constitutional Populist Backsliding. Sydney Law School Research Paper No. 18/01
Safjan M (2018) Domestic infringements of the rule of law as a European Union problem. Osteuropa Recht 64:552–560
Safjan M, Düsterhaus D (2014) A Union of effective judicial protection: addressing a multilevel challenge through the lens of Article 47 CFREU. Yearb Eur Law 33:3–40

Scheppele KL (2015) Understanding Hungary's constitutional revolution. In: von Bogdandy A, Sonnevend P (eds) Constitutional crisis in the European constitutional area: theory, law and politics in Hungary and Romania. C. H. Beck, Hart, Nomos, pp 111–124

Scheppele KL (2016) Enforcing the basic principles of EU law through the systemic infringement procedure. In: Closa C, Kochenov D (eds) Reinforcing rule of law oversight in the European Union. Cambridge University Press, Cambridge, pp 105–132

Scheppele KL (2017) Constitutional coups in EU law. In: Adams M, Meuwese A, Hirsch Ballin E (eds) Constitutionalism and the rule of law: bridging idealism and realism. Cambridge University Press, Cambridge, pp 446–478

Scheppele KL (2018) Autocratic legalism. Univ Chicago Law Rev 85:545–583

Schmidt von Sydow H (2001) Liberté, Démocratie, Droits Fondamentaux et État de Droit: Analyse de l'Article 7 du Traité UE. Revue de droit de l'Union Européenne 2001(2):285–328

Sedelmeier U (2014) Anchoring democracy from above? The European Union and Democratic Backsliding in Hungary and Romania after Accession. J Common Mark Stud 52:105–121

Simon Z (2019) Hungary Becomes First 'Partly Free' EU Nation in Democracy Gauge. Bloomberg News 05/02/2019, https://www.bloomberg.com/news/articles/2019-02-05/hungary-becomes-first-partly-free-eu-nation-in-democracy-gauge (last accessed on 13 Sept 2019)

Sólyom L (2015) The rise and decline of constitutional culture in Hungary. In: von Bogdandy A, Sonnevend P (eds) Constitutional crisis in the European constitutional area: theory, law and politics in Hungary and Romania. C. H. Beck, Hart, Nomos, pp 5–32

Szente Z (2017) Challenging the basic values – the problems with the rule of law in Hungary and the EU's Failure to Tackle Them. In: Jakab A, Kochenov D (eds) The enforcement of EU law and values. Oxford University Press, Oxford, pp 456–475

Timmermans F (2015) The European Union and the Rule of Law. Keynote Speech, Conference on the Rule of Law, Tilburg University, 3 August 2015. https://bit.ly/2Vpkg31 (last accessed on 13 Sept 2019)

Tóth GA (2017) Illiberal rule of law: changing features of Hungarian constitutionalism. In: Adams M, Meuwese A, Hirsch Ballin E (eds) Constitutionalism and the rule of law: bridging idealism and realism. Cambridge University Press, Cambridge, pp 386–416

Tsoukalis L (1981) The European Community and its mediterranean enlargement. Allen & Unwin, Sydney

Vachudova MA, Spendzharova A (2012) The EU's Cooperation and Verification Mechanism: Fighting Corruption in Bulgaria and Romania after EU Accession. European Policy Analysis 2012/1

Varju M, Papp M (2016) The crisis, national particularism and EU law: what can we learn from the Hungarian Case? Common Mark Law Rev 53:1647–1674

von Bogdandy A (2019) Principles and challenges of a European Doctrine of systemic deficiencies. MPIL Research Paper 2019-14

von Bogdandy A, Ioannidis M (2014) Systemic deficiency in the rule of law: what it is, what has been done, what can be done. Common Mark Law Rev 51:59–96

von Bogdandy A, Sonnevend P (eds) (2015) Constitutional crisis in the European constitutional area: theory, law and politics in Hungary and Romania. C. H. Beck, Hart, Nomos

von Bogdandy A, Antpöhler C, Ioannidis M (2017) Protecting EU Values: reverse Solange and the rule of law framework. In: Jakab A, Kochenov D (eds) The enforcement of EU law and values. Oxford University Press, Oxford, pp 218–233

von Toggenburg GN (2001) La crisi austriaca: delicati equilibrismi sospesi tra molte dimensioni. Diritto pubblico comparato ed europeo 2:735–756

Waelbroek M, Oliver P (2017) La crise de l'État de droit dans l'Union Européenne: Que faire?. Cahiers de droit européenne 2017/2:299–342

Weiler JHH (2012) The Schuman declaration as a manifesto of political messianism. In: Dickson J, Eleftheriadis P (eds) Philosophical foundations of European Union law. Oxford University Press, Oxford

Weiler JHH (2016) Living in a Glass House: Europe, democracy and the rule of law. In: Closa C, Kochenov D (eds) Reinforcing rule of law oversight in the European Union. Cambridge University Press, Cambridge, pp 313–326
Wennerås P (2017) Making effective use of Article 260. In: Jakab A, Kochenov D (eds) The enforcement of EU law and values. Oxford University Press, Oxford, pp 79–98
Williams A (2006) The indifferent gesture: Article 7 TEU, the fundamental rights agency and the UK's Invasion of Iraq. Eur Law Rev 31:3–27
Williams A (2009) The ethos of Europe. Cambridge University Press, Cambridge
Wilms G (2017) Protecting fundamental values in the European Union through the rule of law. European University Institute, Florence

Dimitry Kochenov is a Professor of EU Constitutional Law at the University of Groningen.

The Responsibility of Courts in Maintaining the Rule of Law: Two Tales of Consequential Judicial Self-Restraint

Pál Sonnevend

Contents

Abstract Modern constitutionalism is based on the paradigm that courts are inherently entitled and obliged to enforce the constitution of the respective polity. This responsibility of courts also applies in the context of the European Union to both the CJEU and national constitutional courts. The present chapter argues that in the face of constitutional crises the CJEU and the Hungarian Constitutional Court shy away from applying the law as it is to the full. The reasons behind this unwarranted judicial self-restraint are most different: the CJEU aims to avoid conflicts with national

P. Sonnevend (✉)
Eötvös Loránd University, Department of International Law, Budapest, Hungary
e-mail: sonnevend@ajk.elte.hu

A. von Bogdandy et al. (eds.), *Defending Checks and Balances in EU Member States*, Beiträge zum ausländischen öffentlichen Recht und Völkerrecht 298,
https://doi.org/10.1007/978-3-662-62317-6_7

constitutional courts whereas the Hungarian Constitutional Court has been facing a legislative power also acting as constitution making power willing to amend the constitution to achieve specific legislative purposes or to undo previous constitutional court decisions. Yet both courts respond to expediencies that do not follow from the law they are called upon to apply. It is argued that rule of law backsliding requires these courts to abandon the unnecessary self-restraint and exploit the means already available.

1 Introduction

In the past several years, the European Union has been struggling with ensuring respect for the rule of law in all member states. The political mechanism envisaged by Article 7 TEU has thus far proved to be ineffective, there being only two instances of triggering this procedure, on 20 December 2017, by the Commission in respect of Poland,[1] and on 12 September 2018, by the European Parliament in respect of Hungary.[2] No visible progress can be detected in any of these cases. Equally, the Rule of Law Framework set out by the European Commission in 2014 has been activated only once, and even the European Commission acknowledges that 'it did not solve the detected rule of law deficiencies' in Poland.[3] The recent communication of the European Commission on further strengthening the Rule of Law within the Union[4] tries to move forward the debate, but fails to provide any specifics on how the system on enforcing the rule of law may become more effective.

It occurs that the political enforcement mechanisms have failed to deliver a sensible result.[5] This inevitably shifts the focus to the courts that are entrusted with the task of ensuring respect for foundational constitutional values. In the European Union context, this court is most importantly the CJEU which is called upon by virtue of Article 19 (1) TEU to 'ensure that in the interpretation and application of the Treaties the law is observed.' Besides, national constitutional courts also bear responsibility for maintaining the values common to the Member States of the EU, including the rule of law, respect for human rights and democracy. This common responsibility—which is of legal and constitutional nature—applies irrespective of political pressures or eventual repercussions.

[1]Proposal for a Council Decision on the determination of a clear risk of a serious breach by the Republic of Poland of the rule of law (COM(2017) 835 final, 20.12.2017).

[2]European Parliament resolution of 12 September 2018 calling on the Council to determine, pursuant to Article 7(1) of the Treaty on European Union, the existence of a clear risk of a serious breach by Hungary of the values on which the Union is founded (2017/2131(INL)).

[3]Communication from the Commission to the European Parliament, the European Council and the Council, Further strengthening the Rule of Law within the Union, State of play and possible next steps, Brussels, 3.4.2019, (COM(2019) 163 final) p. 3.

[4]Id.

[5]Kochenov and Bárd (2018).

That courts are at the centre of maintaining the rule of law is also recognised by the recent case law of the CJEU on the independence of the national judiciary. Starting with the seminal ASJP judgment on the Portuguese judges association[6] and leading up to the ruling on the Polish law on the Supreme Court[7] the CJEU made it clear that an independent and effective judiciary is indispensable for ensuring the application of EU law in the Member States and ultimately for maintaining the membership of the respective Member States in the EU. Judicial independence, is, however, just a bare minimum which does not on its own guarantee a proper interpretation and application of the law.[8] What if judges respond to unspoken expectations and political realities and fail to exhaust their full capacity to protect the fundamental values they shall maintain in their respective constitutional order? What if courts exercise self-restraint that does not follow from the language and the context of the constitutional document they are supposed to enforce? What if this self-restraint ultimately undermines the coherence of the polity these courts are supposed to serve?

This chapter tells the tale of two courts in utterly different positions yet demonstrating a certain similarity in self-restraint in exploiting the means at their hands. These two courts are, on the one hand, the CJEU, and, on the other, the Hungarian Constitutional Court. It is not submitted that these two courts would have a comparable mandate or an even a vaguely similar political environment. What is common is their reluctance to take the risk inherent in applying the law to the fullest extent. This reluctance has far reaching consequences for both the legal system of the EU and of Hungary.

In the following I shall first outline the interpretation of Article 51 (1) CFR by the CJEU and the consequences of this restrictive interpretation to Hungary in such important areas as the freedom of the press, the independence of the judiciary and of the data protection commissioner (Sect. 2). In the second part of the chapter, I will argue that the Hungarian Constitutional Court still has powerful and mostly unused opportunities at disposal to control the legislative power, even if this legislative power acts most of the time as constitution making power, and frequently amends the Basic Law in order to achieve specific policy objectives or to counter decisions of the Constitutional Court (Sect. 3). In conclusion I submit that rule of law crises call for a more robust and courageous approach by both the CJEU and constitutional courts.

[6]CJEU Case C-264/16, *Associação Sindical dos Juízes Portugueses*, Judgment of the Court of 27 February 2018.

[7]CJEU Case C-619/18, *European Commission v. Poland*, Judgment of the Court of 24 June 2019.

[8]Cf. from the perspective of the internal independence of judges Avbelj (2019).

2 Narrowing the Charter's Applicability: Article 51 (1) CFR

2.1 *Siragusa, Hernández: Context and Consequences*

The evolution of the case law of the CJEU on Article 51 (1) CFR need not be retold here. It is, however, necessary to recall the context and consequences of the shift from the *Åkerberg Fransson* judgment[9] to the *Siragusa and Hernandez* case law in order to assess the implications of this shift for situations in which the rule of law is threatened.

Åkerberg Fransson was certainly an attempt by the CJEU to return to a case law that existed long before the framing of the Charter. Since the *ERT* judgment it has been the consistent case-law that general principles apply to Member States in situations falling within the scope of application of EU law.[10] In fact, the decisive paragraph of the *Åkerberg Fransson* judgment quotes the langue of the *ERT* judgment literally.[11] By that, the CJEU actually followed the explanations to Article 51 (1) CFR which describe the framing of the relevant part of this provision as an expression of the previous case law of the Court.[12]

In contrast, it was submitted especially in German scholarship before[13] and after[14] the *Åkerberg Fransson* judgment that the framers of the Charter intended to correct the breadth of the application of EU fundamental rights suggested by the *ERT* case law by using the term 'implement' in Article 51 (1) CFR. For this view, the explanations to the Charter have a questionable status as on the basis of Article

---

[9]CJEU, Case C-617/10 *Åkerberg Fransson*, Judgment of 26 February 2013, para. 19.

[10]CJEU, Case C-260/89 *ERT*, Judgment of the Court of 18 June 1991, para. 42.

[11]The Court 'has no power to examine the compatibility with the European Convention on Human Rights of national rules which do not fall within the scope of Community law. On the other hand, where such rules do fall within the scope of Community law, and reference is made to the Court for a preliminary ruling, it must provide all the criteria of interpretation needed by the national court to determine whether those rules are compatible with the fundamental rights the observance of which the Court ensures', *ERT*, *supra* note 10, para. 42, *Åkerberg Fransson supra* note 9, para. 19.

[12]Explanations relating to the Charter of Fundamental Rights, Explanation on Article 51—Field of application 'As regards the Member States, it follows unambiguously from the case-law of the Court of Justice that the requirement to respect fundamental rights defined in the context of the Union is only binding on the Member States when they act in the scope of Union law (judgment of 13 July 1989, Case 5/88 *Wachauf* [1989] ECR 2609; judgment of 18 June 1991, Case C-260/89 *ERT* [1991] ECR I-2925; judgment of 18 December 1997, Case C-309/96 *Annibaldi* [1997] ECR I-7493). The Court of Justice confirmed this case-law in the following terms: 'In addition, it should be remembered that the requirements flowing from the protection of fundamental rights in the Community legal order are also binding on Member States when they implement Community rules . . .' (judgment of 13 April 2000, Case C-292/97 [2000] ECR I-2737, paragraph 37 of the grounds)' OJ 14.12.2007 C 303/32.

[13]Huber (2008), p. 197.

[14]Schorkopf (2014), para. 26; also Hancox (2013), p. 1411.

52 (7) CFR they only need be considered to provide guidance in the interpretation of the Charter.[15]

This debate would have not had particular bearings if only the German Bundesverfassungsgericht did not take up the issue only two months after *Åkerberg Fransson* in its judgment on the counter-terrorism database.[16] Here Karlsruhe went as far as to use the term 'ultra vires' in relation to the *Åkerberg Fransson* judgment and advised Luxemburg that '[t]he decision must thus not be understood and applied in such a way that absolutely any connection of a provision's subject-matter to the merely abstract scope of Union law, or merely incidental effects on Union law, would be sufficient for binding the Member States by the Union's fundamental rights set forth in the EUCFR.'[17]

The *Siragusa and Hernandez* judgments can be understood in this context. In *Siragusa* the CJEU in essence requires the assessment of the following for the applicability of the Charter against Member States: whether that legislation is intended to implement a provision of EU law; the nature of that legislation and whether it pursues objectives other than those covered by EU law, even if it is capable of indirectly affecting EU law; and also whether there are specific rules of EU law on the matter or capable of affecting it.[18] In essence it needs be ascertained whether there is an EU law obligation on Member States with regard to the situation at issue.[19] This 'specific obligation' test was soon articulated more clearly in the Hernandez judgment[20] and can now be regarded as the guiding interpretation of Article 51 (1).

It may occur that the CJEU still relies on the *Åkerberg Fransson* doctrine, as the judgment has been referred to in the case law several times even after the *Siragusa* judgment. Nevertheless, a closer look reveals that *Åkerberg Fransson* is not invoked to exploit the 'scope of application' doctrine. Rather, *Åkerberg Fransson* is quoted to deny the applicability of the Charter,[21] or in a solely VAT related context.[22] The only exception to this pattern is *Delvigne*, where the Court ultimately found the Charter to be applicable relying on *Åkerberg Fransson* because the member state in question was implementing its obligation under Article 14(3) TEU and Article 1(3) of the

[15]Schorkopf (2014), para. 26.

[16]BVerfG 133, 277.

[17]BVerfG 133, 277, 316 para. 91. For a detailed analyses and critical appraisal see Thym (2013), p. 391 et seq.

[18]CJEU, Case C-206/13 *Siragusa*, Judgment of the Court of 6 March 2014, para. 25.

[19]*Siragusa*, *supra* note 18, para. 26.

[20]CJEU, Case C-198/13 *Hernández*, Judgment of the Court of 10 July 2014, para. 35.

[21]CJEU, Case C-265/13, *Torralbo Marcos*, Judgment of the Court of 27 March 2014, para. 30; CJEU, Cases C-650/13 and C-395/15 *Mohamed Daouidi v. Bootes Plus SL and Others*, Judgment of the Court of 1 December 2016, paras. 63–64; CJEU, Case C-638/16 PPU, *X and X v. État belge*, Judgment of 7 March 2017, para. 45.

[22]CJEU, Case C-42/17, *M.A.S. and M.B.*, Judgment of 5 December 2017, para. 31.

1976 Act while excluding certain convicted EU citizens from the right to vote in the elections to the European Parliament.[23]

The Court gets closest to applying the 'scope of application' doctrine in cases where it deals with the classic *ERT* scenario in which the member state is relying on grounds envisaged in the TFEU or on overriding reasons in the public interest that are recognised by EU law in order to justify the obstruction of one or more fundamental freedoms by the member state.[24]

It is fair to state that the 'scope of application doctrine' would have given more teeth to the Charter as an instrument of protecting the constitutional values enshrined in Article 2. It may seem somewhat exaggerated to assume that *Åkerberg Fransson* would subject a nearly unlimited breadth of Member States competencies to the application of the Charter.[25] Nevertheless the scope of application doctrine would definitely have yielded a more flexible approach and a far more effective enforcement of the basic values of Article 2 against Member States.

Especially damming are the underlying considerations behind the restrictive 'specific obligations' doctrine. According to *Siragusa*, the reason for pursuing the objective of fundamental rights protection by the EU is 'the need to avoid a situation in which the level of protection of fundamental rights varies according to the national law involved in such a way as to undermine the unity, primacy and effectiveness of EU law.'[26] According to this, the CJEU still seems to regard the protection of fundamental rights as a necessary evil to protect the supremacy of EU law from fundamental rights based challenges by national constitutional courts. Fundamental rights are thus not protected following the mandate of Article 2 TEU, but as a matter of expediency for the uniform application of EU law. To put the message bluntly: the CJEU will protect fundamental rights in order to prevent interferences by the constitutional courts but will not take it as far as to disturb the sensitivity of the very same constitutional courts, especially the Bundesverfassungsgericht.

In the following I shall demonstrate how the restrictive approach of the CJEU in relation to the interpretation of Article 51 (1) impacted the handling the case of Hungary and how it did not serve the promotion of the rule of law in the EU.

---

[23]CJEU, Case C-650/13, *Delvigne*, Judgment of the Court of 6 October 2015, para. 27–33.

[24]CJEU, Case C-201/15, *AGET Iraklis*, Judgment of the Court of 21 December 2016, paras. 62–63; CJEU, Case C-235/17, *Commission v. Hungary*, Judgment of 21 May 2019, paras. 64–65.

[25]Schorkopf (2014), para. 26.

[26]Case C-206/13 *Cruciano Siragusa v. Regione Sicilia – Soprintendenza Beni Culturali e Ambientali di Palermo* Judgment of the Court of 20 March 2014, para. 32 'The reason for pursuing that objective is the need to avoid a situation in which the level of protection of fundamental rights varies according to the national law involved in such a way as to undermine the unity, primacy and effectiveness of EU law.'

2.2 *Consequences of the Restrictive Interpretation of 51 (1) CFR Until 2017 in Hungary*

Against the above outlined background, it does not come as a surprise that until December 2017 the European Commission attempted to intervene with undesired constitutional developments in Hungary by means of an infringement procedure only in three cases. All three cases addressed issues of primary importance for the rule of law and democracy: the freedom of the press, the independence of the judiciary and the independence of the date protection commissioner. Out of these only two made it to a judgment by the CJEU, and none was based on the Charter.[27]

2.2.1 The Media Law

One of the first steps of reshaping the legal landscape in Hungary in 2010 was to adopt new laws on print and electronic media: Act CIV of 9 November 2010 on the freedom of the press and the fundamental rules on media content (Press Freedom Act)[28] and Act CLXXXV of 30 December 2010 on media services and on the mass media (Mass Media Act). These laws raised a number of grave concerns from the perspective of the freedom of the press.[29] To name a few, the new regulation provided for an obligation to register for all media, including print, electronic and online media;[30] it obliged all media to provide balanced coverage;[31] it contained a general, broadly framed content based prohibitions for all media to protect vaguely defined concepts as human dignity,[32] human rights and privacy;[33] it reduced significantly the protection for sources, created the position of a Media Ombudsman giving it vaguely defined sanctioning powers and it authorised the newly created National Media and Infocommunications Authority to impose severe sanctions.[34] The President of the National Media and Infocommunications Authority was to be appointed for the unusually long term of nine years (more than two legislative periods) by the President of the Republic.[35]

[27]Article 47 (2) EU Charter (right to a fair trial before an independent and impartial tribunal); Article 8 (3) EU Charter (guarantee of an independent data protection authority).

[28]For an English translation of the original text see http://cmcs.ceu.hu/sites/default/files/domain-69/cmcs-archive/act_civ_media_content.pdf.

[29]For a critical appraisal see Polyák (2015), p. 125 et seq.

[30]Sec. 41 (4) Mass Media Act as of 31 December 2010.

[31]Sec. 13. Press Freedom Act and Sec. 12 (1) Mass Media Act as of 31 December 2010.

[32]On this specific aspect see Koltay (2013), p. 823 et seq.

[33]Part Two Chapter I Mass Media Act as of 31 December 2010.

[34]Secs. 185–187 Mass Media Act as of 31 December 2010.

[35]Sec. 111/A. (1) Mass Media Act.

It is by no surprise that the European Commission reacted quickly and strongly to the new legislation.[36] Already on 23 December 2010 Neelie Kroes, vice-president of the European Commission addressed her Hungarian counterpart in a letter, stating her concerns in general terms.[37] This letter was followed by a more detailed one on 21 January 2011[38] requiring clarifications of three issues.[39] The Hungarian side gave in rapidly in all points raised by the Commission. Although the amending legislation was only adopted on 7 March and published in the Official Gazette on 22 March 2011,[40] Commission Vice-President Kroes welcomed the planned amendments to Hungarian Media Law already on 16 February in a press release.[41]

Notably, these amendments did not address many general concerns relating to the freedom of the press and focused on those aspects that had a direct link to European Union law.[42] Especially telling is the exclusion of the Charter of the discussion between the Commission and Hungary.

[36]For a highly informative collection of relevant documents, see https://cmcs.ceu.hu/node/26249#euro. See also Hoffmeister (2015), p. 195 et seq.

[37]See http://www.kormany.hu./download/8/01/10000/kroes.pdf. According to the letter: 'Independent regulatory authorities for the broadcasting sector have an important role to play to ensure the existence of a wide range of independent and autonomous media. Concerns have been expressed by numerous commentators that the recently adopted Media Act risks jeopardising the rights by giving very broad competences to the Media Authority. These same commentators also allege that the composition of the Media Authority does not seem to guarantee its independence. In addition, doubts have been raised about some of the provisions of the Act which apparently are applicable to broadcasters established in other Member States, which raises potential questions of coherence with one of the basic principles of the Audiovisual Media Services Directive.'

[38]See http://cmcs.ceu.hu/sites/default/files/domain-69/cmcs-archive/EC_lettertoHungary_2011Jan21.pdf.

[39]These included the obligation to provide balanced coverage applicable to all audiovisual media service providers on the basis of Sec. 13. Press Freedom Act and Sec. 12 (1) Mass Media Act, the power of the National Media and Infocommunications Authority to impose fines and other sanctions on media service providers established in another member states of the EU on the basis of Sec. 176 ad 177 Mass Media Act, as well as the requirement in Sec. 41 Mass Media Act that all media, in particular press and online media be registered. The Commission and the Hungarian authorities held thereafter meetings in Brussels at experts level between on 7th February and 15th February.

[40]A sajtószabadságról és a médiatartalmak alapvető szabályairól szóló 2010. évi CIV. törvény és a médiaszolgáltatásokról és a tömegkommunikációról szóló 2010. évi CLXXXV. törvény módosításáról szóló 2011. évi XIX. törvény.

[41]See http://europa.eu/rapid/press-release_MEMO-11-89_en.htm.

[42]The amendments agreed included the following:

- limitation of the balanced coverage requirements to broadcasting, these no longer apply to on-demand media services;
- broadcasters and other audiovisual media service providers legally established and authorised in other Member States can no longer be fined for breaching the Hungarian Media Law's provisions on incitement to hatred;
- on-demand audiovisual media service providers, media product publishers and ancillary media service providers established in Hungary and in other Member States are no longer subject to prior authorisation by the Hungarian authorities;
- the prohibition not to cause offence to individuals, minorities or majorities is limited to situations of incitement to hatred or discrimination.

In her first relevant letter of 23 December 2010 Vice-President Kroes seemed to take a broader approach which would have warranted the examination of the Hungarian legislation on the basis of the Charter of Fundamental Rights. First, the letter expressed the understanding that the media legislation 'primarily aims to transpose the Audiovisual Media Services Directive (Directive 2010/13/EU)'. It then continued by stating that '[t]he freedom of expression constitutes one of the essential foundations of our democratic societies[...] Media pluralism, freedom of expression and press freedom are underlying elements of European democracy guaranteed by the Charter of Fundamental Rights.'[43] This opening could be understood as paving the way for the application of Art. 51 (1) of the Charter of Fundamental Rights inasmuch it referred to the Hungarian legislation as an implementation of EU law.

In contrast, the following letter of 21 January 2011 took a narrow approach and only relied on specific provisions of the Audiovisual Media Services Directive as well as on the freedom of establishment and the free provision of services guaranteed by Art. 49 and 56 TFEU.[44] This letter made no mention of the Charter of Fundamental Rights whatsoever.

2.2.2 The Forced Retirement of Justices

Until the entry into force of the Basic Law, relevant legislation essentially allowed judges to remain in office until the age of 70. The Basic Law provided in its Article 26(2) that 'with the exception of the President of the Kúria, judges may remain in office until the general retirement age'. This provision was supplemented by Article 12(1) of the Transitional Provisions. With these provisions, applied together with the relevant pension legislation, the constitution-maker tied the cessation of the mandate of the judges to the general retirement age, which in 2012 was 62 years and would progressively increase up until 2022, when it will be 65 years. As a result, around 10% of all judges, including many in leading positions, were forced to leave office within a year.

The Constitutional Court was confronted with the forced retirement of judges in its Decision 33/2012 (VII.17) AB.[45] The Court declared the sudden reduction of the upper age limit for judges unconstitutional on the grounds that it was a breach of judicial independence protected by article 26(1) of the Basic Law. Ultimately, the Decision annulled the statutory provisions on early retirement with *ex tunc* effect. The implementation of this judgment has resulted in considerable legal uncertainty. The legal basis of forced retirement was declared null and void, but this did not directly affect the individual resolutions of the President of Hungary, which actually

---

[43] See http://www.kormany.hu./download/8/01/10000/kroes.pdf.

[44] See http://cmcs.ceu.hu/sites/default/files/domain-69/cmcs-archive/EC_lettertoHungary_2011Jan21.pdf.

[45] Kocsis (2013), p. 556.

dismissed the judges. What is more, the President of the National Judicial Office did not initiate a procedure to reinstate those who had been removed, and without an appropriate proposal the President of the Republic could not repeal the previous decisions. Even if a justice was reinstated, by that time the leading positions were already filled.

The European Commission and the CJEU also reacted to the issue of early retirement, but in a different context. The lowering of the mandatory retirement age of judges from 70 to 62 was addressed by the European Commission as discrimination in the workplace on grounds of age in the light of the rules on equal treatment in employment (Directive 2000/78/EC).[46] The CJEU acceded to the position of the European Commission and ruled that the relevant national legislation gives rise to a difference in treatment on grounds of age which is neither appropriate nor necessary to attain the objectives pursued and therefore does not comply with the principle of proportionality.[47] Judicial independence or Article 47 CFR were not addressed.

In response, Hungary, taking into account the previous decision of the Hungarian Constitutional Court as well, amended the legislation on the legal status of the judges, and it introduced a new method of calculation, setting the retirement age to between 65 and 70, depending on the date of birth of the judge. The law also set forth a unified retirement age calculation method for judges, prosecutors and notaries.[48] Nevertheless, only a small number of judges requested to be reinstated, and none of them regained the leading position they previously possessed.

2.2.3 The Removal of the Data Protection Commissioner

The six-year term of the incumbent Data Protection Commissioner was prematurely terminated by Article 16 of the Transitional Provisions on the day of the entry into force of the Basic Law on 1 January 2012. This came along with the creation of a new National Agency for Data Protection to replace the current Data Protection Commissioner's Office.

This move was challenged by the European Commission before the CJEU. In its action submitted on 8 June 2012, the Commission relied on Article 28(1) of Directive 95/46/EC on the protection of individuals with regard to the processing of

---

[46] Letter from Vice-President Viviane Reding to Vice-Prime Minister Tibor Navracsics (Brussels, 12 December 2011), available at www.lapa.princeton.edu/hosteddocs/hungary/letter_from_vp_of_the_european_commission.pdf. European Commission Press Release, 'European Commission Launches Accelerated Infringement Proceedings against Hungary over the Independence of its Central Bank and Data Protection Authorities as well as over Measures affecting the Judiciary' (Strasbourg, 17 January 2012), available at www.europa.eu/rapid/pressReleasesAction.do?reference=IP/12/24.

[47] C-286/12 *Commission v Hungary*, Judgment of the Court of 6 November 2012, para. 48 et seq.

[48] Act XX of 2013 (2013. évi XX. törvény az egyes igazságügyi jogviszonyokban alkalmazandó felső korhatárral kapcsolatos törvénymódosításokról).

personal data and on the free movement of such data and argued that the removal from office before time of the authority responsible for supervising data protection undermines the independence required by the Directive of that authority.[49] The judgment of the CJEU on 8 April 2014 confirmed this.[50] It is remarkable that the central concern in the case was actually orchestrated as a matter of the personal fate of the previous Commissioner, and not as a matter of principle. Besides, the judgment does not mention Article 8 (3) CFR which, in the light of Article 51 (1) CFR has the potential to be interpreted as referring also to national supervisory authorities.

2.3 *Article 19 (1) TEU as a Partial Supplement for a Broad Interpretation of Article 51 (1)*

By the time Polish constitutional developments took a turn in 2015, the forced retirement of justices and the removal of the data protection commissioner were the only cases where an infringement procedure was initiated against Hungary for concerns relating to the values listed in Art. 2 TEU. They show a pattern which can be best characterised by recourse to narrow internal market related provisions and by strictly avoiding the conflicts that may arise from the application of the Charter to a member state. This approach clearly reflects the *Siragusa and Hernández* line of cases and the expediencies following from the Bundesverfassungsgericht's stance on fundamental rights protection by the CJEU.

By that, the CJEU clearly had ignored that protection against removal from office is one of the most important aspects of independence of the judiciary or of any other independent office. In relation to the judiciary, the European Court of Human Rights has repeatedly made it clear that the irremovability of judges by the executive during their term of office must in general be considered as a corollary of their independence and thus included in the guarantees of the right to a fair trial.[51] This does not necessarily mean that this irremovability must under all circumstances be formally declared in law. It suffices that the irremovability is recognised in fact and that the other necessary guarantees are present.[52] From this it follows that independence presupposes a general protection from removal from office except in cases clearly and narrowly defined by law relating to the misconduct or lack of capabilities of the person bearing the office.

---

[49]CJEU, Case C-288/12, *Commission v Hungary* [2012] OJ C227/15–16.

[50]CJEU, Case C-288/12, *Commission v. Hungary,* Judgment of the Court of 8 April 2014.

[51]ECtHR, *Campbell and Fell v United Kingdom*, Judgment of 28 June 1984, Application no. 7819/77; 7878/77 para. 80.

[52]Id., with reference to ECtHR, *Engel and others*, Judgment of 8 June 1976, Application no 5100/71 para. 68.

Irremovability is also considered an important guarantee of independence under express provisions of EU law. With regard to the CJEU, Art 19 TEU and Art 254 TFEU stipulate the independence of the Justices of the Court. This is supplemented by several provisions of the Statute of the Court of Justice of the European Union. Amongst these, Article 5(1) provides that '[a]part from normal replacement, or death, the duties of a Judge shall end when he resigns'. Article 6 of the Statute only allows for removal from office if a Justice 'no longer fulfils the requisite conditions or meets the obligations arising from his office.' As a procedural safeguard in Article 6 of the Statute, decision on the removal may only be taken by a unanimous Court and all Advocates General. Similar rules apply to members of the European Commission. Article 17(3) III TEU declares that 'in carrying out its responsibilities, the Commission shall be completely independent.' The Commission being a political organ with political responsibility, a motion of censure of the Commission in the European Parliament is possible under Art 18(8) TEU. But the independence of individual commissioners is protected by Art 247 TFEU which only allows for the removal of individual commissioners if he or she 'no longer fulfils the conditions required for the performance of his duties or if he has been guilty of serious misconduct.'

These considerations had to have a bearing as it became clear that Hungary will not remain an isolated case and Poland would use the same legislative means to change the composition of the judiciary. The decision in ASJP[53] and the *Commission v. Poland* case on the Supreme Court[54] clearly indicate this understanding.

Nevertheless Article 19 (1) TEU is not a vehicle to trigger the application of the Charter through Article 51 (1) CFR.[55] Rather, the second subparagraph of Article 19 (1) TEU is a stand-alone guarantee which shall be interpreted in the light of Article 47 CFR. This was the position of the Commission at the hearing in the *Commission v. Poland* case,[56] and this follows from the operative parts of the judgments in the same case and in the ASJP case. In ASJP the requesting court sought an interpretation of Article 19 (1) and Article 47 CFR,[57] but the CJEU merely pronounced on the former.[58] In *Commission v. Poland*, the operative part of the judgment found solely a violation of the obligations following from the second subparagraph of Article 19 (1) TEU, but did not establish a violation of Article 47 CFR.[59] It is to be expected that the cases pending in relation to the judiciary in Poland[60] will be decided along the same lines.

[53]CJEU *Associação Sindical dos Juízes Portugueses*, *supra* note 6.

[54]CJEU *Commission v. Poland*, *supra* note 7.

[55]For a different view see Spieker (2019).

[56]CJEU *Commission v. Poland*, *supra* note 7, para. 32.

[57]CJEU *Associação Sindical dos Juízes Portugueses*, *supra* note 6, para. 1.

[58]CJEU *Associação Sindical dos Juízes Portugueses*, *supra* note 6, operative part.

[59]CJEU *Commission v. Poland*, *supra* note 7, operative part 1.

[60]See the case relating to the law on ordinary courts organisation—CJEU, Case C-192/18, *European Commission v. Republic of Poland*, Opinion of AG Tanchev of 20 June 2019; the case

2.4 Revival of ERT?

It follows that the CJEU regards the independence of the judiciary as an issue completely separated from the application of the Charter to Member States. ASJP thus has not broadened the applicability of the Charter to Member States. It is highly questionable whether other vital elements of the rule of law protected by fundamental rights will still remain within the restraints of the *Siragusa and Hernández* case law.

There are signs that the CJEU might take up the *ERT* case law in the stricter sense and find the Charter applicable in situations where fundamental freedoms are involved and Member States seem to rely on exceptions to such fundamental freedoms. Examples can be found regarding Hungary, in relation to which the European Commission launched three infringement procedures based on fundamental freedoms and the Charter. These include the following: (i) the case relating to the amendment of the Act on National Higher Education affecting foreign universities, most of all the Central European University;[61] (ii) the case relating to the law on the transparency of organisations that receive financial support from abroad;[62] (iii) the case of Act VI of 2018 on the amendment of certain laws relating to measures to combat illegal immigration.[63] Common to these cases is that the European Commission relies on one of the fundamental freedoms and in connection with that provisions of the Charter. In relation to the Act on National Higher Education the freedom to provide services is invoked, and in relation to that Articles 13, 14(3) and 16 CFR. As regards the transparency of foreign funded organisations the vehicle is the freedom of movement of capital, which seems to trigger the application of Articles 7, 8 and 12 CFR. The case of Act VI of 2018 on the amendment of certain laws relating to measures to combat illegal immigration the Commission invokes the freedom of movement, whereas the press release on the reasoned opinion only refers to the Charter in general terms.

As neither the reasoned opinions nor the applications of the Commission to the CJEU are public, it is unclear whether the Commission indeed utilises the *ERT* precedent to trigger the application of the Charter. Yet these cases certainly point in that direction. It would mean that while the CJEU is not ready to apply the 'scope of application' doctrine of the *ERT* and *Åkerberg Fransson* judgment to broaden the applicability of the Charter to Member States in situations sensitive to the rule of law in general, it sticks with the already established precedent of the *ERT* judgment if it is applicable. This conclusion is reinforced by the already mentioned post-*Siragusa*

---

relating to the new disciplinary regime for Polish judges—Reasoned Opinion of the European Commission of 17 July 2019, http://europa.eu/rapid/press-release_IP-19-4189_en.htm.

[61] CJEU, Case C-66/18, *Commission v Hungary*, Action brought on 1 February 2018.

[62] CJEU, Case C-78/18, *Commission v Hungary*, Action brought on 1 June 2018.

[63] Reasoned opinion of the European Commission of 24 January 2019, http://europa.eu/rapid/press-release_IP-19-469_EN.htm.

and Hernández cases not involving systemic rule of law concerns where the CJEU relied on the *ERT* precedent to invite the application of the Charter.[64]

3 Unused Means to Control the Constitution Making Power

3.1 The Convolution of Pouvoir Constituant and Pouvoir Constitué

The circumstances of the activity of the Hungarian Constitutional Court could hardly be more different than those of the CJEU. Out of the past ten years the governing coalition in Hungary had a constitution making majority for about seven years altogether.[65] This majority did not refrain from amending the Constitution and from 2012 the Basic Law. Between 2010 and 2012 the Constitution was amended eight times. Following the adoption of a new Basic Law, seven different amendment thereto were adopted within seven years. In other words, nine years have seen the adoption of a new constitution (the Basic Law) and fifteen constitutional amendments out of which seven affected the brand-new Basic Law.

Not only the statistics suggest a volatile constitutional environment. Almost all constitutional amendments were borne out of immediate political needs and motivations. With a few exceptions, they served to exclude or reduce the possibility of challenging specific legislative projects before the Constitutional Court or attempted to undo the results of previous Constitutional Court decisions.[66] Especially the curtailing of the competences of the Constitutional Court in tax matters by what is now Article 37 (4) of the Basic Law and the Fourth Amendment made it clear that the legislative power is ready to use its constitution making power to combat the Constitutional Court.

As regards Article 37 (4) of the Basic Law, the restriction of the competences of the Constitutional Court is certainly a very serious loophole in the Basic Law. This is because Article 37(4) of the Basic Law excludes a wide range of laws on the central budget, on the implementation of the budget, on central taxes, on duties and on contributions, on customs duties, and on the central conditions for local taxes issues from the competence of the Constitutional Court, and only allows for the review of these on the basis of a limited list of fundamental rights, i.e. the rights to life and human dignity, to the protection of personal data, to freedom of thought, conscience and religion, and the rights related to Hungarian citizenship. This language arose out of a conflict between Parliament and the Constitutional Court over a 98% punitive tax charged on severance payments of dismissed civil servants and public employees

[64]See CJEU *AGET Iraklis, supra* note 24, paras 62–63; C-235/17, CJEU *Commission v. Hungary, supra* note 24, paras. 64–65.

[65]May 2010 to February 2015, May 2018 to present (July 2020).

[66]Vincze (2014), p. 86.

before the adoption of the Basic Law. In its Decision 184/2010 (X.28) AB[67] the Constitutional Court declared this punitive tax to be in violation of the right to property, even though Parliament had previously specifically amended the Constitution to cover the impugned legislation. Apparently, Parliament felt it necessary to protect its prerogatives by stripping the power of the Constitutional Court to adjudicate tax matters in the broad sense, and introduced Article 32/A(2) of the Constitution, the language of which was identical to what is today Article 37 (4) of the Basic Law.[68]

The Fourth Amendment was adopted in reaction to Decision 45/2012 (XII.29) AB of the Constitutional Court which had declared the so-called transitory provisions of the Basic Law unconstitutional. Accordingly, the most important part of the Fourth Amendment was that it incorporated those provisions of the Transitional Provisions into the text of the Basic Law that were previously annulled by the Constitutional Court. These reinstated rules included substantive provisions, such as the reallocation of cases by the President of the National Judicial Office (Article 27(4)), the possibility to reduce pensions of former communist leaders (Article U (5)), and the suspension of the statute of limitations for crimes not prosecuted for political reasons in the communist regime (Article U(6)). Besides these, the Fourth Amendment included in Article U(1) of the Basic Law the previous Preamble to the Transitional Provisions, which declared, inter alia, that the Hungarian Socialist Workers' Party (the communist party before 1989) bears responsibility for different wrongdoings, including 'the systematic destruction of European civilisation, legacy and prominence'. What is more, the newly inserted Article U(1) also declares that the successor of the Hungarian Socialist Workers' Party, the Hungarian Socialist Party (MSZP, which is at the present time the strongest opposition), shares the responsibility of its predecessor.

However, the constitution-making power did not stop at undoing one single Constitutional Court ruling. Rather, the Fourth Amendment basically reversed all politically sensitive decisions handed down by the Constitutional Court after the 2010 elections. This was carried out by including specific exceptions to fundamental rights provisions in the Basic Law based on which laws previously annulled by the Constitutional Court can no longer be regarded as unconstitutional.

For example, the Fourth Amendment inserted the following provision into Article L(1) of the Basic Law: 'Hungary shall protect the institution of marriage as the union of a man and a woman established by voluntary decision, and the family as the basis of the nation's survival. Family ties shall be based on marriage or the relationship between parents and children.'

This was a direct response to Decision 43/2012 (XII.20) AB,[69] in which the Constitutional Court annulled section 7 of the Act on Protection of Families. Section 7 had defined family as a system of relations that generates an emotional

[67]Constitutional Court of Hungary Decision 184/2010 (X.28) AB határozat para 900.

[68]I shall address this conflict in detail below at point 3.2.3.

[69]Constitutional Court of Hungary, Decision 43/2012 (XII.20) AB, para. 296.

and economic community of natural persons, based on the marriage of a man and a woman, next of kinship or adoptive guardianship. The Court found this concept of a family too narrow as the state should also protect long-term emotional and economic partnerships of persons living together (for example, those relationships in which the couples raise and take care of each other's children, or couples who do not have any children or are not able to have any children, grandchildren cared for by grandparents, etc.).

Another reaction to one of the contemporary decisions of the Constitutional Court was the amendment of Article VII(2) and (3) of the Basic Law which authorise Parliament to recognise religious organisations as churches. Just ten days before the adoption of the Fourth Amendment, in its Decision 6/2013 (III.1) AB, the Constitutional Court decided, inter alia, that on the basis of freedom of religion Parliament cannot be authorised to grant church status.[70] Both of these will be elaborated on in more detail in Sect. 3.2.

Similarly, to reverse a Constitutional Court Decision, Article XXII of the Basic Law introduced an obligation of the state and local governments to strive for the protection of homeless persons but at the same time granted authorisation for the Parliament and the local governments to outlaw the use of certain specific sections of public areas for habitation. This amendment was a reaction to Decision 38/2012 (XI.14) AB,[71] in which the Constitutional Court reviewed the Petty Offence Act and stated that the punishment of homeless people for living in a public area is in violation of the right to human dignity. In the Court's view, homelessness is a social problem which the state must handle within the framework of social administration and social care instead of punishment. Ultimately, therefore, the newly introduced Article XXII(3) created an exception to the protection of human dignity concerning homeless people at the level of the Basic Law.

Equally, the Fourth Amendment included a new paragraph in Article IX of the Basic Law which explicitly allows for banning political advertisements from private broadcasting in times of political campaign, thereby reversing Decision 45/2012 (XII.29) AB, discussed above. Besides this, the new Article IX(3) discourages political advertising in private broadcasting by prohibiting media outlets from charging for broadcasting political adverts, should they decide to air these.

What is more, some provisions of the Fourth Amendment relating to hate speech aim to cut back a 20-year-old case law of the Constitutional Court. Between 1992 and 2008, the Constitutional Court found several laws to be unconstitutional that aimed to penalise hate speech.[72] As an answer to this, Article 5(2) of the Basic Law stipulates that: '[t]he right to freedom of speech may not be exercised with the aim of violating the dignity of the Hungarian nation or of any national, ethnic, racial or

[70] Constitutional Court of Hungary, Decision 6/2013 (III.1) AB para. 203.

[71] Constitutional Court of Hungary, Decision 38/2012 (XI.14) AB para. 185.

[72] See Constitutional Court of Hungary, Decision 30/1992 (V.26) AB; Constitutional Court of Hungary, Decision 18/2004 (IV.25) AB; Constitutional Court of Hungary, Decision 95/2008 (VII.3) AB.

religious community. Members of such communities shall be entitled to enforce their claims in court against the expression of an opinion which violates their community, invoking the violation of their human dignity as determined by law.'

In general, reversing several decisions of the Constitutional Court by constitutional amendment resulted in a Basic Law packed with specific exceptions to fundamental rights and provisions that are normally at the level of an ordinary law. Not only did this lower the level of protection of fundamental rights, it also had the aim of reducing the possibility of review by the Constitutional Court. And above all, the Fourth Amendment sent an extraordinary strong message to the Constitutional Court that no other power is supposed to control the legislative and at the same time constitution making branch.

Under these circumstances it is fair to ask what role constitutional adjudication can play. Is it at all possible to maintain a meaningful constitutional review, or is the role of the Constitutional Court necessarily reduced to review politically non-sensitive issues? Do we experience the development of a new, special Eastern European type of the well-known political question doctrine? Naturally this 'new political question' doctrine would not be a constitutional standard, rather the necessity of judicial self-restraint in matters the actual legislative and constitution making power would deem too important to be decided by anybody else than itself.

I submit that even under these difficult circumstances constitutional review is possible. The Hungarian Constitutional Court had developed tools that are, to a certain extent, capable of limiting the constitution making power or enable the Court to adjudicate irrespective of the existing substantive and competence limitations.

As regards the limitation of the constitution-making power, the identity of the Basic Law as well as international *ius cogens* serve as a standard (Sect. 3.2). Constitutional adjudication is further possible in the present setting based on international human rights treaties, especially the European Convention on Human Rights (Sect. 3.3).

3.2 Limits of the Constitution Making Power

The concept of an unconstitutional constitutional amendments is equally fascinating and controversial, especially if the substantive limits to constitutional change are implied[73] and are not foreseen explicitly by the respective constitution. Declaring a constitutional amendment to be unconstitutional by the constitutional court is not only a harsh interference with popular sovereignty, but also comes dangerously close to to a 'juristocracy'[74] and—due to the lacking standards against which constitutional amendments can be reviewed (e.g. an explicit eternity clause)—even judicial arbitrariness. It is therefore tempting for a constitutional court to seek objective and

[73]Jacobsohn (2006), p. 460 et seq.

[74]Hirschl (2007).

relevant criteria in historic documents or European[75] and international law. This temptation may raise questions of legitimacy, but it can help overcoming accusations that the respective constitutional court is inventing standards that do not exist.

It occurs that the case law of the Constitutional Court and ultimately the Basic Law offer two different sets of supraconstitutional norms: the concept of constitutional identity (Sect. 3.2.1) and international law. International law even has a double role to play in this context: it is considered as a binding standard of interpretation of constitutional provisions (Sect. 3.2.2) and constitutional amendments must conform international jus cogens (Sect. 3.2.3).

3.2.1 Constitutional Identity

Constitutional identity is a new phenomenon in Hungarian law. It was first stipulated in Decision 22/2016. (XII. 5.) of the Constitutional Court without an express constitutional foundation and is now codified by the seventh amendment to the Basic Law. The seventh amendment namely included a reference in the Preamble of the Basic Law to the constitutional identity of Hungary. According to this new language, 'We hold that the protection of our identity rooted in our historic constitution is a fundamental obligation of the State'. This is reinforced also in the operative part of the Basic Law, as a new Article R (4) is included stating that '[t]he protection of the constitutional identity of Hungary is an obligation of all organs of the state.'

The contours of constitutional identity are rather vague. Decision 22/2016. (XII. 5.) states that the Constitutional Court 'unfolds the content of this concept from case to case, on the basis of the whole Fundamental Law and certain provisions thereof, in accordance with the National Avowal and the achievements of our historical constitution.'[76] There is thus a close link between constitutional identity and the historic constitution, which may be further reinforced by the seventh amendment to the Basic Law declaring the constitutional identity of Hungary to be rooted in the historic constitutions. Yet, there is a strong consensus in academia that the historic constitution of Hungary is an empty shell, the content of which cannot be reconstructed.[77] What remains at the moment is thus an exemplificatory reference in Decision 22/2016 (XII. 5.) to certain values as part of constitutional identity. These are 'freedoms, the division of powers, republic as the form of government, respect of autonomies under public law, the freedom of religion, exercising lawful authority, parliamentarism, the equality of rights, acknowledging judicial power, the protection of the nationalities living with us.'[78]

[75] On this, see Dupré (2015), p. 351 et seq.

[76] Constitutional Court of Hungary, Decision 22/2016 (XII. 5.) AB para. 64.

[77] Szente (2011), p. 1 et seq.

[78] Constitutional Court of Hungary, Decision 22/2016 (XII. 5.) AB para. 65.

What makes the concept of constitutional identity intriguing is that it seems to have a rank above the Basic Law. This follows from the language of Decision 22/2016. (XII. 5.) according to which 'the constitutional identity of Hungary is a fundamental value which was not created by the Basic Law, it is merely recognised by the Basic Law'[79] This clearly suggests the existence of pre-constitutional values which serve as a standard for the actual written constitution, the Basic Law. And because constitutional identity is defined by reference to the historic constitution, and this concept is capable of having a variety of contents and meanings, the Constitutional Court enjoys a considerable discretion in reviewing constitutional amendments on the basis of constitutional identity.

3.2.2 International Law as a Standard of Interpretation of Constitutional Provisions

For a long time, it seemed unclear, whether from the perspective of the Hungarian constitutional order the role of the jurisprudence of the European Court of Human Rights is merely of non-binding, inspiring character, or whether the case law of the Court should be deemed to define the scope and content of the respective rights, and as such have a binding force.[80]

At the beginning, this question was answered almost unanimously in the negative. Representative of this was the view of the first President of the Hungarian Constitutional Court, who argued that reference to the Strasbourg case law is merely of auxiliary nature besides the reasoning of the Constitutional Court, and such reference might also emphasize the importance of a specific rule of the Constitution.[81] For two decades the Hungarian Court never went as far as to derive binding constitutional standards from the Convention. Only once has the Constitutional Court found that the understanding of the freedom of expression by the European Court of Human Rights is 'forming and binding the Hungarian jurisprudence.'[82] Yet this statement had no consequences in later decisions and the Court continued to refer to the practice of the Convention without declaring them to be binding in the interpretation of the Constitution.

---

[79]Constitutional Court of Hungary, Decision 22/2016 (XII. 5.) AB para. 67.

[80]This approach seems to follow from the Commentaries attached to the Charter of Fundamental Rights. Cf. the comments on Article 52. (3) [2007] OJ C 303/33.

[81]*Sólyom and Brunner* (2000), p. 1317. This view was certainly in line with the case law of the Bundesverfassungsgericht. Cf. BVerfG, Judgement of 14 October 2004, 2 BvR 1481/04, *Görgülü*, para. 30–32, BVerfG, Judgment of 12 June 2018, 2 BvR 1738/12, *Ban on strike action for civil servants*, para. 126: 'Using them as guidelines for interpretation does not require that the statements of the Basic Law and those of the European Convention on Human Rights be schematically aligned or completely harmonised.'

[82]Constitutional Court of Hungary, 18/2004. (V. 25.) AB, ABH 2004, 303, 306. The Constitutional Court referred to a series of judgments in this context, Hungary was not party to any of them.

This picture seems to gradually change by decisions of the Court that actually give effect to judgments of the European Court of Human Rights. The first instance of this was a consequence of the Judgment *Bukta and others v. Hungary*.[83] Here the European Court of Human Rights ruled that the subjection of public assemblies to a prior–authorisation procedure does not normally encroach upon the essence of Article 11 of the Convention.[84] But when an immediate response, in the form of a demonstration, to a political event might be justified, a decision to disband the ensuing, peaceful assembly solely because of the absence of the requisite prior notice, without any illegal conduct by the participants, amounts to a disproportionate restriction on freedom of peaceful assembly.[85] Shortly after this judgment the Constitutional Court decided on the constitutionality of the Act Nr. III of 1989 on the right of assembly in its Decision Nr. 75/2008.[86] This Decision actually comes to the same conclusion as the ECHR. Yet the Hungarian Court merely refers to the *Bukta* judgment in a brief paragraph, and the same paragraph also quotes the jurisprudence of the German Bundesverfassungsgericht. The substantive argument is solely based on Article 62 para. 1 of the Constitution. It appears that the Court did not want to tie its hands for the future, even if it was ready to follow the path of interpretation drawn by the European Court of Human Rights,[87] and even if the Constitutional Court is deciding on a statute the application of which was reviewed by the European Court of Human Rights.

The breakthrough came with Decision Nr. 61/2011.[88] Here the Court declared clearly that it is under an obligation to follow the case law of the Convention in its decisions interpreting the Constitution as long as the language of both corresponds. In the words of the Court: 'In the case of certain fundamental rights the Constitution sets out the essential content of the fundamental right in the same fashion as an international treaty (i.e. the International Covenant on Civil and Political Rights and the European Convention on Human Rights). In these cases, the level of protection for fundamental rights provided by the Constitutional Court may under no circumstances be lower than the level of international protection (typically elaborated by the European Court of Human Rights). Therefore following from the principle of *pacta sunt servanda* [Article 7 (1) Constitution Article Q (2)-(3) Basic Law] the Constitutional Court has to follow the Strasbourg case law and the level of fundamental rights protection defined therein even if this would not be necessitated by its previous 'precedents'.[89] This statement was later referred to in Decision Nr. 166/2011[90] and after the entry into force of the Basic Law in Decision

[83]ECtHR, *Bukta and others v. Hungary*, Judgment of 17 July 2007, Application no. 25691/04.

[84]Id. para. 35.

[85]Id. para. 36.

[86]Constitutional Court of Hungary, 75/2008. (V. 29.) AB, ABH 2008, 651.

[87]Id. 663 et seq.

[88]See Kovács (2013), p. 73 et seq.

[89]Constitutional Court of Hungary, 61/2011. (VII.13.) AB, ABH 2011, 321.

[90]Constitutional Court of Hungary, 166/2011. (XII.20.) AB, ABH 2011, 545.

Nr. 43/2012.[91] It occurs therefore that the rights of the Convention as interpreted by the European Court of Human Rights are obligatory standards of interpretation of the rights of the Basic Law at least in the sense that they provide for a minimum of protection.[92] Absent express provisions to the contrary in the language of the Basic Law this shall help in maintaining European minimum standards domestically.

3.2.3 International Law as a Standard of Legality of the Constitution

The Hungarian Constitutional Court has already relied on international *ius cogens* to define the eternal core of the constitution of Hungary in two of its decisions. Both decisions were made in the context of a controversial constitutional amendment, yet none of them actually found a violation of international *ius cogens*.

Decision 61/2011 (VII.13.) AB was made under the 1989 Constitution in a battle between Parliament and the Constitutional Court over a piece of tax legislation. On 22 July 2010, the Hungarian Parliament adopted several economic and financial Acts. The Act, *inter alia*, introduced a new punitive tax on certain payments for employees of the public sector (civil servants, public servants, etc.) whose employment was terminated. Accordingly, severance payments and other payments related to the termination of employment exceeding a certain amount became subject to a 98% tax. The proposal of the Act justified the punitive tax by reference to the needs of the society to do justice, claiming that under the previous government public employees had been granted immorally excessive severance payments. Although the Act entered into force on 1 October 2010, the punitive tax was to be applied to the relevant incomes starting from 1 January 2010. In order to ensure the constitutionality of this Act, Parliament also amended Article 70/I of the 1989 Constitution by including a new paragraph (2) in the Article that allowed for special taxes.[93]

The punitive tax was challenged before the Constitutional Court within the framework of an *actio popularis*, and the Court found the relevant provisions of the Act to be unconstitutional in its Decision 184/2010 (X.28) AB, because, inter alia, Article 70/I(2) of the Constitution did not cover the retroactive 98% tax.[94]

In response, Parliament reintroduced the 98% tax with certain modifications. At the same time, Parliament modified Article 70/I(2) of the Constitution allowing for retroactive taxation going back five years from the actual tax year. To prevent the Constitutional Court from reviewing the legislation, a limitation was also introduced

[91]Constitutional Court of Hungary, 43/2012. (XII.20.) AB, ABH 2012, 320.

[92]In this sense Kovács (2013), p. 76.

[93]Article 70/I(2) of the Constitution (no longer in force): 'In respect of any remuneration received against the good morals from public funds, or from bodies entrusted to manage state assets and state property, including bodies under majority state ownership or control, tax liabilities of a special extent may be introduced on the strength of law, beginning with the given tax year.'

[94]Constitutional Court of Hungary, Decision 184/2010 (X.28) AB para. 900.

in Article 32/A(2)–(3) of the Constitution, the language of which was basically identical with what is today Article 37(4) of the Basic Law.

The Constitutional Court was confronted with this limitation on its powers in Decision 61/2011 (VII.13.) AB where several petitioners challenged the constitutional amendments that made the new Articles 32/A(2) and 70/I(2) part of the Constitution. The Constitutional Court was not ready to find these amendments unconstitutional but indicated that it might be ready to review constitutional amendments on the basis of international law. The Decision stated that 'norms, principles and fundamental values of *ius cogens* together form a standard which all subsequent constitutional amendments and the Constitution must comply with.'[95]

In spite of this clear language Decision 61/2011 (VII.13.) AB did not state clearly that the Constitutional Court would possess the power to enforce these standards against the constitution-making power. This came only after the entry into force of the Basic Law in Decision 45/2012 (XII. 29.) of the Constitutional Court.

Decision 45/2012 (XII. 29.) concerned the Transitional Provisions to the Basic Law. The Transitional Provisions were a document separate from the Basic Law but it were, according to Point 3 of the Final Provisions of the Basic Law, to be adopted by Parliament according to the rules of the previous Constitution on constitutional amendments. Since these provisions were also the legal basis of the Basic Law itself, it seemed reasonable to suppose that the constitution-maker intended to attribute to the Transitional Provisions a rank similar to that of the Basic Law. This was reinforced by the First Amendment to the Basic Law which inserted Point 5 in the closing provisions of the Basic Law, according to which the Transitional Provisions form an integral part of the Basic Law.

In its Decision 45/2012 (XII.29) AB, the Constitutional Court declared the Transitional Provisions null and void.[96] The core of the Court's argument was that Parliament had overstepped its constitutional authorisation when it implemented regulations in the Transitional Provisions which had no transitional character. It was probably to reduce confrontation with Parliament that the Constitutional Court cautiously framed its ruling as the enforcement of formal rules and emphasised that it did not review the merits of the Transitional Provisions. Still, the Decision also seems to establish the power for itself to review the constitutionality of constitutional amendments in its paragraph 118, which reads as follows: 'Constitutional legality has substantive criteria besides the procedural, formal, public law ones. [These are] [t]he constitutional requirements of the democratic state under the rule of law, constitutional values and principles acknowledged by democratic communities under the rule of law and enshrined in international agreements, as well the so-called *ius cogens*, which partly overlaps with these. Under certain circumstances the Constitutional Court is empowered to review whether the substantive

[95] Constitutional Court of Hungary, Decision 61/2011. (VII.13.) AB, ABH 2011, 321.

[96] Constitutional Court of Hungary, Decision 45/2012 (XII.29) para. 347.

constitutional requirements, guarantees and values of a democratic state under the rule of law are consistently respected and included in the constitution.'[97]

It is remarkable that the Court here not only reiterated its findings on the role of international *ius cogens* as a standard of review of the constitutional amendments, but also claimed the power to carry out a substantive review of norms formally incorporated into the Basic Law.

3.3 The European Convention on Human Rights as a Standard of Review by the Constitutional Court

The Basic Law of Hungary seems to be surprisingly open towards international law. Article Q (2) of the Basic Law provides that 'Hungary shall ensure harmony between international law and Hungarian law in order to fulfil its obligations under international law.' Further, according to Article Q (3) international treaties become part of Hungarian Law upon their promulgation by a piece of Hungarian legislation. From these it follows that international treaties promulgated by an Act of Parliament shall take precedence over domestic legislation. This is supplemented by Section 32 of the Constitutional Court Act which specifically entitles the Constitutional Court to review the conformity of domestic legislation with international treaties. Should such a procedure establish a conflict between an international treaty promulgated by Act of Parliament and a domestic piece of legislation, the Constitutional Court is obliged to declare the domestic law null and void. What is more, the already mentioned limitation on the competences of the Constitutional Court in Article 37 (4) in relation to tax laws does not apply to this type of procedure. In effect, the combination of these provisions enables the Constitutional Court to conduct review on the basis of international law.

The real question is who may initiate this type of review. The European Convention on Human Rights was promulgated in the Hungarian legal order by Act Nr. XXXI of 1993, and therefore can be invoked by individuals before ordinary courts. Yet individuals are not listed in Section 32 (2) amongst those entitled to request the review of conflict with international treaties.[98] Nevertheless concrete, incidental norm control is open under Section 33 (2) of the Constitutional Court Act, which provides that 'judges shall suspend judicial proceedings and initiate Constitutional Court proceedings if, in the course of the adjudication of a concrete case,

---

[97] Id., paras. 347, 403.

[98] Section 32 (2) CC Act 'The proceedings may be requested by one quarter of Members of Parliament, the Government, the President of the Curia, the Prosecutor General or the Commissioner for Fundamental Rights. Judges shall suspend judicial proceedings and initiate Constitutional Court proceedings if, in the course of the adjudication of a concrete case, they are bound to apply a legal regulation that they perceive to be contrary to an international treaty.'

they are bound to apply a legal regulation that they perceive to be contrary to an international treaty.'

As a result, ordinary courts are not only bound to apply the applicable Hungarian laws and interpret them in conformity with the Convention as far as possible.[99] Should a harmonious interpretation not be possible because of the express language of the Hungarian law in question, courts are entitled to call upon the Constitutional Court and ask for a review of the Hungarian piece of legislation on the basis of international treaties, notably the European Convention on Human Rights. In case of a conflict the Constitutional Court is obliged to declare the Hungarian law in question unconstitutional.

4 Conclusions

The present Chapter attempted to demonstrate that the enforcement of the basic values of the EU by courts has unexploited potentials. It occurs that both the legal system of the EU and Hungarian constitutional law offers possibilities that are not used for considerations of non-legal nature.

In the case of the CJEU, deference to constitutional courts, especially the Bundesverfassungsgericht and an outdated approach to fundamental rights protection are a crucial shortcoming. As demonstrated by the *Siragusa* judgment, the CJEU seems to regard the protection of fundamental rights protection as a means of preventing challenges to the supremacy of EU law by national constitutional courts. I submit that this mid 1960s understanding does not fit the state of the EU as it is in the 2010s, at least for two reasons. First, the constitutional foundations of the EU have changed radically. Second, the realities changed with the accession of Member States with more fragile democratic traditions and by the rise of populist parties all over Europe.

As regards the changed constitutional foundations, the express stipulation of constitutional values in Article 2 TEU clearly calls for the application of the Charter as the concretisation of these values also against Member States. Besides, the EU is equipped with far reaching consequences in the field of criminal cooperation and the mandate to facilitate the full application of the principle of mutual recognition by virtue of Article 70 TFEU.

Changed realities are clear from the developments in Hungary, Romania[100] and the subject matter of the present volume, Poland. It occurs that the presumption of an approximately homogenic area of the rule of law no longer applies and certain

[99]Such a harmonious interpretation is a constitutional mandate repeatedly confirmed by the Constitutional Court. Cf. Constitutional Court of Hungary 53/1993 (X. 13.) AB, ABH 1993, 323, 327; Constitutional Court of Hungary, 4/1997. (I. 22.) AB, ABH 1997, 41, 51.

[100]For these see inter alia von Bogdandy and Sonnevend (2015).

Member States do not meet all supposedly common standards of fundamental rights protection and the rule of law.

The implications and eventual perils following from the changed constitutional and sociological realities are aptly demonstrated by the *Aranyosi*[101] and *LM*[102] line of cases. Especially LM demonstrates that mutual recognition and mutual trust presuppose a coherent level of respect for human rights in all EU Member States. If this is missing, the whole fabric of EU law may fall apart. As a result, the protection of fundamental rights by Member States is a common concern.

The situation of the Hungarian Constitutional Court is different in many respects. Constitutional adjudication against the constitution making power is a seemingly insurmountable task, especially when the constitution making power is not separated from the legislative power. This situation requires extreme means like the concept of an unconstitutional constitution. These means are, however, readily available. Both the new concept of constitutional identity and the case law on international *ius cogens* as a binding standard of constitutional provisions offer munition for extreme situations. These possibilities, I believe, exist even in the face of Article 25 (4) of the Basic Law, which enables the Constitutional Court to review the constitutionality of Amendments of the Basic Law only on procedural grounds.[103] In an already extreme situation triggering the application of the constitutional identity of the Basic Law or international *ius cogens* it is possible to argue that any competence limitation in Article 25 (4) of the Basic Law is also in violation of said supra-constitutional norms.

Besides these extreme situations the European Convention on Human Rights offers a perfect secondary tool of constitutional adjudication through the procedure of review of conformity of laws with international treaties. This has remained thus far completely underexplored and unused by the Constitutional Court. This, I submit, is a self-restraint that does not follow from the law as it stands today.

The phenomenon of constitutional adjudication was borne for the first time out of the consideration that courts are inherently called upon to apply the law, and the concept of law necessarily encompasses the constitution. As the US Supreme Court stated in *Marbury v. Madison* '[i]t is emphatically the province and duty of the Judicial Department to say what the law is.'[104] The birth of modern constitutionalism

---

[101] CJEU, Cases C-404/15 and C-659/15 PPU, *Aranyosi and Căldăraru*, Judgment of the Court of 5 April 2016.

[102] CJEU, C-216/18 PPU. *LM*, Judgment of the Court of 25 July 2018.

[103] Article 25 (4) of the Basic Law: 'The Constitutional Court may review the Basic Law and an amendment to the Basic Law only with respect to the procedural requirements set out in the Basic Law pertaining to the adoption and the promulgation of the Basic Law and any amendment thereof. This review may be initiated by:

a) the President of the Republic, in the case where the Fundamental Law or an amendment to the Basic Law was adopted by Parliament but not yet promulgated;
b) the Government, one fourth of all Members of Parliament, the President of the Kúria, President of the Közigazgatási Felsőbíróság, the Prosecutor General, or the Commissioner for Fundamental Rights within thirty days of promulgation.'

[104] *Marbury v. Madison* 5 U.S. 137 (1803).

is thus intimately linked to the responsibility of the courts to enforce the constitutional documents of the respective polity. All courts shall follow the mandate resulting from this and apply all available means in order to preserve the common basic values of constitutionalism.

References

Avbelj M (2019) Judges depending on judges, a missing brick in the CJEU jurisprudence on judicial independence. https://verfassungsblog.de/judges-depending-on-judges/

Dupré C (2015) The unconstitutional constitution: a timely concept. In: von Bogdandy A, Sonnevend P (eds) Constitutional crisis in the European constitutional area, theory, law and politics in Hungary and Romania, p 351

Hancox E (2013) The meaning of 'implementing' EU law under Article 51(1) of the Charter: Åkerberg Fransson. Common Mark Law Rev 50(5):1411

Hirschl R (2007) Towards juristocracy: the origins and consequences of the new constitutionalism. HUP, Cambridge

Hoffmeister F (2015) Enforcing the EU Charter of Fundamental Rights in Member States: How Far are Rome, Budapest and Bucharest from Brussels? In: von Bogdandy A, Sonnevend P (eds) Constitutional crisis in the European constitutional area, theory, law and politics in Hungary and Romaina, p 195

Huber PM (2008) Unitarisierung durch Gemeinschaftsgrundrechte – Zur Überprüfungsbedürftigkeit der ERT-Rechtsprechung, EuR 2008, 190

Jacobsohn GJ (2006) An unconstitutional constitution? A comparative perspective. Int J Const Law 4(3):460

Kochenov D, Bárd P (2018) Rule of law crisis in the New Member States of the EU, The Pitfalls of Overemphasising Enforcement, reconnect Working Paper No. 1 July 2018

Kocsis M (2013) Hungarian Constitutional Court: the mandatory retirement of judges, Judgment of 17 July 2012, Decision 33/2012 (VII 17) (2013). ICL J 7:556

Koltay A (2013) The protection of human dignity in Hungarian media regulation. German Law J 14 (7):823

Kovács P (2013) Az Emberi Jogok Európai Bírósága ítéletére való hivatkozás újabb formulái és technikái a magyar Alkotmánybíróság valamint néhány más európai alkotmánybíróság mai gyakorlatában, Alkotmánybírósági Szemle 2013/2, p 73

Polyák G (2015) Context, rules and practice of the new Hungarian Media Law – how does the Media Law affect the structure and the functioning of publicity. In: von Bogdandy, Sonnevend (eds) Constitutional crisis in the European constitutional area, theory, law and politics in Hungary and Romania, p 125

Schorkopf F (2014) In: Grabenwarter C (ed) Europäischer Grundrechtsschutz EnzEur Bd. 2 (Nomos) § 3

Sólyom L, Brunner G (2000) Constitutional judiciary in a new democracy: the Hungarian Constitutional Court

Spieker LD (2019) Commission v. Poland – a stepping stone towards a strong 'union of values'? https://verfassungsblog.de/commission-v-poland-a-stepping-stone-towards-a-strong-union-of-values/

Szente Z (2011) A historizáló alkotmányozás problémái – a történeti alkotmány és a Szent. Korona az új Alaptörvényben. Közjogi Szemle 2011/3. 1

Thym D (2013) Separation versus fusion – or: how to accommodate national autonomy and the charter? Diverging visions of the German Constitutional Court and the European Court of Justice. Eur Const Law Rev 9:391

Vincze A (2014) Wrestling with constitutionalism: the supermajority and the Hungarian Constitutional Court. ICL J 8:86
von Bogdandy A, Sonnevend P (eds) (2015) Constitutional crisis in the European constitutional area, theory, law and politics in Hungary and Romania

Pál Sonnevend is head of Department of International Law at Eötvös Loránd University, Budapest, Hungary.

Suspending Horizontal *Solange*: A Decentralized Instrument for Protecting Mutual Trust and the European Rule of Law

Iris Canor

Contents

Abstract Mutual trust is the basis on which the Member States' judiciaries are expected to deal with each other in the European Union. By constitutionalizing the principle of mutual trust, the CJEU has introduced an axiological addition to the basic structure of the European Union. From a Union which concentrated on the vertical relationships between each Member State and the central Union's institutions, the Union has turned out to be additionally preoccupied with the horizontal relationships among the Member States, which are based on what might be called a doctrine of Horizontal *Solange*.

I. Canor (✉)
School of Law, Zefat Academic College, Sefad, Israel

School of Law, College of Management, Rishon Le Zion, Israel
e-mail: Canor@colman.ac.il

A. von Bogdandy et al. (eds.), *Defending Checks and Balances in EU Member States*, Beiträge zum ausländischen öffentlichen Recht und Völkerrecht 298,
https://doi.org/10.1007/978-3-662-62317-6_8

According to the principle of mutual trust, each Member State must presume that all other Member States are in compliance with EU law, in particular promote its values and respect European fundamental rights. This presumption, however, can be rebutted in exceptional circumstances. These exceptional circumstances are based on a two-prong test: first, the violation of the values or the fundamental rights must amount to a systemic deficiency; second, there is a need for an assessment whether the individual concerned will be the victim of this systemic deficiency.

This contribution critically analyses these exceptional circumstances. Regarding the first prong, it is argued that the existence of systemic deficiencies should ideally be established by the CJEU via preliminary ruling references or via direct infringement proceedings. Alternatively, such systemic deficiencies may also be established by domestic courts in a host Member State. Regarding the second prong, it is argued that the individual test is redundant in cases where the systemic deficiency imposes challenges to the existing legal order of the Member State in question. Finally, it is argued that the suspension of mutual trust can serve as a decentralized instrument for protecting the European rule of law by pressuring the violating state to restore the rule of law.

1 Introduction

Nowadays, the interstate relationships among the Member States of the European Union are based on the principle of mutual trust. The principle of mutual trust is based on the presumption that there are common values which all Member States recognize and adhere to.[1] In other words, there exists mutual confidence between the Member States that their national legal systems are capable of providing equivalent and effective protection of the values as recognized at the EU level. Since those values are to be presumed as recognized by all Member States, they may not check, save in exceptional circumstances, whether another Member State has actually observed the values guaranteed by the EU. This is especially the case in situations when they are called upon by EU law to assist each other to execute other Member State's judgments.

Such exceptional circumstances can flow from deficiencies in respecting the rule of law. The rule of law is one of the values on which the European Union is founded, as is stated in Article 2 TEU.[2] By now, it is well-established jurisprudence that in

[1]See e.g. CJEU, Opinion 2/13 *Accession of the European Union to the European Convention for the Protection of Human Rights and Fundamental Freedoms*, ECLI:EU:C:2014:2454, para. 168; CJEU, Case C-284/16 *Achmea*, ECLI:EU:C:2018:158, para. 34; CJEU, Case C-128/18 *Dorobantu*, ECLI:EU:C:2019:857, para. 45; CJEU, Case C-314/18 *SF (Mandat d'arrêt européen—Garantie de renvoi dans l'État d'exécution)*, ECLI:EU:C:2020:191, para. 35.

[2]The rule of law is also mentioned in the preambles of the EU Treaty and of the Charter of Fundamental Rights of the European Union. Respect for the rule of law constitutes, moreover, a prerequisite of accession to the European Union, pursuant to Article 49 TEU. The concept of the rule of law is also enshrined in the preamble of the European Convention for the Protection of Human Rights and Fundamental Freedoms.

cases where a Member State systematically violates the rule of law, the trust otherwise conferred upon it by other Member States is to be suspended and the cooperation with its judiciary should be deferred.

This contribution aims to elaborate and assess this relationship between the principle of mutual trust and the value of the rule of law. More concretely, the central question is: what is the potential for a derogation from the principle of mutual trust, because the credentials of one Member State on the rule of law are lacking, to actually enhance adherence to the dictates of the rule of law in this Member State? The Chapter will first examine the manner in which the Court elevated the principle of mutual trust into a constitutional principle of the EU, the content which the Court has poured into the value of the rule of law, and the way mutual trust and the rule of law are intertwined in the jurisprudence of the Court. Finally, the Chapter will critically assess the exceptional circumstances that, according to the Court, justify the suspension of the horizontal cooperation between the Member States, mainly but not exclusively with respect to the European Arrest Warrant. It will be argued that Member States shall be able to freeze their horizontal cooperation with another Member State which, systematically infringes the rule of law, following a less stringent test than the one invoked by the Court. In this way, the principle of mutual trust and its exceptions might encourage the infringing state to amend its ways and adhere again to the rule of law.

2 Mutual Trust: The Path Towards Becoming a Founding Constitutional Principle of the EU

2.1 Mutual Trust: Initial Steps

The term 'mutual trust' appeared in the jurisprudence of the Court as early as 1975.[3] In *Opinion 1/75*, the Court ruled that the power to conclude international agreements on commercial matters could not be a 'concurrent power' because, by using such a power, there was the possibility that the Member States could adopt positions towards third countries which differed from those which the Community would otherwise adopt towards them, thereby calling into question the mutual trust within the Community. In this Opinion, the Court refers to mutual trust as a vertical principle concerning the relationship between the Community and the Member States.

Almost simultaneously, the Court started using mutual trust for the horizontal relationship between Member States in the context of the internal market. In *Bauhuis,* the Court decided, for example, that the European harmonized system of veterinary and public health inspections is 'based on the trust which member states

[3]CJEU, Opinion 1/75 *Arrangement OCDE—Norme pour les dépenses locales*, ECLI:EU: C:1975:145.

should place in each other as far as concerns the guarantees provided by the inspections carried out initially by the veterinary and public health departments.'[4] At issue was the imposition of obligations for the inspections on the exporting state, replacing thereby the systematic inspection measures at the border so as to make multiple border inspections unnecessary. Hence, Member States should trust each other and not monitor compliance with EU law of another Member State.[5]

2.2 *Mutual Trust: A Horizontal Principle of Cooperation Among the Member States' Judiciaries*

Subsequently, the principle of mutual trust has been elaborated by the Court in relation to specific fields of law, mainly European Arrest Warrant, Common European Asylum System, and European private international law and civil procedure. Indeed, in these cases, mutual trust is applied horizontally, regulating the relationships between the Member States in these matters.

Hence, for example, in *Apostolides*, mutual trust 'in the administration of justice in the Union', was invoked to justify, as a rule, the almost automatic recognition and enforcement of judgments given in one Member State in another Member State.[6] The presumption is that, in a common market in which the internal borders were abolished, the legal orders of the Member States have become closely intertwined. Therefore, there is a stronger need to recognize and enforce judgments emanating from another Member State, in comparison to judgments from courts of non-Member States.

Therefore, the judiciary has been elaborating the principle of mutual trust in sync with the principle of mutual recognition. Mutual trust provides for the almost automatic horizontal enforcement of civil judgments among the Member States of the EU. Because of that, a 'fifth freedom', namely the free movement of judgments, was gradually emerging.[7]

Indeed, mutual trust has been the outcome of a long process, practically since the establishment of the European Economic Community, the process of drawing the Member State's legal orders closer together. This process has been taking different forms and has been occurring on different paths. These include the unifying and harmonizing character of EU legislation; the elaboration of the principle of mutual

[4]CJEU, Case C-46/76 *Bauhuis*, ECLI:EU:C:1977:6, para. 21–22.

[5]See also, CJEU, Case C-5/94 *The Queen v. Ministry of Agriculture, Fisheries and Food, ex parte Hedley Lomas*, ECLI:EU:C:1996:205, para. 19, which concerned the European harmonized system of stunning animals before slaughter, which according to the Court, does not allow the Member States to restrict the free movement of goods on the ground of protection of health and life of animals on the basis of Article 36 of the Treaty, as 'the Member States must rely on trust in each other to carry out inspections on their respective territories'; See also Janssens (2014), pp. 28 et seq.

[6]CJEU, Case C-420/07 *Apostolides*, ECLI:EU:C:2009:271, para. 73.

[7]Lenaerts (2017), p. 805.

recognition and the familiarization with the regulatory standards of other Member States; the invocation of comparative law among the Member States' courts when relying on the *acte clair* doctrine; the emergence of constitutional traditions common to the Member States which form part of general principles of European law; and the admission requirement of new states to the European Union regarding their adherence to the European *acquis*.

The result is that the legal orders of the Member States have become more similar and closely intertwined. The Member States have been able to acknowledge that the plurality of responses that each one of them might give to a specific civil conflict do, nevertheless, correspond to a similar legal substructure lurking below. Thus, the plurality of responses is based on a common denominator and would not result in overly divergent responses. This in turn implies that the Member State issuing a judgment (the home State) can be assured that the judgment will be almost blindly and almost automatically recognized and enforced by the executing Member State (the host State), even if the legal norm or the judicial decision to be executed differed from the norm or decision which would otherwise be applied to the same situation by a court in the host State.[8]

While mutual trust is intended to restrain national courts from invoking the doctrine of public policy as a justification for non-enforcement of other Member States' judgments, it has never been intended to be an absolute principle.[9] The Court has ruled in *Apotolides* that mutual trust should be balanced against the possible violation of the rights of the defence of an individual, which would then justify non-enforcement of a judgment.

The principle of mutual trust is playing an important role also in criminal law in matters relating to arrest warrant,[10] or migration law in matters relating to asylum seekers.[11] Hence, this expansion of mutual trust made it mainly relevant to matters within the area of freedom security and justice, that is to areas in which the Member States retain many competences, but which have substantial EU harmonization and a cross-border spillover element.

In this process, mutual trust gained an ever greater importance, culminating in *N.S*, when the Court ruled: 'At issue here is the *raison d'être* of the European Union and the creation of an area of freedom, security and justice and, in particular, the Common European Asylum System, based on mutual confidence and a presumption of compliance, by other Member States, with European Union law and, in particular,

---

[8]Still, it should be noted that the *exequatur* was not fully repealed in the EU, Timmer (2013).

[9]Pergantis (2020), p. 409.

[10]CJEU, Joined Cases C-187/01 and C-385/01 *Gözütok and Brügge*, ECLI:EU:C:2003:87, para. 33; CJEU, Joined Cases C-404/15 and C-659/15 PPU *Aranyosi and Căldăraru*, ECLI:EU:C:2016:198.

[11]See for example, CJEU, Case C-411/10 *N.S. and Others*, ECLI:EU:C:2011:865. For a critique that the Court is using a too broad brush for these different fields, see e.g. AG Bot, CJEU, Joined Cases C-404/15 and C-659/15 PPU *Aranyosi and Căldăraru*, ECLI:EU:C:2016:140, paras. 44–59; Janssens (2014), pp. 315 et seq.; van Ballegooij (2015), pp. 136 et seq.; Lavenex (2007).

fundamental rights.'[12] This line of jurisprudence can be framed as 'horizontal Solange'.[13] The doctrine of 'horizontal *Solange*' is composed of two tiers. The first, substantive, tier forms the *Solange* component. Cooperation between Member States will be maintained as long as all the Member States systematically adhere to core European fundamental rights. If the evidence shows that a systemic violation of core European fundamental rights took place in a Member State, other Member States should suspend their cooperation. The second, institutional, tier forms the 'horizontal' component. The national courts are entrusted with the task of reviewing whether the other Member States abide by the European standard of protection of fundamental rights.

2.3 Mutual Trust: A Constitutional Principle

Eventually, in *Opinion 2/13*, the Court upgraded the principle of mutual trust into an overarching *constitutional* principle of the EU.[14] This judicial upgrade matched the legal emergence of the values on which the EU is founded, and which are common to the Member States, as expressed in Article 2 TEU, as well as the emergence of the Charter of fundamental rights. Once the EU was transformed from a treaty-based market union into a union which is based on values, the ground was laid for this new constitutional principle to emerge.

In Opinion 2/13, the Court mentions among the 'essential characteristics of EU law', 'a structured network of principles, rules and *mutually interdependent legal relations linking* the EU and its Member States, and *its Member States with each other*, which are now engaged, as is recalled in the second paragraph of Article 1 TEU, in a 'process of creating an ever closer union among the peoples of Europe'.'[15] Alongside the classic, long established, characteristic set of principles of the EU: supremacy, direct effect and autonomy, the Court now refers also to the principle of mutual trust.[16] The Court ties together the newly introduced common values mentioned in Article 2 TEU, on which the EU is founded, and which all the Member States *share* and *recognize*, with the principle of mutual trust. The Court rules that there exists a 'premiss [which] *implies* and *justifies* the existence of mutual

---

[12]CJEU, Case C-411/10 *N.S. and Others*, *supra* note 11, para. 83; See also, Canor (2013).

[13]Canor (2013).

[14]Some find the roots of mutual trust in Article 4(3) of the TEU regarding the principle of sincere cooperation.

[15]CJEU, Opinion 2/13 *Accession of the European Union to the European Convention for the Protection of Human Rights and Fundamental Freedoms*, *supra* note 1, para. 167; CJEU, Opinion 1/17 *Comprehensive Economic and Trade Agreement between Canada, on the one part, and the European Union and its Member States, of the other part (CETA)*, ECLI:EU:C:2019:341, para. 109; CJEU, Joined Cases C-585/18, C-624/18 and C-625/18 *A.K.*, ECLI:EU:C:2019:982, para. 156.

[16]CJEU, Opinion 2/13 *Accession of the European Union to the European Convention for the Protection of Human Rights and Fundamental Freedoms*, *supra* note 1, para. 166.

trust between the Member States that those values will be recognised and, therefore, that the law of the EU that implements them will be respected'.[17]

The principle of mutual trust implies that: 'when implementing EU law, the Member States may, under EU law, be required to presume that fundamental rights have been observed by the other Member States, so that not only may they not demand a higher level of national protection of fundamental rights from another Member State than that provided by EU law, but, save in exceptional cases, they may not check whether that other Member State has actually, in a specific case, observed the fundamental rights guaranteed by the EU'.[18] The Court completes its reasoning by emphasizing that: 'it should be noted that the principle of mutual trust between the Member States is of *fundamental importance* in EU law, given that it allows an area without internal borders to be created and maintained.'[19]

By this ruling the Court is, as a matter of fact, depicting the principle of mutual trust as an underlying principle on which the EU has been constructed.[20] The constitutional principle of mutual trust has been transformed into one of the core markers of the EU. It has become one of the guiding principles for contouring and defining the meaning of being a Member States in the EU, in contrast to third countries. It is the principle which justifies that each Member State must give other EU Member States' norms and judicial decisions special treatment in their own legal orders. Member States must introduce these norms and judicial decisions into their own legal orders in cases stipulated by EU law. Yet, mutual trust will not be the underlying principle when a Member State is called to interact with other third states, like, for example, the contracting parties of the Council of Europe or other non-European states. As the Court confirmed in *CETA*, 'that principle of mutual trust ... is not applicable in relations between the Union and a non-Member State'.[21]

As the principle of mutual trust is based on the common values of the Member States, however, the question soon arose, how this principle would be applied in case a host State suspects that a home State is violating these values. This article will focus on the specific question of possible violations of the rule of law by the home State.

---

[17]Id., para. 168. On the circularity of this construction, see e.g. Rizcallah (2019), p. 303: 'En effet, le principe de confiance mutuelle repose sur, en même temps qu'il impose, une présomption de respect, par l'ensemble des États membres, de ces valeurs. En d'autres mots, c'est parce que les ordres juridiques nationaux sont présumés respecter les valeurs de l'article 2 du T.U.E. que les États sont tenus de se faire confiance; mais c'est aussi parce que les États doivent se témoigner une confiance mutuelle qu'ils sont tenus de présumer le respect de ces valeurs par les ordres juridiques des autres États membres.'

[18]CJEU, Opinion 2/13 *Accession of the European Union to the European Convention for the Protection of Human Rights and Fundamental Freedoms*, *supra* note 1, para. 192.

[19]Id., para. 191.

[20]Id., para. 194. See also Lenaerts (2017), von Bogdandy (2018) and Meyer (2017).

[21]CJEU, Opinion 1/17 *Comprehensive Economic and Trade Agreement between Canada, on the one part, and the European Union and its Member States, of the other part (CETA)*, *supra* note 15, para. 129.

3 The Rule of Law and the Jurisprudence of the CJEU

A rule of law crisis is occurring in several Member States of the EU. These Member States, which have authoritarian tendencies, legislate norms and take active measures that undermine the rule of law in their countries. Some of the measures directly aim at undermining the national judiciaries' legitimacy, in particular by interfering with their independence. Indeed, attacks on the judiciary nowadays take many forms. Often, under the pretext of 'reform' of the judiciary, governments aim to cut or distort judicial powers. Budgets are cut, and changes are introduced to the structure of the courts and the judicial proceedings. Also, the nomination and employment conditions and the retirement scheme of judges are interfered with. Structural changes are also introduced, so that the number of judges serving on supreme or constitutional courts is changed, and the case allocation within courts is newly restructured. Likewise, subordinating all judges to disciplinary measures affects the courts' independence.[22] All this hampers the courts' ability to serve as a 'check' over the government.[23]

Such steps are of direct concern to the CJEU, which observes the rule of law principally via the lenses of the rule of law's requirements for courts. Indeed, the notion of the rule of law is broad.[24] Until today, however, the CJEU has mainly focused on issues related to the judiciary. As early as the famous case *Les verts*, the Court ruled that: 'It must first be emphasized in this regard that the European Economic Community is a Community based on the rule of law, inasmuch as neither its Member States nor its institutions can avoid a review of the question whether the measures adopted by them are in conformity with the basic constitutional charter, the Treaty'.[25] Hence, the Court has emphasized the requirement for a review of any EU norm which produces legal effect by a court. Closely related is the Court's ruling that 'the European Union is a union based on the rule of law in which individual parties

---

[22]With regard to Poland, see e.g. the findings of the European Commission, Proposal for a Council Decision on the determination of a clear risk of a serious breach by the Republic of Poland of the rule of law, COM/2017/0835 final. On the new Polish 'muzzling law', see e.g. Venice Commission, Poland—Urgent Joint Opinion on the amendments to the Law on organisation on the Common Courts, the Law on the Supreme Court and other Laws, CDL-PI(2020)002-e (16 January 2020); ODHIR, Urgent Interim Opinion on the Bill Amending the Act on the Organization of Common Courts, the Act on the Supreme Court and Certain Other Acts of Poland, JUD-POL/365/2019 [AlC] (14 January 2020); Polish Commissioner for Human Rights Adam Bodnar, Comments, VII.510.176.2019/MAW/PKR/PF/MW/CW (7 January 2020); Opinion of the Polish Judges' Association 'Iustitia' on the Act of 20 December 2019 amending the Act- the Law on the System of Common Courts, the Act on the Supreme Court and Certain Other Acts (10 February 2020).

[23]See also the contribution of von Bogdandy, in this book.

[24]EGC, Case T-242/16 *Stavytskyi v. Council*, ECLI:EU:T:2018:166, para. 69.

[25]CJEU, Case C-294/83 *Les Verts v. Parliament*, ECLI:EU:C:1986:166, para. 23.

have the right to challenge before the courts the legality of any decision or other national measure relating to the application to them of an EU act'.[26]

Similar emphasis on the judicial aspects of the rule of law, while mainly concentrating on the independence of the Member States' judiciary, has been put forward by the Court more recently when it was called to assess the legality of measures taken by governments with authoritarian tendencies. Of a whole arsenal of measures taken by these governments which has the potential to undermine the rule of law, the Court concentrates distinctively on the independence of national judiciaries. As Lenaerts explains, the absence of independent national judiciaries will undermine the possibility of 'integration through the rule of law'.[27]

The Court's judgments provide substantiated and rather standard minimum requirements for an independent judiciary. The Court outlines two aspects of such independence: one external and one internal. The external requirement focuses mainly on the autonomy of the courts which should be protected against external intervention or pressure.[28] The freedom from such external factors requires certain guarantees to be given to the judges, such as guarantees against removal from office, and guarantees of receipt of a certain level of remuneration.[29] There is also a need to prevent any risk of political control of the content of judicial decisions. The internal requirement is linked to the impartiality of the judges. That aspect requires objectivity and the absence of any interest in the outcome of the proceedings apart from the strict application of the law.[30] The Court further elaborates that those guarantees of independence and impartiality require clear rules, in order to dispel any reasonable doubt in the minds of individuals as to the imperviousness of the court to external factors and its neutrality with respect to the interests before it.[31]

Yet, the independence of the judiciary, although being mentioned by the CJEU as a core aspect of the rule of law, is actually mainly examined by the CJEU via the

---

[26]See, to that effect, judgment of CJEU, Case C-583/11 P *Inuit Tapiriit Kanatami and Others v. Parliament and Council*, ECLI:EU:C:2013:625, paras. 91 and 94. See also CJEU, Case C-64/16 *Associação Sindical dos Juízes Portugueses*, ECLI:EU:C:2018:117, para. 31.

[27]Lenaerts (2020), p. 31. Lenaerts further enumerates the reasons for such undermining: being the inability to refer questions to the CJEU; the inability to recourse to effective remedies for the violation of the EU law; and the challenge for the mutual trust between national courts of other Member States.

[28]See, to that effect, CJEU, Case C-64/16 *Associação Sindical dos Juízes Portugueses*, *supra* note 26, para. 44; CJEU, Case C-216/18 *Minister for Justice and Equality (Deficiencies in the system of Justice)*, ECLI:EU:C:2018:586, para. 63. On this jurisprudence, see Lenaerts (2019), pp. 155–174; Giegerich (2019); Jaeger (2018); Rizcallah and Davio (2019); Zinonos (2019).

[29]CJEU, Case C-64/16 *Associação Sindical dos Juízes Portugueses*, *supra* note 26, para. 45; CJEU, Case C-216/18 *Minister for Justice and Equality (Deficiencies in the system of Justice)*, *supra* note 28, para. 64.

[30]CJEU, Case C-216/18 *Minister for Justice and Equality (Deficiencies in the system of Justice)*, *supra* note 28, para. 52.

[31]CJEU, Case C-222/13 *TDC*, ECLI:EU:C:2014:2265, para. 32; CJEU, Case C-216/18 *Minister for Justice and Equality (Deficiencies in the system of Justice)*, *supra* note 28, para. 66.

lenses of the interpretation of Articles 47 and 48 of the Charter.[32] Specifically, and despite the fact that the CJEU is called upon to frame its decision as primarily concerning the deficit of the rule of law,[33] the Court is probably still conceiving the rule of law in an overly abstract way, and therefore prefers to stick to the legal analysis of the fundamental right closely derived from it.[34] Obviously, the Court identifies the close connection between Article 2 TEU (including the rule of law) and Article 19 TEU, on the one hand, and Article 47 of the Charter on fundamental rights, on the other hand. The CJEU has noted that Article 19 TEU, which gives concrete expression to the value of the rule of law as it appears in Article 2 TEU, entrusts the responsibility for ensuring the full application of EU law in all Member States and judicial protection of the rights of individuals under that law to national courts and to the Court.[35] It further connects Article 19(1) TEU with Article 47 of the Charter for ensuring the principle of the effective judicial protection of individuals' rights under EU law, which is also a general principle of EU law.[36] However, beyond these general observations, the Court often retreats to a detailed examination of Article 47 of the Charter stating, for example, that 'it does not appear necessary to conduct a distinct analysis of Article 2 and the second subparagraph of Article 19 (1) TEU, which can only reinforce the conclusion already set out [in relation to Article 47 of the Charter].'[37] Possibly, injecting content into a concrete fundamental right is regarded by the CJEU as falling more squarely within its judicial competence.[38]

4 Mutual Trust and Its Exceptions

According to the principle of mutual trust, each Member State must presume that all other Member States are in compliance with EU law, promoting its values and respecting fundamental rights. As discussed above, the derivative of this

[32] CJEU, Case C-216/18 *Minister for Justice and Equality (Deficiencies in the system of Justice)*, *supra* note 28, para. 67.

[33] As was recommended by Bárd and van Ballegooij (2018).

[34] Arguably, this gradually changes. The newer judgments of the CJEU rely equally on Art. 19 TEU and Art. 47 of the Charter. However, the relationship of both is not clear yet. See Spieker (2019b); See also Opinion of AG Tanchev, CJEU Case C-192/18, *Commission v. Poland*, ECLI:EU:C:2019:529, paras. 115-16 who proposes a distinction between individualized infringements and 'structural infirmities'; Bonelli and Claes (2018), p. 630; Torres Pérez (2020), p. 112 et seq.

[35] CJEU, Case C-619/18 *Commission v. Poland (Independence of the Supreme Court)*, ECLI:EU:C:2019:531, para. 47.

[36] Id., para. 49. CJEU, Joined Cases C-585/18, C-624/18 and C-625/18 *A.K.*, *supra* note 15, para. 168.

[37] Id., para. 169. But see CJEU, Case C-619/18 *Commission v. Poland (Independence of the Supreme Court)*, *supra* note 35, paras. 72–97 which was decided on the basis of Article 19 TEU.

[38] Spieker (2019a), p. 1186.

presumption is that Member State can very closely cooperate with each other; specifically, each host State should assist each home State in executing norms and judicial decisions stemming from the latter. This presumption, however, can be rebutted in exceptional circumstances. Such exceptional circumstances warrant the departure from the mutual trust principle and would oblige the host State to refuse cooperating with the home State. As a matter of fact, cooperating with the home State, while these exceptional circumstances take place, would amount, in and of itself, to a violation of EU law by the host State. Therefore, defining more clearly these exceptional circumstances is crucial in order to understand the importance of the principle of mutual trust.

4.1 Political Versus Judicial Determination

In elaborating the content of the exceptions, the Court has made a distinction between situations where, one, the political institutions of the EU have taken a position in relation to the level of protection of the principles set in Article 2 TEU in a certain Member State, and, two, courts decide on the same matter. These two situations entail different legal consequences ranging from the suspension of the *whole* mechanism of mutual trust to the denial of *individual* requests for cooperation.

As far as the political institutions are concerned, the Court ruled that once *a serious and persistent breach* by one of the Member States of the principles set out in Article 2 TEU (including the rule of law) is determined by the European Council pursuant to Article 7(2) TEU, with the consequences set out in Article 7(3) TEU, at least regarding arrest warrant matters, the mechanism of mutual trust may be suspended in respect of that Member State without any need for further examination.[39] The executing judicial authority of the host State would be required to automatically refuse to execute any European arrest warrant issued by the home State, without having to carry out any specific assessment of whether, for the individual concerned, there is a real risk that the essence of his or her fundamental right to a fair trial will be affected.[40] Such a determination amounts to exceptional circumstances which will freeze the otherwise almost automatic cooperation.[41]

Hence, a political determination by the Council pursuant to Article 7 TEU will have serious judicial horizontal implications on the cooperation between domestic courts. Such a political decision determines the suspension of the horizontal cooperation between the domestic courts. All the courts in potential host states will be required to stop assisting executing and enforcing the decisions of the home State's

[39]CJEU, Joined Cases C-404/15 and C-659/15 PPU *Aranyosi and Căldăraru*, *supra* note 10, para. 81; CJEU, Case C-216/18 *Minister for Justice and Equality (Deficiencies in the system of Justice)*, *supra* note 28, para. 70.

[40]Id., para. 72.

[41]Id., paras. 71–72.

courts. The home State court's decisions might, therefore, remain largely ineffective to the extent that the execution of these decisions is sought outside the borders of the home State.

To the extent that these political determinations extend beyond the category of arrest warrant matters, they amount to a possible additional sanction to be imposed on the home State, not directly mentioned in, but nonetheless flowing from, Article 7 TEU. In this way, the suspension of the principle of mutual trust might assist in putting a supplementary pressure on the home Member State to mend its violations of the rule of law.[42]

In the absence of such a political determination, the courts of the host State may judicially decide whether the home State is violating the values mentioned in Article 2 TEU, including the rule of law. In order to determine whether such a violation mandates setting aside the principle of mutual trust, the host State's court must undertake a more detailed examination based on a two-prong test: first, it must establish whether the non-independence of the home State's judiciary amounts to a systemic deficiency. Second, a specific and precise assessment is required, specifically, whether the individual concerned will be subject to the risk embodied in the systemic deficiency.[43]

Establishing the existence of a systemic deficiency (the first prong of the test) '*is capable of permitting* the executing judicial authority to refrain, by way of exception, from giving effect to the principle of mutual trust'.[44] In order to refrain from giving effect to the principle of mutual trust, it is requested additionally to determine whether the individual would be concretely subjected to the deficiency (the second prong of the test). A determination by the political institutions of the existence of serious and persistent breach of the rule of law can possibly entail a general suspension of the principle of mutual trust without further ado.[45] By contrast, the CJEU holds that for the courts to suspend mutual trust without such a political determination, further elements are needed. Only if both the systemic and the individual examinations by the host state's court regarding the situation prevailing in the home State reveal problems, cooperation with the home State's courts must be suspended. Otherwise, by continuing to give effect to the home State's judgments in the host state, the latter will implicitly be helping the home State's courts to spread their flawed judgments, which violate the fundamental rights of the affected person, throughout the EU. That would amount to a violation of EU law by the host state, in particular by assisting the home State to violate the fundamental rights of the affected person.

---

[42]Critically with regard to the pressure this might exert, see e.g. Spieker (2019a), p. 1197.

[43]CJEU, Joined Cases C-404/15 and C-659/15 PPU *Aranyosi and Căldăraru*, *supra* note 10, para. 92 (emphasis added); CJEU, Case C-216/18 *Minister for Justice and Equality (Deficiencies in the system of Justice)*, *supra* note 28, para. 68.

[44]CJEU, Case C-216/18 *Minister for Justice and Equality (Deficiencies in the system of Justice)*, *supra* note 28, para. 59 et seq.

[45]Council Framework Decision 2002/584/JHA on the European arrest warrant and the surrender procedures between Member States (2002) OJ L190/1, recital 10 in the preamble.

As exceptions often help to understand the meaning of a rule, this two-prong test for the suspension of mutual trust will now be critically examined.

4.2 Judicial Determination of Systemic Deficiencies

4.2.1 Substantive Matters

First, the courts of the host State must assess whether in general there are deficiencies in respect for fundamental rights' in the home State. These deficiencies have to be systemic.[46]

The question is what will amount to a systemic deficiency, as far as violations of fundamental rights are concerned. The CJEU has ruled that a violation of absolute fundamental rights amounts to a systemic violation.[47] Since no limitation may be imposed upon fundamental rights that are absolute, such as human dignity, the right to life, the prohibition of torture, and the prohibition of inhuman and degrading treatment,[48] the principle of mutual trust may not be interpreted as requiring cooperation with home States which infringe these rights.

Yet, the Court goes beyond that. It rules that the breach of *the essence* of other fundamental rights may also amount to a systemic deficiency. For example, the Court has ruled that the principle of judicial independence is part of the 'essence' of the right to a fair trial enshrined in Article 47 of the Charter. This means that the right to an independent court may not be subject to any limitations, regardless of the public objectives put forward by the national legislature.[49]

Lenaerts, while relying on the notion of the 'essence' of a right as stemming from *Scherms*, explains that 'a measure that compromises the essence of a fundamental right may not be justified on any ground'.[50] Any attempt to compromise the essence of the right will call into question the fundamental right as such.[51] Lenaerts mainly refers to *ne bis in idem* enshrined in Article 50 of the Charter, the *right to vote* in elections to the European Parliament enshrined in Article 39(2) of the Charter and the *principle of non-discrimination* as fundamental rights stemming from the Charter the essence of which cannot be compromised. Hence, one might deduce that a violation of the essence of these fundamental rights may also amount to a systemic deficiency in the home State.

---

[46]The infringements cannot be minor ones, but have to be systemic, see CJEU, Case C-411/10 *N.S. and Others*, *supra* note 11, paras. 85–86.

[47]See, for example, id., para. 86; CJEU, Joined Cases C-404/15 and C-659/15 PPU *Aranyosi and Căldăraru*, *supra* note 10, paras. 84–88.

[48]Lenaerts (2020), p. 783.

[49]CJEU, Case C-216/18 *Minister for Justice and Equality (Deficiencies in the system of Justice)*, *supra* note 28, paras. 47–48.

[50]Lenaerts (2020), p. 782.

[51]Id., p. 784.

It is still unclear whether, according to the CJEU, the violation of the *essence* of a fundamental right will automatically amount to systemic violations. Given the ambitious postulation of the principle of mutual trust as a founding constitutional principle of the EU, which can be set aside only in exceptional situations, it seems to me that the CJEU should take a nuanced approach by further discerning among the different fundamental rights. The Court should identify the essence of those fundamental rights, the violation of which, one, *imposes challenges to an existing legal order* of a Member State, two, are not met with an adequate institutional reaction and, three, produces a problem to another Member State—an interrelated legal order—to cooperate with it.[52] Only a general infringement of the essence of those fundamental rights which cannot be processed as a matter of routine and which have an inter-systemic dimension should amount to a systemic deficiency, which then might justify setting aside the constitutional principle of mutual trust.

4.2.2 Institutional Aspects

By compelling a domestic judge of the host State to assess the possible existence of systemic (or generalized) deficiencies in the legal order of the home State, the Court expands the role of national judges beyond their traditional function of settling an individual dispute coming before them. Admittedly, nowadays, an approach in which a court performs only a single function seems implausibly narrow.[53] Alongside the role of deciding a single dispute, based on a single infringement of a certain fundamental right, there may be an additional role attributed to a national court, namely, its role in controlling another legal order, by examining its systemic approach to the protection of human rights.[54] In this way, a court of a host State may review, and hence legitimize or delegitimize, the home State's legal order as a whole.

Within the EU legal order, judges are not alien anymore to the task of undertaking systemic examinations. This was, for example, a clear expression of the *Solange* model, offered by the German Constitutional Court in relation to the primacy of EU law. The German Constitutional Court undertook a systemic examination of the legal order of the European Communities regarding the protection of fundamental rights and ruled that 'as long as the European Communities and in particular the case law of the European Court, *generally* ensure an effective protection of fundamental rights as against the sovereign powers of the Communities . . . and in so far as they *generally safeguard the essential content of fundamental rights*, the Federal Constitutional Court will no longer exercise its jurisdiction to decide on the applicability of secondary Community legislation cited as the legal basis for any acts of German civil courts or authorities within the sovereign jurisdiction of the Federal Republic of

[52] von Bogdandy (2020), p. 715.
[53] von Bogdandy and Venzke (2014), p. 5.
[54] See, by analogy, id., p. 15.

Germany, and it will no longer review such legislation by the standard of the fundamental rights contained in the Constitution'.[55]

Yet, in my opinion, it is nevertheless questionable whether it is recommendable that the court of a host State should review the existence of systemic deficiencies of another (home) state. Obviously, all the Member States are equal and have the same footing. Therefore, it might be difficult for a home State's judges to pass a judgment on a systemic deficiency of another national legal order.

First, generally, the home State does not usually have the possibility to join the proceedings before the host State and to submit its observations and to defend its position regarding a potential systemic violation of fundamental rights.[56] Indeed, it seems that the Court tries to mitigate this institutional defect by relying on the need to also carry out the examination of the second—individual—prong of the test. At this second stage, the Court instructs that the home State may provide the host State with objective evidence which may rule out the existence of that systemic risk for the individual concerned.[57]

Yet, in my opinion, the home State should have the right to intervene and defend itself before the court which is called upon to decide whether a systemic deficiency occurred. The absence of right to be heard of the home State undermines the general legal principle for fair trial.[58]

Second, the evidence, which the court of the host State may rely on when deciding whether there is a systemic deficiency, amounts, as a matter of fact, to 'out of court' materials. The CJEU expects the national courts to 'assess, on the basis of material that is objective, reliable, specific and properly updated ... whether there is a real risk ... of systemic or generalised deficiencies ...'.[59] Thus, the Court is stating that 'that information may be obtained from, inter alia, judgments of international courts, such as judgments of the ECtHR, judgments of courts of the issuing Member State, and also decisions, reports and other documents produced by bodies

---

[55]GCC, BVerfGE 73, 339; Other courts in other occasions also make similar systemic assessments. See for example the examination carried by the ECHR regarding the role of the CJEU in the EU legal order, ECtHR, *Bosphorus Airways v. Ireland*, Grand Chamber Judgment of 30 June 2005, Application No. 45036/98, paras. 155–156. Although in the latter decision the ECtHR also mentions a case by case examination, the first prong of the decision is institutional, id., para. 156. Similarly, see the examination by the CJEU of the UN sanctions system in CJEU, Case C-402/05 P *Kadi and Al Barakaat International Foundation v. Council and Commission*, ECLI:EU:C:2008:461 and the comparable examination by the ECtHR in ECtHR, *Al-Dulimi and Montana Management Inc. v. Switzerland*, Grand Chamber Judgment of 21 June 2016, Application No. 5809/08.

[56]See also Wendel (2019), p. 43; Spieker (2019a), p. 1197; and the contribution of von Bogdandy, *supra* note 23, section 3.3.

[57]CJEU, Case C-216/18 *Minister for Justice and Equality (Deficiencies in the system of Justice)*, *supra* note 28, para. 77.

[58]Jarass (2016), para 12.

[59]CJEU, Case C-216/18 *Minister for Justice and Equality (Deficiencies in the system of Justice)*, *supra* note 28 paras. 60–61. This standard was also adopted by the ECtHR, *Romeo Castaño v. Belgium*, Second Chamber Judgment of 9 July 2019, Application No. 8351/17, para. 86.

of the Council of Europe or under the aegis of the UN.'[60] This list goes beyond traditional evidence submitted to a court, namely, witnesses or testimonies being subject to examination. This procedure guarantees that the evidence is produced in an objective manner, free from political or other bias, without manipulation, and also gives the state involved the possibility to present its position regarding the evidence.

To take just one example, the CJEU has stated that 'a reasoned proposal recently addressed by the Commission to the Council on the basis of Article 7(1) TEU is particularly relevant for the purposes of that assessment'.[61] With this statement, the CJEU aspires to give 'bite' to the political decision taken on the basis of Article 7 (1) TEU, and indeed such a reasoned proposal is issued after hearing the relevant Member State, but the permission to the national court to rely on a reasoned proposal when determining whether a systemic deficiency occurred in the home State, can nevertheless be criticized: first, given the fact that such a reasoned proposal is solely subject to the CJEU's review regarding the procedural stipulation of Article 7 TEU, but not regarding the substantive determinations;[62] and second, the reasoned opinion is probably not subject to judicial review by the courts of the host State. As a preparatory act without legal effects vis-à-vis third parties, it cannot be challenged neither before the court of the host State nor before the Court of Justice.[63]

I suggest that, in response to these institutional flaws, systemic deficiencies in the home State should only be determined by the CJEU. Whenever a court of the host state suspects that there is a systemic deficiency in the home State, the host State court should seek a preliminary ruling from the CJEU.[64] Only the CJEU has the means to objectively conclude that there is a systemic deficiency at a home State. The CJEU, being a court of the EU as a whole, is able to take a broader perspective and can undertake a more comprehensive examination of the possible existence of a systemic deficiency. Hence, the CJEU can better assess whether the human rights violation which occurred in the home State is a minor one or a systemic one. Moreover, procedurally, the home State can join the proceedings before the CJEU and can argue its position regarding the allegedly systemic deficiency.[65] Finally, by receiving a preliminary ruling on behalf of the Court which will then serve as a precedent to all the courts of the potential hosting states,[66] it will be possible to

[60] CJEU, Joined Cases C-404/15 and C-659/15 PPU *Aranyosi and Căldăraru*, *supra* note 10, para. 89.

[61] CJEU, Case C-216/18 *Minister for Justice and Equality (Deficiencies in the system of Justice)*, *supra* note 28, para. 61.

[62] Article 269 TFEU.

[63] See also Krajewski (2018), p. 801 et seq.

[64] See similarly von Bogdandy and Spieker (2019), p. 396. This was also proposed by Wendel (2019), p. 41 who proposes a division of labor according to the two prongs test. Clearly if the host State reaches the conclusion that there is no systemic deficiency in the home State it does not need to refer a question to the CJEU.

[65] See also Wendel (2019), p. 43; Spieker (2019a), p. 1197; von Bogdandy, *supra* note 23, section 3.5.

[66] CJEU, Case C-283/81 *CILFIT*, ECLI:EU:C:1982:335, paras. 13–14.

isolate the judiciary of the home State, and therefore put pressure on the home State's judges to find a manner to undo the systemic deficiencies.

Alternatively, a ruling about a systemic deficiency in a home State can be rendered by the CJEU via infringement proceedings that may be initiated by the Commission or another EU country.[67] Admittedly, there are differing views whether systemic problems can be addressed by the procedure of infringement proceedings, which is more focused on individual and concrete infringements.[68] Yet, when deciding about a specific infringement of the rule of law, the Court can also take a position regarding the possible systemic dimension of such a specific or individual violation in its ruling.

Thus, the CJEU will be able to assist the court of the host State if the latter is called upon to establish whether systemic deficiencies are present in the home State. Moreover, the courts of the host State, while freezing their cooperation with the home State will be able to potentially assist the CJEU in enforcing its ruling in the infringement proceedings. Such assistance will take place given the fact that, if the home State opted to avoid executing the Court's infringement proceedings' ruling, the host State would be obliged (if also the second prong of the test will also be fulfilled) to sanction the home State by suspending the cooperation with the home State. In this way, I maintain, the vertical ruling in an infringement proceeding by the CJEU is supported by the horizontal ruling of the host State by suspending the cooperation among the Member States.[69]

Yet, even if the determination of systemic deficiencies in a home State is left to be made solely by the courts of the host States, this might entail advantages, too. Before making such a determination, each legal order will be required to take a deep look and complete a profound examination of the other Member State's legal order. The Court is alluding to 'a dialogue between the executing judicial authority and the issuing judicial authority'.[70] Such a dialogue might bring familiarity with the other legal orders and draw all the domestic courts closer together, which helps the aim of 'an ever closer union'. Admittedly, it might be that, given the possible comity among the Member States, domestic courts will be reluctant to pass critical judgments over their counterparts. Indeed, a finding that there exists a systemic deficiency has the potential of stigmatization of the home State. This possibly implies that it will take a considerable amount of time until a uniform approach among the courts of potential host States will be created. This might lead to the result that, sooner or later, the CJEU will in any case be called upon to rule on the matter and settle possible conflicting views among domestic courts.

---

[67]Schmidt and Bogdanowicz (2018) and Kochenov (2015).

[68]Scheppele (2016) and Schmidt and Bogdanowicz (2018).

[69]For a different view according to which the horizontal route of mutual trust is the less preferred route in comparison to the vertical infringement proceedings/preliminary references route, see Kochenov and Bárd (2019), p. 275.

[70]CJEU, Case C-216/18 *Minister for Justice and Equality (Deficiencies in the system of Justice)*, *supra* note 28, para. 77.

Against the approach, and against the horizontal *Solange* doctrine altogether, it has been argued that 'a decentralized control by each Member State might put the functioning of the internal market, if not the very existence of the Union, in jeopardy'.[71] This criticism points also to the inadmissibility of 'self-help' in the context of EU law.[72] Yet, it seems to me that EU law has always advanced through its application by domestic courts. Domestic courts are the real enforcers of EU law. If a court of the host State decides wrongly or controversially in the context of a certain pending case that there are systemic deficiencies in a home State, and if the same matter reappeared before another host State, it is likely that, sooner or later, the matter will likely to be referred to the CJEU for a preliminarily ruling. The Court will then be able to voice itself whether there exists a systemic deficiency in this specific Member State. This ruling must then be followed by all national courts. Indeed, in my opinion, the principle of mutual trust transformed the EU and indirectly introduced into the European legal order the principle of self-help. Due to the systemic deficiency in the home State, the host State might be prevented from being able to perform its own obligations stemming from EU law (i.e., enforce the home State's civil judgments or execution of a European Arrest Warrant, etc.). Therefore, the principle of mutual trust permits the court in the host State to take the law into its own hands and to independently decide to withhold its cooperation with this failing home State. Just like in other cases regarding the interpretation of EU law, a domestic court is not obliged to make a request for a preliminary ruling to the CJEU, except when it decides on the non-application of EU legislation.[73]

4.3 Individual Examination

In the second prong of the two-prong test, the host judicial authority must determine, in the event that cooperation with the home State should take place, whether there are substantial grounds to believe that the person subject to the proceedings will be exposed to a real risk of his or her fundamental rights being violated due to the

[71] Closa et al. (2014), p. 19; Spieker (2019a), p. 1197: 'A decentralized control by each Member State, however, could lead to diverging or incompatible decisions throughout the EU judicial space and jeopardize the uniform application of Union law. Further, bilateral control mechanisms are generally alien to the EU legal order. Therefore, at least the standards for review must be set and strictly defined in a centralized manner and in much greater detail by the CJEU.'

[72] On inadmissibility of 'self-help' in the context of EU law, see, CJEU, Joined cases 90 and 91/63 *Commission v. Belgium and Luxembourg*, ECLI:EU:C:1964:80, p. 631.

[73] See CJEU, 314/85 *Foto-Frost v Hauptzollamt Lübeck-Ost*, ECLI:EU:C:1987:452, para. 15. Therefore, should the ruling by the court in the host State regarding the situation in the home State be convincing, it is likely that it will be followed by other courts of other host States. Should it not be convincing, either it will remain as an isolated violation of EU law, or the matter will be referred to the CJEU, for an authoritative ruling.

systemic deficiency.[74] Only if the risk of such an infringement is established, both in general and in the specific case, the cooperation with the home State must be suspended.

Yet, as already shown by others, this second prong makes the setting aside of mutual trust almost impossible, given that the burden to show how a systemic breach of the rule of law effects his or her case individually might be very high.[75] Hence it was proposed that once the first step of the test is satisfied, the burden of proof of the second prong should shift to the stronger party, namely the home State.[76]

But, even beyond that, it seems to me that the second prong of the test should be put in correlation to the systemic deficit which has been established in the examination of the first prong. Specifically, the more the systemic deficit in the home State is about a serious violation of the rule of law, the less need (or even no need) there should be to insist on the additional fulfilment of the individual prong. The individual prong should only be relevant to systemic deficiencies for infringements of fundamental rights, while having almost no bearing (or even being altogether discarded) when the home State's systemic deficiency relates to how the State is organized.[77]

In order to exemplify this comment, I contrast the decisions of the court regarding the size of prison cells, with the decisions regarding the independence of the judiciary as part of the rule of law. In the decisions regarding the size of prison cells in the home State to which the individual is supposed to be surrendered, the Court acknowledges that, with respect to the individual prong of the test, there is no way that the host State will be able to assess the conditions of detention in all the prisons in which the individual concerned might be detained in the issuing Member State. This is perceived by the Court as an excessive task which would render the operation of the European arrest warrant system wholly ineffective.[78] But that leads the Court to the conclusion that the host State 'will only need to assess the detention conditions in the prisons of the home State, in which according to the information available it is actually intended that the person concerned will be detained, and it is for the home State to guarantee the compatibility of the conditions of detention in the other prisons in which that person may possibly be held at a later state.'[79]

The Court has been giving similar guidelines to the host State's courts regarding the individual prong of the test when the systemic violation related to the breach of the rule of law. The examination requested from the host State's court was relatively

[74]CJEU, Joined Cases C-404/15 and C-659/15 PPU *Aranyosi and Căldăraru*, *supra* note 10, para. 88; CJEU, Case C-216/18 *Minister for Justice and Equality (Deficiencies in the system of Justice)*, *supra* note 28, para. 59.

[75]Kochenov and Bárd (2019), p. 274.

[76]van Ballegooij and Bárd (2016).

[77]Even more broadly, see Bárd and Morijn (2020a, b).

[78]CJEU, Case C-220/18 PPU *Generalstaatsanwaltschaft (Conditions de détention en Hongrie)*, ECLI:EU:C:2018:589, para. 84.

[79]Id., para. 87.

limited. It was called upon to examine whether the absence of the independence of the judiciary is 'liable to have an impact *at the level of that State's courts with jurisdiction over the proceedings* to which the requested person will be subject'.[80] And then, even more specifically, the Court ruled: 'If that examination shows that those deficiencies are liable to affect those courts, the executing judicial authority must also assess, in the light of the specific concerns expressed by the individual concerned and any information provided by him, whether there are substantial grounds for believing that he will run a real risk of breach of his fundamental right to an independent tribunal and, therefore, of the essence of his fundamental right to a fair trial, *having regard to his personal situation, as well as to the nature of the offence for which he is being prosecuted and the factual context that form the basis of the European arrest warrant.*'[81] Hence, the Court demands that the court of the host State must conduct a detailed examination, but, at the same time, it insists on a very limited examination solely of the level of the state's court with direct jurisdiction over the proceedings.[82] By analogy to the size of the prison cells, the Court might expect that if the individual concerned appealed even to the supreme instances of the home State's courts, it would be for the home State to guarantee that the individual would not face a court which will expose him or her to a real risk of the breach of his or her fundamental right to an independent tribunal.

Yet, it seems to me that the Court should have reached the opposite conclusion. When the deficit is systemic, and the host State cannot guarantee the comprehensive protection of a fundamental right which is closely connected to the rule of law in the state, a finding that the state is suffering from a systemic deficiency should suffice for suspending cooperation out of mutual trust. There is no place for the individual test.[83] Accordingly, in *LM*, once it was established that there was a systemic deficiency regarding the independence of the judiciary in the home State (Poland) the host State (Ireland) should not have been required to examine whether the individual to be sent back to Poland would have been brought in front of a judge who would nevertheless be independent. This is because the home State will not be able to categorically guarantee that the individual's fundamental right to an independent court will be protected throughout the court hierarchy, all the way up to the constitutional court, which has evidently been packed by the government.

Accordingly, I suggest a distinction should be drawn between systemic deficiency regarding the custodial conditions of prisoners and systemic deficiency regarding the non-independence of the judiciary. For the first case, examinations should be conducted on an individual basis, but, for the second case, such individual examinations should not be required. Therefore, at least in those systemic violations of fundamental rights which are closely connected to the organization of the State and

[80]CJEU, Case C-216/18 *Minister for Justice and Equality (Deficiencies in the system of Justice), supra* note 28, para. 74.

[81]Id., para. 75.

[82]Spieker (2018), p. 21 et seq.

[83]See also, Krajewski (2018), p. 805 et seq.; Bárd and van Ballegooij (2018); Wendel (2019).

affect the rule of law (like the independence of the judiciary), and which cannot be individually examined, the second prong of the test should not be relevant. Establishing a systemic deficiency in the home State regarding the rule of law should suffice in justifying the suspension of the mutual trust.

4.4 A Horizontal Solange Doctrine

This suggestion mirrors the *Solange* test. Under the *Solange* test, as long as the European system of protection of fundamental rights, as administered by the CJEU, functions to generally ensure an effective protection of fundamental rights, which is to be regarded as substantially similar to the protection offered by the German Constitution, then possible variations regarding the protection of fundamental rights are allowed.[84] In respect of mutual trust, the mirror test would stipulate that once a systemic deficit is established in the home State, even if the latter is willing to guarantee the individual's fundamental rights protection by the court at hand, cooperation with the judiciary of the home State should, nevertheless, stop. There is no requirement to trust a Member State, which does not live up to the rule of law as defined by the Court for Article 2 TEU. The collective suspension of cooperation with the home State's judiciary by the courts of all host States might put pressure on the home State to re-establish the rule of law. A comprehensive shaming effect which such a suspension will entail might also encourage home States' judges to act in this direction and to regain their independence.

Such wide-ranging suspension of cooperation with the national judges of the home State might harm the judges who remain independent in the home State's judicial system and might do them injustice and weaken them to the extent that they try to fight the authoritarian tendencies from within. Yet, in my opinion, the overall discrediting attitude towards the home State, by suspending any possible cooperation with its courts, will be an effective method to assist all those from inside of the home State who fight for the reestablishment of the rule of law.

5 Conclusion

Mutual trust is the basis on which the Member States' judiciaries are expected to deal with each other in the European Union. By constitutionalizing the principle of mutual trust, the CJEU has introduced an axiological addition to the basic structure of the European Union. From a Union which concentrated on the vertical relationships between each Member State and the central Union's institutions, the Union has turned out to be additionally preoccupied with the horizontal relationships among

[84]GCC, *supra* note 55, p. 339.

the Member States, which are based on what might be called a doctrine of Horizontal *Solange*.

According to the principle of mutual trust, each Member State must presume that all other Member States are in compliance with EU law, in particular promote its values and respect European fundamental rights. This presumption, however, can be rebutted in exceptional circumstances. These exceptional circumstances are based on a two-prong test: first, the violation of the values or the fundamental rights must amount to a systemic deficiency; second, there is a need for an assessment whether the individual concerned will be the victim of this systemic deficiency.

This contribution critically analyses these exceptional circumstances. Regarding the first prong, it is argued that the existence of systemic deficiencies should ideally be established by the CJEU via preliminary ruling references or via direct infringement proceedings. Alternatively, such systemic deficiencies may also be established by domestic courts in a host Member State. Regarding the second prong, it is argued that the individual test is redundant in cases where the systemic deficiency imposes challenges to the existing legal order of the Member State in question. Finally, it is argued that the suspension of mutual trust can serve as a decentralized instrument for protecting the European rule of law by pressuring the violating state to restore the rule of law.

Acknowledgements Special thanks are owed to Dimitri Spieker who carefully commented on an earlier draft of this contribution and for Martin Jarrett for his rigorous language editing.

References

Books and Journals

Bárd P, Morijn J (2020a) Luxembourg's unworkable test to protect the rule of law in the EU: decoding the Amsterdam and Karlsruhe Courts' post-LM Rulings (Part I). Verfassungsblog (18 March 2020)

Bárd P, Morijn J (2020b) Domestic Courts pushing for a workable test to protect the rule of law in the EU: decoding the Amsterdam and Karlsruhe Courts' post-LM Rulings (Part II)'. Verfassungsblog (19 March 2020)

Bárd P, van Ballegooij W (2018) Judicial independence as a pre-condition for mutual trust? The ECJ in *minister for justice and equality v. LM*. New J Eur Crim Law 9:353

Bonelli M, Claes M (2018) Judicial serendipity: how Portuguese judges came to the rescue of the Polish judiciary. Eur Const Law Rev 14:622, 630

Canor I (2013) My brother's keeper? Horizontal Solange: 'An ever closer distrust among the peoples of Europe'. Common Market Law Rev 50:383

Closa C, Kochenov D, Weiler JHH (2014) Reinforcing rule of law oversight in the European Union. EUI Working Paper RSCAS 2014/25

Giegerich T (2019) Die Unabhängigkeit der Gerichte als Strukturvorgabe der Unionsverfassung und ihr effektiver Schutz vor autoritären Versuchungen in den Mitgliedstaaten. ZEuS 22:61

Jaeger T (2018) Gerichtsorganisation und EU-Recht: Eine Standortbestimmung. Europarecht 53:611

Janssens C (2014) The principle of mutual recognition in EU law. Oxford University Press, Oxford
Jarass HD (2016) Art. 47 GRCh. In: Jarass HD (ed) Charta der Grundrechte der EU, 3rd edn. C.H. Beck, München, pp 405–427
Kochenov D (2015) Biting intergovernmentalism: the case for the reinvention of Article 259 TFEU to make it a viable rule of law enforcement tool. Hague J Rule Law 7:153
Kochenov D, Bárd P (2019) The last soldier standing? Courts versus politicians and the rule of law crisis in the new member states of the EU. Eur Yearb Const Law 1:243
Krajewski M (2018) Who is afraid of the European Council? The Court of Justice's cautious approach to independence of domestic judges. Eur Const Law Rev 14:792
Lavenex S (2007) Mutual recognition and the monopoly of force: limits of the single market analogy. J Eur Public Policy 14:762
Lenaerts K (2017) La vie après l'avis: exploring the principle of mutual (Yet Not Blind) trust. Common Market Law Rev 54:805
Lenaerts K (2019) On judicial independence and the quest for national, supranational and transnational justice. In: Selvik G et al (eds) The Art of judicial reasoning. Festschrift in Honour of Carl Baudenbacher. Springer, Heidelberg, pp 155–174
Lenaerts L (2020) New horizons for the rule of law within the EU. German Law J 21:29
Meyer F (2017) Der Grundsatz gegenseitigen Vertrauens. Konzeptualisierung und Zukunftsperspektiven eines neuen Verfassungsprinzips. Europarecht 52:163
Pergantis V (2020) The 'sovereignty clause' of the Dublin regulations in the case-law of the ECtHR and the CJEU: the mirage of a jurisprudential convergence? In: Bruno GC et al (eds) Migration issues before international courts and tribunals. CNR Edizioni, Rome, p 409
Rizcallah C (2019) Le principe de confiance mutuelle – une utopie malheureuse. Revue trimestrielle des droits de l'homme:297
Rizcallah C, Davio V (2019) L'article 19 du Traité sur l'Union européenne: sésame de l'Union de droit – Analyse de la jurisprudence récente de la Cour de justice de l'Union européenne relative à l'indépendance des juges nationaux. Revue trimestrielle des droits de l'homme:155
Scheppele KL (2016) Enforcing the basic principles of EU law through systemic infringement actions. In: Closa C, Kochenov D (eds) Reinforcing rule of law oversight in the European Union. Cambridge University Press, Cambridge, pp 105–132
Schmidt M, Bogdanowicz P (2018) The infringement procedure in the rule of law crisis: how to make effective use of Article 258 TFEU. Common Market Law Rev 55:1061–1100
Spieker LD (2018) From moral values to legal obligations – on how to activate the union's common values in the EU rule of law crisis. MPIL Research Paper No. 24, 2018
Spieker LD (2019a) Breathing life into the Union's common values: on the judicial application of Article 2 TEU in the EU value crisis. German Law J 20:1182, 1186
Spieker LD (2019b) Commission v. Poland – a stepping stone towards a strong 'Union of Values'?. Verfassungsblog (30 May 2019)
Timmer LJ (2013) Abolition of *Exequatur* under the Brussels I regulation: ILL conceived and premature? J Private Int Law 9:129
Torres Pérez A (2020) From Portugal to Poland: the Court of Justice of the European Union as watchdog of judicial independence. Maastricht J 27:105
van Ballegooij W (2015) The nature of mutual recognition in European Law. Intersentia, Cambridge
van Ballegooij W, Bárd P (2016) Mutual recognition and individual rights: did the court get it right. New J Eur Crim Law 7:439
von Bogdandy A (2018) Ways to frame the European rule of law: Rechtsgemeinschaft, trust, revolution, and Kantian peace. Eur Const Law Rev 14:675
von Bogdandy A (2020) Principles of a systemic deficiencies doctrine: how to protect checks and balances in the member states. Common Market Law Rev 57:705
von Bogdandy A, Spieker LD (2019) Countering the judicial silencing of critics: Article 2 TEU values, Reverse Solange, and the responsibilities of National judges. Eur Const Law Rev 15:391
von Bogdandy A, Venzke I (2014) In whose name? Oxford University Press, Oxford

Wendel M (2019) Mutual trust, essence and federalism – between consolidating and fragmenting the area of freedom, security and justice after LM. Eur Const Law Rev 15:17
Zinonos P (2019) Judicial independence & national judges in the recent case law of the Court of Justice. Eur Public Law 25:615

Iris Canor is a Professor for European Law at the School of Law, Zefat Academic College, and the School of Law, College of Management, Israel.

Ascertaining the 'Guarantee of Guarantees': Recent Developments Regarding the Infringement Procedure in the EU's Rule of Law Crisis

Matthias Schmidt and Piotr Bogdanowicz

Contents

Abstract This chapter builds on an assessment of infringement proceedings in the EU rule of law crisis that we previously published in the Common Market Law Review. We offer a close reading of two recent prominent infringement cases by the European Commission against Poland (cases C-619/18 and C-192/18). Noteworthy advancements in EU law made with them are in particular a clarification on the parallel use of Articles 7 TEU and 258 TFEU, the use of both interim relief and an expedited procedure prior to the judgment, and, as regards the merits, further substance for the functioning of Articles 19 TEU and 47 of the EU Charter of Fundamental Rights regarding the operationalisation of the rule of law in EU law.

M. Schmidt
Max Planck Institute for Comparative Public Law and International Law, Heidelberg, Germany
e-mail: mschmidt@mpil.de

P. Bogdanowicz (✉)
University of Warsaw, Faculty of Law and Administration, Warsaw, Poland
e-mail: p.bogdanowicz@wpia.uw.edu.pl

A. von Bogdandy et al. (eds.), *Defending Checks and Balances in EU Member States*, Beiträge zum ausländischen öffentlichen Recht und Völkerrecht 298,
https://doi.org/10.1007/978-3-662-62317-6_9

We offer a critical assessment of the Court's findings and contextualise in light of two Commission communications on the rule of law published in 2019.

1 Introduction

When the European Commission published, in March 2014, a communication to introduce a new 'Rule of Law Framework' to complement Article 7 TEU,[1] it created quite a stir, from academic analyses[2] to a legal opinion by the Council's legal service.[3] But no observer, academic or other else, could have imagined the developments over the coming years that have intensified to such a degree that the Commission's First Vice President (now Executive Vice President) Frans Timmermans told the public in April 2019 it was time for the Union's Member States to decide if they wanted to 'bite the bullet' for it.[4] In other words, time had come to act.

It has become common ground in legal practice and academia, as made again evident through this edited volume,[5] that the general development surrounding the 'Rule of Law Framework' condenses in a rule of law crisis exhibited in particular in Hungary and Poland. Among numerous academic debates that followed, two have drawn our particular attention: the debates about which concept could be used to grasp the crisis and which procedure should be used to counteract its most dramatic consequences.

In an article published in 2018 in the *Common Market Law Review*, we took the position that infringement proceedings are an effective option for the Commission in the ongoing rule of law crisis. Building on previous, and what we consider groundbreaking, suggestions,[6] we indicated how the Commission and the Court of Justice could continue on a path already initiated, and pursue systemic deficiencies in the rule of law with the infringement procedure under Article 258 TFEU, notwithstanding the procedure under Article 7 TEU.[7]

---

[1]European Commission, Communication from the Commission to the European Parliament and the Council: A new EU Framework to Strengthen the Rule of Law, COM(2014) 158 final/2 of 19.03.2014.

[2]Cf. in particular, Giegerich (2015), pp. 499–542; Taborowski (2019), pp. 103–140; for the perspective of practitioners see notably Crabit and Bel (2016), pp. 197–206.

[3]Council of the European Union, Opinion of the Legal Service—Commission's Communication for a New Mechanism to Strengthen the Rule of Law, of 27 May 2014, Document no. 10296/14.

[4]'Timmermans invites EU members to 'bite the bullet' on rule of law', Report by EurActiv of 3 April 2019, available at: https://www.euractiv.com/section/justice-home-affairs/news/timmermans-invites-eu-members-to-bite-the-bullet-on-rule-of-law/.

[5]See previously also, for a wider context, Editorial Comments: 2019 shaping up as a challenging year for the Union, not least as a community of values (2019), pp. 3–22; as well as the contributions in Schroeder (2016) and Jakab and Kochenov (2017).

[6]Notably Scheppele (2016), pp. 105–132.

[7]Schmidt and Bogdanowicz (2018), pp. 1061–1100.

While the procedure under Article 7 TEU has remained rather static in the Council despite its launch against Poland and Hungary,[8] infringement proceedings have undergone several remarkable developments.

This justifies a continued focus on infringement proceedings in this article, whereas recent and noteworthy case law justifies the focus on Poland.

This case law has answered several questions raised in academia while the ongoing developments they assess pose new ones. They are accompanied by a large body of other ongoing proceedings in that Member State. Among them are not only infringement proceedings but also a variety of preliminary references from Polish courts, focussing on the independence of the ordinary judiciary and notably of the Supreme Court, referred by the Supreme Court,[9] by the Supreme Administrative Court[10] as well as several lower ordinary courts.[11]

As regards infringement proceedings, the European Commission has brought three actions under Article 258 TFEU before the Court of Justice, two of which have already been decided: one focussing on the lowering of the retirement age of judges of the Supreme Court,[12] and the other one focussing more generally on the ordinary judiciary.[13] A third one, with a specific focus on the new 'Disciplinary Chamber' at the Polish Supreme Court, that is likely to impact the entire judiciary, is pending.[14]

Rather than recapitulating considerations on the doctrinal framework or preceding jurisprudence, for which we refer explicitly to earlier publications,[15] this contribution offers a close-reading of and comments on Case C-619/18 regarding the 'independence of the Supreme Court' and Case C-192/18 on the retirement age differentiation between men and women in the Polish judiciary (Sect. 2). We will focus in particular on the substantive yardstick, for which the Commission, in its action, pleaded to rely on Article 19(1) TEU read together with Article 47 of the EU Charter of Fundamental Rights (hereafter: Charter). We will then contextualise these developments in court in light of recent action by the Commission out of court with

[8]One notable exception is the action brought by Hungary against the decision by the European Parliament to commence an Art. 7(1) procedure against Hungary, see CJEU, Case C-650/18, *Hungary v. European Parliament*, pending.

[9]See e.g. CJEU, Joined Cases C-585/18, C-624/18 and C-625/18, *A.K. (Indépendance de la chambre disciplinaire de la Cour suprême)*, Judgment of 19 November 2019, ECLI:EU:C:2019:982 or CJEU, Case C-487/19, *W.Ż*, pending.

[10]CJEU, Case C-824/18, *A.B. and others*, pending.

[11]See e.g. CJEU, Joined Cases C-558/18 and C-563/18, *Miasto Łowicz and others*.

[12]CJEU, Case C-619/18 *Commission v. Poland (Indépendance de la Cour suprême)*, Judgment of 24 June 2019, ECLI:EU:C:2019:531.

[13]CJEU, Case C-192/18 *Commission v Poland (Indépendance des juridictions de droit commun)*, Judgment of 5 November 2019, ECLI:EU:C:2019:924.

[14]CJEU, Case C-791/19, *Commission v Poland*, Action of 25 October 2019, O.J. (EU) C 413/36 of 9 December 2019.

[15]See, specifically on the infringement procedure Schmidt and Bogdanowicz (2018); on the concept of systemic deficiency von Bogdandy and Ioannidis (2014) and von Bogdandy (2019); on a preliminary stock-taking regarding the crisis von Bogdandy et al. (2018).

reference to its two communications on the rule of law of April and its first-ever public stakeholder consultation on this matter, of July 2019 (Sect. 3). The purpose of this text is therefore to provide a concise overview on either case and to sketch the most recent state of affairs regarding the *Rechtspolitik* surrounding the infringement procedure in the rule of law crisis.

2 The Rule of Law Crisis in Court: The Commission Infringement Cases Against Poland

In this section, we focus on the two recent infringement proceedings pertaining to the rule of law in Poland, i.e. cases C-619/18 and C-192/18. Both cases concern the independence of the judiciary. One has to remember, however, that the crisis in Poland, while affecting its judiciary in particular, is broader, and several actions by constitutional authorities are highly doubtful already under the national constitutional yardstick. This concerns the Polish Parliament, the President and the government, and in substance namely the freedom of the media, the civil service, and the respect for fundamental rights.[16]

2.1 The 'Independence of the Supreme Court Case': C-619/18

Case C-619/18 was filed by the Commission on 2 October 2018[17] after a letter of formal notice of 2 July 2018 with a 1-month deadline for reply by the Polish authorities and a reasoned opinion of 14 August 2018, with the same deadline. Both deadlines were short, demonstrating the determination of the Commission to see the matter through.[18] The subsequent judicial proceedings, which were provided by the Court with the above title, offer—even to the reader familiar with the

[16]Wyrzykowski (2019), pp. 417–418. For a longer analysis, cf. Sadurski (2019). On our observations regarding the concept of 'systemic deficiency' as underpinning this development, see Schmidt and Bogdanowicz (2018), pp. 1080 et seq.

[17]O.J. C 427/30 of 26.11.2018.

[18]This determination appears not lessened by the fact that, in the proceedings concerning the 'Disciplinary Chamber' at the Polish Supreme Court, CJEU, Joined Cases C-585/18, C-624/18 and C-625/18, *A.K. (Indépendance de la chambre disciplinaire de la Cour suprême), supra* note 9, the Commission gave the Polish authorities the 'usual' 2 months, both at the stage of the letter of formal notice and the reasoning opinion, cf. Commission press release, 'Rule of Law: European Commission launches infringement procedure to protect judges in Poland from political control', IP/19/1957 of 3 April 2019.

background—an impressive procedural complexity. In total, three decisions, by the Court's Vice President of October 2018,[19] then the Court's President of November 2018[20] and then the Grand Chamber of December 2018,[21] preceded opinion[22] and final judgment.[23] They were followed by a rectification order[24] concerning the Polish version.

The case was brought by the Commission in light of amendments to the law on the Supreme Court, enacted in 2017 and with effect of 3 April 2018, and one further amendment of 10 May 2018, all concerning the mandatory retirement age of its judges. It had stood, since 2002, at 70 for all judges, with the possibility of extension by the First President of the Supreme Court upon request and provision of a medical certificate by the judge in question. It was lowered on 20 December 2017, the day the Commission commenced in relation to it and other matters the Article 7 TEU procedure against Poland, to 65, applying to all sitting judges. The possibility of asking for an extension for 3 years remained, but authorisation was transferred to the full discretion of the President of the Republic, who had to consult the National Council of the Judiciary (NCJ). Neither the President's decision nor the NCJ's opinion had to be motivated.[25] A second extension was possible. The amended law also provided for two cut-off dates limiting the possibility of requests which ranged, depending on the age of the judge, from 3 months to 12 months. A second amendment of May 2018 clarified certain procedural provisions.[26]

The Commission had voiced concerns primarily because of the effect of the lowering of the retirement age, which, it held, amounted to 'a profound and immediate change in that court's composition'.[27] On 3 July 2018, the day after the Commission had sent its formal notice in the case to Poland,[28] a day that was used by

[19]CJEU, Case C-619/18, *Commission v. Poland*, Order of the Vice President of the Court of 19 October 2019, ECLI:EU:C:2018:852.

[20]CJEU, Case C-619/18, *Commission v. Poland*, Order of the President of the Court of 15 November 2018, ECLI:EU:C:2018:910.

[21]CJEU, Case C-619/18, *Commission v. Poland*, Order of the Court of 17 December 2018 [Text rectified by order of 2 July 2019], ECLI:EU:C:2018:1021.

[22]CJEU, Case C-619/18, *Commission v. Poland*, Opinion of Advocate General Tanchev of 11 April 2019, ECLI:EU:C:2019:325.

[23]CJEU, Case C-619/18, *Commission v. Poland*, *supra* note 12.

[24]CJEU, Case C-619/18 REC, Rectification d'arrêt of 11 July 2019, not published in the digital reports.

[25]Consequently, as dramatically put by Wojciech Sadurski: 'The new law on the [Supreme Court] created severe moral dilemmas for the older judges who faced a choice: either make a request to the president for an 'extension' beyond a newly lowered retirement age or accept the inevitable and step down.' See Sadurski (2019), p. 107.

[26]CJEU, Case C-619/18, *Commission v. Poland*, cf. paras. 6–14, *supra* note 12.

[27]Id., para. 63.

[28]See Commission Press Release of 2 July 2018, 'Rule of Law: Commission launches infringement procedure to protect the independence of the Polish Supreme Court', IP/18/434.

the Court as a reference point,[29] the law affected 27 judges out of 72 who were to be retired under the new rules, including then the Supreme Court's First President, Małgorzata Gersdorf. She and 14 others, i.e. 15 in total, were forced to retire on different formal grounds, having not or not properly submitted a request to stay on. Of the 12 others, another 7 received negative opinions by the NCJ, which the President did not overturn. Thus, 22 judges in total were forced to retire.

The Commission was further concerned because the extension procedure foreseen to possibly remedy the impact of the lowering of the retirement age was not subject to sufficient safeguards, in its opinion. It noted that the Polish President had full discretion to decline a request by a judge and that the NCJ, which provided the basis for an assessment, had in itself undergone a fundamental change by a separate law outside the scope of the proceedings, due to which its judges' members were no longer elected by their peers but instead by the lower house of the Polish parliament, the Sejm. With respect to the integrity of the members of the NCJ after that amendment, the Commission noted drily 'that doubt may be cast on their independence',[30] meaning it now considered the NCJ by-and-large defunct and politicised, so as to rubber-stamp the will of the legislature.

The complaint of the Commission in the main proceedings is rather concise and two-pronged, of which one line of argument can be subdivided into two further parts. It rests solely on primary law. The Commission had submitted that, (a) by lowering the retirement age of judges of the Polish Supreme Court from 70 to 65 for all sitting judges and applying it to judges appointed to the Supreme Court before 3 April 2018 and (b) by granting the Polish President discretion to extend the active mandate of Supreme Court judges upon request and to review the application for renewal, Poland had violated its obligations under Article 19(1) TEU in conjunction with Article 47 of the Charter.

Poland, supported by Hungary, disputed these findings in their entirety. Poland claimed in particular that 'the organisation of the national justice system constitutes a competence reserved exclusively to the Member States, so that the EU cannot arrogate competences in that domain' and that the provisions invoked by the Commission were not applicable since the case was not governed by EU law.[31]

2.1.1 Combined Interim Relief and Expedited Procedure

2.1.1.1 Procedural Novelties

Rather than to provide a chronological summary of either of the three orders prior to the opinion, it makes sense to point out, first, that two of them, the order by the Court's Vice President of October, Silva de Lapuerta,[32] and the order by the Grand

[29] CJEU, Case C-619/18, Order of the Court, para. 14 et seq. *supra* note 21.

[30] CJEU, Case C-619/18, *Commission v. Poland*, para. 100, *supra* note 12.

[31] Id., paras. 38 et seq.

[32] CJEU, Case C-619/18, Order of the Vice President, *supra* note 19.

Chamber of December 2018[33] concern the Commission's application for interim measures, whereas the order published 'in-between', i.e. in November 2018 by the Court's President, Koen Lenaerts,[34] concerns the separate Commission application for an expedited procedure.

The Polish Supreme Court case is therefore a novelty in EU law in several aspects, not only as regards its fundamental legal and political questions, but also its procedural structure. First, because of the combination of interim measures and expedited procedure, for which the Court's President, in his order, cites no precedent,[35] although allowing both to be combined.[36] Secondly, the procedure is noteworthy because there are two orders, not only one, as regards the interim measures, of which one serves as interim injunction until a decision on the interim measures themselves is taken, an 'injunction for an injunction' so to say. Thirdly, because both applications were successful for the Commission, which, given their rare use and a diminished success rate,[37] is remarkable as such.

With the applications for interim relief and the expedited procedure, the case differs from the second one discussed below. The reason for the Commission's decision to file for both measures is found in the facts surrounding the legal amendments on the Supreme Court. As the Court's Vice President reiterated, the Polish President had increased the total number of positions at the Supreme Court from 93 to 120 in March 2018, and 44 new vacancies had been advertised over the summer of 2018.[38] The Commission obviously saw this as a particular danger of being confronted with a *fait accompli*; and the Court agreed.

2.1.1.2 The Application for Interim Relief and the Court's Two Subsequent Orders

The Commission set in motion both interim measures and the expedited procedure with separate applications, all filed on the same day as the application in the main proceedings.

We will devote some space to the application for interim relief, because of its novel use, and because we had called, in our article of 2018, for increased recourse to

[33]CJEU, Case C-619/18, Order of the Court, *supra* note 21.

[34]CJEU, Case C-619/18, Order of the President, *supra* note 20.

[35]Id., paras 26–27.

[36]For further discussion on this point, cf. Castillo de la Torre (2007), pp. 273–353, pp. 808 et seq.; Jaeger (2013), pp. 3–28, p. 26.

[37]Between 2014 and 2018, the last period for which data is available, 17 applications for interim measures were filed, of which 8 in 2018 alone, and none in 2015. In total, 10 were granted, 7 were not granted. In 2014 and 2016, 2 out of 3 and 3 out of 5, respectively, were not granted. In 2018, 6 out of 8 were successful. See Court of Justice, Annual Report 2018, Judicial Activity, Luxembourg, February 2019, p. 139.

[38]CJEU, Case C-619/18, Order of the Vice President, para. 22, *supra* note 19.

the procedure.[39] The Supreme Court case now offers a very good opportunity to assess how Commission and Court are developing this procedural tool.

The Commission's application for interim measures, made pursuant to Article 279 TFEU in conjunction with Article 160(3) of the Rules of Procedure, contained four requests: (a) to order Poland to suspend the national legal amendments in question and to refrain from taking any action to implement them, (b) to assure that all sitting judges of the Supreme Court could continue to exercise their office under the conditions as they stood on 3 April 2018, the day the amendments came into effect, (c) to refrain from any appointment of judges under the new rules on posts becoming vacant because of them, in particular as regards measures to replace the President of the Supreme Court, and finally (d) to keep the Commission appraised of all measures taken in compliance in regular intervals.[40] Sanctions under Article 279 TFEU, such as those that had recently created considerable interest in academia, were not subject of the proceedings.[41]

The Vice President of the Court, based on Article 160 (7) of the Court's Rules of Procedure, decided that the matter was so urgent that it could not even wait until the Grand Chamber had decided on the interim measures but that, more still, interim orders had to be issued until that decision prior to a judgment, i.e. that the above-mentioned 'injunction for an injunction' was necessary.

In relation to the later order of the Grand Chamber, it is evident that the first order remains briefer and necessarily more superficial, which is why we focus on the reasoning of the second order. Nonetheless, there is one point of importance, on the use of the *fumus boni iuris*.

As is the case in many national legal systems, the Court decides on the request for interim relief by means of an ancillary procedure, based on a summary examination, i.e. briefer and less in-depth than in the final judgment. However, the CJEU has varied national blueprints with its own test, which is somewhat distinct and based on three considerations: first, whether 'such an order is justified prima facie in fact and in law' (*fumus boni juris*), secondly, whether the order is required 'to avoid serious and irreparable damage to the applicants' interests' (*urgency*) and thirdly, whether the applicants' interests outweigh the interests of the defendant (*balance of interest*).[42] The assessment of the *fumus boni iuris* appears equivalent to the 'summary assessment' in certain Member States.

---

[39]Schmidt and Bogdanowicz (2018), pp. 1078–1080.

[40]CJEU, Case C-619/18, Order of the Vice President, para. 1, *supra* note 19.

[41]See, on them and the corresponding case, Wennerås (2019), pp. 541–558.

[42]Castillo de la Torre (2007), p. 283. In the concrete case, the Court formulated, at para. 30 of CJEU, Case C-619/18, Order of the Court, *supra* note 21: 'the fumus boni juris requirement is met where at least one of the pleas in law relied on by the applicant for interim measures in support of the main action appears, prima facie, not unfounded.'

With her (the first) order of 19 October, Vice President Silva de Lapuerta adopted this test, but in a considerably condensed form.[43] Her reasoning on the *fumus boni iuris* is particularly noteworthy. She concludes that:

> without it being possible to rule, at the current state of the proceedings, on the question of the merits of these arguments, *let alone on the existence of a fumus boni juris as such*, the [relevant] question must be analysed in detail.[44]

This means that the Vice President granted the request without seriously examining the *fumus boni iuris*, rather refusing to do so in light of the complexity of the case. This approach ought to be contextualised, since it continues a development long observed in academia,[45] by which the Court has almost inversed its initial, very restrictive, approach, having originally required a 'manifest soundness' of an application in interim proceedings to accede to it.[46] Since the Vice President of the Court turns that original test on its head, the application of the Commission is also, with no surprise, granted.

In its second order of December 2018, on the requested interim measures, that follows the result of the first, the Grand Chamber confirmed its willingness to inverse assumptions on the *fumus boni iuris*.[47]

The Grand Chamber extends the initial reasoning of the Vice President in a motivation comprising no less than 118 paragraphs of its order, otherwise sufficient for a full-blown judgment.

In order to assess the *fumus boni iuris*, on which it consecrates a full 29 paragraphs, the Court carefully avoids to deal with the main plea of the Commission, the infringement of Article 19 TEU read together with Article 47 of the Charter. It emphasises instead that this raises 'difficult legal issues',[48] to be reserved for the judgment. This is in line with the general rule in national jurisdictions that the interim measure does not serve to decide already on the merits.

In order to assess the complex situation in Poland *prima facie* nonetheless, the Court uses a three-step test that can be deemed a smart solution.

The Court, after an extensive recapitulation of the parties' arguments, first recalls the importance, relevant jurisprudence, and content of Article 19 TEU and Article 47 of the Charter for Member States, except that the case it knowingly cites in particular, the *LM* case, hardly deals with 'every Member State', as the Court

---

[43]CJEU, Case C-619/18, Order of the Vice President, paras. 15–26, *supra* note 19.

[44]Id., para. 16 (emphasis added, our translation).

[45]Castillo de la Torre (2007), p. 284 et seq.; equally Glawe (2012), pp. 676–683, pp. 681–682.

[46]Cf. CJEU, Joined Cases 43/59 and others, *Eva von Lachmüller and others v. Commission*, Order of the President of the Court of 20 October 1959, para. 11, ECLI:EU:C:1959:24. On this case and the evolution of the fumus boni iuris as part of interim measures, see in detail also Sladič (2008), p. 174 et seq., 178.

[47]CJEU, Case C-619/18, Order of the Court, para. 30, *supra* note 21.

[48]Id., para. 45.

formulates, but no other than the defendant in the present one.[49] It therefore manages to remain abstract and at the same time leave no doubt as to the concrete addressee.

Concentrating on the importance also of 'maintaining the independence of those bodies', i.e. courts and tribunals, the Court, in a second step, recalls that it is 'common ground' that the functioning of the Supreme Court is particularly essential for the Polish judiciary, and that, already for this reason, it is part of the judiciary in the sense of Article 19 (1) TEU.[50] This finding very much predetermines a later confirmation in the judgment, while avoiding to explicitly look at its merits. This assessment does not amount to a reasoning based on general principles or an extensive substantive assessment, but a reduced reiteration of key case law waiting to be further extended and deepened.

The Court then, in a third step, assesses different arguments brought forward by Poland that might rebut the Commission's claim, including that the Commission was barred from invoking objections already made. The Court concludes that none of them convince it *prima facie*, nor that Poland can successfully claim the novelty of the Commission's arguments.[51]

The Court is to be credited for having dwelled on the consequences of this case law ahead of its later judgment, while a strict summary assessment may not have required it.

The Court of Justice then turns to the urgency of the application, which it condenses into the formula whether there is serious damage to be expected from the situation at hand and whether that damage is likely to be irreparable.[52] The Court affirms that this is the case since any endangering of the Supreme Court, as an apex court, is 'likely to have an irreversible effect on the EU legal order'.[53]

As a last step, it agrees that the weighing of interest is in favour of the Commission. In this context it is particularly noteworthy that the Court highlighted, as phrased by Maciej Taborowski, a 'deep interference in national law and with the autonomy of the national law-maker'.[54] The Court rebuts the argument submitted by Poland that the effect of the interim measure suspending the application of the provisions of national legislation would be the creation of a legal lacuna as regards the definition of the retirement age for judges of the Supreme Court. The Court rather underlines that 'granting such interim measures entails an obligation for that Member State immediately to suspend the application of the provisions of national legislation at issue, *including those whose effect is to repeal or replace the previous provisions* governing the retirement age for judges of the Sąd Najwyższy (Supreme Court), so that those previous provisions become applicable again pending delivery

[49]Id., paras. 40–42.

[50]Id., paras. 41–43.

[51]Id., paras. 47 et seq.

[52]Id., para. 70.

[53]Id., para. 71.

[54]Taborowski (2019), p. 250.

of the final judgment.'[55] In other words, provisions that were already repealed have to be brought back into force in such a case.

2.1.1.3 The Application to Expedite the Procedure

Distinct from the Commission's application for interim measures, but equally present in the case at hand, is the possibility for the Commission to request that the main procedure be expedited. The Court decided on this second application of the Commission with its second order of November 2018, based on Article 133 of the Court's Rules of Procedure.

The expedited procedure does not use the same test as the application for interim measures, even though the criteria used by the Court to grant it also rest on an 'intrinsic urgency' test, which bears some resemblance. Decisive here is not the risk for permanent damage, should no interim measure be taken, but the possibility to reduce the risk emanating from the main procedure by speeding it up. Thus, there has to be a particular and intrinsic urgency to the case in the main proceedings.[56]

In contrast to the two orders for interim measures, Court President Lenaerts, who decided on this annex application in the main case, considered also the substantive yardstick found in the Commission's application, but he looked in particular at Article 47 of the Charter and did not relate his findings to Article 19(1)(2) TEU.[57] His decision to grant the request based on urgency rests on two main considerations. He first considered the importance of a functioning apex court, such as the Supreme Court, to guarantee individuals access to an independent court, a right under Article 47 of the Charter, which, he continues, 'forms part of the essence' of the fair trial right under the same norm, and which equally serves to safeguard as a 'guarantee' of 'cardinal importance' to safeguard the Union's values under Article 2 TEU, including the rule of law.[58] That line of argument, we note, is thoughtful and daring at the same time. The Commission had framed its argument much broader and relied on a more objective notion. It had argued that the 'systemic concerns on which those complaints are based' 'hinder the proper functioning of the EU legal order'.[59] While we fully agree with this observation and welcome the use of the concept of systemic deficiency, it was seemingly too early at this stage of the procedure for the Court's President to entertain such a broad concept. Next, Lenaerts considers the amendments in Poland as a possible infringement of a Member State's obligations to guarantee a proper functioning of the preliminary reference procedure, which he elevates to 'the keystone of the EU judicial system',[60] a term later recalled in the

[55]CJEU, Case C-619/18, Order of the Court, para. 95, *supra* note 21.

[56]Barbier de la Serre (2006), p. 804.

[57]CJEU, Case C-619/18, Order of the President, para. 20, *supra* note 20.

[58]Id., paras.19–21.

[59]Id., para. 15.

[60]Id.

judgment.[61] The term is borrowed from the opinion in *Achmea*,[62] but it is the first time that the Court itself used it.

2.1.2 Opinion

The opinion of Advocate General Evgeni Tanchev followed on 11 April 2019.

The main procedural point for Tanchev, before coming to the substance, is the relation of Article 258 TFEU to Article 7 TEU,[63] which the literature had long disagreed on. Tanchev now clarifies that the wording of the treaties, notably in its Lisbon version, does not argue for an exclusion of the infringement action in the area of Article 7 TEU, since today's Article 258 TFEU aims at an infringement of a norm in both treaties, compared to the former Article 226 TEC. Further, he observes a teleological difference, whereas 'Article 7 TEU is essentially a 'political' procedure' while 'Article 258 TFEU constitutes a direct 'legal' route before the Court for ensuring the enforcement of EU law by the Member States'.[64] Article 7 TEU does therefore not act as lex specialis to the infringement action.[65] Rather, and without Article 269 TFEU being an objection, he fittingly concludes that 'the autonomous, indeed complementary, nature of these procedures' mean 'that they may apply in parallel'.[66] This clarification is a major advancement for the interaction of the two procedures in primary law, it was much needed and it is to be expressly welcomed.

The clarification of this very important doctrinal and procedural connection between two core norms of the EU's constitutional supervision system results in the possibility for Tanchev to deal with two substantive points. He first turns to the substantive yardstick of the infringement, for which the Commission, setting the frame under the principle *ne ultra petita*, had aimed at primary law, and had proposed a combined reading of Article 19(1)(2) TEU with Article 47 of the Charter. The opinion now gave a chance to turn to this yardstick more extensively. The importance of both norms, and notably of Article 19(1)(2) TEU as an 'operationalisation' of the rule of law as an EU value enshrined in Article 2 TEU, had arisen against the backdrop of a more complex development, notably through repeated use by the Commission and important case law of the Court of Justice.[67]

---

[61] CJEU, Case C-619/18, *Commission v. Poland*, para. 45, *supra* note 12.

[62] CJEU, Case C-284/16, *Achmea*, Opinion of Advocate General Wathelet of 19 September 2017, ECLI:EU:C:2017:699, para. 84.

[63] CJEU, Case C-619/18, Opinion of Advocate General Tanchev, paras 48-51, *supra* note 22.

[64] Id., para. 50.

[65] Id., para. 49.

[66] Id., para. 50.

[67] See, in detail, Schmidt and Bogdanowicz (2018), pp. 1092 et seq. and the case-law cited, in particular CJEU, Case C-64/16, *Associação Sindical dos Juízes Portugueses (ASJP)*, Judgment of 27 February 2018, ECLI:EU:C:2018:117.

Tanchev dealt a severe blow to the Commission's legal point of view of a combined reading, siding explicitly with the defendant and finding that the Commission could invoke neither Article 19(1) TEU in combination with Article 47 of the Charter, nor the latter by itself, for lack of an implementation of EU law, as required by Article 51 of the Charter.[68] In particular, he held that any

> contrary finding would be apt to undermine the current system of review of the compatibility of national measures with the Charter and open the door for Treaty provisions such as Article 19(1) TEU to be used as a 'subterfuge' to circumvent the limits of the scope of application of the Charter as set out in Article 51(1) thereof.[69]

Moreover, he notes, the Commission could not rely on the Court's assessment of Art. 47 in the *Achmea* case, because, he stated, 'the Court mentioned Article 47 of the Charter and related case-law only to confirm findings made on the basis of Article 19(1) TEU.'[70]

In a similar manner, the Advocate General also ruled out that the Commission could invoke the *ASJP* case[71] as a precedent for its combined reading of both norms. He found that the passages cited by the Commission from that case proved only that the Court relied on Article 47 of the Charter to support the substantive scope of Article 19(1) TEU.[72] In the passages cited by the Advocate General,[73] the Court declares that a previous reading of Art. 19(1) TEU is 'now reaffirmed by Article 47 of the Charter' or that it is 'confirmed by the second subparagraph of Article 47 of the Charter'.

In our view, the precedent in *ASJP* should be read as the Court's opening—through Article 19(1)(2) TEU—of the possibility to apply Article 47 of the Charter in a combined standard required by these two provisions. Where Article 19(1)(2) TEU applies, the substantive yardstick of Article 47 of the Charter can apply as well, without contravening Article 51 of the Charter. In his second opinion in the case discussed below, Tanchev would later underscore that he regards a meaningful separation of the jurisdictions of the Court of Justice, the ECtHR as well as national constitutional courts, as demonstrated by a limited applicability of certain EU norms, i.e. here a 'delimited scope' of Article 19 TEU, to be as important under the rule of law 'as the protection of fundamental rights'.[74] We fully agree with the Advocate General that a meaningful distinction of jurisdictions is important. To commit to a

[68] CJEU, Case C-619/18, Opinion of Advocate General Tanchev, para. 52 et seq., *supra* note 22.

[69] Id., para. 57 et seq.

[70] Id., para. 55 in fine.

[71] See *supra* note 67.

[72] CJEU, Case C-619/18, Opinion of Advocate General Tanchev, para. 55 at footnote 33, *supra* note 22.

[73] CJEU, Case C-64/16, *Associação Sindical dos Juízes Portugueses (ASJP)*, paras. 35, 41, 42, *supra* note 67. We note that, in para. 42, the Court does not again refer explicitly to both norms but continues its reasoning of the previous paragraph.

[74] CJEU, Case C-192/18, *Commission v. Poland*, Opinion of Advocate General Tanchev of 20 June 2019, ECLI:EU:C:2019:529, para. 114.

combined standard of both norms, Article 19 (1) TEU and Article 47 of the Charter, does not mean a hidden attempt to level the obstacle of Article 51 of the Charter. The goal then is not a clandestine extended application of the Charter but a comprehensive objective standard. Further, neither the Court nor the Advocate General eventually disregarded Article 47 entirely, as we will show below. It may have made for a smoother assessment to not bar Article 47 and then requiring to take it into account after all.

We also note that, in at least two cases, the Court appears to support a joint reading. In the *Berlioz* case, the Court had stated that '[t]he obligation imposed on the Member States in the second subparagraph of Article 19(1) TEU, to provide remedies sufficient to ensure effective legal protection in the fields covered by Union law, *corresponds to that right* [scil.: Article 47 of the Charter].'[75] Advocate General Wathelet, in his opinion in that case, had even required a mandatory reading in conjunction, stating that 'Article 47 of the Charter cannot be treated independently of the second paragraph of Article 19 TEU'.[76]

Returning to the opinion in the Supreme Court case, Advocate General Tanchev, having thus narrowed the substantive yardstick for assessment to the 'second subparagraph of Article 19 (1) TEU', assesses two points on the merits: the requirement of judicial irremovability from office and the principle of judicial independence, both in light of the new retirement age at the Polish Supreme Court.

For the concept of judicial independence, the Advocate General reiterates the *ASJP* formula,[77] despite his previous narrow reading of that case.

To ascertain the meaning of irremovability, Advocate General Tanchev cites the opinion of Advocate General Ruiz-Zarabo Colomer in the *De Coster* case. This is a very useful addition, since the opinion appears to have been previously overlooked in the debate at hand. Accordingly, irremovability 'is the basis and the reflection of judicial independence and means that judges cannot be dismissed, suspended, moved or retired except on grounds, and subject to the safeguards, provided by law'.[78] Hence, the distinction for Tanchev is that *irremovability* from office *protects the judicial position as such* once acceded to it, while *judicial independence*, in the specific setting of EU primary law, *protects the proper and unhindered exercise* of said position. That juxtaposition, we observe, finds support in the same passage of the above *De Coster* opinion.

[75] CJEU, Case C-682/15, *Berlioz Investment Fund*, Judgment of 16 May 2017, ECLI:EU:C:2017:373, para. 44.

[76] CJEU, Case C-682/15, *Berlioz Investment Fund*, Opinion of Advocate General Wathelet of 10 January 2017, ECLI:EU:C:2017:2, para. 38.

[77] CJEU, Case C-619/18, Opinion of Advocate General Tanchev, para. 86 and case law cited, *supra* note 22.

[78] Id., para. 55, citing Case C-17/00, *De Coster*, Opinion of Advocate General Ruiz-Zarabo Colomer of 28 June 2001, para. 93.

Tanchev further elaborates the principle of irremovability based on ECtHR case law and various non-binding guidelines by the Council of Europe, including the Venice Commission. He equally cites the CCJE and UN documents,[79] a noteworthy reception of soft law and international law sources, that he would continue in similar fashion in the subsequent case. From them, Tanchev deduces that

> judges should have a guaranteed tenure until a mandatory retirement age or the expiry of their term of office, and can be subject to suspension or removal from office in individual cases only for reasons of incapacity or behaviour rendering them unfit for office. Early retirement should be possible only at the request of the judge concerned or on medical grounds, and any changes to the obligatory retirement age must not have retroactive effect.[80]

The Advocate General finds that, as the Commission has shown, these requirements are not met.[81] Tanchev further finds the principle of irremovability of judges infringed because the termination of office was premature. Relying on precedent case law, he concludes that Poland cannot invoke economic motives to justify the decision.[82]

As regards the second principle in question, judicial independence, Tanchev's position is equally clear:

The Polish legal provisions in question

> expose the Supreme Court and its judges to external intervention and pressure from the President of the Republic in the initial extension and renewal of their mandate which impairs the objective independence of that court and influences the judges' independent judgment and decisions. This is so, especially given that the requirement to apply to the President of the Republic for the extension of retirement age is accompanied by a reduction in the retirement age.[83]

As regards the possibility for extension requests to the Polish President, Tanchev finds that this offers no judicial review and does not rely on binding criteria.[84]

Relying on these findings, the Advocate General therefore suggests to the Court to find that there has been a violation of Article 19(1) TEU.

2.1.3 Judgment

In its judgment of June 2019, the Court's Grand Chamber sides, in the operative part, fully with the Advocate General, even though its reasoning differs in parts.

The Court finds that Poland violated its obligations under Article 19(1)(2) TEU by enacting a law that retroactively lowers the retirement age for judges at the Supreme Court and, secondly, by granting the Polish President discretion to extend

---

[79]Id., para. 72 and references cited at footnote 52 and 53.

[80]Id., para. 72.

[81]Id., para. 73.

[82]Id., para. 72–82.

[83]Id., para. 89.

[84]Id., paras. 90 et seq.

the mandate of its judges beyond the newly fixed retirement age. The applicability of the infringement procedure to the case is not discussed.

Very close to Tanchev's reasoning, the Court rejects Poland's argument that the subsequent amendments of November 2018 to the original law can impact the Court's own competence or indeed the requirement to assess the law in question, recalling clearly that the relevant point in time is the date of the reasoned opinion, even if later retroactive amendments came into effect.[85]

It then deals, as the Advocate General did, with the yardstick for the substantive assessment, Article 19(1) (2) and Article 47 of the Charter. From the outset however, it departs very notably from the Advocate General's point of view; at the same time, it avoids a clear positioning.

The Court uses its power to reformulate the application in a manner that takes away the main point of difference between the Commission's application and the Advocate General's opinion. It finds: 'At the hearing, the Commission stated that, by its action, it is seeking, in essence, a declaration that the second subparagraph of Article 19(1) TEU, *read in the light of Article 47 of the Charter*, has been infringed.'[86] This is clearly not what the Commission had submitted in writing, it had demanded an assessment 'under the *combined provisions* of Article 19(1) (2) TEU and Article 47 of the Charter'.[87]

The Court however does not find that Article 47 of the Charter must *not* be considered. Rather, and now implicitly returning to the reformulated application, it holds: 'that the second subparagraph of Article 19(1) TEU requires Member States to provide remedies that are sufficient to ensure effective legal protection, *within the meaning in particular of Article 47 of the Charter*, in the fields covered by EU law' and that it is assessing the scope of Art. 19(1) TEU 'as confirmed by the second paragraph of Article 47 of the Charter'.[88]

The Court therefore mediates between two positions. Like the Advocate General, it narrows the yardstick, but remains more extensive than Tanchev. From this basis, the Court proceeds to assess the merits.

Before going into the assessment of the application, the Court, in contrast to the Advocate General, adds a section on 'applicability and the scope of the second subparagraph of Article 19(1) TEU'.[89] Given that the scope of assessment had already been established, the Court could have omitted that section without immediate loss to its reasoning. That it decides otherwise is very telling because the Court

[85]CJEU, Case C-619/18 *Commission v. Poland*, paras. 27-33 of the judgment, in particular para. 31, and case law cited, *supra* note 12.

[86]Id., para. 32.

[87]Id., para. 25 of the judgment, emphasis added, *supra* note 12. The French version, lacking the 'in particular' reads 'lu à la lumière de l'article 47 de la Charte.' The German version is yet more explicit, using the verb 'interpret': 'ausgelegt im Licht von Art. 47 der Charta'.

[88]Id., para. 57.

[89]Id., paras. 34 et seq.

uses the following paragraphs for general findings on the normative framework of the case.

Only after these initial normative findings does the Court go into an assessment of Article 19(1) TEU, combining both key findings of its previous judgments in *ASJP* and *LM* into one, central statement:

> Article 19 TEU, [...] gives concrete expression to the value of the rule of law affirmed in Article 2 TEU [and] entrusts the responsibility for ensuring the full application of EU law in all Member States and judicial protection of the rights of individuals under that law to national courts and tribunals and to the Court of Justice.[90]

It coincides with that finding that the Court had included Article 2 TEU as applicable law at the beginning of the judgment.[91] The Court emphasizes that Article 19(1) TEU demands full compliance irrespective of various counterarguments, such as the possible presence of an excessive deficit procedure and 'irrespective of whether the Member States are implementing Union law within the meaning of Article 51(1) of the Charter'.[92] The compliance requirement also does not amount to a transfer of competences from Member States to the Union.[93] The Court then also answers how it intends to read Article 19(1)(2) TEU 'in the light of' Article 47 of the Charter. Accordingly, this combined interpretation requires Member States to provide 'effective judicial protection', and that in turn entails ensuring judicial independence,[94] a finding with which the Court can commence its concrete assessment in the case at hand.

The Court distinguishes two pleas of the Commission and examines them separately.

In its first plea in law, the Commission in essence alleged that the application of the lowering of the retirement age to all sitting judges of the Polish Supreme Court, with two cut-off dates depending on their age, and in addition an increase in the number of judges, leading both to a large number of vacancies, amounted to an impression that the measures were used to 'covertly' change the composition of 'judicial bodies',[95] a term by which the Commission meant the Polish Supreme Court.

Poland, in turn, defended itself by stating that early retirement of judges, with all salaries and immunities kept, did not amount to dismissal, this being the solely prohibited measure in question here under Art. 19(1) TEU and further, that it had only re-established a previously existing, earlier, retirement age, under which several of the sitting judges had served, who were therefore not affected by the current

[90] Id., para. 47.

[91] Id., para. 2.

[92] Id., para. 50 and case law cited.

[93] Id., paras. 49–52.

[94] Id., paras. 54–56.

[95] Id., para. 64.

measures. Further, Poland also claimed that the measures aimed at 'improving the age balance among senior members'.[96] This is an argument with which the Court was familiar, since it was raised, in similar fashion, by Hungary regarding its judiciary in 2012.[97] Hungary, in its support, claimed that the Commission had not proven an impact of the measures in question on the Supreme Court's capacity.[98]

Dealing further with the arguments for the first plea, it is noteworthy that the Court addresses them solely under the principle of independence, to which it attaches the notion of impartiality,[99] whereas the Advocate General had previously addressed either concept separately. The Court also separates the notion of independence (tacitly the operative core of Article 19(1)(2) TEU) into 'two aspects', one, 'which is external in nature' and the other being 'internal in nature'.[100] The latter, internal one, concerns the behaviour and set-up of a bench in relation to concrete proceedings, i.e. 'that an equal distance is maintained from the parties to the proceedings and their respective interests'.[101] It subsequently only assesses the external aspect, the 'freedom of the judges from all external intervention or pressure'[102] for which it adds, for the concrete case:

> the requirement of independence means that the rules governing the disciplinary regime and, accordingly, any dismissal of those who have the task of adjudicating in a dispute must provide the necessary guarantees in order to prevent any risk of that disciplinary regime being used as a system of political control of the content of judicial decisions.[103]

In light of this high bar, the Court sets as a test four elements to find whether the Polish law is compatible with the external aspect of judicial independence, and, consequently, EU law: first, 'a legitimate objective' that is, secondly, 'proportionate in the light of that objective' and, thirdly, 'must not raise reasonable doubt in the minds of individuals as to the imperviousness of the court concerned to external factors' nor, the fourth point, its 'neutrality with respect to the interests before it'.[104]

It is somewhat surprising that the Court never openly finds that this test has not been met. Instead, it speaks of 'doubts', first as regards the retirement as such, secondly, related to the newly introduced possibility to have a mandate extended, thirdly, as regards the combined effect of the measures and lastly, the extent of that combined effect on the Supreme Court.[105] In other places, the Court is more explicit. In particular when it comes to additional material provided by Poland, such as an

[96]Id., para. 80.

[97]Cf. CJEU, Case C-286/12, *Commission v. Hungary*, Judgment of 6 November 2012, ECLI:EU:C:2012:687, para. 25.

[98]CJEU, Case C-619/18 *Commission v. Poland*, paras. 65–70, *supra* note 12.

[99]Id., paras. 73–74.

[100]Id., paras. 71–73.

[101]Id., para. 73.

[102]Id., paras. 74–76.

[103]Id., para. 77.

[104]Id., para. 79.

[105]Id., paras. 82–86.

explanatory memorandum for the Venice Commission, it noted that this could raise serious doubts as to whether the reform of the retirement age of serving judges of the Supreme Court was made in pursuance of legitimate objectives, and not '*with the aim of side-lining a certain group of judges of that court*'.[106] Weighed against the arguments of the defendant the Court first does not accept that some of the judges had originally served under terms meaning a retirement at 65. The Court equally rejected further Polish arguments, such as that the retirement of judges had to be regarded as a right rather than an obligation,[107] as well as the assumption that, in light of the economic situation, the amendments were to mainstream and standardise the retirement age of its judges. The Court is finally almost amused, it seems, by the fourth argument, that the amendments were intended to improve the age balance at the court and to allow positive discrimination.[108] Consequently, the Court approves of the first plea in full.[109]

The second plea of the Commission addressed the discretion granted to the Polish President to extend the term of retired judges for 3 years, and to repeat that extension once upon request.

The Court, rather concise in its reasoning, finds that the President's manner of appointment clearly did not satisfy the requirements it had set and that the NCJ did not meet standards to aptly justify its decisions, which therefore could not rule out the 'imperviousness of the judges concerned to external factors and as to their neutrality with respect to any interests before them.'[110] Interestingly, the Court requires that a body such as the NCJ be itself independent of the legislative and executive authorities and of the authority to which it is required to deliver its opinion.[111] Hence, for the first time in history, the Court specifies the terms for the functioning of a body that is not itself a court but established for the purpose of safeguarding judicial independence. It would return to that problem later.[112]

To conclude its reasoning, the Court reiterates, as the Advocate General had done before, that Member States could not, if not in their own right, point to another Member State to justify their own infringement of EU law, an important argument given Poland's frequent references to legal systems in other Member States, including, but not limited to, Germany and France.[113] As a last point, it notes drily that its own members were appointed for a fixed year term on accord of all Member States

[106]Id., para. 82.

[107]Id., paras. 89–90.

[108]Id., paras. 94–95.

[109]Id., para. 97.

[110]Id., paras. 116–118, para. 118 for the citation.

[111]Id., para. 116.

[112]See CJEU, Joined Cases C-585/18, C-624/18 and C-625/18, *A.K. (Indépendance de la chambre disciplinaire de la Cour suprême)*, paras. 136 et seq., notably 143–145, *supra* note 9.

[113]See e.g. Chancellery of the Polish Prime Minister, White Paper on the Reform of the Polish Judiciary, 7 March 2018.

and of the panel provided for under Article 255 TFEU, to counter the argument by Poland as to its own composition.[114]

2.2 The 'Case on the Independence of the Ordinary Courts': C-192/18

The second important infringement action, *Case C-192/18*, is the 'Case on the Independence of the Ordinary Courts', for which Advocate General Tanchev issued his opinion on 20 June 2019 and the Court handed down its judgment on 5 November 2019. The case offers several interesting findings and complements the case on the independence of the Supreme Court.

The title of the case, again assigned by the Court, is somewhat too narrow as it does not concern only the ordinary courts, but a retirement differentiation according to the sex of the person that concerned, other than ordinary court judges, *mutatis mutandis* equally public prosecutors and Supreme Court judges. This differentiation, according to which men retire in general at the age of 65, whereas women were set to retire at the age of 60, with a possible extension of employment at the discretion of the minister of Justice, had been introduced on 12 July 2017. The Commission was faced with not only having to address the amendment concerning the lowering of the retirement age, but also that new differentiation. It brought a letter of formal notice only 2 weeks later, on 28 July 2017, a record-worthy speediness given its internal procedures and stakeholders involved. The date of that initial decision of the Commission coincided with the last (fourth) 'Rule of Law Recommendation' addressed to Poland and the threat to trigger Article 7 TEU.[115] A reasoned opinion followed on 12 September 2017. Since the case was not subject to an expedited procedure, the Court took considerably longer to decide on it, and concluded the case only in 2019, long after the Commission had taken non-judicial steps also regarding that matter with the launch of Article 7 (1) TEU on 20 December 2017.[116]

The Commission addressed the age differentiation in the Polish law by two pleas, first under the combined primary and secondary law equal treatment provisions (Article 157 TFEU and Articles 5(a) and 9(1)(f) of Directive 2006/54/EC). With the second plea, the Commission again invoked the view that Poland, by the same token, had violated the 'combined provisions' of Article 19(1) TEU and Article 47 of the Charter. For the yardstick, the Commission had limited its action during the

[114]CJEU, Case C-619/18 *Commission v. Poland*, para. 121, *supra* note 12.

[115]Cf. Commission Press Release of 26 July 2017, 'European Commission acts to preserve the rule of law in Poland', IP/17/2161.

[116]Cf. European Commission, Reasoned proposal in accordance with Article 7(1) of the Treaty on European Union regarding the Rule of Law in Poland—Proposal for a Council Decision: On the determination of a clear risk of a serious breach by the Republic of Poland of the Rule of Law, COM (2017) 835 final of 20 December 2017, see in particular mn. 5, point (2), mn. 114 et seq.

hearing to Article 19(1)(2) TEU, *read in the light of Article 47 of the Charter*. The Court understood this to mean a focus only on Article 19 (1) TEU, and did not consider Article 47 further,[117] in contrast to the previous case, where exactly that reasoning had been upheld.[118] The Court is yet to explain this difference.

2.2.1 Opinion

Advocate General Tanchev, also assigned to this case, proposed that the Court should declare that Poland has breached its obligations under Article 157 TFEU, along with Article 5(a) and Article 9(1)(f) of Directive 2006/54/EC, as well as under Article 19(1)(2) TEU. He only briefly considered and rejected the motion by Poland to declare the case hypothetical due to subsequent amendments to the laws in question, for this case of April 2018, in particular because of the fundamental need for clarification by the Court.[119]

As before, and already as discussed above in part, Tanchev remained of the opinion that Art. 47 of the Charter again was not to be considered. He referred for that purpose to his considerations in the above-mentioned case[120] including a polite reservation possibly against previous mediation attempts by the Court: 'I therefore take the view that prudence should be exercised in making direct recourse to Article 47 of the Charter in illuminating the protection with respect to the rule of law provided by Article 2 TEU.'[121]

But he evidently felt the need to return to this point in more detail. As a rule, the Advocate General regards an extensive application of Article 47 of the Charter, even from an objective viewpoint, as non-compliant with the principle of conferral. 'Contrary to the European Court of Human Rights, the Court does not have a specific mandate to penalise all fundamental rights violations committed by the Member States.'[122] But that limitation, he continues, does not mean that the Court cannot consider 'common legal sources',[123] in the assessment of Article 19 (1) TEU. Fundamental rights, notwithstanding their non-applicability to the individual under the Charter in the case at hand in light of its Article 51, are part of these sources, as indicated in particular by Article 6 (3) TEU.[124] They are inherent in the 'content of the guarantee of the rule of law'.[125] Following this logic, as the Advocate General continues, there is necessarily 'a tension inherent in Article 6(1) TEU, in the sense

---

[117] CJEU, Case C-192/18, *Commission v. Poland*, paras. 85–86, *supra* note 13.

[118] Id., paras. 54, 57.

[119] CJEU, Case C-192/18, Opinion of Advocate General Tanchev, paras. 64 to 65, *supra* note 74.

[120] Id., para. 67 et seq. and case-law cited.

[121] Id., para. 99.

[122] Id., para. 70.

[123] Id., para. 71.

[124] Id., para. 96.

[125] Id., para. 96.

that the Charter is, in effect, recognised as a source of fundamental rights guaranteed by the EU legal order, while the same provision also states, [. . .] that the 'provisions of the Charter shall not extend in any way the competences of the Union as defined in the Treaties."[126]

Tanchev's solution for that tension is a novel concept in the Court's terminology: a '*constitutional passerelle*' ('*passerelle constitutionnelle*' in the French version, somewhat weak '*verfassungsrechtliche Verbindung*' in the German version, '*konstytucyjny pomost*' in the Polish version). Reminiscent of the 'passerelle clause' but of an evidently different meaning, the Advocate General uses this concept to point out a necessary connection between both norms, requiring an interpretation 'in harmony'.[127]

As regards the two complaints by the Commission, the Advocate General first assesses and confirms that there has been an unequal treatment between men and women, and in particular also that remunerations in question were to be regarded as pay in the sense of Directive 2006/54/EC on equal opportunities and treatment.[128]

It is the second complaint, and the above considerations, that are of considerably more interest here. The Advocate General examines the fulfilment of both principles, irremovability and independence, according to several subprinciples that he takes from varying sources, including by international organisations.[129] The point of view essential for ascertaining, for each point, whether there has been an interference, is in particular that of general public that is subject to the judiciary, or 'whether the public might legitimately perceive the arrangements in issue to taint the impartiality of proceedings.'[130] The Court would later adopt this viewpoint.

The assessment also condenses into a statement on the material scope of Art. 19 (1) TEU:

> The material scope of Article 19(1), second subparagraph, TEU is confined, in the context of irremovability and independence of judges, to correcting problems with respect to structural infirmity in a given Member State; which is here the case given that the laws challenged by the Commission impact across entire tiers of the judiciary. These might best be termed systemic or generalised deficiencies, which 'compromise the essence' of the irremovability and independence of judges.[131]

This formula adds further substance ('impact across entire tiers of the judiciary') to the concept of 'systemic or generalised deficiencies', which the Court had previously already dwelled on in *LM*, but left in its details to Member State courts.[132] Accordingly, there can be particularly severe, 'structural infirmities' in a Member

---

[126]Id., para. 98.

[127]Id., para. 97.

[128]Id., paras. 74 et seq.

[129]Id., para. 102 et seq.

[130]Id., para. 112.

[131]Id., para. 115.

[132]CJEU, Case C-216/18 PPU, *Minister for Justice and Equality (LM)*, Judgment of 25 July 2018, ECLI:EU:C:2018:586, notably paras. 67–68.

State, which can take the form of 'systemic or generalised deficiencies' and there is a concept of 'essence' of a principle in EU constitutional law, which can be infringed by these phenomena.[133] The Advocate General may still have to further illustrate what difference, if any, he sees between the adjectives 'systemic or generalised' and how the new notion of 'structural infirmity' comes into play.

2.2.2 Judgment

The Court sided with the Advocate General and declared that Poland had breached its obligations under Article 157 TFEU, along with Article 5(a) and Article 9(1)(f) of Directive 2006/54/EC, as well as under Article 19(1)(2) TEU.

As regards the substance of the first plea, the main point of dispute between the Commission and Poland was the scope of application of the Directive or a different legal basis, which would have supposedly granted more leeway to the defendant.[134] The Court dismissed Poland's arguments as fundamentally flawed.[135]

As regards the second plea, the Court spent some time on the 'applicability and the scope of the second subparagraph of Article 19(1) TEU'.[136]

Having repeated its findings on the different aspects of the guarantee of judicial independence, the Court engages in a concrete assessment and clarifies, first, that the main point for objection is not per se the lowering of the retirement age nor in fact the involvement of the Minister of Justice. For both, the Court indicates some leeway for the Member States. Rather, it is the concrete amount of discretion granted to the Minister of Justice and, in return to the Advocate General's reasoning, the impact on concerned individuals in 'that they cannot give rise to reasonable doubts, [...] as to the imperviousness of the judges concerned to external factors and as to their neutrality with respect to the interests before them' that lead the Court to find its yardstick infringed.[137] Among other things, the Court noted that the new system might actually have been intended to enable the Minister for Justice, acting at his discretion, to remove, once the newly set normal retirement age was reached, certain groups of judges serving in the ordinary Polish courts while retaining others of those judges at their post.[138] This reference to the context of the 'reform' of the judiciary spikes Poland's guns by contradicting the claim that nothing special is happening in Poland, at least nothing that would differ Poland from other EU Member States.

---

[133]On the usefulness of the concept of systemic deficiency see recently von Bogdandy and Spieker (2019), p. 425.

[134]Namely Poland has argued that the pension schemes at issue are covered by Council Directive 79/7/EEC of 19 December 1978 on the progressive implementation of the principle of equal treatment for men and women in matters of social security (OJ 1979 L 6, p. 24). CJEU, Case C-192/18 *Commission v. Poland*, para. 52, *supra* note 13.

[135]Id., paras. 66, 73 and 84.

[136]Id., paras. 98–107.

[137]Id., para. 126.

[138]Id., para. 12.

3 Context of the Judgments: The Commission Communications of April and July 2019

The two cases, of which we have offered summaries and close readings above, have not yet settled the rule of law crisis, here in its manifestation in Poland. But they have catapulted the doctrinal understanding of the Court forward on essential points that far exceed the crisis. This is something which many observers, us included, had been advocating for. Both cases have furthered the understanding of the protection of Member States under the infringement action, now fully established in parallel to Article 7 TEU. And they have contributing to the understanding of the overlapping and interaction of Article 19(1)(2) TEU, Article 47 of the Charter, and in particular their relation to Article 2 TEU, now termed a 'constitutional passerelle'.

Both cases, as we said in the beginning, do not stand in isolation. On 19 November 2019, barely two weeks after having decided in the infringement proceedings related to Poland's ordinary judiciary, the Court decided the case of a preliminary reference by the Polish Supreme Court, again concerning the new amendments and flanking the cases portrayed here.[139] The Court, while leaving the final assessment to the referring court, also determined a yardstick for the Polish courts to ascertain whether the new 'Disciplinary Chamber' set up within the Supreme Court, could be deemed independent.[140] It will, in the near future, have to return to this point within the scope set specifically also by the Commission.[141]

We leave this case, since it did not arise from Commission infringement actions, to separate assessment and would rather like to use the remaining space to draw the reader's attention to further Commission measures flanking its own initiatives. They are relevant here because they illustrate, from a perspective that does not solely focus on the Court, that the Commission pursues an integral strategy in dealing with the rule of law crisis, both before and outside the Court of Justice and that it has overcome an ad-hoc use of the infringement procedure in favour of a strategic approach.

Such material is found in particular in two communications of the Commission of April and July 2019. With the first communication,[142] the Commission provides readers with an overarching, analytical, and college-approved document, in which a 'rule of law crisis' is explicitly acknowledged for the first time since the beginning of that crisis. The communication also serves the Commission to take stock of its own actions and suggests that its different steps—such as the reasoned opinion under Art.

---

[139]CJEU, Joined Cases C-585/18, C-624/18 and C-625/18, *A.K. (Indépendance de la chambre disciplinaire de la Cour suprême)*, *supra* note 9.

[140]Id., paras. 131–153, *supra* note 18.

[141]CJEU, Case C-791/19, *Commission v Poland*, Action of 25 October 2019, O.J. (EU) C 413/36 of 9.12.2019.

[142]Communication from the Commission to the European Parliament, the European Council and the Council, Further strengthening the Rule of Law within the Union: State of play and possible next steps, COM(2019) 163 final of 3.4.2019.

7 TEU, its infringement actions, as well as various other measures—form part of a coherent legal regime, a 'rule of law toolbox'.[143] In the literature, we observe, a more doctrinal concept that is explored elsewhere, that of a nascent 'constitutional supervision' serves a similar purpose of combining these different measures into a logical whole.[144]

The Commission also introduces the concept of 'rule of law-related infringement actions',[145] reminiscent of the earlier concept of 'values-related infringement actions', for which the Commission submitted to the Council background information in particular on Hungary in late 2018.[146] To us, it is evident that the cases analysed above constitute prime examples of this category of infringement proceedings.

At the end of the communication of April 2019, the Commission issued, in a remarkable move, a call for stakeholders and interested parties of various backgrounds to provide it with contributions on 'three pillars for future action – promotion, prevention and response'. It received around 60 replies to this call, including non-papers from several Member States' governments and in part other public bodies, from Poland and Hungary included, which have been made publicly available.[147] While it is difficult to summarise them here, a recurrent topic, alongside the Commission's suggested structure, is the way forward by means of supplementing additional measures. Some suggestions have dwelled in particular on infringement proceedings. Sweden and France e.g. both suggested to boost the reactivity of the Court within the procedure by further developing notably the expedited procedure and interim measures.[148] Other interesting suggestions abound. Germany reiterated, alongside Belgium, its desire to install a proposed 'periodic peer review' mechanism

---

[143]Id., p. 3 et seq.

[144]Briefly Schmidt and Bogdanowicz (2018), p. 1071; for earlier mentioning, Zuleeg (2000), pp. 2846–2851, p. 2850 (for the Art. 7 TEU procedure) and Giegerich (2015), p. 520. Cf. further: Matthias Schmidt, Verfassungsaufsicht in der Europäischen Union, forthcoming.

[145]European Commission, State of play Communication, p. 3 et seq., *supra* note 142.

[146]Council of the European Union, 'Commission non-paper providing factual information on the values-related infringement proceedings in relation to Hungary', Document No. 14022/18 of 8 November 2018, made publicly available via: https://www.asktheeu.org/en/request/6115/response/19716/attach/6/st14022.en18.pdf.

[147]Cf. https://ec.europa.eu/info/publications/stakeholder-contributions_en.

[148]Swedish input to the European Commission Communication on Further strengthening of the Rule of Law within the Union (COM(2019) 163 final), p. 2 (no page nos.); Communication de la Commission du 3 avril 2019 sur l'État de droit. Non-papier de la France, p. 6.

for the rule of law in the Council,[149] and France suggested to 'codify' (i.e. possibly transfer into primary law) the Rule of Law Framework of the Commission.[150]

The Commission reacted by a second communication of July 2019, in which it introduces the idea of a 'blueprint for action'[151] and structures the different procedures of what it had previously identified as a toolbox into a multi-procedural and multi-actor scheme, consisting of a preventive and a reactive arm, and announcing both its own actions as well as seeking the support of other actors. The preventive arm, and a novelty, to be set apart notably from procedures in the Council, is the idea of a 'rule of law review cycle',[152] that is in part reminiscent of the background analysis already carried out during the Rule of Law Framework. The reactive arm is in particular an explicitly more 'strategic use' of the infringement procedure.[153] How this might look is still to be developed but in previous communications, such as in 2016, the Commission has provided some material.[154]

As regards the substance of such more strategic action, the Commission appears focussed notably on the Union's budget and financial interests, which is why here it may be engaged, as it was in the summer of 2017 when it first brought up the yardstick of Article 19(1) TEU in conjunction with Article 47 of the Charter, in another attempt to further operationalise Union values. In its Toolbox Communication, the Commission states that '[t]he Commission will further build on the recent case law of the Court, for example in relation to the independence of national courts *and to the effective protection of financial interests of the Union*'.[155] This links to the Commission's regulation proposal in relation to generalised deficiencies in the rule

[149] Input of the Federal Government regarding the Communication from the Commission to the European Parliament, the European Council and the Council 'Further strengthening the Rule of Law within the Union – State of play and possible next steps' of 3 April 2019, p. 3 (no page nos.), 'Communication of the European Commission of the 3rd of April 2019 "Further strengthening the Rule of Law within the Union – State of play and possible steps" – Belgian elements', p. 2 (no page nos.). See also 'Discours du Ministre D. Reynders lors de la 5ème Conférence belgo-allemand [sic] (Debeko), axée cette année sur les thèmes de la digitalisation, l'énergie et le transport', of 18 March 2019, p. 5, available at: https://diplomatie.belgium.be/sites/default/files/downloads/discours_debeko_20190318.pdf; 'Opening speech by Minister of State for Europe Michael Roth at the Peer-Review-Workshop on Rule of Law', of 7 November 2018, available at: https://www.auswaertiges-amt.de/en/newsroom/news/-/2158210.

[150] Communication de la Commission du 3 avril 2019 sur l'État de droit. Non-papier de la France, p. 6.

[151] European Commission, Communication from the Commission to the European Parliament, the European Council, the Council, the European Economic and Social Committee and the Committee of the Regions, Strengthening the rule of law within the Union: A blueprint for action of 17 July 2019, COM(2019) 343 final.

[152] Id., p. 9 et seq.

[153] Id., p. 14 and 16.

[154] Communication from the Commission, C/2016/8600, OJ C 18 of 19 January 2017, p. 14.

[155] European Commission, State of play Communication, p. 13, emphasis added, *supra* note 142.

of law and the protection of the EU budget, as well as a new 'Commission Anti-Fraud Strategy' (CAFS).[156]

In its 'Blueprint Communication', the Commission moreover included, as an 'obiter dictum', a sentence that may be the start of a distinct policy development or, not unlike before as regards Article 19 (1) TEU and Article 47 of the Charter, another operationalisation attempt of an underlying value:

> There is also an evolving jurisprudence of the Court highlighting how systematic problems related to the rule of law may have a specific impact in the area of Union finances.[157]

The Commission relies here on Article 325 TFEU,[158] under which the Union has developed its comprehensive policy for the protection of financial interests. This provision is already creating scholarly interest. It has e.g. recently been suggested that Article 310 (6), read together with Article 325 TFEU, could provide a legal basis for further Commission action.[159] If so, this also could be the start of further action before the Court in appropriate cases.

The preventive arm of the new blueprint, the 'rule of law review cycle', including an announced 'Annual Rule of Law Report', also surely deserves further elaboration. The Commission ought to make concrete, in particular, how such a report feeds into decisions before the Council or the Court, in order to have added value. In short, any report must provide sharp and notably original analysis and clear recommendations, to which the Commission should feel encouraged.[160] For such purposes, a 'Rule of Law Report', must also clearly set apart systemic deficiencies, creating spill-over effects on European level, from discrepancies or reform processes of judicial systems in Member States of varying kind and severity but to be left to their own

---

[156]Id. It is to be noted, though, that the CAFS in its current form, Communication from the Commission to the European Parliament, the Council, the European Economic and Social Committee, the Committee of the Regions and the Court of Auditors: 'Commission Anti-Fraud Strategy: enhanced action to protect the EU budget', COM(2019) 196 final of 29.04.2019, lacks such a link.

[157]European Commission, Blueprint Communication, p. 13, *supra* note 151.

[158]Id., p. 13, at footnote 46.

[159]Brauneck (2019), in particular pp. 57–59.

[160]Looking for guidance outside the European Union, we suggest that the United States Department of State's annual 'Country Reports on Human Rights Practices', even though created with a different angle, might offer an example. They are available under: https://www.state.gov/reports-bureau-of-democracy-human-rights-and-labor/country-reports-on-human-rights-practices/ for almost all countries worldwide and regular used by U.S. decision-makers.

resolve. Germany,[161] France[162] and Spain[163] provide recent examples of such non-systemic controversies.[164]

4 Conclusions

This article has offered a close reading of two recent Court of Justice judgments regarding the EU's rule of law crisis in its manifestation in particular in Poland.

In the previous section, the purpose of looking at two recent Commission communications rather than other recent case law was to contextualise the use of the infringement procedure by the Commission, and to 'feel its pulse' where it may take the procedure in the near future. The material here proves that Commission and Court are now fully engaged in effectively using the infringement procedure for the defence of the rule of law, being, as aptly put by *Emmanuel Crabit* and *Anna Perego*, the 'guarantee of guarantees'[165] in EU constitutional law. This is also what we had advocated for previously.

In particular the case concerning the independence of the Polish Supreme Court can be considered a landmark decision. The case presented the Court with the opportunity to decide, for the first time within the context of an infringement action under Article 258 TFEU, on the compatibility of national measures concerning the organisation of its judicial system with the standards set down in EU law to ensure the respect for the rule of law in the Union's legal order. For the very first time, the Court has found a Member State to have failed in its obligations under Art. 19(1)

---

[161] See CJEU, Joined Cases C-508/18 and C-82/19 PPU, *OG and PI (Public Prosecutor's Office of Lübeck),* Judgment of 27 May 2019, ECLI:EU:C:2019:456, concerning in essence a pre-constitutional and dormant interference power of the Ministers of Justice of the Federation and the Länder with their respective prosecution services, for a comment see Graf von Luckner (2019). For the reaction of the German federal legislature, see now in particular the draft act on the amendment of the Act on International Mutual Assistance in Criminal Matters, Bundesrat-Drucksache 195/20 of 24 April 2020, p. 15. *Mutatis mutandis* for Lithuania see Case C-509/18, *PF (Procureur général de Lituanie),* Judgment of 27 May 2019, ECLI:EU:C:2019:457.

[162] See Loi n° 2019-222 du 23 mars 2019 de programmation 2018-2022 et de réforme pour la justice, not yet in effect, and the French government's information website: https://www.gouvernement.fr/action/reforme-de-la-justice; for the fierce domestic debate on this reform see e.g. Jean-Baptise Jacquin, 'Menace de blocage à l'heure de la rentrée judiciaire', Le Monde of 14 January 2019.

[163] GRECO evaluation regarding, among other things, the Spanish Council for the Judiciary, see the press report 'El Consejo de Europa avala las reformas emprendidas por España contra la corrupción en la justicia y el ámbito parlamentario', available at https://elderecho.com/consejo-europa-avala-las-reformas-emprendidas-espana-la-corrupcion-la-justicia-ambito-parlamentario.

[164] This article could not take into account the extensive novelties and analyses provided by the European Commission in its 2020 Rule of Law Reports for all Member States, now available under https://ec.europa.eu/info/publications/2020-rule-law-report-communication-and-countrychapters_en.

[165] Crabit and Perego (2019), p. 7.

(2) TEU. Contrary to submissions of the Polish and Hungarian government, the Court has confirmed that it has the competence to address issues of the internal organisation of a Member State's judiciary. While the cases can only close a chapter in the development of the crisis, that chapter can at least end with a more positive outlook than before.

Acknowledgments We would like to thank Armin von Bogdandy for his advice and Juliane Dieroff for comments. The usual disclaimer applies.

References (Primary Sources, Links and Jurisprudence Omitted)

Brauneck J (2019) Gefährdung des EU-Haushalts durch rechtsstaatliche Mängel in den Mitgliedstaaten? Europarecht 53:37–61

Castillo de la Torre F (2007) interim measures in community courts: recent trends. Common Market Law Rev 44:273–353, 808 ff

Crabit E, Bel N (2016) The EU rule of law framework. In: Schroeder W (ed) Strengthening the rule of law in Europe: from a common concept to mechanisms of implementation. Hart, Oxford, pp 197–206

Crabit E, Perego A (2019) L'État de droit: une politique de l'Union européenne. Revue du Droit de l'Union européenne 20:7–14

de la Serre EB (2006) Accelerated and expedited procedures before the EC Courts: a review of its practice. Common Market Law Rev 43:783–815

Editorial Comments (2019) Common Market Law Rev 56:3–22

Giegerich T (2015) Verfassungshomogenität, Verfassungsautonomie und Verfassungsaufsicht in der EU: Zum 'neuen Rechtsstaatsmechanismus' der Europäischen Kommission. In: Calliess C (ed) Herausforderungen an Staat und Verfassung: Völkerrecht – Europarecht – Menschenrechte: Liber Amicorum für Torsten Stein zum 70. Geburtstag. Nomos, Baden-Baden, pp 499–542

Glawe RAP (2012) Das System des einstweiligen Rechtsschutzes in der Praxis von EuGH und EuG. Wirtschaftsrechtliche Blätter 676–683:681–682

Graf von Luckner J (2019) German Prosecutors are insufficiently independent to issue European arrest warrants. European Law Blog 11.06.2019. https://europeanlawblog.eu/2019/06/11/german-prosecutors-are-insufficiently-independent-to-issue-european-arrest-warrants/

Jaeger M (2013) Eilverfahren vor dem Gericht der Europäischen Union. Europarecht 48:3–28, 26

Jakab A, Kochenov D (eds) (2017) The enforcement of EU law and values: ensuring member states' compliance. Oxford University Press, Oxford

Sadurski W (2019) Poland's constitutional breakdown. Oxford University Press, Oxford

Scheppele KL (2016) Enforcing the basic principles of EU law through systemic infringement actions. In: Carlos C, Kochenov D (eds) Reinforcing rule of law oversight in the European Union. Cambridge University Press, Cambridge, pp 105–132

Schmidt M, Bogdanowicz P (2018) The infringement procedure in the rule of law crisis: how to make effective use of Article 258 TFEU. Common Market Law Rev 55:1061–1100

Schroeder W (ed) (2016) Strengthening the rule of law in Europe: from a common concept to mechanisms of implementation. Hart, Oxford

Sladič J (2008) Einstweiliger Rechtsschutz im Gemeinschaftsprozessrecht: Eine Untersuchung des EG/EU-Prozessrechts. Nomos, Baden-Baden

Taborowski M (2019) Mechanizmy ochrony praworządności państw członkowskich w prawie Unii Europejskiej. Studium przebudzenia systemu ponadnarodowego. Wolters Kluwer, Warsaw, pp 103–140

von Bogdandy A (2019) Principles and challenges of a European doctrine of systemic deficiencies. In: MPIL research paper series 14

von Bogdandy A, Ioannidis M (2014) Systemic deficiency in the rule of law: what it is, what has been done, what can be done. Common Market Law Rev 51:59–96

von Bogdandy A, Spieker LD (2019) Countering the judicial silencing of critics: Article 2 TEU values, reverse solange, and the responsibilities of national judges. Eur Const Law Rev 15:391–426

von Bogdandy A, Bogdanowicz P, Canor I, Taborowski M, Schmidt M (2018) Guest editorial: a potential constitutional moment for the European rule of law – the importance of red lines. Common Market Law Rev 55:983–996

Wennerås P (2019) Saving a forest and the rule of law: Commission v. Poland Case C-441/17 R, Commission v. Poland, Order of the Court (Grand Chamber) of 20 November 2017, EU: C:2017:877. Common Market Law Rev 56:541–558

Wyrzykowski M (2019) Experiencing the unimaginable: the collapse of the rule of law in Poland. Hague J Rule of Law 11:417–418

Zuleeg M (2000) Die föderativen Grundsätze der Europäischen Union. Neue Juristische Wochenschrift 55:2846–2851

Matthias Schmidt is a research fellow at the Max Planck Institute for Comparative Public Law and International Law, Heidelberg.

Piotr Bogdanowicz is an associate professor at the Faculty of Law and Administration of the University of Warsaw.

Defending Union Values in Judicial Proceedings. On How to Turn Article 2 TEU into a Judicially Applicable Provision

Luke Dimitrios Spieker

Contents

Abstract This chapter centres on the question of how to address violations of EU values in judicial proceedings before the Court of Justice. Instead of relying on fundamental freedoms, EU secondary legislation or the Charter, this chapter explores a more promising path—engaging with Article 2 TEU itself. Yet this path rests on a crucial premise: the judicial applicability of the values enshrined in Article 2 TEU. Such a judicial applicability is far from self-evident and needs to be carefully construed. Based on recent jurisprudential developments, this chapter will propose ways to operationalise Article 2 TEU without curtailing its unrestricted scope of application. The judgments of *Associação Sindical dos Juízes Portugueses*,

This chapter draws on Spieker (2019a) and von Bogdandy and Spieker (2019).

L. D. Spieker (✉)
Max Planck Institute for Comparative Public Law and International Law, Heidelberg, Germany
e-mail: spieker@mpil.de

A. von Bogdandy et al. (eds.), *Defending Checks and Balances in EU Member States*, Beiträge zum ausländischen öffentlichen Recht und Völkerrecht 298,
https://doi.org/10.1007/978-3-662-62317-6_10

Minister for Justice and Equality (*L.M.*) and *Commission v. Poland* will be at the heart of this contribution.

1 Introduction

As evidenced by many contributions in this volume,[1] the developments in several EU Member States have consolidated to a larger illiberal turn posing a systemic threat to the values enshrined in Article 2 TEU. Especially the governing parties in Poland and Hungary started rejecting the model of a liberal democracy and attacking checks and balances of the political process. Much has been written on *whether* the Union should act[2] and if so, how to *institutionally* and *procedurally* address these issues.[3] Yet one thing seems almost certain: any path requiring unanimity in the Council (Article 7 TEU) or a Treaty change[4] seems to be a political pipe dream. Since backsliding Member States will be watching each other's backs, these paths are barred.[5]

This political petrification reminds a well-known pattern of European integration: In times, when the necessary actions were not pursued in the realm of politics, the CJEU stepped in as an 'engine of integration' to safeguard the European integration agenda.[6] In the late 1960s, it was the Court that compensated the political stagnation with its constitutionalizing jurisprudence.[7] In the face of a growing legitimacy deficit on the Community level, it was the Court that developed fundamental rights as general principles.[8] And when facing the political inertia in constructing the internal market, it was the Court that stepped in with its doctrine of mutual recognition.[9]

[1]See e.g. the contributions of Beata Bakó and Marcin Wiącek in this volume.

[2]On the EU's mandate and legitimacy to intervene, see von Bogdandy (2020), pp. 711–715; Maduro and Menezes Queiroz (2020), pp. 370–371; Iliopoulou-Penot (2019); Hillion (2016), pp. 60–64; Closa (2016), pp. 15–22. Critically with regard to the Union's own democracy and justice deficits, see among many others Weiler (2016a).

[3]For a comprehensive assessment, see the individual contributions to Jakab and Kochenov (2017), Closa and Kochenov (2016a) and Schroeder (2016a). See further Möllers and Schneider (2018), Skouris (2018), Waelbroeck and Oliver (2017), Pech et al. (2016) and Schorkopf (2016).

[4]For an amendment of Art. 7 TEU or 51(1) CFR, see e.g. Reding (2013).

[5]See e.g. Orbán (2017): 'a campaign of inquisition against Poland will never succeed, because Hungary will resort to all the legal mechanisms offered by the European Union in order to show its solidarity with the Polish people.'

[6]Lenaerts (1992), pp. 2, 10 et seq. See already Pescatore (1974), p. 89; Lecourt (1976), pp. 306 et seq. Critically, Rasmussen (1986), p. 61.

[7]CJEU, Case C-26/62 *Van Gend en Loos*, ECLI:EU:C:1963:1; Case C-6/64 *Costa/E.N.E.L.*, ECLI: EU:C:1964:66; Mancini (1989), p. 612.

[8]CJEU, Case C-29/69 *Stauder*, ECLI:EU:C:1969:57, para. 7; Case C-11/70 *Internationale Handelsgesellschaft*, ECLI:EU:C:1970:114, para. 4; de Búrca (2011), pp. 475 et seq.

[9]CJEU, Case C-120/78 *Rewe*, ECLI:EU:C:1979:42; Pescatore (2008).

When it comes to countering the illiberal turn in several Member States, a similar inertia seems to beset the political plane and especially the Council as the key decision maker under the Article 7 TEU procedure. Therefore, many argued to concentrate on judicial mechanisms, to employ the infringement procedure under Article 258 TFEU[10] or to interact with brave national courts via the preliminary reference procedure (Article 267 TFEU).[11]

Although it might place an immense burden on the Court's legitimacy,[12] there are solid arguments for involving the Court of Justice. First, the appearance of legality is crucial for governments in backsliding Member States.[13] Since the CJEU enjoys considerable trust from both national courts and the public,[14] an authoritative judgment declaring the attacks on domestic checks and balances illegal would constitute a severe set-back. Further, any non-compliance with these judgments would not only damage the façade of legality but lead to a new stage of escalation.[15] Second, governments in backsliding Member States try to shift the debate on their value-compliance into the sphere of moral and ideological convictions. Such conflicts can easily turn heated and trigger antagonism or polarisation.[16] Judicial procedures may help shifting the discourse to *legal* principles and thus into more rational channels. Third, a frequent objection of backsliding Member States is that the European Commission is ideologically biased seeking to force its own conception of the Union's common values on the Member States.[17] Being a court, the CJEU might seem more neutral than the 'politicized' Commission. As some observed in the context of the Euro-crisis, procedures before the Court have the potential to depoliticize conflicts and unfold an integrating potential.[18] Finally, the political Article 7 TEU procedure reveals severe shortcomings with regard to procedural

---

[10]See e.g. Schmidt and Bogdanowicz (2018), pp. 1073–1080; Scheppele (2016). Critically, see Kochenov and Bárd (2019), pp. 264 et seq.

[11]See e.g. Blauberger and Kelemen (2017), pp. 325–326. See already von Bogdandy et al. (2012).

[12]Möllers and Schneider (2018), pp. 107, 147; Blauberger and Kelemen (2017), p. 331.

[13]See e.g. Jakab (2020), pp. 12 et seq. See further Scheppele (2018), Bernatt and Ziółkowski (2018) and Landau (2013).

[14]In 2012, the CJEU was 'the only European institution that is trusted by a majority', see European Commission, Standard Eurobarometer 78 (Autumn 2012), p. 73 (after 2012, the Eurobarometer does not include data specifically on trust in the CJEU anymore). On the trust of national judges in the CJEU, see Mayoral (2016).

[15]On the general Member State compliance with CJEU decisions and the very limited number of Article 260(2) TFEU procedures, see e.g. European Commission, Monitoring the Application of Union Law, 2018 Annual Report, Part I: General statistical overview, p. 22. Critically with regard to the reliability of this data, see e.g. Falkner (2018).

[16]See von Bogdandy's contribution in this volume.

[17]See e.g. Press Release, 'They want to make Soros's man the President of the Commission' (2 July 2019), www.miniszterelnok.hu/they-want-to-make-soross-man-the-president-of-the-commission/. See also Mendelski (2016).

[18]Krenn and Farahat (2018). Cautious, see Everling (2015). On the depoliticising potential of court proceedings more generally, see Sunstein (1999), pp. 24 et seq.; Möllers (2013), pp. 92 et seq., 96 et seq. as well as Easton (1965), pp. 262, 264; Luhmann (1989), pp. 121 et seq.

guarantees.[19] As emphasised by Armin von Bogdandy, however, the fairness of European responses is of essence.[20] Such fairness is assured in CJEU procedures by granting the defendant Member State a full set of procedural rights and guarantees.

So far, jurisprudential solutions seem to have proven successful, as the Polish example demonstrates. Many Polish courts submitted references concerning the Polish reforms curtailing the judiciary.[21] Further, the Commission successfully launched several infringement procedures.[22] Already after the Court ordered interim measures,[23] the Polish government reversed some parts of its reforms.[24] This shows that even governments in backsliding Member States remain responsive to CJEU decisions.

This leads to the following question, which will be at the heart of this chapter: What happens when a case, in which Union values are at stake, reaches the CJEU? What substantive provisions can be invoked? The preliminary problem is that important parts of the Polish or Hungarian reforms seem to escape the scope of EU law. As such, provisions of the EU *acquis*, like fundamental freedoms or

---

[19]See e.g. Niedobitek (2018), p. 241.

[20]See von Bogdandy's contribution in this volume.

[21]See e.g. *A. K. (Indépendance de la chambre disciplinaire de la Cour suprême)* (Joined Cases C-585/18, C-624/18 and C-625/18) and *Miasto Łowicz* (Joined Cases C-558/18 and C-563/18). See also the references by the Polish Supreme Court in *W.Ż.* (Case C-487/19), *Prokurator Generalny* (Case C-508/19) and *Getin Noble Bank* (Case C-132/20), by district courts in *Prokuratura Rejonowa w Słubicach* (Case C-623/18) and *Prokuratura Rejonowa w Mińsku Mazowieckim* (Joined Cases C-748/19 to C-754/19), by the Polish Supreme Administrative Court in *A.B. u.a. (Nomination des juges à la Cour suprême—Recours)* (Case C-824/18) and by the Disciplinary Court of the Bar Association (Warsaw) in *Ministerstwo Sprawiedliwości* (Case C-55/20). See further the preliminary references concerning judicial independence by a Hungarian Court in *IS* (Case C-564/19) and by Romanian courts in *Asociația "Forumul Judecătorilor Din România"* (Joined Cases C-83/19, C-127/19 and C-195/19), *SO* (Case C-291/19), *Asociația "Forumul Judecătorilor din România"* (Case C-355/19), *DNA- Serviciul Teritorial Oradea* (Case C-379/19), *Statul Român—Ministerul Finanțelor Publice* (Case C-397/19), *Asociația "Forumul Judecătorilor din România"* (Case C-547/19), *Ministerul Public* (Case C-811/19). Finally, there are references from a German Court in *Land Hessen* (Case C-272/19) and a Maltese court in *Repubblika* (Case C-896/19).

[22]See CJEU, Case C-619/18 *Commission v. Poland (Indépendance de la Cour suprême)*, ECLI:EU:C:2019:531; Case C-192/18 *Commission v. Poland (Indépendance des juridictions de droit commun)*, ECLI:EU:C:2019:924. Another procedure has been initiated against the disciplinary regime for judges, see *Commission v. Poland*, Case C-791/19. Further, infringement proceedings were successfully initiated against the Hungarian foreign-NGO and higher-education laws, see CJEU, Case C-66/18 *Commission v. Hungary (Enseignement supérieur)*, ECLI:EU:C:2020:792; Case C-78/18 *Commission v. Hungary (Transparency of associations)*, ECLI:EU:C:2020:476.

[23]CJEU, Order of 19 October 2018 (ECLI:EU:C:2018:852) and 17 December 2018 (ECLI:EU:C:2018:1021) in *Commission v. Poland (Indépendance de la Cour suprême)*, *supra* note 22.

[24]On 21 November 2018 the Polish Sejm passed an act reinstating the previous retirement age for judges, see the Press Release (17 December 2018), see www.president.pl/en/news/art,926,president-signs-bill-amending-law-on-supreme-court.html.

secondary legislation, cannot capture these measures.[25] And even if some developments might fall within the scope of these provisions, the infringement procedures against Hungary illustrate that relying on them can lead to superficial, eventually unsuccessful results.[26] The scope of the Charter of Fundamental Rights (CFR) is equally limited. On one hand, the Charter's applicability to Member State actions is limited to 'situations ... within the scope of European Union law'.[27] This excludes purely internal situations, areas of not actually exercised EU competences[28] and purely hypothetical links.[29] On the other hand, threats to democracy and the rule of law are not always depictable as fundamental rights violations. Though being essentially interrelated,[30] democracy and the rule of law go beyond the protection of fundamental rights and include structural or institutional elements that affect the organization of State.[31] So what is the alternative?

Taking up the latest jurisprudential developments, this chapter explores a more promising path: relying on Article 2 TEU itself. That provision states at a prominent position: 'The Union is founded on the values of respect for human dignity, freedom, democracy, equality, the rule of law and respect for human rights ... These values are common to the Member States ...'. Article 2 TEU presents two features qualifying it especially for countering the illiberal tendencies in EU Member States. First, it has an unrestricted scope of application—it applies to *any* Member State act irrespective of *any* link to (other) EU law.[32] Second, it is not confined to ensuring

---

[25]For examples of how these developments can still be addressed under fundamental freedoms and secondary legislation, see the grounds on which the Commission based its infringement procedures against Hungary, *supra* note 22. For a further discussion of this path, see e.g. Dawson and Muir (2013).

[26]CJEU, Case C-286/12 *Commission v. Hungary*, ECLI:EU:C:2012:687. See further Halmai (2017).

[27]CJEU, Case C-617/10 *Åkerberg Fransson*, ECLI:EU:C:2013:105, paras. 18 et seq. For attempts to systematise the post-*Fransson* case law, see e.g. Lazzerini (2018), pp. 183 et seq.; Safjan et al. (2016); Spaventa (2016). Many argue that the Charter's scope can only be triggered by a specific provision of EU law actually applying in the case at hand, see e.g. Borowsky (2014), para. 30b; Safjan (2014), pp. 4 et seq.; Sarmiento (2013), p. 1279; Ladenburger (2012), p. 163; Rosas (2012), p. 1284.

[28]CJEU, Case C-370/12 *Pringle*, ECLI:EU:C:2012:756, paras. 180–181; Case C-198/13 *Hernández*, ECLI:EU:C:2014:2055, para. 36.

[29]CJEU, Case C-299/95 *Kremzow*, ECLI:EU:C:1997:254, para. 16; Case C-40/11 *Iida*, ECLI:EU:C:2012:691, para. 77.

[30]Habermas (2005). See further Carrera et al. (2013), p. 30.

[31]EU Fundamental Rights Agency (2014), p. 10.

[32]See in rare agreement European Commission, A new EU Framework to strengthen the Rule of Law, COM(2014) 158, p. 5 and Council of the European Union, Opinion of the Legal Service: Commission's Communication on a new EU Framework to strengthen the Rule of Law: compatibility with the Treaties, 10296/14, para. 17. See further European Commission, Communication on Art. 7 of the Treaty on European Union (15 October 2003), COM(2003) 606 final, p. 5; European Convention, Praesidium: Presentation of an initial draft set of Articles of Part I of the Constitutional Treaty, CONV 528/03, p. 11; Klamert and Kochenov (2019), p. 25; Hilf and Schorkopf (2020), para. 18; Calliess (2016), para. 10.

'respect for human rights', but also threats to democracy and the rule of law in their structural, institutional dimension.

Yet this path rests on a central premise: the judicial applicability of the values enshrined in Article 2 TEU. This applicability, however, is far from self-evident and needs to be carefully construed. While much has been written on the Union's common values,[33] their position in EU law and how they feature in the CJEU's jurisprudence,[34] there still remains a plethora of uncertainties. As such, this chapter will first address uncertainties related to the values' legal nature, their direct effect and the jurisdiction of the Court (Sect. 2). Based on the CJEU's recent jurisprudence, this contribution will then propose ways to operationalise Article 2 TEU without curtailing its unrestricted scope of application (Sect. 3). The judgments of *Associação Sindical dos Juízes Portugueses* (ASJP),[35] *Minister for Justice and Equality* (L.M.),[36] and *Commission v. Poland*[37] will be at the heart of this analysis. Placing an activated Article 2 TEU in the hands of Luxembourg will most certainly raise doubts and criticism. Therefore, this chapter will close by anticipating likely objections and advancing possible rejoinders (Sect. 4).

2 Uncertainties Surrounding the Judicial Application of Article 2 TEU

Before engaging with the most recent case law, it seems worthwhile to analyse the uncertainties and potential shortcomings that might prevent a judicial application of Article 2 TEU. These uncertainties can be narrowed down to three key points: Its nature (Sect. 2.1), direct effect (Sect. 2.2), and the jurisdiction of the CJEU (Sect. 2.3).

2.1 Nature: Do Article 2 TEU Values Have Any Legal Effect?

Scott Shapiro once wrote that 'there is often no way to resolve specific disagreements about *the* law without first resolving disagreements about the *nature* of law'.[38] This holds especially true for an overarching provision like Article 2 TEU. By using the term 'value', the Treaty drafters introduced a rather ambiguous notion into EU

[33]See among many others Schorkopf (2020), Levits (2018a), Voßkuhle (2017), Kochenov (2017a), Weiler (2016b), von Bogdandy (2010), Calliess (2009) and Williams (2009).

[34]See e.g. Rossi (2020), Cannizzaro (2018), Baratta (2018), Lenaerts (2017a) and Nicolosi (2015).

[35]CJEU, Case C-64/16 *Associação Sindical dos Juízes Portugueses*, ECLI:EU:C:2018:117.

[36]CJEU, Case C-216/18 PPU *Minister for Justice and Equality*, ECLI:EU:C:2018:586.

[37]CJEU, *Commission v. Poland (Indépendance de la Cour suprême)*, *supra* note 22.

[38]Shapiro (2011), p. 28.

primary law.[39] Values are widely used in very different contexts: law, politics, economics, philosophy, ethics, religion, sociology, psychology ... Values are very close to what Uwe Pörsken called 'plastic words'[40]—empty formulas that mean everything and nothing. As context-dependent shapeshifters, they can be used in different fields with different meanings.

In law, values are generally juxtaposed with 'principles' and 'rules',[41] and in the Treaties especially with 'competences' and 'objectives'.[42] Yet values somehow transcend these dichotomies without revealing their precise character. One might justifiably ask why the drafters burdened the Treaties with such a can of worms. Unfortunately, analysing the European Convention's *travaux* is of no further use. Although several members saw the uncertainties tied to values and suggested replacing them with principles,[43] the term remained in the draft without being grounded in a solid theory of what they were supposed to be.[44]

As such, it is not self-evident that Article 2 TEU values unfold legal effects. Some even doubt their status as *law*.[45] Such doubts, however, are hardly convincing. The values of Article 2 TEU are laid down in the operative part of a legal text. They are applied in legally determined procedures by public institutions (Article 7 and 49 (1) TEU) and their disregard leads to sanctions, which are of legal nature.[46] In fact,

---

[39]See already draft Art. I-2 of the Constitution of Europe. Before the Constitution, the term 'principles' was used, see Art. 6(1) TEU-Nice, Art. F(1) TEU-Maastricht. See however the reference to 'values' in the context of the Austria crisis, Martti Ahtisaari, Jochen Frowein and Marcelino Oreja, Report of 8 September 2000, paras. 115, 117 and of EU enlargement, see e.g. Declaration on European Identity (Copenhagen, Dec. 14, 1973), 1973 Bull. EC 12/118.

[40]See Pörsken (2004), pp. 22, 26 placing 'values' in one line with notions like 'identity' or 'substance'.

[41]On how to distinguish these categories, see e.g. Habermas (1996), pp. 255 et seq.; Alexy (2009), pp. 86 et seq.; Dworkin (2013), pp. 38 et seq. Critically with regard to these distinctions, see Jakab (2016), p. 368.

[42]See Larik (2014).

[43]European Convention, Praesidium: Reactions to draft Articles 1 to 16 of the Constitutional Treaty, CONV 574/1/03, REV 1, pp. 17 et seq. See e.g. the suggestions for amendment by Ernâni Lopes and Manuel Lobo Antunes: 'Human dignity, liberty ... are principles and not mere values. Only principles may be legally binding and its violation invoked before a Court'; suggestion for amendment by Meglena Kuneva: 'Il serait préférable de garder la notion de 'principes', bien connue du droit communautaire et qui est employée par l'article 6 du TUE.' See also Plenary Session: Debate on Draft Articles 1 to 16 (27–28 February 2003). The minutes are accessible here: www.europarl.europa.eu/Europe2004/textes/verbatim_030227.htm. See e.g. 4-018 – Einem (Parl.-AT): 'Herr Präsident! ... wir treten dafür ein, lieber von Grundsätzen – principles – statt von Werten – valeurs – zu sprechen' or 4-083 – Kutskova (Gouv.-BG): 'Concerning Article 2, we consider it preferable to keep the notion of principles typical of the acquis'.

[44]Hilf and Schorkopf (2020), para. 21; von Bogdandy (2010), p. 21.

[45]Such uncertainties are provoked first and foremost by the Commission itself, European Commission, Reasoned Proposal in Accordance with Article 7(1) of the Treaty on European Union Regarding the Rule of Law in Poland, COM (2017) 835 final, para. 1: 'The Commission, beyond [!] its task to ensure the respect of EU law, is also responsible ... for guaranteeing the common values of the Union' (emphasis added). See further Möllers and Schneider (2018), p. 125.

[46]Dumbrovsky (2018).

the legal framing of the Union's values seems almost inevitable. The rule of law warrants that normative requirements enforced by public institutions are laid down in the form of law. Otherwise, the mechanisms of Article 7 or Article 49 TEU would provide political morality with public authority without making it subject to any constitutional limitations.[47] For this reason, Article 2 TEU values are necessarily part of EU *law*.

Yet, the views on their exact nature differ considerably. First, Article 2 values can be understood as 'rules', as they form legal parameters relevant for both the sanctioning mechanism under Article 7 and the admission procedure under Article 49 TEU. Second, one could argue that values are in fact 'principles'.[48] Indeed, the Treaty drafters used both notions in a rather undifferentiated way.[49] Further, the 'values' enshrined in the first sentence of Article 2 TEU were termed 'principles' in Article 6(1) TEU-Nice/Amsterdam, which is generally understood as a predecessor of Article 2 TEU. Finally, one could perceive Article 2 TEU as a *new* form of legal category, which still has to be determined. Whatever the response to this question might be, one thing seems rather clear: Article 2 TEU does not only contain a set of rough ideals or solemn aspirations—it unfolds *legal* effects.

2.2 Direct Effect: Are Article 2 TEU Values Directly Applicable?

Nevertheless, the acknowledgment of legal effects does not necessarily entail Article 2 TEU's direct applicability (or even justiciability).[50] Indeed, the values—for example, the rule of law—are extremely vague and open.[51] Hence, it is not entirely clear whether Article 2 TEU fulfils the essential criteria for direct effect: A Treaty provision must be precise, clear, and unconditional.[52] While these rigid criteria have often been criticized,[53] recent jurisprudential developments indicate a more nuanced understanding of direct effect. Concerning the direct effect of Charter rights, the

---

[47] von Bogdandy (2020), p. 716.

[48] See e.g. von Bogdandy (2010), p. 22; Mangiameli (2012); Streinz (2018); Pérez de Nanclares (2019), p. 136.

[49] This becomes especially apparent in the preamble to the TEU. On one hand, the Treaty drafters draw 'inspiration from the . . . universal *values* of the inviolable and inalienable rights of the human person, freedom, democracy, equality and the rule of law' on the other hand, they confirm 'their attachment to the *principles* of liberty, democracy and respect for human rights . . . and of the rule of law'.

[50] Kochenov and Pech (2015), p. 520.

[51] On the need for a 'non-controversial' and thus deliberately open set of values, see European Convention, *supra* note 32, p. 11.

[52] See e.g. CJEU, Case C-176/12 *Association de médiation sociale*, ECLI:EU:C:2014:2, para. 36. Further Craig and de Búrca (2020), p. 223.

[53] See e.g. Wohlfahrt (2016) and Pescatore (1983).

Court started to distinguish between two categories:[54] first, 'mandatory effect', meaning that a provision is sufficient in itself to entail a right or obligation;[55] and second, the 'unconditional nature', meaning that a right does not need 'to be given concrete expression by the provisions of EU or national law'.[56]

According to this recent understanding, the application of Article 2 TEU faces three options. First, Article 2 TEU could be perceived as mandatory *and* unconditional and thus apply as a self-standing provision.[57] Second, Article 2 TEU could lack a mandatory effect but still be unconditional. In this case, Article 2 TEU could be considered by the CJEU or national courts through some sort of (non-binding?) value-oriented interpretation of EU and national law. A third option would be that Article 2 TEU is mandatory but not unconditional. It would need to be applied with a more specific provision giving concrete expression to the values enshrined in Article 2 TEU.[58] Such a combined approach could be construed in two ways: On one hand, Article 2 TEU could be applied directly but *informed* by a more specific provision. On the other hand, one could apply a specific provision of EU law *giving expression* to a value enshrined in Article 2 TEU and thus operationalizing the latter.

2.3 Jurisdiction: Does the Court Have Competence to Review the Member States' Value Compliance?

Even if we assume that Article 2 TEU has direct effect and creates directly applicable (and thus in principle justiciable) *obligations* for the Member States, it is not said that the CJEU has *jurisdiction* to assess and enforce Article 2 TEU compliance in the Member States. Generally, the Court's competence encompasses the interpretation and assessment of the 'law' (Article 19(1)(1) TEU). This includes Union law in all its shapes, forms, and manifestations.[59] In this light, it seems very likely that the

---

[54]See e.g. CJEU, Case C-684/16 *Max-Planck-Gesellschaft*, ECLI:EU:C:2018:874, para. 74; Case C-569/16 *Bauer*, ECLI:EU:C:2018:871, para. 85: 'Article 31(2) of the Charter, is thus, as regards its very existence, *both* mandatory *and* unconditional in nature' (emphasis added).

[55]CJEU, Case C-414/16 *Egenberger*, ECLI:EU:C:2018:257, paras. 76–77; Case C-193/17 *Cresco Investigation*, ECLI:EU:C:2019:43, para. 77.

[56]CJEU, *Max-Planck-Gesellschaft*, *supra* note 54, paras. 74, 78; *Bauer*, *supra* note 54, paras. 85, 89.

[57]For an approach relying directly on Art. 2 TEU yet specified i.a. via the Copenhagen Criteria, see Hillion (2016), pp. 66 et seq. This is further what the proposal of an 'systemic infringement action' boils down to, see Scheppele et al. (2020); Scheppele (2016); Skouris (2018), p. 50.

[58]For first sketches, see Cannizzaro (2018); Closa and Kochenov (2016b), pp. 182–184; Pech et al. (2016), p. 198.

[59]The CJEU has assessed recommendations (CJEU, Case C-322/88 *Grimaldi*, ECLI:EU:C:1989:646, paras. 7-8; Case C-16/16 P *Belgium v. Commission*, ECLI:EU:C:2018:79, para. 44), communications (CJEU, Case C-57/95 *France v. Commission*, ECLI:EU:C:1997:164, para. 23), guidelines (CJEU, C-233/02 *France v. Commission*, ECLI:EU:C:2004:173, para. 40), memoranda

Court has a competence to interpret and assess Article 2 TEU as well. Yet it is highly debated whether the Article 7 TEU procedure and the Court's limited competence to review the latter (Article 269 TFEU) bar an assessment and enforcement of Article 2 TEU values via the Article 258 or 267 TFEU procedures[60]—especially beyond the scope of application of (other) EU law.[61]

Nevertheless, there are good arguments in favour of the Court's jurisdiction. While the former Treaties have kept the EU's foundational principles out of the Court's reach,[62] the Lisbon Treaty does not contain any comparable limitation with regard to Article 2 TEU. First, Article 269 TFEU is an exception to the CJEU's general competence under Article 19(1)(1) TEU, which must be interpreted narrowly. Second, the political Article 7 TEU and the judicial Article 258/267 TFEU procedures have very different objects and consequences. Article 7 TEU concentrates on a political situation and entails, as a last resort, the suspension of Member States' rights. In contrast, the Court adjudicates an individual case and its sanctioning powers are limited to Article 260 TFEU (penalty payments).[63] For this reason, there seems to be no identity between the judicial and the political procedures that would afford exclusivity to the latter.

3 Turning Article 2 TEU into a Judicially Applicable Provision

In an emerging line of jurisprudence, the CJEU could be seen as resolving these uncertainties by developing Article 2 TEU into a judicially applicable provision justiciable before the Court. The *pierre fondatrice* of this emerging jurisprudence is the judgment in *Associação Sindical dos Juízes Portugueses* (*ASJP*). In this seminal case, the Court established the Member States' obligation to guarantee the judicial independence of virtually the whole national judiciary irrespective of any specific

(CJEU, Case C-258/14 *Florescu*, ECLI:EU:C:2017:448, para. 30) and even mere announcements (CJEU, Case C-62/14 *Gauweiler*, ECLI:EU:C:2015:400, para. 27).

[60]Arguing in favour of the Court's jurisdiction, see e.g. the Opinion of AG Tanchev in Case C-619/18, *Commission v. Poland (Indépendance de la Cour suprême)*, para. 50; Rossi (2020), pp. 655–666; Giegerich (2019), p. 80; Skouris (2018), pp. 50 et seq.; Schmidt and Bogdanowicz (2018), pp. 1069–1073; Franzius (2018), p. 386; Hilf and Schorkopf (2020), para. 46; Waelbroeck and Oliver (2017), p. 335; Hillion (2016), pp. 71–73; Scheppele (2016), p. 114. Arguing for a restriction, see Levits (2018a), p. 521; Martenczuk (2018), pp. 46 et seq.; Nicolosi (2015), p. 643.

[61]Against the Court's jurisdiction outside the scope of EU law, see Lenaerts and Gutiérrez-Fons (2017), p. 774.

[62]According to Art. 46(d) TEU-Nice the CJEU was only competent for what was then Art. 6(2) TEU-Nice but not for the 'principles' laid down in Art. 6(1) TEU-Nice. The CJEU nonetheless relied on them, see CJEU, Case C-402/05 P *Kadi*, ECLI:EU:C:2008:461, para. 303.

[63]This becomes most visible in *L.M.*, where the Court rejected to generally suspend the EAW Framework with regard to Poland, see CJEU, *Minister for Justice and Equality*, *supra* note 36, paras. 70 et seq.

link to EU law (Sect. 3.1). Although this stance can also be reconstrued as a manifestation of the well-established *effet utile* rationale (Sect. 3.2), I propose a reading relying on Article 2 TEU. According to my understanding, the Court opted for a combined approach, operationalising Article 2 TEU through a specific provision of EU law (here Article 19(1)(2) TEU). This operationalisation, it is argued, leads to a 'mutual amplification' of both provisions: While the specific provision of EU law translates Article 2 TEU into a judicially applicable legal obligation, the operationalized Article 2 TEU charges and eventually extends the scope of application of the specific provision. Such a reading kills two birds with one stone: it leads to the judicial application of Article 2 TEU without limiting its unrestricted scope. As such, it allows reviewing and sanctioning *any* Member State action violating the Union's common values in judicial proceedings before the CJEU—irrespective of any link to other EU law. Finally, this approach is not confined to Article 19 TEU but could be extended to any provision giving expression to a value enshrined in Article 2 TUE (Sect. 3.3).

3.1 The Groundbreaking Judgment in ASJP

On its face, *ASJP* seems like a rather innocent case. A Portuguese court asked the CJEU whether salary reductions for judges adopted in the context of an EU financial assistance program violated judicial independence. Generally, there are two Treaty provisions guaranteeing judicial independence: Article 47 CFR and Article 19(1)(2) TEU. The former only operates under the scope defined in Article 51(1) CFR. The salary reductions were part of spending cuts conditional for financial assistance under the EU financial crisis mechanisms. Since the Court already applied the Charter in comparable situations,[64] Advocate General Øe proposed to grasp this thin material link and rely on the CFR.[65] The CJEU could have followed this approach and *ASJP* would have disappeared discreetly as another clarification of the meandering post-*Åkerberg Fransson* case law. Yet, this is not what happened. The Court referred to Article 19(1)(2) TEU, which stipulates that 'Member States shall provide remedies sufficient to ensure effective legal protection in the fields covered by Union law.' Such effective legal protection presupposes an independent judiciary.[66]

According to the Court, this obligation applies '*irrespective* of whether the Member States are implementing Union law, within the meaning of Article 51(1).'[67] This is already indicated by the different wording of both provisions. Article 19(1)(2) TEU limits its scope to 'the fields covered by Union law', whereas the

[64]See e.g. CJEU, *Florescu*, *supra* note 59.

[65]Opinion of AG Saugmandsgaard Øe, Case C-64/16, paras. 43–53.

[66]CJEU, *Associação Sindical dos Juízes Portugueses*, *supra* note 35, para. 36.

[67]Id., para. 29 (emphasis added).

Charter applies to 'situations ... within the scope of European Union law'.[68] 'Fields' are different from 'situations'. According to this semantic difference, 'fields covered by Union law' could be understood in a more extensive manner.[69] But how broad should the scope of Article 19(1)(2) TEU be? The Court refers to the preliminary ruling mechanism under Article 267 TFEU: '[T]hat mechanism may be activated only by a body *responsible* for applying EU law which satisfies, *inter alia*, that criterion of independence'.[70] 'Responsible for applying EU law' includes all authorities which are *potentially* in the situation of applying it.[71] This means practically *every* Member State court.[72] For Article 19(1)(2) TEU to be triggered, it is not necessary that the respective Member State court *actually* adjudicates a matter of EU law in the specific case at hand; the mere *potentiality* of dealing with such matters suffices.

After the Court's stance in *ASJP*, Article 19(1)(2) TEU reaches even situations which do not present any other link to EU law. Accordingly, *ASJP* has been interpreted as establishing a 'quasi-federal standard'[73] for judicial independence. How does the Court justify this ample scope? A thorough analysis of *ASJP* reveals two (complementary) rationales, a *functional* and *axiological* one.[74] A similar reading has been advanced by Advocate General Tanchev in *Miasto Łowicz*. According to him, the ample scope is justified because

> Article 19 TEU is a concrete manifestation of the rule of law, one of the fundamental values on which the European Union is founded under Article 2 TEU, *and* Member States are bound under the second subparagraph of Article 19(1) TEU to 'provide remedies sufficient to ensure effective legal protection'. Structural breaches of judicial independence inevitably impact on the preliminary ruling mechanism under Article 267 TFEU and therefore on the capacity of Member State courts to act as EU Courts.[75]

In this sense, the CJEU's broad interpretation of Article 19(1)(2) TEU can be justified both by a recourse to the functioning of the EU's judicial system and the values enshrined in Article 2 TEU.

---

[68]CJEU, *Åkerberg Fransson*, *supra* note 27, para. 19. More recently, CJEU, Case C-117/14 *Nisttahuz Poclava*, ECLI:EU:C:2015:60, para. 29. But see *Egenberger* where the Court referred to Charter rights as applying 'in a field covered by EU law', *supra* note 55, para. 76. See also CJEU, Case C-68/17 *IR*, ECLI:EU:C:2018:696, para. 69.

[69]See for this interpretation Lenaerts (2019a); id. (2019b); Giegerich (2019), p. 76; von Danwitz (2018); Levits (2018b); Pech and Platon (2018), p. 1837; Miglio (2018), p. 426. On the problematic doctrinal implications of diverging scopes under Art. 19(1)(2) TEU and the Charter, see Spieker (2019b); Bonelli and Claes (2018), pp. 630–632.

[70]CJEU, *Associação Sindical dos Juízes Portugueses*, *supra* note 35, para. 43 (emphasis added).

[71]See also CJEU, *Commission v. Poland (Indépendance de la Cour suprême)*, *supra* note 22, para. 51; AG Tanchev in Case C-558/18, *Miasto Łowicz*, paras. 87–88, 94, 125.

[72]Similarly, von Danwitz (2018); Pech and Platon (2018), p. 1838; Bonelli and Claes (2018), p. 623.

[73]Pech and Platon (2018), p. 1847; Adam and Van Elsuwege (2018), p. 341.

[74]See also von Bogdandy and Spieker (2019), pp. 413 et seq.

[75]Opinion of AG Tanchev in Case C-558/18, *Miasto Łowicz*, para. 92 (emphasis added).

3.2 First Rationale: Securing the Functioning of the EU's Judicial System

At first sight, the CJEU seems to employ the well-established *effet utile* rationale. First, the Court refers to the functioning of the preliminary reference procedure in Article 267 TFEU. National courts have an indispensable position in the effective and uniform application of EU law.[76] As they are obliged to apply EU law in the respective Member States even where it may conflict with national law, they are considered to be the first 'Union courts'[77] and as such an arm of EU law.[78] Such a system cannot work if Member State courts are not independent. Not without reason, one of the key pre-conditions for a court to be eligible for launching preliminary references is its independence.[79] Second, the rationale behind Article 19(1)(2) TEU supports the Court's findings. Despite a limited extension of the demanding *locus standi* criteria for individual actions before the CJEU (see Article 263(4) TFEU),[80] the drafters of the Lisbon Treaty retained the decentralized judicial system based on both the CJEU and Member State courts.[81] The function of Article 19(1)(2) TEU is to ensure that this diffused judicial system works and that no protection gaps arise.[82] This necessarily enables the CJEU to specify and harmonize Member States' provisions regarding judicial remedies and procedures.[83] These two considerations seem to strongly indicate that the CJEU is relying on its well-known *effet utile*

---

[76]See e.g. CJEU, Case C-284/16 *Achmea*, ECLI:EU:C:2018:158, para. 36; Opinion 2/13 *Accession of the EU to the ECHR II*, para. 176; Opinion 1/09 *Agreement creating a Unified Patent Litigation System*, ECLI:EU:C:2011:123, paras. 84–85.

[77]See CJEU, Case C-106/77 *Simmenthal*, ECLI:EU:C:1978:49; Case C-294/83 *Les Verts v. Parliament*, ECLI:EU:C:1986:166; *Unified Patent Litigation System, supra* note 76, para. 80. See further Fennelly (2013).

[78]Lenaerts (2019b).

[79]For cases, in which the CJEU actually assessed the independence of the referring entity, see CJEU, Case C-203/14 *Consorci Sanitari del Maresme*, ECLI:EU:C:2015:664, para. 19; Case C-222/13 *TDC*, ECLI:EU:C:2014:2265, paras. 28–36; Joined Cases C-58/13 and C-59/13 *Torresi*, ECLI:EU:C:2014:2088, paras. 18–25; Case C-109/07 *Pilato*, ECLI:EU:C:2008:274, paras. 21–30; Case C-506/04 *Wilson*, ECLI:EU:C:2006:587, paras. 49 et seq.; Case C-53/03 *Syfait*, ECLI:EU:C:2005:333, paras. 29, 31; Case C-516/99 *Schmid*, ECLI:EU:C:2002:313, paras. 35 et seq.; Case C-407/98 *Abrahamsson and Anderson*, ECLI:EU:C:2000:367, paras. 29–37; Case C-103/97 *Köllensperger and Atzwanger*, ECLI:EU:C:1999:52, paras. 19–24; Case C-54/96 *Dorsch Consult*, ECLI:EU:C:1997:413, paras. 34–36. More generally, see Broberg and Fenger (2014), pp. 62 et seq.

[80]For a sharp critique of these demanding criteria, see the Opinion of AG Jacobs in Case C-50/00 P, *Unión de Pequeños Agricultores*, paras. 36–49; Konstadinidis (2017), pp. 111 et seq.

[81]See e.g. Tridimas (2013).

[82]See Lenaerts (2007), pp. 1629–1630.

[83]See e.g. CJEU, Case C-432/05 *Unibet*, ECLI:EU:C:2007:163, paras. 40-43; Case C-213/89 *Factortame I*, ECLI:EU:C:1990:257, paras. 19 et seq. See further da Cruz Vilaça (2013), pp. 300 et seq.; Lenaerts et al. (2014), pp. 107 et seq.

argument.[84] In this light, *ASJP* could be read as an important step in the jurisprudential line of *Simmenthal*, *Opinion 1/09* and *Unibet*.

3.3 Second Rationale: Operationalizing the Values in Article 2 TEU

Yet there is another, potentially groundbreaking explanation for the ample scope of Article 19(1)(2) TEU leaving the beaten tracks and venturing into uncharted territories of EU law. In the crucial passage of *ASJP*, the Court states that 'Art. 19 TEU … gives *concrete expression* to the value of the rule of law stated in Article 2'.[85] According to my understanding, this recourse to values lays the groundworks for the judicial applicability of Article 2 TEU. The Court implicitly rejected a self-standing application of Article 2 TEU and opted for a combined approach (see *supra* Sect. 2.2). It operationalizes Article 2 TEU through a specific provision of EU law (here Article 19(1)(2) TEU).[86] How does this operationalization work and what is its effect?

Like the Charter, Article 19(1)(2) TEU's scope of application is a *derived* one. It only applies within the 'fields covered by Union law'.[87] This means, however, that some kind of 'Union law' is needed to trigger its scope. Since Article 2 TEU presumably lacks direct effect and is thus no self-standing provision either, it would per se not allow for such a triggering.[88] Taken in isolation, both provisions are therefore not applicable: Article 19 because of its derived scope and Article 2 TEU because of its lacking direct effect. What could be a way out of this impasse?

At first glance, Article 19(1)(2) TEU would have to be triggered by *other* Union law (e.g. a directive or fundamental freedoms). In consequence, Article 2 TEU operationalized by Article 19(1)(2) TEU would depend on the scope of *other*

---

[84]For such a 'functional' interpretation of *ASJP*, see also Schill and Krenn (2020), paras. 102 et seq.; Jaeger (2018), pp. 615 et seq. On a 'functional' scope of Art. 19(1)(2) TEU, see also Bonelli and Claes (2018), p. 631; Mickonyte (2019), pp. 830 et seq.

[85]CJEU, *Associação Sindical dos Juízes Portugueses*, *supra* note 35, para. 32 (emphasis added). Similarly, CJEU, *Commission v. Poland (Indépendance de la Cour suprême)*, *supra* note 22, para. 47; *Commission v. Poland (Indépendance des juridictions de droit commun)*, *supra* note 22, para. 98; Joined Cases C-585/18, C-624/18 and C-625/18 *A.K. (Indépendance de la chambre disciplinaire de la Cour supreme)*, ECLI:EU:C:2019:982, para. 167. See also Opinion of AG Tanchev in Case C-192/18, *Commission v. Poland (Indépendance des juridictions de droit commun)*, ECLI:EU:C:2019:529, para. 71; Opinion of AG Tanchev in Joined Cases C-585/18, C-624/18 and C-625/18, *A.K. (Indépendance de la chambre disciplinaire de la Cour supreme)*, para. 77; Opinion of AG Tanchev in Case C-558/18, *Miasto Łowicz*, para. 92.

[86]von Bogdandy et al. (2018).

[87]On Art. 19(1)(2) TEU as a self-standing provision, see Pech and Platon (2018), pp. 1838, 1848.

[88]For a triggering relationship between Art. 2 TEU and Art. 51(1) CFR, see Jakab (2017), p. 255.

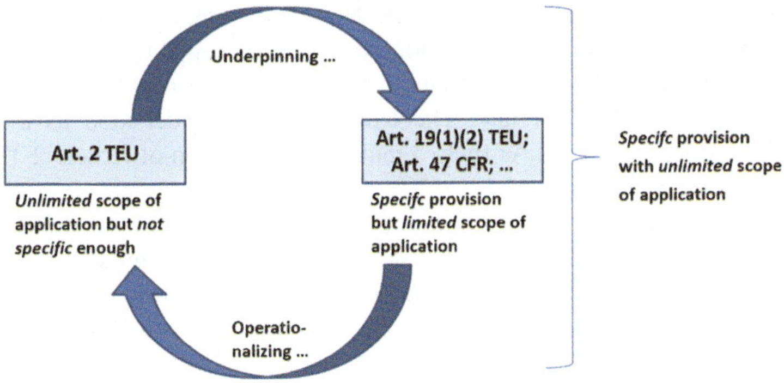

Fig. 1 Mutual amplification

Union law and could not operate beyond that.[89] Such a limitation, however, seems to severely neglect Article 2 TEU's foundational character and its unrestricted scope of application: The Member States are bound by it even in areas not covered by any (other) Union law.[90] Limiting Article 2 TEU to the scope of other Union law would frustrate its overarching importance and deprive the recourse to Union values of any added-value.

And indeed, the CJEU did not seem to have limited the scope of Article 19(1)(2) TEU (operationalizing Article 2 TEU) to the scope of any other Union law applying. It established standards for practically *any* Member State court. How does the Court reach this conclusion? According to my understanding, the combined reading of Article 2 TEU with a specific provision leads to a cumulation of their legal effects—a *mutual amplification*: While the specific provision of EU law (here Article 19 TEU) translates Article 2 TEU into a specific legal obligation, the operationalized Article 2 TEU triggers and determines the scope of application of the specific provision.[91] In this interplay, each contributes what the other lacks—specificity *and* scope (see Fig. 1).

As it is Article 2 TEU, which determines the scope, the operationalized obligations can apply beyond the scope of any other Union law to *any* Member State action. In this sense, the idea of mutual amplification kills two birds with one stone: It allows for the judicial applicability of Article 2 TEU through a specific provision without losing its unrestricted scope.

---

[89]This would also be the case if Article 2 TEU was operationalized by other provisions, like Charter rights or a specific directive.

[90]See *supra* note 32.

[91]See already Spieker (2019a), pp. 1204 et seq.; von Bogdandy and Spieker (2019), pp. 416 et seq. See also Rossi (2020), p. 650: 'c'est en réalité l'ancrage à l'article 2 et à ses valeurs suprêmes qui a permis de donner à l'article 19, paragraphe 1, ... un épaisseur et une portée qu'avant l'arrêt *Juízes Portugueses* il aurait été difficile à imaginer. Il s'agit donc d'une "concretisation" au moins réciproque.'

Eventually, this approach could be extended to *any* norm of EU law containing a specific obligation and 'giving expression' to values enshrined in Article 2 TEU. As already mentioned, Article 2 TEU contains the values of 'respect for human rights,' democracy, and the rule of law. The Charter can be understood as a specific realisation of these values.[92] As such, a mutual amplification of Article 2 TEU and Charter rights seems possible.

The Court's judgment in *L.M.* could be a first, careful step in this direction. The case dealt with the surrender of a Polish national, who is wanted to face trial in Poland and was arrested in Ireland based on an European Arrest Warrant (EAW). The referring Irish High Court asked whether the surrender could be denied on the basis that the rule of law in Poland has been systematically damaged and the respective person would thus face trial in a jurisdiction where an independent judge is not guaranteed. The CJEU applied the two-pronged *Aranyosi*-test[93] and extended it to violations of the essence of the right to a fair trial (Article 47 CFR).

While the CJEU left the final assessment of the situation in Poland to the referring court, this test eventually allows reviewing the conformity of a situation which falls at first glance *beyond* the scope of Union law with the essence of a Charter right. Although the issue of an EAW is clearly *within* the scope of Union law as defined by Article 51(1) CFR, this is not the case for *what is scrutinized* under the *Aranyosi*-test. In *L.M.*, neither the Polish judicial reforms nor the specific domestic criminal proceedings presented any apparent link to EU law—except for Article 2 TEU. Nevertheless, the referring Court is under the obligation to examine this situation for its compliance with *EU standards* (the essence of Article 47 CFR). One could of course argue that this review competence is a result of the specificities of mutual recognition regimes or that the assessment of the internal situation in Poland is only conducted indirectly in order to determine whether the EAW has to be executed or denied. Yet, similar to *ASJP*, the Court establishes a nexus between the essence of Article 47 CFR and Article 2 TEU:

> Judicial independence forms part of the essence of the fundamental right to a fair trial ... which is of cardinal importance as a guarantee ... that the values common to the Member States set out in Article 2 TEU, in particular the value of the rule of law, will be safeguarded.[94]

In this spirit, the Court started to increasingly connect Article 2 TEU and Charter rights in its recent case law. In *Tele2 Sverige*, for instance, the Court established a continuum between the freedom of expression under Article 11 CFR and the value of

[92] Voßkuhle (2017), p. 114; Hilf and Schorkopf (2020), para. 36; Rossi (2020), p. 653.

[93] First, the applicant must demonstrate systemic deficiencies amounting to a real risk of inhumane and degrading treatment. Second, there must be 'substantial grounds to believe that the individual concerned will be exposed to that risk', see CJEU, Joined Cases C-404/15 and C-659/15 PPU, *Aranyosi and Căldăraru*, ECLI:EU:C:2016:198, paras. 89, 92.

[94] CJEU, *Minister for Justice and Equality*, *supra* note 36, para. 48. On this continuum between Art. 47 CFR and Art. 2 TEU, see also Wendel (2019), pp. 27–29.

democracy under Article 2 TEU.[95] In light of these links, one could argue that the concept of mutual amplification is not limited to the situation in *ASJP*, but instead open to all provisions of EU law giving concrete expression to Article 2 TEU values.

4 Anticipating Objections and Advancing Rejoinders

In sum, the Court's stance in *ASJP* could be interpreted as making the values in Article 2 TEU judicially applicable through a mutual amplification with a specific provisions of EU law. The decisions following *ASJP* reveal a twofold development. First, the Court is willing to scrutinize and sanction Member State actions under the operationalised Article 2 TEU. Although the CJEU refrained from finding any violation in *ASJP*, the judgment served as a stepping stone for the infringement proceedings against Poland.[96] Second, the CJEU seems to develop the diffused and decentralized EU judicial network into a value monitoring and enforcement mechanism. Today, violations of operationalised Union values can reach the CJEU not only via infringement proceedings initiated by the Commission (constellation in *Commission v. Poland*) but also through preliminary reference procedures—either by 'brave' national courts directly against national measures (constellation in *ASJP* or *A.K.*) or by courts in *other* Member States assessing cooperation with backsliding Member States under mutual recognition regimes (constellation in *L.M.*).

Without a doubt, the proposed reading of *ASJP* and its progenies leads to a considerable development of the law. It seems to immensely extend the scope of Union law and the Court's jurisdiction. Indeed, no Member State area seems to escape the obligations stemming from Article 2 TEU. As such, Article 2 TEU could become the core of a European Constitution with federalizing potential, threatening the federal equilibrium established by the Treaties. Therefore, this proposal of activating Article 2 TEU will most certainly raise doubts and criticism. The following section aims at anticipating some of this critique by referring to one of the CJEU's most accomplished national counterparts—the *Bundesverfassungsgericht* (BVerfG).

[95] CJEU, Joined Cases C-203/15 and C-698/15 *Tele2 Sverige*, ECLI:EU:C:2016:970, para. 93: '[t]hat fundamental right, guaranteed in Article 11 of the Charter, constitutes one of the essential foundations of a pluralist, democratic society, and is one of the values on which, under Article 2 TEU, the Union is founded'. See also CJEU, Joined Cases C-511/18, C-512/18 and C-520/18 *La Quadrature du Net*, ECLI:EU:C:2020:791, para. 111; Case C-623/17 *Privacy International*, ECLI:EU:C:2020:790, para. 62; Case C-163/10 *Patriciello*, ECLI:EU:C:2011:543, para. 31. See further the connection between Art. 47 CFR and Art. 2 TEU in CJEU, Case C-72/15 *Rosneft*, ECLI:EU:C:2017:236, paras. 72–73.

[96] CJEU, *Commission v. Poland (Indépendance de la Cour suprême)*, *supra* note 22.

4.1 Framing Possible Objections

Generally, it seems uncontested that EU primary law is characterised by a special, evolutive dynamic[97] and has to be interpreted accordingly.[98] Due to the partial incompleteness of the EU legal order, the creative judicial development of the law[99] has been an accepted feature of the CJEU's legal reasoning since the very beginning.[100] This must apply especially in situations of new and unprecedented challenges that threaten the EU's very foundations.

There are, however, two key limits to such a judicial development of the law, which the BVerfG sketched out in *Honeywell*:[101] Horizontally, the Court should respect the inter-institutional separation of powers. Accordingly, '[t]he Court of Justice is . . . not precluded from refining the law by means of *methodically bound* case-law' respecting its judicial function.[102] '[A]s long as the Court of Justice applies *recognised methodological principles*', the judicial development of the law by the CJEU has to be accepted.[103] Vertically, a 'major limit on further development of the law by judges at Union level is the principle of conferral'.[104] Under this premise, it is essential to anchor the proposed reading of *ASJP* and the idea of mutual amplification carefully in the Court's case law and established methods of legal reasoning. At the same time, its impact must be strictly limited in order to safeguard the Union's federal equilibrium epitomised by Articles 4(2) or 5(1) TEU.

4.2 Methodologically Unsound?

Despite evident difficulties in agreeing on a common European legal methodology,[105] the CJEU's interpretation generally revolves around 'the spirit, the general scheme and the wording of the Treaty'[106] and concentrates especially on a mixture

---

[97]See e.g. the characterisation as 'Wandel-Verfassung' by Ipsen (1983), pp. 32, 51.

[98]Martens (2013), p. 475; Itzcovich (2009), pp. 549 et seq.; Bengoetxea (1993), pp. 251 et seq.

[99]The CJEU does not distinguish between 'interpretation' ('Auslegung') and 'development of the law' ('Rechtsfortbildung'), see Martens (2013), p. 503; Jestaedt (2014), p. 33.

[100]See BVerfG, 2 BvR 687/85, *Kloppenburg*, Judgment of 8 April 1987, paras. 58–60. See further Lecourt (1976), p. 236; Everling (2000); Lenaerts and Gutman (2006), p. 7.

[101]BVerfG, 2 BvR 2661/06, *Honeywell*, Order of 6 July 2010. See also Calliess (2005), p. 930; Lenaerts and Gutman (2006), pp. 45 et seq.; Roth (2011), p. 834.

[102]BVerfG, *Honeywell*, *supra* note 101, paras. 62, 64 (emphasis added).

[103]BVerfG, 2 BvE 13/13, *OMT*, Judgment of 21 June 2016, para. 161 (emphasis added). See also BVerfG, 2 BvR 859/15, *PSPP*, Judgment of 5 May 2020, para. 112.

[104]Id., para. 65.

[105]Dann (2005). In EU private law, see Fleischer (2011).

[106]CJEU, *Van Gend en Loos*, *supra* note 7. For a typology, see Lenaerts and Gutiérrez-Fons (2014) and Itzcovich (2009).

of systematic and teleological considerations.[107] On one hand, the Court can consider the *telos* of a respective provision itself. On the other hand, it can refer to a *telos* detached from said provision by referring to objectives or principles of the EU legal order. This second type could be described as systematic or meta-teleological interpretation.[108] In this light, there is a twofold, interlocking methodological justification for the idea of mutual amplification between Article 2 TEU and a specific provision of EU law.

First, the Court can rely on a teleological, concretizing, or gap-filling interpretation of Article 2 TEU itself—a practice accepted, for example, by the BVerfG as a methodologically sound endeavour.[109] Specifying the obligations enshrined in Article 2 TEU by relying on existing provisions of the *acquis* not only provides such specificity, but is also much more restrained than filling the gap solely based on case law and praetorian principles. In doing so, a parallel could be drawn to the Court's case law on Union objectives. Although these objectives do not have any direct effect,[110] the Court found ways to make them judicially applicable. It stated that the Union's objectives 'are necessarily applied *in combination* with the respective chapters of the EC Treaty intended to *give effect* to those principles and objectives'.[111]

Second, the Court can employ a systematic or meta-teleological interpretation of the specific provision operationalizing Article 2 TEU (e.g. Article 19(1)(2) TEU, Charter rights or any other provision giving specific expression to Article 2 TEU). Although the existence of hierarchies in EU primary law is highly disputed,[112] some provisions—like objectives—seem to have been treated as *primus inter pares* and served as guiding stars for its interpretation.[113] After Lisbon, objectives seem to have been placed behind the Union's common values. Article 2 TEU symbolises a 'shift from a legal entity that ... exists to strive for certain goals to one which, above all, expounds what it stands for.'[114] This shift should find its expression in the Court's

---

[107]See e.g. CJEU, Case C-283/81 *CILFIT*, ECLI:EU:C:1982:335, para. 20. On the difficulties to separate teleological and systemic interpretation, see Lenaerts and Gutiérrez-Fons (2014), p. 17.

[108]Maduro (2007), p. 5.

[109]BVerfG, *Honeywell*, *supra* note 101, para. 64: 'There is particular reason for further development of the law by judges where programmes are fleshed out, gaps are closed ...'.

[110]See e.g. CJEU, Case C-339/89 *Alsthom Atlantique*, ECLI:EU:C:1991:28, paras. 8-9. See also Case C-260/89 *ERT*, ECLI:EU:C:1991:254, paras. 39–40.

[111]See e.g. CJEU, Case C-484/08 *Caja de Ahorros*, ECLI:EU:C:2010:309, para. 46 (emphasis added); Case C-293/03 *My*, ECLI:EU:C:2004:821, para. 29.

[112]Hinting towards the existence of hierarchies, see *Kadi*, *supra* note 62, para. 303; Opinion 1/91 *EEA I*, ECLI:EU:C:1991:490, para. 6. See further, Rosas and Armati (2018), pp. 53–55. Similarly, with regard to the former Art. I-2 of the European Constitution and Art. 6(1) TEU-Nice/Amsterdam, see Tridimas (2007), p. 16; Peters (2000), pp. 341 et seq.; Gaudin (1999), p. 6. Critically concerning any hierarchies in EU primary law, see Nettesheim (2006), pp. 740 et seq.

[113]See e.g. CJEU, Case C-85/76 *Hoffmann-La Roche*, ECLI:EU:C:1979:36, para. 125; Case C-53/81 *Levin*, ECLI:EU:C:1982:105, para. 15; Case C-6/72 *Continental Can*, ECLI:EU:C:1973:22, para. 24.

[114]Larik (2014), p. 951.

legal methodology. Hence, it does not seem far-fetched to propose a new kind of meta-teleological interpretation—not in light of the Union's objectives, but in light of its common values: An axiological interpretation.[115] Under this method, the specific provision would be interpreted in light of the Union's founding values as enshrined in Article 2 TEU. In case of specific provisions, which have no derived (like Article 19(1)(2) TEU or the Charter) but nonetheless a limited scope of application (e.g. cross-border requirements), this could lead to a careful teleological reduction of their restricted scope insofar as Article 2 TEU values are at stake.[116]

Eventually, the idea of a mutual amplification—two mutually complementing and reinforcing provisions—is not unprecedented in the Court's case law. In a rather recent line of cases, the Court had to decide on the interplay of rights stemming from directives and Charter rights in horizontal situations between private parties. These cases concerned the question of whether a national provision in a case between two individuals conformed with EU law—first with rights stemming from specific directives and second with EU fundamental rights. Directives do not apply horizontally.[117] The fundamental rights at issue apply horizontally[118]—yet they are accessory to the scope of Union law (Art. 51(1) CFR). Thus, the Charter applies only in case its scope is triggered by the directive.[119] Taken in isolation, neither of them is applicable. The Court, however, relied on a creative solution based on the notorious *Mangold* judgment.[120] Taken together, both the directive as well as the fundamental right contribute to what the other lacks: Scope and horizontal effect. The directive, although not directly applicable, has 'the effect of bringing within the scope of European Union law the national legislation at issue . . ., which concerns a matter governed by that directive'.[121] Once the scope is triggered, it is the Charter right that applies horizontally in the case at hand. To add another layer to this complex interplay, the Court applies the Charter right (or the general principle) in a manner that is exactly equivalent to the right enshrined in the directive. This becomes most apparent in *Kücükdeveci*, where the Court stated that Directive 2000/78 'gives

[115] On such a 'value-oriented' interpretation, see von Bogdandy and Spieker (2019), Potacs (2016) and Calliess (2009).

[116] On the high burdens for justifying the use of this method, see Jakab (2016), p. 19.

[117] See e.g. CJEU, Case C-122/17 *Smith*, ECLI:EU:C:2018:631, paras. 42–44.

[118] This has been confirmed by the CJEU in *Bauer*, *supra* note 54, paras. 79–90; *Max-Planck-Gesellschaft*, *supra* note 54, paras. 75–79; *Egenberger*, *supra* note 55, para. 76; *Cresco Investigation*, *supra* note 55, para. 76; *Association de médiation sociale*, *supra* note 52, para. 47; with regard to general principles CJEU, Case C-441/14 *Danks Industri*, ECLI:EU:C:2016:278, para. 27; Case C-555/07 *Kücükdeveci*, ECLI:EU:C:2010:21, para. 51; Case C-144/04 *Mangold*, ECLI:EU:C:2005:709, para. 77.

[119] On Article 51(1) CFR requiring an obligation of EU law actually applying in the case at hand, see *supra* note 27.

[120] *Mangold*, *supra* note 118, para. 75; *Kücükdeveci*, *supra* note 118, para. 23. Critically BVerfG, *Honeywell*, *supra* note 101; Danish Supreme Court, 15/2014, *Dansk Industri (DI) acting for Ajos A/S*, Judgment of 6 December 2016.

[121] *Kücükdeveci*, *supra* note 118, para. 25. Similarly, *Bauer*, *supra* note 54, para. 53; *Max-Planck-Gesellschaft*, *supra* note 54, para. 50.

specific expression' to the general principle of non-discrimination.[122] The Court *de facto* applied the Directive as the principle's (or right's) specific expression.[123] As such, this reasoning is a perfect example for the cumulation of legal effects sketched out above: The general principle allows for the horizontal application, while the Directive triggers the scope of Union law and provides for specificity.

4.3 *Pretext for a Power Grab?*

Naturally, the bold reading of the Court's case law as proposed above has the potential of severely upsetting the Union's federal equilibrium epitomised by Articles 4(2) or 5(1) TEU.[124] Therefore, it is essential to put safeguards in place ensuring that Article 2 TEU does not become the 'pretext for a power grab'.[125] These essential safeguards, however, should not be applied in a way that frustrates the respect for Article 2 TEU values either. Both considerations have to be carefully balanced against each other. In my view, the outcome of this balancing exercise could be a threefold limitation ensuring Article 2 TEU's function and simultaneously providing a safety net for the 'federal bargain'.

Limiting the Obligations Enshrined in Article 2 TEU First, Article 2 TEU must be interpreted in a restrictive manner as being triggered only in exceptional situations. On the one hand, Article 2 TEU cannot impose *high* standards upon the Member States, since such an interpretation could not be squared with the legally guaranteed constitutional autonomy of the Member States.[126] Concerning the 'respect for human rights', some have proposed operating with the concept of 'essence'.[127] Insofar as the 'essence' of Charter rights is concerned, they are also protected as

---

[122] *Kücükdeveci, supra* note 118, para. 21. See further CJEU, *Cresco Investigation, supra* note 55, para. 75; Case C-68/17 *IR*, ECLI:EU:C:2018:696, para. 67; *Egenberger, supra* note 55, paras. 47, 75; *Dansk Industri, supra* note 118, para. 35; Case C-447/09 *Prigge*, ECLI:EU:C:2011:573, para. 48; Case C-297-298/10 *Hennigs and Mai*, ECLI:EU:C:2011:560, para. 68. Similarly, *Max-Planck-Gesellschaft, supra* note 54, para. 72; *Bauer, supra* note 54, para. 83.

[123] See even CJEU, Case C-132/11 *Tyrolean Airways Tiroler Luftfahrt Gesellschaft*, ECLI:EU:C:2012:329, para. 23: 'to be examined *solely* in the light of Directive 2000/78' (emphasis added).

[124] See e.g. the arguments of Poland in CJEU, *Commission v. Poland (Indépendance de la Cour suprême), supra* note 22, paras. 39–40.

[125] Kochenov (2017b), p. 443.

[126] For similar conceptions, see Voßkuhle (2017), p. 117 ('essential content'); Schroeder (2016b), p. 11 ('minimum standards'); Toggenburg and Grimheden (2016), p. 221 ('minimum constitutional cohesion'). See also European Convention, *supra* note 32, p. 11: 'This Article can thus only contain a *hard core* of values meeting two criteria at once: on one hand, they must be *so fundamental* that they lie at the very heart of a peaceful society practicing tolerance, justice and solidarity; on the other hand, they must have a *clear non-controversial* legal basis so that the Member States can discern the obligations resulting therefrom'.

[127] von Bogdandy et al. (2012), pp. 509 et seq.; on the notion of 'essence', see further Brkan (2018); Lenaerts (2019c). See further the special issue in 20 *German Law Journal* 763 (2019).

values under Article 2 TEU, while Article 51(1) CFR continues to delimit the application of the *full* fundamental right *acquis*. On the other hand, Article 2 TEU can hardly force *detailed* obligations upon the Member States, because this would ignore the actually existing constitutional pluralism in the Union. Due to the practically countless possibilities of how to bring the abstract values to life, Article 2 TEU cannot—from a mere practical perspective—be understood as containing very detailed obligations.[128] Accordingly, Article 2 TEU's high degree of abstraction necessarily correlates with a lower degree of review by the Court. Where does that leave us? One feasible solution could be to understand Article 2 TEU as establishing only a regime of 'red lines'.[129] On a conceptual level, Article 2 TEU would determine *negatively* what is not allowed, without *positively* determining how things should be instead. In a nutshell, Article 2 TEU would apply only in *exceptional* situations and only in the form of 'red lines'.

Limiting the EU's Competence Second, I argue that the Union's '*Verbandskompetenz*' (its competence as a legal order) to enforce Member State's Article 2 TEU compliance beyond the scope of (any other) Union law is limited to the thresholds of Article 7 TEU. Indeed, the only provision explicitly empowering the EU legal order to enforce EU values or sanction violations thereof beyond the scope of (any other) Union law is Article 7 TEU. Hence, this provision contains a strong indication that the EU's *Verbandskompetenz* is limited at least to the *substantive* thresholds triggering Article 7 TEU (a 'serious and persistent breach').[130] This could provide the starting point for a workable restriction operating in form of a sliding scale (see Fig. 2): The more or the clearer a situation falls within the scope of

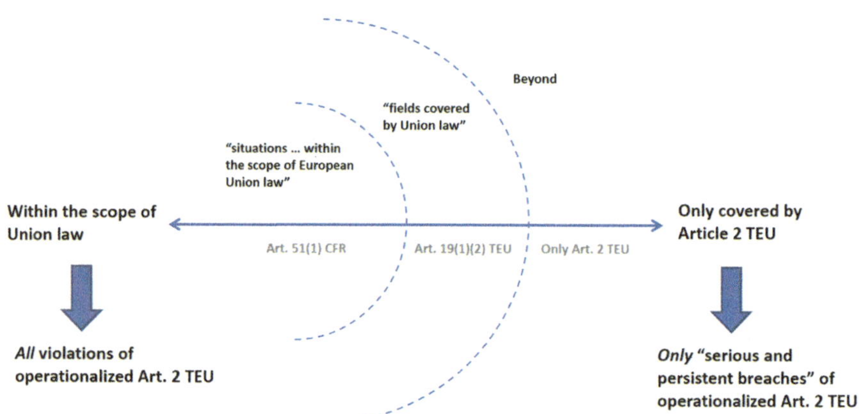

Fig. 2 Sliding Article 7 TEU scale

[128]von Bogdandy (2010), p. 40.

[129]von Bogdandy et al. (2018).

[130]See similar Council of the European Union, Opinion of the Legal Service, *supra* note 32, para. 17.

other EU law, the more the EU and the less the respective Member State is affected. This means that in case of a clear link to EU law, *every* violation of Article 2 TEU values can be sanctioned by EU institutions (e.g. under the Charter). If the link is weaker or nonexistent, it approaches the confines of Article 7 TEU. To assess and sanction every violation in such situations would exceed the EU's *Verbandskompetenz*. Therefore, the more the situation departs from the scope of Union law and comes solely under Article 2 TEU, the more a violation must reach the thresholds of Article 7, and the more it must constitute a 'serious and persistent' breach to be claimed before the CJEU.

Limiting the Exercise of the CJEU's Jurisdiction Finally, there are several ways in which the CJEU might limit the exercise of its jurisdiction over Article 2 TEU: First, as proposed by the *Reverse Solange* doctrine, the Court could introduce a presumption of value compliance accompanied by a high threshold for its rebuttal. Such a threshold could be fixed on the level of systemic deficiencies—a notion which is well-established throughout the European legal space.[131] Therefore, simple and isolated infringements upon the values enshrined in Article 2 TEU would not suffice to rebut the proposed presumption. The justification for such a presumption could be derived from the principle of mutual trust. Although mutual trust has been invoked only horizontally between the Member States,[132] this does not mean that it is excluded in the vertical relationship of EU and Member States. Indeed, mutual trust is based on or at least intrinsically linked to the principle of loyal and sincere cooperation in Article 4(3) TEU.[133] The principle of mutual loyalty, however, expressly extends to Union institutions and hence the CJEU as well.[134] Similar developments could be predicted for the principle of mutual trust.

A second option could consist of a more deferential approach, leaving the final determination of value compliance in the hands of national courts—at least in case of preliminary references. Indeed, the Court can vary and adjust the degree of specificity it applies.[135] While it sometimes leaves the final determination to the referring court,[136] it can also fully assess the situation in the respective Member

---

[131] See von Bogdandy and Spieker (2019), p. 424; further von Bogdandy and Ioannidis (2014).

[132] CJEU, *Associação Sindical dos Juízes Portugueses*, *supra* note 35, para. 30; *Minister for Justice and Equality*, *supra* note 36, para. 35.

[133] See e.g. CJEU, Case C-5/94 *Hedley Lomas*, ECLI:EU:C:1996:205, para. 19. See further AG Ruiz-Jarabo Colomer in Case C-297/07, *Bourquain*, para. 45: 'experience shows that mutual trust applies ... fulfilling a role similar to that of loyal cooperation'. See also Meyer (2017), pp. 179 et seq.; Prechal (2017), pp. 90–92; Gerard (2016), p. 76. But see Lenaerts (2017b), p. 807 who derives it from the principle of equality between the Member States.

[134] See the wording of Article 4(3) TEU. See further CJEU, Case C-339/00 *Ireland v. Commission*, ECLI:EU:C:2003:545, para. 72; Case C-197/13 *Spain v. Commission*, ECLI:EU:C:2014:2157, para. 87.

[135] On deference in the CJEU's jurisprudence, see e.g. Zglinski (2018).

[136] See e.g. *Minister for Justice and Equality*, *supra* note 36.

State.[137] These variations are no random exercise but a conscious judicial choice.[138] A differential approach can not only lead to a burden sharing between the interacting courts but is also more respectful towards national autonomy.[139] The Court's stance in *L.M.* and in *A.K.* especially could be understood as an expression of this deferential attitude. Yet deference does not come without risks. In *A.K.*, for instance, the Court left the final decision of whether the new Polish disciplinary chamber violates judicial independence to the referring court.[140] Thus, both the Polish government as well as the affected judiciary tried to capitalize on the judgment and claimed it as a victory.[141] The referring court decided that the disciplinary chamber does not comply with the standards of independence set out by the CJEU.[142] Instead of changing the problematic appointment procedures, however, the Polish government countered with a new bill aimed at tightening its control over the judiciary and preventing judges from questioning the independence of peers.[143] Further, it increased its disciplinary proceedings against critical judges.[144] As these continuing attacks demonstrate, deference is a two-edged sword: While it shows greater respect for national autonomy and diversity, it risks leaving affected national courts with a burden too heavy to shoulder. In this sense, the CJEU will have to carefully assess the situation in the respective Member State before determining the degree of deference applied.

---

[137]See e.g. CJEU, *Associação Sindical dos Juízes Portugueses, supra* note 35. Concerning systemic deficiencies, see e.g. CJEU, Joined Cases C-411/10 and C-493/10 *N.S. and Others*, ECLI:EU:C:2011:865; Case C-220/18 PPU *Generalstaatsanwaltschaft (Conditions de détention en Hongrie)*, ECLI:EU:C:2018:589.

[138]Tridimas (2011), p. 749.

[139]See also Schiffauer (2019), p. 568.

[140]CJEU, *A.K. (Indépendance de la chambre disciplinaire de la Cour supreme), supra* note 85.

[141]For the statements of the Minister of Justice, see e.g. Ziobro o wyroku TSUE: Wielka porażka nadzwyczajnej kasty, *Do Rzeczy* (19 November 2019), dorzeczy.pl/kraj/120931/ziobro-o-wyroku-tsue-wielka-porazka-nadzwyczajnej-kasty.html.

[142]Polish Supreme Court, Judgment of 5 December 2019, Case III PO 7/18; Judgments of 15 December 2020, Cases III PO 8/18 and III PO 9/18. See also the Resolution of three joint chambers of the Polish Supreme Court of 23 January 2020, Case BSA I-4110-1/20. In two rulings, however, the captured Polish Constitutional Tribunal declared the resolution to be unconstitutional, see Polish Constitutional Tribunal, Decision of 21 April 2020, Kpt 1/20; Decision of 20 April 2020, U 2/20. See further European Commission, 2020 Rule of Law Report Country Chapter on the rule of law situation in Poland (30 September 2020), SWD(2020) 320 final, pp. 4 et seq.

[143]For critical accounts, see e.g. Venice Commission, Poland—Urgent Joint Opinion on the amendments to the Law on organisation on the Common Courts, the Law on the Supreme Court and other Laws, CDL-PI(2020)002-e (16 January 2020); ODHIR, Urgent Interim Opinion on the Bill Amending the Act on the Organization of Common Courts, the Act on the Supreme Court and Certain Other Acts of Poland, JUD-POL/365/2019 [AlC] (14 January 2020); Polish Commissioner for Human Rights Adam Bodnar, Comments, VII.510.176.2019/MAW/PKR/PF/MW/CW (7 January 2020).

[144]See e.g. PACE, Report—The functioning of democratic institutions in Poland, Doc. 15025 (6 January 2020), paras. 95 et seq. See further Gajda-Roszczynialska, Markiewicz (2020).

5 Conclusion

In entering the European Union and opening their respective legal orders for direct effect and primacy, the Member States simultaneously accepted an openness towards internal developments and decisions taken by other Member States. The EU does not only extend the 'transnational reach' of each Member State, but also creates a situation of mutual vulnerability.[145] Internal developments in one Member State can lead to spill-over effects in all other Member States. The complex network of cooperation created by the European Union is not only enabling, it is transmitting and intensifying these effects. Especially through the introduction of majority decisions in the Council, each Member State partially and indirectly governs all others. As Commissioner Jourova put it: 'the EU is like a chain of Christmas lights. When one light goes off, others don't light up and the chain is dark.'[146] Therefore, it is of utmost importance to secure Member States' adherence to the Union's common values as an underlying basis and essential safety net on which cooperation can take place.

The last 2 years have shown that the Court seems more than willing to protect this common value basis against the illiberal turn in some Member States. The judgment in *ASJP* especially represents a veritable stepping stone towards a strong union of values—a judgment on par with *van Gend en Loos, Costa/ENEL*, or *Les Verts*.[147] With *ASJP*, the Court turned Article 2 TEU into a judicially applicable provision and paved the way for its activation in the EU value crisis. According to the interpretation advanced in this chapter, the Court renders Article 2 TEU applicable by operationalizing it through specific provisions of EU law without, however, losing its unrestricted scope. Due to this mutual amplification, *any* Member State act can be scrutinized under the operationalised Article 2 TEU—albeit under very restrictive conditions and only in very exceptional circumstances. As such, Article 2 TEU has become the Archimedean point for judicial proceedings against backsliding Member States.

Acknowledgments I am grateful to the *Dienstagsrunde*, especially Armin von Bogdandy, Iris Canor, Pedro Cruz Villalón, Michael Ioannidis, Christoph Krenn and Eva Neumann as well as Lukas Huthmann, Nicole Lazzerini, Andreas Orator, Anca Mihaela Rusu, Marie-Sophie Schäfer, and Pál Sonnevend for their comments and inspirations on this chapter and earlier drafts.

References

Adam S, Van Elsuwege P (2018) L'exigence d'independance du juge, paradigme de l'Union européenne comme union de droit. J de droit européen:334–343

Alexy R (2009) A theory of constitutional rights. Oxford University Press, Oxford

[145]For an analysis of these effects, see Somek (2010).

[146]Jourova (2017).

[147]For this perception, see Lenaerts (2019d).

Baratta R (2018) La 'communauté de valeurs' dans l'ordre juridique de l'Union européenne. Revue des affaires européens:81–91

Bengoetxea J (1993) The legal reasoning of the European Court of Justice. Oxford University Press, Oxford

Bernatt M, Ziółkowski M (2018) Statutory anti-constitutionalism. Wash Int Law J 28:487–526

Blauberger M, Kelemen RD (2017) Can courts rescue national democracy? J Eur Public Policy 24:321–336

Bonelli M, Claes M (2018) Judicial serendipity: how Portuguese judges came to the rescue of the Polish judiciary. Eur Const Law Rev 14:622–643

Borowsky M (2014) Art. 51 – Anwendungsbereich. In: Meyer J (ed) Charta der Grundrechte der Europäischen Union, 4th edn. Nomos, Baden Baden

Brkan M (2018) The concept of essence of fundamental rights in the EU legal order: peeling the onion to its core. Eur Const Law Rev 14:332–368

Broberg M, Fenger N (2014) Preliminary references to the European Court of Justice, 2nd edn. Oxford University Press, Oxford

Calliess C (2005) Grundlagen, Grenzen und Perspektiven europäischen Richterrechts. NJW 58:929–933

Calliess C (2009) The transnationalization of values by European Law. German Law J 10:1367–1382

Calliess C (2016) Art. 2 EUV. In: Calliess C, Ruffert M (eds) EUV/AEUV, 5th edn. C.H.Beck, Munich

Cannizzaro E (2018) I ruolo della Corte di giustizia nella tutela dei valori dell'Unione europea. In: Liber Amicorum Antonio Tizzano. Giappichelli, Milan, pp 159–169

Carrera S, Guild E, Hernanz N (2013) The triangular relationship between fundamental rights, democracy and the rule of law in the EU. European Parliament, LIBE Committee. www.europarl.europa.eu/RegData/etudes/etudes/join/2013/493031/IPOL-LIBE_ET(2013)493031_EN.pdf. Accessed 20 Oct 2020

Closa C (2016) Reinforcing EU monitoring of the rule of law, normative arguments, institutional proposals and the procedural limitations. In: Closa C, Kochenov D (eds) Reinforcing rule of law oversight in the European Union. Cambridge University Press, Cambridge, pp 15–35

Closa C, Kochenov D (eds) (2016a) Reinforcing rule of law oversight in the European Union. Cambridge University Press, Cambridge

Closa C, Kochenov D (2016b) Reinforcing the rule of law oversight in the European Union: key options. In: Schroeder W (ed) Strengthening the rule of law in Europe. Hart, Oxford, pp 173–196

Craig P, de Búrca G (2020) EU law, 7th edn. Oxford University Press, Oxford

da Cruz Vilaça JL (2013) Le principe de l'effet utile du droit de l'Union dans la jurisprudence de la Cour. In: Rosas A, Levits E, Bot Y (eds) The Court of Justice and the construction of Europe. T.M.C. Asser Press, The Hague, pp 279–308

Dann P (2005) Thoughts on a methodology of European constitutional law. German Law J 6:1453–1473

Dawson M, Muir E (2013) Hungary and the indirect protection of EU fundamental rights and the rule of law. German Law J 14:1959–1979

de Búrca G (2011) The evolution of EU human rights. In: Craig P, de Búrca G (eds) The evolution of EU law, 2nd edn. Oxford University Press, Oxford, pp 464–498

Dumbrovsky T (2018) Beyond voting rights suspension. Tailored sanctions as democracy catalyst under Article 7 TEU. In: Hatje A, Tichý L (eds) Liability of member states for the violation of fundamental values. Europarecht Beiheft 1/2018. Nomos, Baden Baden, pp 201–228

Dworkin R (2013) Taking rights seriously. Bloomsbury, London. (reprint of 1978)

Easton D (1965) A systems analysis of political life. University of Chicago Press, Chicago

EU Fundamental Rights Agency (2014) Fundamental rights: challenges and achievements in 2013 – annual report 2013

Everling U (2000) On judge-made law of the European community's courts. In: O'Keeffe D (ed) Judicial review in European Union law. Kluwer Law International, The Hague, pp 29–44
Everling U (2015) Justizielle Krisenbewältigung: Der EuGH als Garant des europäischen Rechts. In: Hatje A (ed) Verfassungszustand und Verfassungsentwicklung der Europäischen Union. Europarecht Beiheft 2/2015. Nomos, Baden Baden, pp 86–103
Falkner G (2018) A causal loop? The Commission's new enforcement approach in the context of non-compliance with EU law even after CJEU judgments. J Eur Integr 40:769–784
Fennelly N (2013) The national judge as judge of the European Union. In: Rosas A, Levits E, Bot Y (eds) The Court of Justice and the construction of Europe. T.M.C. Asser Press, The Hague, pp 61–70
Fleischer H (2011) Europäische Methodenlehre: Stand und Perspektiven. Rabel J Comp Int Private Law 75:700–729
Franzius C (2018) Der Kampf um Demokratie in Polen und Ungarn – Wie kann und soll die Europäische Union reagieren? Die Öffentliche Verwaltung 71:381–388
Gajda-Roszczynialska K, Markiewicz K (2020) Disciplinary proceedings as an instrument for breaking the rule of law in Poland. Hague J Rule Law
Gaudin H (1999) Amsterdam: l'échec de la hiérarchie des normes? Revue trimestrielle de droit européen 35:1–20
Gerard D (2016) Mutual trust as constitutionalism? In: Brouwer E, Gerard D (eds) Mapping mutual trust. Understanding and framing the role of mutual trust in EU LAW. EUI Working Papers MWP 2016/1, Florence. Cadmus, Port Angeles, pp 69–79
Giegerich T (2019) Die Unabhängigkeit der Gerichte als Strukturvorgabe der Unionsverfassung. ZEuS 22:61–112
Habermas J (1996) Between facts and norms. Polity Press, Cambridge
Habermas J (2005) On the internal relation between the rule of law and democracy. In: Cronin C, De Greiff PP (eds) The inclusion of the other. Studies on political theory. Polity Press, Cambridge, pp 253–264
Halmai G (2017) The case of the retirement age of Hungarian judges. In: Nicola F, Davies B (eds) EU law stories. Contextual and critical histories of European jurisprudence. Cambridge University Press, Cambridge, pp 471–488
Hilf M, Schorkopf F (2020) Art. 2 EUV. In: Grabitz E, Hilf M, Nettesheim M (eds) Das Recht der Europäischen Union. C.H. Beck, Munich
Hillion C (2016) Overseeing the rule of law in the EU: legal mandate and means. In: Closa C, Kochenov D (eds) Reinforcing rule of law oversight in the European Union. Cambridge University Press, Cambridge, pp 59–81
Iliopoulou-Penot A (2019) La justification de l'intervention de l'Union pour la garantie de l'Etat de droit au sein des pays membres. Revue des affaires européennes:7–16
Ipsen HP (1983) Die Verfassungsrolle des Europäischen Gerichtshofs für die Integration. In: Schwarze J (ed) Der Europäische Gerichtshof als Verfassungsgericht und Rechtsschutzinstanz. Nomos, Baden Baden, pp 29–67
Itzcovich G (2009) The interpretation of community law by the European Court of Justice. German Law J 10:537–560
Jaeger T (2018) Gerichtsorganisation und EU-Recht: Eine Standortbestimmung. Europarecht 53:611–653
Jakab A (2016) European constitutional language. Cambridge University Press, Cambridge
Jakab A (2017) Application of the EU CFR by national courts in purely domestic cases. In: Jakab A, Kochenov D (eds) The enforcement of EU law and values. Oxford University Press, Oxford, pp 252–262
Jakab A (2020) What can constitutional law do against the erosion of democracy and the rule of law? On the interconnectedness of the protection of democracy and the rule of law. Const Stud 6:5–34
Jakab A, Kochenov D (eds) (2017) The enforcement of EU law and values. Oxford University Press, Oxford

Jestaedt M (2014) Luxemburger Richterrecht. In: Hillgruber C (ed) Gouvernement des Juges – Fluch oder Segen. Schöningh, Paderborn, pp 21–44
Jourova V (2017) Speech at the high level seminar: Finland 100 years – Finnish and European perspectives to the Rule of Law (31 October 2017)
Klamert M, Kochenov D (2019) Article 2 TEU. In: Kellerbauer M, Klamert M, Tomkin J (eds) The Treaties and the Charter of fundamental rights – a commentary. Oxford University Press, Oxford, pp 22–30
Kochenov D (2017a) The acquis and its principles, the enforcement of the 'Law' versus the enforcement of 'Values' in the EU. In: Jakab A, Kochenov D (eds) The enforcement of EU law and values. Oxford University Press, Oxford, pp 9–27
Kochenov D (2017b) The EU and the rule of law – Naïveté or a grand design? In: Adams M, Anne Meuwese A, Hirsch Ballin E (eds) Constitutionalism and the rule of law. Cambridge University Press, Cambridge, pp 419–445
Kochenov D, Bárd P (2019) The last soldier standing? Courts versus politicians and the rule of law crisis in the new member states of the EU. Eur Yearb Const Law 1:243–287
Kochenov D, Pech L (2015) Monitoring and enforcement of the rule of law in the EU: rhetoric and reality. Eur Const Rev 11:512–540
Konstadinidis T (2017) The rule of law in the European Union: the internal dimension. Hart, Oxford
Krenn C, Farahat A (2018) Der Europäische Gerichtshof in der Eurokrise: eine konflikttheoretische Perspektive. Der Staat 57:357–385
Ladenburger C (2012) European Union institutional report. In: Laffranque J (ed) Protection of fundamental rights post-Lisbon. Reports of the XXV FIDE congress. Tartu University Press, Tallinn, p 141
Landau D (2013) Abusive constitutionalism. UC Davis Law Rev 47:189–260
Larik J (2014) From speciality to a constitutional sense of purpose: on the changing role of the objectives of the European Union. Int Comp Law Q 63:935–962
Lazzerini N (2018) La Carta dei Diritti Fondamentali dell'Unione Europea. I Limiti di Applicazione. Franco Angeli, Milan
Lecourt R (1976) L'Europe des juges. Bruylant, Brussels. (reprint 2008)
Lenaerts K (1992) Some thoughts about the interaction between judges and politicians in the European community. Yearb Eur Law 12:1–34
Lenaerts K (2007) The rule of law and coherence of the judicial system of the European Union. Common Market Law Rev 44:1625–1659
Lenaerts K (2017a) Die Werte der Europäischen Union in der Rechtsprechung des Gerichtshofs der Europäischen Union. Europäische Grundrechte-Zeitschrift 44:639–642
Lenaerts K (2017b) La vie après l'avis: exploring the principle of mutual (yet not blind) trust. Common Market Law Rev 54:805–840
Lenaerts K (2019a) Upholding the rule of law through judicial dialogue. Yearb Eur Law 38:3–17
Lenaerts K (2019b) On judicial independence and the quest for national, supranational and transnational justice. In: Selvik G et al (eds) The art of judicial reasoning. Festschrift in Honour of Carl Baudenbacher. Springer, Heidelberg, pp 155–174
Lenaerts K (2019c) Limits on limitations: the essence of fundamental rights in the EU. German Law J 20:779–793
Lenaerts K (2019d) Upholding the rule of law within the EU. Speech held at the RECONNECT conference 'Democracy and the Rule of Law in the EU', 5 July 2019. reconnect-europe.eu/events/conference-2019/
Lenaerts K, Gutiérrez-Fons JA (2014) To say what the law of the EU is: methods of interpretation and the European Court of Justice. Columb J Eur Law 20:3–61
Lenaerts K, Gutiérrez-Fons JA (2017) Epilogue on EU citizenship: hopes and fears? In: Kochenov D (ed) EU citizenship and federalism. The role of rights. Cambridge University Press, Cambridge, pp 751–781

Lenaerts K, Gutman K (2006) 'Federal Common Law' in the European Union. Am J Comp Law 54:1–122
Lenaerts K, Maselis I, Gutman K (2014) EU procedural law. Oxford University Press, Oxford
Levits E (2018a) L'Union européenne en tant que communauté de valeurs partagées: les conséquences juridiques des articles 2 et 7 du traité sur l'Union européenne pour les États membre. In: Liber Amicorum Antonio Tizzano. Giappichelli, Milan, pp 509–522
Levits E (2018b) Die Europäische Union als Wertegemeinschaft. In: Jaeger (ed) Europa 4.0. Jan Sramek Verlag, Wien, pp 239–270
Luhmann N (1989) Legitimation durch Verfahren, 2nd edn. Suhrkamp, Frankfurt am Main
Maduro MP (2007) Interpreting European Law: judicial adjudication in a context of constitutional pluralism. Eur J Legal Stud 1:1–21
Maduro MP, Menezes Queiroz B (2020) A hard law approach to states systemic violations of Article 2 of the Treaty of the European Union. Reasons and means. In: Fisher E, King J, Young A (eds) The foundations and future of public law. Oxford University Press, Oxford, pp 363–380
Mancini GF (1989) The making of a constitution for Europe. Common Market Law Rev 26:595–614
Mangiameli S (2012) The Union's homogeneity and its common values in the Treaty on European Union. In: Blanke H-J, Mangiameli S (eds) The European Union after Lisbon. Springer, Heidelberg, pp 21–46
Martenczuk B (2018) Art. 7 EUV und der Rechtsstaatsrahmen als Instrument der Wahrung der Grundwerte der Union. In: Kadelbach S (ed) Verfassungskrisen in der Europäischen Union. Nomos, Baden Baden, pp 41–60
Martens SAE (2013) Methodenlehre des Unionsrechts. Mohr Siebeck, Tübingen
Mayoral JA (2016) In the CJEU judges trust: a new approach in the judicial construction of Europe. J Common Market Stud 55:551–568
Mendelski M (2016) Das europäische Evaluierungsdezifit der Rechtsstaatlichkeit. Leviathan 44:366–398
Meyer F (2017) Der Grundsatz gegenseitigen Vertrauens – Konzeptualisierung und Zukunftsperspektiven eines neuen Verfassungsprinzips. Europarecht 52:163–185
Mickonyte A (2019) Effects of the rule-of-law crisis in the EU: towards centralization of the EU system of judicial protection. ZaöRV 79:815–840
Miglio A (2018) Indipendenza del giudice, crisi dello stato di diritto e tutela giurisdizionale effettiva. Diritti Umani e Diritto Internazionale 12:421–432
Möllers C (2013) The three branches: a comparative model of separation of powers. Oxford University Press, Oxford
Möllers C, Schneider L (2018) Demokratiesicherung in der Europäischen Union. Studie zu einer europäischen Aufgabe. Mohr Siebeck, Tübingen
Nettesheim M (2006) Normenhierarchien im EU-Recht. Europarecht 41:737–772
Nicolosi SF (2015) The contribution of the Court of Justice to the codification of the founding values of the European Union. Revista De Derecho Comunitario Europeo 19(51):613–643
Niedobitek M (2018) Right and duty to pursue the 'wrongdoer' and a possible abuse of Art. 7 TEU. In: Hatje A, Tichý L (eds) Liability of member states for the violation of fundamental values. Europarecht Beiheft 1/2018. Nomos, Baden Baden, pp 233–242
Orbán V (2017) Speech at the 28th Bálványos Summer Open University (22 July 2017)
Pech L, Platon S (2018) Judicial independence under threat: the Court of Justice to the rescue in the ASJP case. Common Market Law Rev 55:1827–1854
Pech L et al (2016) An EU mechanism on democracy, the rule of law and fundamental rights, European Parliament, EPRS. www.europarl.europa.eu/EPRS/EPRS_STUD_579328_annexI_EU_Mechanism_MILIEU.pdf. Accessed 27 Oct 2020
Pérez de Nanclares JM (2019) La Unión Europea como comunidad de valores: a vueltas con la crisis de la democracia y del Estado de Derecho. Teoría y Realidad Constitucional 43:121–159
Pescatore P (1974) The law of integration. Emergence of a new phenomenon in international relations, based on the experience of the European Communities. A.W. Sijthoff, Leiden

Pescatore P (1983) The doctrine of direct effect: an infant disease of community law. Eur Law Rev 8:155–177
Pescatore P (2008) La carence du législateur communautaire et le devoir du juge (1983). In: Picod F (ed) Études de droit communautaire européen 1962–2007. Bruylant, Brussels, pp 613–636
Peters A (2000) Elemente einer Theorie der Verfassung Europas. Duncker&Humblot, Berlin
Pörsken U (2004) Plastic words: the tyranny of a modular language. The Pennsylvania State University Press, Pennsylvania
Potacs M (2016) Wertkonforme Auslegung des Unionsrechts? Europarecht 51:164–176
Prechal S (2017) Mutual trust before the Court of Justice of the European Union. Eur Papers 2:75–92
Rasmussen H (1986) On law and policy in the European Court of Justice. Martinus Nijhoff, Dordrecht
Reding V (2013) The EU and the rule of law – what next? http://europa.eu/rapid/press-release_SPEECH-13-677_en.htm. Accessed 27 Oct 2020
Rosas A (2012) When is the EU Charter of fundamental rights applicable at national level? Jurisprudencija/Jurisprudence 19:1269–1288
Rosas A, Armati L (2018) EU constitutional law, 3rd edn. Hart, Oxford
Rossi LS (2020) La valeur juridique des valeurs. L'article 2 TUE: relations avec d'autres dispositions de droit primaire de l'UE et remèdes juridictionnels. Revue trimestrielle de droit européen:639–657
Roth WH (2011) Verfassung und europäische Methodenlehre. Rabel J Comp Int Private Law 75:787–844
Safjan M (2014) Fields of application of the Charter of fundamental rights and constitutional dialogues in the European Union, EUI Distinguished Lecture 2014/02
Safjan M, Düsterhaus D, Guérin A (2016) La Charte des droits fondamentaux de l'Union européenne et les ordres juridiques nationaux. Revue trimestrielle de droit européen:219–247
Sarmiento D (2013) Who's afraid of the Charter? The Court of Justice, national courts and the new framework of fundamental rights protection in Europe. Common Market Law Rev 50:1267–1304
Scheppele KL (2016) Enforcing the basic principles of EU law through systemic infringement actions. In: Closa C, Kochenov D (eds) Reinforcing rule of law oversight in the European Union. Cambridge University Press, Cambridge, pp 105–132
Scheppele KL (2018) Autocratic legalism. Univ Chicago Law Rev 85:545
Scheppele KL, Kochenov D, Grabowska-Moroz B (2020) EU values are law, after all: Enforcing EU values through systemic infringement actions by the European Commission and the member states of the European Union. Yearb Eur Law 38 (forthcoming)
Schiffauer P (2019) Ein Anker von Rechtsstaatlichkeit in der Europäischen Union durch den Verbund der Verfassungs- und Obersten Gerichte. Neue Begründungswege in der jüngsten Rechtsprechung des EuGH zur Reform des polnischen Justizsystems. Europäische Grundrechtezeitschrift 46:549–571
Schill S, Krenn C (2020) Art. 4 EUV. In: Grabitz E, Hilf M, Nettesheim M (eds) Das Recht der Europäischen Union. C.H. Beck, Munich
Schmidt M, Bogdanowicz P (2018) The infringement procedure in the rule of law crisis: how to make effective use of Article 258 TFEU. Common Market Law Rev 55:1061–1100
Schorkopf F (2016) Wertesicherung in der Europäischen Union. Prävention, Quarantäne und Aufsicht als Bausteine eines Rechts der Verfassungskrise? Europarecht 51:147–164
Schorkopf F (2020) Value Constitutionalism in the European Union. German Law J 21:956–967
Schroeder W (ed) (2016a) Strengthening the rule of law in Europe. Hart, Oxford
Schroeder W (2016b) The European Union and the rule of law – state of affairs and ways of strengthening. In: Schroeder W (ed) Strengthening the rule of law in Europe. Hart, Oxford, pp 3–34

Shapiro S (2011) Legality. Harvard University Press, Cambridge
Skouris V (2018) Demokratie und Rechtsstaat. C.H. Beck, München
Somek A (2010) The argument from transnational effects I. Eur Law J 16:315–344
Spaventa E (2016) The interpretation of Article 51 of the EU Charter of fundamental rights. European Parliament, PETI Committee. www.europarl.europa.eu/RegData/etudes/STUD/2016/556930/IPOL_STU(2016)556930_EN.pdf. Accessed 27 Oct 2020
Spieker LD (2019a) Breathing life into the Union's common values: on the judicial application of Article 2 TEU in the EU value crisis. German Law J 20:1182–1213
Spieker LD (2019b) Commission v. Poland – a stepping stone towards a strong 'Union of Values'? Verfassungsblog, 30 May 2019
Streinz R (2018) Principles and values in the European Union. In: Hatje A, Tichý L (eds) Liability of member states for the violation of fundamental values. Europarecht Beiheft 1/2018. Nomos, Baden Baden, pp 11–22
Sunstein CR (1999) One case at a time. Judicial minimalism on the Supreme Court. Harvard University Press, Cambridge
Toggenburg GN, Grimheden T (2016) Managing the rule of law in a heterogeneous context: a fundamental rights perspective on ways forward. In: Schroeder W (ed) Strengthening the rule of law in Europe. Hart, Oxford, pp 221–241
Tridimas T (2007) The general principles of EU law, 2nd edn. Oxford University Press, Oxford
Tridimas T (2011) Constitutional review of member state action: the virtues and vices of an incomplete jurisdiction. ICON 9:737–756
Tridimas T (2013) Bifurcated justice: the dual character of judicial protection in EU law. In: Rosas A, Levits E, Bot Y (eds) The Court of Justice and the construction of Europe. T.M.C. Asser Press, The Hague, pp 367–380
von Bogdandy A (2010) Founding principles. In: Bast J, von Bogdandy A (eds) Principles of European constitutional law, 2nd edn. Hart, Oxford, pp 11–54
von Bogdandy A (2020) Principles of a systemic deficiencies doctrine: how to protect checks and balances in the member states. Common Market Law Rev 57:705–740
von Bogdandy A, Ioannidis M (2014) Systemic deficiency in the rule of law: what it is, what has been done, what can be done. Common Market Law Rev 51:59–96
von Bogdandy A, Spieker LD (2019) Countering the judicial silencing of critics. Article 2 TEU values, Reverse Solange, and the responsibilities of national judges. Eur Const Law Rev 15:391–426
von Bogdandy A et al (2012) Reverse Solange – protecting the essence of fundamental rights against EU member states. Common Market Law Rev 49:489–519
von Bogdandy A et al (2018) Guest editorial: a potential constitutional moment for the European rule of law – the importance of red lines. Common Market Law Rev 55:983–995
von Danwitz T (2018) Values and the rule of law: foundation of the European Union – an inside perspective from the ECJ. Revue du droit de l'Union européenne 4:263–270
Voßkuhle A (2017) The idea of the European community of values. Thyssen Lectures. Bittner, Cologne
Waelbroeck M, Oliver P (2017) La Crise de l'État de Droit dans l'Union Européenne: Que Faire? Cahiers de droit européen 26:299–342
Weiler JHH (2016a) Epilogue: living in a glass house: Europe, democracy and the rule of law. In: Closa C, Kochenov D (eds) Reinforcing rule of law oversight in the European Union. Cambridge University Press, Cambridge, pp 313–326
Weiler JHH (2016b) Taking (Europe's) values seriously. In: Hofmann R, Kadelbach S (eds) Law beyond the state. Campus, Frankfurt, pp 93–150
Wendel M (2019) Mutual trust, essence and federalism – between consolidating and fragmenting the area of freedom, security an justice after LM. Eur Const Law Rev 15:17–47
Williams AT (2009) Taking values seriously: towards a philosophy of EU law. Oxf J Legal Stud 29:549–577

Wohlfahrt C (2016) Die Vermutung unmittelbarer Wirkung des Unionsrechts. Plädoyer für die Aufgabe der Kriterien hinreichender Genauigkeit und Unbedingtheit. Springer, Heidelberg
Zglinski J (2018) The rise of deference: the margin of appreciation and decentralized judicial review in EU free movement law. Common Market Law Rev 55:1341–1385

Luke Dimitrios Spieker is a PhD Candidate and Research Fellow at the Max Planck Institute for Comparative Public Law and International Law, Heidelberg.

Suspension of EU Funds Paid to Member States Breaching the Rule of Law: Is the Commission's Proposal Legal?

Justyna Łacny

Contents

This chapter is a result of the research project No 2019/35/B/HS5/01024 financed by the National Science Centre, Poland.

J. Łacny (✉)
Department of Administration and Social Sciences, Warsaw University of Technology, Warsaw, Poland
e-mail: justyna.lacny@pw.edu.pl

A. von Bogdandy et al. (eds.), *Defending Checks and Balances in EU Member States*, Beiträge zum ausländischen öffentlichen Recht und Völkerrecht 298,
https://doi.org/10.1007/978-3-662-62317-6_11

Abstract The existing scale of violations of the rule of law by some Member States, including capturing judicial independence by their governments, is a relatively new phenomenon for the EU; the one for which the EU based on the EU common values (Article 2 TEU) originally was not prepared to effectively deal with. The EU reacts to current rule of law crisis by using different legal methods and instruments: it *inter alia* applies existing procedures (Article 7 TEU procedure and with more success general infringement procedure under Articles 258-260 TFEU) and struggles to develop new ones. This contribution is focused on the new EU legislative initiative of connecting in the Multiannual Financial Framework (MFF) 2021–2027 transfers of EU funds to Member States with their observance of the rule of law. Or to put it differently, this legislative initiatives would authorize the EU institutions to suspend regular transfers of EU funds to Member States that systematically breach the rule of law.

1 Introduction

Although in many people's views the EU was established to achieve individual and common interests of the Member States, it would be over simplistic to recognise the EU only as the community of interests. The EU is, if not primarily, the community of values such as human dignity, freedom, democracy, equality, the rule of law and respect for human rights (Article 2 TEU). If these values are put at risk or violated and the mutual trust among the Member States is hence infringed, possibilities of identifying and accomplishing common European interests are weakened. This may undermine legitimacy and rationality of the whole 'European project'. Therefore the protection of the common European values (Article 2 TEU) lies at the heart of the EU integration process.

This chapter presents the latest Commission's proposal aimed to ensure the Member States' respect of the rule of law—one of the common values on which the EU is based. The Commission intends to make regular transfers of EU funds to Member States paid from the EU budget for the implementation of different EU policies (mainly the agriculture and the cohesion policies) conditional upon their respect of the rule of law (known as 'the conditionality mechanism'). This contribution comments on the Draft Regulation as first proposed by the Commission (hereinafter: Commission version[1]) and amended during the first reading by the European Parliament (hereinafter: European Parliament version[2]). This mechanism

[1]Proposal for a regulation of the European Parliament and of the Council on the protection of the Union budget in the event of generalized gaps in the rule of law in the Member States (COM(2018) 324 final). See Halmai (2018).

[2]European Parliament legislative resolution of 4 April 2019 on the proposal for a regulation of the European Parliament and of the Council on the protection of the Union's budget in case of generalised deficiencies as regards the rule of law in the Member States (COM(2018) 324 final).

toward Member States and relations between this mechanism and other EU Treaties procedures aimed at stopping breaches of the rule of law (the Article 7 TEU procedure) and the general infringements procedure (Article 258-260 TFEU).

2 Conditionality Mechanism in EU Law

2.1 The Conditionality Mechanism in EU Internal and External Relations

The conditionality mechanism is an EU policy tool which has been in use since the late 1980s.[3] It is based on the assumption that the Member States and third countries are prompted to comply with requirements established under EU law in return for the advantages obtained. Or in other words, they would adhere to EU law due to the risk of losing advantages, particularly financial ones.

Initially, the conditionality mechanism was applied in the EU's external relations, in international agreements in which the EU made the granting of humanitarian aid to third countries conditional upon their respect for human rights.[4] It continues to be so applied at present. To give some examples. If countries participating in the European Neighbourhood Policy[5] implement actions agreed upon with the EU, in return they receive financial assistance and the trade and visa facilitation from the EU.[6] As another example, if candidate countries want to join the EU, they must have institutions which guarantee a stable democracy, the rule of law, respect for human and minority rights as well as market economy allowing the national producers to cope with competitive pressure and market forces within the EU (the so called 'Copenhagen criteria').

Increasingly, the conditionality mechanism is being used in the EU's internal relations as well, in legal acts governing relations between the EU and its Member States. For example, the macroeconomic conditionality mechanism was introduced in 1994 to support the establishment of the European Monetary Union. It conditioned access of the less developed Member States (then Greece, Ireland, Spain and Portugal) to the Cohesion Fund on the adoption by these States of economic convergence plans and their compliance with the EU budgetary deficit rules. It has

[3]For more on the concept of the conditionality see: Vita (2017).

[4]Fierro (2003), Bartels (2005), McKenzie and Meissner (2017) and Cornelius (2016).

[5]Through its European Neighbourhood Policy, the EU works with its southern and eastern neighbours to foster stabilisation, security and prosperity, in line with the Global Strategy for the EU Foreign and Security Policy. See: https://eeas.europa.eu/diplomatic-network/european-neighbourhood-policy-enp/330/european-neighbourhood-policy-enp_en; Joint Communication to the European Parliament, the Council, the European Economic and Social Committee and the Committee of the Regions, *A review of the European Neighborhood Policy* (JOIN (2015) 50 final).

[6]Council Implementing Decision 2012/156/EU of 13 March 2012 suspending commitments from the Cohesion Fund for Hungary with effect from 1 January 2013, OJ L 78/19.

been enforced only once, against Hungary in 2011, albeit without leading to an actual cut-off in funding.[7] As another example, in order to address the 2008 financial crisis in the EU and support those Member States with major budgetary difficulties, the EU made the financial assistance granted to them conditional on their compliance with the macro-economic convergence criteria.[8]

It has been observed that the increasing use of the conditionality mechanism in the EU's internal relations marks a shift towards a generalised 'conditionality culture' in the relationship between the EU and its Member States. The compliance function that the conditionality mechanism was aimed to ensure in the EU's external relations was—in the EU's internal relations—initially supposed to be fulfilled primarily by the principle of sincere cooperation between the EU and the Member States.[9] If a Member State breaches its EU obligation(s), the principle of sincere cooperation does not allow the EU institutions themselves or other Member States to deprive the State in breach of its EU benefits; however the Commission or another Member State can take the case against this State to the CJEU, and as a last resort financial sanctions may be imposed on the breaching State.[10] Based on this principle, the compliant Member States must continue to comply with their EU obligations, even if others do not. It has been observed that the shift from the principle of loyal cooperation to the conditionality mechanism in the EU's internal relations was brought about by the 2004 enlargement, with its attendant concerns that some 'new' Member States might decline to fulfil their EU obligations.[11] Calls for the establishment of the conditionality mechanism, allowing for the suspension of EU funding to Member States breaching the rule of law (discussed further on in this chapter), may be considered as proof that these concerns related with 'new' Member States were correct. That could mean that we are heading toward a new era of conditionality in the EU.

2.2 The Financial Conditionality Mechanisms in EU Secondary Law on EU Funds

In the debate on the Draft Regulation introducing a new conditionality mechanism to EU law it is rightly noted that there already exists a legal basis that the Commission could apply to suspend transfers of EU funds to Member States violating the rule of law.[12] It has been claimed that such an opportunity is provided by the Common

[7]Council Implementing Decision 2012/156/EU of 13 March 2012 suspending commitments from the Cohesion Fund for Hungary with effect from 1 January 2013, OJ L 78/19.

[8]Atik (2016) and Louis (2010).

[9]Article 4 (3) TEU.

[10]Article 258-260 TFEU.

[11]Cremona (2005).

[12]Butler (2018), Scheppele et al. (2018) and Kelemen and Scheppele (2018).

Provisions Regulation (hereafter: CP Regulation)[13] containing rules on spending the European Structural and Investment Funds (hereafter: ESIF) which finance implementation of the cohesion policy in the Member States. Similar rules also allow for the suspension of EU funds transferred to Member States for implementation of Common Agricultural Policy (CAP).[14]

Under the CP Regulation, the Member States spending ESIF must establish a management and control system and ensure its effective functioning.[15] This system is comprised of the bodies designated by the Member States (e.g. the managing authorities, audit institutions), tasks they carry out in relation to EU funds (e.g. carrying out controls, making payments, imposing sanctions) and tools allowing for proper management and control of EU funds (e.g. databases, computer systems). This system should guarantee that these funds are spent in the Member States in accordance with EU law and that the risk of their losses is minimised. If the Commission finds a serious deficiency in the effective functioning of the management and control system in the Member State, which has put at risk the EU funds, it is authorised to suspend the payments of these funds transferred to this State.[16] It may also recover them[17] by imposing financial corrections on this State which leads to definitive loss of the amount of the EU funds imposed as corrections. It is claimed in the EU legal doctrine that systemic violations of the rule of law by a Member State, e.g. undermining of judicial independence, can be classified as a serious deficiency in the effective functioning of the management and control system in such State. In such a case, the Commission could suspend the EU funds transferred to this State, or recover them by imposing financial correction on this State. So far, the Commission has not explored either of these possibilities.[18]

Another example provided by the CP Regulation relates to the national system of legal complaints. Under this Regulation, the Member States must ensure they have effective arrangements for the examination of complaints concerning the EU funds.[19] They thus must ensure the access of natural and legal persons to remedies

[13] Articles 23-24 Regulation No 1303/2013 of the European Parliament and of the Council of 17.12.2013 laying down common provisions on the European Regional Development Fund, the European Social Fund, the Cohesion Fund, the European Agricultural Fund for Rural Development and the European Maritime and Fisheries Fund and laying down general provisions on the European Regional Development Fund, the European Social Fund, the Cohesion Fund and the European Maritime and Fisheries Fund and repealing Council Regulation (EC) No 1083/2006 (OJ L 347, 20.12.2013, p. 320).

[14] Article 58 (2) Regulation No 1306/2013 of the European Parliament and of the Council of 17 December 2013 on the financing, management and monitoring of the common agricultural policy and repealing Council Regulations (EEC) No 352/78, (EC) No 165/94, (EC) No 2799/98, (EC) No 814/2000, (EC) No 1290/2005 and (EC) No 485/2008 (OJ L 347, 20.12.2013, p. 549).

[15] Articles 72–74 and Article 122 (1) CP Regulation. The same concerns the agricultural spending, see: Article 58 (2) 2 and Articles 67–73 Regulation No 1306/2013.

[16] Article 142 (a) CP Regulation.

[17] Article 144 (1) (a) CP Regulation.

[18] Kelemen and Scheppele (2018).

[19] Article 74 (3) CP Regulation.

allowing effective legal protection in cases concerning these funds, including access to independent and impartial tribunals.[20] For a Member State with an established record of breaching the rule of law, including capturing an independent prosecution and judiciary, it could be difficult to prove that it fulfils this requirement.

So far the Commission has not applied the possibilities offered by the CP Regulation to try to influence on Member States breaching the rule of law. Therefore, the real problem may be not the lack of adequate legal tools, but the lack of political will on the part of the Commission to use the tools that already exist. Instead, the Commission has proposed the Draft Regulation establishing the conditionality mechanism which is commented on in this chapter.

3 The Conditionality Mechanism Applied for Breaches of the Rule of Law

The EU is a community of law and its values constitute the very basis of its existence. Respect for these values must be ensured throughout all EU policies, including the EU budget.[21] Having this in mind the Commission presented the Draft Regulation to respond to the common diagnosis that the EU lacks effective legal instruments to stop systemic breaches of the rule of law by Member States.[22] It claimed that it cannot be accepted any longer and that these breaches damage the financial interests of the EU.[23] Some authors point out a paradox: that the EU transfers the largest amounts of EU funds to governments of the Member States with a history of long-standing violations of the rule of law,[24] for example to

[20]Article 19(1) TEU and Article 47 of the Charter of Fundamental Rights. See: CJEU, Case C-562/12, *Liivimaa Lihaveis MTÜ*, ECLI:EU:C:2014:2229, paras 67–75.

[21]Communication from the Commission. A new, modern Multiannual Financial Framework for a European Union that delivers efficiently on its priorities post-2020. COM(2018) 98 final.

[22]Closa and Kochenov (2016), Jakab and Kochenov (2017), Schroeder (2016), Hatje (2018), Costa (2017) and Konstadinides (2017).

[23]The Commission based the Draft Regulation on Article 322 (1) (a) TFEU which authorises the European Parliament and the Council to adopt regulations containing financial rules determining *inter alia* procedures for establishing and implementing the EU budget. This Article is commonly applied as a legal basis for adopting Financial Regulations—the main EU secondary budgetary law (presently binding Financial Regulation no 2018/1046). Selection of this legal basis could indicate that the Commission finds the conditionality mechanism as an instrument ensuring sound implementation of the EU budget (Article 317 TFEU). This is, however, in contradiction with the overall assumption expressed in the Draft Regulation that its primary objective is to protect the financial interests of the EU against damages resulting from the breaches of the rule of law by the Member States. Protection of these interests would require that the Draft Regulation would be adopted based on Article 325 (4) TFEU. Under both articles (Article 322 (1) (a) TFEU and Article 325 (4) TFEU) legal acts are adopted by the European Parliament and the Council in accordance with the ordinary legislative procedure after consulting the Court of Auditors.

[24]Kelemen and Scheppele (2018) and Peel et al. (2019).

Poland—the largest overall recipient taking in 86 billion EUR from various ESIF in the Multiannual Financial Framework (MFF) 2014–2020; and Hungary—the largest recipient of EU funds on a *per capita* basis, with more than 95% of all public investment in MFF 2014–2020 having been co-financed by the EU.[25] The conditionality mechanism proposed to be introduced by the Draft Regulation is supposed to remedy this situation. Before discussing this, it is necessary to engage in some terminological explanations.

3.1 The Notion of 'the Rule of Law'

Understandably, the key notion '*the rule of law*' was defined in the Draft Regulation with regard to the Union values enshrined in Article 2 TEU.[26] They include the principles of legality, implying a transparent, accountable, democratic and pluralistic process for enacting laws; legal certainty; a prohibition of arbitrariness of executive powers; effective judicial protection by independent courts, including protection of fundamental rights; separation of powers; and equality before the law. On top of this the European Parliament proposed to include the 'Copenhagen criteria' in this notion, which candidate countries must fulfil in order to accede to the EU. They include, beyond the rule of law, the stability of the institutions guaranteeing democracy, respect for and protection of human rights and minorities, and further a functioning market economy and the capacity to cope with the competition and market forces, as well as the ability to meet the obligations of Union membership.[27]

3.2 The Notion 'Generalised Deficiency As Regards the Rule of Law in a Member State'

A key notion of the Draft Regulation is '*the generalised deficiency as regards the rule of law in a Member State*'.[28] Detection of such a deficiency in a Member State is a necessary premise to apply the conditionality mechanism to this State.

A generalised deficiency as regards the rule of law in a Member State is defined as a widespread or recurrent practice or omission, or a measure by public authorities which violates the rule of law and affects or risks affecting the principle of sound

[25] It has been noted that the situations of Poland and Hungary differ, since there are no well-proven cases that breaches of the rule of law by the Polish authorities have led to the misspending of EU funds (von Brauneck 2019), while such is the case in Hungary (Kelemen and Scheppele 2018) and Romania (Pech et al. 2019).

[26] Article (a) Draft Regulation (Commission proposal).

[27] Article 49 TEU.

[28] On similar notion of 'systemic deficiency as regards the rule of law' see: von Bogdandy (2019).

financial management or the protection of the financial interests of the EU.[29] Some clarification is necessary as regards the principle of sound financial management and the protection of the financial interests of the EU.

3.2.1 The Principle of Sound Financial Management (Article 317 TFEU)

The '*principle of sound financial management*', as set forth in the TFEU,[30] relates to the EU budget and its implementation. The Financial Regulation no 2018/1046[31]—the main EU secondary budgetary law act—provides explanations on the meaning of these terms.

The EU budget forecasts and authorises for each financial year all revenue and expenditures considered necessary for the EU. Implementation of this budget requires the carrying out of activities related to the management, monitoring, control and auditing of EU appropriations, undertaken in accordance with the relevant methods of its implementation.[32] The TFEU entrusts responsibility for the implementation of the EU budget to the Commission.[33] The latter is obliged to implement the EU budget in cooperation with the Member States, on its own responsibility and within the limits of the appropriations, having regard to the principles of sound financial management. Member States must cooperate with the Commission during implementation of the EU budget in order to ensure that the appropriations are used in accordance with this principle.[34] When the European Court of Auditors (the ECA) undertakes its core tasks and examines how the Commission implements the EU budget, it checks, *inter alia*, whether the financial management has been sound.[35]

According to Financial Regulation no 2018/1046,[36] the principle of sound financial management—one of the EU budgetary principles[37]—requires that the EU budget is implemented in accordance with the principles of economy, efficiency,

---

[29] Article 2 (b) Draft Regulation.

[30] Article 287 (2) 2 TFEU, Article 310 (5) TFEU and Article 317 TFEU.

[31] Regulation (EU, Euratom) 2018/1046 of the European Parliament and of the Council of 18 July 2018 on the financial rules applicable to the general budget of the Union, amending Regulations (EU) No 1296/2013, (EU) No 1301/2013, (EU) No 1303/2013, (EU) No 1304/2013, (EU) No 1309/2013, (EU) No 1316/2013, (EU) No 223/2014, (EU) No 283/2014, and Decision No 541/2014/EU and repealing Regulation (EU, Euratom) No 966/2012, OJ L 193, 30.7.2018, p. 1, hereafter Financial Regulation no 2018/1046.

[32] Article 2 (7) Financial Regulation no 2018/1046.

[33] Article 310 (5) TFEU.

[34] Article 317 TFEU.

[35] Article 287 (2) TFEU.

[36] Article 2 (59), Article 6 and Article 33 Financial Regulation no 2018/1046.

[37] Next to principles of unity, budgetary accuracy, annuality, equilibrium, unit of account, universality, specification, and transparency.

and effectiveness.[38] The CJEU claims that the principle of sound financial management (applied in area of the EU funds) corresponds to the principles of sincere co-operation (applied in general terms of EU law[39]). The CJEU often recalls this principle in the context of EU rules establishing tasks related to the management and spending of EU funds, to underline the necessity to protect them.[40]

3.2.2 Protection of the Financial Interests of the Union (Article 325 TFEU)

The objective of the conditionality mechanism, eventually to be established by the Draft Regulation, is to protect the financial interests of the Union (the EU budget) against damages deriving from breaches of the rule of law by the Member States. This fact is stipulated in the title of this Draft (Regulation on the protection of the Union's budget) and in its provisions.[41] They foresee that this Draft would establish rules necessary for the protection of the Union's budget in the case of generalised deficiencies as regards the rule of law in the Member States.[42] What's more, a generalised deficiency as regards the rule of law in a Member State—a premise necessary to launch the conditionality mechanism—was defined as a common national practice violating the rule of law and affecting or risking to affect the protection of the financial interests of the EU.[43]

---

[38]The principle of economy stipulates that the resources used by the EU institutions concerned in the pursuit of its activities are made available in due time, in appropriate quantity and quality, and at the best price. The principle of efficiency concerns the best relationship between the resources employed, the activities undertaken and the achievement of objectives. The principle of effectiveness concerns the extent to which the objectives pursued are achieved through the activities undertaken.

[39]Article 4 (3) TEU.

[40]CJEU, Cases C-138/03, C-324/03 and C-431/03 *Italy v. Commission*, ECLI:EU:C:2005:714, para. 44; CFI, Case T-345/03 *Evropaïki Dynamiki v. Commission*, ECLI:EU:T:2015:168, para. 77; CFI, Case T-549/08 *Luxemburg v. Commission*, ECLI:EU:T:2010:244, para. 47; Court, Case T-265/08 *Germany v. Commission*, ECLI:EU:T:2012:434, para. 40; CJEU, Case C-500/99 *P Conserve Italia v. Commission*, ECLI:EU:C:2002:45, para. 88; CFI, Case T-308/05, *Italy v. Commission,* ECLI:EU:T:2007:382, para. 109; opinion of AG Trstenjak, Case C-539/09 *Germany v. Commission*, ECLI:EU:C:2011:345, para. 95.

[41]See also paras 9–11, opinion of the Court of Auditors No 1/2018 concerning the proposal of 2 May 2018 for a regulation of the European Parliament and of the Council on the protection of the Union's budget in case of generalised deficiencies as regards the rule of law in the Member States, hereafter: ECA opinion No 1/2018.

[42]Article 1 Draft Regulation.

[43]Article2 (b) Draft Regulation.

The notion '*protection of the financial interests of the Union*', is used in the TFEU,[44] defined in EU secondary law,[45] and clarified by the CJEU.[46] The '*financial interests of the Union*' encompass revenues, expenditures, and assets covered by the EU budgets, the budgets of the EU institutions, bodies, offices and agencies established under the EU Treaties, and budgets directly or indirectly managed and monitored by them. Article 325 TFEU, the main Treaty provision regarding financial interests of the Union, obliges the Member States and the EU institutions to counter fraud and any other illegal activities affecting these interests through deterrent measures that should ensure their effective protection. In turn, the Member State on their side should take the same measures to counter fraud affecting the financial interests of the EU as they take to counter fraud affecting their own financial interests (the assimilation principle).

To sum up, a generalised deficiency as regards the rule of law, the existence of which in a Member State is a necessary premise of launching the conditionality mechanism, indicates (1) a common conduct on the part of public authorities of the Member States that (2) violate the rule of law, which (3) adversely affects or is likely to affect the EU funds (the financial interests of EU, Article 325 TFEU) or its management (the sound financial management of the EU, Article 317 TFEU).

3.2.3 Types of Generalised Deficiency As Regards the Rule of Law

Presented definition of 'a generalised deficiency as regards the rule of law' was formulated broadly-worded. To give some examples of these generalised deficiencies and to limit the scope of interpretation of this notion at the same time, the Commission and the European Parliament established their specific types.

The Commission provided for two lists of generalised deficiency as regards the rule of law. The first list includes, generally speaking, the conduct of national authorities (administrative, investigative, and judicial) related to EU funds. The list is left open. Deficiencies included there do not have to be serious, since they include, e.g., practices on the part of a national authority affecting the effective and timely cooperation with the European Anti-Fraud Office (OLAF) or the European Public Prosecutor's Office.[47] Detection of these types of deficiencies as regards the rule of law in the Member States *leads to*[48] the launching of a conditionality mechanism. In contrast, the second list of generalised deficiencies as regards the rule of law indicates conducts on the part of national administration that *may lead*[49] to the initiation of the conditionality mechanism. In this case the deficiencies are related

[44]Article 310 (5) and Article 325 TFEU.

[45]Article (1) (a) Directive (EU) 2017/1371.

[46]Opinion of AG Jacobs in Case C-11/00 *Commission v. ECB*, ECLI:EU:C:2002:556.

[47]Article 3 (1) (f) Draft Regulation (Commission proposal).

[48]Article 3 (1) Draft Regulation (Commission proposal).

[49]Article 3 (2) Draft Regulation (Commission proposal).

merely to the national judiciary and concern its constitutional determinants (e.g. judicial independence), administration (e.g. lack of relevant financial and human resources), and actions performed (e.g. prosecuting, sanctioning). There is, however, no requirement that these deficiencies must or may affect the financial interest of the Union.

The European Parliament's approach was similar, as it also created two lists of generalised deficiencies as regards the rule of law. The first, also open list, relates to the conduct of national administration and justice and includes, e.g., failing to prevent, correct and sanction arbitrary or unlawful decisions made by public authorities; limiting the availability and effectiveness of legal remedies, including through restrictive procedural rules; lack of implementation of judgments or limiting the effective investigation, prosecution and sanctioning of breaches of law. This list includes *inter alia* 'endangering the administrative capacity of Member States to respect the obligations of Union membership, including the capacity to effectively implement EU law'. Last but not least, measures that weaken the protection of confidentiality of communications between lawyers and clients were also included on this list.[50] The second list includes generalised deficiencies as regards the rule of law that endanger or risk to endanger financial interests of the Union.[51] This list includes general deficiencies included on the Commission's first list,[52] as well as two new breaches, concerning among other Copenhagen criteria[53] and fundamental rights.[54]

To sum up deliberation on the notion of '*a generalised deficiency as regards the rule of law*'—the premises necessary to launch a conditionality mechanism, it can be said that it has been formulated extremely broadly, and its scope is virtually impossible to determine. The general wording leaves the Commission and the Council—the EU institutions that would launch the conditionality mechanism—with a wide margin of discretion, which is undesirable, especially from the point of view of the principles of legal certainty and legality of sanctions. This principle requires that any provision imposing sanctions on entities must be formulated clearly and precisely, so that they can determine with certainty the scope of their rights and

[50] Article 2 (a) Draft Regulation (European Parliament proposal).

[51] Article 3 Draft Regulation (European Parliament proposal).

[52] Article 3 (1) Draft Regulation (Commission proposal).

[53] Distortion or risk of distortion of proper functioning of the market economy and effective implementation of obligations of membership, including adherence to the aim of political, economic and monetary union could constitute generalised deficiencies as regards the rule of law (Article 3 (1) aa Draft Regulation, European Parliament proposal).

[54] This same classification could be given to the shortages in proper implementation of the EU budget following a systemic violation of fundamental rights (Article 3 (1) fa Draft Regulation (European Parliament proposal).

obligations and take appropriate actions.[55] As required by the CJEU, this principle should be rigorously observed, particularly in the case of provisions that have or may have a financial impact. Viewed in this light, it may be stated that the notion of a generalised deficiency as regards the rule of law is neither clear nor precise. Its strict formulation is even more necessary if one takes into account the oppressive nature that the conditionality mechanism may have on the Member State and beneficiaries (see Sect. 5.2). It seems highly undesirable that the EU institutions, in taking actions against Member States for breaching the rule of law, may itself frustrate this rule by applying premises which are formulated (too) broadly. The wide scope of the competences conferred on the EU institutions under the conditionality mechanism has also been criticized by the ECA, which recommended to the EU legislator to establish precise criteria defining the concept of a generalised deficiency as regards the rule of law, and to specify measures to be taken in this framework. The suggested clarifications, sharpening the Draft Regulation, could satisfy the principle of legal certainty and legality of sanctions as well as limit the scope of the EU institutions' discretion.[56]

4 Measures Applied Under the Conditionality Mechanism

The conditionality mechanism is a general term under which specific measures would be imposed on the Member States breaching the rule of law. These measures would depend on which method of implementing the EU budget is used for spending the EU funds. These methods—namely direct, shared, and indirect management—require different entities incurring expenditures financed from the EU budget (EU funds) to comply with related tasks and responsibilities established in EU law, and authorise the Commission to take supervisory actions to ensure their proper spending.[57] These methods vary according to which entity is spending the EU funds. In the case of direct management, the funds are spent by the Commission, through its departments and executive agencies; in the case of shared management—by the Member States; and in the case of indirect management—by third countries, international organizations, and other entities.[58]

[55]CJEU Cases: 70-83, *Kloppenburg*, ECLI:EU:C:1984:71; 325/85, *Ireland v. Commission*, ECLI:EU:C:1987:546, para. 18; C-143/93, *Gebroeders van Es Douane Agenten*, ECLI:EU:C:1996:45, para. 27; C-177/96, *Banque Indosuez*, ECLI:EU:C:1997:494; C-439/01, *Cipra, Kvasnicka*, ECLI:EU:C:2003:31, para. 49; C-110/03, *Belgium v. Commission*, ECLI:EU:C:2005:223, para. 30; C-158/06, *Stichting ROM-projecten*, ECLI:EU:C:2007:370, paras 25–26.

[56]ECA opinion No 1/2018, paras 12-16, 19.

[57]The methods of implementation of the EU budget is determined by Financial Regulation 2018/104, Article 62.

[58]Financial Regulation 2018/1046, Article 62 (1) (c).

Here we focus on shared management,[59] under which the EU funds are spent for the implementation of the CAP and the cohesion policy, altogether constituting about 70% of the EU's budgetary expenditures.[60] If the EU funds are spent under shared management, the following measures can be applied under the conditionality mechanism: suspension of approval of programs or amendments thereof; suspension of commitments; reduction of commitments, including through financial corrections or transfers to other spending programs; reduction of pre-financing; an interruption of payment deadlines; and suspension of payments.[61]

The Draft Regulation does not establish how these measures should operate in practice, nor even provide their general legal characteristics. There is also no guidance as to which types of the above-mentioned measures should be applied in the case of certain generalised deficiencies as regards the rule of law. The Draft Regulation simply refers to the names of particular measures, which may suggest the essence of the activities undertaken. Very general information is given in the preamble, which states that these measures should include the suspension of payments and of commitments, a reduction of funding under existing commitments, and a prohibition on concluding new commitments with recipients.[62]

The application of these measures requires recourse to the EU sectoral Regulations, which provide specific rules for the spending of the EU funds for EU policies, e.g. for the CAP and the cohesion policy. Surprisingly, the Draft Regulation does not mention such a reference. It must also be noted that, at present, a detailed and final assessment of these sectoral Regulations is not possible since they are undergoing legislative processes in the EU institutions heading the new MFF 2021–2027.[63] At this point in time, it can only be stated that these measures can be taken at various stages of the implementation of EU policies: from the stage of approval of national programs by the Commission to the stage of making legal commitments by the Commission, followed by the payments of the EU funds to the Member States. It is clear however that one of these measures consists of suspending the payment of EU funds,[64] and this is what the remainder of this contribution will mainly focus on.

The undefined nature of the measures to be imposed under the conditionality mechanism deserves the same criticism which was already formulated towards the

[59]Craig (2012), p. 27; Hofmann et al. (2012); Schöndorf-Haubold (2011).

[60]Communication from the Commission. A new, modern Multiannual Financial Framework for a European Union that delivers efficiently on its priorities post-2020. COM(2018) 98 final.

[61]Article 4 (1) (b) Draft Regulation (Commission proposal).

[62]Recital 13 preamble Draft Regulation (Commission proposal).

[63]Proposal for a Regulation of the European Parliament and of the Council on the financing, management and monitoring of the common agricultural policy and repealing Regulation (EU) No 1306/2013 (COM(2018)393 final) and proposal for a Regulation of the European Parliament and of the Council laying down common provisions on the European Regional Development Fund, the European Social Fund Plus, the Cohesion Fund, and the European Maritime and Fisheries Fund and financial rules for those and for the Asylum and Migration Fund, the Internal Security Fund and the Border Management and Visa Instrument (COM(2018)375 final).

[64]See point 7 ECA opinion No 1/2018.

vagueness of the premise of its application, namely notion of 'a generalised deficiency as regards the rule of law' (see: Sect. 3.2 above). Principles of legal certainty and legality of sanctions must be recalled once again to evoke that any provision imposing sanctions must be formulated clearly and precisely.[65] The CJEU requires that these principle should be rigorously observed, particularly in the case of provisions that have or may have a financial impact. Viewed in this light, it may be stated that neither the premise of launching the conditionality mechanism (the notion of 'a generalised deficiency as regards the rule of law') nor measures imposed under this mechanism are clear nor precise. Its strict formulation is even more necessary if one takes into account the oppressive nature that the conditionality mechanism may have on the Member State and beneficiaries (see Sect. 6).

What's important and deserves credit, the Draft Regulation provides rules which the EU institutions (the Commission or the Council) should take into account when imposing measures under the conditionality mechanism.[66] They would be obliged to ensure that these measures should be proportionate to the nature, gravity, and scope of the generalised deficiency as regards the rule of law. These measures also should, insofar as possible, target the EU actions affected or potentially affected by that deficiency. The requirement of proportionality between the generalised deficiency as regards the rule of law, that is EU law infringement leading to launching of the conditionality mechanism on one side, and measures adopted under this mechanism on the other side signifies that these measures are deemed as sanctions imposed upon the Member State for breaching the rule of law. Under EU law, the principle of proportionality is the *sine qua non* condition of adoption of any sanctions imposed as the result of an infringement of a law.

To sum up this sub-section, the Draft Regulation provides generally-formulated premises for launching the conditionality mechanism together with their very specific examples, which can lead to measures of a really unknown (as yet) character. This extremely broad formulation of provisions defining prohibited infringements of the law and sanctions imposed for their perpetration raises concerns as to their legality. It is because it cannot be claimed that these provisions are clear and or precise, as the principles of legal certainty and legality of sanctions would require. No matter how challenging this may be, respect for the principles of legality and legal certainty would require the premises for launching the conditionality mechanism to be formulated more unequivocally. Provisions of the Draft Regulation should clearly indicate major types and a closed list of examples of systematic breaches of the rule of law that could lead to the activation of this mechanism.

[65]CJEU Cases: 70-83, *Kloppenburg*, ECLI:EU:C:1984:71; 325/85, *Ireland v. Commission*, ECLI:EU:C:1987:546, para. 18; C-143/93, *Gebroeders van Es Douane Agenten*, ECLI:EU:C:1996:45, para. 27; C-177/96, *Banque Indosuez*, ECLI:EU:C:1997:494; C-439/01, *Cipra, Kvasnicka*, ECLI:EU:C:2003:31, para. 49; C-110/03, *Belgium v. Commission*, ECLI:EU:C:2005:223, para. 30; C-158/06, *Stichting ROM-projecten*, ECLI:EU:C:2007:370, para. 25–26.

[66]Article 4 (3) Draft Regulation (Commission proposal) and Article 5a Draft Regulation (European Parliament proposal).

These provisions should be formulated taking into account the standards established in the case-law of the CJEU and the ECtHR for the imposition of sanctions.

5 The Procedure for Adoption of a Decision Applying the Conditionality Mechanism

While the proposals lodged by the Commission and the European Parliament concerning premises for launching the conditionality mechanism are generally in line with each other, their proposals for procedural rules to be applied to this end differ considerably. Disparities concern the key issue, namely determining the EU institution that would adopt a decision applying the conditionality mechanism and the procedural steps that would be taken in this regard. While the Commission proposed that this decision should be adopted by the Council, on a request from the Commission, according to the European Parliament this decision should be adopted by the Commission, with a right of the European Parliament and the Council to oppose it or change it. These issues are presented below.

5.1 Initiation of the Procedure

According to the Draft Regulation, initiation of the conditionality mechanism would require a determination that there is at least one generalised deficiency as regards the rule of law in the Member State targeted (see Sect. 3.2).

The Commission proposes that it would conduct an inquiry by itself and that if it found a generalised deficiency, it would indicate it in a written notification submitted to the Member State concerned. The Commission could request additional information from this State, including proposals for remedial measures. The Member State would have to provide the Commission with information within the time-limits set by the Commission, not less than 1 month from the date of the written notification. When assessing the existence of a generalised deficiency as regards the rule of law, the Commission could take into account all information, including judgments of the CJEU, reports of the ECA, and recommendations of international organizations.[67]

The European Parliament has proposed two modifications to this procedure. The first concerned the establishment of an advisory panel of independent experts (hereafter: Panel) that would assist the Commission in assessing the existence of a generalised deficiency as regards the rule of law in a given Member State. The second one concerns obliging the Commission to take into account certain Copenhagen criteria while making such an assessment.

[67] Article 5 Draft Regulation (Commission proposal).

The primary function of the Panel would be to assist the Commission in identifying generalised deficiencies as regards the rule of law in the Member States.[68] This function would be achieved in a twofold manner. Firstly, the Panel would adopt *ad hoc* opinions concerning generalised deficiencies as regards the rule of law as examined by the Commission. Secondly, the Panel would annually assess situations in all Member States as regards their respect for the rule of law and would make a public summary of its findings each year. The Draft Regulation thus would create a new body—the Panel—entrusted with the task of continuous monitoring of the rule of law situation in all the Member States.

As regards the Copenhagen criteria, the European Parliament proposes that the Commission should examine them when assessing the existence of generalised deficiencies as regards the rule of law in a Member State. The criteria should include: chapters of the *aquis* on judiciary and fundamental rights, justice, freedom and security; financial control and taxation; as well as guidelines used in the context of the Cooperation and Verification Mechanism (CVM).[69] The idea to link the compliance with the rule of law with the Copenhagen criteria may raise concerns. It is not evident why and how the compliance of the Member States with the legal principle (the rule of law) could be assessed by evaluation of political criteria, in some cases not even substantially related with the rule of law (e.g. financial control and taxation).

5.2 *Who Adopts the Decision?*

The subsequent action, after the Commission finds a generalised deficiency as regards the rule of law in the Member State, consists of the adoption of a decision launching the conditionality mechanism (see Sect. 4). The Commission's and the European Parliament's proposals considerably differ as to who should adopt this decision.

---

[68]The Panel would be established by the Commission from specialists of constitutional law and financial and budgetary matters. Each national parliament of the Member States would nominate one expert to this Panel and the European Parliament would appoint five experts. Representatives of relevant organisations and networks could be invited to the Panel as observers. Article 3a Draft Regulation (European Parliament proposal).

[69]CVM is a transitional measure established by the Commission to assist Romania and Bulgaria in progress after their accession to the Union in the fields of judicial reform, corruption and organised crime. The Commission assesses progress under CVM based on benchmarks established for each State. The benchmarks for Romania concern effectiveness and transparency of the judicial system and the fight against and prevention of corruption. The benchmarks for Bulgaria deal with the independence, professionalism, and efficiency of the judicial system and the fight against corruption and organised crime. The Commission reports on developments on a regular basis. For more, see: https://ec.europa.eu/info/policies/justice-and-fundamental-rights/upholding-rule-law/rule-law/assistance-bulgaria-and-romania-under-cvm/cooperation-and-verification-mechanism-bulgaria-and-romania_en.

The Commission proposes that if it detects a generalised deficiency as regards the rule of law in a Member State, it would submit to the Council a proposal for a decision imposing measures on this State, e.g. suspending its payments from the EU funds.[70] This decision would be deemed to have been adopted unless the Council rejects it by a QMV within 1 month of the Commission's submission of its decision.[71] The Council may also amend this proposal by a QMV, with no time limits established for amendment.

The European Parliament proposal differs, as it foresees the adoption of two decisions, both by the Commission. In the first decision, addressed to the Member State concerned, the Commission indicates a measure to be imposed on this State under the conditionality mechanism (e.g. suspension of EU funds). In the second decision, addressed to the European Parliament and to the Council (the EU budgetary authorities), the Commission indicates an amount equivalent as a measure adopted in the first decision (e.g. amount of EU funds suspended). Then this amount is classified as a EU budgetary reserve. The idea to adopt the latter decision, regulating the legal and financial status of the amount concerned under the conditionality mechanism, fills the gap in the Commission proposal, which would not determine what would in legal terms happen to these funds. Both decisions are considered to be adopted unless the European Parliament (acting by majority of the votes cast) or the Council (acting by QMV), amend or reject it within 4 weeks of its receipt.[72]

5.3 Voting in the Council by Reverse QMV

The procedure to be followed by the EU institutions to adopt a decision launching the conditionality mechanism is peculiar and therefore deserves attention. This decision is *not* adopted under the standard legislative procedures provided by the EU Treaties (most commonly applied—the ordinary and special legislative procedures[73]), but under a peculiar procedure created by the Draft Regulation. The same concerns the voting cast in the Council. The Council would *not* vote on this decision by the simple majority votes or by the *ordinary* QMV, the latter being the standard cast provided for the Council's voting by the EU Treaties,[74] but by *reverse* QMV—not foreseen by the EU Treaties.

---

[70] Article 5 (6-8) Draft Regulation (Commission proposal).

[71] The Council votes on the Commission's proposal by *reverse* QMV. For more on this, see Sect. 5.3 below.

[72] Article 5 (6 a) (6 b) (6 c) Draft Regulation (European Parliament proposal).

[73] Articles 289 and 294 TFEU.

[74] Qualified majority votes is the 'standard' voting method in the Council used when the Council takes decisions during the ordinary legislative procedure. About 80% of all EU legislation is adopted with this procedure. A qualified majority is reached in the Council if 55% of Member States vote in favour (16 out of 28) and the proposal is supported by the Member States representing at least 65% of the total EU population. The blocking minority includes at least four Council members representing more than 35% of the EU population (Article 238 TFEU).

In general, when the Council votes by the *ordinary* QMV, obtaining this majority leads to the adoption of a legal act. In the case of voting by *reverse* QMV the logic is different—a proposal submitted by an applicant (in our case—the Commission) is adopted unless the legislator (the Council) *rejects* or *amends* it acting by *standard* QMV in a vote held in a given period. Following this period, a decision is considered adopted. Thus, in the case of *reverse* QMV—a failure to obtain the *standard* QMV necessary to block or change a proposal results in its *adoption* (in the wording of the Draft Regulation 'the decision shall be deemed to have been adopted'), while this majority is necessary to reject or amend it. Under *reverse* QMV abstention counts as positive votes, forcing the Member States to take a clear position and obliging them to explicitly vote against the proposal, rather than following a more politically expedient route of abstaining.

It can therefore be concluded that if the Commission sought to suspend EU funds to a Member State for breaching the rule of law, but it was not convinced of the Council's support, it would much easier achieve its intention under the *reverse* QMV then under the *ordinary* QMV. This is because in the case of voting by *reverse* QMV the decision would only require that the Council would not *reject* it by *ordinary* QMV (within 1 month) or otherwise amend it by such QMV. So, if there is no *ordinary* QMV to reject (within 1 month) or amend the decision, it would be adopted. In contrast, if this decision would be voted by ordinary QMV, to be adopted, it would have to be *approved* by *ordinary* QMV.

According to the Commission, the idea that the Council would vote on a decision launching the conditionality mechanism by *reverse* QMV is dictated by the necessity to protect the financial interests of the Union (in short—the EU funds).[75] It seems rather unthinkable to claim that necessity to protect the EU funds requires circumvention of the EU legislative procedure. It is not the first time in history of the EU when voting in the Council by *reverse* QMV is to be introduced as a remedy allowing an effective implementation of the EU policies. Such voting was already established in 2011 when rules aimed to strengthen effective enforcement of the EU fiscal policy were agreed. Under EU fiscal rules (Article 126 TFEU), the euro area Member States must avoid excessive government deficit (3% of GDP), debt (60% of GDP) and maintain sound and sustainable public finance. The Stability and Growth Pact (the SGP) was signed by all Member States based on Articles 121 and 126 TFEU to facilitate and maintain these rules. The SGP provides for fiscal monitoring of the Member States' budgetary situation by the Commission and the Council. It purpose was to ensure that the Member States maintain and enforce EU fiscal rules and do not exceed budgetary deficit and debt limits. Under the SGP ('preventive arm') each year all Member States submit a compliance report presenting expected fiscal development for the current and subsequent 3 years ('stability programmes' for eurozone Member States and 'convergence programmes' for non-eurozone Member States). If a Member State does not comply with the EU fiscal rules, an 'Excessive Deficit Procedure' (EDP) is initiated under the SGP

---

[75]Recital 15 preamble Draft Regulation. See critics: ECA opinion No 1/2018, para. 12.

('dissuasive arm'). If this situation continues to remain despite multiple warnings, sanctions can be imposed on this Member State. In 2011, in the face of the world financial crisis, enforcement of the SGP was strengthened by the adoption of '*Six Pack*', '*Two Pack*' and '*Fiscal Compact*'. These acts provided for automaticity of sanctions, including interest-bearing deposits, non-interest-bearing deposits and fines to be imposed on the Member States for recurrent breaches of the EU fiscal rules.[76] These sanctions are imposed based on the *reverse* QMV in the Council. The Commission can impose them unless the Council decides by the *reverse* QMV to reject the Commission recommendation within a specified period (usually 10 days). Adoption of these sanctions thus requires a minority of the Member States to agree on the Commission proposal or alternatively an *ordinary* QMV to block or change this proposal.[77] Legality of imposing sanctions on the Member States by voting in the Council by the *reverse* QMV was not contested in action brought before the CJEU. Therefore the position of the CJEU on this issue is unknown.

Coming back to the conditionality mechanism, it can be stated that the logic applied in 2011 in the '*Six Pack*', '*Two Pack*' and '*Fiscal Compact*' in area of sanctions to be imposed for breaching—by the Member States—the EU fiscal rules established under Article 126 TFEU and the SGP was reused in 2018 in the Draft Regulation (the Commission proposal) providing for suspension of EU funds transferred to the Member States systematically breaching the rule of law. In both cases the procedural peculiarities facilitate a procedure of adopting EU secondary acts imposing sanctions on the Member States and strengthen the procedural role of the Commission *vis à vis* a Member State suspected to breach the EU law (the EU fiscal rules or the rule of law). Procedural peculiarities concern both the type of a legislative procedure to be followed to adopt a decision initiating the conditionality mechanism (a special procedure established by the Draft Regulation) and the necessary vote cast in the Council to adopt it (*reverse* QMV). As regards the legislative procedure (adoption of a decision by the Council) the EU Treaties neither provide it as one of the standard legislative procedures that the EU institutions apply to adopt EU secondary law (e.g. legislative, delegated, implementing acts and acts 'without adjective') nor authorise the EU institutions to apply it. So, the Draft Regulation establishes a legislative procedure specially for the sake of the conditionality mechanism, which remains outside of the EU Treaties regime. The same can be said about voting by the Council under the *reverse* QMV to adopt a decision launching the conditionality mechanism. Such a majority is not foreseen under the

---

[76]Articles 4-6 Regulation No 1173/2011 of the European Parliament and of the Council of 16 November 2011 on the effective enforcement of budgetary surveillance in the euro area (OJ L 306, 23.11.2011, p. 1); Article 3 Regulation No 1174/2011 of the European Parliament and of the Council of 16 November 2011 on enforcement measures to correct excessive macroeconomic imbalances in the euro area (OJ L 306, 23.11.2011, p. 8); Article 10 (4) Regulation No 1176/ 2011 of the European Parliament and of the Council of 16 November 2011 on the prevention and correction of macroeconomic imbalances (OJ L 306, 23.11.2011, p. 25); Article 7 Treaty on Stability, Coordination and Governance in the Economic and Monetary Union (Fiscal Compact).

[77]Van Aken and Artige (2013), p. 131; Chalmers et al. (2015), p. 751.

EU Treaties. Just to remind Article 16 (3) TEU foresees that the Council act by a *standard* QMV except where the Treaties provide otherwise. There is no provision under the Treaties which authorise the Council to vote under *reverse* QMV. These doubts inevitably lead to a question of legality of the Draft Regulation establishing procedural conditions of adopting a decision initiating the conditionality mechanism, not mentioned nor foreseen under EU Treaties.

5.4 Decision Lifting the Measures

The Member State against whom the conditionality mechanism was initiated is authorized at any time to provide the Commission with evidence that it has remedied or eliminated the generalised deficiency as regards the rule of law. On this base the Commission assesses the situation in this State with a view toward adopting a decision lifting the conditionality mechanism.[78] This formula was presented by the Commission, and the European Parliament subsequently added two elements to it. The first is that·the Commission should assess the situation in the Member State taking into account the opinion of the Panel (see Sect. 5.1) and second, that the Commission should act within 1 month and in any case within a reasonable timeframe from the date of receipt of the notification from the Member State.[79]

A decision lifting the conditionality mechanism would be issued by the EU institutions that have adopted it—by the Council (as the Commission proposes) or by the Commission (as the European Parliament proposes). The same procedure would apply *mutatis mutandis.*[80]

6 Impact of the Conditionality Mechanism

The key issue related to the conditionality mechanism concerns its real financial impact. In the public debate it is frequently claimed that its essence is a temporary suspension of transfers of EU funds to the Member State breaching the rule of law. However, analysis of the Draft Regulation reveals that this diagnosis seems overly simplistic, and launching of the conditionality mechanism may end up as well in a definitive loss of the EU funds by the Member State in question. What's more, this may also affect individuals. These issues are presented below.

[78] Article 6 (2) Draft Regulation (Commission proposal).

[79] Article 6 (2) Draft Regulation (European Parliament proposal).

[80] Article 6 (2) Draft Regulation (Commission proposal and European Parliament proposal).

6.1 *Impact of the Conditionality Mechanism on the Member States*

According to the Draft Regulation, if EU funds are suspended under the conditionality mechanism, the amounts corresponding to the suspended commitments are re-entered into the EU budget subject to the Article 7 Draft Multiannual Financial Framework Regulation[81] (the Draft MFF Regulation). Re-entering allows reallocation and future reutilisation of the EU funds in question (see Sect. 5.2). What is important, the Article 7 Draft MFF Regulation proposes that commitments suspended in year 'n' due to a generalised deficiency as regards the rule of law in a Member State may not be re-entered into the EU budget later than in the year 'n'+2.[82] The Draft Regulation contains a similar provision, stipulating that suspended commitments for year 'n' may not be entered into the EU budget beyond year 'n'+2.[83] On the top of this, from year 'n'+3, amounts corresponding to the suspended commitments should be entered in the Union Reserve for Commitments (hereafter: Union Reserve).[84] This Reserve is a new financial instrument which would be financed from, *inter alia*, funds committed to the EU budget but ultimately not spent for the implementation of EU programmes and thus de-committed. Amounts of the Union Reserve would be made available for the Member State in the new MFF 2021–2027.

In should be thus reminded that according to political declarations and its common understanding by the public, the conditionality mechanism is supposed to only lead to a temporary suspension of EU funds of the Member States breaching the rule of law, thus motivating them to eliminate the breaches promptly. If that is the case, the funds should be returned to these States. However, this may not happen because of the 'n+2' rule contained in the Draft Regulation and in the Draft MFF Regulation. Application of the conditionality mechanism may thus relatively easily result not in the suspension, but in the permanent loss of EU funds by the Member States.[85] This is because these Drafts introduce the 'n+2' rule which authorizes the Commission to enter into the EU budget only the amounts corresponding to the amounts suspended under the conditionality mechanism which were lifted within 2 years (year 'n'+2) from the year they were suspended (year 'n'). After the elapse of these 2 years, the Commission will have no legal basis to enter these amounts into the EU budget anymore. From year 'n'+3 these amounts would be entered into the Union Reserve and could be allocated to the Member States—all Member States, not only the one on which the conditionality mechanism was applied and spend in the MFF 2021–2027.

---

[81] Article 6 (3) Draft Regulation (Commission proposal).

[82] Proposal for a Council Regulation laying down the multiannual financial framework for the years 2021 to 2027 (COM(2018) 322 final).

[83] Article 6 (3) Draft Regulation (Commission proposal).

[84] Article 12 Draft MFF Regulation.

[85] Para. 8 ECA opinion No 1/2018.

This indicates that a Member State whose EU funds were suspended under the conditionality mechanism practically has 2 years from the year of suspension (year 'n') to remedy the generalised deficiency as regards the rule of law and to request the EU institutions to lift the suspension and re-enter the amounts corresponding to the suspended commitments to the EU budget.[86] If the Member State fails to undertake these actions during the 2-year period, it loses the possibility to benefit from the suspended EU funds. Conducting all these actions within 2 years can be extremely difficult, taking into account that the elimination of rule of law breaches is usually time-consuming and in addition further time is needed to complete the proceedings in the EU institutions to lift the suspension.

6.2 Impact of the Conditionality Mechanism on the Beneficiaries of EU Funds

In principle, the conditionality mechanism should solely affect those Member States breaching the rule of law, and the consequences of the suspension of EU funds should not in any way influence the beneficiaries of these funds (e.g. farmers, entrepreneurs).[87] To achieve this objective, the Commission foresees, in the Draft Regulation, that unless the decision adopting the measures imposed under the conditionality mechanism provides otherwise, its adoption does not affect the obligation of the Member States to implement the programme or fund those affected by the measures, and in particular the obligation to make payments to the beneficiaries of EU funds (hereafter: beneficiaries).[88] In other words, despite the fact that the regular transfer of the EU funds from the EU budget to Member States' budget is suspended under the conditionality mechanism, this State is nevertheless obliged to continue to implement programmes financed from these funds and make payments to beneficiaries. It could be assumed that since the Commission recognized the need to protect the beneficiaries against the possibility that Member States will cease to make payments to them due to the suspension of EU funds under the conditionality mechanism, it should also specify in the Draft Regulation legal measures that beneficiaries could apply against the Member States if this should occur. However, the Commission has not done so.[89]

[86]Article 6 Draft Regulation (Commission proposal).

[87]The European Parliament formulated this assumption in its resolution of 14 March 2018 on the MFF (2017/2052(INI)). The Commission also pointed out that beneficiaries of EU funding must not be affected by breaches of the rule of law by Member States. See page 2 of the Draft Regulation.

[88]Article 4 (2) Draft Regulation (Commission proposal).

[89]See critics: ECA opinion No 1/2018, point 27.

The European Parliament has tried to remedy this deficiency and strengthen the legal protection of beneficiaries against the misconduct of Member States.[90] It proposed that the Commission should provide information and guidance *via* a website or internet portal for beneficiaries on the obligations of Member States to implement the programme, in particular to make payments to them. The Commission should also provide, on the same website or portal, adequate tools allowing beneficiaries to inform it of any breaches of these obligations by the Member States. The information provided by the beneficiaries may only be taken into account by the Commission if it is accompanied by a proof that they have lodged a complaint to the competent national authority. Beneficiaries informing the Commission would be protected under the proposed Directive on whistle-blower protection.[91]

The above-mentioned rules establish communication channels between the Commission and beneficiaries enabling them to exchange information on any eventual negative effects experienced by the latter due to Member States stopping to make the payments of EU funds. It is, however, doubtful whether such communication itself may effectively protect beneficiaries, without being accompanied by any formal legal actions. Three solutions appear to exist. Firstly, beneficiaries could apply legal remedies established under the national law to claim continuation of payments of EU funds from national authorities. This may however be challengeable or even unattainable in Member States in which an illiberal democracy has captured the national administration and independent prosecution and judiciary. Secondly, the beneficiaries could initiate an action for damages against the Member State claiming the State has infringed its obligation under the Draft Regulation to make payments of EU funds (*Francovich* liability). The success of this claim may still however depend on the effectiveness and independence of the national judiciary, which could and is troublesome in the case of some Member States. The Commission's legal position is more meaningful, as it could—as a third solution—initiate a general infringement action (Article 258 TFEU) against a Member State who breaches the Draft Regulation by ceasing to make the payments of EU funds to beneficiaries.

It is important to note that the Draft Regulation has equipped the Commission with competences that may help to ensure that beneficiaries would receive their EU funds if its transfer would be suspended on a national level. These competences depend on the method under which the EU budget is implemented (see Sect. 4). Two possibilities exist in this respect, since these EU funds may be spent under indirect management[92]—by public and private law Member States' organisations—or under shared management[93]—by Member States, mostly for implementation of CAP and the cohesion policy. If EU funds are spent under indirect management (by public and

[90]Recital 14 preamble and Article 4 (3) (a) and (3) (b) Draft Regulation (European Parliament proposal).

[91]Proposal for a Directive on the protection of persons reporting on breaches of Union law COM (2018)218 final.

[92]Article 62 (1) (c) of the Financial Regulation no 2018/1046.

[93]Article 62 (1) (b) of the Financial Regulation no 2018/1046.

private law Member State organisations), the Commission may recover the payments directly made to these organisations for an amount equivalent to the amount not paid to beneficiaries.[94] When EU funds are spent under shared management (by the Member States), the Commission may impose a financial correction[95] on them to recover the EU funds from these State. In both cases amounts recovered by the Commission are transferred to the Union Reserve.[96]

These provisions, however, do not change the general rule describe above according to which the Member States are obliged to make payments to beneficiaries despite the transfer of EU funds to these States is suspended under the conditionality mechanism. In other words, suspension of EU funds transferred to a Member State does not change a legal situation of beneficiaries who can claim payments of these funds only from the national administration, not from the Commission.

6.3 Impact of the Conditionality Mechanism on Relations Between the National Authorities

Independently of the financial losses that the conditionality mechanism causes to the Member State (Sect. 6.1) and may cause to beneficiaries (Sect. 6.2), it may also affect internal relations within the national administration. More specifically, it may lead to conflicts between the central government of the Member State (the addressee of the EU decision suspending the EU funds) and public authorities functioning on the lower levels in the structure of this State. This is because the Draft Regulation imposes the obligation to make payments to beneficiaries not only on the central government of the Member States, but also on 'government entities', which, as defined, include all public authorities at all levels of government, i.e. national, regional, and local authorities as well as Member State organizations.[97] It can thus be predicted that if transfers of EU funds would be suspended under the conditionality mechanism, these funds would not be paid to the government of a Member State, whereas the obligation to pay them to beneficiaries would still rest on government entities, e.g. local authorities and national organisations, which are defined broadly. This could easily give rise to internal domestic conflicts.

---

[94] Article 12 draft MFF Regulation.

[95] Article 98 of CP Regulation, COM(2018) 375 final.

[96] Article 12 (2) (a) draft MFF Regulation.

[97] Article 2 (c) Draft Regulation (Commission proposal).

7 The Conditionality Mechanism and Other Rule-of-Law Mechanisms

The verification of Member States' compliance with the rule of law that would be performed under the conditionality mechanism if the Draft Regulation is adopted may also be checked under other legal procedures established in EU Treaties. The most important are: the Article 7 TEU procedure and the general infringement procedures (Articles 258-260 TFEU). Since the Draft Regulation does not specify the relationship between the proposed conditionality mechanism and these procedures, this may lead to major legal disputes[98] and require some clarifications.

7.1 The Article 7 TEU Procedure

Article 7 TEU allows the EU institutions to examine whether the Member States respect the values on which the EU is based (Article 2 TEU) which include, *inter alia*, the rule of law. Article 7 TEU foresees a procedure to be followed and measures to be adopted if a breach of these values is detected. This procedure has already been launched against Poland (in 2017) and Hungary (in 2018).

The Article 7 TEU procedure consists of two stages: '*the preventive stage*', where decisions are taken by the Council;[99] and *'the sanctioning stage'*, which belongs to the European Council and the Council.[100] At '*the preventive stage*' of the Article 7 TEU procedure, the Council hears the Member State, addresses recommendations to it, and determines whether there is a clear risk of a serious breach by this State of the rule of law.[101] At '*the sanctioning stage*' of the Article 7 TEU procedure, the European Council determines the existence of a serious and persistent breach of the rule of law by this State.[102] After that, the Council may decide to suspend certain rights of this State deriving from the application of the Treaties, including the voting rights of the representative of the government of this Member State in the Council.[103] In response to changes in the situation which led to the imposition of the above measures, the Council may decide to alter or revoke them.[104] As regards the judicial control of actions taken based on Article 7 TEU, the CJEU decides only on

[98]Taborowski (2019), pp. 205–207.

[99]Article 7 (1) TEU.

[100]Article 7 (2) and (3) TEU.

[101]The Council acts by a majority of 4/5 of its Members, on a reasoned proposal of 1/3 of the Member States, by the European Parliament or by the Commission, after obtaining the consent of the European Parliament.

[102]In this stage the European Council acts unanimously, on a proposal from 1/3 of the Member States or by the Commission, after obtaining the consent of the European Parliament.

[103]The Council acts by QMV.

[104]The Council acts by QMV.

the legality of the procedural stipulations contained in this Article,[105] with no substantive control of measures (e.g. sanctions) adopted.

Article 7 (3) TEU, which allows the Council to suspend certain rights of the Member States deriving from the application of the Treaties, deserves a closer look inasmuch as actions undertaken on its basis *prima facie* may be similar to actions performed under the Draft Regulation. The legal nature of actions undertaken based on Article 7 (3) TEU is not determined by the Treaties. These provisions simply indicate the essence of such actions (suspension of rights deriving from the application of the Treaties) and provide one example (suspension of the voting right in the Council); otherwise they describe such actions by using the neutral term '*measure'*. The scope of competences conferred on the Council based on Article 7 (3) TEU have given rise to a heated debate, in which it is commonly accepted that the Council's actions constitute political sanctions imposed on Member States for breaching the values on which the EU is founded.[106] It should thus be determined whether, based on Article 7 (3) TEU, the Council is authorized to suspend the EU funds of a Member State found to be in breach of the rule of law. In other words, is it true that the competences to be created under the conditionality mechanism (the Draft Regulation) already exist under Article 7 (3) TEU?

Given that under Article 7 (3) TEU the rights of a Member State deriving from the application of the Treaties may be suspended, it should also be possible to suspend transfers of EU funds to this State on this basis.[107] Undoubtedly, receipt of the EU funds is a right that the Member States benefit from as a result of their EU membership, and the amounts received are set out in the MFF Regulations based on political agreements reached by all Member States. It can therefore be stated that by suspending transfer of the EU funds, the Member State is temporarily deprived of the possibility to enjoy its right deriving from the Treaties.

It thus follows that the suspension of the EU funds of Member States breaching the rule of law is possible both under Article 7 (3) TEU and would be under the conditionality mechanism as well if the Draft Regulation is adopted. It has already been pointed out that the Draft Regulation does not specify the relationship between the Article 7 TEU procedure and the conditionality mechanism. This silence calls for an analysis in which two options should be taken into consideration.

The first option, based on the hierarchy of EU legal norms, is that the Article 7 TEU procedure and the conditionality mechanism are interdependent. The Article 7 TEU procedure (regulated by EU Treaty) has a primary role and the conditionality mechanism (regulated in the Draft Regulation) supplements it. The Article 7 TEU procedure provides a general framework for a suspension of EU funds for breaches of the rule of law, and the Draft Regulation ensures its practical implementation. Based on this reasoning, in legal terms the suspension of EU funds under the conditionality mechanism would constitute a '*measure'* within the meaning of

[105] Article 269 TFEU.

[106] Geiger (2015), Mangiameli and Saputelli (2013), Besselink (2017) and Dumbrovský (2018).

[107] Taborowski (2019), pp. 194–197.

Article 7 (3) TEU. Following this logic, the suspension of EU funds would have to be first imposed under Article 7 (3) TEU and only then under the conditionality mechanism. In this scenario, however, one breach of the rule of law would be double-checked in two different procedures—first under the Article 7 TEU procedure and then under the conditionality mechanism. At a glance, this seems counterproductive. It may not be also excluded that decisions made under the Article 7 TEU procedure and under the conditionality mechanism would differ, depending on the political ambience, not to mention how unpractical and time-consuming this may be. If one recalls that the reasons to create the conditionality mechanism regulated by the EU secondary law was to overcome the political difficulties or even impossibility of conducting the Article 7 procedure, proven by the unsuccessful proceedings launched against Poland and Hungary, the idea to merge the Article 7 TEU procedure and the conditionality mechanism multiplies existing difficulties. Therefore the second option requires scrutiny.

The second option is based on the argument of procedural effectiveness, or the *effet utile* principle. Under this option the Article 7 TEU procedure and the conditionality mechanism are parallel and independent of each other, because their legal nature is different. The Article 7 TEU procedure is a political one, while the conditionality mechanism is a legal proceeding. In the Article 7 TEU procedure decisions are made by a political body (the Council) based on political assessments. Judicial control of the legality of these decisions performed by the CJEU is limited only to reviewing the procedural requirements stipulated in Article 7 TEU. This procedure aims exclusively to eliminate breaches of values on which the EU is based, including the rule of law. In contrast, the objective of the conditionality mechanism is more clear-cut, as it should safeguard the EU funds, or more precisely their sound management[108] and protection[109] against damages resulting from systematic breaches of the rule of law in the Member State. In this procedure decisions are made based on an assessment of the legal (and not political) criteria established under the Draft Regulation, namely the existence of a generalised deficiency as regards the rule of law in the Member State as defined in this Draft (see Sect. 3.2). The key decisions are taken by the Commission,[110] which is the guardian of the EU Treaties,[111] also responsible for the EU budget.[112] The legality of these decisions is fully checked by the CJEU under an action for annulment.[113] This kind of jurisdiction of the CJEU significantly strengthens the legal situations of the Member States in comparison to the purely procedural checks of decisions performed by the CJEU under the Article 7 TEU procedure.[114] In conclusion, it is thus justified to claim the

[108]Article 317 TFEU.

[109]Article 325 TFEU.

[110]The European Parliament proposal.

[111]Article 17 TEU.

[112]Article 317 TFEU.

[113]Article 263 TFEU.

[114]Article 269 TFEU.

Article 7 TEU procedure and the conditionality mechanism are parallel and independent of each other.

One could imagine to attack the Draft Regulation as an illegal circumvention of the Article 7 TEU procedures. However, Article 7 TEU does not contain an explicit statement as to whether other Union institutions may defend European values using other instruments. Thus, the general rules apply. It is well established that a specific procedure designed to deal with a certain problem does not exclude developing other instruments,[115] a core doctrine since the *Van Gend en Loos* judgment.[116] Accordingly, it is, in principle, admissible to develop new instruments,[117] such as the Commission's Rule of Law Framework, or to use the budget to defend European values.

7.2 *The General Infringement Procedure (Arts. 258-260 TFEU)*

The general infringement procedure is another legal proceeding that can be initiated against a Member State's breaching the rule of law. Under this procedure, if the Commission considers that a Member State has failed to fulfil its obligation under the Treaties it may bring the matter before the CJEU. If the CJEU finds that the Member State indeed infringed provisions of EU law, it confirms its finding in a judgment.[118] The Member State is then obliged to eliminate the infringement found, and if it does not do so the CJEU may impose financial penalties on this State.[119]

The possibilities offered by the general infringement procedure (Article 258-260 TFEU) in the context of rule of law breaches have already been described by legal scholars.[120] Unlike the Article 7 TEU procedure fruitlessly conducted against Poland and Hungary, the general infringement procedure has already been successfully completed in 2019 in cases against Poland. In case C-192/18 *Commission v. Poland* the CJEU ruled that by establishing a different retirement age for men and women judges and prosecutors in Poland, Poland has failed to fulfil its obligations under Article 157 TFEU and Articles 5(a) and 9(1)(f) of Anti-Discrimination Directive 2006/54/EC. In addition, by granting the Minister for Justice the right to authorise judges to continue to carry out their duties beyond the new retirement age, Poland has failed to fulfil its obligations under Article 19 (1) TEU.[121] In similar cases C-619/18 *Commission v. Poland* the CJEU also ruled that Poland had failed to fulfil

[115]Bast (2006), pp. 60–63.

[116]CJEU, Case C-26/62, *Van Gend en Loos*, ECLI:EU:C:1963:1, para. 26.

[117]Bast (2006), pp. 42–67.

[118]Article 258 TFEU.

[119]Article 260 TFEU.

[120]Wennerås (2017), Gormley (2018), Schmidt and Bogdanowicz (2018) and Taborowski (2019).

[121]CJEU Cases C-192/18, *Commission v. Poland,* ECLI:EU:C:2019:924.

its obligations under Article 19 (1) TEU by lowering the retirement age of the judges of the Supreme Court and by granting the President of Poland the discretion to extend the period of their judicial activity beyond the newly fixed retirement age.[122] In 2019 the Commission brought another case against Poland (C-791/19 *Commission v. Poland)* concerning disciplinary proceedings against judges also with charges of breaching Article 19 (1) TEU. Although the charge of breaching the rule of law was not explicitly raised in that case, it concerned judicial independence, which is a key element of the rule of law.[123]

All in all, the general infringement procedure (Article 258-260 TFEU) and the conditionality mechanism (Draft Regulation) are initiated by the Commission against Member States in cases of possible breaches of the EU law, with a view toward eliminating them. However, these procedures significantly differ.

While the general infringement procedure is regulated by EU primary law (Arts. 258-260 TFEU), the conditionality mechanism will be regulated by EU secondary law (the Draft Regulation). Litigation is also resolved differently. In the case of the general infringement procedure, the dispute between the Commission who brings charges and the accused Member State is resolved by the CJEU. Under the conditionality mechanism, the CJEU is involved only if a Member State—an addressee of a decision launching the conditionality mechanism—challenges its legality in the front of the CJEU under action for annulment (Articles 263 TFEU).

Last but not least, while the general infringement procedure is of a horizontal nature, as it may concern all different kinds of violations of EU law (including breaches of the rule of law), the conditionality mechanism is of a sectoral nature, since its concerns only one specific EU law violation, namely a breach of the rule of law detrimental to EU funds. The relationship between the general infringement procedure (Articles 258-260 TFEU) and the sectoral procedures provided in EU regulations allowing the Commission to protect the EU funds has already been analysed by the CJEU. In cases concerning EU funds, the Member States have claimed that if the Commission finds that expenditures financed by EU funds were incurred in breach of EU law, it should initiate the general infringement procedure against them (Article 258 TFEU), under which the CJEU would assess the charges and legality of EU expenditures. By this approach the Member States opposed the Commission's practice to initiate, in such cases, '*the clearance of accounts procedure'*, regulated in the CAP regulations. In these procedures, now already also conducted in the cohesion policy, if the Commission detects irregular EU expenditures incurred in a Member State, it adopts a decision imposing financial corrections on said State, which obliges it to return the irregularly spent EU funds to the EU budget. The CJEU did not share the Member States' argumentation and ruled that infringements of EU law related to the illegal spending of EU funds should be decided within the framework of sectoral procedures and not under the general

[122]CJEU Cases C-619/18, *Commission v. Poland,* ECLI:EU:C:2019:53, see: Wyrzykowski (2018), Waelbroeck and Oliver (2018), Kmieciak (2019) and Klatt (2019).

[123]Bárd and Ballegooij van (2018).

infringement procedure (Article 258 TFEU).[124] The practice of bringing cases involving the irregular spending of EU funds under sectoral procedures, developed in, e.g., agriculture and cohesion regulations, is currently applied today. In such cases the Commission does not bring general infringement proceedings against the Member States (Arts. 258-260 TFEU) but applies procedures established under EU secondary law regulations. The question that can be asked is whether the above-mentioned case-law of the CJEU would apply to the conditionality mechanism. *Prima facie* there are no legal obstacles excluding such a possibility.

8 Conclusions

Analyses of rule of law instruments established under EU law, analysed in this chapter, lead to the following conclusions.

Practice of conducting the Article 7 TEU procedure—the main EU Treaties procedure aimed to protect the 'European values', including the rule of law (Article 2 TEU) is disappointing. After few years from initiating it against Poland (in 2017) and Hungary (in 2018) there is hardly any real progress made. With more success the general infringement procedure is conducted (Article 258-260 TFEU)—in 2019 two cases were settled by the CJEU (C-192/18 *Commission v. Poland* and C-619/18 *Commission v. Poland)* and one case was brought (C-791/19 *Commission v. Poland*), all concerning capturing judicial independence of Polish courts. For some (unknown) reasons, the possibilities offered by the EU secondary law, namely the CP Regulation on the EU funds, allowing for the suspension and recovery of the EU funds from the Member State infringing EU law, have not been tested yet by the Commission. Instead the Draft Regulation establishing the conditionality mechanism allowing for the suspension of EU funds transferred to the Member State breaching the rule of law (commented on in this chapter) was put on the table. Scrutiny of this Draft lead to the following conclusions. Two most important remarks concern legality of (1) (too) generally formulated premises for applying of the conditionality mechanism and unknown shape of measures to be imposed under this mechanism and (2) launching this mechanism by the Council by the *reverse* QMV.

First of all, premises for applying the conditionality mechanism were set out extremely broadly, to the extent that their exact meaning and scope is extremely difficult to determine (see Sect. 3.2). Their very essence is 'a generalised deficiency as regards the rule of law' defined as widespread or recurrent practice of public authorities which violates the rule of law and affects or risk affecting the EU funds—their sound financial management (Article 317 TFEU) or the protection (Article

---

[124] CJEU Cases: 15 and 16-76, *France v. Commission*, ECLI:EU:C:1979:29, paras 22-35, C-247/98, *Greece v. Commission*, ECLI:EU:C:2001:4, paras 13-14; C-332/00, *Greece v. Commission*, ECLI:EU:C:2002:235, para. 46.

325 TFEU). To make this abstract notion of a 'generalised deficiency' more pragmatic, the Draft Regulation provided some of their examples. This list contains, on the one hand, such explicit infringements as e.g. ineffective and late cooperation of national authorities with OLAF and EPP; or breaches of confidentiality of communication between lawyers and clients. On the other hand, the list also contains very general breaches, e.g. limiting the effective investigation, prosecution and sanctioning of breaches of EU law; jeopardizing judicial independence; or endangering capacity of the Member State to respect the obligations of EU membership, including the capacity to effectively implement EU law. Instead of legal certainty, this list creates further legal confusion. This lack of precision in formulation of premises to apply the conditionality mechanism is problematic, if one takes into account that the CJEU consequently requires that the principle of legal certainty should be respected particularly rigorously in the case of sanctions and provisions having financial implications. It is clear that the Draft Regulation establishing conditionality mechanism consists of sanctions that would have a financial impact on the Member States breaching the rule of law. This is its essence and *raison d'être*. Therefore, it can be claimed that excessively general phrasing of premises necessary to launch the conditionality mechanism frustrates the principle of legal certainty.

The same can be said about specific measures (e.g. suspension of EU funds, their recovery) to be imposed under the conditionality mechanism (see Sect. 4). These measures are not regulated by the Draft Regulation, but under EU sectoral Regulations that would establish EU spending rules to be applied in MFF 2021–2027 in specific EU policies (e.g. agricultural, cohesion). Since these Regulations are presently under EU legislative processes run independently from legislative works on the Draft Regulation, the final outcome and impact of the conditionality mechanism, depended on this sectoral rules, cannot be presently assessed. Surprisingly, the Draft Regulation does not mention such reference. What's striking, in the legal debate on the conditionality mechanism a legal relation between the EU sectoral Regulations and the Draft Regulation is often missed with the effect that the conditionality mechanism is described as the self-regulatory one. This is an evident omission.

Secondly, serious legal doubts concern peculiar procedure of adoption of a decision launching the conditionality mechanism. This decision is not adopted under the standard procedure and vote cast established by the EU Treaties but under the specific procedures provided by the Draft Regulation in which the Council votes by the *reverse* QMV. A proposal of a decision launching a conditionality mechanism submitted by the Commission is adopted unless the Council *rejects* it within 1 month or otherwise amend it by *ordinary* QMV. This procedure places the Commission in a privileged position and facilitates the adoption of decisions. If the Council is unable to obtain *ordinary* QMV to reject the decision (within a month), the Commission's proposal would become a legally binding decision. After 1 month the decision may be however changed, if the Council votes on it by *ordinary* QMV. At this point in time, it is difficult to definitively assess the legality of this procedure, given the fact that the CJEU has not expressed its view on legality of voting by the Council by *reverse* QMV. Establishing the legislative procedure and vote cast remaining outside the EU Treaties toolbox may, however, raise serious legal concerns. To conclude this part, there is a strong evidence in the above-mentioned parts of the Draft Regulations concerning (1) premises for applying the conditionality mechanism and measures to be imposed under it as well as (2) voting by the Council by the *reverse* QMV to initiate this mechanism violates the EU Treaty. Despite these reservations, other provisions of the Draft Regulation can also be critically assessed.

Despite the common narration that the conditionality mechanism should only lead to suspension of EU funds, it is clearly regulated in the Draft Regulation that a Member State whose EU funds were suspended under the conditionality mechanism can easily lose them forever (see Sect. 6.1). This will happen if, within 2 years from the year of their suspension, this State will not remedy the breach of the rule of law and convince the EU institution to lift (or alter) the suspension. In such a case the Commission would not be authorised to re-enter the suspended amounts in the EU budget. Because of this serious and automatic effect, the conditionality mechanism may turn out to be a far more severe and detrimental financial penalty than perhaps is envisioned. For this reason formulating precise premises for the adoption of the conditionality mechanism, as stated above, is even more important.

The Draft Regulation provides beneficiaries of EU funds with a weak legal protection if the Member States whose EU funds were suspended under the conditionality mechanism stop making payments to them (see Sect. 6.2). The E-communication channel foreseen would rather not suffice. Thus in effect the real financial impact of suspension in some cases may be passed on beneficiaries. Then the most effective legal remedy they could undertake would probably be an action for damages brought against a Member State breaching the EU law (the *Francovich* liability). From its side, the Commission could bring to the CJEU a general infringement action (Article 258-260 TFEU) against this State.

The Draft Regulation does not specify the relationship between the conditionality mechanism and other EU Treaties procedures (the Article 7 TEU procedure and general infringement procedure under Articles 258-260 TFEU) that may be applied in cases of breaching the rule of law by the Member States (see Sect. 7). There are, *prima facie*, no legal obstacles to introduce the conditionality mechanism to EU law, as its legal construction (objectives, premises and procedure) significantly differs from the EU Treaties procedures aimed at safeguarding the rule of law. While the Article 7 TEU procedure is political in nature, the general infringement procedure (Articles 258-260 TFEU) is aimed at any kind of infringement of EU law. In contrast, the conditionality mechanism is a clear-cut procedure, regulated by the EU secondary law, aimed to safeguard the EU funds from damages resulting from systemic infringements of the rule of law by the Member States. It is mainly in the hands of the Commission, as it is the guardian of the EU Treaties (Article 17 TEU) and also responsible for management of the EU budget (Article 317 TFEU). In case of doubts, any legal disputes arising from the application of the conditionality mechanism are to be settled by the CJEU under the action for annulment (Article 263 TFEU).

To conclude the thoughts concerning the Draft Regulation it can be claimed that the important issue to be tackled during coming legislative works on it would be to finding a way to ensure the protection of the rule of law without compromising this rule and other values on which the EU is based.

References

Atik J (2016) From 'no bailout' to the European stability mechanism. Fordham Int Law J 39 (5):1201
Bárd P, Ballegooij van W (2018) The AG Opinion in the Celmer case: why lack of judicial independence should have been framed as a rule of law issue. https://verfassungsblog.de/the-ag-opinion-in-the-celmer-case-why-lack-of-judicial-independence-should-have-been-framed-as-a-rule-of-law-issue/
Bartels L (2005) Human rights conditionality in the EU's international agreements. Oxford University Press, Oxford
Bast J (2006) Grundbegriffe der Handlungsformen der EU. Springer, Heidelberg
Besselink L (2017) The bite, the bark and the howl: Art. 7 TEU and the rule of law initiatives. In: Jakab A, Kochenov D (eds) The enforcement of EU law and values, ensuring member states' compliance. Oxford University Press, Oxford, pp 128–144
Butler I (2018) Two proposals to promote and protect European values through the multiannual financial framework: conditionality of EU funds and a financial instrument to support NGOs. Liberties, 7.03.2018, https://www.liberties.eu/en/news/european-vaues-fund-two-proposals-mff/14471
Chalmers D, Davies G, Monti G (2015) European Union Law: text and materials. Cambridge University Press, Cambridge
Closa C, Kochenov D (2016) Reinforcing rule of law oversight in the European Union. Cambridge University Press, Cambridge
Cornelius J (2016) The European Union development policies are based on European values, democracy, respect for the rule of law and human right. In: Goudappel F, Hirsch B (eds) Democracy and rule of law in the European Union. T.M.C. Asser, The Hague, pp 109–126
Costa M (2017) The accountability gap in EU law. Routledge, London
Craig P (2012) EU administrative law. Oxford University Press, Oxford
Cremona M (2005) EU enlargement: solidarity and conditionality. Eur Law Rev 30(1):19
Dumbrovský T (2018) Beyond voting rights suspension. Tailored sanction as democracy catalyst under Article 7 TEU. In: Hatje A, Tichý L (eds) Liability of member states for the violation of fundamental values of the European Union. Nomos, Baden-Baden, pp 203–228
Fierro E (2003) The EU's approach to human rights conditionality in practice. Martinus Nijhoff Publishers, The Hague
Geiger R (2015) Commentary to Article 7 TEU in: European Union treaties. Commentary. Beck, München
Gormley L (2018) Infringement proceedings. In: Jakab A, Kochenov D (eds) The enforcement of EU law and values, ensuring member states' compliance. Oxford University Press, Oxford, pp 65–78
Halmai G (2018) The possibility and desirability of economic sanction: the rule of law against the EU Member States. 2018/06, EUI Working Paper Law, http://cadmus.eui.eu/handle/1814/51644
Hatje A (2018) Liability of member states for the violation of fundamental values of the European Union. Nomos, Baden-Baden
Hofmann HCH, Rowe GC, Türk AH (2012) Administrative law and policy of the European Union. Oxford University Press, Oxford
Jakab A, Kochenov D (2017) The enforcement of EU law and values: ensuring member states' compliance. Oxford University Press, Oxford

Kelemen D, Scheppele KL (2018) How to stop funding autocracy in the EU. Verfassungsblog, 10.9.2018, https://verfassungsblog.de/how-to-stop-funding-autocracy-in-the-eu/
Klatt MK (2019) Herabsetzung des Ruhestandsalters für Richter in Polen. Neue Zeitschrift für Verwaltungsrecht 2019:1109–1118
Kmieciak Z (2019) Ochrona tymczasowa w sprawie ze skargi Komisji przeciwko Polsce dotyczącej przepisów ustawy obniżającej wiek przejścia w stan spoczynku sędziów SN. Glosa do postanowienia TSUE z 19.10.2018 r., C-619/18 R. Państwo i Prawo 2019:143–150
Konstadinides T (2017) The rule of law in the European Union. Hart Publishing, Oxford
Louis J-F (2010) The no-bailout clause and rescue packages. Common Market Law Rev 47(4):971
Mangiameli S, Saputelli G (2013) Commentary to Article 7 TEU. In: Blanke H-J, Mangiameli S (eds) The treaty on European Union. Springer, Berlin, p 350
McKenzie L, Meissner K (2017) Human rights conditionality in European Union trade negotiations. J Common Market Stud 55(4):832–849
Pech L, Perju V, Platon S (2019) How to address rule of law backsliding in Romania: the case for an infringement action based on Article 325 TFEU. Verfassungsblog, 2019.5.29, https://verfassungsblog.de/how-to-adress-rule-of-law-backsliding-inromania, https://doi.org/10.17176/20190529-121940-0
Peel M, Hopkins V, Shotter J (2019) Finland to push EU budget rule of law clampdown. Financial Times, September 8 2019, https://www.ft.com/content/c3d655fe-cfe7-11e9-99a4-b5ded7a7fe3f
Scheppele KL, Pech L, Kelemen RD (2018) Never missing an opportunity to miss an opportunity: the council legal service opinion on the Commission's EU budget-related rule of law mechanism. Verfassungsblog, 2018.11.12, https://verfassungsblog.de/never-missing-an-opportunity-to-miss-an-opportunity-the-council-legal-service-opinion-on-the-commissions-eu-budget-related-rule-of-law-mechanism, https://doi.org/10.17176/20181115-215538-0
Schmidt M, Bogdanowicz P (2018) The infringement procedure in the rule of law crisis: how to make effective use of Article 258 TFEU. Common Market Law Rev 55:1061–1100
Schöndorf-Haubold B (2011) Common European administration: the European structural funds. In: Jansen O, Schöndorf-Haubold B (eds) The European composite administration. Intersentia, Antwerp, p 25 et seq
Schroeder W (2016) Strengthening the rule of law in Europe. Hart Publishing, Oxford
Taborowski M (2019) Mechanizm ochrony praworządności państw członkowskich w prawie Unii Europejskiej. Studium przebudzenia systemu ponadnarodowego. Wolters Kluwer, Alphen aan den Rijn
Van Aken W, Artige L (2013) Reverse majority voting in comparative perspective: implications for fiscal governance in the EU. In: de Witte B, Héritier A, Trechsel A (eds) The Euro crisis and the state of European democracy. European University Institute, Fiesole, p 129 et seq
Vita V (2017) Revisiting the dominant discourse on conditionality in the EU: the case of EU spending conditionality. Camb Yearb Eur Legal Stud 19:136
von Bogdandy A (2019) Principles and challenges of a European Doctrine of systemic deficiencies. MPIL Research Paper No. 2019-14, https://ssrn.com/abstract=3431303 or https://doi.org/10.2139/ssrn.3431303
von Brauneck J (2019) Gefährdung des EU-Haushalts durch rechtsstaatliche Mängel in den Mitgliedstaaten? Europarecht (EuR) 2019:37–60
Waelbroeck M, Oliver P (2018) Enforcing the rule of law in the EU: what can be done about Hungary and Poland? https://blogdroiteuropeen.com/2018/01/31/enforcing-the-rule-of-law-in-the-eu-what-can-be-done-about-hungary-and-poland-par-michel-waelbroeck-et-peter-oliver/
Wennerås P (2017) Making effective use of Article 260 TFEU. In: Jakab A, Kochenov D (eds) The enforcement of EU law and values, ensuring member states' compliance. Oxford University Press, Oxford, pp 79–98

Wyrzykowski M (2018) Rule of law: European Commission v. Poland. In: Hatje A, Tichý L (eds) Liability of Member States for the violation of fundamental values of the European Union. Nomos, Baden-Baden, pp 169–199

Justyna Łacny is Professor at the Warsaw University of Technology.

The Rule of Law Framework in the European Union: Its Rationale, Origins, Role and International Ramifications

Artur Nowak-Far

Contents

Abstract At present, the European rule of law enforcement framework under Article 7 TEU (RLF) is vulnerable to unguaranteed, discretionary influences of the Member States. This vulnerability arises from its procedural format which requires high thresholds in decision-making with the effect that this procedure is prone to be terminated by the EU Member States likely to be scrutinized under it, if only they collude. Yet, the Framework may prove effective to correct serious breaches against human rights (in the context of ineffective rule of law standards). The European Commission is bound to pursue the RLF effectiveness for the sake of achieving relative uniformity of application of EU law (at large), and making the European Union a credible actor and co-creator of international legal order. The RLF is an

A. Nowak-Far (✉)
Institute of Law, SGH-Warsaw School of Economics, Warsaw, Poland
e-mail: artur.nowak-far@sgh.waw.pl

A. von Bogdandy et al. (eds.), *Defending Checks and Balances in EU Member States*, Beiträge zum ausländischen öffentlichen Recht und Völkerrecht 298,
https://doi.org/10.1007/978-3-662-62317-6_12

important tool for the maintenance of relative stability of human rights and the rule of law in the EU despite natural divergence propensity resulting from the procedural autonomy of the EU Member States. By achieving this stability, the EU achieves significant political weight in international dialogue concerning human rights and the rule of law and preserves a high level of its global credibility in this context. Thus, RLF increases the EU's effectiveness in promoting the European model of their identification and enforcement.

1 Introduction

The Rule of Law Framework (here referred to as 'RLF' or 'the Framework') is a contingency procedure adopted to reflect on these processes of political (and legal constitutional) developments in the European Union Member States which give rise to significant enough doubts of whether these developments are in line with the fundamental standards set forth in the EU Treaties, i.e. the Treaty on the European Union (TEU) and the Treaty on the functioning of the European Union (TFEU). In the context of the RLF, the most important provisions of these two legal instruments are those which specify the constitutional standard values of the European Union as an international organisation and those which provide for a legal basis of the RLF.

For the sake of analysis, two distinctive forms of RLF are distinguished:

(a) RLF *sensu largo*—which should be construed under Articles 2 and 7 TEU and which includes all other legal vehicles adopted to enforce these two provisions;
(b) RLF *sensu stricto*—which, for analytical purposes, can be considered the mechanism of enforcement of Article 7 TEU designed by the European Commission and adopted pursuant to its communication of 19 March 2014 (further referred to as 'the RLF communication').[1]

The objective of this Chapter is to verify the following hypotheses:

1. In the RLF, the political element dominates over the legal one as much of the Framework is owned by the EU Member States rather than by an independent judiciary; in consequence, the very rationale of the RLF is contradictory: at the material level, it is to protect the rule of law where the role of independent judiciary is enshrined, whereas at the procedural level, its fundamental mechanisms rely upon the political will of the EU Member States to protect them; this makes the RLF a relatively easy prey for at least two European Union Member States prone to collude in the situation where, at the same time, they may find themselves within remit of the Framework because of their defiance of the EU Treaty values.

[1]Communication from the Commission to the European Parliament and the Council: A New EU Framework to Strengthen the Rule of Law, 10 March 2014, document COM (2014) 158 final/2.

2. Despite this vulnerability, the RLF has significant systemic value as it is able to put on a check all EU Member States' practices which manifestly contravene the values enshrined in the Treaties, including the rule of law; moreover, the RLF is not a final format and is very likely to be further developed into a more stringent, and legally certain construct—which is the area where the European Commission evidently sees its significant role in the future, and where it nurtures its powers *vis-à-vis* other EU institutions and the Member States.
3. The Commission is bound to pursue its active and, in terms of competences, rather expansionary policy in order to ensure uniformity of EU law enforcement internally and to preserve a high level of EU credibility as a globally significant promotor of human rights.

2 Rule of Law Framework *sensu largo*: Articles 2 and 7 TEU

2.1 The Benchmark: Article 2 TEU

The RLF is meant to assure enforcement of EU values enshrined in Article 2 TEU. Article 2 provides that:

> The Union is founded on the values of respect for human dignity, freedom, democracy, equality, the rule of law and respect for human rights, including the rights of persons belonging to minorities. These values are common to the Member States in a society in which pluralism, non-discrimination, tolerance, justice, solidarity and quality between women and men prevail.

The provision was adopted originally in the Treaty of Amsterdam in 1997. It was intended to provide for the axiological foundations of the European Union. In the post-Lisbon setting (i.e. after 2008) this provision was meant to create—together with the Charter of Fundamental Rights (which in the Treaty of Lisbon was given binding force) and other, already existing, provisions of EU law (pertaining especially to EU citizenship)—a set of overarching systemic reference for any other EU law provision, if only it concerned rights of individuals.

Article 2 TEU has its direct equivalent in Article I-2 of the Treaty establishing the Constitution for Europe, i.e. the EU treaty of 2004 which had been intended to replace the then present EU Treaty framework but had failed as a result of lack of ratifications in all the EU Member States.

In the EUCJ's jurisprudence of recent years, the question of the interpretation of Article 2 TEU has been deliberated quite frequently especially in the context of mutual trust of judicial systems. Thus, in its opinion 2/13[2] (EU accession to the

[2]CJEU, Opinion 2/13 of 18 December 2014, *Accession of the European Union to the European Convention for the Protection of Human Rights and Fundamental Freedoms*, ECLI:EU:C:2014:2454.

European Convention of Human Rights), the Court suggested that this mutual trust required that fundamental to the EU legal system values would be recognized in each and every EU member states as a precondition to the proper implementation of EU law;[3] this requirement was construed as a straightforward product of the very fabric of EU law which represents 'a structured network of principles, rules and mutually independent legal relations linking the EU and its Member States'.[4] In the judgment of 27 February 2018 in case C-64/16 *Associaçao Sindicos dos Juízes Portugueses (ASJP),*[5] the Court held that Article 2 was a pivotal provision for the mutual trust of national judiciaries in the EU jurisdictional system construed pursuant to Article 19 (1) TEU to consist also of national courts.[6] Thus, guarantees of judicial independence are required also at the national level.[7] The Court also upheld that the interpretation of art. 19(1) TEU could be rendered independently of whether, in a given situation, Article 51(1) CFR applies.[8] The issue has also been quite extensively discussed in a series of illustrious opinions presented by Advocate General Evgeni Tanchev.[9] AG Tanchev adopted a broader, systemic view of respective elements of judiciary reform in Poland (such as, especially, setting forth a lowered cap on the retirement age of judges during their tenure or subjecting the access to judicial positions or advancement in it to a scheme *de facto* controlled by the executive). In his opinions, he assessed them as contributing to an extensive systemic overhaul of the judiciary defying the relevant EU standards enshrined in the EU Treaty, thus undermining mutual trust principle. All these recent developments has proved to be a departure from a narrower analytical concept which had been adopted by the EU Court of Justice in the case C-286/12 *Commission v. Hungary,*[10] where the question of judiciary-concerned regulation on judges' age of retirement had been assessed in terms of its compliance with the EU principle of proportionality.

No doubt, the systemic position of Article 2 TEU and the exact content of values it enshrines has also been extensively debated in rule of law-concerned publications. Many of them considered *ASJP* judgment to have 'conceptional' importance for the whole rule of law discourse in the context of modifications of judiciary systems in some EU member states.[11] It has been argued in literature that the existing

[3]Id., para. 168.

[4]Id., para. 167.

[5]ECLI:EU:C:2018:117.

[6]Id., para. 30.

[7]Id., para. 42.

[8]Id., para. 29.

[9]Opinions in cases C-619/18 *Independence of the Polish Supreme Court* of 11 April 2018, ECLI:EU:C:2019:325; C-192/18 (retirement age of judges) of 20 June 2019, ECLI:EU:C:2019:529; C-585/18, C-524/28, C-625/18 *Polish National Judiciary Council, Disciplinary Chamber of the Supreme Court* of 27 June 2019, ECLI:EU:C:2019:551.

[10]Judgment of 6 November 2012, ECLI:EUI:C:2012:687.

[11]Pech and Platon (2018), pp. 1827–1854; Krajewski (2018), pp. 395–405; Bonelli and Claes (2018), pp. 622–643.

infringement procedures proved to be badly needed to defend basic principles of EU law and that they are paramount for the development of the underlying legal concept.[12] Some authors argued that the rule of law procedures were important to maintain the EU axiological system intact despite possible or existing stresses arising from the ever-changing political strains in the EU member states.[13] The TEU arrangements for the protection of rule of law were interpreted as unique as they were meant to provide for cooperation and axiological consensus instrumental for the EU to maintain its character as a polity of constitutional quality able to effectively protect its citizens whenever whey happen to enjoy EU law rights.[14]

Systemic approach and adequate institutional arrangements were considered to be of acute importance for the effectiveness of the existing EU rules meant to promote and/or protect EU values.[15] It has been argued that a causal model of infringement of values enshrined in Article 2 TEU was needed to make liability of the Member State possible under art. 7 TEU.[16]

2.2 *Two-Stage Procedure Under Article 7 TEU*

A rough equivalent of Article 7 appeared in the EU legal system in 1997, with the successful ratification of the Treaty of Amsterdam. Now it is one of the provisions of the Treaty of Lisbon. Article 7 can be applied in two distinctive situations emerging in the EU Member States:

(a) in a situation of a 'clear risk of a serious breach (...) of the values referred to in Article 2';
(b) in a situation of a 'serious and persistent breach (...) of the values referred to in Article 2'.

These two situations are addressed upon in two distinctive provisions of Article 7: its paragraph 1 and 2, respectively. Depending on specific circumstances, these provisions can be applied one after another, or—if the gravity of the situation commends it—just paragraph 2 can apply even from the very outset. In the former case, the two paragraphs concerned represent a two-stage description of the situation in which the breach of the values referred to in Article 2 has persisted over sufficiently long time or even aggravated.

For each of the so distinguished stages, different modes of situation identification and application of corrective measures apply. In each of these models a fairly

[12] Prete (2017), pp. 6–10, 301–304.
[13] Kochenov (2017), pp. 9–27.
[14] Tichý (2018), pp. 85–108.
[15] Itzcovich (2017), pp. 28–43; Schmidt and Bogdanowicz (2017), pp. 1069–1073.
[16] Bagińska and Majkowska-Szulc (2018), pp. 125–144.

complex and subtle interplay of the European Commission, the European Parliament, the Council, the European Council and the Member States is granted.

The procedure of Article 7(1) is initiated by $^{1}/_{3}$ of the EU Member States, or the European Parliament of the European Commission; under Article 7(2) the mode of the initiation is the same, with the exception that the European Parliament cannot trigger the procedure. The core institution making the pivotal decision for each procedure is different for paragraph 1 and 2. In Article 7(1) procedure, the decision is made by the Council (in its General Council formation, i.e. in the format made up of the European affairs ministers from all EU Member States) acting with a very challenging $^{4}/_{5}$ majority of votes. In contrast, in Article 7(2) procedure, the decision on the existence of 'a serious and persistent breach (. . .) of values referred to in Article 2' is to be made by the European Council. Only within the procedure under Article 7(1), the Council may address to the Member State (under the preliminary RLF scrutiny) its corrective recommendations prior to the determination that this Member State experiences a situation of 'a clear risk of a serious breach of the values referred to in Article 2'. The European Council is not empowered to take a similar step under Article 7(2).

The procedures of Article 7(1) and Article 7(2) can be distinguished also by their different outcomes. Under Article 7(1), the Council is invested with the right to regularly verify whether the grounds on which the Member State considered was determined to experience 'a clear risk of a serious breach (. . .) of values referred to in Article 2'. In contrast, in the aggravated situation falling within the ambit of Article 7 (2), the outcome of the procedure is that the Council would now be empowered (pursuant to Article 7(3)) to decide (by a qualified majority) 'to suspend certain of the rights deriving from the application of the Treaties to the Member States in question'. This coercive suspension may take the form of excluding the Member State's representative from voting in the Council; the suspension can as well involve any negative deformation of the regular rights of the Member State under the TEU and TFEU. The only limitations applicable to the power of the Council in this context is that—under Article 7(3) TEU—it should 'take into account the possible consequence of such a suspension on the rights and obligations of natural and legal persons'. Because of a high position of general principles of law in the EU legal system, the Council should also make its measures applied under Article 7(3) in line with these principles, especially with the principle of proportionality. Yet, as any overview of the Court of Justice jurisprudence may indicate, only serious, 'manifest' errors in this principle application are most likely to make the measures so adopted subject to annulment by the Court of Justice.[17] Moreover, these measures may escape any EU Court of Justice's scrutiny initiated by natural and legal persons, as under the well-established *Plaumann* doctrine they are required to substantiate that the contested measures are uniquely applicable to the person challenging them—which is a difficult task. In other words, the decisions adopted under Article 7(3) are

[17]See the judgment in the case 25-62 *Plaumann & Co. v. Commission*, ECR [1963] 95. See also: Arnull (2006), pp. 41–49.

bound to be quite enduring in the EU legal system.[18] The RLF Treaty procedures specified in Article 7 is graphically depicted in Fig. 1.

The Treaty does not offer any further or more detailed elaboration of the system of Article 7 enforcement. This implies that neither does it give any guidelines which may apply to the systematic monitoring of the situation in respective Member States prior to the application of Article 7. This shortage is quite striking when the system of Article 7 TEU is compared with the EU system of enforcement of rules of economic governance set forth in Articles 121 and 126 TFEU as the latter system is elaborated in a significant number of secondary legal acts which set forth detailed rules on the evaluation of relevant criteria and procedural aspects of their application.

The Treaty model of RLF, as it is, is quite vulnerable to the Member States' collective will to trigger its respective stages even in a rather hypothetical situation of serious infringements of any of them against the values enshrined in Article 2 TEU. This vulnerability arises from the very demanding unanimity threshold for the decision made under Article 7(2), i.e. the one which would determine 'serious and persistent breach of the values referred to in Article 2' by one of the EU Member States. It is therefore enough that two EU countries will simultaneously be subject to the RLF procedure to make it manifestly ineffective as each of these countries would be able to vote on the case of another. Such a voting 'complot' is not a novelty in the EU: e.g. exactly this type of cooperative behavior prevented the Council from making its decision effective in the seemingly much less vulnerable system of economic governance.[19]

2.3 *Rule of Law Framework sensu stricto in the Preparatory Stage: Its Origins and Formula*

European Union statutory law does not contain any specific provisions concerning the evaluation of the situation in any Member States with regard to Article 7 TEU. In other words, the initiation criteria for the RLF or the procedure applicable to the initiation of Article 7 application have not been detailed in the Treaties or any legislative legal acts. The fact that the EU law falls short of expectations with regard to the enforcement mechanisms of Article 7 (in connection with Article 2) TEU has not gone unnoticed to many actors of the EU legal system. The most pronounced political initiative to improve this situation was undertaken by a group of Northern EU Member States: Denmark, Finland, Germany, and the Netherlands which advocated for the development of an instrument which would make it possible to monitor the internal rule of law in EU Member States on a permanent basis. In the programming document of this initiative, a 2013 report titled 'Respect and Justice for All',

[18]Tridimas (2000), pp. 89–123.

[19]See the judgment in the case C-27/04 *Commission v. Council*, ECR [2004] I-6649. See also e.g. Andersen (2012), p. 27.

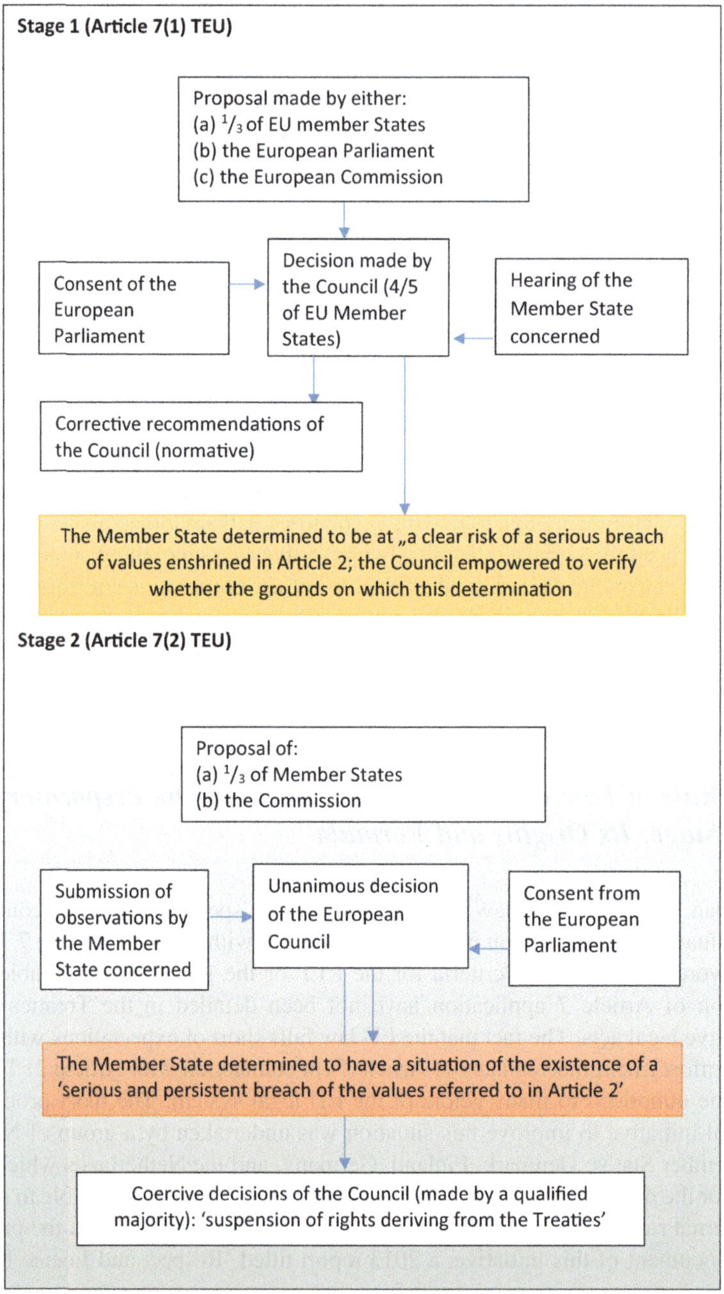

Fig. 1 Procedure of Article 7 paragraphs 1–2 TEU (Treaty of Lisbon). Source: Artur Nowak-Far

the Dutch Ministry of Foreign Affairs explained the rationale of the initiative in the following way:

> ...the rule of law does not always function sufficiently well, even within EU member states. To strengthen the rule of law within Europe, the government seeks to promote transparent governance, independent judiciaries, respect for human rights, antidiscrimination policy and legislation to curb corruption and conflicts of interest (...) Countries wanting to join the EU must comply with strict accession criteria in the realm of the rule of law and human rights (the Copenhagen criteria[20]) (...) At the moment, there are still too few resources to call member states to account after their accession to the EU. Ideally, there should be a mechanism within the EU enabling member states to remind each other of their obligations on the basis of equality. There is already a system of this kind in the framework of the United Nations, but the EU also has a responsibility to tackle problems in its own house on a political level.[21]

The initiative coincided with some actions undertaken in the EU institutions: In June 2013 the Justice and Home Affairs Council and the European Parliament, respectively. The former called on the Commission 'to take forward the debate in line with the Treaties on the possible need for and shape of a collaborative and systematic method' to monitor the observance of EU values in respective EU Member States and address detected departures from the generally accepted standards.[22] The European Parliament requested that 'Member States be regularly assessed on their continued compliance with the fundamental values of the Union and the requirement of democracy and the rule of law.'[23]

The said RLF initiative did not earn any firm enough support from other Member States which remained neither neutral or negative to it. The Hungarian government already feared that the procedure would be used against it; some governments (like the Polish one, at least for some time) perceived it as an 'elitist' procedure which would be used by the 'better' states (most likely the 'old' EU members) to scrutinize political practices of the 'worse' countries (most likely to be the 'new' EU Member States, i.e. the ones which acceded past 2004 and which, indeed, had to meet the Copenhagen criteria). Some other Member States perceived the RLF as a tool to expand the European Commission's realm of authority—something they were reluctant to easily accept.

Regardless of these hurdles, in response to these initiatives, the European Commission came up with its own communication concerning the procedure which could be used for activating the mechanisms foreseen in Article 7 TEU.[24] According to the Commission's own statement, the proposed rules were to 'precede and complement

---

[20]For the explanation of this point refer to the next section of this chapter.

[21]Ministry of Foreign Affairs of the Netherlands (2013), p. 20.

[22]Press release 3244th Council Meeting – Justice and Home Affairs, Luxembourg 6–7 June 2013, document 10461/13 (OR.en).

[23]European Parliament, Committee on Civil Liberties, Justice and Home Affairs, Report of 17 February 2014 on evaluation of justice in relations to criminal justice and the rule of law, rapporteur Kinga Göncz, document A7-0122/2014.

[24]See *supra* Fig. 1.

Article 7 TEU mechanisms'; their application was to be 'without prejudice to the Commission's powers to address specific situations falling within the scope of EU law by means of infringement procedures under Article 258 TFEU' (i.e. its powers to start up an EU law infringement procedure before the European Union Court of Justice). Where there are clear indications of a systemic threat to the rule of law in a Member State, the Commission can launch a 'pre-Article 7 Procedure' by initiating a dialogue with that Member State through the Rule of Law Framework.

According to the Commission communication, the RLF procedure has three stages:

(a) the assessment stage—where the Commission collects and examines all the relevant information and assesses whether there are clear indications of a systemic threat to the rule of law; at this stage, if the Commission's concerns have been substantiated, it would initiate a dialogue with the Member State concerned by sending its 'Rule of Law Opinion' to that state;
(b) the recommendation stage—where the Commission would address its 'Rule of Law Recommendation' to the Member State concerned, in which this EU institution would make public expected actions and their applicable time-frame-work—all meant to improve the situation in the Member State concerned,
(c) the follow-up stage—where the Commission would monitor the Member State's action and, if it found the State's performance unsatisfactory, it would trigger Article 7 procedure—either on its own, or by prompting $^1/_3$ of the Member States or the European Parliament to do so.

The RLF (*sensu stricto*) can thus be interpreted also as a system of structured discourse as it involves a continuous dialogue and exchange or views between the Commission and the Member State concerned and between the European Parliament and the Member States (represented within the Council).

3 Exposition of EU Axiological Basis in the Treaties and Its Procedural Ramifications

3.1 Driving Forces

The idea to expose the EU axiological basis in a EU treaty has been on the agenda for a long time prior to the entry into force of the Treaty of Lisbon (in December 2009). The sense of urgency with regard to this exposition emerged as a result of the following two phenomena:

(a) the EU enlargement negotiations which started in 1998 and were successfully concluded in 2004 and resulted in accepting a group of Central and Eastern European countries as new Member States of the EU,
(b) the emergence of the authoritarian right-wing coalition in Austria (in the period of 2000–2002).

One of the challenges of the EU enlargement negotiations which involved a group of Central and Eastern European countries (i.e. Czech Republic, Estonia, Latvia, Lithuania, Hungary, Poland, Slovakia, Slovenia) was their authoritarian heritage (in fact, a little bit less extensive for the Czech Republic, as prior to WWII, it had been a fully-feathered liberal democracy). All these 8 countries had a Communist past, the Baltic States (i.e. Estonia, Latvia, and Lithuania) were even the component republic of the USSR until 1991. For this reason, the rule of law and other EU democratic values were included in the EU membership criteria negotiation package, most importantly in the form of the so called 'Copenhagen Criteria'. These were set forth by the European Council in its summit Conclusions of June 21–22 1993. The most relevant requirement was formulated in the following way:

> Membership requires that the candidate country has achieved stability of institutions guaranteeing democracy, the rule of law, human rights and respect for and protection of minorities, the existence of a functioning market economy as well as the capacity to cope with competitive pressure and market forces within the Union. Membership presupposes the candidate's ability to take on the obligations of membership including adherence to the aims of political, economic and monetary union.[25]

Thus, throughout the negotiations, the incumbent States were required to modify their institutional and legal systems in a way which could guarantee that the Copenhagen Criteria were met. Interestingly, the question of meeting the Copenhagen Criteria had not been an issue in the 1995 EU enlargement which included Austria, Finland, and Sweden, but had again been quite important in the 2007 EU enlargement onto Bulgaria and Rumania and in 2013 when they were again applied to Croatia. The problem with the sheer application of the Copenhagen Criteria was, however, that—from the perspective of the EU legal order—these criteria represent non-binding set of rules (which does not mean that they cannot be considered to form contractual obligations-reference under international law). This means that they could effectively be applied whenever, in the context of EU membership negotiations, there was enough conditionality to enforce adequate standards in the EU membership-aspiring countries; yet this element was lost whenever they entered the EU as the European Council's presidency conclusions of 1993 were not even their own original political commitment but rather something imposed 'from outside'. Thus, in order to avoid departures from the negotiated standards, an adequate amendment of the Treaty appeared to be badly needed.

As it has already been said, the other phenomenon which prompted the process of adoption of adequate Treaty standards of democracy, the rule of law, human rights, and the protection of minorities was that of the political rise of right, authoritarian parties in Austria. The phenomenon found its pivotal moment after the 1999 parliamentary elections in Austria when the radical right party, Freedom Party of Austria (*Freiheitliche Partei Österreichs, FPÖ*), was able to create a coalition with the mainstream Social Democrats (*Sozialdemokratische Partei Österreichs, SPÖ*).

[25]European Council in Copenhagen. Conclusions of the Presidency, June 21–22, 1993, document SN 180/1/93 REV 1, p. 14.

What now (unfortunately) appears not so unusual anymore, had in 2000 come as a surprise because of a controversial, nationalistic, anti-immigration, and authoritarian penchant of the controversial FPÖ's leader Jörg Haider. The resulting situation made it visible, that the only pressure other EU Member States could exert on the EU country whose policy might not be completely in line with the EU values was the political pressure (in fact, intra-EU cooperation with the Austrian government then was limited), but no firm legal tool could be used.

The first ever legislative reaction to the threat of rightist populists was the amendment of the Treaty introduced by the Treaty of Amsterdam (1997), often referred to as '*Lex Austria*'. Namely, in Article F.1, the Treaty was given a new provision which provided that:

> The Union is founded on the principles of liberty, democracy, respect for human rights and fundamental freedoms and the rule of law, principles which are common to the Member States.

It is quite striking that, when compared to Article 2 of the present TUE, Article F (1) TUE (the Amsterdam version) made its reference to a narrower catalogue of values. Moreover, it made a reference to liberty which is not made any more in the present Treaty. Its reference to human rights goes together with the reference to fundamental freedoms—whereas the present Treaty does not contain a reference to the latter value. Most importantly, Article F(1) TUE does not contain any specific catalogue of values which pertain to the societies of the Member States (such as pluralism, non-discrimination, tolerance, justice, solidarity, and equality between women and men); rather, it points out an axiological network which should be 'common the Member States' but which apparently 'stem from the fundamental EU legal order'.

In Article F.1., the Amsterdam Treaty set forth, for the first time, a RLF procedure, yet it was quite distinctive from the present one. The most important difference is that the Amsterdam RLF was a single-stage procedure with the pivotal role of the Council, acting in a very special format (not used anymore in the EU institutional order) of the heads of states or governments (i.e. with no participation of the President of the Council nor any of its own President, as this position had never existed for this very special type of the Council). The Council was to act by unanimity on a proposal by 1/3 of the Member States or by the Commission and after obtaining the assent of the European Parliament—which is the same arrangement as the one used now (also with respect to the majority requirements). Article F.1 provided also that the Council's decision should be made only after inviting the Member State concerned to submit its observations. The procedure was to be concluded with the determination by the Council of 'the existence of a serious and persistent breach by a Member State of principles mentioned in Article F(1)'. When such a conclusion had been adopted in the decision, the Council, acting by a qualified majority, might decide to suspend certain of the rights deriving from the application of this Treaty to the Member State in question, including the voting rights of the representative of the government of that Member State in the Council. The Amsterdam RLF procedure is depicted in Fig. 2.

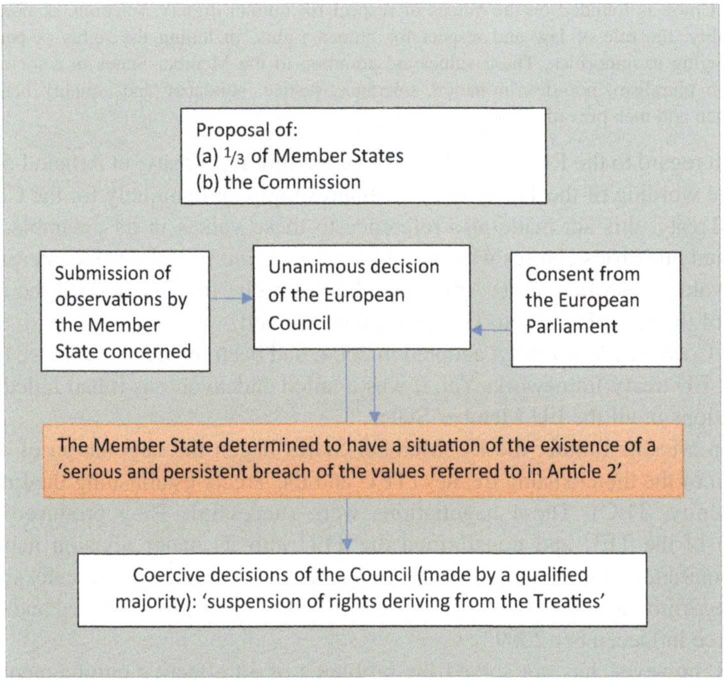

Fig. 2 Single stage RLF procedure of Article 7 TEU (Article F.1. of the Treaty of Amsterdam). Source: Artur Nowak-Far

Article F.1. TEU contained the same modalities as the present Article 7(2). Namely, the Council decision on the suspension of rights of the Member State put under the RLF scrutiny had to take into account 'the possible consequences of such a suspension on the rights and obligations of natural and legal persons'. It could also, acting by a qualified majority, decide to vary or revoke measures originally adopted with respect to that Member States—reflecting on changes in the underlying situation.

The RLF procedure specified in the Amsterdam Treaty was quickly considered too rigid and inflexible as it did not allow for any preliminary stage where the Member State concerned could be involved in a dialogue on its practices. Thus, Article 7 TUE was amended in the subsequent revision of the TEU, now in the Treaty of Nice (2000).

The rule of law became an important element of the agenda within the negotiation of the EU Constitutional Treaty, which, in Article I-2 enshrined it together with other values deemed inextricably interwoven with it: democracy and the human rights. Moreover, it contained a clause not only stating that the EU-specific values listed in it are 'common' to the EU Member States, but also formulating requirements concerning the axiological fabric of their societies—all in the format which was later adopted in the Treaty of Lisbon as well. Thus, the wording of Article I-2 of the Constitutional Treaty was as follows:

> The Union is founded on the values of respect for human dignity, freedom, democracy, equality, the rule of law and respect for human rights, including the rights of persons belonging to minorities. These values are common to the Member States in a society in which pluralism, non-discrimination, tolerance, justice, solidarity and equality between women and men prevail.

With regard to the RLF procedure, the Constitutional Treaty, in Article I-59, took over the wording of the Treaty of Nice. Interestingly and uniquely for the Constitutional Treaty, this act made also reference to these values in its preamble. It also contained numerous clauses which provided significant guidelines for interpretation of the values enshrined in its Article I-2. Interestingly, it also extended the requirements of the rule of law onto EU institutions, as well.

The Constitutional Treaty, adopted in 2004, had been intended to replace the then present EU treaty framework. Yet, it was a failed endeavor—as it had failed to win ratifications in all the EU Member States.

Soon after its failure, the EU Member States began the negotiation of a major revision of the then existing treaties (TEU and the Treaty establishing the European Community, TEC). These negotiations were successful. They produced a new version of the TEU and transformed the TEC into its major revision named the Treaty on functioning of the European Union. The new treaties (technically speaking resulting from the accord called the Treaty of Lisbon), were duly ratified and entered into force in December 2009.

This, however, has not solved the problems of an effective enforcement of the rule of law in the EU. A possibility for the EU venue to achieve a high enough standard in this area would be to accede to the European Convention of Human Rights and Fundamental Freedoms (ECHR). Yet, the EU failed to do it. The EU failure to make an accession to the European Convention of Human Rights and Fundamental Freedoms (ECHR) occurred despite the fact that the Convention is referred to in Article 6 TEU which

(a) in its paragraph 2 provides that the Union shall accede to the ECHR, yet that 'such accession shall not affect the Union's competences as defined in the Treaties',
(b) in its paragraph 3, provides that fundamental rights, as guaranteed by the Convention shall (together with the fundamental rights resulting from constitutional traditions common to the Member States) constitute general principles of the EU law.

The former provision was intended to defy the Court of Justice's negative opinion issued in 1994 (i.e. the opinion 2/94[26]) which upheld that with no express legal Treaty basis, the Community was not entitled to accede to the ECHR. This 'defying' effect seemed to be even reinforced by a modification of the ECHR itself, by the introduction of the Protocol No. 14, which in Article 17 provided for a change in Article 59(2) ECHR with the effect that it now expressly foresaw the EU accession to

---

[26]CJEU, Opinion 2/94, ECLI:EU:C:1996:140.

the Convention. The process of accession seemed to be reinforced by the fact that, by virtue of the Lisbon Treaty, the EU Chapter of Fundamental Rights (CFR) had been included into the EU legal system as a binding instrument.[27] As such, it required that the rights enshrined in it be identical with the rights arising from the ECHR (Article 52(3) CFR), yet with an important reservation that these rights be not interpreted in departure from the established EU law, international public law (at large) and international conventions to which the Union or all its Member States were counterparties (Article 53 CFR).

The specific conditions on which the EU was to accede to the ECHR were set forth in the Protocol No. 8 attached to the Treaty of Lisbon. This Protocol set forth the following principles applicable to the accession:

(a) the principle of inter-semiotic retention (set forth in Article 1), i.e. the requirement that the accession should make it possible to retain specific features of the EU and the EU legal system (especially with regard to the participation of the EU in controlling mechanisms of the ECHR);
(b) the principle of non-modification of external and internal powers of the EU (Article 2, first sentence),
(c) the principle of non-modification of the status of the EU Member States in the ECHF legal order (Article 3, second sentence);
(d) the principle of exclusive competence of the EU Court of Justice with regard to disputes concerning the interpretation and application of EU Treaties (Article 3 of the Protocol in connection with Article 344 TFEU).

In its opinion 2/13,[28] the EU Court of Justice upheld that the already negotiated agreement on the EU accession to the ECHR should not be signed. One of the most significant arguments which prompted the Court to conclude negatively was that the accession to the ECHR would result in a deformation of the principle of mutual trust inherent in the EU legal system. This principle implies that the Member States should not double-check, in any legal action context, whether other Member States observe fundamental rights guaranteed by the Union.[29] Nevertheless, such rights should be interpreted 'within the framework of the structures and objectives of the Union'[30] which are determined by EU substantive law. In the case of doubt, national courts can refer to the Court of Justice within the preliminary questions procedure

[27]The Chapter of Fundamental Rights had been considered to have just a 'declaratory' value before.

[28]CJEU, Opinion 2/13 of 18 December 2014, *Accession of the European Union to the European Convention for the Protection of Human Rights and Fundamental Freedoms*, ECLI:EU:C:2014:2454.

[29]Id, para. 191 of the Opinion 2/13, *supra* note 2. See also the CJEU's judgment of 25 June 2018 in the case C-216/18 PPU *LM*, ECLI:EU:C:2018:586 in which the Court upheld that such a double-checking should guarantee rights conferred to EU citizens under Article 47 CFR; the CJ emphasized that the check should be based on specific and detailed analysis of the underlying situation and should take into account the specific situation of an individual concerned as well as the information provided for by the Member State whose legal system is to be trusted.

[30]Id, para. 170.

under Article 267 TFEU. This important legal arrangement cannot be reconciled with the mechanisms of application of ECHR, as—among others—any interpretation offered by the EU Court of Justice could not be binding to the separate Court of Justice operating under the Convention. Instead, judiciary decisions of that latter court would be binding onto the EU Court of Justice which could undermine the principles set forth in Protocol No. 8.

Interestingly, this does not mean that the EU Treaties and the ECHR represent two legal systems immune from each other. In practice, they are in a constant intersemiotic dialogue (i.e. the dialogue in which two separate, yet interlegible 'institutional languages' are employed) as the judgments under the ECHR are often treated as a type of preliminary rulings by the EU Court of Justice.[31] In turn, the ECHR Court sometimes invokes the EU preliminary questions procedure under Article 267 TFEU considering denial of its application a breach of the ECHR (i.e. its Article 6(2) which prohibits denial of justice).[32] However, regardless of this dialogue, the linkage between the ECHR and the EU legal order proved to be insufficient to provide for a stronger enforcement mechanism of the EU values, especially those enshrined in the Charter of Fundamental Rights and in Article 2 TEU.

3.2 Legal Interpretation of the RLF *sensu stricto*

The legal meaning of the procedure set forth in Article 7 TEU does not yield any specific concerns as to its legal binding force. In contrast, the RLF *sensu stricto* does give rise to some concerns about its legal force which would likely be raised by the Member States subject to any form of the European Commission's scrutiny in the context of Article 7.

Admittedly, the RLF *sensu stricto* was set forth in the European Commission communication (i.e. the RLF communication). The communication is not included in the list of binding legal acts specified in the Treaties; most importantly, it is not covered by Article 288 TFUE, which provides that regulations, directives and decisions have binding force in the EU legal system. Thus, the RLF communication can be considered an act of soft law.

The European Commission was empowered to make the RLF communication as it was meant to 'precede and complement Article 7 TEU mechanisms' and provide transparency in the Commission's own actions—as such a specification can be

[31]See e.g. the judgment in the case C-404/15 and C/659/15 *Criminal Proceeding against Pál Aranyosi and Robert Căldăraru,* ECLI:EU:C:2016:198 (where the Court upheld that the European Arrest Warrant can be denied effect with respect to the Member State being persistently in contravention of the ECtHR—what has already been confirmed in the ECtHR judgments in *Vociu v. Rumania,* Application No. 22015/10, *Bujorean v. Rumania,* Application No. 13054/12, *Varga et al. v. Hungary,* Applications No. 14097/12, 45135/12, 73712/12, 34001/13, 44055/13, 64586/13.

[32]ECtHR *Dhahbi v. Italy,* Application No. 17120/09.

considered a specification of the Commission's general powers arising from this Treaty provision. The rules set forth in the RLF communication can be interpreted as a measure to eliminate uncertainty of law resulting from the incompleteness of rules specified in Article 7 with regard to the triggering of the mechanism of RLF (*sensu largo*). Thus, the procedure foreseen in it is meant to produce legal (and at the end of the day, binding) effect, yet the RLF rules (*sensu stricto*) are deprived of a binding force. In the terminology developed by Susan Senden, the RLF communication can be classified as a decisional communication (as contrasted to informational or interpretative ones), i.e. a communication which provides for general rules regarding the way in which the already existing implementing powers will be exercised, in particular, indicating, how the Commission will apply binding law provisions in respective cases and how it will make use of the applicable discretion at its disposal.[33] Decisional communications are not binding but are apt to produce legal effects by virtue of some other rules to which they pertain and to which they pragmatically relate. In the specific RLF (*sensu stricto*) context, the RLF communication derives its legal effectiveness from the fact that it is meant to make sure that the application of Article 7 should commence on a well-reasoned and adequately substantiated basis. As such, the RLF *sensu stricto* could make the application of Article 7 much more informed than without it. Moreover, as it performs an obvious signaling element, the RLF *sensu stricto* guarantees that the Member States concerned would not be surprised with the decision to become subject to measures under Article 7. More than that—they will have a chance to get involved in a dialogue with the Commission where they would be able to submit their own argumentation concerning the rule of law situation.

It is a matter of serious doubt whether the Member States subjected to the RLF *sensu stricto* would be able to challenge the recommendations addressed to them within this procedure before the EU Court of Justice (under Article 263 TFEU, i.e. within the action of annulment of an EU legislative act). The doubt arises from at least two issues:

(a) the formal one, which is based on an argument that Article 263 TFEU overtly excludes annulment actions brought against Commission's recommendations,
(b) the material one, which is based on an argument that, even if Article 263 TFUE were applicable (as—because of the clear intention to produce legal effect—the 'recommendations' under the RLF could be re-interpreted as acts falling within the remit of actions for annulment[34]), at the end of the day, they could not be challenged as they do not represent a final measure, but are rather steps in a procedure to be completed and to involve challengeable legal acts.[35]

---

[33]Senden (2004), pp. 148–149.

[34]See e.g. the EU Court of Justice judgment in the case C-362/08 *P Internationaler Hilfsfonds eV v. Commission*, ECLI:EU:C:2010:40, para. 52; 22/70 *Commission v. Council*, ECLI:EU:C:1971:32, para. 42.

[35]The argument *per analogiam* based on the EU Court of Justice (the Court of First Instance) judgment in the case T-126/95 *Dumez v. Commission*, ECLI:EU:T:1995:189.

Not being able to challenge the RLF recommendations, the Member States concerned, if only determined enough, would likely disregard them (as it was recently the case with Poland). Since (genuine) recommendations are not binding legal acts, the Commission will not be able to bring an action against the Member States concerned (under Article 258 TFEU) for not fulfilling them. Yet, this non-fulfillment will be a significant evidence in any further proceedings under Article 7.

This conclusion is in the same time an argument supporting the Commission's competence to issue the RLF recommendations. In the context of the entire RLF, they represent an important element of the dialogue between the Commission and the Member State concerned. The fact that the Member State ignored them (if this is the case) becomes an element of the argumentation sued for triggering the Article 7 procedure against this state.

4 The Content of the Rule of Law Under the RLF

To complete the analysis presented in this article, it is quite essential to identify what exactly is meant under the term 'rule of law' in the context of the RLF, regardless of its narrow or broader form. As the term does not have any Treaty definition, it is quite in place to rely on the legal doctrine and the EU Court of Justice's jurisprudence to answer this question.

4.1 The Legal Doctrine

More is known about what the rule of law is not than what it exactly is—especially in national contexts. Yet, basic conditions for the rule of law can be identified in the existing body of literature.[36] It is most often held that the rule of law is achieved whenever the following requirements are met:

(a) law generality—law should be general; particular regulation should be avoided;
(b) law publicity—law should be made public, known to those whom it concerns;
(c) law non-retroactivity—law should not act retroactively;
(d) law cataphaticity—law should be understandable to its primary stakeholders;
(e) law relative stability—law should be kept stable, whenever there are not good reasons to amend it;
(f) systemic consistency—legal norms of the system should be consistent with each other;
(g) law observability—it should be possible for law stakeholders to observe it;

[36]See e.g. May (2014), pp. 33–56; Sanchez-Cuenca (2003), pp. 62–93.

(h) behavioral congruence between legal norms and stakeholders' actions—all stakeholders should effectively observe the law.

Adriaan Bedner divided the features/requirements of the rule of law into three classes:

(a) procedural:

- the presence of the rule by law, i.e. the situation where the state actions are subject to law;
- the law formalization, which requires that it is understandable, stable and predictable);
- the creation of law in democratic procedures, i.e. under conditions requiring that the legislative consent should determine or at least influence legal actions)

(b) substantive:

- the law subordination to justice;
- the protection of individual rights and liberties;
- the respect to human rights and group rights

(c) controlling:

- the independence of judiciary;
- the responsibility of administrative and other independent bodies for reviewing legal process.[37]

Interestingly, most of these requirements are primarily addressed to law-makers. Some of them require a good *ex ante* foresight into the expected perceptions/reactions of those who would be most likely and/or most strongly concerned with a given piece of law. It is striking that all of these requirements are formulated in procedural terms or, if they concern the content, they are highly abstract. As a result, the question about the 'content' law under the rule of law is quite justified.

One possible answer to this question is that the rule of law is about providing for conditions in which 'right' relationships between the government and citizens as well as between each and every citizen is set. 'Right' means, that the resulting setting is capable to protect and enforce individual rights and to give framework for a large degree of responsibility and accountability in the government. Some answers aspire even higher, as they would consider the 'real' rule of law to guarantee a perfect impartiality of the law-making system.

---

[37]Bedner (2010), pp. 56–69.

4.2 The EU Court of Justice Jurisprudence

The rule of law was highlighted in the European Union relatively often in various forms. Most importantly in 1986, in its enshrined judgment in the case 294/83 *Parti écologiste 'Les Verts' v. European Parliament,*[38] the Court of Justice held that the Community was a 'community of law'—and reminded that it required the consistency of all law (including national law) with the Treaty serving as a 'basic constitutional charter' (i.e. the systemic anchor of the entire, so defined, legal system). In 1993, the European Council formulated the so called 'Copenhagen Criteria' applicable to all states aspiring for EU membership, in which conformity with the 'rule of law' was enshrined. In 1997, the Treaty of Amsterdam made referrals to rule of law in Article 6 and the new suspension mechanism of Article 7 (so called *Lex Austria*). On some occasions, the Court of Justice upheld the idea that the EU was also subject to the rule of law. In its judgment in the case C-50/00 *P Unión de Pequeños Agricultores v. Council,*[39] the CJ stated that rule of law required consistency of EU secondary law with fundamental rights (see also similarly in joint cases C-402/05 P and C-415/05 *P Yassin Abdullah Kadi and Al Barakaat International Foundation v. Council and Commission*[40]). As it has already been argued, the most recent CJ's jurisprudence has contributed significantly to this rather rudimentary understanding of the concept of rule of law—most importantly in the realm of judiciary. The most recent development of CJ jurisprudence established a link between Article 2 TEU and Article 19(1) TEU as well as the due process standard set forth in Article 47 CFR (concerning the right to an effective remedy and to a fair trial). The CJ construed the EU legal system as the one which is complete and fully capable to enforce all rights conveyed by the EU law onto EU citizens or undertakings, provided that the Member States effectively ensure judicial protection of these rights.[41] In such a complete system, the respective judicial systems, at both national and supranational levels, sport mutual trust to each other.[42] Yet, this trust is subject to the results of a careful double-checking procedure which can be triggered by national courts whenever there are substantiated grounds that the values enshrined in Article 2 TEU are not fully observed or implemented in another Member State.[43] The issue can be expected to be developed further as many cases concerning the rule of law issue are still pending. So far, they have been extensively discussed in a series

[38]ECLI:EU:C:1986:166.

[39]ECLI:EU:C:2002:462.

[40]Judgment of 3 September; ECLI:EU:C:2008:461.

[41]Judgment of 6 March 2018 in the case C-284/16 *Slovak Republic v. Achmea BV*, ECLI:2018:158; see especially para 36.

[42]E.g. Opinion 2/13 of 18 December 2014, *supra* note 2; judgment of 27 February 2018 in case C-64/16 *Associaçao Sindical dos Juízes Portugueses (ASJP),* ECLI:EU:C:2018:117, para. 39.

[43]Judgment of 5 April 2016 in the case C-404/15 and C-659/15 PP *Aranyosi and Câldâraru*, ECLI: EU:C:2016:198, para 104; judgment of 25 June 2018 in the case C-216/18 PPU *LM*, *supra* note 29, para 23.

of illustrious opinions presented by Advocate General Evgeni Tanchev,[44] who adopted a broader, systemic approach in reviewing judiciary system quality in a Member State.

All these actions have contributed to the understanding of the EU concept of the rule of law. Yet, they definitely are not sufficient to make it possible to construe an independent, EU-specific definition of it. The wording of Article 2:

> The Union is founded on the values of respect for human dignity, freedom, democracy, equality, the *rule of law* and respect for human rights, including the rights of persons belonging to minorities... (emphasis added)

suggests that the rule of law is one of the values on which the EU is founded and that it is somehow different from other values enshrined in this particular provision of the Treaty. We also know (from other provisions of the Treaty as well as from the CJ jurisprudence) that the principle of procedural autonomy applies to the EU Member States. In the procedural realm, its rectifications in CJ's judgments in e.g. cases 21-24/72 *International Fruit Company NV et al. v. Produktschap voor Groenten en Fruit,*[45] C-188/89 *A. Foster et al. v. British Gas plc,*[46] 103/88 *Fratelli Costanzo v. Comune di Milano*[47] indicate that its major aspect is the Member States' free hand in shaping their basic constitutional (institutional) order. This means that also the rule of law (as it has been construed under Article 2 TEU) can be applied in divergent procedural settings of now numerous EU Member States. As a result, uniformity of application of 'the rule of law' (and almost all other standards of EU law) in the European Union is far from an ideal pattern attempted by the EU Court of Justice. In consequence, 'uniform EU law' is—by definition—divergent in real settings, where real interests of EU citizens are at stake. In other words, there is a great deal of intersemiotic discourse of EU Member States' judicial and administrative systems over EU law purported to be 'uniform'. Nevertheless, the already discussed recent developments in CJ's jurisprudence clearly indicated that the substantive concept of rule of law heavily relies on the judiciary independence of the executive.

[44]Opinions in cases C-619/18 *Independence of the Polish Supreme Court* of 11 April 2018, ECLI: EU:C:2019:325; C-192/18 (retirement age of judges) of 20 June 2019, ECLI:EU:C:2019:529; C-585/18, C-524/28, C-625/18 *Polish National Judiciary Council, Disciplinary Chamber of the Supreme Court* of 27 June 2019, ECLI:EU:C:2019:551.

[45]Judgment of 12 December 1972; ECLI:EU:C:1972:115.

[46]Judgment of 12 June 1990: ECLI:EU:C:1990:313.

[47]Judgment of 22 June 1989; ECLI:EU:C:1989:256.

5 The International Dimension of the EU Rule of Law Framework

5.1 The Rule of Law Importance for the EU Common Foreign and Security Policy

The fact that the initiative for increased enforcement of the rule of law within the Treaty of Lisbon system was promoted by the foreign affairs services of a group of the EU countries is quite telling about the significance of that idea for the EU external policy. It is enough to say that the TEU (in Article 21(1)) requires the EU foreign service (operating within the framework of the EU Common Foreign and Security Policy, CFSP[48]) to consider the rule of law to be one of its guiding principles (together with democracy, the universality and indivisibility of human rights and fundamental freedoms, respect for human dignity, the principles of equality and solidarity and respect for the Principles of the UN Charter and international law). Pursuant to Article 21(2) TEU, the Union shall define and pursue international common policies and actions which, *inter alia*, consolidate and support democracy, the rule of law, human rights and the principles of international law. As a result, the rule of law has become an idea well pronounced at various levels and in various fora where the EU is represented.

As a matter of fact, in the international sphere, the EU promotes its own model of human rights and—within it—the rule of law. Generally speaking, this model emphasizes the importance of the individual's dignity and individual rights—the ideas deeply rooted in the European Enlightenment. The rule of law can be considered a comprehensive instrument of safeguarding these rights and enforcing them in a uniform manner. Thus, the RLF mechanisms are vital for assuring that—despite the existing procedural divergences in respective EU Member States' legal systems—the EU preserves the integrity of the EU human rights model, and that the EU as an actor of international relations, maintains its high credibility in promoting this model. In other words, the RLF is meant to curb the existing divergence and achieve some uniform standards in the system of enforcement of human rights in order to attract global adherence.

The problem of a proper (i.e. complete and functional) intersemiotic translation of international human rights standards into domestic ones (i.e. the transposition of one legal-pragmatic model of making them reality into another) is pronounced even in systems of common legal tradition and philosophy. With regard to the relationship between legal systems of the Western legal and political tradition, Ernest A. Young noticed, that even when we looked to such systems which, with no doubt, shared common heritage and reflected the same or significantly similar axiological fundaments, we saw 'divergence rather than convergence on many aspects of values and

[48] I.e. the subject matter of the provisions of Title V TEU.

political culture'.[49] This not very encouraging conclusion is even more applicable to the relationship between the Western legal and political traditions and its more distant counterparts. The underlying prevalent local social circumstances, moral attitudes and customs may determine a significant gap between the Western concept of human rights and their popular/political acceptance beyond the Western world. This gap may also serve as a political excuse for a national policy of not pursuing any ambitious programme of human rights promotion. Moreover, the recent tensions within the EU which urged the Commission to make recourse to the RLF with respect to Poland were fundamentally caused by the fact that the present Polish government emphasized its different stance to human rights—as it does not seem to share the respect too common to most EU states legal tradition and philosophy stemming strongly from the ideas of the European Enlightenment. Instead, it prefers to derive its legitimacy from rather obscure and unclear ideas of social collectivism and Catholic nationalism.

In order to be effective, international human rights (that is the rights adopted in a context of an international agreement for the purpose of their more or less universal application), must be suitable for their at least relatively equivalent intersemiotic translation—that is their transformation into legal norms expressed in an international statute into legal norms of a given national system.[50] As a result, international standards will only be 'common' either if the transformation system is apt to act effectively and efficiently and/or if translated common standards represent a low enough denominator (which could be detrimental to the international level of human rights protection). Irrespective of the systemic capacity of intersemiotic translation or structural complexity of norms being translated, a firm and welcoming constitutional approach is required to make human rights enshrined in an international law instrument subject to such a translation. The resulting divergence eliminates 'an axiological common ground' to which respective EU Member States could refer in their EU wide and global discourse on human rights. As a result, this discourse could be deprived of important common reference framework which could have brought these counterparties closer to each other and make legal measures reconciliation more likely to achieve.

It is obvious that this problem is not only bilateral. In the globalized world, bilateral reciprocity shortages become aggregated so that they are increasingly likely to cause acute frictions between legal systems which tend to be more often exposed in the area of consular protection and asylum granting. As a result, they may become a source of a wide dispute over the general roles of the state needed to make the international order an effective and efficient system in which various communities and individuals can achieve levels of welfare not achievable under non-cooperative conditions. In respective areas relevant for the formulation and implementation of national and/or regional public policies, such a lack of reciprocity and the resulting inter-systemic friction would reduce effectiveness of these policies, thus reducing an

---

[49]Young (2005), pp. 161–166 (referring to the *Thompson* judgment, 487, US 830).

[50]See, e.g. Tiefenbrun (2010), pp. 263–280.

aggregate level of total global welfare which—under more concurrence and cooperation—might have reached higher levels.

5.2 International Law Interpretation of the RLF

In legal terms, the modern European human rights concept (including its procedural frameworks such as RLF) represents a departure from a 'traditional bottom line' standard defining inter-relational aspects of international law set forth in the 1927 PCIJ *Lotus* judgment[51] holding that international law (and thus, the human rights-relevant international law) is essentially about relations among states. Today, international law, and especially human rights and the rule of law component of it is a law about global governance which is a concept extending well beyond the relationships amongst states. Global governance can be defined as 'the sum of many ways individuals and institutions, public and private, manage their common affairs'.[52] The practice follows this approach putting in the radar of both international law and human rights (being its significant element) not only states but also non-state actors (especially individuals and their more or less formalized groupings). It does so through the application of international law norms conceived not only as a result of state consent but also of general pressure resulting from a broad consent of all legitimate international law and human rights stakeholders to pursue basic common values of humankind. In modern times such a pressure has become a driving force for shaping international normative agenda.[53]

Having said that, it is important to emphasize that states still play the most important role as international law operators and human rights guarantors (through their own substantive and procedural guarantees producing the rule of law). Thus, at the end of the day, their consent to any conceived norms in these realms still plays the dominant role in legitimating a broad enough and effective (judiciable) recourse to those values in an international scale (in state-setting). To some extent, this pronounced role of states represents an argument usually somehow less pronounced but worth mentioning that only effective assets of international relations really count in international law and human rights promotion.

The essential problem of today's international relations, international law and thus human rights defined in broad terms (i.e. also as a source of potential inspiration for a global governance practice) is at what level of aggregation of their respective standards should be conceived and, consequently, how universally, they can or should be applied and enforced. In such a context, the EU effort to maintain some uniformity in its human rights and the rule of law context can be interpreted as an

[51][1927] PCIJ 10 Series A, 18.

[52]Commission on Global Governance (1995), *Our Global Neighbourhood: The Report of the Commission on Global Governance*.

[53]See discussion presented in: Thirlway (2014), pp. 8–16.

effort to achieve significant 'weight' able to attract other, non-EU states to follow the European pattern or at least to become an important reference point for the international discussion on the nature, scope of application and the mode of enforcement of human rights.

6 Conclusions

1. The Rule of Law Framework (*sensu largo*) is vulnerable to unguaranteed, discretionary influences of the Member States. This vulnerability arises from its procedural format which requires high thresholds in decision making—with unanimity applicable to the decision which could make it possible for the EU institutions to effectively address any situation in a EU Member States where the rule of law standards have been considered unsatisfactory. With such a mode of the applicable decision-making, RLF procedures are prone to be terminated as a result of collusions made by EU Member States likely to be scrutinized, if at least two of them wish to cooperate with each other in order to abort the RLF procedure brought against one of them.
2. Yet, any serious breaches of an EU Member State of human rights (in the context of ineffective rule of law standards) could single it out within the Union. As a result, in breaches of significant gravity, such a state would not be able to attract cooperation needed for the collusive termination of the RLF. Thus the Framework can have some positive impact on respective EU Member States' behaviour with regard to their respect to human rights.
3. This effect is even reinforced by an active stance of the European Commission which is bound to pursue the RLF effectiveness for the sake of achieving relative uniformity of application of EU law (at large), and making the European Union a credible actor and co-creator of international legal order. The Commission is determined to play an active role also because this allows it to make an important statement on its own institutional powers *vis-à-vis* other EU institutions and the EU Member States.
4. The RLF is an important tool for the maintenance of relative stability of human rights and the rule of law in the EU despite natural divergence propensity resulting from the procedural autonomy of the EU Member States. By achieving this stability, the EU achieves significant political weight in international dialogue concerning human right and the rule of law and preserves a high level of its global credibility in this context. Thus, RLF increases the EU's effectiveness in promoting the European model of their identification and enforcement.
5. It is rather difficult to judge about the universal acceptability of the European evolving concept of human rights. Admittedly, they may be considered attractive because of the universality of their underlying axiology and their comprehensiveness as a legal concept reflexing the Western idea of broadly understood individual and collective welfare. Such general elements can be considered sufficient to serve as a low enough denominator which is widely acceptable to

serve as an element of the 'international order' and to enforce other elements of it. Moreover, high standards of protection of a vast catalogue of human rights in the Western world have contributed to the effectiveness and efficacy of its political and economic systems. They have done so by reinforcing largely adequate mechanisms of public choice generally based on the determination of prevailing preferences *via* political elections, protection of minority groups, and on the well-functioning system of balance of powers. As soon as the prevailing preferences are unveiled, they have to be translated into respective public policies formulated and implemented at various stages of the organization of polity. This has an important bearing on the content of public policies: in their goals, objectives and instruments which—under such a system—take a proper account of human rights.

References

Andersen S (2012) Enforcement of European Union law: the role of the European Commission. Oxford University Press, Oxford

Arnull A (2006) The European Union and its Court of Justice. Oxford University Press, Oxford

Bagińska E, Majkowska-Szulc S (2018) Causation as a requirement for the Member State liability under Art. 7 TEU in conjunction with Art. 2 TEU. In: Hatje A, Tichý L (eds) Liability of Member States for the violation of the fundamental values of the EU. Nomos, Baden-Baden, pp 125–144

Bedner A (2010) An elementary approach to the rule of law. Hague J Rule Law 2(1):48–74

Bonelli M, Claes MN (2018) Judicial serendipity: how Portuguese judges came to rescue the Polish judiciary. Eur Const Law Rev 14(3):622–643

Commission on Global Governance (1995) Our global neighbourhood: the report of the commission on global governance. Oxford University Press, Oxford

European Council in Copenhagen. Conclusions of the Presidency, June 21–22, 1993, document SN 180/1/93 REV 1

European Parliament, Committee on Civil Liberties, Justice and Home Affairs, Report of 17 February 2014 on evaluation of justice in relations to criminal justice and the rule of law, rapporteur Kinga Göncz, document A7-0122/2014

Itzcovich G (2017) On the legal enforcement of values: the importance of the institutional concept. In: Jakab A, Kochenov D (eds) The enforcement of EU law and values: ensuring Member States' compliance. Oxford University Press, Oxford, pp 28–43

Kochenov D (2017) The *Acquis* and its principles: the enforcement of the 'law' vs. the enforcement of 'values' in the European Union. In: Jakab A, Kochenov D (eds) The enforcement of EU law and values: ensuring Member States' compliance. Oxford University Press, Oxford, pp 9–27

Krajewski M (2018) *Associaçao Sindicos dos Juízes Portugueses:* the Court of Justice and Athena's dilemma. Eur Pap 3(1):395–405

May C (2014) The rule of law: the common sense of global politics. Edward Elgar, Cheltenham

Ministry of Foreign Affairs of the Netherlands (2013) Human Rights Policy – Respect and Justice for All. The Hague

Pech L, Platon S (2018) Judicial independence under threat: the Court of Justice to the rescue in the ASJP case. CLMR 55(6):1827–1854

Press release 3244th Council Meeting – Justice and Home Affairs, Luxembourg 6–7 June 2013, document 10461/13 (OR.en)

Prete L (2017) Infringement proceedings in EU law. Kluwer Law Int 6–10:301–304

Sanchez-Cuenca I (2003) Power, rules, and compliance. In: Maravall JM, Przeworski A (eds) Democracy and the rule of law. Oxford University Press, Oxford
Schmidt M, Bogdanowicz P (2017) The infringement procedure in the rule of law crisis. In: Closa C, Kochenov D (eds) Reinforcing rule of law oversight in the European Union. OUP, Oxford, pp 1069–1073
Senden S (2004) Soft law in European Community law. Hart Publishing, Oxford
Thirlway H (2014) The sources of international law. Oxford University Press, Oxford
Tichý L (2018) The nature and requirements for liability of a Member State under Article 7. In: Hatje A, Tichý L (eds) Liability of Member States for the violation of the fundamental values of the EU. Nomos, Baden-Baden
Tiefenbrun S (2010) Decoding international law: semiotics and the humanities. Oxford University Press, Oxford
Tridimas T (2000) The general principles of EC law. Oxford University Press, Oxford
Young EA (2005) Foreign law and the denominator problem. Harv Law Rev 119(148):148–167

Artur Nowak-Far is senior researcher and director of the Institute of Law, SGH-Warsaw School of Economics.

The Rule of Law and the Roll of the Dice. The Uncertain Future of Investor-State Arbitration in the EU

Wojciech Sadowski

Contents

Abstract Investment treaty law and EU law began to develop in the same era and share some important philosophical and axiological foundations. The pressure on the

All opinions expressed herein are personal to the author and should not be attributed to Queritius or its clients.

W. Sadowski (✉)
Queritius, Warsaw, Poland
e-mail: wojciech.sadowski@queritius.com

A. von Bogdandy et al. (eds.), *Defending Checks and Balances in EU Member States*, Beiträge zum ausländischen öffentlichen Recht und Völkerrecht 298,
https://doi.org/10.1007/978-3-662-62317-6_13

CEE countries to enter into numerous bilateral investment treaties in late 80s and early 90s, in the context of the EU accession aspirations of the former communist countries, was likely to result, eventually, in a conflict between EU law and investment treaty law. The conflict could have been managed in three different ways, yet the CJEU decided in *Achmea* to declare an undefined volume of intra-EU arbitrations to be incompatible with EU law. This important judgment, which delivered an outcome desired by the European Commission and a number of Member States, is based on questionable legal reasoning that creates high uncertainty in this area of law. The doubts include the scope of application of *Achmea*, which is now a highly debatable issue. The CJEU itself saw it necessary to limit the scope of *Achmea* by declaring in Opinion 1/17 (*CETA*) that the legal reasoning of *Achmea* did not apply to investment protection treaties with third countries. The Member States of the EU remain politically divided in their views as to whether *Achmea* applies to the Energy Charter Treaty. And while the problems with the rule of law and independence of the judiciary in certain Member States continue to grow, *Achmea* has left an important gap for which there is no substitute in the current architecture of the EU legal system.

1 Introduction

Yogi Berra, a baseball player and coach, once famously said it was difficult for him to make predictions, especially about the future. His job should be easier in legal studies, since law is supposed to be a set of rules intended to yield reasonably high predictability of result. A frequent connotation of the rule of law is that legal matters should unfold in an orderly and foreseeable fashion, instilling the sense of certainty in legal subjects. When it comes, however, to the interactions between EU law and investor-state arbitration, predictability of outcome has been rather low lately. Politics clearly trumps technical legal reasoning in this field. This should probably be of little wonder. International investment protection law has always been a highly political issue. In the early 90s, investment protection treaties were used in Europe as a way to foster economic expansion of Western European companies to the former Soviet bloc, without much technical legal thought being given to the long-term consequences of creating this new legal order in Europe and its relation to EU law.

The potential for conflict between EU law and investment treaty law was not identified at that time, though it was eventually unavoidable. When these two worlds finally came to a clash, their confrontation could have been managed in several different ways. Advocate-General Wathelet made an ingenuous proposal in *Achmea*,[1] which could have established harmonious co-existence of both legal systems, and at the same time, surrender intra-EU investment treaty tribunals to

[1]CJEU, Case C-284/16, *Achmea*, ECLI:EU:C:2017:699.

the functional supremacy of the CJEU.[2] The CJEU, however, chose a radically different approach, declaring an undefined volume of intra-EU arbitrations to be incompatible with the EU law.[3] That decision elated certain European Governments, but not necessarily those most adherent to the rule of law. The CJEU then purported to clarify in *Opinion 1/17* that only the investor-state dispute resolution clauses in intra-EU treaties should be deemed incompatible with EU law, and not those in the treaties with third countries.[4] In the latter case, the outcome seems to depend on whether a treaty in question complies with the threshold criteria defined by the CJEU in *Opinion 1/17*. By declaring that the CETA[5] complied with such criteria, the CJEU cleared the path to the ratification and entry into force of that treaty. *Opinion 1/17* reads as if the pendulum swang in the direction opposite to *Achmea*, since the position the CJEU took in it contradicts in many important aspects the legal reasoning underlying the *Achmea* judgment.[6] Nonetheless, the CJEU confirmed in *Opinion 1/17* that *Achmea* applies broadly to intra-EU proceedings, but sought to distinguish it from the case of treaties with third countries.[7] As shall be shown below, however, the distinction between the intra-EU and extra-EU investment treaties is not sufficient to justify the contradictory conclusions reached by the CJEU in these two decisions. A more plausible explanation is that in either case the delivered outcome was conforming to the existing political expectations, which in each case were different. In *Achmea*, the expectation was to do away with investment treaty arbitration in Europe.[8] In *Opinion 1/17*, to confirm the ability of the EU to create a new system of international justice in investment matters, featuring the Investment Court System.[9]

Because of these important decisions, the EU is now facing three important challenges. *Firstly*, the elimination of intra-EU investment arbitrations has left an important gap in the legal protection of individuals in Europe. There is no substitute for it in the current architecture of the EU legal system.[10] At the time when certain illiberal governments pursue systemic actions intended to undermine the

[2]See Buczkowska et al. (2017).

[3]CJEU, Case C-284/16, *Achmea*, ECLI:EU:C:2018:158.

[4]CJEU, Opinion 1/17 *Comprehensive Economic and Trade Agreement between Canada, on the one part, and the European Union and its Member States, of the other part*, ECLI:EU:C:2019:341, see dispositive part and paras. 126–129.

[5]See http://trade.ec.europa.eu/doclib/docs/2014/september/tradoc_152806.pdf. Last accessed on 17 July 2019.

[6]Koutrakos (2019), pp. 239–294.

[7]CJEU, Opinion 1/17, *supra* note 4, paras. 126–127.

[8]See Hartley (2019), p. 335: 'It will be clear from the cases discussed that the law in this area is almost entirely based on policy. The Treaty provisions are important, but they are regarded simply as underpinning the wider policies inherent in the EU Treaties.[...] it would be futile to search for a narrow formula which encapsulates the law.'

[9]See http://europa.eu/rapid/press-release_IP-19-2334_en.htm. Last accessed on 17 July 2019.

[10]Which is admitted even by the enthusiastic supporters of the *Achmea* judgment, see e.g. Hindelang (2019), p. 383.

independence of the judiciary in certain EU countries, it is also riskier than ever to assume that state courts in these countries can remain capable of providing effective protection of EU rights to individuals.[11] *Secondly*, *Achmea* has created significant uncertainty as to its exact meaning and scope. Its reasoning is far from clear and the judgment itself is based on seemingly mistaken assumptions.[12] Even the EU Member States differ among themselves in their official positions as to the impact of *Achmea* on the Energy Charter Treaty.[13] *Achmea* also creates a conflict between international and EU law. In particular, it puts EU Member States in a delicate situation, since they are obliged to comply with existing arbitral awards in accordance with the investment protection treaties, but *Achmea* prevents them from complying voluntarily. This may create real practical problems especially outside the EU, where local courts seized with requests for enforcement against state assets do not necessarily have to recognize the principles of primacy and autonomy of EU law.[14] Thirdly, *Achmea* creates lingering problems for the ambitious plans of the EU to reform the investor-state dispute resolution system globally, in particular through the creation of a multinational investment court.[15] *Opinion 1/17* resolves this problem only partially and superficially. Future arbitrations under the CETA shall likely lead to the situation in which the CJEU's position taken in *Opinion 1/17* may have to be revisited in light of the views expressed in *Achmea*. Predictability in this area of law has been reduced to a roll of the dice.

[11]See Sadowski (2018), pp. 1025–1060.

[12]As the Arbitral Tribunal in ICSID Case No. ARB/15/15, *9REN Holding S.À.R.L. v. Spain*, award of 31 May 2019, para. 150, put it: 'The Tribunal has attempted, with the Parties' assistance, to understand the truncated reasoning in the CJEU's decision in *Achmea*. There is much to understand.'

[13]Compare the Declarations of the Member States of 15 and 16 January 2019 on the legal consequences of the *Achmea* judgment and on investment protection, available at https://ec.europa.eu/info/publications/190117-bilateral-investment-treaties_en, last accessed on 20 June 2019.

[14]The U.S. courts currently seem to be the principal extra-EU destination of EU investors who were awarded damages by investment treaty tribunals against Spain. See, for example, N*extEra Energy Global Holdings B.V. and NextEra Energy Spain Holdings B.V. v. Kingdom of Spain*, Petition to Confirm International Arbitral Award Pursuant to the 1965 ICSID Convention of 3 June 2019, Case no. 1:19-cv-01618, https://www.italaw.com/sites/default/files/case-documents/italaw10570.pdf, last acceded on 17 July 2019.

[15]Lavranos and Singla (2018), p. 351 et seq.

2 From Friends to Foes

2.1 Early Co-existence

Modern investment treaty law and European integration have contemporaneous origins. The 1959 treaty between Germany and Pakistan,[16] regarded as the first bilateral investment treaty worldwide, was adopted just 2 years after the Treaty of Rome was signed. The arbitration between a UK company *AAPL and Sri Lanka* in the late 80s was the first dispute in which an arbitration agreement conferring jurisdiction on an arbitral tribunal, was construed from a combination of a provision in an international treaty and the express or implied will of an investor.[17]

When the CEE countries began the process of their association with the EEC (later the EU) in the 90s, it was the European Commission which requested them, in the so-called Europe Agreements, to enter into bilateral investment treaties with the then Member States.[18] This is the explanation of the high number of bilateral investment treaties between Eastern and Western European countries. The European Union and its Member States also adopted the Energy Charter Treaty, which provides for the settlement of a broad range of investor-state disputes through international arbitration.[19] There does not seem to be evidence that at the time these treaties were signed, serious discussions were held as to whether international investment law and investor-state arbitration were compatible with EU law, or whether candidate Member States from Central and Eastern Europe should renounce these treaties once they are admitted to EU membership.

---

[16]Treaty for the Promotion and Protection of Investments (with Protocol and exchange of notes), Germany and Pakistan, 25 November 1959, 457 U.N.T.S. 24 (entered into force 28 November 1962), available at http://treaties.un.org/Pages/showDetails.aspx?objid=0800000280132bef, last accessed on 20 June 2019.

[17]Arbitral Tribunal, *Asian Agricultural Products Ltd. v. Republic of Sri Lanka*, ICSID Case No. ARB/87/3, Final Award of 27 June 1990.

[18]See, e.g., Article 72(2) of the Europe Agreement establishing an association between the European Communities and their Member States, of the one part, and the Republic of Hungary, of the other part, signed in Brussels on 16 December 1991, OJ 1993 L 347/2; see also: CJEU, Case C-284/16, *Achmea*, ECLI:EU:C:2017:699, footnote 41 for similar examples concerning Poland, Romania, Slovakia or Croatia.

[19]The text of the Energy Charter Treaty is available at https://energycharter.org/fileadmin/DocumentsMedia/Legal/ECTC-en.pdf, last accessed on 20 June 2019. The (non-exhaustive) list of investment treaty arbitration initiated under the ECT is available here: https://energycharter.org/what-we-do/dispute-settlement/all-investment-dispute-settlement-cases/, last accessed on 20 June 2019.

2.2 Rise in Intra-EU Arbitrations

The surge in investor-state arbitrations, which began worldwide in late 90s, did not spare Central and Eastern Europe.[20] In fact, the economic and legal transformation, including massive privatization plans and the process of adaptation of the CEE legal systems to the requirements of the European Union were fruitful grounds for numerous treaty claims related to that part of the world.[21] Following the accessions of 2004 and 2007, new Member States were among the first ones to note the potential conflict between EU law and investment protection treaties. Defending themselves against treaty claims, they started to raise, in various shapes and forms, objections related to the alleged incompatibility of the two legal regimes. The European Commission also stepped in to support these contentions. Arbitral tribunals, often composed of prominent international judges and scholars in public international law, consistently rejected, however, jurisdictional objections based on EU law.[22]

The arguments in favour and against the 'EU objection' were rehearsed so many times and from so many angles that the matter can now be said to have been profoundly examined and discussed by arbitral tribunals. The case law which emerged from those decisions could be regarded as *jurisprudence constante* in investment treaty law. The unequivocal conclusion was that neither the accession of the new Member States to the EU, nor the inherent features of the EU legal system, deprived arbitral tribunals of the jurisdiction conferred upon them by investment protection treaties.

2.3 Game-Changing Catalysts

Three catalysts then played a major role in undermining the position of investment treaty arbitration in Europe. The first one was the emergence of cases, which, rightly or wrongly, were considered to threaten the autonomy of the EU legal order. These

[20]See e.g. UNCTAD Fact Sheet on Investor–State Dispute Settlement Cases in 2018, available at https://unctad.org/en/PublicationsLibrary/diaepcbinf2019d4_en.pdf, last accessed on 20 June 2019, p. 1.

[21]See UNCTAD Fact Sheet on Investor–State Dispute Settlement Cases in 2018, p. 2. Czechia and Poland have been among the most frequently sued countries, along Ukraine and Russia.

[22]Among many decisions preceding the CJEU judgment in *Achmea*, see e.g. Arbitral Tribunal, SCC Case No. 088/2004, *Eastern Sugar B.V. v. Czech Republic*, Partial Award of 27 March 2007; *Jan Oostergetel and Theodora Laurentius v. Slovak Republic*, UNCITRAL, Decision on Jurisdiction of 30 April 2010; PCA Case No. 2008-13, *Achmea B.V. (formerly Eureko) v. Slovak Republic*, Award on Jurisdiction, Arbitrability and Suspension of 26 October 2010; ICSID Case no. ARB/07/19, *Electrabel S.A. v. Republic of Hungary*, Decision on Jurisdiction, Applicable Law and Liability of 30 November 2012; ICSID Case No. ARB/05/20, *Ioan Micula, Viorel Micula, S.C. European Food S.A, S.C. Starmill S.R.L. and S.C. Multipack S.R.L. v. Romania*, Final Award of 11 December 2013 et al.

included *Micula v. Romania*, which was often presented as a clear example that investment treaty arbitration could be used to circumvent the EU rules on state aid.[23] Such statement was inaccurate with respect to *Micula*, since the facts of that case concerned the consequences of the benefits, which were withdrawn *before* Romania joined the EU and started to be bound by the *acquis communautaire*. By implication, since the alleged internationally unlawful act occurred before the accession, the alleged liability in damages of the respondent state also arose before that date. These points were correctly identified by the General Court of the EU in its judgment of 18 June 2019, which annulled the decision of the European Commission (EU) 2015/1470 of 30 March 2015 on State aid SA.38517 (2014/C) (ex 2014/NN) implemented by Romania—Arbitral award *Micula v. Romania* of 11 December 2013.[24] Indeed, it should not be a controversial issue that benefits withdrawn 2 years before Romania's accession to the EU should not be regarded as state aid under EU law.[25] However, the perception impact of the *Micula* case had already taken its toll and influenced the development of international investment law.[26] Furthermore, it is not inconceivable that in another case with a different set of facts, a conflict between EU state aid law and an investment protection treaty could actually arise.

The second catalyst was the emergence of high profile disputes related to politically or socially sensitive matters. This includes, for example, the *Vattenfall* arbitration concerning the consequences of the uncompensated phasing out of nuclear power plants in Germany.[27] Along with a small number of other high profile cases, including the *Philip Morris* arbitrations concerning the plain tobacco packaging rules in Australia and Uruguay,[28] *Vattenfall* attracted considerable interest

---

[23]*Micula, supra* note 22.

[24]GCEU, Cases T-624/15, T-694/15 and T-704/15, *European Food SA and Others v. European Commission, ECLI:EU:T:2019:423*. See also Croisant (2019) and Bakos (2019).

[25]Interestingly, the Arbitral Tribunal in the *Micula* award calculated the amount of damages due to the investors on the basis of hypothetical assumption that the benefits would remain in force also beyond the date of the Romania's accession to the EU. The Court noted that point, but ruled that since the Commission did not draw a distinction, among the amounts to be recovered, between those falling within the period predating accession and those falling within the period subsequent to accession, the decision by which it classified the entirety of the compensation as aid is necessarily unlawful (GCEU, *European Food, supra* note 24, para. 108).

[26]See e.g. Art. 8.9.4 of the CETA: 'nothing in this Section shall be construed as preventing a Party from discontinuing the granting of a subsidy or requesting its reimbursement where such measure is necessary in order to comply with international obligations between the Parties or has been ordered by a competent court, administrative tribunal or other competent authority, or requiring that Party to compensate the investor therefor.' A footnote to that provision explained that with respect to EU, subsidies also embrace state aid. See also e.g. Article 2.2.4 of the Investment Protection Agreement between the European Union and its Member States, of the one part, and the Socialist Republic of Viet Nam, of the other part.

[27]See the official explanation of Vattenfall for the reasons of its action: https://group.vattenfall.com/press-and-media/news%2D%2Dpress-releases/newsroom/2016/why-vattenfall-is-taking-germany-to-court, last accessed on 20 June 2019.

[28]Arbitral Tribunal, ICSID Case No. ARB/10/7, *Philip Morris Brands Sàrl, Philip Morris Products S.A. and Abal Hermanos S.A. v. Oriental Republic of Uruguay* (formerly *FTR Holding SA, Philip*

within the civic societies of Western European states. These cases spurred protests against the then ongoing negotiations of the trade and investment agreements with Canada (CETA) and the US (TTIP).[29]

Thirdly, the global financial crisis required some Member States to intervene on its financial markets or to implement austerity measures, in particular with respect to certain ill-conceived public support schemes for the renewable energy sector. That led to more arbitrations where, for the first time, some of the Western European states found themselves on the receiving end and began to reconsider the risks and benefits of intra-EU investment treaty disputes.[30] These cases, too, have had an impact on the further erosion of the investors' rights in the newest generation of investment protection treaties.[31]

2.4 Achmea

Such was the landscape on 6 March 2018, when the CJEU rendered its judgment in *Achmea*. The case concerned an action brought by Slovakia to German courts to set aside a jurisdiction award of an arbitral tribunal, in a relatively low profile and low-value dispute between a Dutch insurance company and Slovakia over regulatory measures in the life insurance sector. The German Supreme Court, which referred the preliminary questions to the CJEU, considered that it essentially had no major doubts that the provisions of the Netherlands-Slovakia bilateral investment agreement conferring jurisdiction on the arbitral tribunal were compatible with EU law, but asked the CJEU to confirm that view. In the proceedings before the CJEU, the intervening Member States formed two opposing camps. The polarization of views

---

Morris Products S.A. and Abal Hermanos S.A. v. Oriental Republic of Uruguay) and PCA Case No. 2012-12.*Philip Morris Asia Limited v. The Commonwealth of Australia*, UNCITRAL.

[29]The TTIP negotiations were launched in 2013 and ended without conclusion at the end of 2016, see: http://ec.europa.eu/trade/policy/in-focus/ttip/index_en.htm, last accessed on 20 June 2019. This happened due to a wave of civil opposition in various EU countries, including massive street protests. See e.g. https://www.theguardian.com/business/2016/sep/17/ttip-protests-see-crowds-take-to-streets-of-seven-german-cities, last accessed on 20 June 2019.

[30]Spain is by far the most-frequently sued EU Member State and the second most-often sued country in the world with 49 known cases, closed or pending, by the end of 2018. Among other 'old' Member States, Italy follows with 11 cases, followed by Greece (4 cases) and Germany (3 cases), see UNCTAD Fact Sheet on Investor–State Dispute Settlement Cases in 2018, available at https://unctad.org/en/PublicationsLibrary/diaepcbinf2019d4_en.pdf, last accessed on 20 June 2019, pp. 11–13.

[31]See note 23 above. The problem, from the investors' perspective, is that the ability of the states to freely withdraw subsidies incentives states to play the bait-and-switch, i.e. to first lure investors to make heavy capital expenditures in order to create the required infrastructure in exchange for a promise of long-term subsidy scheme, and then cancel the scheme shortly after the investment is completed. This is particularly problematic in sectors such as renewable energy, or water and sewage distribution and collection systems, which require very high initial capex, but then do not generate high operating costs.

in Europe was manifest, and the dividing lines were clearly marked between the capital-exporting, and capital-importing states, the latter category supported by the Member States with a high number of pending investment treaty claims.[32]

Arguably, the CJEU could have dealt with the alleged potential incompatibility between EU law and investment treaty law in three different ways. Firstly, it could have agreed with the *Bundesgerichtshof* and declare investment treaty arbitration to be compatible with EU law. This may have left unresolved the problem of potential future clashes between EU and investment treaty law in some borderline scenarios. Secondly, the CJEU could have created a framework for dialogue between arbitral tribunals and the CJEU on issues related to the application and interpretation of the EU law. To that effect, the CJEU could have recognized investment treaty tribunals as 'courts or tribunals' in the sense of Article 267 TFUE. This was exactly what Advocate General Wathelet was suggesting to the CJEU in his opinion in the *Achmea* case. The third option, and the one chosen by the CJEU, was to declare investment treaty arbitration incompatible with the EU law. In its judgment, the CJEU said it considered intra-EU investment treaty arbitration as threatening the autonomy of the EU legal order. The CJEU considered arbitral tribunals sitting under the intra-EU bilateral investment treaties to be trespassing on its own exclusive jurisdiction and refused to enter into a dialogue with them under the auspices of Article 267 TFUE. As a consequence, it ruled that the EU law 'precludes' the investor-state arbitration provisions such as the one in the treaty between the Netherlands and Slovakia.

2.5 Reception of Achmea by Arbitral Tribunals

Contrary perhaps to the CJEU's expectations, its judgment has not brought investment treaty arbitration to a halt, although the number of new claims has dropped considerably. However, arbitral tribunals have so far failed or refused to give broad effects to the *Achmea* judgment.[33] Not a single arbitral tribunal after the 6 March 2018 declined jurisdiction because of *Achmea*, although the *Bundesgerichtshof*

[32]This polarization was recorded in paras. 34 and 35 of the Opinion of Advocate General Wathelet in *Achmea*, *supra* note 1.

[33]Among others, see: Arbitral Tribunal, ICSID Case No. ARB/13/31, *Antin Infrastructure Services Luxembourg S.à.r.l. and Antin Energia Termosolar B.V. v. Kingdom of Spain*, Award of 15 June 2018; PCA Case No. 2014-0, *Antaris Solar GmbH and Dr. Michael Göde v. Czech Republic*, Award of 2 May 20181; ICSID Case No. ARB/14/1, *Masdar Solar & Wind Cooperatief U.A. v Kingdom of Spain*, Award of 16 May 2018; ICSID Case No. ARB/13/35, *UP and C.D. v Hungary*, Award of 9 October 2018; SCC Arbitration V 2015/150, *Greentech Energy Systems A/S et al. v Kingdom of Spain*, Award of 23 December 2018; ICSID Case No. ARB/13/30, *RREEF Infrastructure (G.P.) Limited and RREEF Pan-European Infrastructure Two Lux SARL*, Award of 30 November 2018; SCC Case No. 2015/063, *Novenergia II—Energy & Environment (SCA) (Grand Duchy of Luxembourg), SICAR v The Kingdom of Spain*, Award of 15 February 2018; ICSID Case No. ARB/15/15, *9REN Holding S.À.R.L. v. Spain*, *supra* note 12.

eventually annulled the *Achmea* award as a consequence of the CJEU decision.[34] Arbitral tribunals recurred to various legal reasons in order not to give effect to *Achmea*. Most notably, the arbitral tribunal in *Vattenfall* issued a lengthy and thoroughly reasoned decision in which it declared that *Achmea* should not apply to arbitrations based on the Energy Charter Treaty.[35] Given that at least several dozen cases brought under the Energy Charter Treaty are currently pending against various EU Member States, the *Vattenfall* decision is of clear importance to the future of investment-treaty arbitrations in Europe.

In reaction to the *Vattenfall* decision and the general pushback from arbitral tribunals, on 15 and 16 January 2019, all EU Member States adopted three, partially concurring declarations on the *effects* of the *Achmea* judgment.[36] More than anything else, these declarations are strong political statements against investment-treaty arbitration in Europe. However, these declarations also include specific promises, such as an undertaking to deposit their instruments of ratification, approval or acceptance of a plurilateral treaty or of any bilateral treaty terminating bilateral investment treaties between Member States, by 6 December 2019.[37]

In parallel to, and somehow in spite of, its quest against the intra-EU investment protection treaties, the European Commission has launched an ambitious initiative to reform the global investor-state dispute resolution system through the creation of a multilateral investment court.[38] Such court would be intended as a dispute resolution forum, including between the EU or its Member States and investors of the other contracting parties to the investment protection and trade agreements. There are many problems how to conciliate the functioning of such system with *Achmea*. More broadly, the reasons underlying *Achmea* should also be seen as the legal obstacles to investment protection treaties with third countries. This is why Belgium (on behalf of Wallonia) questioned the compatibility of the EU-Canada trade and protection

---

[34] Order of the *Bundesgerichtshof* of 31 October 2018, file no. I ZB 2/15, available at: http://juris.bundesgerichtshof.de/cgi-bin/rechtsprechung/document.py?Gericht=bgh&Art=en&nr=89393&pos=0&anz=1, last accessed on 20 June 2019.

[35] Arbitral Tribunal, ICSID Case No. ARB/12/12, *Vattenfall AB and others v. Federal Republic of Germany*, Decision on the Achmea Issue of 31 August 2018; *9REN Holding S.À.R.L. v. Spain*, *supra* note 12.

[36] See: https://energycharter.org/what-we-do/dispute-settlement/all-investment-dispute-settlement-cases/, last accessed on 20 June 2019. See also e.g. Power (2019).

[37] See https://ec.europa.eu/info/sites/info/files/business_economy_euro/banking_and_finance/documents/190117-bilateral-investment-treaties_en.pdf, last accessed on 20 June 2019. The Agreement for the termination of Bilateral Investment Treaties between the Member States of the European Union was signed on 5 May 2020 (OJ L 169, 29.5.2020, p. 1–41) by 23 Member States and enterd into force for the first time on 29 August 2020.

[38] The European Commission proposed a new Investment Court System for TTIP and other EU trade and investment negotiations already in September 2015, see: http://europa.eu/rapid/press-release_IP-15-5651_en.htm. This model was initially included in the series of bilateral trade and investment agreements which the EU was negotiating with Singapore, Canada and Vietnam. Subsequently, on 20 March 2018, the Council authorised negotiations for a treaty establishing a multilateral investment court (MIC).

agreement with the TFEU. Notwithstanding, the CJEU followed the opinion of Advocate-General Bot[39] and ruled on 30 April 2019 that the CETA is compatible with EU law.[40] This is a good outcome for the future of investment treaty arbitration in Europe, but it fails to provide legal certainty and bears an inherent risk of being revisited once the actual cases under the CETA (or another similar treaty) are decided one day.

3 Three Question Marks About *Achmea*

The root of all uncertainty is obviously *Achmea.* The judgment provoked diagonally opposite emotions and reactions worldwide. It came as a blessing to the governments of the EU Member States with large numbers of pending arbitrations or unenforced awards, and as a curse to entrepreneurs who had made substantial long-terms investment in Europe. It has already been addressed by multiple articles[41] and arbitral awards.[42] However, even the supporters of *Achmea* recognize its ambiguities, and there are many. This chapter purports to deal with only three of them.

3.1 Scope of Application

Firstly, it is unclear to which investment protection treaties *Achmea* applies. The dispositive part of *Achmea* reads: 'Articles 267 and 344 TFEU must be interpreted as precluding a provision in an international agreement concluded between Member States, such as Article 8 of the Agreement on encouragement and reciprocal protection of investments between the Kingdom of the Netherlands and the Czech and Slovak Federative Republic, under which an investor from one of those Member States may, in the event of a dispute concerning investments in the other Member State, bring proceedings against the latter Member State before an arbitral tribunal whose jurisdiction that Member State has undertaken to accept.' Thus, the interpretation rendered by the CJEU does not seem to be confined to the specific treaty in question, but is likely to extend to other international treaties concluded between Member States which include provisions 'such as' the provision analysed by the CJEU in *Achmea*. Now, at the time of the judgment there were close to 300 bilateral investment treaties between Member States, which significantly differed from each other. Remarkably, the CJEU failed to notice these differences in *Achmea*, and it did

---

[39]CJEU, Opinion 1/17 *Accord ECG UE-Canada*, ECLI:EU:C:2019:72.

[40]Id.

[41]Among others, see Hess (2018); Lavranos and Singla (2018), pp. 348–357; Berger (2017), pp. 282–291; Hartley (2019), pp. 321–337.

[42]*Supra* note 33.

not explain which criteria should be taken into account to determine whether a dispute resolution clause in a given treaty was 'such as' Article 8 of the Netherlands-Slovakia BIT.

This omission could create significant lack of legal certainty. However, EU Member States have addressed this problem with the subtleness of Alexander the Great approaching the Gordian knot. Their declarations of 15 and 16 January 2019 start from the assumption that *Achmea* applies to *all* bilateral investment treaties between EU Member States, no matter how similar or different they could be from the Netherlands-Slovakia BIT.[43] Moreover, although the CJEU did not pronounce in *Achmea* over the conformity of substantive provisions of the bilateral investment treaties with EU law and confined its decision only to the jurisdictional aspects of the Netherlands-Slovakia treaty, the Member States went further in their declarations. They undertook to terminate all intra-EU investment protection treaties by way of a treaty, they promised to adopt still in 2019. This step was clearly not required by the *Achmea* judgment and should rather be considered a political decision, for which *Achmea* provides a convenient supportive argument. It lead to the adoption of a treaty which shall likely have the effect of immediate termination of all intra-EU bilateral investment treaties, notwithstanding the existence of sunset clauses in many of such treaties.[44] Accordingly, the uncertainty concerning the scope of the *Achmea* judgment in practice may be limited to intra-EU arbitrations, which were pending at the time of its entry into force, and to enforcement of awards rendered to date under intra-EU BITs.

3.2 Energy Charter Treaty

Secondly, it is unclear whether *Achmea* extends onto intra-EU disputes under the Energy Charter Treaty. Here, the positions of EU Member States seem to be divided, although a large majority of them (22 out of 27) thinks that *Achmea* has such effect. Five other Member States, namely Finland, Luxembourg, Malta, Slovenia and Sweden, noted however, that *Achmea* is silent on the Energy Charter Treaty. They referred to the fact that while a number of international arbitration tribunals post the *Achmea* judgment have concluded that the Energy Charter Treaty contains an investor-State arbitration clause applicable between EU Member States, this interpretation was contested before a national court in a Member State. Against this background, those Member States considered that it would be inappropriate, in the absence of a specific judgment on this matter, to express views as regards the compatibility with EU law of the intra EU application of the Energy Charter

[43] *Supra* note 37.

[44] *Supra* note 37.

Treaty.[45] One Member State, i.e. Hungary, went against the wind and declared that in its view, the *Achmea* judgment concerns only the intra-EU bilateral investment treaties and it 'does not concern any pending or prospective arbitration proceedings initiated under the ECT'. Hungary also stated that the ongoing and future applicability of the ECT in intra-EU relations requires further discussion and individual agreement amongst the Member States. Indeed, the revision process of the Energy Charter Treaty has already started[46] and it cannot be excluded that this treaty could prospectively be changed so as to limit or exclude admissibility of intra-EU claims based on its provisions. This, however, should not have an impact on the legal ramifications of the claims brought before any such future change takes place. As of the time present, arbitral tribunals accept ECT claims brought by EU investors against EU Member States and EU national courts have not taken any firm position on this point.

3.3 Commercial Arbitration

The *third* area of ambiguity resulting from *Achmea* concerns commercial arbitration. Namely, although the CJEU made a very clear distinction between commercial and investment state arbitration in *Achmea*, some of the reasons and arguments underlying the approach that the CJEU took with respect to investment treaty arbitration also extend logically to commercial arbitration. Similar to investment treaty tribunals, arbitral tribunals in commercial matters also cannot refer questions to the CJEU pursuant to Article 267 TFEU. The position of the Court in this respect is well settled.[47] Similar to investment treaty arbitration, commercial arbitration also derogates from jurisdiction of national courts of EU Member States, certain matters in which EU law could be interpreted or applied. Awards of arbitral tribunals sitting in commercial matters, and awards of arbitral tribunals sitting in non-ICSID investment treaty matters are subject to the same scope and degree of review from EU national courts in the context of actions for annulment or applications for enforcement. Therefore, although it results from *Achmea* that the same standard of review is

[45]Declaration of the Representatives of the Governments of the Member States, of 16 January on the Enforcement of the Judgment of the Court of Justice in Achmea and on Investment Protection in the European Union, available at https://www.regeringen.se/48ee19/contentassets/d759689c0c804a9ea7af6b2de7320128/achmea-declaration.pdf, last accessed on 24 June 2019.

[46]See Modernisation of the Energy Charter Treaty (ECT), TDM 2019(1), https://www.transnational-dispute-management.com/journal-browse-issues-toc.asp?key=83%20; see also https://energycharter.org/fileadmin/DocumentsMedia/CCDECS/2018/CCDEC201818_-_STR_Modernisation_of_the_Energy_Charter_Treaty.pdf and Negotiating directives for the European Commission issued by Council on 2 July 2019, https://data.consilium.europa.eu/doc/document/ST-10745-2019-ADD-1/en/pdf, last acceded on 17 July 2019.

[47]CJEU, Case C-102/81 *Nordsee*, ECLI:EU:C:1982:107 and CJEU, Case C-126/97 *Eco Swiss*, ECLI:EU:C:1999:269.

sufficient to ensure autonomy of EU law in commercial matters and insufficient in investment treaty matters, it is completely unclear why. Some could argue this is because of the reportedly sensitive nature of the matters, which are dealt with in investment treaty matters. But if these matters are sensitive, they are typically sensitive to particular national interests and national policies of EU Member States and not of the EU. On the other hand, EU law expressly approves and endorses commercial arbitration in matters involving EU competition law.[48] There could be hardly anything more sensitive in the entire body of EU law, yet the CJEU is satisfied with the limited purview of national courts in these matters.

Another attempt to justify the distinction of investment treaty arbitration and commercial arbitration under *Achmea* has been to show that in investment treaty arbitration it is a treaty between the EU Member States that is the reported source of the derogation of the jurisdiction of national courts. Accordingly, some authors purported to claim that the existence of such treaty collides with Article 344 TFEU and thus creates the problem. This argument, however, does not justify the distinction with commercial arbitration and is incorrect for a number of reasons. Firstly, in order for jurisdiction of an investment treaty tribunal to arise (and thus to derogate any existing competence of national state courts), also the investor needs to give its consent. Accordingly, an investment treaty is not *per se* the autonomous and enforceable basis for jurisdiction of investment treaty tribunals. Rather, the treaty is a set of mutual undertakings of the contracting states that each of them should respect and honour future decisions of eligible investors to refer disputes to international arbitration (and not to state courts). However, an arbitration agreement is perfected between the state and the investor.[49] Secondly, in commercial arbitration, the derogation of competence of state courts in favour of arbitral tribunals has dual basis. On the one hand, such derogation is governed by national arbitration laws. On the other, the derogation is rooted in Article 2 of the New York Convention on the Recognition and Enforcement of Foreign Arbitral Awards,[50] which obliges the

[48]See e.g. *Eco Swiss*, *supra* note 47, where the CJEU agreed that matters of EU competition law were arbitrable and was satisfied that proper application of EU competition law could be ensured by national courts reviewing arbitral awards as part of the action for enforcement or annulment of award. It is simply illogical and inconsistent on the part of the CJEU, to accept in *Eco Swiss* that annulment proceedings before national courts offer sufficient guarantees of proper application of EU law by commercial arbitral tribunals, and to claim at the same time in *Achmea* that they do not. Commercial arbitration is also widely used and promoted in the EU as legal remedy for parties injured by anti-competitive behaviour of parties abusing dominant position. See e.g. Commission Decision of 24.5.2018 relating to a proceeding under Article 102 of the Treaty on the Functioning of the European Union (TFEU) and Article 54 of the EEA Agreement Case AT.39816—Upstream Gas Supplies in Central and Eastern Europe. See also e.g. recital (48) of the Directive 2014/104/EU of the European Parliament and of the Council of 26 November 2014 on certain rules governing actions for damages under national law for infringements of the competition law provisions of the Member States and of the European Union, OJ L 349, 5.12.2014, 1–19, which expressly admits private enforcement of infringements of EU competition law through arbitration.

[49]See e.g. Wychera and Mimnagh (2019), pp. 395-419.

[50]https://www.uncitral.org/uncitral/en/uncitral_texts/arbitration/NYConvention.html.

contracting parties to honour and give effect to the arbitration agreements in derogation of national courts. The question following *Achmea* therefore is whether the New York Convention, insofar as it was made between the EU Member States, also should be reviewed in the light of Article 344 TFEU.[51]

In addition, the logic of *Achmea* may likewise apply to the individual applications to the European Court of Human Rights, which are based on a similar mechanism that intra-EU bilateral investment treaties. Member States have agreed among themselves to authorize individuals to refer issues which may involve the application or interpretation of EU law, to an international court. Moreover, the CJEU has already precluded the possibility of the EU's accession to the European Convention of Human Rights in *Opinion 2/13*. It also held there that inter-state applications under Article 33 of the Convention would not be compatible with Article 344 TFEU.[52] It may now be an open, but still unaddressed question whether and to which extend *Achmea* takes the conclusions of *Opinion 2/13* another step further, to individual applications under Article 34.

4 Investor, Mind the Gap

4.1 How EU Law Purports to Replace Intra-EU BITs...

Assuming for a moment that *Achmea* could indeed achieve its political objective, which is to eradicate investment treaty arbitration from within the EU, the judgment would create a gap in the system of judicial protection in Europe.[53] This would be its natural consequence. For so long, investment treaty arbitration and EU law have co-existed and provided complementary protection to the beneficiaries of the four fundamental freedoms in Europe that there were no demands for an extension of EU law onto guarantees similar to those offered under investment treaties. Then in the aftermath of *Achmea*, a sudden realization came that the judgment of the CJEU could deprive a large number of EU investors of important substantive rights they required in order to maintain and develop their cross-border investments. The pressure was such that within 4 months after *Achmea*, the European Commission prepared and submitted to the European Parliament and Council, the Communication on Protection of intra-EU investment.[54]

The document opened with a bold statement that the 'European Union's single market is a unique area of investment opportunities'. The European Commission

---

[51]See also further Paschalidis (2019), pp. 219–236.

[52]CJEU, Opinion 2/13 *Accession of the EU to the ECHR*, ECLI:EU:C:2014:2454, see para. 213.

[53]See e.g. Balthasar (2018), pp. 227–233.

[54]European Commission, Communication on Protection of intra-EU investment, 19.7.2018 COM (2018) 547 final.

then went to declare it 'is committed to preserving and improving both a predictable, stable and clear regulatory environment and the effective enforcement of investors' rights.' It failed to mention that at the time of the communication, EU Member States were respondents in over 100 investment treaty disputes,[55] the majority of which related to allegations of unpredictability, instability or lack of clarity of the regulatory framework in the energy,[56] financial[57] or mining sectors.[58]

The European Commission was presumably mindful of those claims, but it nonetheless declared in the Communication that 'EU laws allows for markets to be regulated to pursue legitimate public interests such as public security, public health, social rights, consumer protection or the preservation of the environment, which may have consequences also for investments. Public authorities of the EU and of the Member States have a duty and a responsibility both to protect investment and to regulate markets. Therefore, the EU and Member States may legitimately take measures to protect those interests, which may have a negative impact on investments.'[59] This statement, again, did not take into account that in many cases the EU Member States were declared to be in breach of their international law obligations and obliged to pay damages.

The European Commission went on to recognize that 'In the aftermath of the Achmea judgment, the unlawfulness of intra-EU investor-State arbitration may result in the perception that EU law does not provide for adequate substantive and procedural safeguards for intra-EU investors. However, the EU legal system protects cross-border investors in the single market, while ensuring that other legitimate interests are duly taken into account. When investors exercise one of the fundamental freedoms, they benefit from the protection granted by: (1) the Treaty rules establishing those freedoms; (2) the Charter of Fundamental Rights of the European Union ("Charter"); (3) the general principles of Union law; and iv) extensive sector-specific legislation covering areas.'[60]

The Communication went on to demonstrate with examples that EU protects intra-EU investors with respect to the acts of investing in, acquiring and setting up companies; the right to acquire, use or dispose of immovable property; the repurchase of shares and bonds dealt in and quoted on a stock exchange; the receipt

---

[55]According to UNCTAD, there are currently 105 known pending investment treaty arbitrations against EU Member States (https://investmentpolicy.unctad.org/investment-dispute-settlement/advanced-search, acceded on 16 July 2019). This does not take into account unreported arbitrations.

[56]E.g. see cases *The PV Investors v. Spain, Vattenfall v. Germany, CSP Equity Investment v. Spain, Europa Nova v. The Czech Republic, EVN v. Bulgaria, I.C.W. v. The Czech Republic, MOL v. Croatia, Natland and others v. Czech Republic, Photovoltaik Knopf Betriebs-GmbH v. The Czech Republic, RREEF v. Spain, Voltaic Network v. The Czech Republic, InfraRed and others v. Spain* or *NextEra v. Spain.*

[57]E.g. cases *Cyprus Popular Bank v. Greece, Adamakopoulos and others v. Cyprus, UniCredit Bank and Zagrebačka Banka v. Croatia* or *Addiko Bank v. Croatia.*

[58]E.g. case *Gabriel Resources v. Romania, Lumina Copper v. Poland* or *Corcoesto v. Spain.*

[59]European Commission, *supra* note 54, p. 1.

[60]European Commission, *supra* note 54, p. 3.

of dividends and interest; the commercial grant of credits (including consumer credits); the acquisition of units of an investment fund; mortgages, legacies and loans, etc. and the acquisition of patents, trademarks and other intellectual property rights.

4.2 ... And Why It Fails

The point is, however, in what the Communication did not show. Notably, it did not show that the EU protects investors against unfair or unfavourable treatment at the hands of the Member State, that it protects them against breach of legitimate expectations, instability, arbitrariness, or polititcally charged measures. That EU procedural law offered a one-stop-court in the event of a concerted action of various state organs targeting a single investor. It also failed to show that EU national courts could effectively protect the investors' rights including by way of award of damages commessurate with the loss suffered.

The point is, EU law—including the specific instances featured by the European Commission in the Communication—protects intra-EU investors from a different angle and at a different level than bilateral investment treaties. To use an example invoked in the Communication, the taxation which was found by the CJEU to be incompatible with EU law in C-493/09 *Commission v. Portugal*[61] would not need to be declared incompatible with a bilateral protection treaty.[62] On the other hand, investment treaty law could protect an investor against an oppressive and harassing tax enforcement proceedings or unjustified freezing of assets in the course of tax proceedings related to the collection of that tax, while EU law would not.

The differences in the protection of investors between EU law and bilateral investment agreements can also be shown on the example of the joined cases C-52/16 and C-113/16 *SEGRO and Horváth,*[63] which are being regarded by the European Commission as a reportedly apposite example of the ability of EU law instruments to protect investors in the EU.[64] In that matter, amendments to the relevant Hungarian law in 2013 extinguished all usufructuary rights on arable land, unless it could be proven that they were created between members of the same family. Consequently, the rights of the EU foreigners concerned were

[61]ECLI:EU:C:2011:635.

[62]In that matter, the CJEU dealt with discriminatory taxation which exempted Portuguese-based pension funds from corporate income tax which was applied on dividends, when this tax was applied to pension funds from other EU Member States. If that matter had been referred to an investment treaty tribunal under a bilateral investment treaty, the questions for the tribunal to consider would include e.g. whether the foreign-seated fund could demonstrate to have an investment in Portugal and whether the tribunal's jurisdiction was not excluded or restricted in tax-related matters.

[63]ECLI:EU:C:2018:157.

[64]European Commission, *supra* note 54, p. 14.

cancelled from the property register. The CJEU, responding to the preliminary question of Hungarian courts, declared that the legislation infringed the provisions on the free movement of capital. In a subsequent judgment of 21 May 2019, the CJEU also confirmed that by adopting the contested legislation, Hungary was in breach of its obligations under the TFEU.[65]

The outcome of *SEGRO* can be, in many respects, more favourable for investors than the outcome of a theoretical investment treaty claim in a parallel case. First of all, the claimants could eventually receive restitution, i.e. its rights should be returned to it. This would not be possible in investment treaty arbitration, where damages would be the principal remedy.[66] Proceedings before Hungarian courts, even including the reference to the CJEU, would be cheaper, and not necessarily longer than an investment treaty arbitration. On the other hand, claimants in the SEGRO-type scenario *depend* on the willingness of national courts to refer matters to the CJEU, and sometimes national courts can bend over backwards to arrive at an interpretation that would deny the claimants their relief in spite of the CJEU decision.[67] Also, because of the sectoral and limited jurisdiction of national courts, as well as the limited scope of application of EU law, the SEGRO-type scenario is not apposite for complex factual patters, where claimant is affected by various measures taken by different state organs. Thus, despite the attempts of the European Commission to prove the contrary, the EU law cannot effectively make up for the legal vacuum that shall be created when the system of intra-EU investment treaty protection is terminated.

5 Triumph of Hope Over Experience

5.1 Risk of Conflicting Decisions

Another risk created by *Achmea* is that in the future, this judgment may undermine the attempts of the EU to create a new mechanism of resolution of investor-state disputed, involving a multilateral investment court and, more broadly, call into question the trade and investment agreements which are now being negotiated by the EU. This may be the situation e.g. when an arbitral tribunal established under one of these treaties comes to conclusion that conflicts with the interpretation of EU law

[65]CJEU, Case C-235/17 *Commission v. Hungary* (Usufruct of agricultural land), ECLI:EU:C:2019:432.

[66]But see Arbitral Tribunal, ICSID Case No. ARB/11/23, *Mr. Franck Charles Arif v. Republic of Moldova*, Award of 8 April 2013.

[67]See e.g. CJEU, Cases C-213/11, C-214/11 and C-217/11 *Forta, Fortuna and Grand*, ECLI:EU:C:2012:495 and the subsequent case law of the Polish courts, such as the judgment of the Constitutional Court of 11 March 2015, file no P 4/14 (accessible at www.trybunal.gov.pl) and resolution of the Supreme Administrative Court of 16 May 2016, II GPS 1/16 (accessible at http://orzeczenia.nsa.gov.pl/doc/98C5206CE9).

provided by the CJEU. So far, and for some unexplained reason, the European Commission and the CJEU seem to believe that the EU or its Member States would never lose a dispute under such treaties and that in any event, no friction between such treaties and the TFEU could arise.[68] In the light of *Micula*, *Achmea* and the numerous cases confirming the breach of international law standards by EU Member States, this optimism is difficult to understand.[69]

The core of the *Achmea* reasoning is that an arbitral tribunal could misinterpret or misapply EU law and therefore affect its autonomy. Accordingly, it is—according to *Achmea*—wrong to derogate investor-state disputes from national courts (who can ask questions by virtue of Article 267 TFEU) and to refer these disputes to arbitral tribunals (who cannot ask such questions). But if so, would not the same concerns arise if a matter is referred to an arbitral tribunal (or a multilateral investment court) established to resolve investment treaty dispute on the basis of a treaty between the EU and a third country?

5.2 *Application of EU Law As Facts?*

An arbitral tribunal, or a multilateral investment court seized with a dispute under the investment treaty between the EU and a third country shall likely have to apply or interpret provisions of EU law just to the same extent as the arbitral tribunal would under the Netherlands-Slovakia bilateral investment treaty. In *Opinion 1/17*, the CJEU purported to distinguish the arbitral tribunal under the CETA from investment tribunals sitting under intra-EU bilateral investment treaties by pointing to the explicit provision of the CETA (Article 8.31.2) pursuant to which a CETA tribunal would have to evaluate EU law merely as a fact. Whereas, in the view of the CJEU expressed in *Achmea*, bilateral investment tribunals *could* apply EU law *qua* law and not *qua* facts. The distinction is not persuasive for many reasons. Firstly, not all bilateral investment treaties have had similar choice of law clauses, and in many instances domestic and EU law of the EU Member States would be regarded as facts.

---

[68] See in particular CJEU, Opinion 1/17, *supra* note 4, paras. 152 and 153. The CJEU has focused on the fact that according to its provisions, the CETA 'cannot be interpreted in such a way as to prevent a Party from adopting and applying measures necessary to protect public security or public morals or to maintain public order or to protect human, animal or plant life or health, subject only to the requirement that such measures are not applied in a manner that would constitute a means of arbitrary or unjustifiable discrimination between the Parties'. On that basis, the CJEU declares in para. 153 of Opinion 1/17 that the CETA Tribunal 'has no jurisdiction to declare incompatible with the CETA the level of protection of a public interest established by the EU measures specified in paragraph 152'. This conclusion not only confuses the question of jurisdiction with the decision on merits, but more importantly it overlooks that it will be for the CETA tribunal to decide what was necessary for the Member States to pursue a public interest and whether its actions were not arbitrary, disproportionate or abusive.

[69] On Opinion 1/17 see e.g. Koutrakos (2019), p. 294 who refers to the approach of the CJEU in Opinion 1/17 as to a leap of faith.

Secondly, even if an arbitral tribunal under a BIT were to interpret EU law *qua* law, it would not differ in such operation from an arbitral tribunal resolving a commercial dispute under national law of an EU Member State. Thirdly, such interpretation would not in any event be binding on the CJEU.

The point is, regardless of whether EU law is applied as law or as facts, it does always require certain interpretation on the part of the arbitral tribunal, whether under the CETA or not. It is not possible to assume that a future CETA tribunal would not have to review the conduct of an investor, or state authorities, against the yardstick defined in an act of EU law. Nor that in view of conflicting submissions of the parties as to whether each side could reasonably rely on its own interpretation of that act, assess that conduct. Such assessment could then be contrary to an anterior or posterior interpretation given to that act by the CJEU. Alternatively, it could well happen that a CETA tribunal would find that an interpretation given by the CJEU to a particular provision of the EU law constitutes a breach (or part of a breach) of the CETA provision.

Two other arguments have been used to distinguish between intra and extra EU situations. They are the principle of mutual trust and involvement of the EU as the contracting party to the treaty. Starting with the latter argument, it goes only as far as Article 344 TFEU is concerned. However, the fact that the involvement of the EU as a party may do away with the issue of an Article 344 violation is irrelevant for the principal problem, which is the risk of incompatibility of the award with the principle of autonomy of EU law. As far as the problem concerns the autonomy of EU law, it is immaterial who the parties to the treaty are. The point is, even the EU cannot enter into an international treaty that would be incompatible with the TFEU.

5.3 Role of Mutual Trust

Turning to mutual trust, this principle merely means that a court of a Member State should assume that courts of another Member State can be trusted to comply with a minimum (*nota bene*, vague and undefined) standard of due process. The argument to be built on the principle of mutual trust is that in an intra-EU context, it is not necessary to take a dispute out of the purview of the courts of a Member State because it is supposed that those courts would ensure due process of law. But in relation with third countries, the principle of mutual trust simply implies that courts of *all* Member States seen as one, are deemed to offer the same type of due process guarantees and be subject to the supervision of the CJEU. Accordingly, a provision in an investment protection treaty with a third country conferring jurisdiction onto an arbitral tribunal operating outside the judicial structures of the Member States, logically implies that the EU would agree to waive these guarantees which are presumed to exist (pursuant to the mutual trust principle) in the entire EU. Such provision also implies the waiver of the power of the CJEU to ensure that an arbitral tribunal properly applies and/or interprets EU law.

The justification given in *Opinion 1/17* for these concessions was that respect for the rule of law could not be presumed in the third countries with whom such treaties are made.[70] Accordingly, it seems following *Achmea* and *Opinion 1/17* that the CJEU is prepared to sacrifice the autonomy of EU law and limit the jurisdiction of national courts because certain third countries may have inadequate judicial systems, but is not prepared to accept investment treaty arbitration in a purely intra-EU context, where the risk of an actual conflict between a decision of an arbitral tribunal with EU law would be much lower. The reasoning here is plainly incoherent and the issue would have to be revisited by the CJEU at some point in the future.

In summary, the derogation of a dispute from Member State courts in favour of an international court or tribunal (one of the key reasons why the CJEU declared intra-EU arbitration to be incompatible with EU law in *Achmea*), could create similar legal issues in an intra-EU as in an extra-EU dispute.[71] Moreover, an international investment court could even declare that the CJEU acted in violation of the respective investment protection treaty through the adoption of a particular judgment on the interpretation or application of EU law. All these points, adopting the logic of *Achmea*, would strongly advocate against alleged conformity of extra-EU investment protection treaties with EU law. One would therefore think that following the decided stance taken in *Achmea*, the CJEU should take the next logical path and decide in *Opinion 1/17* that investment treaty arbitration is likewise prone to undermine the effectiveness of EU law in the non-intra EU context. As we have seen, this did not happen. But this does not mean that the issue will not be revisited one day.

6 Simply Bad Outcome for Europe

6.1 Imprudence of Trusting National Courts Only

Putting aside the technical legal flaws in the reasoning of *Achmea*, it is submitted that the judgment was also imprudent from the perspective of protection of the rule of law in Europe. At the time when independence of the judiciary is under attack from illiberal governments, promoting judicial monopolism is not the best strategy. Thus, while *Achmea* strengthens the position of the CJEU and national courts, a better route to defend the rule of law precisely in those Member States where it most needs to be protected would be to allow for a multiplicity of legal remedies at the choice of

[70]Expressed clearly in para. 82 of the opinion of AG Bot, supra 40, and implied in paras. 128–129 of Opinion 1/17, *supra* note 4.

[71]Admittedly, the conferral of jurisdiction would take place pursuant to an agreement entered into not by and between EU Member States, but pursuant to a treaty entered into by the EU and the Member States with a third country. This, however, only addresses the concerns raised by the CJEU in *Achmea* in relations to Article 344 TFEU, but not these related to Article 267 TFEU nor these related to Article 19 TEU and the principle of autonomy of EU law.

the aggrieved party. A useful analogy is the engineering concept of redundancy. In a technical context, redundancy is understood as duplication of critical components or functions of a system with the intention of increasing reliability of the system in the event of a failure or break-down.[72] Thanks to redundancy, for example, passenger airplanes may safely continue a flight even in the case of the breakdown of one (or more) engines. Similarly, multiple safeguards are routinely put in place to ensure safety in air traffic. In law, redundancy is intuitively regarded as unwelcome as it entails the risk of multiplicity of proceedings and conflicting judgments. As a result, duplications in legal systems are eliminated. This, however, exposes the critical components of the legal infrastructure designed to protect the rule of law to the risk of a single successful attack from an illiberal or autocratic political power.

The existing system of investment treaty arbitration in Europe not only offered a choice but was importantly different from proceedings before state courts and more immune to current threats. International investment law enforces the rule of law principally through non-state, apolitical *quasi*-judicial bodies, notably international arbitral tribunals, which are constituted on an *ad hoc* basis for the limited purpose of determining the outcome of a single case. The decentralized, dispersed system of arbitration results more resilient to the potential attacks to which national courts may be exposed from illiberal governments. Additionally, investment treaty arbitration enables individuals to bypass national courts and assert their claims directly before supra-national *quasi*-judicial bodies, which they cannot do under EU law.

6.2 Three Salient Advantages of Investment Treaty Arbitration

Three specific features of international investment arbitration make it more attractive for investors than any remedy available under EU law. Firstly, international arbitration under investment protection treaties typically allows creating a level playing field for the individual and the government with respect to the composition of the arbitral tribunal. From the perspective of an individual claimant, this is a remarkable advantage, which is simply not available elsewhere. In national courts, judges are appointed exclusively by the competent organs of the executive power.[73] Individuals

[72] Adams (2017), p. 77.

[73] The perceived bias of domestic courts is typically indicated as one of the reasons that investors prefer international arbitration to litigation before domestic courts, see e.g. Brower and Steven (2001), p. 196. This phenomenon was also recognized by the European Commission in the 2013 Factsheet Investor-State Dispute Settlement, http://trade.ec.europa.eu/doclib/docs/2013/october/tradoc_151791.pdf (last visited on 18 July 2019), in which it stated at p. 2: 'Firstly, the investor may not want to bring an action against the host country in that country's courts because it might think they are biased or lack independence. Secondly, investors might not be able to access the local courts in the host country. There are examples of cases where countries have expropriated foreign investors, not paid compensation and denied them access to local courts. In such situations,

are similarly disadvantaged in proceedings before permanent international courts, to which judicial candidates are often nominated by states. In international arbitration, however, an individual and a state are on a par regardless of whether each party appoints a co-arbitrator (and the president of the tribunal is appointed by those two or by an arbitral institution) or the entire arbitral panel is chosen from among neutrals by an arbitral institution.

Secondly, investment arbitral tribunal can be harsher to respondent states with respect to damages. Domestic courts often feel constrained from ruling against states with respect to the consequences of measures taken in pursuit of their sovereign powers. Therefore, even in high value disputes, high damages are rare. In proceedings before the European Court of Human Rights, settled case law regarding a taking in breach of Article 1 of Protocol No. 1 confirms that the compensation need not be full.[74] Confronted with such benchmarks, the prevailing approach in investment treaty arbitration favoring the full compensation model[75] is attractive to investors. It allows to assume that owners of a business project frustrated by unlawful acts of a state could receive compensation calculated on the basis of expected future streams of revenue that were missed because of the contested measures.

Thirdly, enforcement of investment arbitral awards need not take place in the territory of the Member State concerned. Arbitral awards are enforced either pursuant to the Washington Convention[76] or the New York Convention,[77] which implies that the grounds for refusal of enforcement on the leading international financial markets is very limited. This poses an important risk to the states that refuse to settle the awards voluntarily. The existence of a number of unsettled awards may create problems for a state when seeking to gain access to international funding. It can also increase the perceived political risk of doing business within that state, thus affecting the inflow of foreign investments and augmenting the cost of service of sovereign debt. Furthermore, the very prospect of being engaged in costly arbitration proceedings is a nuisance to the states.[78] In the end, the disadvantages of investment treaty arbitration proved in the past to have a chilling effect on the attempts of various states to take measures inconsistent with the rule of law.

---

investors have nowhere to bring a claim, unless there is an ISDS provision in the investment agreement.'

[74]ECtHR, *Lithgow and others v. United Kingdoms,* Judgment of 8 July 198, *Applications nos. no. 9006/80; 9262/81; 9263/81; 9265/81; 9266/81; 9313/81; 9405/81.*

[75]PCIJ, the *Chorzów Factory* case (*Germany v. Poland*), Judgment of 13 September 1928, P.C.I.J., Series A, No. 17, p. 47.

[76]Convention on the Settlement of Investment Disputes Between States and Nationals of Other States, Washington D.C., 18 March 1965, 575 UNTS 159.

[77]Convention on the Recognition and Enforcement of Foreign Arbitral Awards, New York, 10 June 1958, 330 UNTS 38.

[78]Pelc (2017), p. 567 estimates the average defence cost for a state per case at approximately USD 5.5 million.

For aforementioned reasons, investment treaty arbitrations played an important role in the European Union as a tool of fostering and enforcing the rule of law. Member States of the EU, particularly in Central and Eastern Europe, felt there was real risk of facing adverse financial consequences if they would adopt measures that are incompatible with the rules laid down in the investment protection treaties. Investors could assume that if they did not trust local courts in that part of the world,[79] they had recourse before an international forum. Following *Achmea*, the accuracy of that assumption was undermined. Following *Opinion 1/17*, it has been partially restored, as it seems that the CJEU shall tolerate—at least for some time—recourse to arbitration by investors from Canada (and possibly also other jurisdictions) or their EU subsidiaries,[80] against EU Member States.

7 Conclusions

The decisions in *Achmea* and *Opinion 1/17* have critical importance for the future of cross-border investment protection in Europe. Their political manifesto is clear. Protection of cross-border investments within the EU should not take place pursuant to current investment protection treaties, and should not involve international arbitration as it has been known to date. With respect to investments involving third countries, the EU has green light to engage in trade and investment protection treaties, provided that investor-state dispute resolution provisions in such treaties comply with certain conditions believed to preserve the autonomy of EU law. However, the technical legal analysis used by the CJEU to justify these conclusions is wanting in many important aspects and it is internally incoherent. Therefore, it undermines legal certainty and meets with considerable pushback from international arbitral tribunals and international business community.

The source of these problems is clearly *Achmea*. The principal issue with this judgment is that it purports to deliver a simplified political message that all investor-state arbitrations based on intra-EU BITs are reportedly unlawful. By doing so, *Achmea* overlooks not only the legal and factual niceties concerning almost 300 potentially affected international treaties which were formally in force at the time when the judgment was issued, but also the potential collateral effect which the legal reasoning employed in that judgment may have e.g. for commercial arbitration or the European Convention of Human Rights.

[79]The situation in national judicial systems in many EU Member States if far from ideal, which is being admitted even by the European Commission. See e.g. the 2018 EU Justice Scoreboard, https://ec.europa.eu/info/sites/info/files/justice_scoreboard_2019_en.pdf.

[80]See Article 8.23.1. (b) of the CETA.

The timing of *Achmea* could not be worse as it coincided with the systemic actions taken in countries such as Poland to undermine the independence and efficiency of the national judicial system and to subjugate it to the political will of the executive branch.[81] It is of course most desirable that the CJEU intervenes to protect the rule of law by supporting the independence of the judicial systems of the Member States. However, the contested legislative acts in Poland, and earlier in Hungary, were not a result of innocent errors of the national legislator. They were undertaken in wilful disregard of due process of law and they were intentional. As of today, the jury on the future of judiciary in Poland is still out. It also seems that the procedure under Article 7 TEU has encountered serious difficulties and it is uncertain whether it can be completed at all.[82] Given the continuing rise of populism and extremism in Europe is may be that also other political powers are watching the space closely. In these circumstances, cutting the intra-EU investors off from an alternative way of pursuing their legal claims and referring them before the mandatory jurisdiction of national courts was not a prudent move.

The same arguments which served to justify the decision in *Achmea* can also turn in the future against the trade and investment agreements which have been entered into, or are currently being negotiated by the EU. As long as these treaties provide for access of investors to international arbitration, they will incentivize EU investors to bypass *Achmea* by setting up subsidiaries in such third countries parties to these treaties. Clearly, there is a tendency in the current international investment and tax law to deprive post-box (or conduit) companies of the benefits of preferential tax treatment[83] and investment protection. This, however, makes it only harder—but not impossible—to engage in jurisdiction shopping and treaty planning.

Finally, *Achmea* puts EU Member States into a position of conflicting obligations. On the one hand, the intra-EU treaties remain in force and create certain obligations for these Member States under public international law, which may benefit third parties (investors). On the other, under the interpretation of *Achmea* as the Member States adopted on 15 and 16 January 2019, they are constrained from complying with these obligations voluntarily. What results is an increasing mass of

[81]See e.g. CJEU, Case C-619/18 *Commission v. Poland (retirement of Supreme Court judges)*, judgment of 24 June 2019, ECLI:EU:C:2019:531; CJEU, Case C-192/18 *Commission v. Poland (retirement rules for Polish judges)*, AG Opinion of 20 June 2019, ECLI:EU:C:2019:529; CIEU, Joined Cases C-585/18, C-624/18 and C-625/18 *Krajowa Rada Sądownictwa and Others*, AG Opinion of 27 June 2019, ECLI:EU:C:2019:551.

[82]The process was brought to a stall in 2018. Moreover, senior EU officials admit the procedure has had limited impact on Poland's behaviour, see https://www.reuters.com/article/us-poland-katainen-eu/eus-katainen-says-article-7-procedure-against-poland-has-had-little-impact-idUSKCN1S73C6; last acceded on 17 July 2019.

[83]See e.g. CJEU, Joined Cases C-116/16 and C-117/16, *Skatteministeriet v. T Danmark and Y Denmark Aps*, ECLI:EU:C:2019:135.

unpaid awards rendered against EU Member States that one day shall reach the gravitas required for the problem to be resolved at a political, and not legal level. How and when can this may happen remains to be seen.

References

Adams H (2017) Systemic decision making: fundamentals for addressing problems and messes. Springer, Heidelberg

Bakos A (2019) Schrödinger's investment: the EU's General Court considers that the compensation ordered by the Micula tribunal is not a form of state aid (Although it Might as Well Have Been). EFILA Blog, https://efilablog.org/2019/06/26/schrodingers-investment-the-eus-general-court-considers-that-the-compensation-ordered-by-the-micula-tribunal-is-not-a-form-of-state-aid-although-it-might-as-well-have-been/. Last acceded on 17 July 2019

Balthasar S (2018) Investment protection in Europe: international investment treaties, the European Convention on Human Rights and the need for reform at EU level. SchiedsVZ 4:227–233

Berger J (2017) Intra-EU investor-state arbitration: the uncertainty continues – unpacking the advocate general's opinion in Case C-284/16 (Achmea). SchiedsVZ 15:282–291

Brower C, Steven LA (2001) Who then should judge? Developing the international rule of law under NAFTA Chapter 11. Chicago J Int Law 2:193–202

Buczkowska E, Treder P, Sadowski W (2017) The house always wins remarks on AG Wathelet's opinion in the C-284/16 Achmea case. Kluwer Arbitration Blog, 22 November 2017, http://arbitrationblog.kluwerarbitration.com/2017/11/22/house-always-wins-remarks-ag-wathelets-opinion-c-28416-achmea-case/. Last accessed on 17 July 2019

Croisant G (2019) Micula Case: the general Court Quashes the Commission's decision and rules that the award is not state aid. Kluwer Arbitration Blog, 19 June 2019, http://arbitrationblog.kluwerarbitration.com/2019/06/19/micula-case-the-general-court-quashes-the-commissions-decision-and-rules-that-the-award-is-not-state-aid

Hartley TC (2019) The European Court, the rule of law and the reach of judicial power in the European Union. Law Q Rev 135:321–337

Hess B (2018) The fate of investment dispute resolution after the Achmea decision of the European Court of Justice. MPILux Research Paper 2018/3. Available at https://doi.org/10.2139/ssrn.3152972

Hindelang S (2019) Conceptualisation and application of the principle of autonomy of EU law – the CJEU's Judgement in Achmea put in perspective. Eur Law Rev 3:383–400

Koutrakos P (2019) More on autonomy – opinion 1/17 (CETA). Eur Law Rev 3:293–294

Lavranos N, Singla T (2018) Achmea: groundbreaking or overrated. SchiedsVZ 17:348–357

Paschalidis P (2019) Chapter 14: challenges under EU law to the enforcement of arbitral awards under the New York Convention. In: Fach Gomez K, Lopez-Rodriguez AM (eds) 60 years of the New York convention: key issues and future challenges. Kluwer, Alphen aan den Rijn, pp 219–236

Pelc K (2017) What explains the low success rate of investor-state disputes. Int Organ 71:559–583

Power R (2019) The (Final?) death of intra-EU investor-state arbitration. Kluwer Arbitration Blog of 28 January 2019, http://arbitrationblog.kluwerarbitration.com/2019/01/28/the-final-death-of-intra-eu-investor-state-arbitration/. Last acceded on 17 July 2019

Sadowski W (2018) Protection of the rule of law in the European Union through investment treaty arbitration: is judicial monopolism the right response to illiberal tendencies in Europe. Common Market Law Rev 55:1025–1060

Wychera B, Mimnagh W (2019) Chapter IV: investment arbitration, the nature of state consent expressed in BITs. Austrian Yearb Int Arbitr:395–419

Wojciech Sadowski is partner at Queritius.

Sounding the Alarm: The Council of Europe As the Guardian of the Rule of Law in Contemporary Europe*

Jörg Polakiewicz and Julia Katharina Kirchmayr

Contents

1 Introduction

The Council of Europe was founded upon the Rule of Law as one of its three core principles. This transpires from the preamble of the Council's Statute and the requirements for membership, as enshrined in Article 3 where "every member of the Council of Europe must accept the principles of the *Rule of Law* [emphasis added] and of the enjoyment by all persons within its jurisdiction of human rights

*This submission was completed on 23 August 2019 and thereby only reflects upon the developments up and until this date.

J. Polakiewicz (✉)
Europainstitut of the University of Saarbrücken, Saarbrücken, Germany

Directorate of Legal Advice and Public International Law (Legal Adviser), Council of Europe, Strasbourg, France
e-mail: Jorg.Polakiewicz@coe.int

J. K. Kirchmayr
European Commission, Brussels, Belgium
e-mail: Julia.Kirchmayr@ec.europa.eu

A. von Bogdandy et al. (eds.), *Defending Checks and Balances in EU Member States*, Beiträge zum ausländischen öffentlichen Recht und Völkerrecht 298,
https://doi.org/10.1007/978-3-662-62317-6_14

and fundamental freedoms, and collaborate sincerely and effectively in the realisation of the aim of the Council."[1]

Respect for the Rule of Law is a precondition for the accession of States to the Organisation. The Rule of Law is of the upmost importance for the Council, so much that if a member State were to consistently fail to uphold this principle, it may trigger the application of Article 8 which would not only provide for the suspension of a State's right to representation, but also its eventual expulsion if the systematic violations continued to persist. The relevant Committee of Minister's decisions require a mere two-thirds majority (as defined by Article 20 (d) of the Statute).[2]

The Parliamentary Assembly disposes of a range of measures in the context of its own monitoring procedure. Based on the procedure to challenge the credentials of national delegations, it may choose to suspend the voting and participatory rights of a delegation.[3] These powers have been subject to criticism on both political and legal grounds.[4] Following the adoption of the decision by the Committee of Ministers at its 129th Session (Helsinki, 17 May 2019) on "A shared responsibility for democratic security in Europe – Ensuring respect for rights and obligations, principles, standards and values", the Assembly modified its sanctions regime. Henceforth, the members' right to vote, to speak and to be represented in the Assembly and its bodies shall not be suspended or withdrawn in the context of a challenge to or reconsideration of the credentials of these members.[5] Should a member State continue to persistently disrespect its commitments, the Assembly may address a recommendation to the Committee of Ministers requesting it to take action in accordance with the provisions of Articles 7 and 8 of the Statute. Both organs are currently in the process of setting up, in addition to the existing procedures, a joint reactionary procedure to serious violations of the Organisation's fundamental principles and values, including the Rule of Law, which could be triggered by the Parliamentary Assembly, the Committee of Ministers or the Secretary General.

So far, no member State has ever been sanctioned for showing a blatant disregard for the Rule of Law. Attempts to open 'monitoring procedures' in respect to Hungary[6] and Malta[7] failed in April 2013 and June 2019. Yet, on 24 April 2017, the Assembly chose to reopen a monitoring procedure regarding Turkey citing

[1]*Statute of the Council of Europe*, ETS No 001, London, 5 May 1949.

[2]Ibid.

[3]See Evans and Silk (2013).

[4]See 'Role and responsibilities of the Council of Europe's statutory organs with special emphasis on the limitation of membership rights' DLAPIL 18/2018 of 25 September 2018.

[5]Parliamentary Assembly Resolution 2287 (2019) of 25 June 2019.

[6]Parliamentary Assembly, *PACE Committee Recommends Monitoring of Hungary*, 25 April 2013.

[7]A motion presented in the context of 'Daphne Caruana Galizia's assassination and the rule of law in Malta and beyond: ensuring that the whole truth emerges' (Report by P Omtzigt, doc. 14906) failed, but Resolution 2293 (2019) was adopted and states *inter alia* that "the rule of law in Malta is seriously undermined by the extreme weakness of its system of checks and balances."

"serious concerns"[8] over a number of human rights, democracy and Rule of Law related issues.

This contribution addresses the Council of Europe's various mechanisms designed to strengthen the Rule of Law before examining our cooperation with the European Union and in particular, the European Commission, who in light of the serious breaches of the Rule of Law has initiated infringement proceedings against Poland and referred two cases to the European Court of Justice[9] in addition to asking the Council of the European Union to adopt a decision under Article 7 of the Treaty on European Union.[10]

2 The Venice Commission and its Rule of Law Checklist

The 'European Commission for Democracy through Law', otherwise known as the Venice Commission is an independent consultative body established through an enlarged Council agreement. The Commission has 61 members, the 47 Council of Europe member States and 14 other countries including Algeria, Brazil, Chile, Costa Rica, Israel, Kazakhstan, the Republic of Korea, Kosovo, Kyrgyzstan, Morocco, Mexico, Peru, Tunisia and the US. The Commission has in the past been publicly referred to as the "custodian of constitutional probity all over Europe."[11]

For more than 20 years, the Venice Commission has supported and advised individual countries on the Rule of Law in order to strengthen democratic institutions and protect human rights. As one of its primary objectives, the Commission promotes the Rule of Law as a basic feature of the European constitutional order through recommendations and opinions on draft constitutions and legislation. The Venice Commission can be seized by the Committee of Ministers, the Parliamentary Assembly, the Congress of Local and Regional Authorities of Europe, the Secretary General or by a participating State, international organisation or body to provide an opinion.[12] It may also carry out research on its own accord; prepare studies and draft guidelines, laws and international agreements.[13] Its flexible and ad-hoc character allows the Venice Commission to react swiftly to threats posed to the Rule of Law and ensures the Commission's relevance, in the midst of unfolding crises as the most

---

[8]Parliamentary Assembly, *PACE reopens monitoring procedure in respect of Turkey,* 25 April 2017.

[9]CJEU, Case C-619/18 *Commission v Poland*, ECLI:EU:C:2019:531. CJEU, Case C-192/18 *Commission v Poland* ECLI:EU:C:2019:529.

[10]European Commission, *Rule of Law: European Commission acts to defend judicial independent in Poland*, 20 December 2017.

[11]Gardner (6 April 2017).

[12]Council of Ministers, Resolution (2002) 3, Article 3(2).

[13]Ibid, Article 3 (1).

recent events in Hungary, Poland, Romania, the Ukraine and Turkey, have illustrated.

In 2007, the Parliamentary Assembly called upon the Venice Commission to assist in the offering of further reflections on the Rule of Law in Europe. Following thorough deliberations, the Venice Commission published a 'Report on the Rule of Law' in 2011, in which it sought to identify a consensual definition of the Rule of Law in order to assist "international organisations and both domestic and international courts in interpreting and applying this fundamental value"[14] and distinguish the Rule of Law from a rule *by* law. The report concluded that, despite a variety of opinions a consensus, regarding the core formal and substantive elements that compromise the Rule of Law could, nonetheless, be found.

During its plenary session in March 2016, the Venice Commission adopted its 'Rule of Law Checklist' a practical, accessible and user-friendly instrument intended to be used by a broad breadth of actors, including national authorities, international and non-governmental organisations, academics and ordinary citizens. Designed as a precise enough tool to allow for the application of the Rule of Law principles in an objective, in-depth, and transparent manner, the Checklist is, when applied, meant to benefit from the broad involvement of interested stakeholders.[15]

The Checklist is neither exhaustive nor final; rather, it aims to cover a series of core elements of the Rule of Law whilst taking into account the diversity of Europe's legal systems and traditions.[16] The Checklist translates five principles of the Rule of Law (legality; legal certainty; prevention of abuse of power; equality before the law and non-discrimination; and access to justice) into concrete questions with the intention of applying these to evaluate and assess the country-specific circumstances of its members. It also offers concrete examples of particular challenges with which the Rule of Law is, at times confronted with, such as claims of corruption and conflicts of interest[17] or the collection of personal data and surveillance.[18]

In order to understand the practical value of the Rule of Law Checklist, one should consider the following example: Access to Justice. Access to Justice is an essential requirement to ensure that we do not find ourselves living in a world dominated by *lex imperfecta* and yet, it remains a broad, perhaps even vague principle and should thus be divided into two sub-principles: (a). independence and impartiality and (b). fair trial. Both of these sub-principles are still quite general in their nature and thus require further elaboration. The principle of independence and impartiality for example, includes *inter alia* the independence of the judiciary and of individual judges, the impartiality of the judiciary, the autonomy of the prosecution service and the independence and impartiality of the Bar. Whilst the

---

[14]Venice Commission, *Venice Commission Report on the Rule of Law*, 4 April 2011, paragraph 3.

[15]Ibid, paragraph 24.

[16]For more information on the Rule of Law Checklist, see also Drzemczewski (2018), pp. 179–184.

[17]Venice Commission Report on the Rule of Law, *supra* (note 16), paragraph 114.

[18]Ibid, paragraph 117.

abovementioned components are, at their core still 'principles' they are nonetheless much more precise than the umbrella terms: independence and impartiality.

The Checklist includes a number of more detailed questions regarding the independence of the judiciary:[19] one general question and a number of specific follow-up questions regarding the independence of individual judges:[20]

a) General: Are there sufficient constitutional and legal guarantees for the independence of individual judges?[21]
b) Specific: Are judicial activities subject to the supervision of higher courts (outside the appeal framework), court presidents, the executive or other public bodies? Does the Constitution guarantee the right to a competent judge ("natural judge pre-established by law")? Does the law clearly determine which court is competent? Does it set rules to solve any conflicts of competence? Does the allocation of cases follow an objective and transparent criteria? Is the withdrawal of a judge from a case excluded (other than in cases where a recusal by one of the parties or by the judge him/herself has been declared)?

These questions aim to decipher the country-specific status of the Rule of Law, once they are answered, it becomes easier to identify possible shortcomings and subsequently, (hopefully!) remedy them.

With the adoption of the Rule of Law Checklist in March 2016, the Venice Commission established "one of the few widely accepted conceptual frameworks for the Rule of Law in Europe."[22] The Checklist has been formally endorsed by the Committee of Ministers in September 2016 and a month later, by the Congress of Local and Regional Authorities. The Parliamentary Assembly of the Council of Europe also approved the Rule of Law Checklist during its plenary session in October 2017.[23] The resolution foresees a systematic use of the Checklist by the Assembly, in particular in relation to the preparation of reports by the Committee on Legal Affairs and Human Rights and the Committee on the Honouring of Obligations and Commitments by Member States of the Council of Europe (Monitoring Committee).[24] Furthermore, the Parliamentary Assembly invited national parliaments, governmental bodies and ministries, regional and international organisations, and civil actors to refer to the Checklist when contemplating legislative reform and carrying out their respective activities.[25]

---

[19]Ibid, paragraph II. E.1.a.

[20]Ibid, paragraph II. E.1.b.

[21]Ibid, paragraph 85 b.

[22]Carrera et al. (2013), p. 17.

[23]Parliamentary Assembly, Venice Commission's "Rule of Law Checklist", 11 October 2017, Resolution 2187 (2017).

[24]Ibid, paragraph 6.2.

[25]Ibid, paragraph 6.3–6.5.

According to the former UN Secretary-General Ban Ki-moon, "the Rule of Law is like the rule of gravity."[26] Gravity is, however a scientifically defined concept which describes a universally applicable, naturally existing phenomenon. The Rule of Law, by contrast, is a set of principles describing ideals that every society must freely choose to adopt and adapt to their precise juridical, historical, political and social contexts; thus the effective realisation of the Rule of Law very much depends upon the commitment of civil society. Moreover, the diversity of Europe's legal systems and traditions, must be taken into account when discussing the application of the Venice Commission's Checklist.

Legal discourse at a European level rarely reaches the same breadth and depth as at national level which, as Dieter Grimm observed, takes place in a much closer context of participation and responsibility.[27] International judges enjoy, in a certain sense, a greater level of freedom than their national counterparts and thus try to counterbalance this by respecting national judicial identities. This acknowledgment is also reflected in the justifications for the ECtHR (The European Court of Human Rights)'s recourse to the margin of appreciation and the principle of subsidiarity. A good example of this is the 'measuring' of the 'fairness' of a procedure or system, a task which can only be accomplished with reference to its particular context and through the weighing of different factors which feed into this complex assessment. In order to fully appreciate the significant role played by the national context for this assessment, one may look towards the election procedure of judges in different member States. Whilst the election of judges by citizens is a well-established practice in Switzerland,[28] the same approach would be unimaginable in a country with a recent history of interethnic warfare, like Bosnia and Herzegovina.

3 Overview of the Council of Europe Rule of Law Related Activities[29]*

According to the European Convention on Human Rights, the Rule of Law famously forms part of "the common heritage"[30] of its members, it is a principle inherent to the very soul of the Convention.

The Court used the concept of "prééminence du droit" or "rule of law" for the first time in *Golder v. United Kingdom* in February 1975,[31] basing its interpretation of

---

[26]GA/11290, 'World Leaders Adopt Deceleration Reaffirming Rule of Law as Foundation for Building Equitable State Relations, Just Societies', 24 September 2012.

[27]Grimm (2016), p. 171.

[28]Though not uncontested, see Lübbe-Wolff (2019), Available via https://verfassungsblog.de/richterwahlen-in-der-schweiz-wo-liegt-das-problem/. Accessed 26 August 2019.

[29]For more information please see Polakiewicz and Sandvig (2016), pp. 115–134.

[30]Preamble of the European Convention on Human Rights, Rome 4 November 1950.

[31]ECtHR, *Golder v. United Kingdom*, Judgment of 21 February 1975, Application no. 4451/70.

Article 6 of the Convention (right to a fair trial) on the reference to the Rule of Law in the Convention's Preamble. It emphasised that this principle should not merely be seen as a "more or less rhetorical reference",[32] devoid of relevance for those interpreting the Convention. One of the reasons for why the signatory Governments decided to "take the first steps for the collective enforcement of certain of the rights stated in the Universal Declaration"[33] was their profound belief in the Rule of Law. Since then, the Rule of Law has become a guiding principle for the Court which "inspires the whole Convention"[34] by being "inherent in all the Articles of the Convention."[35] In this context, the Court has offered further clarification on a number of key themes which underpin the Rule of Law, including: (1). the separation of powers, (2). the role of the judiciary, (3). impunity, (4). a tribunal established by law, (5). sufficiently accessible and foreseeable law, (6). the scope of legal discretion, (7). *nullum crimen sine lege* and *nulla poena sine lege*, (8). legal certainty, (9). the execution of final domestic judgments, (10). equality before the law, (11). the judicial control of the executive, (12). positive obligations of the state in the form of procedural requirements and safeguards, (13). the right of access to a court, (14). the right to an effective remedy, and finally (15). the right to a fair trial.

The Court has emphasised that democracy is inseparably linked to the Rule of Law, the concept implying the existence of a separation of powers, institutional guarantees for an independent and impartial judiciary, as well as the judicial oversight of the executive.[36] Already in 2002, the Court itself noted that "the notion of separation of powers between the executive and the judiciary has assumed growing importance in the case-law of the Court."[37] This principle is also of relevance with regard to the appointment and selection of judges, whilst the executive and legislative branches may be involved in the appointment, the procedure must be free from undue pressure and interference.[38]

In the case of *Baka v. Hungary*, the Court recognised the growing importance which international and more specifically, the Council of Europe's legal instruments, case law and bodies attach to procedural fairness in cases concerning the removal and dismissal of judges.[39] Regarding legal certainty, the Court in *Brumărescu v. Romania* found that "one of the fundamental aspects of the rule of law is the

---

[32] Ibid, paragraph 30.

[33] Ibid, paragraph 34.

[34] ECtHR, *Engel and Others v. the Netherlands,* Judgement of 8 June 1976, Application no. 5100/71; 5101/71; 5102/71; 5354/72; 5370/72, paragraph 69.

[35] ECtHR, *Amuur v. France*, Judgment of 25 June 1996, Application no. 19776/92, paragraph 50.

[36] Steiner (2016), p. 154.

[37] ECtHR, *Stafford v. the United Kingdom*, Grand Chamber Judgment of 28 May 2002, Application no. 46295/99, paragraph 78.

[38] See the overview over relevant case-law in the Background Document to the 2018 Judicial Seminar at the Court entitled 'The Authority of the Judiciary', available at: https://www.echr.coe.int/Documents/Seminar_background_paper_2018_ENG.pdf.

[39] ECtHR, *Baka v. Hungary,* Grand Chamber Judgment of 23 June 2016 Application no. 20261/12, paragraph 172.

principle of legal certainty, which requires, inter alia, that where the courts have made a final determination of an issue, their ruling should not be called into question."[40] More recently, the Court in Guðmundur Andri Ástráðsson addressed at length the principle of the separation of powers and judicial independence and impartiality, specifying that "the Court places emphasis on the importance in a democratic society governed by the rule of law of securing the compliance with the applicable rules of national law in the light of the principle of the separation of powers."[41]

The right of access to a court, fair trial and an effective remedy were similarly further elaborated upon by the Court within its growing body of case law. The Court established the basis for the principle of the right of access to a court in the abovementioned case of *Golder*, when it held that in order to give effect to the procedural guarantees contained within Article 6 of the Convention, the right of access to a court must be provided for.[42] In *Sunday Times* Strasbourg not only underlined the fundamentality of public confidence in the judiciary and the importance of the Court's role as a guarantor of justice for the Rule of Law, but also emphasised that the principle implies the need for a fair trial.[43] In relation to the remedy required by Article 13, the Court perceived an effective remedy as "either [to] prevent the alleged violation or its continuation or prove adequate redress for any violation that had already occurred."[44] The Court has also elaborated upon what it understands as the criteria for the phrase 'prescribed by law': "[f]irstly, the law must be adequately accessible... Secondly, a norm cannot be regarded as a "law" unless it is formulated with sufficient precision to enable the citizen to regulate his conduct: he must be able - if need be with appropriate advice - to foresee, to a degree that is reasonable in the circumstances, the consequences which a given action may entail."[45]

The ECtHR thus has, and continues to hold, a crucial function in safeguarding the Rule of Law by fleshing out this principle through relevant case-law.

Furthermore the Committee of Ministers' supervision of the execution of ECtHR judgments constitutes as an invaluable source of information as to the efforts made by member States to remedy both individual and systemic ECHR violations, including those related to the Rule of Law. The Secretary General's annual report on the 'State of Democracy, Human Rights and the Rule of Law in Europe' similarly draws upon the involvement of the Committee of Ministers. In 2017, the Committee was

---

[40]ECtHR, *Brumărescu v. Romania*, Grand Chamber Judgment of 28 October 1999, Application no. 28342/95 Reports, paragraph 61.

[41]ECtHR, *Guðmundur Andri Ástráðsson,* Judgment of 12 March 2019, Application no. 26374/18, paragraph 122.

[42]ECtHR, *Amuur v. France, supra* (note 37) paragraph 72.

[43]ECtHR, *Sunday Times v. United Kingdom (No.1)*, Judgement of 26 April1979, Application no. 6538/74, paragraph 55.

[44]ECtHR, *Kudla v. Poland*, Judgment of 26 October 2000, Application no. 30210/96, paragraph 158.

[45]Ibid, paragraph 49.

asked to examine a report entitled 'Populism – How strong are Europe's checks and balances' which takes the Venice Commission's Rule of Law Checklist into account. Chapter 1, for instance, emphasised that efficient, impartial and independent judiciaries "are the cornerstone of any functioning system of democratic checks and balances. They are the means by which powerful interests are restrained, according to the laws of the land. They guarantee that all individuals, irrespective of their backgrounds, are treated equally before those laws."[46] As a follow-up to this second report, which had identified the lack of judicial independence in several European countries as being one of the most serious challenges to a democratic society, the Committee of Ministers adopted the 'Plan of Action on Strengthening Judicial Independence and Impartiality' with the intention of implementing it within the next 5 years (by April 2021).[47]

Apart from the Council of Europe's statutory organs and the Venice Commission, there are various other technical bodies dealing with, in one way or another Rule of Law related issues. In particular, one must mention the Commission for the Efficiency of Justice (CEPEJ), the Consultative Council of European Judges (CCJE) and the Consultative Council of European Prosecutors (CCPE).[48]

The CEPEJ was established to improve the efficiency and functionality of justice in the member States. Through its work, the CEPEJ strengthens the mutual confidence between judicial professionals and promotes the public service of justice. Furthermore, the CEPEJ's evaluation of judicial systems, through the analysis and collection of quantitative and qualitative data offers a reference point for the execution of judicial reforms across Europe. The CEPEJ's work provides a deeper understanding of the day-to-day functioning of courts, the main trends evidenced by the evolution of judicial systems with a view of improving the quality, fairness and efficiency of the public service of justice. In a nutshell, the CEPEJ provides the fertile soil necessary for the Rule of Law to flourish within the judicial and civil fabric of member States.

The work undertaken by the CCJE and CCPE incorporates the perspectives of serving judges and prosecutors throughout Europe. In 2016, the two bureaus drew a comprehensive review of the challenges for judicial independence and impartiality, in which they jointly recognised the public perception of corruption within the justice system to be one of the most serious challenges for the maintenance of public trust and confidence in the independence and impartiality of judges and prosecutors.[49]

---

[46] Report of the Secretary General of the Council of Europe, 'State of Democracy, Human Rights and the Rule of Law' 2017, page 15.

[47] Committee of Ministers, *Plan of Action on Strengthening Judicial Independence and Impartiality*, CM(2016)36 final.

[48] For more information on this topic, see Drzemczewski (2018), pp. 184–198.

[49] Consultative Council of European Judges, *Challenges for judicial independence and impartiality in the member States of the Council of Europe* SG/Inf(2016)3, 15 January 2016, paragraphs 310 and 313.

Let us not forget that the effective realisation of fundamental values, such as democracy and the Rule of Law depend upon a number of institutional actors, women and men, taking ownership and enforcing these at a national level. It is for this reason, that the cooperative activities which assist member States in their efforts to adapt legislation, practices and institutions to European standards are so vital for the realisation of these values.

The Council of Europe's judicial reform projects aim to assist governments in putting into place laws and practices to address the outcomes and findings of ECtHR's judgments, Venice Commission opinions, CEPEJ reports, Committee of Minister's recommendations as well as the standards developed by the CCJE and the CCPE. The Council of Europe is currently managing projects in the Eastern Partnership countries, the Western Balkans as well as in Turkey, Latvia, Slovakia, Kazakhstan, Kosovo, Morocco, Tunisia and Jordan. These projects seek to address judicial self-governance, time management, the role and status of the legal professionals (judges, prosecutors and lawyers), access to justice and the delivery of legal aid.

4 Case Studies: Poland and Romania

4.1 Poland

The Council of Europe has closely been following the events transpiring in Poland, concerning the government's plans to reform the Constitutional Tribunal and the National Council of the Judiciary. Over the last few years, Poland has adopted more than thirteen laws which aim to transform the judicial system and have had a far-reaching impact upon the Constitutional Tribunal, the Supreme Court, the ordinary courts, the National Council for the Judiciary, the prosecution service and lastly the National School of Judiciary. In a recent public address, the First President of the Supreme Court of Poland, described the reform package as a "coup d'état against the structure of one of the most important State institutions . . . not with the armed force or the paramilitary troops but 'only' by misusing legal institutions."[50]

In March 2016, the Venice Commission issued an opinion at the request of the Polish Minister of Foreign Affairs, in which it underlined the crucial role assumed by an effectively functioning Constitutional Court in order for a State to be governed by the tenets of the Rule of Law. As regards to the amendments adopted on 22 December 2015, the Commission concluded that the different measures included therein, especially in their combined effect, would slow down the work of the Constitutional Tribunal and render it ineffective.

[50]Professor Dr. M. Gersdorf, *Address by the Frist President of the Supreme Court on the reforms of the judiciary in Poland*, 22.12.2017.

The Venice Commission was also severely critical of the new composition of the Tribunal, as the Draft Act of the National Council of the Judiciary (NCJ) would alter the election method of the judicial members to allow for the Sejm to elect a total of 15 members, thus skewing the balance of power and effectively politicising the body.[51] As for the Prime Minister's refusal to publish the Constitutional Tribunal's judgement of 9 March 2016 on the constitutionality of the Act, the Commission held that "a refusal to publish...would not only be contrary to the Rule of Law, such a unprecedented move would further deepen the constitutional crisis triggered by the election of judges ... not only the Polish Constitution but also European and international standards require that judgments of a Constitutional Court be respected."[52]

On 14 October 2016, the Venice Commission published a second Opinion in relation to the Act on the Constitutional Tribunal, in which it examined whether its previous recommendations on the effective functioning and independence of the Constitutional Tribunal had been respected by the Government when it adopted the revised text of the Act. The Commission found that "individually and cumulatively, these shortcomings show that instead of unblocking the precarious situation of the Constitutional Tribunal, the Parliament and Government continue to challenge the Tribunal's position as the final arbiter of constitutional issues and attribute this authority to themselves."[53]

The Venice Commission also examined the new Act on the Constitutional Tribunal which entered into force on the 16 August 2016, despite the judgment given by the Polish Constitutional Tribunal which had annulled several provisions of the Act. In its most recent opinion, published in December 2017, the Commission chose to address the merging of the Office of the Public Prosecutor General with that of the Minister of Justice, noting that "...the Minister has a vested interest in the court proceedings, and, at the same time, has important powers vis-à-vis the courts and individual judges."[54]

Following a letter by the Chairman of the National Council of the Judiciary of Poland in April 2017, the CCJE urgently adopted an opinion on the Draft Act on the NCJ and certain other acts, underlining that the Draft Act was in a number of respects, incompatible with the European standards on judicial independence.[55]

---

[51] *Venice Commission Opinion on the Act on the Constitutional Tribunal*, 14 October 2016, paragraph 19.5.

[52] Ibid, paragraph 143.

[53] *Venice Commission Opinion on the Act on the Constitutional Tribunal, supra* (note 53), paragraph 128.

[54] *Venice Commission Opinion on The Draft Act, Amending The Act On The National Council Of The Judiciary, On The Draft Act Amending The Act On The Supreme Court, Proposed By The President Of Poland And On The Act On The Organisation Of Ordinary Courts*, 8–9 December 2017, paragraph 99.

[55] Consultative Council of European Judges, *Opinion of the CCJE Bureau following the request of the Polish National Council of the Judiciary to provide an opinion with respect to the Draft Act of 23 January 2017, latest amended on 3 March 2017, amending the Act of 12 May 2011 on the Polish*

The CCJE Bureau issued a second statement in July 2017 stating that it "deeply regretted the adoption by the Polish Parliament of the Act on the Polish National Council of the Judiciary."[56] In September 2017, the President of Poland proposed a revised version of the Draft Acts on the NCJ and the Supreme Court, for which a second CCJE opinion was requested. Once more the CCJE concluded that the amendments proposed "would jeopardize the independence of a body whose main purpose is to guarantee judicial independence in Poland. The new draft does not in any way change this."[57] In November 2017, the CCJE released a statement regarding the "critical situation affecting the rule of law and independence of the judiciary in Poland."[58]

In May 2017, the Parliamentary Assembly's Monitoring Committee issued an information note on 'The functioning of democratic institutions in Poland' in which it voiced its concerns regarding the "political and constitutional crisis"[59] following the 2015 parliamentary elections and the new government's subsequent reform plans for the Constitutional Tribunal and the judiciary. The Monitoring Committee asked the Venice Commission to prepare an opinion on the amendments to the law regarding the NCJ, the Act on the Supreme Court, and the Organisation of Ordinary Courts and their compatibility with the relevant European standards on the Rule of Law, democracy and best practices. The Venice Commission found that even the new Proposal for the election of members of the judiciary to the NCJ by a three-fifths majority was "still at odds with the European standards"[60] as the "proposed reform will lead to a NCJ dominated by political nominees."[61] With regard to the Draft Act on the Supreme Court, which foresaw the creation of two new chambers for the hearing of disciplinary cases against Supreme Court judges and other "extraordinary appeals" and another chamber, for the hearing of electoral and other public law disputes, the Venice Commission concluded that despite slight improvements the

National Council of the Judiciary and certain other acts, 7 April 2017, CCJE-BU(2017)5REV, paragraph 26–30.

[56]Consultative Council of European Judges, *Opinion of the request of the Polish National Council of the Judiciary to provide an opinion with respect to the Draft Act of September 2017 presented by the President of Poland amending the Act on the Polish National Council of the Judiciary and certain other acts,* 12 October 2017, CCJE-BU(2017)9REV, paragraph 5.

[57]Ibid, paragraph 15.

[58]Consultative Council of European Judges, *Statement of the CCJE as regards the situation on the independence of the judiciary in Poland,* 10 November 2017, CCJE(2017)9.

[59]Parliamentary Assembly, *The functioning of democratic intuitions in Poland,* 9 May 2017, AS/Mon(2017)14, paragraph 3.

[60]*Venice Commission Opinion on The Draft Act, Amending The Act On The National Council Of The Judiciary, On The Draft Act Amending The Act On The Supreme Court, Proposed By The President Of Poland And On The Act On The Organisation Of Ordinary Courts, supra* (note 56), paragraph 24.

[61]Ibid.

draft still raised concerns in relation to its "compliance with ... European standards."[62]

The Act also lowered the age of retirement for a significant number of currently sitting judges and intends to involve parliamentarians in the proceedings of the Extraordinary Chamber, which possesses the power to review the final and legally binding judgements issued by the other chambers of the Court (even some five or—during the transitional period—20 years after the judgment has been made!).[63] The Commission maintained that this restructuring would establish a hierarchical formation of "courts within the court," a practice not foreseen for by the Polish Constitution. Moreover, according to the Draft the composition of these two new chambers could, almost completely be determined by the President of the Republic thus "making electoral judges particularly vulnerable to political influence"[64] which "creates a serious risk for the functioning of Polish democracy."[65] As to the Draft's proposal for the lowering of the retirement age of judges and the provisions which enable the extension of tenure beyond the retirement age at the discretion of the President of the Republic, the Commission questioned these practices, arguing that they would undermine the "security of tenure and the independence of the SC [Supreme Court] in general."[66]

The Venice Commission criticized the introduction of an Extraordinary Chamber which in effect may "reopen *any* case decided in the country ... on virtually any ground ... it means that no judgment in the Polish system will ever be 'final' anymore."[67] It is difficult to reconcile the proposed mechanism with the fundamental principles of the Rule of Law, including *res judicata*, legal certainty and non-retroactivity. In relation to the powers of the President of the Republic vis-à-vis the Supreme Court, the Commission concluded that the "proposed reform, if implemented, will not only threaten the independence of the judges of the SC [Supreme Court], but also create a serious risk for the legal certainty and enable the President of the Republic to determine the composition of the chamber dealing with the politically particularly sensitive electoral cases."[68] The Venice Commission came to the conclusion that the combined effect of the draft acts and their respective proposals allow the Polish legislative and executive authorities to severely and capaciously intrude upon the administration of justice, thus threatening judicial independence and the Rule of Law.[69]

In 2018, the Council of Europe's Group of States against Corruption (GRECO) published its first ever ad-hoc procedure report, as a response to the "exceptional

[62]Ibid, paragraph 34.

[63]Ibid, paragraph 53.

[64]Ibid, paragraph 53.

[65]Ibid, paragraph 43.

[66]Ibid, paragraph 48.

[67]Ibid, paragraph 58.

[68]Ibid, paragraph 89.

[69]Ibid, paragraph 129.

circumstances" and "serious violations" of anti-corruption standards.[70] GRECO stressed that "several basic principles of the judicial system had been affected in such a critical way and to such an extent that the assessment made in GRECO's Fourth Round Evaluation Report on Poland in 2012 as far as it concerns corruption prevention in respect of judges is no longer pertinent in crucial parts."[71]

On 8 March 2018, the Polish government published a White Paper on the Reform of the Polish Judiciary, in order to "explain that the criticism of the reforms is unfounded, but primarily to clear any doubts our European partners may have about the rule of law in Poland."[72] The Paper was sharply criticised by the First President of the Supreme Court for including "distorted and even untrue information which must be corrected."[73] Similarly, in its response to the Government's White Paper, the Polish Judges Association 'Iustitia' emphasised that the information the White Paper relied upon was "presented in an extremely biased manner, and does not paint a truthful image of the Polish judicial system in the European context."[74] In particular, Iustitia denounced the practice of 'cherry-picking', that is the "drawing of comparisons with selected elements forming part of more complex mechanisms and legal institutions, without regard for their normative environment."[75] The Association concluded that the reforms stipulated in the White Paper "have led to a change in the system of justice and the erosion of guarantees for the independence of the judiciary"[76] and furthermore, that this change was made "without changing the letter of the Constitution."[77]

---

[70]Council of Europe's Group of States against Corruption, 'Poland: Judicial reforms violate anti-corruption standards, say Council of Europe experts' (Press Release, 29 March 2018) https://www.coe.int/en/web/greco/-/poland-judicial-reforms-violate-anti-corruption-standards-say-council-of-europe-experts last accessed 23 August 2019.

[71]Council of Europe's Group of States against Corruption, *Ad hoc Report on Poland*, 19–23 March 2018, Greco-AdHocRep(2018)1, paragraph 57.

[72]The Chancellery of the Prime Minister, *White Paper on the Reform of the Polish* Judiciary, 7 March 2018, 5.

[73]Professor Dr. M. Gersdorf, *Opinion on the White Paper on the Reform of the Polish Judiciary*, 16 March 2018, page 1.

[74]Iustitia Polish Judges Association, *The Response of the Polish Judges Association 'Iustitia' To The White Paper on the Reform of the Polish Judiciary Presented to the European Commission by the Government of the Republic of Poland*, Warsaw 2018, page 9.

[75]Ibid, page 28.

[76]Ibid, page 104.

[77]Ibid.

4.2 Romania

The Venice Commission and GRECO have also adopted a number of opinions and recommendations regarding the reforms initiated by the Romanian government.[78] GRECO has expressed its criticism of a series of proposed amendments to the Romanian justice system, including to the criminal justice system, which if viewed alone but especially in the face of the current political climate are likely to undermine the independence of the Romanian judiciary, weaken the public's confidence, and impair the effectiveness of the criminal justice system and the fight against corruption. Their opinions and recommendations[79] pay tribute to the core concepts that underpin the Rule of Law, including:

- the legislative process should be inclusive and transparent involving effective consultations of all stakeholders and meaningful discussions (which are impossible if the process is excessively fast and non-transparent);
- emergency ordinances and expedited procedures should be the exception, not the rule;
- the principles of legal clarity and certainty and in particular the principle of *res judicata* must be respected;
- not only judges, also the prosecution service and individual prosecutors should enjoy some independence from interference by the government;
- judges and prosecutors are entitled to freedom of expression; a reasonable balance needs to be struck between the degree to which judges may be involved in society and the need for them to be and to be seen as independent and impartial in the discharge of the duties;
- judges and prosecutors must not be prevented from engaging in debates about the adequate functioning of the justice system; fear of sanctions may have a chilling effect which is detrimental to society as a whole;
- corruption leads to arbitrariness and abuse of powers; it undermines the very foundations of the Rule of Law;
- effectively preventing and sanctioning corruption-related acts are vital anticorruption measures and obligations under Council of Europe conventions against corruption to which Romania is a party.

While GRECO and the Venice Commission acknowledge the need to reform the judiciary and prosecution services, in order to adapt it where necessary to new challenges and realities, such important reforms should not be rushed through Parliament, but be based on an inclusive, vetted procedure. In a state governed by the Rule of Law, it is important to play by the rules, and not with the rules.

---

[78] Council of Europe's Group of States against Corruption, *Follow- up Report to the Ad hoc Report on Romania*, 17–21 June 2019, Greco-AdHocRep(2019)1.

[79] All opinions and recommendations can be found at the Venice Commission's https://www.venice.coe.int/webforms/events/ and GRECO's https://www.coe.int/en/web/greco websites.

The Council of Europe will continue to monitor developments in Poland and Romania. The Secretary General and the Council's various other bodies remain at the disposal of the national authorities to provide further assistance if so requested.

5 Cooperation with the European Union

The 2007 Memorandum of Understanding between the Council of Europe and the European Union recognises the Rule of Law as a priority for matters of common interest and encourages both institutions to commit to the development of common standards to promote "a Europe without dividing lines."[80] In particular, it provides that:

> [t]he Council of Europe and the European Union will endeavour to establish common standards thus promoting a Europe without dividing lines, without prejudice to the autonomy of decision. Bearing this in mind, legal co-operation should be further developed between the Council of Europe and the European Union with a view to ensuring coherence between Community and European Union law and the standards of Council of Europe conventions. This does not prevent Community and European Union law from adopting more far-reaching rules.[81]

The three pillars of our "strategic partnership" namely political dialogue, cooperation projects and legal cooperation have led to collaborations "of unprecedented intensity."[82]

It was against this background that the the 'Council of the European Union's Conclusions on Fundamental Rights and the Rule of Law' emphasised the importance of "mak[ing] full use of existing mechanisms and cooperate with other relevant EU and international bodies, particularly with the Council of Europe, in view of its key role in relation to promotion and protection of human rights, democracy and the Rule of Law, in order to avoid overlaps."[83]

Referring specifically, to proposals which called for a EU Framework on the Rule of Law to be established, the Committee of Ministers stressed in February 2014 that it "fully supports the efforts deployed by the Secretary General, who has intensified his political consultations with the EU institutions, emphasising in particular the message that a possible future EU framework should take into account the instruments and expertise of the Council of Europe and co-operate closely with it."[84]

---

[80] Council of Europe and the European Union, *Memorandum of Understanding between the Council of Europe and the European Union*, paragraph 23.

[81] Ibid, paragraph 23–24.

[82] Committee of Ministers, 'Report on co-operation between the Council of Europe and the European Union' 12 May 2017, CM(2017)28-final.

[83] Council of the European Union, *Conclusions on Fundamental Rights and the Rule of Law*, June 2013.

[84] In its reply to Parliamentary Assembly Recommendation 2027 (2013).

The Council of Europe welcomed the European Commission's understanding of the Framework as a complementary component to "all the existing mechanisms already in place at the level of the Council of Europe to protect the Rule of Law."[85] During the assessment phase of the Rule of Law Framework, the Commission may refer to the expertise of different parties where necessary, including the Council of Europe's Venice Commission. The Communication from the Commission on the Rule of Law Framework noted that the European Commission "will as a rule and in appropriate cases seek the advice of the Council of Europe and/or its Venice Commission."[86] The Commission reiterated and developed these ideas in two further communications issued in April[87] and July 2019.[88] It notably committed to the "strengthen[ing] cooperation with the Council of Europe, including the Venice Commission and GRECO, and explore further support to it in relation to EU priorities on the rule of law."[89]

One might be tempted to argue that the more instruments and institutions there are to protect and promote the Rule of Law, the better for the purpose of ensuring that governments act in conformity with the Rule of Law. In October 2016, the European Parliament endorsed the Committee on Civil Liberties, Justice and Home Affair's legislative initiative report calling for the establishment of a new binding mechanism to monitor the Rule of Law, democracy and the fundamental rights' situation in Europe. The mechanism aims to ensure compliance with EU values through preventative, corrective and sanctioning measures. It is composed of four core elements: an annual European report to identify possible breaches (the European DRF report) which includes country-specific and general recommendations, an annual inter-parliamentary debate on the abovementioned report, proposals to remedy possible risks and violations as provided for by the relevant treaties, and lastly a monitoring cycle (DRF policy cycle) within the main EU institutions. Whilst the Commission expressed its support for the Parliament's objective, particularly the fostering of an inter-parliamentary dialogue on democracy, the Rule of Law and fundamental rights, it was more sceptical of the need and feasibility of an annual independent expert report on the Rule of Law.[90]

In addition to the Commission's hesitant appraisal of the EP's initiative, one must not ignore the genuine risk of a duplication of standards and actors, which may lead to serious inconsistencies and forum-shopping practices, an outcome that cannot be seen to be in the interest of either citizens or governments. As a means of avoiding

---

[85]Communication from the Commission to the European Parliament and the Council a New EU Framework to Strengthen the Rule of Law, COM/2014/0158 final of 11 March 2014, page 6.

[86]Ibid, page 9.

[87]'Further Strengthening the Rule of Law within the Union - State of play and possible next steps' COM(2019)163 final of 3 April 2019.

[88]'Strengthening the rule of law within the Union - A blueprint for action' COM(2019) 343 final of 17 July 2019.

[89]Ibid, page 8.

[90]Communication from the Commission to the European Parliament and the Council a New EU Framework to Strengthen the Rule of Law *supra* (note 87) page 6.

such overlaps, the Council and the relevant European institutions abide by a general policy of cooperation such as exemplified by the European Commission and the CEPEJ, where the EU justice scoreboard relies upon the information provided by the CEPEJ, thereby avoiding any potential duplication and confirming the CEPEJ's status as a common reference point for justice evaluations. The DRF report similarly refers to "cooperation envisaged with the Council of Europe and other bodies."[91] In April 2019, the Parliamentary Assembly examined 'the establishment of a European Union mechanism on democracy, the rule of law and fundamental rights'. The Assembly voiced concern "that, in the long run, the variety of the rule of law related initiatives involving different European Union institutions may jeopardise both the Memorandum of Understanding's declared objective of ensuring the coherence of the standard-setting system in Europe, and the complementarity and efficiency of mechanisms in upholding the shared values of human rights, democracy and the rule of law which exist within the two institutions with regard to States which are members of both the Council of Europe and the European Union."[92] The Assembly invited the European Union, in the framework of its existing procedures and its initiatives to ensure compliance with the values guaranteed in Article 2 of the Treaty on European Union, to:

- "support the effective application of benchmarks at European level, using the Council of Europe's 'rule of law standards', including the case law of the European Court of Human Rights, relevant recommendations of the Committee of Ministers, standards and opinions of the Venice Commission (including the 'Rule of Law Checklist') and recommendations, opinions and/or conclusions of other relevant Council of Europe bodies;
- use the available reports, opinions or recommendations of the Council of Europe's advisory or monitoring bodies, not only citing them as references in the documents produced by the European Union bodies, but taking into account the conclusions of these bodies in the assessment by the institutions of the European Union to determine whether a rule of law issue has arisen, as well as to guide proposals for any action to be taken;
- when assessing whether a rule of law deficiency has been remedied or has ceased to exist, liaise with the relevant Council of Europe bodies which issued the opinion or the recommendation to ensure consistency of views and conclusions. The initiative for political action in the event of alleged non-compliance with the European Union legal framework would remain with the European Union, with the Council of Europe offering legal and technical assessment in accordance with its monitoring or advisory bodies' competences;
- provide for safeguards in all mechanisms of the European Union to ensure that the assessment or action of the European Union will not affect existing procedures arising from Council of Europe advisory or monitoring mechanisms, along

[91]Ibid, page 7.

[92]Parliamentary Assembly, *Establishment of a European Union Mechanism on Democracy, the Rule of Law and Fundamental Rights*, Recommendation 2151 (2019), paragraph 7.

similar lines to Article 53 of the Charter of Fundamental Rights of the European Union."[93]

With the next Commission, headed by Ursula von der Leyen due to take office at the end of 2019, Brussels has indicated that it intends to remain tough on the Rule of Law. In turn, the joint Belgian-German proposal, to subject all EU countries to an annual Rule of Law monitoring procedure has been favourably received by the Commission[94] and presents an excellent opportunity to establish new modes of collaboration and mutual-reinforcement between the Council of Europe and the European Union.

6 Concluding Remarks

The Council of Europe is neither rich nor particularly powerful. In 2019, the Council of Europe's budget totalled some € 437 million. If divided between every single European citizen, this would amount to less than € 2 per person, as much as a cup of coffee, which leads one to conclude that the Council is, on the balance of probabilities, a worthwhile investment.

First and foremost, the Council does not embody one particular political or governmental vision but draws upon the experiences, skills and knowhow of the national experts from 47 member States. Somehow, almost paradoxically, its comparative weakness as a political actor provides legitimacy in relation to the formulation of legal standards and recommendations and thus the Council is perceived as a more neutral political actor than for example, the European Union.

These attributes allow the Council to engage in a dialogue with its member States and to openly and constructively address emerging issues in order to avoid division. The Council's main working asset is its credibility and trust acquired through 70 years of successful cooperation. Indeed, it this deep cooperation between the Council of Europe and the EU which is necessary for the promotion and safeguarding of the Rule of Law. In order to properly function, both institutions require that their respective members share a common understanding of the values and principles which define the Rule of Law.

Various forms of successful cooperation on Rule of Law related issues are already taking place, including most notably the Venice Commission, Group of States against Corruption (GRECO), the CEPEJ and the work undertaken by the Human Rights Commissioner. Thus, any initiative to set up new Rule of Law related mechanisms within the EU should take into account the existing Council of Europe

[93]Parliamentary Assembly, *Establishment of a European Union Mechanism on Democracy, the Rule of Law and Fundamental Rights*, Resolution 2273 (2019), paragraph 16.1–16.4.

[94]European Commission Press Release, "Strengthening the Rule of Law through increased awareness, an annual monitoring cycle and more effective enforcement" (17 July 2019) https://ec.europa.eu/commission/presscorner/detail/en/IP_19_4169.

instruments, in particular the Rule of Law Checklist. The fact that the Council's mechanisms are not limited to the EU-28 but practically cover the entire continent should not be regarded as a weakness but rather as a strength, as this provides for a more consistent approach to the Rule of Law.

The existing cooperative relationship between the Council and the EU should be strengthened by increasing the EU's contribution in order to ensure that the conclusions and recommendations of the Council's Rule of Law mechanisms are implemented by the EU's Member States. Secondly, the EU could join a number of selected mechanisms as a full member, such as GRECO[95] or the Venice Commission and thereby fully utilise the Council's instruments with a view of better safeguarding the Rule of Law within the EU, particularly in situations where the EU's competences are limited. Lastly, for the purpose of upholding the Rule of Law within Europe, it is of the upmost importance that the EU finally makes good on its promises and accedes to the ECHR.

The resilience of the Polish democracy must not be underestimated. Poland has one of the oldest democratic traditions in Europe with a written constitution dating back to the 3 May 1791, which is widely considered to be Europe's first codified constitution (and the world's second). According to King Stanisław August Poniatowski, it was "founded principally on those of England and the United States of America, but avoiding the faults and errors of both, and adapted as much as possible to the local and particular circumstances of the country."[96]

Whereas the transition towards democracy was a peaceful one for most countries behind the iron curtain, the price paid by civil society in Romania was a particularly high one. It is perhaps for this reason that the Romanian people have taken to the streets in their tens of thousands to protest against the Rule of Law backsliding of their country. Prompted by the largest street protests since the fall of Communism, President Klaus Iohannis decided to couple the recent European elections with a referendum on the controversial justice reforms. Romanian's were asked: "1). Do you agree with banning amnesty and pardon for corruption offenses? 2). Do you agree with banning the adoption by the Government of emergency ordinances in the area of crimes, punishment and judiciary organizations, and with extending the right to challenge ordinances directly at the Constitutional Court." An overwhelming 84% answered in the affirmative. If anything, the situation in Romania demonstrates the importance of a strong, engaged and informed civil society for the protection of the Rule of Law and democratic values.

Whatever constitution a country chooses to adopt, checks and balances between State powers remain crucial for every democracy. A modern constitution has to guarantee both effective democratic decision-making according to the majorities' will and the protection of individuals and minorities against the dangers of a

---

[95] On 10 July 2019, the EU has been granted observer status with GRECO, see Committee of Ministers' decision CM/Del/Dec(2019)1351bis/11.1.

[96] Barentine (2015), p. 394.

majoritarian rule.[97] In that context, the role of an independent judiciary cannot be overstated. Their work reinforces democracy and promotes the Rule of Law by guaranteeing free elections, clearing the political space for the freedom of association, expression and religion, combating discrimination, and enabling political change. Therefore, whilst Poland and Romania are free to reform their judicial systems, they should do so in a manner which is consistent with the Rule of Law and does not threaten the independence of the judiciary, the separation of powers, the principle of *res judicata* or legal certainty.

References

Barentine CJ (2015) The lost constellations: a history of obsolete, extinct, or forgotten star lore. Springer International Publishing, New York

Carrera S, Guild E, Hernanz N (2013) The triangular relationship between fundamental rights, democracy and the rule of law in the EU. Available via https://www.ceps.eu/ceps-publications/triangular-relationship-between-fundamental-rights-democracy-and-rule-law-eu-towards-eu/. Accessed 21 Aug 2019

Drzemczewski A (2018) European Commission for democracy through law (Venice Commission). Human Rights Law J 37:184–198

Evans P, Silk P (2013) The Parliamentary assembly – practice and procedure, 11th edn. Council of Europe, Strasbourg

Gardner D (6 April 2017) A breach between Turkey and the EU that suits both sides, Financial Times. p. 6

Grimm D (2016) Europa ja – aber welches? Zur Verfassung der europäischen Demokratie. Verlag C.H. Beck, Munich

Huber P (2016) The principle of proportionality. In: Schroeder W (ed) Strengthening the rule of law in Europe, 1st edn. Hart Publishing, Oxford, p 111

Lübbe-Wolff G (2019) 'Richterwahlen in der Schweiz: Wo liegt das Problem?' VerfBlog, Available via https://verfassungsblog.de/richterwahlen-in-der-schweiz-wo-liegt-das-problem/. Accessed 26 Aug 2019

Polakiewicz J, Sandvig J (2016) The Council of Europe and the rule of law. In: Schroeder W (ed) Strengthening the rule of law in Europe, 1st edn. Hart Publishing, Oxford, pp 115–134

Steiner E (2016) The rule of law in the jurisprudence of the European Court of Human Rights. In: Schroeder W (ed) Strengthening the rule of law in Europe, 1st edn. Hart Publishing, Oxford, p 154

Jörg Polakiewicz is a Professor at the *Europainstitut* of the University of Saarbrücken and Director of Legal Advice and Public International Law (Legal Adviser), Council of Europe. This contribution was written in a strictly personal capacity and does not necessarily reflect the official position of the Council of Europe.

[97] Huber (2016), p. 111.

Julia Katharina Kirchmayr holds a Master of Laws from the University of Edinburgh and is a Legal Officer at the European Commission. This contribution was written in a strictly personal capacity and does not necessarily reflect the official position of the European Commission.

Part III
Dissecting the LM Case

A Potential Constitutional Moment for the European Rule of Law: The Importance of Red Lines

Armin von Bogdandy, Piotr Bogdanowicz, Iris Canor, Giacomo Rugge, Matthias Schmidt, and Maciej Taborowski

Contents

Abstract This contribution deals with the current European rule of law crisis. It does so by analyzing the recent CJEU's judgment in re *LM* and by considering its possible ramifications for the future of the rule of law in the EU. In particular, it is argued that, as a result of this judgment, the European rule of law as provided for by Art. 2 TEU has become a legally enforceable value. The CJEU has indeed made clear that this value features a set of minimum standards that the Member States cannot bluntly disregard. In the present context, which is characterized by the inaction of the supranational and national political institutions, a prominent role in safeguarding a liberal understanding of the European rule of law is played by the

An earlier version has been published in the Common Market Law Review.

A. von Bogdandy (✉) · G. Rugge · M. Schmidt
Max Planck Institute for Comparative Public Law and International Law, Heidelberg, Germany
e-mail: sekreavb@mpil.de; rugge@mpil.de; mschmidt@mpil.de

P. Bogdanowicz · M. Taborowski
Faculty of Law and Administration, University of Warsaw, Warsaw, Poland
e-mail: p.bogdanowicz@wpia.uw.edu.pl; maciej.taborowski@brpo.gov.pl

I. Canor
School of Law, Zefat Academic College, Sefad, Israel

School of Law, College of Management, Rishon Le Zion, Israel
e-mail: canor@colman.ac.il

A. von Bogdandy et al. (eds.), *Defending Checks and Balances in EU Member States*, Beiträge zum ausländischen öffentlichen Recht und Völkerrecht 298,
https://doi.org/10.1007/978-3-662-62317-6_15

entire European judiciary (the so-called '*Gerichtsverbund*'), including national courts and tribunals.

1 What Is at Stake?

The Union's 'rule of law crisis' is a multi-faceted phenomenon.[1] Of particular concern are Member States where ruling majorities wilfully uproot the separation of powers. The current focus is very much on Poland. The Polish government has taken extensive measures that have undermined the independence of the Constitutional Tribunal. It has strengthened its influence on the National Council of the Judiciary, which selects the judges. It has dismissed more than 150 (out of 700) presidents and vice presidents of ordinary courts. It has forced almost 40% of Supreme Court judges to retire.[2] It has raised the overall number of Supreme Court judges, thereby creating the need for up to 70 new nominations. It has established a new disciplinary chamber as well as an extraordinary appeals procedure before the Supreme Court, which has the potential to subdue independent-minded judges.[3] Yet other Member States should not be forgotten either, such as Hungary. The latter is even said to have become a rather hopeless case—with some involuntary help from Brussels, e.g., through its funds.[4] Hopefully, the recent adoption by the European Parliament of a reasoned proposal under Article 7 (1) TEU will help improve the situation in Hungary. But, should these authoritarian measures remain unopposed, it will be hard to argue in the future that they are at odds with the European values as enshrined in Article 2 TEU.[5]

European institutions have started to react far more determinedly than in the Hungarian case. This is to be welcomed. At the same time, the European reactions raise the stakes dramatically. We might even witness a 'constitutional moment'. This term indicates a situation that deeply impacts on the future path of a constitutional

[1]Editorial Comments (2015), pp. 619, 625–627; Editorial Comments (2016), p. 597; Editorial Comments (2017), p. 1309; on the academic debate Bonelli (2017), p. 793.

[2]COM(2017) 835 final, 'European Commission, Reasoned Proposal in accordance with Article 7 (1) of the Treaty on European Union regarding the rule of law in Poland: Proposal for a Council Decision on the determination of a clear risk of a serious breach by the Republic of Poland of the rule of law', at p. 21, para. 116.

[3]Act on the Supreme Court of 8 December 2017, Journal of Laws (2018), item no. 5.

[4]For a dire picture, Charlemagne, The Economist, April 5, 2018. Halmai (2018), p. 85. See also European Parliament, Committee on Civil Liberties, Justice and Home Affairs, 25th June 2018 (Result of roll-call votes), http://www.europarl.europa.eu/committees/en/libe/votes-in-committee.html.

[5]See for a comprehensive description Matczak (2018); 'Opinion on the Draft Act amending the Act on the National Council of the judiciary; on the Draft Act amending the Act on the Supreme Court, proposed by the President of Poland, and on the Act on the organisation of ordinary courts', adopted by the Commission at its 113th Plenary Session (Venice, 8-9 December 2017), http://www.venice.coe.int/webforms/documents/default.aspx?pdffile=CDL-AD(2017)031-e.

order without formally amending it.[6] At issue is whether illiberal democracies become part of the European public order as laid out in Article 2 TEU, or are opposed by it. In any event, the consequences could be truly far-reaching. In the first case, the conventional self-understanding of Europe cannot be maintained any longer, because the European rule of law would cover—and thus legitimize—what is currently happening in Poland and Hungary. This would have tremendous implications, for example for the European stance towards critical developments in other Member States or the Union's external policy (Turkey!). In the second case, the European rule of law would be supplemented by 'red lines'. That would also amount to a 'constitutional moment' because it would add substance and bite to the European values.

To advance the second case, the European institutions are to be commended for reacting fiercely. The Commission's actions, in particular its Article 7 TEU proposal, merit support, also for good legal reasons. At the same time, much will depend on the judicial branch. It is indeed no coincidence that a first, important opportunity to draw such red lines has arisen in the context of legal proceedings, more precisely in the context of what is now known as the *LM* case.[7] Initiated by the Irish High Court through a request for a preliminary ruling, this case concerned the interpretation of Article 1(3) of the European Arrest Warrant Framework Decision (hereinafter: EAW Framework Decision). More specifically, the Irish judge asked whether that provision of the Framework Decision could be so construed as to exclude the execution of a EAW in case of 'cogent evidence that conditions in the issuing Member State are incompatible with the fundamental right to a fair trial because the system of justice itself in the issuing Member State is no longer operating under the rule of law'.

This case will be analysed in greater detail in what follows. It has to be said, though, that no European political measure or judicial decision can, by or of itself, restore the separation of powers in a Member State. They can only contribute to Polish self-healing through its internal constitutional process. However, their importance is not limited to this, as they are crucial for upholding European liberal constitutionalism in the rest of the Union. In fact, it is in this light that the *LM* case must be read. But before examining the case, some introductory remarks are in order.

[6]Ackerman (1991), Vol 1, 6. Note that the original articulation of this term by Ackerman has a more specific meaning. For further analysis, Klarman (1992), pp. 759–797.

[7]Case C-216/18 PPU, *Reference for a preliminary ruling from the High Court (Ireland) made on 27 March 2018 – Minister for Justice and Equality v LM*, (pending), http://www.courts.ie/Judgments.nsf/0/FD843302847F2E228025825D00457F19. This case is based on a referral from the Irish High Court 2013 295 EXT;2014 8 EXT; 2017 291 EXT *The Minister for Justice and Equality v. Celmer*, [2018] IEHC 119, http://www.courts.ie/Judgments.nsf/0/578DD3A9A33247A38025824F0057E747. See also Case C-216/18 PPU, *Reference for a preliminary ruling from the High Court (Ireland) made on 27 March 2018 — Minister for Justice and Equality v LM*, Opinion of Advocate General Tanchev, ECLI:EU:C:2018:517. 28th June 2018.

2 Operationalizing the Value of the Rule of Law

By now, much has happened to operationalize—i.e., interpret, apply and even impose—the rule-of-law value. Confuting many who consider the rule-of-law value of Article 2 TEU an all too vague political statement, the guardians of the Treaties have developed it in a way that allows for a juridical assessment of Member States' activities. To be clear, the institutions have not set out to demarcate the value by creating definitions that can be applied in a formalistic manner, but have rather linked the value of the rule of law to well-established principles. Their application requires much contextualization and circumspection and will inevitably contain political, i.e., discretionary, evaluative and opportunistic, elements. But that is the path of the law, in particular when it comes to 'constitutional moments'.

A ground-breaking contribution to the operationalization of the rule-of-law value can be found in the CJEU's recent decision in the case of *Associação Sindical dos Juízes Portugueses* (*ASJP*). Its interpretation of Article 19 TEU covers the institutional dimension of domestic judicial independence.[8] The European rule of law has thus become justiciable vis-à-vis the Member States.[9] The Commission contributes to this development by compiling relevant principles into a sensible whole, in particular in its Rule of Law Framework.[10] It relies on many sources: the Court's rulings, but also decisions and opinions of other institutions, in particular the European Court of Human Rights and the European Commission for Democracy through Law (the Venice Commission). Such a broad spectrum contributes significantly to the legitimacy of its endeavour.

The Commission's Rule of Law Framework is an important step with regard not only for the interpretation but also, possibly, for the normativity of the rule of law. Although it shows some weaknesses, for example by making it almost indistinguishable from the values of democracy and human rights, it seems a convincing operationalization that is in tune with the *acquis* of European public law. The Commission has reiterated the Framework's interpretation in its Reasoned Proposal under Article 7(1) TEU regarding the Rule of Law in Poland.[11] Moreover, it referred to the rule-of-law value in its 2018 Justice Scoreboard for 'monitoring of justice reforms at EU level' as well as in its last Country Report on Poland under the European Semester.[12] The Commission's recent regulation proposal on 'the

---

[8]CJEU, Case C-64/16, *Associação Sindical dos Juízes Portugueses*, ECLI:EU:C:2018:117.

[9]CJEU, Case C-477/16 PPU, *Kovalkovas*, ECLI:EU:C:2016:861; Case C-452/16 PPU, *Poltorak*, ECLI:EU:C:2016:858.

[10]COM(2014) 158 final/2, 'European Commission, Communication from the Commission to the European Parliament and the Council: A new EU framework to strengthen the rule of law' p. 4, and Annex I.

[11]*Supra* note 2, p. 1, para. 1.

[12]SWD(2018) 219 final, 'Commission Staff Working Document, Country Report Poland 2018 accompanying the document Communication from the Commission to the European Parliament, the Council, the European Central Bank and the Eurogroup: 2018 European Semester: Assessment

protection of the Union's budget in case of generalised deficiencies as regards the rule of law in the Member States' even provides a definition for the threshold of 'generalised deficiencies' of the rule of law.[13] Operationalization can also be helped by a newly suggested 'Justice, Rights and Values' Fund with a total volume of 947 million euros.[14] Already in force—albeit not yet enforced—is the Union's Regulation on European Political Parties, which permits reviewing whether a European party complies with Article 2 TEU.[15]

Notwithstanding a number of doctrinal issues that remain open, at least the basis for legally assessing Member States using the rule-of-law value is now fairly well-established. From the Polish 'White Paper on the Judiciary', one can deduce that not even the Polish government puts that into question, since it defends its measures on the merits of the European rule of law.[16] The impressive rebuttal of that 'White Paper' by the Polish Judges Association as well as by the Polish Supreme Court also shows a well-established juridical link between the vague rule-of-law value and crucial features of the domestic judiciaries.[17] The European rule of law has thus become an operational principle in European political and legal controversies.

3 The Political Branch in Troubled Waters

Opposing the Polish measures is extremely sensitive because it implies going against a democratically elected government that is transforming basic features of its constitutional order. For that reason it is to be welcomed that the European political

---

of progress on structural reforms, prevention and correction of macroeconomic imbalances, and results of in-depth reviews under Regulation (EU) No 1176/2011', p. 3, 29.

[13]COM(2018) 324 final, 'European Commission, Proposal for a Regulation of the European Parliament and of the Council on the protection of the Union's budget in case of generalised deficiencies as regards the rule of law in the Member States', at Art. 2(b).

[14]COM(2018) 321 final, 'Annex to the Communication from the Commission to the European Parliament, the European Council, the Council, the European Economic and Social Committee and the Committee of the Regions, A modern budget for a Union that protects, empowers and defends: The multiannual financial framework for 2021-2027', p. 48.

[15]OJ 2011 L 317/1, 'Regulation (EU, EURATOM) No. 1141/2014 of the European Parliament and of the Council of 22 October 2014 on the statute and funding of European political parties and European political foundations', at Art. 3(1)c, Art. 6(1).

[16]Chancellery of the Prime Minister of Poland, 'White Paper on the Reform of the Polish Judiciary', 7 March 2018, https://www.premier.gov.pl/files/files/white_paper_en_full.pdf, para. 166.

[17]Iustitia (Polish Judges Association), 'Response to the White Paper Compendium on the reforms of the Polish justice system, presented by the Government of the Republic of Poland to the European Commission', 17 March 2018, https://twojsad.pl/wp-content/uploads/2018/03/iustitia-response-whitepaper.pdf; Gersdorf (First President of the Supreme Court), 'Opinion on the White Paper on the reform of the Polish judiciary, 16 March 2018, https://archiwumosiatynskiego.pl/images/2018/04/Supreme-Court-Opinion-on-the-white-paper-on-the-Reform-of-the-Polish-Judiciary.pdf.

branch has become active. Since the lessons have been learnt from the miserable action national governments undertook against Austria in 2000, the institutional activities are so far concentrated in the Council of Europe's and the Union's institutions. The European Commission in particular tries to position itself as a defender of European values, thereby responding to the harsh criticism levelled against its earlier reluctance. In the Polish case, it has deployed two core instruments for the first time. This is significant in and of itself, as the first usage of an instrument often impacts on its further utilisation. Unfortunately, there is a clear and serious risk of failure, with a possibly calamitous impact on the European rule of law.

One instrument is the Commission's already mentioned 'Rule of Law Framework' of 2014, which was designed as an instrument whose quick implementation can avoid escalating the situation into Article 7 TEU territory. Read as an '*a maiore ad minus*' approach that is permissible under Article 7(1) TEU and Article 292 TFEU,[18] it provides the Commission with a procedure for engaging—through an opinion and later recommendations—in a dialogue with a Member State in case of an observed 'systemic threat to the rule of law'. To date, the use of the Framework has not yielded tangible results, which casts much doubt on the instrument's capacity to impose results. Despite several Commission's recommendations, the Polish authorities have not undertaken any remedial action and have merely made some minor concessions of an illusory nature and clearly no practical consequence.

The Commission then introduced the second instrument to show it 'meant business'. On 20 December 2017, it launched the procedure under Article 7 (1) TEU for the first time ever. It finds that there is a clear risk of a serious breach of the rule of law in Poland, indicates rather precisely which steps need to be taken, and asks that the Council recommend Poland take such steps.[19] It hereby confutes a statement by its former President Barroso, who depicted Article 7 TEU as the 'nuclear option',[20] a statement that evidently delegitimizes the use of this instrument. The legitimacy of its use is corroborated by the European Parliament[21] as well as the Committee of the Regions,[22] which support the Commission and call upon the Council to quickly follow up on the Commission's action.

The Commission's proposal merits close attention. It is detailed and extensive. It integrates the findings of other institutions, such as the Council of Europe or the

[18]Giegerich (2015), pp. 499, 535–536. For the opposing view, 10296/14 Legal Service of the Council, 'Commission's Communication on a new EU Framework to strengthen the rule of law: – compatibility with the Treaties', 27 May 2014, http://data.consilium.europa.eu/doc/document/ST-10296-2014-INIT/en/pdf.

[19]*Supra* note 2.

[20]SPEECH/13/684, Barroso (President of the European Commission), 'State of the Union address 2013', 11 September 2013, http://europa.eu/rapid/press-release_SPEECH-13-684_en.htm.

[21]P8_TA-PROV(2018)0055, 'European Parliament resolution of 1 March 2018 on the Commission's decision to activate Article 7(1) TEU as regards the situation in Poland (2018/2541(RSP)'.

[22]RESOL-VI/30, 6391/18, 'Determination of a clear risk of a serious breach by Poland of rule of law – Resolution of the European Committee of the Regions of 22 February 2018'.

United Nations as well as civil-society organizations.[23] This fends off accusations that the findings are partisan. By demonstrating that many institutions share its findings, the Commission makes itself the voice of a broad institutional alliance. At the same time, it underlines the legal dimension of the issue by making its proposal resemble a reasoned opinion in infringement proceedings. The Commission's proposal thus evidently aims to be two things at the same time: a convincing *political* value judgment as well as a *legally* sound analysis. This is not paradoxical; rather, it corresponds to how political institutions should decide.

The legal reasoning of the Commission as to why there is a clear risk of serious breach might appear somewhat 'thin', as it does not really develop what the threshold requires. However, one needs to consider that institutional developments towards an authoritarian regime are regularly hard to grasp from a legal standpoint because legal analysis focusses on individual acts. Taken individually, such measures lend themselves more easily to justification (although most of the Polish measures against the Constitutional Tribunal seem rather clear cases).[24] Indeed the Polish government tries to defend its measures through legal comparison with 'unsuspicious' countries.[25] Therefore, to convincingly determine a 'clear risk of a serious breach' of an Article 2 TEU value, all Polish measures affecting the judiciary must be considered together, with due regard to the overall political and social conditions in the country. Such determination inevitably entails an important discretionary and evaluative dimension, which strictly doctrinal arguments cannot fully guide.

It is now for the Council to act, which would require the approval of four fifths of its members, i.e., 22 Member States. The Council has debated the matter in the General Affairs Council on numerous occasions, most recently in April.[26] But it is distinctly possible that the Council will not decide on the matter, for instance in order to keep the Union united in difficult times (just consider Brexit!). However, such an omission could be used as an argument that the Council—and hence the Member States—do not deem the policies of the Polish government, in particular the changes to the Polish judiciary identified in the Commission's Proposal, an infringement of Article 2 TEU. Accordingly, such policies could more easily be presented as conforming to the founding values of the European Union. They could possibly even be considered an expression of the European rule of law. However, it should not be forgotten that there are also the courts. As so often in European crises, much will depend on the Court of Justice of the European Union as well as on the domestic courts—in short, on the entire judiciary in the European legal space.

[23] *Supra* note 2, para. 183 and the respective footnotes.

[24] Iustitia, *supra* note 17, p. 92; Venice Commission, 'Opinion on Amendments to the Act of 25 June 2015 on the Constitutional Tribunal of Poland', Opinion no. 833/2015, CDL-AD(2016) 001, paras. 126, 137, 138.

[25] 'White Paper on the Reform of the Polish Judiciary', *supra* note 16. But see also the rebuttal *supra* note 17.

[26] General Affairs Council, 'Rule of law in Poland', 9 April 2019: https://www.consilium.europa.eu/media/39196/st08130-en19.pdf.

4 The Judicial Branch: 'I Love You, Like I Love Ireland'

Contrary to the Council, courts cannot refrain from making a decision. What might help the courts is the realisation that they will be heavily criticised regardless of how they adjudicate the Polish situation.[27] Still, the courts should seize any opportunity to draw red lines for the European rule of law.[28] Within the complex European judicial system, it is for the CJEU to decide if Poland infringes a European value. Domestic courts should decide this issue only if the CJEU does not do so.

The CJEU might be called upon either via infringement proceedings initiated by the Commission or via preliminary-ruling requests referred to it by national courts, i.e., in top-down or bottom-up proceedings. The traditional path for judicially supervising the Member States is the infringement proceedings, the standard interaction between the two guardians of the Treaties. The infringement procedure should hence also play a vital part in the rule-of-law crisis.[29] The values in Article 2 TEU are subject to the Court's jurisdiction and thus to its mandate to ensure that 'the law is observed' (Article 19(1) TEU), and the Court now seems ready to use this mandate.[30] Article 7 TEU does not preclude parallel infringement proceedings, as the *Van Gend en Loos* precedent exemplifies.[31] How to frame a possible case is more problematic; after all, the Polish situation is triggered by a combination of measures that are as diverse as they are numerous. However, the Court has already held that it can use infringement proceedings to make a finding of general and continuous deficiencies in a Member State,[32] thereby overcoming its normal focus on an individual and concrete setting.

If infringement proceedings are therefore legally viable, one should nevertheless consider that it is a mighty burden for the CJEU to have to decide whether the Polish measures violate the European rule of law. However, this burden can be shared among several courts if the issue is handled via a preliminary-ruling procedure, as

---

[27] The new Vice President of the Polish Constitutional Tribunal has already stated that he would consider any CJEU decision against Poland illegitimate, Muszyński (2018).

[28] The Advocate General in the case indeed addresses the Polish situation. However, he does so only in terms of human rights and thereby fails to fully meet the challenge, *supra* note 7, para. 39.

[29] The Commission initiated two successfull infringement procedures based on Article 19(1) TEU and Article 47 CFR against Poland, see Case C-619/18, *Commission v. Poland (Indépendance de la Cour suprême)*, ECLI:EU:C:2019:531 and Case C-192/18, *Commission v. Poland (Indépendance des juridictions de droit commun)*, ECLI:EU:C:2019:924. A further infringement procedure is currently pending before the Court, see Case C-791/19, *Commission v. Poland.* See also the pending infringement proceedings against Hungary, Case C-66/18, *Commission v. Hungary (Enseignement supérieur)* and Case C-78/18, *Commission v. Hungary (Transparence associative).*

[30] *Supra* note 8. In the infringement proceedings against Hungary concerning judicial independence, (Case C-286/12, *Commission v. Hungary*, ECLI:EU:C:2012:687) the Commission and the Court were criticized for framing and deciding the case on the grounds of discrimination rather than Article 2 TEU, Halmai (2017), p. 471.

[31] Case C-26/62, *Van Gend en Loos* v. *Administratie der Belastingen*, ECLI:EU:C:1963:1. In detail, Scheppele (2016), p. 105.

[32] Case C-494/01, *Commission* v. *Ireland*, ECLI:EU:C:2005:250, para. 36.

the CJEU then responds to the concerns of national courts. Deciding the issue in a preliminary-ruling procedure would also continue the European tradition that most decisions of deep constitutional impact are taken in the European *Gerichtsverbund*, the European union of courts. Indeed, the *LM*[33] case, which was referred to the CJEU by the Irish High Court, is a first example. As the vivid Polish reactions to this referral show,[34] it has the potential to become a landmark decision on the issue.

The *LM* case originates from a negative appraisal made by the Irish judicial authority as regards the rule of law in Poland. In other terms, it has its origins in a country with which Poland has always had a special relationship. A big hit of Polish rock music of the 1990s, with the title 'I love you, like I love Ireland', is a perfect example of that relationship. As the main vocalist of the group 'Kobranocka' affirmed, 'Ireland [...] had a similar history, just like us they fought for independence. We loved them for that. I loved them and love them to this day.'[35] In Polish, to 'love somebody like Ireland' means to love someone deeply. Apart from this curious note, the referral in the *LM* case demonstrates, in broader terms, that it is inevitable that national courts become involved to vindicate the rule of law in the European legal space.[36]

The concrete problem addressed in the preliminary reference was whether Ireland may refuse to surrender a Polish citizen to Poland following a European arrest warrant (EAW) because of a systemic deficiency in the rule of law in that Member State. More specifically, through its referral, the Irish High Court asked the CJEU to interpret Article 1(3) of the EAW Framework Decision, which lays down the obligation to comply with fundamental rights when executing a European arrest warrant.[37] In formulating its questions, the referring court made clear that, in its opinion, the recent reforms of the Polish judiciary jeopardize some fundamental values, such as 'the independence of the judiciary and respect for the Constitution', and amount to 'systemic breaches of the rule of law' as well as 'fundamental defects in the system of justice',[38] thereby prospecting a real risk for the protection of the individual's fundamental right to a fair trial. In the circumstances, instead of asking the CJEU to assess the compatibility of the Polish reforms with the European rule of

[33] *Supra* note 8.

[34] See in this respect the statement of the Association of Judges of Ireland in defence of the referring judge https://aji.ie/communications/press-release-2018-03-15/.

[35] Interview with the leader of 'Kobranocka', Andrzej Kraiński, http://gazetapraca.pl/gazetapraca/1,68946,3425292.html (in Polish only).

[36] Canor (2013), p. 383.

[37] O.J. 2002, L 190/1 'Council Framework Decision 2002/584/JHA of 13 June 2002 on the European arrest warrant and the surrender procedures between Member States' as amended by O.J. 2009, L81/24, 'Council Framework Decision 2009/299/JHA amending Framework Decisions 2002/584/JHA, 2005/214/JHA, 2006/783/JHA, 2008/909/JHA and 2008/947/JHA, thereby enhancing the procedural rights of persons and fostering the application of the principle of mutual recognition to decisions rendered in the absence of the person concerned at the trial'.

[38] Joined Cases C-404/15 and C-659/15 PPU, *Aranyosi and Căldăraru*, ECLI:EU:C:2016:198, para. 140.

law, the Irish court asked whether, in situations akin to those in the case pending before it, judicial authorities can refrain from executing a EAW or whether, similarly to how decided in the *Aranyosi and Căldăraru* judgment, they need to carry out a specific and precise assessment as to the exposure of the individual concerned to the risk of unfair trial.

It is worth recalling that, in the *Aranyosi and Căldăraru* judgment, the CJEU had been asked to decide on the possibility for national judges to derogate from the principles of mutual recognition and mutual trust in case of alleged violations of human rights in the Member State issuing a EAW. More specifically, the referring judge had asked the Court whether, to the extent that national judicial authorities possess 'solid evidence' that detention conditions in the issuing Member State are incompatible with fundamental rights, they may or must refuse to execute a European arrest warrant. According to the CJEU, an interpretation of the EAW Framework Decision, which takes into account the absolute prohibition of inhuman or degrading treatment or punishment as set out in Article 4 CFR, implies the obligation for the national judicial authorities not to execute a EAW. However, such a decision can be taken only if 'there are substantial grounds to believe that, following the surrender of that person to the issuing Member State, he will run a real risk of being subject in that Member State to inhuman or degrading treatment'.

In other words, national judicial authorities must run a two-phase test. For starters, they need to assess whether there are systemic or generalised deficiencies as regards the detention conditions in the prison system of the issuing Member State. This appraisal must rely on 'information that is objective, reliable, specific and properly updated', including—but not limited to—'judgments of the ECtHR, judgments of courts of the issuing Member State, and also decisions, reports and other documents produced by bodies of the Council of Europe or under the aegis of the UN'. Then, national judicial authorities must 'make a further assessment, *specific and precise*, of whether there are substantial grounds to believe that the *individual concerned* will be exposed to that risk because of the conditions for his detention envisaged in the issuing Member State'. To carry out this assessment, the executing judicial authority must ask the issuing Member State for all necessary supplementary information, as provided for by Article 15(2) of the EAW Framework Decision.

Now, in the *LM* case, the Irish High Court submitted two questions to the CJEU. First of all, it asked whether, in the presence of cogent evidence of systemic violations of the rule of law in the issuing Member States, the executing judicial authority is in fact obliged to carry out a two-phase test similar to that devised in the *Aranyosi and Căldăraru* judgment. If so, the second question was if the executing judicial authority is to revert to the issuing judicial authority for any further necessary information and, as a result, 'what guarantees as to fair trial would be required'.

After summarising the facts underlying the request for a preliminary ruling and the objectives and principles governing the EAW Framework Decision, the CJEU affirmed that, according to settled case-law (i.e. *Opinion 2/13* and *Aranyosi and Căldăraru*), the principles of mutual recognition and mutual trust among Member States can be abridged only 'in exceptional circumstances'. However, unlike the *Aranyosi and Căldăraru* judgment, which concerned an absolute prohibition

(Article 4 CFR: prohibition of inhuman or degrading treatment or punishment), the *LM* case concerned the right to a fair trial. Hence the question: does a systemic violation of the right to a fair trial amount to an 'exceptional circumstance' that may justify the abridgment of the principles of mutual recognition and mutual trust? The CJEU replied in the affirmative, stating that the independence of the judiciary is part of the essence of the fundamental right to a fair trial and that the defence of the common value of the rule of law depends, in all respects, on the effective protection of that right. Thus, in case of a real risk of violation of the right to a fair trial in the issuing Member State, the executing judicial authorities must refrain, under Article 1 (3) of the EAW Framework Decision, from surrendering the requested person.

As is clear to see, the Court did not rely on the fundamental right to a fair trial, as suggested by the Advocate General, but on the rule of law value itself. Or, to put it better: the CJEU first linked the fundamental right to a fair trial to the value of the European rule of law, and it then adopted such value as normative yardstick against which to respond to the referring court. This emerges, for instance, in paragraph 50 of the judgment, where the Court referred to Article 19 TEU as 'giv[ing] concrete expression to the value of the rule of law affirmed in Article 2 TEU' and cited the precedent in *Associação Sindical dos Juízes Portugueses*. As a result, due to its being a constitutional value common to the EU and its Member States, the European rule of law must be interpreted, applied and safeguarded also by national judges.

Subsequently, the CJEU affirmed that the entire surrender procedure between Member States must be carried out under judiciary supervision and that, for this to happen, national judges must be fully independent. Thus, when the requested person argues that there are systemic or generalised deficiencies which are liable to affect the independence of the judiciary in the issuing Member State, the executing judicial authority must run a two-phase test similar to that devised in the *Aranyosi and Căldăraru* judgment.

It first has to ascertain whether, due to systemic or generalised deficiencies connected to the independence of the judiciary in the issuing Member State, there is indeed a 'real risk' that the requested person's fundamental right to a fair trial be violated. When carrying out this assessment, the executing judicial authority must rely on 'objective, reliable, specific and properly updated' material and consider both the external and the internal dimensions of independence, notably the autonomy of the judges (i.e., the absence of any hierarchical constraint and any form of subordination vis-à-vis other powers) and their impartiality (i.e., the equal distance from the parties to the proceedings and their respective interests). Should it come to the conclusion that there indeed exists a real risk, the executing judicial authority must then assess 'specifically and precisely' whether there are 'substantial grounds' for believing that the requested person will *actually* run that risk. The CJEU justified the necessity of a two-phase test by referring to recital (10) of the EAW Framework Decision. According to this recital, the mechanism of the European arrest warrant can be suspended only when the Council determines, under Article 7(2) and (3) TEU, the existence of a serious and persistent breach by one of the Member States of the principles set out in Article 2 TEU. Thus, lacking such a determination by the Council, national authorities may refrain from executing a EAW only after carrying out an individual and specific assessment of the concrete risks faced by the person concerned.

5 From the *Maastricht Urteil* to the *LM* Case

Despite the generic nature of the preliminary questions put forth by the Irish judge, the CJEU did not miss out on the opportunity to make some specific considerations on the rule of law crisis in Poland and to draw some red lines. Different reasons spoke in favour of an intervention of the Court. To begin with, it was important that these red lines were drawn in a process that itself respected these European founding values, including the right to a fair hearing. Therefore, Poland had to be granted a formal role in the proceedings and be represented by its legitimate government. A domestic court could have hardly provided for that. Second, given that the recent reforms in Poland encroach significantly on the independence of judges and that—as stated in paragraph 54 of the judgment—such independence is 'essential to the proper working of the judicial cooperation system embodied by the preliminary ruling mechanism', the dispute before the Irish High Court presented such a connection with EU law as to justify the intervention of the Court. Third, and more generally, a systemic rule of law problem with judicial independence impinges on the effectiveness of the entire EU legal system; thus, an overall European assessment of the matter was necessary.

That said, one could arguably maintain that the judgment in *re LM* is too abstract. We disagree with this argument. For instance, when explaining the first stage of the two-phase test, the Court specifies that, to assess the existence of a real risk for the rule of law value in a Member State, the executing judicial authority can rely, among other things, on the information laid down in a reasoned proposal by the Commission under Article 7(1) TEU. These acts are, according to the Court, of particular relevance for the purposes of that assessment, especially if they refer to judgments or opinions by other European and international institutions, like in the case of Poland (e.g. the United Nations Human Rights Committee, the European Council, the ECtHR, the Venice Commission etc.). This increases the soundness and legitimacy of the Commission's and, by extension, of the executing authority's findings. Moreover, as regards the disciplinary chamber mentioned in the introduction, the CJEU takes a clear stance against its compatibility with the European value of the rule of law. Finally, within the limits allowed by the specific case, the Court provides national judges with a range of criteria to be followed when carrying out the second stage of the two-phase test. The executing authorities must in fact consider the personal situation, as well as the nature of the offence for which the requested person is being prosecuted and the factual context that form the basis of the European arrest warrant.

Now, from a broader perspective, the judgment in *LM* has (at least) two distinguishing features. First, it involves overcoming the notion that the defence of the European common values is an exclusive preserve of the European political institutions under Article 7 TEU. Second, it posits a pivotal role of the individuals in the protection of the European rule of law value.

As for the first feature, the Court makes clear that the defence of the European common values is also a task for the courts, especially national courts. Consistently with its role in the preliminary ruling procedure, the CJEU does not express a conclusive opinion on the Polish reforms of the judicial system. Rather, it lets the referring court decide if—and to what extent—these reforms amount to a violation of the European rule of law value. For any such decision requires much legitimacy and is likely to be highly contested, it seems wise to share this burden among several courts, national and supranational. In that respect, one might criticize the initial 'if' in paragraph 68 of the judgment for leaving that difficult task too much on the shoulders of the national judge. After all, the formulation 'systemic and generalised deficiencies' is, for all intents and purposes, a European concept, which calls for a more incisive intervention of the CJEU.

As regards the second feature, an increased involvement of national courts implies, by extension, the empowerment of individuals in the protection of the European rule of law value. By linking this value to the essence of the fundamental right to a fair trial, the Court makes a doctrinal move similar to the one the German Federal Constitutional Court undertook in its Maastricht decision. It remains to be seen if the CJEU thereby aims at a similar position as the German court in framing the founding principles of the polity. What is clear, however, is that, from here on, 'the vigilance of the individual' is core not only for the 'supervision' of European law, as famously stated by the Court in *Van Gend en Loos*, but also of the European rule of law value. In addition, upon jointly reading the Court's judgments in *LM* and in *Associação Sindical dos Juízes Portugueses*, it clearly emerges that the European rule of law value can be used as a weapon by the very same judges whose independence is at stake. The recent request for a preliminary ruling of the Polish Supreme court bear witness to that.

At this point, the next question is what impact the *LM* judgment will have in the overall context of the rule of law crisis management. We believe that the impact of this judgment will be colossal and will by far exceed that of the *N.S.*[39] or the *Aranyosi* case.[40] These two latter cases dealt with a particular violation of a certain human right under specific circumstances. The *LM* case, by contrast, deals with a comprehensive violation of the value of the rule of law. It is about a Member State suffering from a systemic deficiency in upholding the rule of law, because the independence of the judiciary has been undermined. That could have the broadest implications and could possibly affect the fundamental principle of mutual trust on which the entire judicial cooperation in the European legal space rests. Not only will criminals not be surrendered on the basis of an EAW but asylum seekers will not be transferred on the basis of the Dublin mechanism; moreover, civil judgments

[39]Joined Cases C-411/10 and C-493/10, *N.S. and Others* v. *Secretary of State for the Home Department*, ECLI:EU:C:2011:865.

[40]*Supra* note 38.

originating from this state will possibly not be enforced by the national courts of all the other States.

By significantly reducing horizontal judicial cooperation, the *LM* case could therefore isolate Poland within the European legal space, although hopefully only temporarily. This is a harsh consequence, but a number of reasons speak for it. The respect of the rule of law value is a precondition for membership (Article 49 TEU), for mutual trust,[41] for all fundamental rights, for the entire European edifice.[42] If that is not enough: the future of the European rule of law, as Europe thought it knows it, is at stake if no one opposes the developments in Poland. All this would justify significantly reducing *horizontal* cooperation with Poland.

At the same time, this solution does not foreclose *vertical* cooperation, as it allows national courts to continue using the preliminary-ruling procedure. This is particularly important, because the CJEU and valiant Polish courts can thereby continue to fight jointly for the European rule of law or the rights of Union citizens.[43] In other words, the fact that the independence of the Polish judiciary as a system is compromised does not exclude recognizing the independence of individual courts.

The different functional logic of the preliminary ruling procedure, on the one hand, and horizontal judicial cooperation, on the other hand, allows for this distinction. In a preliminary ruling procedure, the CJEU can assess the referring court in light of its case law on judicial independence, a review that is more difficult in the case of horizontal cooperation. Moreover, the CJEU merely interprets EU law in a preliminary ruling procedure, leaving the national court to apply it to the facts, whereas horizontal judicial cooperation directly affects individuals: while horizontal cooperation subjects an individual to the authority of another Member State, a preliminary ruling procedure can in fact help an individual vis-à-vis the authority to which he or she is already subjected.

This leads to the critical issue of the threshold for non-cooperation. In the *LM* case, the Court decided to follow the approach devised in its *Aranyosi* case-law.[44] Accordingly, non-cooperation requires ‘substantial grounds to believe’ that the requested person’s right to a fair trial ‘will run a real risk’, for which there is no evidence in the *LM* proceedings. This choice, however, appears inadequate to tackle the rule of law crisis in Poland. Since the Polish government’s measures undermine the independence of the entire judiciary, there is little or no point in conducting an individual and specific assessment of the concrete risks the person concerned faces. As things stand, there is always the danger that any case might at some point come before a compromised judge. This circumstance should have prompted the Court to

[41] CJEU, Opinion 2/13, *Opinion on the Draft Agreement on the Accession of the European Union to the Convention for the Protection of Human Rights and Fundamental Freedoms*, ECLI:EU:C:2014:2454, para 168.

[42] *Supra* note 8, paras. 41 and 43.

[43] In detail, von Bogdandy et al. (2012), p. 489.

[44] *Supra* note 7, para. 5.

follow the test developed in *N.S.*,[45] according to which the abstract risk for the individual concerned should suffice to refuse a surrender. From a systemic standpoint, the refusal to surrender on the basis of a merely abstract risk is justified by the urgent need for red lines. From a practical perspective, it is difficult to imagine how the 'dialogue' on judicial independence between the executing authority, on the one hand, and the issuing judicial authority and its government, on the other hand, can meaningfully take place. At the same time, it is clear that once a systemic deficiency has been established, the burden of proof shifts to the country issuing the EAW. *In dubio pro libertate.*

6 Conclusion

For more than two decades, the constitutional developments in Central and Eastern European countries were mainly considered a constitutional sideshow, that depicted countries 'catching up' with their luckier neighbours who had never suffered Soviet occupation. Now, these countries stand in the limelight: much of the future path of European constitutionalism depends on how their peoples decide.

The rest of Europe cannot do a great deal for those countries' constitutionalism. One cannot expect from the deployment of the instruments analysed in this chapter a 'solution' to the crisis. None but the citizens of those countries themselves can restore the separation of powers among their countries' institutions. The decisions taken by EU institutions can only contribute 'to creating a situation where self-healing through domestic processes is still possible'.[46]

However, one needs to look beyond those countries to understand the importance of using these instruments now. European decisions confronting the Polish Government are crucial to uphold a liberal and democratic self-understanding of European constitutionalism throughout Europe. Otherwise, the current Polish undermining of the independence of its judiciary is likely to count towards defining the European rule of law, facilitating similar developments in other places and compromising large parts of European foreign policy. Much is at stake. Yet, as the Polish anthem goes, 'Poland Is Not Yet Lost'; and nor is the constitutional European project, if the institutions act wisely.

References

Ackerman B (1991) We the people: foundations, vol 1, 6. Harvard University Press, Cambridge

Bonelli M (2017) From a community of law to a Union of values. Eur Const Law Rev 13:793–816

---

[45] *Supra* note 39.

[46] Sonnevend (2017), pp. 123, 145.

Canor I (2013) My brother's keeper? Horizontal Solange: 'An ever closer distrust among the peoples of Europe'. Common Mark Law Rev 50:383–421

Charlemagne (2018) The EU is tolerating – and enabling – authoritarian kleptocracy in Hungary. The Economist, April 5

Editorial Comments (2015) Safeguarding EU values in the Member States – is something finally happening? Common Mark Law Rev 52:619–628

Editorial Comments (2016) The rule of law in the Union, the rule of Union law and the rule of law by the Union: three interrelated problems. Common Mark Law Rev 53:597–605

Editorial Comments (2017) About Brexit negotiations and enforcement action against Poland: the EU's own song of ice and fire. Common Mark Law Rev 54:1309–1317

Giegerich T (2015) Verfassungshomogenität, Verfassungsautonomie und Verfassungsaufsicht in der EU: Zum 'neuen Rechtsstaatsmechanismus' der Europäischen Kommission. In: Calliess C (ed) Herausforderungen an Staat und Verfassung: Liber Amicorum für Torsten Stein zum 70. Geburtstag. Nomos, Baden-Baden, pp 499, 535–536

Halmai G (2017) The early retirement age of the Hungarian judges. In: Nicola F, Davies B (eds) EU law stories. Cambridge University Press, New York, pp 471–488

Halmai G (2018) Illiberal constitutionalism? The Hungarian constitution in a European perspective. In: Kadelbach S (ed) Verfassungskrisen in der Europäischen Union. Nomos, Baden-Baden, pp 85–104

Klarman MJ (1992) Constitutional fact/constitutional fiction: a critique of Bruce Ackerman's theory of constitutional moments. Stanford Law Rev 44:759–797

Matczak M (2018) 10 Facts on Poland for the Consideration of the European Court of Justice. VerfBlog, 13 May 2018. https://verfassungsblog.de/10-facts-on-poland-for-the-consideration-of-the-european-court-of-justice/

Muszyński M (2018) Polski Trybunał w unijnej rzeczywistości. http://www.rp.pl/Opinie/303229983-Polski-Trybunal-w-unijnej-rzeczywistosci%2D%2D-Mariusz-Muszynski-o-mocy-wyrokow-TSUE-w-Polsce.html (in Polish only)

Scheppele KL (2016) Enforcing the basic principles of EU law through systemic infringement actions. In: Closa C, Kochenov D (eds) Reinforcing rule of law oversight in the European Union. Cambridge University Press, Cambridge, pp 105–132

Sonnevend P (2017) Preserving the acquis of transformative constitutionalism in times of constitutional crisis: lessons from the Hungarian case. In: von Bogdandy A, Ferrer Mac-Gregor E, Morales Antoniazzi M, Piovesan F (eds) Transformative constitutionalism in Latin America. Oxford University Press, Oxford, pp 123, 145

von Bogdandy A, Kottmann M, Antpöhler C, Dickschen J, Hentrei S, Smrkol M (2012) Reverse *Solange* – protecting the essence of fundamental rights against EU Member States. Common Mark Law Rev 49:489–519

Armin von Bogdandy is Director at the Max Planck Institute for Comparative Public Law and International Law, Heidelberg.

Piotr Bogdanowicz is Assistant Professor, Faculty of Law and Administration, Warsaw University.

Iris Canor is Professor, School of Law, Zefat Academic College, Israel; School of Law, College of Management, Israel.

Giacomo Rugge is Research Fellow, Max Planck Institute for Comparative Public Law and International Law, Heidelberg.

Matthias Schmidt is Research Fellow, Max Planck Institute for Comparative Public Law and International Law, Heidelberg.

Maciej Taborowski is Assistant Professor, Faculty of Law and Administration, Warsaw University.

The Assessment of Judicial Independence Following the CJEU Ruling in C-216/18 LM

Stanisław Biernat and Paweł Filipek

Contents

Abstract In the *LM* ruling, the Court of Justice developed the *Aranyosi and Căldăraru* test and indicated it as the one to be applied for the assessment of judicial independence and fair trial guarantees in the context of executing European Arrest Warrants. Although serious threats to the rule of law and judicial independence in some EU countries, like Poland, have been documented over recent years, no warrant has so far been definitely rejected as a consequence of the application of the *LM* test, although there are cases in which the execution of warrants to Poland has been suspended. This naturally raises questions as to whether the mechanism proposed by the Court responds to the need of protecting the right to a fair trial and

S. Biernat (✉)
Jagiellonian University, Krakow, Poland
e-mail: stanislaw.biernat@uj.edu.pl

P. Filipek
University of Economics, Krakow, Poland

A. von Bogdandy et al. (eds.), *Defending Checks and Balances in EU Member States*, Beiträge zum ausländischen öffentlichen Recht und Völkerrecht 298,
https://doi.org/10.1007/978-3-662-62317-6_16

safeguarding judicial independence. In this contribution we evaluate the mechanism devised by the Court, taking into account the available judicial practice after the *LM* ruling. We point out that the almost automatic transfer of a mechanism proposed to evaluate the functioning of a prison system to that evaluating a fair trial and judicial independence has not been fully successful. The mechanism proposed by the Court reveals a number of problematic issues and proves to be insufficient and not entirely adequate to assess judicial independence and guarantees of a fair trial.

1 Introduction

Immediately after its publication, the judgment in Case C-216/18 *LM*[1] generated different reactions in Poland and abroad.[2] Some commentators treated the judgment as a general vote of no confidence in the Polish judiciary and especially with regard to the changes made into it in the recent years. Others, including the Minister of Justice, found it to be a defeat of the Irish court which referred the case to the CJEU, as the latter did not share all the suggestions made by the referring court. The *LM* case and the Court's judgment have been used as an argument in the current political debate. Because of the CJEU approach to certain significant issues, the judgment received equivocal interpretation, and its full consequences may become apparent only after a certain period of time and in the light of the post-*LM* judicial practice of domestic courts.

The wish of some political actors for the Court of Justice to provide an explicit negative assessment of the rule of law in Poland did not come true. Such anticipations did not take account of the specific nature of the preliminary ruling procedure. The *LM* judgment essentially maintained the standard division of roles between the CJEU and national courts. CJEU is to provide interpretation of EU law and give guidance to national courts.[3] In turn, the national courts are to pass judgments in the domestic proceedings, yet having regard to this guidance. A separate question is, whether the result of this division of roles and the actual instructions issued in the *LM* ruling can prove satisfactory in practice.

There is no doubt that the judgment is of a certain significance for the development of EU case law and the arguments set forth therein may potentially apply to various situations and proceedings. Because of that, some of the findings of the

[1]CJEU, Case C-216/18 PPU, *Minister for Justice and Equality (Deficiencies in the system of justice)*, ECLI:EU:C:2018:586. The case is regularly referred to, in an abridged form, as the *'LM case'*. The text builds on previous publications of the authors: Biernat (2018), Filipek (2018), Filipek (2019).

[2]See. *i.a.* the debate on Verfassungsblog: https://verfassungsblog.de/category/debates/after-celmer/ (Accessed 20 Jul 2019); Bogdanowicz and Taborowski (2018a), Grabowska-Moroz (2018a).

[3]See e.g. CJEU, Recommendations to national courts and tribunals in relation to the initiation of preliminary ruling proceedings (2019) C380/1, especially paras. 1, 5 and 11.

CJEU were formulated in a more general manner, especially in respect of two major perspectives. First, the Court developed and supplemented the arguments invoked in the Case C-64/16 *Associação Sindical dos Juízes Portugueses*,[4] concerning the notion and meaning of independence of national courts in the light of EU law. Secondly, the Court continued to set the limits of mutual trust and exceptions to the principle of mutual recognition of court decisions on account of the denial of fundamental rights in the context of executing a European Arrest Warrant.[5] In doing so, the CJEU developed its earlier ruling in cases C-404/15 and C-659/15 PPU *Aranyosi and Căldăraru* on a number of issues.[6] In this chapter we focus on some points of the *LM* judgment from the first of the aforementioned perspectives taking account of the domestic judicial practice that has followed the CJEU ruling.

2 The CJEU Concept of Judicial Independence

A central notion in the *LM* ruling is the independence of the judiciary. In the Court's view, the requirement of judicial independence forms part of the essence of the fundamental right to a fair trial. The right is of cardinal importance as a guarantee that all the rights which individuals derive from EU law will be protected and that the values common to Member States set out in Article 2 TEU, in particular the value of the rule of law, will be safeguarded. (para. 48). It is clear, the independence of the judiciary forms the essence of a fair trial and the right to effective judicial protection. At the same time, it lies in the very heart of the rule of law.[7] Without judicial independence, the state legal system can only provide an illusion of the rule of law.

In recent years, however, in some EU Member States, we have been witnessing the undermining of the role of independent judiciary. Without it, the protection of all human rights is impaired, including the right to a fair trial. Yet, respect for the right to effective judicial protection is a necessary and inalienable prerequisite for the protection of all other fundamental rights.[8] From the perspective of threats to the protection of judicial independence and thus to the rule of law and to fundamental rights, the *LM* ruling marks a further step towards building and consolidating the defense of the EU legal order and Union values against states that seem to be

[4]CJEU, Case C-64/16 *Associação Sindical dos Juízes Portugueses v. Tribunal de Contas*, ECLI: EU:C:2018:117.

[5]In this regard, see *i.a.* Grzelak (2018), especially pp. 51–54, 57–63; Xanthopoulou (2018), Lenaerts (2017), Anagnostaras (2016).

[6]CJEU, Case C-404/15 and C-659/15 PPU, *Pál Aranyosi and Robert Căldăraru v. Generalstaatsanwaltschaft Bremen*, ECLI: EU:C:2016:198.

[7] *'The very existence of effective judicial review designed to ensure compliance with EU law is of the essence of the rule of law.'*, CJEU, *Associação Sindical, supra* note 4, para. 36.

[8]See e.g. Górski (2016), p. 37; Safjan (2018), pp. 559–560; Safjan (2019), pp. 5 and 10.

abandoning them and threaten the entire European project.[9] A new, specific point which was made by the CJEU is the following: if the national court executing the European Arrest Warrant finds that there are substantial grounds for believing that the person in respect of whom that warrant has been issued, will—following his surrender to the issuing judicial authority—run a real risk of breach of his fundamental right to an independent tribunal and, therefore, of the essence of his fundamental right to a fair trial, it may ultimately refrain to give effect to the warrant (para. 73).

In developing the understanding of judicial independence, the CJEU relied on the concept worked out in its previous case law and voiced i.a. in the *Associação Sindical* judgment. In the *LM* ruling, the Court broadened its view on the elements that make up and substantiate judicial independence (para. 63–67). This is one of the most important aspects of the judgment whose relevance goes beyond the specific case brought by the Irish High Court.

The notion of 'court' was elaborated in CJEU jurisprudence in the context of the preliminary reference procedure.[10] The CJEU enjoys the power to verify whether a request for a ruling comes from an authorised body, i.e. a 'court or tribunal'. It is empowered to do so both on party's request or of its own motion, when deciding the admissibility of the preliminary ruling request. The Treaty does not determine which body is to be considered a court, yet the Court of Justice has consistently pointed to a number of criteria which it takes into account when assessing if a body is in fact a 'court or tribunal'. The traditional Court's formula reads as follows:

> the factors to be taken into account in assessing whether a body is a 'court or tribunal' include, inter alia, whether the body is established by law, whether it is permanent, whether its jurisdiction is compulsory, whether its procedure is *inter partes*, whether it applies rules of law and whether it is independent.[11]

It is thus not the formal denomination as a 'court' that is decisive for the actual classification of the body admitted under Article 267 TFEU. What matters most of all is whether it carries out the function of adjudicating; if it acts as a *judicial* body. This entails a number of elements. The court proceedings are initiated by action of a party that wants to have a dispute settled. Bringing the case to the court results in the *lis pendens*, and precludes autonomous action in another ordinary court.[12] In most

---

[9] *'The collapse of the rule of law in any member state is tantamount to the rupture of a legal space in the entire European Union.'*, Safjan (2019), p. 7.

[10] See e.g. Lenaerts et al. (2014), p. 52 et seq.; Dashwood et al. (2011), pp. 214–216; Schütze (2018), pp. 389–391; Schwarze (2012), pp. 2234–2235. On the legitimacy of a uniform understanding of the term 'court' both in Article 267 TFEU and Article 47 Charter, see *i.a.*: Pech (2014), p. 1251; Górski (2016), p. 39; Bogdanowicz and Taborowski (2018a), p. 9. For an in-depth discussion of the differences in the concept of a 'court' under both articles see Grzeszczak and Krajewski (2014), pp. 5–11.

[11] CJEU, *Associação Sindical, supra* note 4, para. 38; almost identical with the original formula CJEU, Case C-54/96 *Dorsch Consult Ingenieurgesellschaft mbH*, ECLI:EU:C:1997:413, para. 23.

[12] CJEU, Case C-503/15 *Ramón Margarit Panicello v. Pilar Hernández Martínez*, ECLI:EU:C:2017:126, para. 34.

cases, judicial proceedings are by nature adversarial, and are characterised by opposing positions of the parties. The proceedings eventually lead to a binding ruling.[13] Furthermore, the court cannot refrain from taking a position on the case; it is entitled and, at the same time, called upon to consider and decide the case.[14] The final ruling of the court has the effect of *res judicata*.[15]

It is clear that the independence of the body belongs to the constitutive elements of a 'court' and is intrinsic to the very basic idea of adjudication. This is why it forms an essential requirement of the right to an effective remedy provided for by Article 19 TEU and Article 47 EU Charter of Fundamental Rights. As such it must be guaranteed both at the EU level, within the CJEU, but equally by the Member States at the national level with respect to domestic courts.[16] The Court of Justice in the *Associação Sindical* case proclaimed a general obligation of EU members to guarantee and respect independence of their judiciaries.[17] Domestic courts once they are qualified as a 'court or tribunal' under EU law and are empowered to rule on EU legal issues, have become 'European courts' ('Union courts') whose independence is now protected by the Union, its institutions and the Union's legal system.[18]

The guarantees of judicial independence are intended to protect both the courts and judges as well as those whose cases they handle. Firstly, they create an environment for the judge that enables him[19] to carry out the judicial function being confident about professional and personal safety. The judge must not fear that another public authority will not appreciate the court's decision and that he may suffer some negative consequences for that reason. Secondly, the guarantees of judicial independence provide the parties with a sense of confidence and certitude that the court will keep equal distance from the parties.[20] The facts of the case and the

---

[13]See also Lenaerts et al. (2014), p. 53.

[14]*'It is called upon to give judgment in proceedings intended to lead to a decision of a judicial nature'*, CJEU, *Panicello*, *supra* note 12, para. 28.

[15]Id., at 34; see also Górski (2016), pp. 39–40; Wachowiec (2019), pp. 568–571; for a critical review of these criteria see Grzeszczak and Krajewski (2014), pp. 7–9.

[16]See CJEU, *Associação Sindical, supra* note 4, para 42.

[17]See Pech and Platon (2018), p. 1828.

[18]See also Lenaerts (2018), p. 8.

[19]We use the pronoun 'he' throughout the text, and not the longer formula 'he or she', only for the reasons of readability.

[20]*'Guarantees of independence and impartiality require rules (. . .) in order to dismiss any reasonable doubt in the minds of individuals as to the imperviousness of that body to external factors and its neutrality with respect to the interests before it'*, CJEU, Case C-506/04 *Graham J. Wilson v. Ordre des avocats du barreau de Luxembourg*, ECLI:EU:C:2006:587, para. 53; see also recent CJEU rulings related to Polish courts: CJEU, Case C-619/18, *Commission v. Poland (Independence of the Supreme Court)*, ECLI: EU:C:2019:531, paras. 74, 111; CJEU, Case C-92/18 *Commission v. Poland (Independence of ordinary courts)*, ECLI:EU:C:2019:924, paras. 111, 124; CJEU, Case C-585/18, C-624/18 and C-625/18 *A.K. and Others v. National Council of Judiciary and Supreme Court (Independence of the Disciplinary Chamber of the Supreme Court)*, ECLI:EU: C:2019:982, paras. 128, 153.

applicable law are of sole relevance to the court, and it shall not take into account other considerations. When, in the end, the court delivers a judgment, it is indeed the very law that speaks.[21]

2.1 Autonomy of Courts

Unquestionably, there is a need to assess the independence of the national judiciary on the basis of a common EU standard. In its case law, the Court of Justice identified external (objective) and internal (subjective) aspects of independence, that to a large extent remain in line with the set of criteria indicated by the European Court of Human Rights.[22] They consist in guaranteeing, on the one hand—the autonomy of the court and, on the other—the objectivity and impartiality of the judge. In a similar way, judicial independence is understood in the jurisprudence of the Polish Constitutional Tribunal.[23]

Judicial independence sets the limits of political influence on the judiciary.[24] When considering a case, the court must remain autonomous. It must be free from outside influence, is protected *'against external intervention or pressure liable to jeopardise the independent judgment of its members as regards proceedings before them'*.[25] It is presumed that *'the court exercises its functions wholly autonomously, without being subject to any hierarchical constraint or subordinated to any other body and without taking orders or instructions from any source whatsoever'*.[26]

These preconditions are ensured by the principle of separation of powers, organizational and functional autonomy of courts which are entrusted with the task of

---

[21] Only in exceptional cases accepted the Court of Justice as a *'court or tribunal'* a body that was not fully independent. It occurred in some cases of administrative bodies which were also acting in a judicial capacity. In such situations the Court required the separation of functions between the departments responsible for administrative tasks and the departments vested with judicial functions. The judicial activities by the latter should be carried out without receiving any instruction from the former. See e.g. CJEU, Case C-110/98 *Gabalfrisa SL and Others v. Agencia Estatal de Administración Tributaria (AEAT)*, ECLI:EU:C:2000:145, para. 39.

[22] For an in-depth analysis of ECHR case law on judicial independence, see *i.a.* Hofmański and Wróbel (2010), pp. 314–325; Lawson (2018), Sillen (2019).

[23] *'Legislative and executive powers cannot exercise judicial power or interfere in areas in which judges are independent'*, Constitutional Tribunal (Judgment), Case Kp 1/15, Law on the Organization of Ordinary Courts, OTK ZU 147/9A/2015, para. III.2.4; *'Independence comprises many elements, namely: (1) impartiality vis-à-vis the parties to the proceedings; (2) independence from non-judicial bodies (institutions); (3) autonomy of the judge in relation to the authorities and other judicial organs; (4) independence from political factors; (5) internal independence of the judge. The independence of a judge is not only the right of a judge but also his constitutional duty, as is the constitutional duty of the legislature and judicial administration bodies to protect the independence of a judge'*, id., para. III.2.5; see also Constitutional Tribunal (Judgment), Case K 47/15 *Novelization of the Act on the Constitutional Tribunal*, OTK ZU 31/A/2018, para. III.6.1.7.

[24] See Lenaerts (2018), p. 5.

[25] CJEU, *Wilson, supra* note 20, para. 51; CJEU, *LM, supra* note 1, para. 63.

[26] CEU, *Panicello, supra* note 12, para. 37; CJEU, *LM, supra* note 1, para. 63.

administering justice. Other public bodies should be deprived of instruments by which they could exert pressure on courts to comply with their instructions or expectations.

In *Commission v. Hungary* the Court of Justice addressed the issue of political influence. It held that the mere risk that political influence could be exercised is enough to hinder the body in the independent performance of its tasks.[27] It continued by indicating a particular example of such influence: a threat of a premature termination of the body's term of office. This could lead to 'prior compliance' that would be incompatible with the requirement of independence.[28] In this case, the Court of Justice was not referring to a national court, but to a supervisory authority for the protection of personal data, which in accordance with Directive 95/46[29] was required to exercise its functions 'with complete independence'. There is no good reason why the protection of the independence of judicial bodies should deserve anything less.[30]

The current lack of effective separation of powers and the undermining of judicial independence, especially in the absence of guarantees of constitutional review, jeopardises the protection of human rights and disrupts the balance of powers. The consequences of the above deficiencies may be severe and far-reaching, beginning with a *de facto* change of a state's political and legal system. As the conduct of the parliamentary majority over the last few years in Poland demonstrates, the Constitution may be ignored or interpreted in a hostile manner.[31]

2.2 *Objectivity and Impartiality of Judges*

The second aspect of judicial independence embraces the impartiality and objectivity of the members of the court. As the CJEU pointed out, it '*seeks to ensure a level playing field for the parties to the proceedings and their respective interests with regard to the subject-matter of those proceedings. (...)* [it] *requires (...) the absence of any interest in the outcome of the proceedings apart from the strict application of the rule of law.*'[32]

In its previous case law the Court recognised a number of personal and institutional guarantees of independence and impartiality, in particular with respect to: court composition; appointment of judges; length of their service; grounds for

[27]CJEU, Case C-288/12 *Commission v. Hungary*, ECLI:EU:C:2014:237, para. 53.

[28]Id., para. 54.

[29]Directive (EC) 95/46 on the protection of individuals with regard to the processing of personal data and on the free movement of such data (1995) OJ L281/31.

[30]Likewise, Bogdanowicz and Taborowski (2018a), pp. 9–10.

[31]See also i.a. Łętowska (2018), p. 614 et seq.; Wyrzykowski (2017), p. 831 et seq.; Sadurski (2018, 2019).

[32]CJEU, *Wilson*, *supra* note 20, para. 52.

abstention, rejection and dismissal; protection against removal from office[33] (in particular, the dismissals of members of that body should be determined by express legislative provisions);[34] or remuneration of judges which should correspond to their function.[35]

A new accent in the *LM* judgment that expands the Court's perception of guarantees of judicial independence is the incorporation of some qualitative features of disciplinary proceedings against judges. It can be presumed that this is related to the Polish context. The Court pointed out that the system of disciplinary measures should be regulated in such a way that it cannot be used for political control of the content of court rulings. In this context, the Court stressed the need for a normative definition of: the conduct constituting disciplinary offences; the disciplinary penalties; the defendant's right to defence; and the right to appeal against a disciplinary ruling. This point of the *LM* judgment can be seen as a response to the reasoned proposal made by the European Commission under Article 7(1) TEU.[36] It is worth noting that, in addition to the legislative dimension, the actual application of the disciplinary regime to individual judges should equally be taken into account. Even if the disciplinary system met the criteria provided in the *LM* ruling at a normative level, its application in individual cases should be also taken into consideration. It is apparent that the situations, the manner and the context in which disciplinary proceedings against judges are instituted, or even the very incidents where judges are threatened with disciplinary responsibility, may intentionally lead to an oppressive effect and interfere with judicial independence. It is expected that the standards of disciplinary regime for judges will be further developed in the course of the infringement action brought in October 2019 by the European Commission against Poland under Article 258 TFEU. The Commission made an evaluation of disciplinary investigations in Poland and concluded that they may be triggered by the content of judicial decisions. This clearly undermines judicial independence and puts judges at risk of political control. The Commission claimed breach of Article 19 (1) TEU—effective judicial protection, and Article 267 TFEU—the right of a domestic court to refer questions for a preliminary ruling, because of the possibility of the initiation of a disciplinary proceeding if the court exercises that right.[37]

A further contribution to the development of the European concept of judicial independence was made by the CJEU in two recent infringement cases on the independence of the Polish Supreme Court[38] and the independence of ordinary courts[39] initiated by the European Commission on the basis of Art. 258 TFEU. In

[33]Id., paras. 51 and 53.

[34]CJEU (order), Case C-109/07 *Jonathan Pilato v. Jean-Claude Bourgault*, ECLI:EU:C:2008:274, para. 24.

[35]CJEU, *Associação Sindical, supra* note 4, para. 45.

[36]Taborowski (2019), p. 397.

[37]CJEU, Case C-791/19 *Commission v. Poland*, ECLI:EU:C:2020:277.

[38]CJEU, *Independence of the Supreme Court, supra* note 20.

[39]CJEU, *Independence of ordinary courts, supra* note 20.

both of them the Court of Justice found that Poland failed to fulfil its obligations to ensure effective judicial protection. In the course of time, there will be more and more CJEU rulings concerning the effects of changes in the Polish judiciary, as a number of Polish courts have referred questions to the Court for a preliminary ruling. The Court has recently responded to first of these questions (the case *A.K. and Others*).[40]

In both infringements rulings the CJEU underlined the protection of the judges against removal from office, and analysed the mechanism to extend judge's mandate after reaching the retirement age. The Court of Justice emphasised that the principle of irremovability requires that judges may remain in post provided that they have not reached the obligatory retirement age or until the expiry of their mandate, where that mandate is for a fixed term.[41] Though the CJEU admitted that the protection against the removal is not absolute, it nonetheless stressed that the interference with the principle can only be justified on *'legitimate and compelling grounds'* and must satisfy the proportionality test.[42] Whether these substantive and formal conditions are met may now clearly be subject to European scrutiny.

The Court examined in detail the mechanism for extending the active service of a judge. The mechanism is acceptable and it is the exclusive competence of the Member State to decide whether to make use of it in the domestic system. However, EU members are not free to impose arbitrary conditions and rules of such prolongations; their competence is limited by the requirement to ensure that the procedure does not undermine judicial independence. Indeed, neither the rule of law nor the principle of judicial independence prohibits the use of such a procedure, even if the non-judicial (e.g. executive) bodies are involved in its application. Yet, it is prohibited to shape the procedure in such a way that it may interfere with the independence of a judge by tempting him or her, even potentially, to give in to external intervention or pressure.[43] A judge who considers himself to be fit to continue in active service may be inclined to rule in conformity with the expectations of those who will examine the request and/or decide on the prolongation. Recognising the deficiencies of the procedures to extend the mandate of the Supreme Court judges by the President of the Republic and the judicial activity of ordinary courts judges by the Minister of Justice, the CJEU pointed to the discretionary nature of the President's and Ministerial powers, the lack of objective and verifiable criteria for their decisions, no obligation to state reasons for the decision and the lack of a judicial remedy against a possible refusal.[44]

---

[40]CJEU, *A.K. and Others*, *supra* note 20.

[41]Id., para. 76; CJEU, *Independence of ordinary courts*, *supra* note 20, para. 113.

[42]Id.

[43]See CJEU, *Independence of the Supreme Court*, *supra* note 20, paras. 110–112; CJEU, *Independence of ordinary courts*, *supra* note 20, paras. 118–120.

[44]CJEU, *Independence of the Supreme Court*, *supra* note 20, para. 114; CJEU, *Independence of ordinary courts*, *supra* note 20, para. 122. It was a paradox that a judge could have appealed from a preparatory, non-binding opinion of the National Council of the Judiciary which was to advise the President on whether to prolong the judge's mandate; while he could not have appealed against a final negative decision.

Another aspect of the *Independence of the Supreme Court* ruling which deserves special emphasis is that the examination whether judicial independence is preserved in a Member State, may also include checking what were the true aims of judicial reforms.[45] This is the case when serious doubts arise as to whether the aims declared by the government (e.g. standardizing the retirement age; improving the age balance of judges) justify the implementation of the specific measures, e.g. lowering the retirement age of judges, or granting a discretionary power to the political body to extend the active service of a judge. After all, a premature dismissal of judges appears not to be a very subtle means by the government to fill the 'vacated' judicial posts with their own appointees.[46] The examination of the actual aims focuses on the justification and the proportionality of the measures adopted. It covers not only the grounds for their application and the degree of discretion conferred on state bodies, but equally, other modalities of their implementation, e.g. compulsory nature, discriminatory effect, or retro-active application, as well as the results they may lead to (i.e. the removal of judges from the office).

In the most recent judgment *A.K. and Others*, delivered in the preliminary ruling procedure, the CJEU developed a method for assessing the independence of a judicial body.[47] Referring to the functioning of the newly established Disciplinary Chamber of the Supreme Court, but also to the National Council of the Judiciary, which participated in its staffing, the CJEU indicated the criteria for assessing, whether the body preserves its independence, ergo, whether it is in fact a court in the meaning of EU law.[48] In keeping with the terms of the judicial dialogue based on Article 267 TFEU, the CJEU left it up to the national court to carry out the assessment and draw conclusions.[49] The consequences of the CJEU ruling and the subsequent domestic judgments will be of major importance for both national and European administration of justice.

---

[45]CJEU, *Independence of the Supreme Court, supra* note 20 paras. 82 et seq. Twenty years ago, in *Köllensperger and Atzwanger*, the CJEU declared a request for a preliminary ruling from the *Tiroler Landesvergabeamt* admissible despite the fact that the provisions on the removal of its members were vague; the Court applied a general presumption that public authorities act in compliance with the national constitution and the rule of law; Case C-103/97 *Josef Köllensperger GmbH & Co. KG and Atzwanger AG v. Gemeindeverband Bezirkskrankenhaus Schwaz*, ECLI:EU:C:1999:52, para. 21 and 24.

[46]See also Kuijer (2018), pp. 532–533.

[47]CJEU, *A.K. and Others, supra* note 20.

[48]These criteria include the circumstances in which the body was set up, its characteristics and nature, the manner in which it operates and the public perception of its work; see CJEU, *A.K. and Others, supra* note 20, paras. 143–153.

[49]The domestic court made such an assessment in a judgment of 5 December 2019. The three-person panel of the Polish Supreme Court (Chamber of Labour and Social Security) ruled that the National Council of the Judiciary is not an impartial and independent body, and the Disciplinary Chamber of the Supreme Court is not a court within the meaning of EU law (case ref. no. III PO 7/18).

3 The LM Test

The general views of the CJEU on judicial independence set out above have been concretised in the *LM* case with regard to the EAW mechanism. The concretisation concerns the extent of obligations incumbent on judicial authorities which decide to execute the EAW at the request of judicial authorities of Member States with regard to which allegations of breach of the rule of law have been made, including interference with judicial independence. These obligations then consist in carrying out an independence test and ensuring that the fundamental right of the requested person to a fair trial is not at risk.

In the *LM* ruling the Court of Justice confirmed, in a different context, the essential application of the *Aranyosi and Căldăraru* mechanism to assess the risk of a breach of a fundamental right.[50] Ergo, the test applies also when the doubts are raised with respect to judicial independence and the fairness of a court trial.

In the operative part of the *LM* judgment, the Court reiterated the two tests introduced in *Aranyosi and Căldăraru*: the general test and the individual one (paras. 68, 79, and the conclusion). It is a *prima facie* conclusion when reading literally the wording of the judgment itself. This is also how most of the literature commented on this ruling. Yet, a more profound analysis brings us to the point that we may distinguish indeed, not a two- but a three-step test, which more accurately reflects the process of verifying the conditions for the execution of the EAW. The CJEU adapted the original test, by introducing an intermediate stage between a general and the individual risk assessment (para. 74). That stage comprises the assessment of judicial independence of the very courts which are competent to hear the individual case of the requested person. The Court thus indicated that the fair trial guarantees should be considered at three levels: general, intermediate and individual, accordingly making a distinction of: (1) a general risk assessment; (2) the assessment of particular courts competent to deal with proceedings concerning the person covered by the EAW; and (3) the individual risk assessment.

(1) The general test of *Aranyosi and Căldăraru* was left unchanged. It is used to determine whether there is a real risk that the fundamental right to a fair trial may be breached on account of systemic or generalised deficiencies concerning the judiciary, such as to compromise judicial independence in the Member State that issued the arrest warrant (para. 68).
(2) The next is the test of particular courts, i.e. the courts which have jurisdiction over the proceedings for which the individual person was requested by the warrant. At this stage, the executing court should determine to what extent systemic or generalised deficiencies in judicial independence (that were identified under the general test) may affect these courts (para. 74). The introduction of

[50] See also Taborowski (2019), p. 394 et seq.; Taborowski (2018), p. 73 et seq.; Bogdanowicz and Taborowski (2018b), Lewandowski (2019), p. 10; Frąckowiak-Adamska (2018b), p. 98 et seq.; Krajewski (2018), p. 796; Grabowska-Moroz (2018b), p. 21; Nita-Światłowska (2018), p. 8.

the intermediate stage is justified by the subject-matter of the assessment which is different from the other tests and, consequently, by the nature of questions that the executing court needs to consider. Only if the existence of such an impact is confirmed, the judicial authority can take the final test.

(3) The third test in the CJEU mechanism is the individualised test in relations to the specific case and the individual person being prosecuted. It aims to answer the ultimate question, whether there is a real risk of a breach of the fundamental right to a fair trial of the person subject to the arrest warrant. In making this assessment, the executing court should take into account the specific concerns of the person prosecuted and his personal situation, the nature of the offence, the circumstances in which it was committed and the context in which the EAW was issued (para. 75).

The evolution of the two-step *Aranyosi and Căldăraru* test into the three-step *LM* test has already been explicitly reflected in national court decisions taking into account the *LM* judgment. Indeed, the Irish High Court followed the three-stage pattern in its ruling to surrender the suspect.[51] Then, the Supreme Court of Ireland which considered the appeal from the High Court's ruling applied the three-step approach as well and concluded that *'although there was clear evidence of breach of Poland's Charter and Treaty obligations (. . .) and further evidence leading the trial judge to conclude that a breach of the principle of independence did operate at the level of the courts involved, the available evidence did not, on its own, satisfy the third stage of the test set out by the C.J.E.U. (. . .)'.*[52]

The consecutive steps of the *LM* test require further analysis and more detailed commentary, which will be made in the following section.

4 Implementation of the LM Test

Judicial independence is an undisputed legal standard of the European Union. Member States have the primary responsibility for ensuring it.[53] The verification of whether Member States fulfil this responsibility can be centralised, *i.e.* carried out by the EU institutions in the framework of political procedures (e.g. the protection of the rule of law, Art. 7 TEU) or judicial proceedings (e.g. an infringement action, Art. 258 TFEU).

Since the *LM* ruling, it has become apparent that the courts in other Member States also have the right and the duty to play an active role in safeguarding the

[51]High Court (Judgment of 19 November 2018), *The Minister for Justice and Equality v. Artur Celmer (No. 5)*, [2018] IEHC 639, paras. 92-98 and 117.

[52]Supreme Court (Judgment of 12 November 2019, *The Minister for Justice and Equality v. Artur Celmer*, S:AP:IE:2018:000181, para. 85.

[53]See CJEU, *LM, supra* note 1, paras. 52–57; CJEU, *Independence of the Supreme Court, supra* note 20, para. 71.

proper standard of judicial independence in the European legal area. The competence of domestic courts in this area is deemed to be a 'safety valve'[54] and a means to protect the EU legal order against the destructive influence of action of certain Member States which are not compliant with the rule of law.[55] The Court of Justice has therefore recognised that this responsibility is also decentralised and lies with all 'Union' courts, including national judiciaries.

4.1 General Risk Assessment

Concerns can be raised in relation to each of the steps of the above test. The mechanism established by the Court of Justice is complex and multilevel. It also appears to be difficult to implement in practice and the degree of difficulty increases with passing to the subsequent levels. From a methodological perspective, the easiest stage to carry out seems the first level: the general test. It may require a considerable amount of work on the part of the executing authority, as it consists in gathering and assessing the information on the general situation in the judiciary of the issuing state.

In this context, the question may be asked: what is the significance of the reasoned proposal of the European Commission opening the proceedings pursuant to Article 7 (1) TEU?[56] Would a similar document, if prepared by the European Parliament, e.g. a resolution on Hungary,[57] or filed by Member States, have a role to play? The Court held in the *LM* ruling that the information provided by the Commission in the proposal is 'particularly relevant' for the purposes of the general risk assessment (para. 61). Thus, the national court is to take account of the information contained in the Commission document.[58]

Nonetheless, it is to be noted that such a document will not be issued in future in each case of suspicion of the risks discussed. After all, in the history of the Union to date, it has only happened once (or twice, if the EP resolution on Hungary is to be counted). In the specific situation in which the Irish High Court was to take the decision, there were no obstacles to relying on the findings and conclusions of the Commission. In particular, no obstacle stemmed from the fact that the Commission proposal was adopted under a different procedure of a political rather than judicial nature; or from the fact that the decision of the Council under Article 7 (1) TEU had

54Taborowski (2019), p. 49, 375 et seq.

55See Barcz (2019), pp. 4, 12–13.

56European Commission, Reasoned proposal in accordance with Article 7 (1) of the Treaty on European Union regarding the rule of law in Poland, 20 December 2017, COM(2017) 835 final.

57European Parliament, Resolution on a proposal calling on the Council to determine, pursuant to Article 7(1) of the Treaty on European Union, the existence of a clear risk of a serious breach by Hungary of the values on which the Union is founded, 12 Sep 2018, P8_TA(2018)0340.

58See also Taborowski (2019), p. 399.

not been taken before the national court reached its decision on the execution of the warrant.

However, may the national court fully rely on the information presented in the Commission's proposal or perhaps it should verify or supplement it? The CJEU judgment is vague in this regard (cf. para. 61, 69, 73, 79). Yet, it seems justified that the national court may rely on the proposal of the Commission bearing in mind its detailed nature and extensive documentation. It should not, however, be confined to the Commission's document only. It should verify whether this document is up to date and, if necessary, gather further material.

The reference by the Court to the Commission's reasoned proposal should be seen as a recognition of the document as a source of information ensuring a high standard of reliability. Nonetheless, it is left to the executing authority to choose and evaluate the sources of information. The CJEU indicated the qualitative criteria of the information on which the executing authority should base its evaluation: the information should be objective, reliable, specific and properly updated (para. 61). In principle, any sources which provide information helpful for the general risk assessment can be used by the national court. The executing court should examine them, so that its determination is based on accurate, complete and exhaustive information that gives a true representation of the situation.

4.2 Assessment of Particular Courts

Further doubts arise in relation to the next levels of the assessment procedure, i.e. the determination whether there are serious and proven grounds to conclude, in the circumstances of the given case, that the prosecuted person will be exposed to the risk of a breach of the right to a fair trial as a result of being surrendered to the issuing state. The doubts concern both the procedural and the substantive aspects of the mechanism devised by the CJEU.

The executing judicial authority is required to assess whether the general or systemic deficiencies in judicial independence indeed affect the courts which have jurisdiction in criminal cases against the persons requested by the EAW. In the first place, it needs to identify the courts in the issuing state which have jurisdiction to rule on the matters in question. This will require to apply the rules of criminal procedure of that state, either by the executing court itself or with the assistance of other authorities, including the issuing court, e.g. through the judicial dialogue (Art. 15 (2) EAW Framework Decision). In principle, the courts' jurisdiction can be established before the person is transferred to the issuing state. In situations specified by the law in force, it may nevertheless be subject to change after the person's transfer. The risk of the potential change of jurisdiction after the surrender of the person prosecuted creates the danger that the assessment made by the executing authority will not be correct. It is equally difficult for the executing authority to predict later developments in the case. Assessment of the independence of the specific courts competent to carry out proceedings against the person wanted, is therefore only of limited usefulness to safeguard the fair trial guarantees to the individual person.

The example of the manner in which the *Oberlandesgericht* in Karlsruhe dealt with a EAW case (Ausl 301 AR 95/18), provide an interesting illustration of the difficulties that the executing courts may encounter when assessing the guarantee of the independence of judges by whom the requested persons would supposedly be tried after the transfer. Initially, the German court held a dialogue with the Polish court to clarify the doubts that had arisen and to gather additional information with regard to judicial independence in Poland. In doing so, it followed the formula indicated by the CJEU (see *infra*). The correspondence with the Polish counterpart did not allow to clarify all doubts of the German court. In the course of the dialogue, the *Oberlandesgericht* asked specifically for a binding assurance under international law that no disciplinary proceedings will be instituted against judges with regard to the content of their decisions taken during the trial of the requested person.[59] After having received a reply that such an assurance is not possible, the court then decided to make the consent for the surrender of the requested Latvian citizen subject to the assurances that the German ambassador or a person authorised by him will be entitled to be present at the trial conducted with respect to that person and, in the event of a conviction, to visit him in custody.[60] By proceeding in that way, the *Oberlandesgericht* apparently went beyond the formula outlined by the Court of Justice.

4.3 Individual Risk Assessment

The Court of Justice's test as proposed in the *LM* ruling, raises the most serious concerns as regards the final test: the examination of the individual risk. At this stage, the executing judicial authority is to make a final determination as to whether the requested person's fundamental right to a fair trial is at risk. The executing judicial authority ought to take into consideration: the specific concerns expressed by the person prosecuted as well as his personal situation, e.g. the political pressure to prosecute or punish him; possible negative statements by state officials about the person wanted; his possible membership of political opposition, social or ethnic minority; or media activities critical of political power, etc. In addition, the judicial authority should take account of the nature of the offence, the circumstances in which it was committed as well as the context in which the arrest warrant was issued,

[59]Oberlandesgericht Karlsruhe (Decision of 31 October 2018), Ausl 301 AR 95/18, para. 33.
[60]Oberlandesgericht Karlsruhe (Decision of 7 January 2019), Ausl 301 AR 95/18, para. 70.

e.g. the political nature of the act; or the fact that the act was committed in connection with the exercise of the freedom of expression or the freedom of assembly, etc.[61]

Taking the individual test means that the foreign national court has already carried out the two previous stages. It must have then established that judicial independence is endangered in the Member State which requested the surrender of the person, and it must have further recognised that this danger exists also in relation to the particular courts that are to try the person requested. At this stage, there should be therefore no doubt that the Member State whose judicial system is subject to such an examination does not respect the values of the Union, in particular the principle of the rule of law and its fundamental element: judicial independence. Some legal scholars suggested that refusal to execute EAWs should take place after general or systemic deficiencies in judicial independence in the given Member State had been identified.[62] However, this was not enough for the CJEU to complete the test. This is where the Court of Justice came to the rescue of the principle of mutual trust and the mutual recognition of judicial decisions. By protecting the EAW cooperation mechanism by requiring all three levels of the *LM* test to be carried out, the CJEU *de facto* accepted that judicial independence was threatened in the Member State which issued the warrant. This is perhaps the most controversial outcome of the *LM* ruling.[63]

The Court of Justice assumed that the actual realisation of the standard of judicial independence in a given Member State may vary. Moreover, this variation may occur at different levels, corresponding to the levels of the *LM* test. The existence of systemic or generalised deficiencies in the judiciary (the general test) may affect national courts to a differing degree: some courts may be affected, while some others not (the intermediate test). Furthermore, the determination that these deficiencies do have an impact on a particular court still does not preclude, in the Court's view, that in such a court a certain person in a specific criminal proceedings may be tried in accordance with the European standard of judicial independence (the individual test).[64] Therefore,

---

[61]CJEU, *LM, supra* note 1, para. 75. See also written observations in the *LM* case of the European Commission of 30 April 2018, paras. 23-24; CJEU, Case C-216/18, *LM*, Opinion of Advocate General E. Tanchev, ECLI:EU:C:2018:517, para. 103.

[62]E.g. Bárd and van Ballegooij (2018a) Judicial Independence; von Bogdandy (2018), Krajewski (2018), p. 805; Pech and Wachowiec (2019).

[63]See also *i.a.* von Bogdandy (2018), Frąckowiak-Adamska (2018a), Scheppele (2018), Grabowska-Moroz (2019), p. 427; Pech and Wachowiec (2019). It is suggested that in addition to preserving the mutual recognition mechanism, the CJEU intended to distinguish its responsibility (to protect the right to a fair trial in individual cases, based on Art. 19 (1) TEU and Art. 47 Charter), from that of the Council and the European Council (to oversee the systemic compliance of domestic judicial systems with the rule of law, stemming from Art. 7 TEU); see CJEU, *LM, supra* note 1, paras. 70–72; CJEU (opinion), *LM, supra* note 63, paras. 40, 42 and 44; Frąckowiak-Adamska (2018a), Krajewski (2018), p. 797.

[64]The Court clearly followed the line suggested by the European Commission and supported by the Advocate General; see European Commission (Written observations of 30 April 2018), para. 19; CJEU (opinion), *LM, supra* note 63, para. 108. See also Bárd and van Ballegooij (2018b) The AG Opinion, para. 2.2; Taborowski (2019), pp. 400–401.

the third stage of the *LM* test is indeed decisive. It makes the test highly rigorous and extreme, to the point that it becomes rather challenging to justify a refusal to execute a European Arrest Warrant.

The Court will soon re-examine the methodology indicated in the LM ruling following two new preliminary references brought by the Amsterdam Court (C-354 and 412/20). The Court in Amsterdam has asked how to deal with Polish warrants, once it has concluded that the independence of every court in Poland is at risk due to systemic deficiencies caused by changes introduced in recent years, including the possibility of initiating disciplinary proceedings for the content of judicial decisions.

There is another crucial aspect of the *LM* ruling that will definitely have far-reaching consequences for the EAW mechanism. It is the obligation of the executing court to request the issuing authority to provide additional information that it considers necessary for assessing whether there is a risk to a fair trial (the Q&A mechanism). The CJEU stated so in both *Aranyosi and Căldăraru* (para. 95), and *LM* (para. 76) cases. The Court of Justice applied the modal verb 'must' in the context of requesting additional information, which suggests that this horizontal judicial dialogue is of a compulsory nature and national courts cannot derogate from this duty. Such interpretation has been expressly accepted by some executing authorities.[65] Indeed, especially the second and third stages of the procedure developed by the CJEU will generally require launching of a Q&A mechanism. The detailed information that would be needed to carry out the assessment of particular courts as well as the specific case and individual situation of the suspect, usually, will not be fully known to the executing court. However, it should be left to the discretion of the executing authority to decide whether the information in its possession is sufficient for taking a decision about the execution of a EAW, or whether any supplementary information is needed.

The horizontal judicial dialogue is based on Article 15 (2) of the EAW Framework Decision[66] and is intended to allow the collection of 'necessary supplementary information', in particular as regards the grounds for non-execution of the warrant, the guarantees to be provided for its execution or the warrant's content or form. The issuing judicial authority may provide the executing court with any objective material in relation to any changes concerning the conditions for protecting the guarantee of judicial independence in the issuing Member State, which may rule out the existence of that risk for the individual concerned (para. 77). The issuing body may as well seek assistance, if need be, from the central authority or one of the central authorities of the issuing Member State (para. 78). Yet, both the CJEU approach to the formula of judicial dialogue and a relatively short practice of its use reveal a number of issues concerning the way in which it is actually carried out.

---

[65]See e.g. Rechtbank Amsterdam (Decision of 16 April 2019), ECLI:NL:RBAMS:2019:2721, section 4.4.

[66]Council Framework Decision 2002/584/JHA on the European arrest warrant and the surrender procedures between Member States, OJ L190/1.

5 Judicial Dialogue of National Courts

This part of the contribution presents the experience gained so far in the dialogue between the executing judicial authorities of different Member States and the issuing judicial authorities in Poland. It covers the dialogue not only of the particular courts which were competent in the case which led to the *LM* judgment, but also of other courts which applied the mechanism prescribed by the Court of Justice in other EAW cases. Most of the documents were obtained via the access to public information mechanism;[67] occasionally, some answers of Polish courts to the questions asked by the executing authorities were also made available on the respective courts' websites. The information obtained can be regarded as representative of other cases of judicial dialogue inspired by the *LM* judgment. They follow a similar pattern and show fairly common deficiencies. It should be noted, however, that this mechanism is still at its debut and may be subject to further evolution.

Following the CJEU ruling in the *LM* case, the Irish High Court complied with the requirements set out by the Court of Justice. It twice requested the supplementary information from Polish courts that issued the arrest warrants. In the end, the court in Dublin decided to execute all three warrants and ordered the surrender of the person wanted to Poland.[68] The Irish court confirmed its earlier assessment of the existence of a general risk of breach of the right to a fair trial due to systemic or general deficiencies in judicial independence in Poland.[69] It also concluded that these deficiencies will affect the courts before which the person wanted will be tried.[70] Ergo, it did determine that two out of the three tests of the *LM* ruling were met. Nonetheless, with respect to the last one: the final assessment of the existence of an individualised risk for the prosecuted person, the Court held that this risk was not proven.[71] The prosecuted person filed an appeal from the High Court's judgment which was examined by the Supreme Court of Ireland. The Supreme Court shared the assessment of the lower instance and eventually ruled in November 2019 to dismiss the appeal.[72]

The dialogue carried out in the *LM* case illustrated some problems of the Q&A mechanism established by the CJEU, which will be addressed below. The analogous judicial dialogue initiated in other EAW cases, e.g. by the courts of Madrid,

[67] The courts were asked for information twice: in November 2018 and in June/July 2019. While in the first round only about half of the courts replied, in the second round the success rate of the requests increased to some 80%. Perhaps this should be linked to the paper, which was the result of the first series of inquiries and was published in a legal periodical regularly consulted by judges; see Filipek (2019).

[68] *Celmer No. 5*, *supra* note 53, para. 123.

[69] Id., para. 93.

[70] Id., para. 97.

[71] Id., para. 117.

[72] Supreme Court, *supra* note 54, para. 88.

Amsterdam or Karlsruhe, also shows that the mechanism is deficient and the 'Union courts' are not fully capable to make use of it.

The questions posed by different courts varied greatly in terms of the content and the level of detail: from the most general questions from the Spanish court to inquisitive, detailed sets of questions from the Dutch and German courts. The most frequent questions concerned systemic, structural issues of the Polish judiciary, including the autonomy of courts in performing their tasks, the irremovability of judges, the composition of adjudicating panels, the available legal remedies, the dismissal of presidents and vice-presidents of courts, disciplinary proceedings, etc.[73] Questions referring directly to particular courts that have jurisdiction to hear the case of the person wanted were less frequent. Questions of this kind were raised primarily by the courts of Amsterdam and Karlsruhe (including: indication of competent bodies, changes in court's staff, recent retirement or transfer of judges in the competent courts, allocation of cases, rules on case resolution, disciplinary proceedings, or measures to protect the right to an independent court).[74] Some of the questions on particular courts were indeed of a general nature. In fact, there were only occasional questions related to the last stage of the *LM* test: the personal situation and concerns of the person prosecuted, or the nature of the offence and the circumstances in which it was committed. The latter category included questions about statements made by the deputy minister of justice referring to the person prosecuted as a dangerous offender, which the Irish court interpreted as likely to undermine the presumption of innocence of the person prosecuted.[75]

The analysis of the responses of Polish courts indicates that they may assist the executing authority in taking a decision to surrender a person prosecuted only to a limited extent. Many replies consisted mainly in a brief presentation of general legal rules concerning the judiciary: provisions of the Constitution/statutes and the submission of some basic data requested by the foreign court. In fact, this kind of replies prevailed. Occasionally, they were supplemented with some superficial conclusions, e.g.: *'In Poland, legal norms exclude threats to the independence of judges'*.[76] Only a few answers of the courts (judges) were explicitly critical, and negatively assessed the existing situation and expressed doubts about the independence of judges. In this context, in particular, disciplinary proceedings against judges were mentioned regularly. Other issues raised by the responding courts included: the non-transparent allocation of cases by a classified algorithm, the excessive influence of the Minister of Justice on the functioning of courts through administrative supervision, as well as

[73]*Celmer No. 5*, *supra* note 53, para. 3; High Court (letter of 8 August 2018); Juzgado Central de Instrucción (letter of 24 September 2018).

[74]Rechtbank Amsterdam (Decision of 4 October 2018), ECLI:NL:RBAMS:2018:7032, para. 4.4.3; Oberlandesgericht Karlsruhe (Decision of 31 October 2018), Ausl 301 AR 95/18, paras. 21–33.

[75]High Court (Judgment of 1 August 2018), *The Minister for Justice and Equality v. Artur Celmer (No. 4)*, [2018] IEHC 484, paras. 37, 40–41, 47.

[76]Regional Court in Warsaw (Letter of 26 September 2018). http://bip.warszawa.so.gov.pl/attachments/download/7511. Accessed 20 July 2019, p. 9.

the premature, arbitrary dismissal and appointment of (vice-)presidents of courts or the politicised composition of the National Council of the Judiciary. In turn, some replies were limited to expressing views in line with the official stance of the government (e.g. *'the National Council of the Judiciary is the independent body responsible for guaranteeing [judge's] rights'*).[77] or individual, hopeful opinions of the responding judge *('I would like to express my conviction that the majority of judges in the Republic of Poland stand up for their independence')*.[78]

Some of the answers were laconic or evasive and, in the opinion of the requesting court, contributed very little to the understanding of the general situation in Poland.[79] Some courts invoked the lack of a formal competence to provide answers in the required material scope (e.g. concerning the general situation of the rule of law in Poland, disciplinary proceedings against judges, the dismissal of presidents and vice-presidents of ordinary courts, the use of the extraordinary appeal, the evaluation of politicians' statements, the position of the Minister of Justice towards statements of his deputy etc.) or the lack of knowledge (e.g. about the disciplinary proceedings, the employment of assessors or judges' assistants, the extraordinary appeal, the statements of the deputy minister etc.). Sometimes both the lack of competence and the lack of knowledge were invoked simultaneously. In situations where the court is not capable of responding to some questions raised by the executing authority, it should perhaps approach the authority (or person) that has such knowledge or competence rather than ignore the questions or leave them unanswered. Excessive brevity or the lack of answer may make the requesting authority repeat or reformulate the questions, which will generate unnecessary additional communication and negatively affect the length of the proceedings. In ten very similar decisions of early 2019, the court in Amsterdam held that the answers of the Polish courts were insufficient to decide on the surrender of the persons wanted, and resolved to continue the dialogue.[80] This mainly consisted in urging the requested court to provide or supplement the answers to the previously transmitted questions.[81]

Over time, the judicial dialogue began to involve other bodies in Poland, apart from the regional courts (*sądy okręgowe*), as the ones entitled to issue European arrest warrants. The communication also included district courts (*sądy rejonowe*, e.g. in questions about assessors), courts of appeal, the Supreme Court (e.g. with

---

[77]Regional Court in Świdnica (Letter of 8 October 2010), p. 2.

[78]Regional Court in Rzeszów (Letter of 8 October 2010), p. 5.

[79]*Celmer No. 5*, *supra* note 53, para. 90.

[80]Rechtbank Amsterdam (Decisions of 4 January 2019), ECLI:NL:RBAMS:2019:33, 2019:42–2019:44, 2019:46–2019:51.

[81]In some cases, the second round of Polish courts' replies also left the EAW executing court unsatisfied; in a series of decisions it requested once again that the replies be supplemented; see Rechtbank Amsterdam (Decisions of 16 April 2019), ECLI:NL:RBAMS:2019:2750, 2019:2760, 2019:2792, 2019:2793, 2019:2801.

regard to extraordinary appeals) and the disciplinary bodies (e.g. the scope of disciplinary proceedings with regard to individual judges).[82]

In April 2019, in some cases, after a second round of dialogue, the court of Amsterdam decided to surrender the persons requested. Similarly to the Irish court, the *Rechtbank* Amsterdam acknowledged the general concerns in respect of the impact of the changes in Poland on the rule of law as well as the concerns with regard to the right to a fair trial before the courts in which the transferred person will be tried.[83] That means that, again, two out of three tests were met. It considered, however, that the risk of breaching the right of the individual person to a fair trial was not demonstrated. It held that neither the personal circumstances of the suspect nor the nature of the offences for which he would be tried justifies a negative decision. The court concluded that the charges related to common criminal offences, so the suspect as well as the type of offences were not in any way in the special attention of the ruling politicians in Poland so as to give rise to inappropriate influence on the judges.[84]

6 Evaluation of the CJEU Mechanism for the Assessment of Judicial Independence

6.1 Nemo Iudex in Causa Sua

In the *Aranyosi and Căldăraru* cases, the answers to be given by national courts within the judicial dialogue mechanism were intended to refer to the conditions under which a custodial sentence was to be served. Thus they related to the area for which a separate branch of public administration was responsible: the prison authorities that remain outside the judiciary. In contrast, in the *LM* case while it concerned a fair trial and judicial independence, national courts were requested to comment on themselves. A domestic judicial authority may be asked to assess particular courts of its own country (the ones having jurisdiction to try the case of the person being prosecuted) or the judiciary in general. Ergo, the court is being asked about a branch of the state structure of which it forms a part, within which it is established. This

[82]The survey of correspondence between courts shows that, occasionally, the understanding (translation) of the correspondence between courts could be a problem. Misunderstandings concerned some issues of importance, e.g.: which court will have jurisdiction to rule on the transferred person's case? Which court is actually giving the answer? (district or regional); Were the individual courts' presidents dismissed or they left due to the expiry of their term of office? Does the question relate to assessors or court assistants?

[83]See e.g. Rechtbank Amsterdam (Judgments of 16 April 2019), ECLI:NL:RBAMS:2019:2722, para. 5.4.1; 2019:2751, para. 5.4.1; 2019:2794, para. 6.4.2; 2019:2795, para. 4.4.1; 2019:2799, para. 4.4.1.

[84]ECLI:NL:RBAMS:2019:2722, *supra* note 85, para. 5.4.2; 2019:2751, para. 5.4.2; 2019:2794, para. 6.4.3; 2019:2795, para. 4.4.2; 2019:2799, para. 4.4.2.

gives rise to potential conflicts unknown to the previously examined cases relating to prison conditions.[85] In this context some difficult questions arise. Will such information meet the standard set by the Court of Justice? Will such information be objective and adequate? Will the assessment be fully reliable? Does a judge (court) who does not recognise any threats to the independence of the judiciary, contrary to the widely expressed and well-documented concerns, remain fully independent? How about a judge whose answers comply with to the expectations of political decision-makers, bearing in mind that their voice could have an impact on the judge's career? Would a judge admit receiving explicit or implicit instructions, suggestions or perhaps 'friendly advice' from the executive or other political actors? Answers to these questions can be challenging. On the other hand, how about a judge who provides critical comments on fair trial guarantees? Could he be afraid of condemnation, intimidation, legal harassment or threats of disciplinary proceedings on account of the answers he has given? These are legitimate concerns.

6.2 Who Shall Answer?

It is not clear who should answer the questions raised by the executing authority: the judge issuing the arrest warrant, the head of the court's department or the president of the court. The *LM* ruling indicates, in general, that the issuing judicial authority should be addressed. The EAW Framework Decision only in general specifies as the addressee of the questions: the court issuing the EAW. It may seem a minor issue, yet in practice, the actual respondent may be of crucial significance to the content of the answers. It actually did happen that competing answers were provided to the same questions by different judges of the same court: the court's president and the judge who issued the warrant.[86] An additional issue in the specific perspective of the *LM* case was that the warrants to surrender the person were issued by three different Polish courts. The cooperation of the executing court with several issuing authorities, with regard to a single wanted person, may lead the former court to ambiguous conclusions.

In practice, questions from a foreign court are generally answered either by court presidents or heads of court departments or sometimes individual judges indicated by them. Occasionally, questions from the foreign court have been answered by the individual judges who actually issued the arrest warrant; this happened when expressly requested by the court executing the EAW. A review of the current practice of judicial dialogue suggests that when answers are given by court presidents or heads of departments, they are more often abbreviated and kept to a minimum. Their actual usefulness for the executing authority may therefore be limited. On the other hand, in the rare cases where answers are given by the

[85]See also *i.a.* Pech and Wachowiec (2019).

[86]For details see Filipek (2019), p. 29.

individual judge who issued the warrant, these are usually more comprehensive, straightforward, and critical. It should be kept in mind that a number of courts' presidents were appointed by the Minister of Justice during a six-month period, when he enjoyed a fully discretionary power to replace presidents and vice-presidents of courts, or who were appointed by him following the expiry of their predecessor's term of office. The Minister, who is responsible for the changes in the Polish judiciary, is inclined to appoint persons who share his point of view.

6.3 *Material Scope of Judicial Dialogue*

Further concerns arise with regard to the scope of the questions asked by the judicial authorities executing arrest warrants and the stage at which the Q&A mechanism should be employed.[87] Could these be general questions, which concern systemic issues and therefore serve to perform a general assessment, the first stage of the tests pointed to by the Court of Justice? Or should these questions relate to the individualised courts which are competent to deal with the case of the person prosecuted after his transfer to the requesting country? Or, should they perhaps be limited mostly to the specific case and the person being prosecuted, and therefore serve the purpose of the ultimate individualised risk assessment?

The executing authority may indeed like to obtain information from the issuing court concerning a general or systemic situation in the Member State. This may be the case in particular with regard to the updating of existing information and cover recent legislative amendments, the development of case law or the administrative practice or any incidents that may be relevant to the assessment of threats to judicial independence. However, this possibility should be considered an exception. The executing authority should not make an initial effort to find and verify information simply by addressing, in the first place, the issuing judicial authority. The assessment of the fair trial guarantees and judicial independence by the executing court is also intended to apply to the responding court. The responding body is therefore in a difficult situation, as it speaks *pro domo suo*.

The judicial dialogue indicated by the Court of Justice should primarily serve the purpose of an individualised test carried out by the court executing the warrant, in which it assesses whether the particular person to whom the warrant refers, will be at risk of a breach of the right to a fair trial. A review of the existing practice indicates, however, that the executing courts do not refrain from asking general questions.[88] In

[87]Doubts about the absence of a more precise indication by the CJEU of what the supplementary information should concern were already raised after the *Aranyosi and Căldăraru* judgment, see *i.a.* Kamiński (2019), p. 59.

[88]It would be advisable for judicial authorities from other Member States to use for the first and second stage of the *LM* test, the available, general and up-to-date information from reliable sources, instead of referring to the Polish courts in the first place. Such sources include reports, analyses, opinions or recommendations from the international expert bodies: the Venice Commission, the UN

fact, they are much more frequent than questions about the person prosecuted and his individual case. Nonetheless, there are also such courts, e.g. the London Court, according to which the requests for further information are appropriate only in relation to particular circumstances affecting the person requested by the EAW.[89]

7 Final Remarks

The mechanism of horizontal judicial dialogue between executing and issuing authorities has some potential to permit the gathering and verification of information on the Member State which issued the EAW, and to clarify doubts related to fair trial guarantees in that State. However, it is a deficient instrument which is not fully capable of examining judicial independence and threats to the rule of law. Its functioning so far raises a number of issues: is it mandatory or optional? What should be its material scope? Who should respond to the questions of the foreign court? Is it appropriate and credible to ask the judge to evaluate his own independence and the attitude of fellow judges?

The above considerations illustrate inherent limitations and substantial inadequacy of the model of supplementary questions to assess judicial independence and decide on the execution of the EAW in relation to fair trial standards. This mechanism assumes that judicial authorities will carry out a self-assessment of their independence and share it with foreign authorities. The adequacy and credibility of such an exercise may be disputed. Despite detailed guidance from the Court (or perhaps: due to them), such a procedure does not seem to be able to lead to a satisfactory result in many or perhaps in most cases.

In view of emerging difficulties, a question may arise whether it would not be a better idea to stick exclusively to the general test: i.e. the examination of the systemic risk of breach of independence of the courts following the formula set in the context of asylum law in the judgment in Case C-411/10 and C-493/10 *N.S.*[90] This could lead to a quasi-automatic refusal to execute arrest warrants issued by Polish courts, and *de facto* result in the full exclusion of Poland's participation in the EAW mechanism. Such a solution would be questionable though. Its consequences could prove too far-reaching and hard to accept as it would not allow a more nuanced response to different specific circumstances of EAW cases.

In Poland's current situation, a general exclusion of all courts from judicial cooperation within the EU would result in a vote of no confidence against the

---

Special Rapporteur on the independence of judges and lawyers; the judges' associations: 'Iustitita', 'Themis'; or the civil society organisations: the Helsinki Foundation, the Batory Foundation, etc.

[89]London High Court of Justice (Judgment of 31 October 2018), *Pawel Lis and others*, [2018] EWHC 2848, postscript.

[90]CJEU, Case C-411/10 and C-493/10, *N.S. v. Secretary of State for the Home Department and M. E. and Others*, ECLI:EU:C:2011:865. See also *i.a.* von Bogdandy (2018), Frąckowiak-Adamska (2018a), Pech and Wachowiec (2019).

entirety of the Polish judiciary. However, a prevailing majority of the total of more than 10,000 judges maintain their independence in difficult conditions, both legal and psychological, which they face in their daily work.

Another observation comes to mind relating to the extensive reach of the Court's arguments going beyond the framework of the case presented by the Irish Court, but being of relevance for the scope of judicial cooperation. The independence of national courts is also required when they refer questions for a preliminary ruling. Such a position was emphasized by the CJEU in its judgment in the *Associação Sindical* case,[91] and repeated in the *LM* judgment discussed here (para. 54). It means that in the case of each reference for a preliminary ruling from Poland (or from another Member State in which there are corresponding doubts as to the respect of the fundamental right to a fair trial) it will be necessary for the Court of Justice to begin with a full test of independence of the referring court in the manner specified in the *LM* case. Did the Court in Luxembourg realise that its judgment might have such consequences?

In the context of a new category of questions referred for a preliminary ruling to the Court of Justice, in which national courts ask for an evaluation of their own independence, we may be soon witnessing new developments. Such questions have recently been referred to the CJEU by the courts in Germany (*Verwaltungsgericht Wiesbaden*)[92] and Hungary (*Central District Court in Pest*).[93] A new element is that the CJEU's reply and its appraisal is to apply to the very courts submitting the questions on judicial independence. This situation poses new challenges. First, if the Court of Justice were to answer the questions in the negative, i.e. if it considered that there is, indeed, a lack of a proper standard of judicial independence in the cases referred, the national court would then in fact not be entitled to ask a question for a preliminary ruling at all. In such cases, the answer on the substance of the question simultaneously becomes the answer on its admissibility. Would the Court of Justice therefore make an exception and admit the question on judicial independence from a non-independent court?, or would it rather declare the question inadmissible, yet pointing to the lack of independence of the requesting court?

Secondly, would the CJEU evaluate the independence of those courts by adapting the *LM* test? Not likely. In both cases of the German and Hungarian courts, the questions were asked in the context of individual cases pending before the national court. However, the questions referred to Luxembourg did not directly concern the private party's right to a fair trial, that is, the individual fundamental right. Instead, they dealt with a more general, constitutional issue: the independence of the court. The latter does not have to be linked to the specific case of a particular person. In

---

[91] CJEU, *Associação Sindical, supra* note 4, para. 43.

[92] CJEU, Case C-272/19, *Land Hessen*. The Wiesbaden Court's self-evaluation of its independence from the viewpoint of EU standards was negative: *'Nach alledem dürfte das vorlegende Gericht die europarechtlichen Vorgaben nach Art. 47 Abs. 2 GrCH eines unabhängigen und unparteiischen Gerichts nicht in diesem Sinne erfüllen.'*, Verwaltungsgericht Wiesbaden (Decision of 28 March 2019), 6 K 1016/15. https://openjur.de/u/2169849.html. Accessed 20 July 2019.

[93] Biró (2019) and Szabó (2019).

principle, therefore, there would be no need for a final (third) *LM* test: the individual assessment of the specific case and the risks related to the party of the national proceeding. The Court of Justice could make a ruling after carrying out: (1) the general assessment of the existence of systemic or generalised deficiencies in the Member State's judiciary, and (2) the impact of these deficiencies on the particular courts, namely those which submitted the questions.

If such a scenario were to materialise, it could also be followed by the courts of the Member States deciding on the execution of the EAW. They could start asking questions not just about the protection of the individual's right of the requested person to a fair trial, but at a more general level about the independence of the court that is supposed to hear the case, after the person were transferred. Such an approach would safeguard the individual right to a fair trial while guaranteeing the independence of national courts and protecting the rule of law more effectively than in the *LM* ruling.

References

Anagnostaras G (2016) Mutual confidence is not blind trust! Fundamental rights protection and the execution of the European arrest warrant: Aranyosi and Căldăraru. Common Mark Law Rev 6:1675–1704

Barcz J (2019) Unia Europejska wobec niepraworządnego państwa członkowskiego. Państwo i Prawo 1:3–23

Bárd P, van Ballegooij W (2018a) Judicial independence as a precondition for mutual trust. Verfassungsblog. https://doi.org/10.17176/20180410-104826

Bárd P, van Ballegooij W (2018b) The AG opinion in the Celmer case: why lack of judicial independence should have been framed as a rule of law issue. Verfassungsblog. https://doi.org/10.17176/20180702-173606-0

Biernat S (2018) How to assess the independence of Member State Courts? Verfassungsblog. https://doi.org/10.17176/20180730-100627-0

Biró M (2019) Hungarian judge requests European Court of Justice to examine his own independence. Index.hu. index.hu/english/2019/07/17/hungary_judicial_independence_european_court_of_justice_suspended_case. Accessed 20 July 2019

Bogdanowicz P, Taborowski M (2018a) Brak niezależności sądów krajowych jako uchybienie zobowiązaniu w rozumieniu art. 258 TFUE (cz. I). Europejski Przegląd Sądowy 1:4–11

Bogdanowicz P, Taborowski M (2018b) Wyrok Trybunału Sprawiedliwości w sprawie 'Celmer'. Analiza w 10 punktach. https://archiwumosiatynskiego.pl/wpis-w-debacie/wyrok-trybunalu-sprawiedliwosci-w-sprawie-celmer-analiza-w-10-punktach. Accessed 20 July 2019

Dashwood A, Dougan M, Rodger B, Spaventa E, Wyatt D (2011) Wyatt and Dashwood's European Union law, 6th edn. Hart, Oxford

Filipek P (2018) Challenges to the rule of law in the European Union: the distressing case of Poland. Revista do Instituto Brasileiro de Direitos Humanos 17(18):221–248

Filipek P (2019) Rozproszona europejska kontrola przestrzegania prawa do rzetelnego procesu sądowego w świetle zasady wzajemnego zaufania i wyroku C-216/18 PPU, LM. Europejski Przegląd Sądowy 2:14–31

Frąckowiak-Adamska A (2018a) Drawing red lines with no (significant) bite – why an individual test is not appropriate in the LM case. Verfassungsblog. https://doi.org/10.17176/20180730-104735-0

Frąckowiak-Adamska A (2018b) Następstwa wyroku w sprawie LM (Celmer) i postępowania na podstawie art. 7 TUE dla funkcjonowania sądów polskich w ramach wspólnoty prawnej UE. In: Barcz J, Zawidzka-Łojek A (eds) Sądowe mechanizmy ochrony praworządności w Polsce w świetle najnowszego orzecznictwa Trybunału Sprawiedliwości UE. Warszawa, pp 89–105
Górski M (2016) Prawo do skutecznego środka prawnego w art. 47 Karty Praw Podstawowych UE – znaczenie i deficyty. Europejski Przegląd Sądowy 8:37–44
Grabowska-Moroz B (2018a) Co orzekł Trybunał Sprawiedliwości w sprawie Celmer? https://archiwumosiatynskiego.pl/wpis-w-debacie/co-orzekl-trybunal-sprawiedliwosci-w-sprawie-celmer. Accessed 20 July 2019
Grabowska-Moroz B (2018b) Zaufanie bez wzajemności – czyli europejski nakaz aresztowania w czasach kryzysu praworządności. Refleksje na kanwie sprawy Celmer. Kwartalnik o Prawach Człowieka 1–2:16–26
Grabowska-Moroz B (2019) Sądowa kontrola Trybunału Sprawiedliwości UE w zakresie zmian dotyczących niezależności sądownictwa w państwie członkowskim UE – uwagi na tle Polski i Węgier. In: Bojarski Ł et al (eds) Konstytucja. Praworządność. Władza sądownicza. Aktualne problemy trzeciej władzy w Polsce, Warszawa, pp 403–430
Grzelak A (2018) Wzajemne zaufanie jako podstawa współpracy sądów państw członkowskich UE w sprawach karnych (uwagi na marginesie odesłania prejudycjalnego w sprawie C-216/18 PPU Celmer). Państwo i Prawo 10:50–66
Grzeszczak R, Krajewski M (2014) 'Sąd' w świetle przepisów art. 47 KPP oraz art. 267 TFUE. Europejski Przegląd Sądowy 6:4–14
Hofmański P, Wróbel A (2010) Komentarz do art. 6 EKPC. In: Garlicki L (ed) Konwencja o Ochronie Praw Człowieka i Podstawowych Wolności. Tom I. Komentarz do artykułów 1–18. Warszawa, pp 241–461
Kamiński IC (2019) Unijna zasada praworządności (państwa prawa) i uprawnienia sądów. In: Bojarski Ł et al (eds) Konstytucja. Praworządność. Władza sądownicza. Aktualne problemy trzeciej władzy w Polsce, Warszawa, pp 35–64
Krajewski M (2018) Who is afraid of the European Council? The Court of Justice's Cautious approach to the independence of domestic judges. Eur Const Law Rev 4:792–813
Kuijer M (2018) The rule of law in crisis? – some observations from the perspective of the Venice commission. Osteuropa Recht 4:530–551
Lawson R (2018) Protecting the independence of the judiciary: possibilities and limits of the European Convention on Human Rights. Revista do Instituto Brasileiro de Direitos Humanos 17(18):249–264
Lenaerts K (2017) La vie après l'avis: exploring the principle of mutual (yet not blind) trust. Common Mark Law Rev 3:805–840
Lenaerts K (2018) The Court of Justice and national courts: a dialogue based on mutual trust and judicial independence. http://www.nsa.gov.pl/download.php?id=753. Accessed 20 July 2019
Lenaerts K, Maselis I, Gutman K (2014) EU procedural law. Oxford University Press, Oxford
Łętowska E (2018) Convulsions in the rule of law. Osteuropa Recht 4:607–623
Lewandowski W (2019) Pomiędzy Scyllą zawieszenia wzajemnego zaufania i Charybdą fragmentaryzacji standardu ochrony prawa podstawowego – dylematy Trybunału Sprawiedliwości w wyroku C-216/18 PPU, LM. Europejski Przegląd Sądowy 2:4–13
Nita-Światłowska B (2018) Europejski nakaz aresztowania – ograniczona zasada wzajemnego zaufania. Kwartalnik o Prawach Człowieka 1–2:5–16
Pech L (2014) Commentary to Art. 47. In: Peers S et al (eds) The EU Charter of fundamental rights. A commentary. Hart, Oxford
Pech L, Platon S (2018) Judicial independence under threat: the Court of Justice to the rescue in the ASJP case. Common Mark Law Rev 6:1827–1854
Pech L, Wachowiec P (2019) 1095 Days later: from bad to worse regarding the rule of law in Poland (Part II). Verfassungsblog. https://doi.org/10.17176/20190211-221846-0
Sadurski W (2018) Anti-constitutional transformation in Poland: dimensions, sources, and prospects. Osteuropa Recht 4:624–636

Sadurski W (2019) Poland's constitutional breakdown. Oxford University Press, Oxford
Safjan M (2018) Domestic infringements of the rule of law as a European Union problem. Osteuropa Recht 4:552–560
Safjan M (2019) Rządy prawa a przyszłość Europy. Europejski Przegląd Sądowy 8:4–11
Scheppele KL (2018) Rule of law retail and rule of law wholesale: the ECJ's (Alarming) 'Celmer' decision. Verfassungsblog. https://doi.org/10.17176/20180730-095958-0
Schütze R (2018) European Union law, 2nd edn. Cambridge University Press, Cambridge
Schwarze J (2012) Kommentar zu Art. 267. In: Schwarze J (ed) EU-Kommentar, 3rd edn. Nomos, Baden-Baden
Sillen J (2019) The concept of 'internal judicial independence' in the case law of the European Court of Human Rights. Eur Const Law Rev 1:104–133
Szabó DG (2019) A Hungarian Judge Seeks Protection from the CJEU – Part I. Verfassungsblog. https://verfassungsblog.de/a-hungarian-judge-seeks-protection-from-the-cjeu-part-i. Accessed 20 July 2019
Taborowski M (2018) Naruszenie elementów zasady państwa prawa (art. 2 TUE) jako ograniczenie zasady wzajemnego zaufania w prawie Unii Europejskiej (w świetle wyroku LM (Celmer). In: Barcz J, Zawidzka-Łojek A (eds) Sądowe mechanizmy ochrony praworządności w Polsce w świetle najnowszego orzecznictwa Trybunału Sprawiedliwości UE, Warszawa, pp 73–88
Taborowski M (2019) Mechanizmy ochrony praworządności państw członkowskich w prawie Unii Europejskiej. Studium przebudzenia systemu ponadnarodowego, Warszawa
von Bogdandy A et al (2018) Drawing red lines and giving (some) bite – the CJEU's deficiencies Judgment on the European rule of law. Verfassungsblog. https://doi.org/10.17176/20180730-102416-0
Wachowiec P (2019) Pojęcie na gruncie traktatów unijnych. Polski wkład do redefinicji? In: Bojarski Ł et al (eds) Konstytucja. Praworządność. Władza sądownicza. Aktualne problemy trzeciej władzy w Polsce, Warszawa, pp 565–579
Wyrzykowski M (2017) 'Wrogie przejęcie' porządku konstytucyjnego. In: Bernatt M et al (eds) Wyzwania dla ochrony konkurencji i regulacji rynku, Warszawa, pp 831–853
Xanthopoulou E (2018) Mutual trust and rights in EU criminal and asylum law: three phases of evolution and the uncharted territory beyond blind trust. Common Mark Law Rev 2:489–510

Stanisław Biernat is a Professor of European law at the Jagiellonian University, Krakow.

Paweł Filipek is an Associate Professor at the University of Economics, Krakow.

The Rule of Law, Fair Trial and Human Dignity: The Protection of EU Values After *LM*

Catherine Dupré

Contents

Abstract The 2018 CJEU ruling in *LM* highlighted the importance of judicial independence for the rule of law and protection of the right to fair trial. In so doing, the judgment raised problematic questions about the relationship between Article 2 values and the EU Charter rights, and their connection with mutual trust. This chapter considers these issues through the lens of human dignity, which is both the first foundational value under Article 2 and the first right in the EU Charter. By discussing how the *LM* judgment raises the constitutional status of the right to a fair trial, this chapter argues that a focus on human dignity could effectively link Article 2 values with EU Charter rights and facilitate assessment of their respective breach.

1 Introduction

The design faults of Article 7 TEU proceedings and the delayed responses of EU institutions to the rapid deterioration of democratic standards in Hungary and Poland have triggered renewed interest in the mainstream EU judicial procedures as possible

This is a reworked version of 'Individuals and Judges in Defense of the Rule of Law', *Verfassungsblog* (28 July 2018).

C. Dupré (✉)
University of Exeter, Exeter, UK
e-mail: c.c.l.dupre@exeter.ac.uk

A. von Bogdandy et al. (eds.), *Defending Checks and Balances in EU Member States*, Beiträge zum ausländischen öffentlichen Recht und Völkerrecht 298,
https://doi.org/10.1007/978-3-662-62317-6_17

channels to address some of these concerns. The European Court of Justice (CJEU) Grand Chamber judgment of 25 July 2018 in *LM*[1] was promptly dissected by commentators across Europe.[2] In many ways, this case illustrates EU constitutionalism at its best: despite not being obliged to do so, the Irish judge made a request under Article 267 TFEU, bringing together concerns raised by the pending Article 7 TEU procedure against Poland and the more technical and narrow issue of fair trial under Article 47 EU Charter. The CJEU addressed these following the urgent procedure. Seizing the first opportunity to intervene on an issue directly relevant to the ongoing Article 7 TEU procedure against Poland,[3] the CJEU stayed on the path opened by *Aranyosi*[4] as a way of seeking to address the problematic issue of judicial independence at the core both of the preliminary ruling reference and of the Article 7 TEU procedure against Poland.

At first glance, in *LM* the CJEU appeared to make decisive strides with regard to the rule of law, stepping up as a prominent participant in the discussion triggered by reforms to the judiciary in Poland and Hungary. Notably the CJEU did not wait for Article 7 TEU proceedings to come to an end[5] in order to devise its own tests and assessment mechanisms, inviting Member States' courts to apply them. The *LM* case can certainly therefore be understood as promoting the role of Member States' courts in assessing what are generally referred to as the rule of law crises and related attacks on judicial independence in fellow Member States. The message of the CJEU is clear. When there is a 'real risk of systemic or generalised deficiencies' affecting the principle of judicial independence constructed by the Court as the 'essence' of the right to a fair trial under Article 47 EU Charter, the presumption of mutual trust that underpins the European Arrest Warrant (EAW) system can be rebutted by the executing authorities (i.e. the domestic courts) unless they are satisfied that the essence of the applicant's right under Article 47 will be protected in the issuing Member State. In carrying out the *LM* abstract test, the Irish High Court predictably found that there was a 'real risk connected with a lack of independence of the courts in Poland on account of systemic or generalised deficiencies'.[6] Predictably too, the Irish High Court did not find that in the concrete situation faced by the applicant upon his being surrendered to Poland he would be exposed to a breach of his right to a fair trial under Article 47.2 EU Charter and to a flagrant denial of justice.[7] This anti-climactic outcome of the Irish High Court judgment brings into sharp relief

[1]CJEU, Case C-216/18 PPU, *Minister for Justice and Equality*, ECLI:EU:C:2018:586.

[2]von Bogdandy et al. (2018) and Peers (2018).

[3]Kochenov et al. (2017).

[4]CJEU, Cases C-404/15 and C-659/15 PPU *Aranyosi and Caldararu*, ECLI:EU:C:2016:198.

[5]At the time of delivery only a reasoned proposal had been issued by the EU Commission in December 2017.

[6]Irish High Court, *Minister for Justice and Equality v. Artur Celmer* (No. 5) [2018] IEHC 639, para. 93.

[7]Irish High Court, *Minister for Justice and Equality v. Artur Celmer* (No. 5) [2018] IEHC 639, paras. 105 and 117.

some of the shortcomings of the CJEU's judgment in *LM* and points to the ruling's potentially wider significance in relation to safeguarding the EU foundational values under Article 2 TEU.

2 Article 7 TEU and *LM:* Questionable Overlaps

In its *LM* judgment the CJEU managed to connect Article 7 TEU and preliminary proceedings while keeping the two avenues on parallel tracks (paragraphs 70–72). First, the CJEU noted the 'particular relevance' of a reasoned proposal of the Commission against Poland adopted under Article 7(1) TEU (paragraph 61). The reasoned proposal is one of the materials that have to be 'objective, reliable, specific and properly updated concerning the operation of the system of justice in the issuing Member State' that may be considered in this process by the executing authority (paragraph 61). On its own, however, it is not sufficient to establish the 'real risk' and the executing court is required to make a wider investigation, with the assessment having to be carried out on the basis of the right to a fair trial (Article 47 EU Charter), and not of the EU value under Article 2 (paragraph 62). The second element shared by the Article 7 TEU procedure and the *LM* tests is the principle of judicial independence, a phrase not used by the Irish High Court in its preliminary reference, which focussed on the fundamental right to a fair trial and on a 'real risk of flagrant denial of justice' (paragraph 25). The two are easily related, but the CJEU's switch to judicial independence is arguably strategic as it makes it possible to establish a hermeneutic continuum between Article 2 TEU, which mentions the rule of law, and Art. 47 EU Charter, which protects the right to a fair trial:

> In that regard, it must be pointed out that the requirement of judicial independence forms part of the essence of the fundamental right to a fair trial, a right which is of cardinal importance as a guarantee that all the rights which individuals derive from EU law will be protected and that the values common to the Member States set out in Article 2 TEU, in particular the value of the rule of law, will be safeguarded. (paragraph 48)

In the above, the CJEU noted that the right to a fair trial under Article 47 EU Charter is included under the scope of Article 2 TEU, referred to in Council Framework Decision 2002/584/JHA of 13 June 2002, about which the Irish High Court sought clarification. In so doing the CJEU justified its entry into the territory of Article 2 TEU, from which it is excluded by Article 7 TEU, which promotes an exclusively political approach to breaches of Article 2 TEU values. The CJEU language however keeps clear boundaries between the two territories: rule of law issues fall under Article 7 TEU, and fair trial can—and should—be addressed by courts. Having established the principle of judicial independence as a bridge between the two, the CJEU provided guidance to domestic courts for determining the quality of judicial independence. In this respect, the CJEU arguably came very close to encouraging domestic courts to substitute Article 7 TEU, with the two procedures being at the very least mutually complementary. The reasoned proposal produced under Article 7.1 TEU will certainly be useful for domestic courts' determination of a 'real risk of systemic or generalised deficiencies'. Repeated positive findings by domestic courts against Poland under the second test of *LM* could potentially provide further evidence to feed into the Article 7 TEU procedure, thus possibly encouraging speedier action through this channel.

If it is certainly well-intentioned, i.e. encouraging action in a situation of a real risk of deficiencies in judicial independence, this promotion of judicial involvement in Articles 2 and 7 TEU territory is not unproblematic. Firstly, the complex pluralism in relation to judicial independence across the EU has been highlighted as rendering any assessment of its 'systemic' quality in a given Member State (abstract test) an arduous task to say the least.[8] As will be recalled from the early stages of pre-Article 7 proceedings, identifying and gathering appropriate documentation on the quality of the rule of law in Poland and Hungary have not been easy tasks, and that is for institutions that are much better equipped than any domestic court being invited to perform that test. Therefore, in this respect *LM* does not provide much clarification, as the reasoned proposal is considered as just one of the possible materials at the disposal of domestic courts. In addition, the abstract test arguably creates a wide power gap between a single court (and a single judge in many cases) and the issuing Member State, subject to the early stage of Article 7 TEU proceedings. Secondly, the executing Member State court's task of checking the quality of judicial independence in the issuing Member State with regards to the pending EAW before them (concrete test) amounts to what was evocatively compared to 'herculean hurdles'.[9] In particular, while the CJEU in *LM* appeared keen to promote a 'dialogue between the executing judicial authority and issuing judicial authority' (paragraph 77), scepticism has been expressed about this, with scholars noting that such a dialogue might not go so smoothly in practice.[10] If a court-to-court exchange of information can be workable, the Irish High Court's effort to engage in this arguably confirmed the difficulty in obtaining unequivocal answers from the issuing authorities in a situation of real risk of systemic or generalised deficiencies.[11] Thirdly, domestic courts having to determine single-handedly the quality of judicial independence and of the right to a fair trial in the issuing Member State is likely going to delay the procedure of EAW and generate extra costs, which would somehow have to be absorbed by the executing judicial authority. Paradoxically, this might trigger a knock-on effect for fair trial in the executing Member State, depending on the volume of EAW with Poland (or Hungary) going through its court system. In this situation, one possible silver lining might come from recent CJEU case law according to which the host state has to cover the cost for granting asylum seekers

[8]Kosar (2016).

[9]Bard and Ballegooij (2018), pp. 8–9.

[10]Bracken (2018) and Biernat (2018).

[11]Irish High Court, *Minister for Justice and Equality v. Artur Celmer* (No. 5) [2018] IEHC 639, paras. 85–91.

'the minimum conditions for reception' pending their application.[12] In relation to the EAW, the extra cost for the executing Member State might, so it could be hoped, alert the Member States' authorities to the seriousness of the situation and encourage them to be more pro-active at the EU level, including through Article 7 TEU. Fourthly and finally, in its endeavour to bring Article 47 EU Charter closer to Article 2 TEU, the CJEU forgot to draw on Article 6 European Convention on Human Rights (ECHR). This apparent forgetfulness is odd considering the EU Charter's requirements under Article 52 paragraph 3 and Article 53 that the CJEU refer to ECHR case law when there is a correspondence between the EU Charter and ECHR rights. It becomes odder considering that the Irish High Court had phrased its Article 267 TFEU question with explicit reference to the 'flagrant denial of justice' test developed by the European Court of Human Rights under Article 6 ECHR (paragraph 25). As a result of this omission, the CJEU's focus on the 'essence of the right to a fair trial' arguably made a complicated situation even more complicated, leading to the Member State's court having to work out the questionable distinctions between the CJEU and the ECHR thresholds for an acceptable quality of fair trial.

3 Sowing the Seeds of Constitutional Distrust?

In *LM* the CJEU widened the possibility of rebutting the mutual trust presumption, while emphasising its 'fundamental importance' (paragraph 36) and defining it as the 'cornerstone' of judicial cooperation in criminal matters (paragraph 41). The CJEU had recognised this possibility in previous case law,[13] however, in *LM* it did so for the first time in relation to a non-absolute right, namely the right to a fair trial. The CJEU was cautious to ring-fence this exceptional approach by requiring that both steps of the *Aranyosi* test be taken in this context too. The pending Article 7 TEU proceeding against Poland was no doubt one of the reasons for extending the *Aranyosi* and *NS* tests involving absolute rights (human dignity, and the prohibition of torture, inhuman or degrading treatment). Nevertheless, as mentioned above, on its own, the existence of a reasoned proposal under Article 7 is not a sufficient criterion for finding a clear risk of systemic or generalised deficiencies, it only forms part of the material that the executing authority can consider in its assessment. This arguably makes mutual distrust a possibility for other situations of systemic deficiencies affecting other non-absolute EU Charter rights. This is all the more possible as mutual trust is a core principle in numerous other EU procedures,[14] therefore likely to concern a range of fundamental rights. In addition, the mutual trust standard

---

[12]CJEU, Case C-179/11 *Cimade and GISTI v Ministre de l'Intérieur, de l'Outre-Mer, des Collectivités Territoriales et de l'Immigration*, ECLI:EU:C:2012:594.

[13]CJEU, Case C-411/10 *N.S. and Others*, ECLI:EU:C:2011:865 and CJEU, Cases C-404/15 and C-659/15 PPU *Aranyosi and Caldararu*, *supra* note 4. Korenica and Coli (2016), p. 542.

[14]Frackowiak-Adamska (2018).

in *LM* (i.e. a real risk of systemic or generalised deficiencies in the protection of Article 47 paragraph 2) appears to be lower than under the EAW Framework Decision 2002/584 which stays within the Article 7 TEU perimeter, requiring a 'serious and persistent breach' of one of the foundational values under Article 2 TEU (paragraph 10).

This has further ramifications as mutual trust (and mutual recognition which derives from it) lies at the core of the whole EU constitutional framework and is anchored in the principle of sincere cooperation of Article 4 paragraph 3 TEU. This therefore arguably raises the question whether *LM* is planting the seeds of constitutional distrust, fighting fire with fire, and undermining ultimately the constitutional principle of mutual trust, without which the EU cannot operate effectively. The CJEU seems to be well aware of this risk, as evidenced by its focus on an essentialist definition of the right to a fair trial, and its connection to Article 2 TEU values. Even so, the scope for mutual distrust remains wide as non-absolute rights represent the vast majority of the EU Charter rights, and Article 2 TEU foundational values are numerous, creating the possibility for an even greater number of combinations between the two. Moreover, this risk of encouraging mutual distrust has to be seen in the current political context of a series of unprecedented crises, which have in common a radical questioning of, and distrust in, the EU's ability to fulfil its own mission and/or to fulfil a mission that Member States would like it to fulfil. In addition, and in relation to the rule of law crises, pre-Article 7 proceedings and Article 7 have created a general climate of deep distrust between the EU on the one hand, and Poland[15] and Hungary[16] on the other. This sentiment flourishes on a widespread resentment and sense of deep social injustice among Central Europeans many of whom feel they have been treated as second class citizens by the EU since joining it. Finally, it must be borne in mind that the CJEU itself might not be viewed by Poland nor Hungary with the greatest level of trust. The few rulings it delivered on the issue of judicial independence had little effect on remedying the problem, especially in the early stages of the Hungarian situation,[17] but they were given great publicity as the first unequivocal condemnation of the judicial reforms by an EU institution. Concerns about the possible germination of this seed of constitutional distrust are therefore not unrealistic, especially as the tension between the EU and Central and Eastern European Member States increases.[18] As the rebuttability of

[15]'Poland Cries Foul as EU Triggers 'Nuclear Option' over Judicial Independence', The Guardian 20 December 2017: https://www.theguardian.com/world/2017/dec/20/eu-process-poland-voting-rights.

[16]Interview with Hungarian Foreign Affairs Minister, Péter Szijjarto, with Le Monde: 'La procédure de sanction est une revanche contre la Hongrie', 14 December 2018.

[17]E.g. CJEU, Case C-286/12 *Commission v. Hungary*, ECLI:EU:C:2012:687.

[18]See e.g. European Parliament Resolution of 12 September 2018 calling for Art. 7 proceeding, P8-TA-PROV (2018) 0340; CJEU, Case C-619/18 *European Commission v Poland*, ECLI:EU:C:2018:910. The EU's relationships with Romania are also marked by a 'climate of defiance': 'La Roumanie en pleine dérive illibérale: Bucarest assure au 1 Janvier sa première présidence de l'UE, dans un climat de défiance inédit avec Bruxelles', Le Monde, 1–2 January 2019.

mutual distrust ultimately rests on the right to a fair trial, the constitutional status of this right therefore requires closer attention.

4 Abstract Versus Concrete Test: *In Dubio pro Dignitate*

It is suggested here that one way of resolving the mutual trust conundrum is to seek to ensure that its rebuttal promote a constitutional good of higher importance or status than mutual trust. This is perhaps what the CJEU has sought to achieve, albeit incompletely, in its *LM* judgment by emphasising the definition of the right to a fair trial as the essence of judicial independence and its connection to Article 2 TEU. Therefore an alternative, or perhaps complementary, approach might arguably be to take the lesson of *NS* and *Aranyosi* a step further. This could involve joining the dots between the right to a fair trial and human dignity which is codified both under Article 1 EU Charter[19] and Article 2 TEU. This would give the right to a fair trial an elevated constitutional status, i.e. close if not identical to that of ‘inviolable human dignity’. As such it would arguably be robust enough to provide a suitable ground for rebutting the presumption of mutual trust, considered both in its specific (e.g. EAW) embodiment and in its constitutional dimension under Article 4 paragraph 3 TEU. This would therefore legitimise constitutional distrust in situations of systemic or generalised deficiencies.

This suggestion needs unpacking. Firstly, this follows *NS* and *Aranyosi* in which the mutual trust presumption gave way to the protection of human dignity in the form of the prohibition of torture and inhuman and degrading treatment, considered under Article 1 and Article 4 EU Charter (*NS*), and under Article 4 EU Charter (*Aranyosi*). This makes both practical and theoretical sense. Practically, the treatments involved under Article 4 EU Charter are the most violent and brutal ones falling short of killing a human being; and this therefore arguably legitimises an executing judicial authority’s decision to suspend the surrendering of a person to another Member State if that person faces a real risk of being subjected to Article 4 EU Charter types of treatment. Theoretically, the Article 4 EU Charter absolute prohibition is the strongest prohibition of the EU human rights system, and this status is further strengthened by Article 15 ECHR according to which Article 3 ECHR (Article 4 EU Charter counterpart) may never be curtailed even in emergency situations. As a result, it is argued that there may not, and should not, be any mutual trust towards Member States where people face a real risk of being tortured or subjected to inhuman and degrading treatment or punishment, due to systemic or generalised deficiencies. Finally and importantly, breaches of Article 4 EU Charter do not only result in violations of this person’s human dignity under the EU Charter, they also attack human dignity as the first foundational value of the EU under Article 2 TEU and the principle of inviolability of human dignity codified under Article 1 EU Charter. As

[19]Dupré (2014), pp. 3–24.

such, the commitment to human dignity holds together the EU's first foundational value under Article 2 TEU and the most important fundamental right of the EU Charter (from which all the other rights flow), therefore bringing together the realms of values and rights. It is suggested that the presumption of mutual trust can therefore be rebutted not only because of the real risk of treatments contrary to Article 4 EU Charter in situations of systemic and generalised deficiencies, but also because the considered Member State might be breaking the EU foundational promise never again to destroy humanity as codified both under Article 2 TEU and the EU Charter.[20]

The connection between the commitment to protect human dignity and the right to a fair trial is not made explicit in *LM*, but it arguably lies very close to the surface of the judgment. Drawing it out would therefore strengthen the legitimacy of extending the rebuttability of the mutual trust presumption in the specific case of the non-absolute right to a fair trial. Many, if not all, non-absolute EU Charter rights can be related in one way or another to human dignity which is, as the 2017 Report on the Application of the EU Charter reminds us, 'the basis of all fundamental rights' and 'part of the essence of all other rights'.[21] It has to be noted, however, that the right to a fair trial stands out as a *sine qua non* condition for the respect of human dignity, as only if it exists can human dignity (and rights) victims be heard, effectively seek justice and ultimately start healing the violation. Moreover, it is argued that the right to a fair trial plays a crucial (if not exclusive) role in making it possible for a democracy to learn from its mistakes, and to seek to prevent further breaches of human dignity and of human rights from occurring again. Above all, grounding the rebuttability of the mutual trust presumption in human dignity considered in its inviolable (Article 1 EU Charter) and foundational (Article 2 TEU) natures has another benefit, as this explicitly limits the situations in which the presumption can be rebutted, therefore addressing the concern of constitutional distrust discussed above. Namely, it might be rebutted only when the four rights codified under the dignity title of the EU Charter face a real risk of being breached. This, it is suggested, limits the problematically wide scope of pluralist definitions and practices of judicial independence, which could easily lead to double standards in addition to problems of identification in a given situation of alleged breach of this principle. Moreover and crucially, this draws attention to other situations in which

[20]Dupré (2015), pp. 66–74.

[21]'Human dignity, as protected under Art. 1 of the Charter, is *the basis of all fundamental rights*. It guarantees the protection of human beings from being treated as mere objects by the state or by their fellow citizens. It is a right, *but also part of the essence of all other rights*. Therefore it must be respected when any other rights are restricted. All subsequent rights and freedoms on dignity, such as the right to life and the prohibition of torture and slavery, add specific protection against violations of dignity. They must be equally upheld in order to protect other rights and freedoms in the Charter, for example the freedom of expression and the freedom of association. None of the rights laid down in the Charter may be used to harm the dignity of another person.' 2017 Report on the Application of the EU Charter of Fundamental Rights, SWD (2018) 304 final, p. 12. Emphasis added.

the presumption of mutual trust may be legitimately rebutted, such as those of servitude, slavery, forced labour and human trafficking which are absolutely banned under Article 5 EU Charter (the last right of the dignity title).

As a result, the *LM* judgment can be read in two ways. One, as the judgment through which the CJEU opened the gates to mutual distrust in instances of a real risk of breach of (potentially all) non-absolute EU Charter rights. Alternatively, *LM* can be read as elevating the constitutional status of the right to a fair trial to a level close (if not totally similar) to the absolute protection of human dignity. In this reading, it is suggested that the CJEU builds on the EU commitment to making human dignity inviolable by securing the strongest possible constitutional basis for a key procedural mechanism required for its effective protection. Exploring this interpretation might give the CJEU the opportunity to shed light on what is at stake with a breach of Article 2 TEU values, which arguably goes far beyond the significance of the rule of law and judicial independence, to include the constitutional ontology and *raison d'être* of a democratic European Union anchored in the dignity promise.

Finally, drawing out the connection between the foundational commitment to protect human dignity and the right to a fair trial makes it possible to address the shortcomings of the *LM* two-stage test. This can arguably be achieved, by reverting to the approach put forward in *NS*.[22] Namely, the presumption that in situations of systemic deficiencies in conditions of reception for asylum seekers (*NS*), and, by extension, of judicial independence (*LM*) in fellow Member States, issuing Member States 'cannot be unaware' of the risk of breaches to Article 4 TEU (*NS*) and by extension to Article 47 TEU (*LM*). This double negative presumption has three main advantages over the two-stage test advocated in *LM*. First, by rendering the *LM* two-stage test unnecessary, it prevents the constitutionally awkward positioning of the executing Member State courts (a single judge in most cases), both vis-à-vis the issuing Member State and vis-à-vis Article 7 TEU (abstract test). In an Article 7 TEU context, the existence of a reasoned proposal would be sufficient for confirming the double negative presumption, while keeping Member State courts outside the boundaries of Article 7 TEU. Second, adopting the *NS* approach would contribute to addressing the nonsensical second and concrete stage of the *LM* test, whereby the executing Member State court is expected to trust the information provided by the issuing Member State court, about which it has just established that the mutual trust presumption may not apply. Third, considering the foundational nature of human dignity (Article 2 TEU) and its paradigmatic function in shaping human rights in the EU (Article 1 EU Charter), it would be wise not to dilute human dignity in chance concretisations depending in part on the judges' subjectivity, but to retain it as a whole in its abstraction and as the foundational promise on which the EU project rests.

---

[22]CJEU, Case C-411/10 *NS and Others*, ECLI:EU:C:2011:865, para. 91.

5 Conclusion

Disappointing for some, exciting for others, the ultimate significance of the *LM* judgment might not mainly lie in its connections with Article 7 TEU, and in its ability to offer new tools or new channels for Member States' courts to address the systemic deterioration of the rule of law in fellow Member States. Rather, this judgment's principal merit might prove to be the connections it established between the set of foundational values under Article 2 TEU and rights contained in the EU Charter, therefore bringing the Charter and its rights to the political core of the EU.

At least two questions remain at this stage. One is whether the hermeneutic route taken by *LM* from Article 2 EU to EU Charter rights can be reversed, namely whether the judicial finding of systemic and generalised deficiencies of the *NS* and *Aranyosi* type in relation to the right to a fair trial, and in relation to one or all of the dignity rights under Title 1 EU Charter might be one of the factors for triggering pre-Article 7 or Article 7 proceedings. The other question is about which institution is best placed to safeguard the foundations of a constitutional order such as the EU. In the framework of European constitutionalism developed on the basis of a collaboration between the EU, the Council of Europe and their common Member States, safeguarding the foundational values in any of these orders has not been left to that order alone. Rather, protection of their foundational values has been entrusted to a dynamic equilibrium of sovereignty.[23] In this respect, the EU still has a way to go. As *LM* shows, despite its visible endeavour to draw red lines, the judicial collaboration between the CJEU and Member States' courts at the heart of the preliminary reference process cannot effectively address the shortcomings of Article 7 TEU mechanisms for the protection of the EU foundational values. Even in the event of a negative finding by the issuing court, implementing *LM* does not contribute to advancing Article 7 TEU. If anything, the Irish High Court ruling arguably weakens Article 7 TEU by demonstrating that when there is a proven 'real risk of systemic or generalised deficiencies' in relation to the right to a fair trial, it can still be appropriate to surrender applicants in individual instances. An appropriate custodian for the EU foundational values, together with procedural avenues to access it effectively by those who need it most, remain therefore to be imagined and designed.

Failing an institutional reform, hermeneutic connections with the ECHR case law is a necessary and simple step for the CJEU to take towards protecting its foundational values and safeguarding democracy in the EU. The ECHR is not just a convenient—and illusory—safety net for the protection of fair trial when the EU mechanisms fail, as pointed out by the Irish High Court.[24] As will be recalled, the ECHR case law is a valuable source of inspiration for interpreting EU Charter rights and ensuring that standards of protection are consistent across the EU and the Council of Europe. Arguably, it is also a keystone for European constitutionalism,

---

[23] Dupré (2015), p. 5.

[24] Irish High Court, *Minister for Justice and Equality v. Artur Celmer* (No. 5) [2018] IEHC 639, para. 124.

which brings together the constitutional orders and the EU and its Member States through their respective commitment to it.[25] Ultimately, the ECtHR provides the overarching narrative as to why it is important to protect these rights and these values in a democratic society. By omitting to refer to ECHR case law under Article 6 ECHR, the CJEU might have missed a golden opportunity to take part in this powerful narrative and to give meaning to the EU democratic project at a time where it faces its greatest challenges.

Acknowledgments I am grateful to Gabor Halmai and Stephen Skinner for their comments on earlier versions of this chapter.

References

Bard P, Ballegooij W (2018) Judicial independence as a precondition for mutual trust? The CJEU in Minister for Justice and equality v LM. New J Crim Law:1–13

Biernat S (2018) How to Assess the Independence of Member State Courts? Verfassungsblog, 28 July 2018. https://verfassungsblog.de/how-to-assess-the-independence-of-member-state-courts/

Bracken C (2018) Episode 5 of the Celmer Saga – The Irish High Court Holds Back. Verfassungsblog, 28 November 2018. https://verfassungsblog.de/episode-5-of-the-celmer-saga-the-irish-high-court-holds-back/

Dupré C (2014) Article 1: human dignity. In: Peers S, Hervey T, Kenner J, Ward A (eds) The EU Charter of fundamental rights: a commentary. CH Beck/Hart/Nomos, Oxford, pp 3–24

Dupré C (2015) The age of dignity: human rights and constitutionalism in Europe. Bloomsbury/ Hart, Oxford

Frackowiak-Adamska A (2018) Drawing Red Lines with No (Significant) Bite – Why an Individual Test is not Appropriate in the LM Case. Verfassungsblog 30 July 2018. https://verfassungsblog.de/drawing-red-lines-with-no-significant-bite-why-an-individual-test-is-not-appropriate-in-the-lm-case/

Kochenov D, Pech L, Scheppele KL (2017) The EU Commission's Activation of Art. 7: better late than never?, EU Law Analysis, 23 December 2017. http://eulawanalysis.blogspot.com/2017/12/the-european-commissions-activation-of.html

Korenica F, Coli D (2016) No more unconditional 'mutual trust' between the Member States: an analysis of the landmark decision of CJEU in Aranyosi and Caldararu. Eur Human Rights Law Rev 21:542

Kosar D (2016) Perils of judicial self-government in transitional societies: holding the least accountable branch to account. Cambridge University Press, Cambridge

Peers S (2018) Mutual trust and independence of the judiciary after the CJEU judgment in LM – a new era or business as usual?, EU Law Anal 15 August 2018. http://eulawanalysis.blogspot.com/2018/08/mutual-trust-and-independence-of.html

von Bogdandy A, Bogdanowicz P, Canor I, Schmidt M, Taborowski M (2018) Drawing Red Lines and Giving (some) Bite – the CJEU's Deficiencies Judgment on the European Rule of Law. Verfassungsblog, 3 August 2018. https://verfassungsblog.de/drawing-red-lines-and-giving-some-bite-the-cjeus-deficiencies-judgment-on-the-european-rule-of-law/

[25]Dupré (2015), pp. 179–183.

Catherine Dupré is an Associate Professor of Comparative Constitutional Law at the University of Exeter, UK.

Drawing Red Lines with No (Significant) Bites: Why an Individual Test Is Not Appropriate in the *LM* Case

Agnieszka Frąckowiak-Adamska

Contents

Abstract This contribution argues that an obligation for an executing court to conduct an individual assessment in case of systemic deficiencies of the judiciary in other Member States is not an adequate tool for ensuring the respect for the rule of law. Infringements of the independence of the judiciary require other legal mechanisms of protection than fundamental rights. Moreover, individual test is often not feasible in the European judicial area as some other acts providing for recognition of judgments in the EU do not contain the mechanisms of refusal of recognition or execution. A breach of the obligation to ensure independence of the courts should logically result in suspending the participation of a given Member State in the EU policy area at stake.

This Chapter draws on 'Drawing Red Lines With No (Significant) Bites—Why An Individual Test Is Not Appropriate in the LM Case', Verfassungsblog (30 July 2020) and 'Mutual trust and independence of the judiciary after the CJEU judgment in LM – new era or business as usual?', EU Law Analysis (15 August 2018).

A. Frąckowiak-Adamska (✉)
University of Wrocław, Wrocław, Poland
e-mail: agnieszka.frackowiak-adamska@uwr.edu.pl

A. von Bogdandy et al. (eds.), *Defending Checks and Balances in EU Member States*, Beiträge zum ausländischen öffentlichen Recht und Völkerrecht 298,
https://doi.org/10.1007/978-3-662-62317-6_18

1 Introduction

The judgment in the *LM*[1] case was much expected as the first opportunity for the Court of Justice of the EU to assess the consequences of the systemic changes restricting judicial independence in Poland. The sequence of laws adopted in 2015–2018[2] in this State has been assessed commonly by various external and internal institutions as '[enabling] the legislative and executive powers to interfere in a severe and extensive manner in the administration of justice and thereby [posing] a grave threat to the judicial independence as a key element of the rule of law'.[3] These reforms are problematic for the EU as the national courts shall ensure an 'effective legal protection in the fields covered by Union law'.[4] But they also pose a problem for other Member States because of mechanisms of judicial cooperation established by the EU in last 19 years as a part of area of freedom, security and justice.

The open questions are whether these reforms should have consequences for the position of Poland in the EU and if yes, who should draw them and how. To protect the rule of law in Europe, the European Commission submitted for the first time in its history a reasoned proposal activating the Article 7 TEU mechanism.[5] The proceedings against Poland based on Article 258 TFEU are also ongoing.[6] The *LM* case hinges on the horizontal aspect of the changes—verifying the state of the rule of law

---

[1]CJEU, Case C-216/18 PPU, *Minister for Justice and Equality (LM)*, ECLI:EU:C:2018:586.

[2]Described in Report of the Stefan Batory Foundation Legal Expert Group on the impact of the judiciary reform in Poland in 2015–2018.

[3]CDL-AD(2017)031-e Poland—Opinion of the European Commission For Democracy Through Law on the Draft Act amending the Act on the National Council of the Judiciary; on the Draft Act amending the Act on the Supreme Court, proposed by the President of Poland, and on the Act on the Organisation of Ordinary Courts, adopted by the Commission at its 113th Plenary Session (Venice, 8–9 December 2017). Similar opinions were expressed i.a. by the European Commission, the Executive Board of the European Network of Councils for the Judiciary (ENCJ), www.encj.eu/articles/96, Polish Supreme Court, Polish faculties of law, independent nongovernmental organisations.

[4]Article 19 (1) TEU. See also CJEU, Opinion 1/09, ECLI:EU:C:2011:123, para. 68: 'it is for the national courts and tribunals and for the Court of Justice to ensure the full application of European Union law in all Member States and to ensure judicial protection of an individual's rights under that law' and para. 69: 'The national court, in collaboration with the Court of Justice, fulfils a duty entrusted to them both of ensuring that in the interpretation and application of the Treaties the law is observed'.

[5]European Commission, Reasoned proposal of 20 December 2018 in accordance with Article 7 (1) of the Treaty on European Union regarding the rule of law in Poland, COM(2017) 835 final.

[6]At the time of deciding the *LM* case, the case C-192/18 on the law on the ordinary courts organisation was already pending before the CJEU (action brought on 15 March 2018). And infringement procedure regarding the Polish law on the Supreme Court was launched by the Commission only on 2 July 2018. At the time of deciding the *LM* case it was thus at the pre-trial stage and it was not evident at all that the Commission will decide to bring an action to the court. Finally, the action was brought on 2 October 2018 and registered as Case C-619/18 *Commission v. Poland.*

by courts of the other Member States. In the case, in which the European Arrest Warrant (EAW) was issued by a Polish judicial authority against a person prosecuted for a drug-related crime, the defendant argued before an Irish court that due to the reforms of the Polish judiciary there is a risk of denial of justice if he is transferred to Poland.

Has the Court of Justice (hereinafter CJEU), in deciding the *LM* case, drawn red lines for Member States in the context of the rule of law? It could be admitted that it set 'a limit beyond which someone's [Member State's] behavior is no longer acceptable'[7] but it could also be argued that it did not establish adequate consequences of crossing it. The Luxemburg court focused on the protection of individuals, leaving the issue of systemic consequences to the Council acting on the basis of Article 7 TEU. This contribution argues that an individual test required by the *LM* judgment is not an adequate tool for ensuring the respect for the rule of law.

2 Potential Solutions in the LM Case

The Irish question was based on the CJEU's case law relating to the protection of fundamental rights in the context of mutual recognition of judgments in criminal matters (*Aranyosi*[8]). According to the latter case, if a court taking the decision on extradition on the basis of an EAW possesses evidence of systemic or generalised deficiencies in the protection of fundamental right in the issuing Member State, it should postpone the execution and assess whether the individual concerned will be exposed to a real risk of inhuman or degrading treatment because of the conditions during detention. The CJEU in the *LM* case had three main options: (1) to refrain from assessing the impact of the restriction of judicial independence on the EAW mechanism (following Poland's argument that it is possible only by the Council on the basis of Article 7 TEU), (2) to follow the *Aranyosi* pattern or (3) to introduce a new mechanism if the independence of the courts is doubtful in the Member State issuing the judicial decision (building on its recent decision in the case *Associação Sindical dos Juízes Portugueses*,[9] in which it stated that Member States are obliged to ensure independence of the courts).

The *LM* judgment treated an issue of judicial independence as a part of a right to a fair trial protected by Article 47 of the Charter. It allowed the CJEU to follow the *Aranyosi* path and base its answer on a similar pattern: if the court executing an EAW from another Member State possesses the information that there is a real risk of a breach of the fundamental right to fair trial due to systemic or generalised

[7]See Cambridge Dictionary, see dictionary.cambridge.org/pl/dictionary/english/red-line.

[8]CJEU, Joined Cases C-404/15 and C-659/15 PPU, *Aranyosi and Căldăraru*, ECLI:EU:C:2016:198.

[9]CJEU, Case C-64/16, *Associação Sindical dos Juízes Portugueses*, ECLI:EU:C:2018:117, para. 37.

deficiencies concerning the independence of the issuing Member State's judiciary, it shall assess whether the person incurs such a risk if he is surrendered to that State (individual or specific assessment).[10] The CJEU indicated that the suspending of the mechanism of recognition is possible only if the decision is taken on the basis of Article 7(2) TEU.[11] Until this moment even if a Member State is the subject of a reasoned proposal as referred to in Article 7(1) TEU, the 'executing judicial authority must refrain from giving effect to the European arrest warrant' only if there are substantial grounds for believing that that person will run a real risk of breach of the fundamental right to a fair trial.[12]

3 Individual Test

An executing judicial authority conducting an individual test should verify firstly 'to what extent the systemic or generalised deficiencies are liable to have an impact at the level of that State's courts with jurisdiction over the proceedings to which the requested person will be subject'. Then it should verify whether there is a real risk of breach of his fundamental right to an independent tribunal having regard to his personal situation, the nature of the offence for which he is being prosecuted and the factual context that forms the basis of the European arrest warrant. The sources of knowledge are: (1) specific concerns expressed by the individual concerned and any information provided by him, (2) any supplementary information obtained from the issuing judicial authority in the answer to the (mandatory) request made by the executing authority, (3) (optional) assistance from the central authority or one of the central authorities of the issuing Member State.[13] If the information obtained in such a way by the executing judicial authority 'does not lead the latter to discount the existence of a real risk [for the individual concerned] (...) the executing judicial authority must refrain from giving effect to the European arrest warrant'.[14]

4 Critical Assessment of an Individual Test

It can be argued that an obligation for an executing court to conduct an individual assessment in case of systemic deficiencies of the judiciary in other Member States reverses the logic of the mutual trust developed by the CJEU (Sect. 4.1). Furthermore it is not the proper test to protect the rule of law due to two reasons. Firstly

[10]CJEU, *LM*, *supra* note 1, para. 79.

[11]Id., paras. 71–73.

[12]Id., paras. 78 and 59.

[13]Id., paras. 75–78.

[14]Id., para. 78.

(Sect. 4.2), there is a substantial difference between fundamental rights and the independence of the judiciary. Infringements of the latter require other legal mechanisms of protection deterring a Member State from restricting judicial independence. Secondly (Sect. 4.3), the individual test is often not feasible in the European judicial area as some other acts providing for recognition of judgments in the EU do not contain the mechanisms of refusal of recognition or execution. A broader perspective should be taken as Polish institutional changes affecting judicial independence may influence all twenty-six EU acts providing for mutual recognition of judgments.

4.1 Regular Mutual Control Contrary to the Spirit of Mutual Trust

According to the CJEU the principle of mutual trust has a fundamental importance and 'requires (...) each of those States, save in exceptional circumstances, to consider all the other Member States to be complying with EU law and particularly with the fundamental rights recognised by EU law'.[15] But according to para. 69 of the *LM* judgment, when the issuing Member State has been the subject of a (well) reasoned proposal adopted by the Commission pursuant to Article 7(1) TEU,[16] the executing court is obliged to pursue a regular control. The fact of starting the Article 7 TEU procedure thus rebuts the presumption of mutual trust as the individual assessment is required in every case in which the person subject to EAW pleads it.[17]

Perhaps the CJEU treated this obligation as a tool of pressure on the Member State restricting the independence of the judiciary contrary to the recommendations of the Commission—applied until the decision on the basis of Article 7(2) TEU is taken. But a regular control of judicial decisions from other Member States reverses the logic of mutual trust and can impair it in the long term (as taking a decision on the basis of Article 7(2) TEU which requires unanimity is not very probable). From the perspective of mutual trust a better solution would be if a decision of a Member State to restrict the independence of the courts (assessed as systemic deficiencies) implied a temporary suspension of its participation in all legal acts based on mutual trust in the administration of justice.

[15]CJEU, Opinion 2/13 *Accession of the EU to the European Convention for the Protection of Human Rights and Fundamental Freedoms*, ECLI:EU:C:2014:2454, para. 191.

[16]Based on actions impairing the independence of national courts.

[17]CJEU, *LM*, *supra* note 1, paras. 60 and 68–69.

4.2 Substantial Difference Between Fundamental Rights and the Independence of the Judiciary

The answer in the *LM* judgment was based on the interpretation of Article 1 (3) of the EAW framework decision which states that this act shall not modify 'the obligation to respect fundamental rights and fundamental legal principles as enshrined in Article 6 [TEU]'.[18] But there is a substantial difference between fundamental rights and the independence of the judiciary. Both values are certainly interconnected: the independence of the judiciary is in particular a part of the right to effective judicial protection. But it is not limited to this aspect. Fundamental rights are entitlements of individuals and it is therefore possible to verify whether they are ensured in individual situations. The independence of the judiciary is important in an individual case, but it also remains a key element of the State's system, indispensable to ensuring the right balance between public and private interests. In the EU, it also guarantees securing effective legal protection in the fields covered by Union law. It is important especially if the executive power in a Member State openly declares the protection of its own nationals and ignores the European citizenship context. For example, in the case of a child abduction to another State the principle is that the authority shall order the return of the child forthwith save for exceptional cases.[19] But the Polish government treats children who have a Polish parent as Polish children (ignoring the parent of other nationality) and does not hide the wish that they stay in Poland. A law on the central authority in family matters[20] was recently adopted to enable the Ministry of Justice to supervise judicial proceedings in child abduction cases.[21] It provides, amongst others, for the right of the Ministry to inquire courts about pending cases and for the obligation of the courts to answer immediately.[22] The purpose of such supervision is clear from the title of a Ministry leaflet—'Stop transferring Polish children abroad'.[23] The influence of the executive on the judiciary can diminish the protection of rights stemming from EU law including the right to equal treatment.

[18] It is interesting to note that the CJEU did see in this provision also the reference to Article 2 TEU (CJEU, *LM*, *supra* note 1, para. 45) while Article 1(3) mentions only Article 6 TEU.

[19] Art. 12(2), 13 and 20 Convention of 25 October 1980 on the Civil Aspects of International Child Abduction, complemented by Council Regulation (EC) 2201/2003 concerning jurisdiction and the recognition and enforcement of judgments in matrimonial matters and the matters of parental responsibility, repealing Regulation (EC) No 1347/2000, (2003) OJ L338/1.

[20] Ustawa z dnia 26 stycznia 2018 r. o wykonywaniu niektórych czynności organu centralnego w sprawach rodzinnych z zakresu obrotu prawnego na podstawie prawa Unii Europejskiej i umów międzynarodowych, Dz.U. 2018 poz. 416 (law on the central authority in family matters).

[21] Information from the Polish Ministry of Justice website explains that 'Under current law Ministry of Justice has not had possibilities of efficient supervision on such cases. (...) It is time to finish with it. State must protect Polish children', see www.ms.gov.pl/pl/informacje/news,8926, chronimy-prawa-dzieci-w-postepowaniach.html.

[22] Law of 26 January 2018 on the central authority in family matters, *supra* note 20, Art. 15.

[23] See www.ms.gov.pl/Data/Files/_public/aktual/2018/2_years_eng_ms.pdf.

In *LM* the CJEU could have stated that the European area of justice is based on a high level of mutual trust in the administration of justice, but at the same time on the responsibility of Member States to ensure independence of the courts. Such an obligation was recently confirmed by the CJEU in the case *Associação Sindical dos Juízes Portugueses* (*ASJP*).[24] In this case the judicial independence was derived mainly from Articles 2, 4(3) and 19 TEU, while Article 47 of the Charter was treated only as a subsidiary source. The *LM* judgment takes Article 2 TEU as a starting point,[25] repeats the statements of the *ASJP* judgment[26] and confirms the importance of judicial independence in the context of the EAW.[27] But these general statements do not find expression in the conclusions of the *LM* case. In the answer given to the Irish court, judicial independence is reduced to the right of an individual to an independent court as a part of a right to a fair trial.[28] It is a step back in comparison to the *ASJP* judgment.

Fortunately, a broader perspective on the independence of the judiciary is taken by the CJEU in a subsequent case relating to the rule of law deficiencies in Poland. A judgment in the *Commission v. Poland*[29] case confirms the importance of Article 19 (1) TEU as a main source of obligation of maintaining independent courts by Member States. The most important consequence is a broader scope of application. While fundamental rights (including Article 47 of the Charter) are applied only when Member States are implementing Union law,[30] Article 19(1) TEU 'refers to 'the fields covered by Union law', irrespective of whether the Member States are implementing Union law within the meaning of Article 51(1) of the Charter'.[31] The CJEU explained explicitly that the national body falls within the fields covered by EU law if it may be called upon to rule, as a court or tribunal, on questions concerning the application or interpretation of EU law.[32] As almost any court in Member States can nowadays rule on questions of EU law, each Member State is obliged to ensure that its judiciary as a whole must meet the requirements of effective judicial protection. The CJEU underlined the interdependence between the requirement of independence of the courts stemming from Article 19(1) TEU and the right to effective judicial protection[33] but the *Commission v. Poland* judgment shows clearly that the former is something more than the fundamental right of an individual.

---

[24]CJEU, *Associação Sindical dos Juízes Portugueses*, *supra* note 9, para. 37.

[25]CJEU, *LM*, *supra* note 1, para. 35.

[26]Id., paras. 51–54.

[27]Id., paras. 55–58.

[28]Id., paras. 59–60.

[29]CJEU, Case C-619/18, *Commission v. Poland*, ECLI:EU:C:2019:531.

[30]Article 51 of the Charter.

[31]CJEU, *Commission v. Poland*, *supra* note 29, para. 50.

[32]Id., paras. 51 and 56.

[33]Id., para. 58.

4.3 Individual Assessment Often Not Feasible in the European Judicial Area

The Irish question relates only to the EAW, but a broader perspective shall be taken as the restriction of independence of the judiciary has a potential impact on at least 25 acts providing for mutual recognition of judgments. Mutual trust in the administration of justice is the guiding principle of nine framework decisions, two directives related to mutual recognition in criminal matters, and 14 regulations governing mutual recognition in civil matters. In criminal matters there are in chronological order: Directives on European Investigation Order[34] and European protection order[35] and framework decisions on: mutual recognition of decisions on supervision measures,[36] decisions rendered in the absence of the person concerned at the trial,[37] recognition of judgments imposing custodial sentences,[38] supervision of probation measures and alternative sanctions,[39] taking account of convictions in the course of new criminal proceedings,[40] confiscation orders,[41] mutual recognition to financial penalties,[42] orders freezing property or evidence,[43] European arrest warrant.[44] In

[34]Directive (EU) 2014/41 of the European Parliament and of the Council regarding the European Investigation Order in criminal matters (2014) OJ L130/1.

[35]Directive (EU) 2011/99 of the European Parliament and of the Council on the European protection order (2011) OJ L338/2.

[36]Council Framework Decision (JHA) 2009/829 on the application, between Member States of the European Union, of the principle of mutual recognition to decisions on supervision measures as an alternative to provisional detention (2009) OJ L294/20.

[37]Council Framework Decision (JHA) 2009/299 amending Framework Decisions 2002/584/JHA, 2005/214/JHA, 2006/783/JHA, 2008/909/JHA and 2008/947/JHA, thereby enhancing the procedural rights of persons and fostering the application of the principle of mutual recognition to decisions rendered in the absence of the person concerned at the trial (2009) OJ L81/24.

[38]Council Framework Decision (JHA) 2008/909 on the application of the principle of mutual recognition to judgments in criminal matters imposing custodial sentences or measures involving deprivation of liberty for the purpose of their enforcement in the European Union (2008) OJ L327/27.

[39]Council Framework Decision (JHA) 2008/947 on the application of the principle of mutual recognition to judgments and probation decisions with a view to the supervision of probation measures and alternative sanctions (2008) OJ L337/102.

[40]Council Framework Decision (JHA) 2008/675 on taking account of convictions in the Member States of the European Union in the course of new criminal proceedings (2008) OJ L220/32.

[41]Council Framework Decision (JHA) 2006/783 on the application of the principle of mutual recognition to confiscation orders (2006) OJ L328/59.

[42]Council Framework Decision (JHA) 2005/214 on the application of the principle of mutual recognition to financial penalties (2005) OJ L76/16.

[43]Council Framework Decision (JHA) 2003/577 on the execution in the European Union of orders freezing property or evidence (2003) OJ L196/45.

[44]Council Framework Decision (JHA) 2002/584 on the European arrest warrant and the surrender procedures between Member States—Statements made by certain Member States on the adoption of the Framework Decision (2002) OJ L190/1.

civil matters there are regulations on: insolvency proceedings,[45] general civil matters (the so-called Brussels I[46]), parental responsibility and divorce (Brussels II bis),[47] the European Enforcement Order (EEO),[48] the European Order for Payment (EOP),[49] small claims,[50] maintenance obligations,[51] the Brussels I bis Regulation,[52] the succession,[53] the European protection order,[54] European Account Preservation Order,[55] new regulation on insolvency proceedings,[56] matrimonial property regimes,[57] property consequences of registered partnerships.[58]

All acts introducing mutual recognition of judgments relate to judgments of courts/tribunals[59] or judicial authority.[60] This notion was considered by the CJEU

---

[45]Council Regulation (EC) 1346/2000 on insolvency proceedings (2000) OJ L160/1.

[46]Council Regulation (EC) 44/2001 on jurisdiction and the recognition and enforcement of judgments in civil and commercial matters (2001) OJ L12/1.

[47]Council Regulation (EC) 2201/2003 concerning jurisdiction and the recognition and enforcement of judgments in matrimonial matters and the matters of parental responsibility, repealing Regulation (EC) No 1347/2000, (2009) OJ L347/32.

[48]Regulation (EC) 805/2004 of the European Parliament and of the Council creating a European Enforcement Order for uncontested claims (2004) OJ L143/15.

[49]Regulation (EC) 1896/2006 of the European Parliament and of the Council creating a European order for payment procedure (2006) OJ L399/1.

[50]Regulation (EC) 861/2007 of the European Parliament and of the Council establishing a European Small Claims Procedure (2007) OJ L199/1.

[51]Council Regulation (EC) 4/2009 on jurisdiction, applicable law, recognition and enforcement of decisions and cooperation in matters relating to maintenance obligations (2009) OJ L7/1.

[52]Regulation (EU) 1215/2012 of the European Parliament and of the Council on jurisdiction and the recognition and enforcement of judgments in civil and commercial matters (recast) (2012) OJ L351/1.

[53]Regulation (EU) 650/2012 of the European Parliament and of the Council on jurisdiction, applicable law, recognition and enforcement of decisions and acceptance and enforcement of authentic instruments in matters of succession and on the creation of a European Certificate of Succession (2012) OJ L201/107.

[54]Regulation (EU) 606/2013 of the European Parliament and of the Council on mutual recognition of protection measures in civil matters (2013) L181/4.

[55]Regulation (EE) 655/2014 of the European Parliament and of the Council establishing a European Account Preservation Order procedure to facilitate cross-border debt recovery in civil and commercial matters (2014) OJ L189/59.

[56]Regulation of the European Parliament and of the Council (EU) 2015/848 on insolvency proceedings (2015) OJ L141/19.

[57]Council Regulation (EU) 2016/1103 implementing enhanced cooperation in the area of jurisdiction, applicable law and the recognition and enforcement of judgments in matters concerning matrimonial property regimes (2016) OJ L183/1.

[58]Council Regulation (EU) No. 2016/1104 implementing enhanced cooperation in the area of jurisdiction, applicable law and the recognition and enforcement of judgments in matters concerning the property consequences of registered partnerships (2016) OJ L183/30.

[59]According to Article 2(a) Brussels I bis: "judgment' means any judgment given by a court or tribunal of a Member State, whatever the judgment may be called'.

[60]Article 1(1) of Framework Decision 2002/584: 'The European arrest warrant is a judicial decision issued by a Member State (...)'. Article 6 of the same act: '1. The issuing judicial authority shall be

as an autonomous notion of EU law and interpreted several times in both civil and criminal cases. In the cases *Ibrica Zulfikarpašić*[61] and *Pula Parking*,[62] the Luxembourg Court stated that, due to mutual trust, EU regulations require 'that judgments the enforcement of which is sought in another Member State [be] delivered in court proceedings offering guarantees of independence and impartiality'. In two cases relating to criminal matters—*Kovalkovas*[63] and *Poltorak*[64]—the CJEU stated that the term 'judiciary' 'must (...) be distinguished, in accordance with the principle of the separation of powers which characterises the operation of the rule of law, from the executive'. These requirements are difficult to reconcile with the statement of the Venice Commission quoted at the beginning of this chapter that Polish reforms 'enable the legislative and executive powers to interfere in a severe and extensive manner in the administration of justice'.

The most important issue is that a level of integration in the field of judicial cooperation is so high that the judgments issued in one Member State have full effects in other Member States. In civil cases the majority of judgments are automatically recognised and enforceable in the other Member States. In all EU acts on mutual recognition, the review of jurisdiction of another Member State or of the content of the judgment to be recognized is prohibited. In some legal instruments, there are even no legal mechanisms allowing recognition/execution to be refused (for example in the case of maintenance or Article 42 of 2201/2003 regulation relating to child return decisions). The courts in Member States are thus often defenceless to judgments coming from other Member States as there is no proceeding in which they could conduct an individual assessment. An obligation of individual assessment is not suitable to protect other Member States which are obliged to recognise judgments originating from a Member State restricting judicial independence.

5 Conclusions

A breach of the obligation to ensure independence of the courts should logically result in suspending the participation of a given Member State in the EU policy area at stake, not (only) because the individual right can be impaired but because the EU should deter a Member State from restricting independence of the judiciary and protect other Member States which are obliged by EU law to recognise and enforce judgments from a Member State breaching the rule of law. It is probable that in the

the judicial authority of the issuing Member State which is competent to issue a European arrest warrant by virtue of the law of that State.'

[61] CJEU, Case C-484/15 *Ibrica Zulfikarpašić*, ECLI:EU:C:2017:199, para. 43.

[62] CJEU, Case C-551/15 *Pula Parking*, ECLI:EU:C:2017:193, para. 54.

[63] CJEU, Case C-477/16 PPU *Kovalkovas*, ECLI:EU:C:2016:861, para. 36.

[64] CJEU, Case C-452/16 PPU *Poltorak*, ECLI:EU:C:2016:784, para. 35.

majority of cases Polish judges will resist the political influence. But the courts in other Member States will never know whether this actually is the case. They would have to make difficult[65] investigations about the substantial issues of the cases and of the division of powers in Poland. The regular individual assessment can contravene the spirit of mutual trust between the courts and often will be impossible in practice.

Moreover, the non-execution of EAWs can save some individuals but is not capable of resolving the essence of the problem. Firstly, the *Aranyosi* test can protect one's fundamental rights only partly. This became apparent in the judgment in the *ML*[66] case, which limits an obligation to assess detention conditions in the issuing Member State to the first prisons in which it is intended that the person concerned will be held just after the surrender. The CJEU admitted that 'a person who is the subject of a European arrest warrant can, as a general rule, be detained in any prison in the territory of that State. It is generally not possible at the stage of executing a European arrest warrant to identify all the prisons in which such a person will actually be detained'.[67] It means that in reality the individual is not wholly protected against inhuman treatment.

The ideal tool to protect judicial independence would be the one which could solve the source of the problem. And there is a clear difference between prison conditions and the independence of the judiciary. In the *Aranyosi* judgment, the reason lying at the heart of the breach was a serious, structural incapacity of some Member States to ensure the proper standard of protection in prison. Improvement of the situation is a long, costly and complicated process which the EU could stimulate and support. Differently, in the *LM* case, the source of the problem has been the will of the governing party. The problem could be very easily and quickly resolved by amending the laws on courts according to the recommendations of the Venice Commission and the European Commission. The only thing that the EU can (and should) do is to set clear limits and the consequences in the case of violations. If the EU had addressed the Hungarian case more promptly, the Polish government would probably not have dared to follow the Hungarian path.

In the *LM* case the CJEU acted like a human rights court. This circumstance is always very welcome. Perhaps, future cases—especially those based on Article 258 TFEU and on the preliminary reference request from the Polish Supreme Court—will present the Luxembourg court with the opportunity to look at the judicial deficiencies from a broader constitutional perspective and stand up against the destruction of the rule of law in Europe.

[65]Rizcallah (2018).

[66]CJEU, Case C-220/18 PPU, *ML*, ECLI:EU:C:2018:589, para. 87.

[67]Id., para. 81.

Reference

Rizcallah C (2018) 'Dear Colleague, Are You Independent Enough?' The fate of the principle of mutual trust in case of systemic deficiencies in a Member State's System of Justice. EU Law Analysis Blog 4 July 2018

Dr. hab. Agnieszka Frąckowiak-Adamska assistant professor, Chair of European and International Law, University of Wrocław, Poland.

Intermezzo in the Rule of Law Play: The Court of Justice's *LM* Case

Matteo Bonelli

Contents

Abstract In the *LM* case, the CJEU was called to decide on whether systemic rule of law deficiencies in Poland could lead to the suspension of EU cooperation based on mutual trust, in particular under the European Arrest Warrant system. Building on its earlier decision in *Aranyosi*, the Court concluded that EAWs may be suspended only after the executing authority conducts a general analysis of the situation in the country concerned *and* an individual assessment of the specific situation of the applicant. For some, the decision was a disappointing one, as the Court failed to take a clear stance on the Polish constitutional crisis. This chapter argues, on the other hand, that the Court reached a balanced decision: while it is true that it confirmed the strict *Aranyosi* test, it also sent some key messages on the crucial importance of the rule of law and judicial independence for the EU and underlined the red lines of European constitutionalism. Furthermore, a different line of cases that originated from the groundbreaking decision of the Court in the 'Portuguese

This contribution draws on 'The Deficiencies Judgment: Postponing the Constitutional Moment', *Verfassungsblog* (27 July 2018) and was finalized in September 2019.

M. Bonelli (✉)
Maastricht University, Faculty of Law, Maastricht, The Netherlands
e-mail: matteo.bonelli@maastrichtuniversity.nl

A. von Bogdandy et al. (eds.), *Defending Checks and Balances in EU Member States*, Beiträge zum ausländischen öffentlichen Recht und Völkerrecht 298,
https://doi.org/10.1007/978-3-662-62317-6_19

judges' case seems much more promising for the protection of EU values. Thus, rather than a constitutional moment for the Union, *LM* was ultimately an intermezzo between the two main acts of the rule of law play before the Court of Justice.

1 Introduction

The decision of the Court of Justice in the *LM* case was one of the most eagerly anticipated of 2018.[1] The preliminary reference of the Irish High Court brought to the attention of the CJEU two of the thorniest issues of European constitutional law: the EU's reaction to Polish constitutional backsliding[2] and the operation of the principle of mutual trust, in particular the European Arrest Warrant system (EAW). Many wished the Luxembourg court would take a strong stance on the Polish situation, even suspending the operation of the EAW and possibly other instruments based on mutual trust in Poland.[3] In any event, the Court of Justice was called to strike an undoubtedly difficult compromise, one bound to be controversial. Unsurprisingly, the ruling delivered on July 25 was welcomed with mixed reactions.[4] Although generally perceived as a step forward compared to the Opinion of Advocate General Tanchev,[5] some authors considered the decision of the Court ultimately too timid and insufficient to address the fundamental challenges posed by the Polish judicial reforms.[6]

This contribution takes a different line. First, it argues that, despite some loose ends in its reasoning, the Court's approach and the compromise it reached were ultimately quite solid;[7] secondly and more broadly, the way in which the *LM* case was framed was simply not suitable for a bold intervention of the Court in the Polish crisis.[8] The attempt of Justice Donnelly of the referring Irish High Court to bring to the attention of the Court of Justice her concerns for the Polish rule of law situation was certainly respectable and even courageous. Yet, the line of cases based on Article 19 TEU that initiated with the ruling in the 'Portuguese judges' (or *ASJP*) case[9] seems much more promising for the protection of the rule of law and judicial

---

[1]CJEU, Case C-216/18 PPU *LM*, ECLI:EU:C:2018:586.

[2]See Sadurski (2019) and Pech and Scheppele (2017).

[3]See e.g. von Bogdandy et al. (2018).

[4]For an overview of the first reactions, see the contributions to the Verfassungsblog debate 'The CJEU's Deficiencies Judgment', available at www.verfassungsblog.de/category/themen/after-celmer/.

[5]CJEU, Case C-216/18 PPU *LM*, Opinion of Advocate General Tanchev, ECLI:EU:C:2018:517.

[6]See e.g. Bard and van Ballegooij (2018), Krajewski (2018) and Scheppele (2018).

[7]On the 'elegant compromise' reached by the Court, see also Sonnevend (2018).

[8]For a similar argument, see Kosar (2018), who argued that 'neither the preliminary reference procedure nor the fundamental right to the fair trial are good 'vehicles' for addressing the Polish structural judicial reforms'.

[9]CJEU, Case C-64/14 *Associação Sindical dos Juízes Portugueses*, ECLI:EU:C:2018:117.

independence in Poland and across the Union. The landmark ruling of the Court of Justice in the infringement action on the reform of the Polish Supreme Court[10] very well demonstrates the potential of this new approach to Article 19 TEU and offered a perfect moment for the Court of Justice to finally enforce the red lines of European constitutionalism.[11] Further opportunities to advance this line of cases will come in the next months: a second infringement action,[12] as well as a series of preliminary references coming from Polish courts,[13] are now pending in Luxembourg.

All considered, rather than a decisive moment of the Court of Justice's rule of law play,[14] the *LM* case could be best seen as an *intermezzo* between the two key acts: the 'Portuguese judges' decision, in which the Court, offering an extensive interpretation of Article 19 TEU, set the scene for its intervention; and then the infringement procedure on the Supreme Court, as well as the other forthcoming rulings on the Polish judiciary, in which the Court took the next step and began enforcing the EU judicial independence standards. At the same time, it should not be forgotten that it is unlikely that legal mechanisms alone could address crises such as the Polish or the Hungarian ones. The procedures under Article 7 TEU against both Member States might prove equally, if not more, important than the Court's decisions, and the Court itself seems to be aware of the importance of political mechanisms.

The chapter develops these points in the following paragraphs, starting from a brief analysis of the *LM* case (Sect. 2), then taking a step back to the 'Portuguese judges' case (Sect. 3) and one forward to the Article 19 cases on the Polish judiciary and in particular the infringement action on the Supreme Court (Sect. 4). Having done so, the contribution explains why *LM* can therefore be best seen as an intermezzo in the Court's play (Sect. 5): the framing of the case did not offer to the Court the best opportunity for a strong intervention in the Polish constitutional crisis. Nonetheless, the Court still sent some clear messages to Polish authorities and the European public, making it clear that European constitutionalism contains red lines against threats to democracy and the rule of law. Furthermore, the Court

---

[10]CJEU, Case C-619/18 *Commission v. Poland (Supreme Court)*, ECLI:EU:C:2019:53. See also the two previous interim orders: CJEU, Case C-619/*18 Commission v. Poland*, Order of 19/10/2018, ECLI:EU:C:2018:852 and Order of 17/12/2018, ECLI:EU:C:2018:1021.

[11]On red lines, von Bogdandy et al. (2018).

[12]See CJEU, Case C-192/18 *Commission v. Poland (Law on the Organisation of Ordinary Courts)* (pending), and the Opinion of Advocate General Tanchev in the same case. In July 2019, the Commission has also opened another infringement action regarding the new disciplinary regime for Polish judges: see European Commission, Press Release—Rule of Law: European Commission takes new step to protect judges in Poland against political control, Brussels, 17 July 2019. The case was decided in November 2019, after the submission of this contribution.

[13]See Opinion of Advocate General Tanchev in Joined Cases C-585/18, C-624/18 and C-625/18 *A. K. (C-585/18) v Krajowa Rada Sądownictwa and CP (C-624/18) DO (C-625/18) v Sąd Najwyższy (C-624/18 and C-625/18)*, ECLI:EU:C:2019:551. These joined cases were also decided in November 2019, after the submission of this contribution.

[14]Even more drastically, Avbelj (2018) concluded that the *Celmer* case was *not* 'a landmark ruling' and that its impact will not be 'of seismic constitutional proportions'.

restated the need for parallel political procedures that can give further bite to the red lines.

2 The Court of Justice's Ruling in *LM*

As described in other contributions to this volume, the *LM* case originated in Ireland, where the High Court was called to give execution to a EAW issued by Poland against Mr. Artur Celmer, accused of drug-related offences. The Irish Court doubted whether, in view of the systemic deficiencies with the rule of law in Poland, the execution of the EAW could lead to the violation of the applicant's fundamental right to a fair trial, protected by the Irish Constitution, the ECHR and the EU Charter of Fundamental Rights. It is worth underlining a few key elements of the Irish High Court's referral, in order to illustrate how the latter framed the case and how this influenced the proceedings before the Court of Justice.

Generally and most importantly, the Irish Court built its questions on the basis of the previous *Aranyosi* decision of the Court of Justice.[15] In this landmark case, the CJEU acknowledged for the first time that the execution of EAWs could be suspended in case of systemic deficiencies in the issuing Member State. Following the *Aranyosi* approach, the Irish Court in the first place directly assumed the existence of systemic rule of law problems in Poland and did not call the CJEU to reflect on that matter.[16] In *Aranyosi*, in fact, the CJEU left to the referring court to determine whether the deficits of prisons facilities in Hungary and Romania amounted to a systemic problem.[17] Second, the Irish Court brought to the attention of the Court the position of the specific individual concerned by the surrender request and his fundamental right to a fair trial. This is to say that the referring court wanted to understand what would be the effects of the assumed breach of the common values on the specific situation of the applicant, and in particular whether they could amount to a 'flagrant denial of justice' for the individual.[18] Third, the Irish

[15]CJEU, Case C-404/15 *Aranyosi and Câldâraru*, ECLI:EU:C:2016:198.

[16]Irish High Court, *The Minister for Justice and Equality and Artur Celmer*, Record no. 2013 EXT 295, 12 March 2018, para. 123: the Commission reasoned that a proposal under Art. 7 is considered a 'shocking indictment of the status of the rule of law', illustrating 'what appears to be the deliberated, calculated and provocative legislative dismantling by Poland of the independence of the judiciary. In the next paragraph, the Irish High Court then '*concludes* . . . that the rule of law in Poland has been *systematically damaged*' and further adds (para. 135) that 'the common value of the rule of law in Poland has been breached'.

[17]See also the Opinion AG Tanchev in *Celmer*, *supra* note 5, para. 35: 'it is not for the Court to rule on whether there is a real risk of breach of the right to a fair trial on account on deficiencies in the Polish system of justice . . . It is for *the executing judicial* authority to rule on the existence of such a risk'.

[18]Irish High Court, *The Minister for Justice and Equality and Artur Celmer*, *supra* note 16, para. 137. On flagrant denial of justice, see para. 107: it constitutes the standard for extradition cases both under Irish law and under the ECHR.

Court asked a very specific question to the Court of Justice, all imprinted on the applicability of the *Aranyosi* test and in particular of its second prong, namely the individual part of the test.[19] While the Irish judge considered conducting an individual test 'unrealistic' and 'difficult' in the situation she was confronted with,[20] it was precisely on this matter—the necessity to conduct an individual test even after establishing the existence of a systemic problem—that the Court of Justice was called to intervene and clarify the landscape. The answers given by the Advocate General and the Court of Justice were thus necessarily informed by the referring courts' questions and analysis, as it is true for any preliminary reference to the CJEU under Article 267 TFEU.

In substance, Advocate General Tanchev and the Court of Justice reached similar conclusions, confirming the applicability of both prongs of the *Aranyosi* test: an individual assessment of the specific situation of the applicant is required after establishing that the situation amounts to a systemic threat to the rule of law, which has negative repercussions on Article 47 of the Charter protecting the fundamental right to a fair trial.[21] Yet, the overall approach and tone of the Advocate General and the Court were not identical. The Advocate General's Opinion considered the possibility of refusing to execute the EAW absolutely exceptional. More precisely, Advocate General Tanchev argued that not *any* breach of Article 47 of the Charter could lead to postpone the execution of an EAW. Postponement, in his view, would only be possible when 'there is a real risk that [the individual] will be exposed in the issuing Member State to a *flagrant denial of justice*';[22] in turn, problems with the independence and impartiality of a court could only amount to a flagrant denial of justice when they '[destroyed] the fairness of the trial'.[23] While the Opinion argued that it should be left to the referring court to determine whether the Polish situation reached that level, it established an extremely high threshold already for the first, general part of the *Aranyosi* test.

The ruling of the Grand Chamber of the Court of Justice, while fairly similar in the operative part—confirming in particular the need for the individualized assessment, the second prong of the *Aranyosi* test—showed more explicitly the judges' concerns with the Polish situation. Overall, the Court's reasoning and the underlying tone are more convincing. Both in the specific response to the referring court and in the message sent to the European public eagerly waiting for the decision, the Court tried to find a balance between, on the one hand, emphasizing the importance of the

---

[19]Irish High Court, *The Minister for Justice and Equality and Artur Celmer*, *supra* note 16, see para. 145. The second question is on a more specific aspect of the individual prong, namely whether the referring court has to contact the issuing judicial authority in order to obtain further necessary information.

[20]Irish High Court, *The Minister for Justice and Equality and Artur Celmer*, *supra* note 16, paras. 141 and 142.

[21]This was also the view expressed by the Commission in the case: see Opinion AG Tanchev in *Celmer*, *supra* note 5, para. 103.

[22]Opinion AG Tanchev in *Celmer*, *supra* note 5, para. 69.

[23]Opinion AG Tanchev in *Celmer*, *supra* note 5, para. 93.

common values of the rule of law and fundamental rights for the Union as a whole and, on the other, protecting the smooth operation of mutual trust instruments. The Court reached that balance using different languages and techniques.

On the one hand, the Court reinstated some of its traditional mutual trust arguments.[24] By making a textbook reference to *Opinion 2/13*,[25] the Court repeated that mutual trust is a principle of fundamental importance for the Union's legal order that can only cease to operate in 'exceptional cases'.[26] As a rule, judicial authorities are thus 'require[d] to execute any European arrest warrant on the basis of the principle of mutual recognition'; refusals are, on the other hand, exceptions 'which must be interpreted strictly'.[27] The crucial importance of the principles of mutual trust and mutual recognition led the Court to confirm the need for the individual assessment of the specific situation of the applicant, which remains necessary even after establishing the existence of a systemic problem. At the same time, in *LM*, for the first time, the Court extended the *Aranyosi* approach to a non-absolute right such as the right to a fair trial. Furthermore, it lowered the strict requirements posited by the Advocate General,[28] and generally granted a broad discretion to the executing authorities in conducting both parts of the assessment. In particular, the Court left to the executing authority the task to evaluate whether the possible systemic deficiencies generated a real risk to the fundamental right to a fair trial[29] and only made general references to the facts to be considered in conducting the second part of the assessment, which include the personal situation of the applicant, the 'nature of the offence', and the 'factual context' in which the EAW was issued.[30] National authorities are thus granted a wide margin of action in taking their final decision on the execution of the warrant and they could easily play with the Court's criteria in order to justify a possible suspension of cooperation.[31]

The Court then went even a step further. Several paragraphs of the rulings can be read as implicit messages that the Court considers the Polish situation deeply problematic. The first message is the importance given to the concept of judicial independence, a point on which the Court departs from the approach of the Advocate General. The Opinion had indeed considered that problems with judicial independence could amount to a 'flagrant denial of justice' only when they radically destroyed the fairness on the trial. The Court thinks differently. It held that judicial

[24]CJEU, *LM*, *supra* note 1, see paras. 35–37.

[25]CJEU, Opinion 2/13 *Accession of the EU to the ECHR*, ECLI:EU:C:2014:2454, in particular para. 192.

[26]CJEU, *LM*, *supra* note 1, para. 37.

[27]CJEU, *LM*, *supra* note 1, para. 41.

[28]See also Konstadinides (2019), p. 745.

[29]CJEU, *LM*, *supra* note 1, para. 61.

[30]CJEU, *LM*, *supra* note 1, para. 75.

[31]It is not be noted, however, that the Irish High Court ultimately did not suspend the transfer: Irish High Court *The Minister for Justice and Equality v. Celmer No. 5*, Record no. 2018 IEHC 639, 19 November 2018. The decision has been appealed in the meantime.

independence 'forms part of the essence of the fundamental rights to a fair trial',[32] which seems to mean that any breach of that requirement should be considered a breach of the essence of Article 47 of the Charter, thus in principle able to lead to the suspension of a EAW transfer, following the two steps of the assessment. Moreover, with references in particular to the cases *ASJP*, *Wilson*,[33] and *TDC*,[34] the Court summarized its case law setting the EU law requirements of judicial independence and generally pointed at the crucial relevance of judicial independence for the Union constitutional order.[35] Crucially, independence is one of the conditions for participation to the preliminary reference system, the 'keystone'[36] of the EU judicial system: the Court of Justice has since long maintained that only 'independent' bodies can send preliminary questions to the Court of Justice under Article 267 TFEU.

The Court sent a second signal in paragraph 61 of the ruling, where it gave instructions to the referring court on the materials to be evaluated in determining the existence of systemic deficiencies (the first part of the *Aranyosi* test).[37] The Court affirmed that the Commission's reasoned proposal under Article 7(1) TEU 'is particularly relevant' for that assessment. When taking also into account the long summary of the Commission's document in the first part of the ruling,[38] it becomes evident that the Court wanted to underline the importance of the document adopted by the Commission, suggesting that the concerns expressed by the Commission are at least well founded. All in all, the Court's analysis strived to find a delicate balance: protecting the smooth functioning of mutual trust and thus of the European legal order, while remarking that the rule of law and judicial independence are of the outmost importance for the EU. In doing so, the Court further bolstered the expectations for its following rulings on the Polish judiciary, discussed later in this contribution.[39]

Nonetheless, as already mentioned above, the decision was not universally praised. There are two main strands of criticism. The first concentrates on the feasibility of conducting an individual assessment in cases where judicial independence is at stake.[40] The task of the executing judicial authority, it is said, is excessively complex, especially because it cannot truly rely on the authorities of the issuing Member State, as they are the direct targets of the reforms in question and may thus have a stake in the process. The second strand of criticism, on the other hand, looks at *LM* and at the Court's approach mostly as a missed opportunity in the

---

[32]CJEU, *LM*, *supra* note 1, para. 48.

[33]CJEU, Case C-506/04 *Wilson*, ECLI:EU:C:2006:587.

[34]CJEU, Case C-22/13 *TDC*, ECLI:EU:C:2014:2265.

[35]CJEU, *LM*, *supra* note 1, paras. 63–67.

[36]CJEU, Case C-284/16 *Achmea*, ECLI:EU:C:2018:158.

[37]CJEU, *LM*, *supra* note 1, para. 61.

[38]CJEU, *LM*, *supra* note 1, paras. 18–21.

[39]See Sect. 4.

[40]See e.g. Bard and van Ballegooij (2018).

rule of law play.[41] It is said, for example, that by sticking to the question referred and thus focusing on the individual fundamental right to a fair trial, rather than on the rule of law in general, the Court failed to take a clearer stance against Polish constitutional backsliding.

There is certainly some truth in both assertions. The individual assessment national courts are called to do is much more complex than the already difficult analysis they were asked to pursue in the *Aranyosi* situation.[42] While evaluating the fundamental rights' conditions of specific detention centers is, although not easy, still feasible—and the Court of Justice has further helped to clarify the procedure [43]—assessing whether a trial could be fair, despite the structural changes to a rule of law regime, is a much more difficult and speculative exercise. It demands that judges try to grasp and assess the functioning of other legal orders they are not necessarily familiar with.[44] There is also a higher risk of receiving conflicting information and that the authorities to which clarifications are asked are already compromised, i.e. not independent. The Court perhaps downplayed the difficulties in applying the *Aranyosi* test to a different context. Offering more guidance to national courts could have been an option to pursue—for example further clarifying the factors to be taken into account for the individual assessment—but the Court preferred to follow the opposite approach, namely granting them a wide margin of discretion, which may also be used for refusing surrenders when issuing authorities do not give sufficient assurances on the individual trial.

As for the 'missed opportunity' critique, the Court of Justice could certainly have been more explicit in pointing out the systemic threats to the rule of law in Poland, as it did for example in *N.S.* on the systemic problems of the Greek asylum system.[45] Furthermore, there is no doubt that a more centralized system of assessment at least of the 'systemic' part of the test would certainly have significant benefits.[46] However, that was not the issue the Irish Court referred to Luxembourg: the questions concentrated on the applicability of the *second* part of the *Aranyosi* test. More generally, the task of the Court in preliminary references, according to Article 267 TFEU, is to rule on the interpretation and validity of EU law, not to assess the factual situation in a Member State. While the Court has always interpreted its powers under Article 267 TFEU in a fairly broad manner,[47] it remains that there are limits to what it can do in the context of a preliminary reference.

---

[41]See Krajewski (2018), Pech and Wachowiec (2018), Scheppele (2018) and Wendel (2019).

[42]On the complexity of the test, see Lazowski (2018), p. 14.

[43]See CJEU, Case C-220/18 PPU *Conditions de détention en Hongrie*, ECLI:EU:C:2018:589.

[44]On this difficulty, see Krajewski (2018) and Konstadinides (2019).

[45]CJEU, Joined Cases C-411/10 and C-493/10, *N.S. and Others*, ECLI:EU:C:2011:865. In *N.S.* the Court found that systemic problems in the asylum system of a Member State, creating a real risk of inhuman or degrading treatment, prevent asylum transfers under the Dublin regulation. An individual assessment of the specific situation of the applicant is not necessary in those circumstances.

[46]See Wendel (2019).

[47]In general, see Broberg and Fenger (2014).

Hence, the framing of the case did not offer the best opportunity for the Court to take a clear stance on the Polish crisis. Rather than a sign of a timid approach of Luxembourg towards cases of constitutional backsliding, the decision can be best seen as an *intermezzo* in the Court's rule of law play, which took place between the two main acts: the ruling in the 'Portuguese judges' and then a set of more precise and targeted decisions on the Polish situation, which has started with the key ruling in the Supreme Court case. To better understand *LM*, thus, it seems necessary to, first, take a step back and look at the decision in *Associação Sindical dos Juízes Portugueses*, and then a step forward, analyzing the 'Supreme Court' ruling and then the other forthcoming decisions on the Polish judiciary, mapping out the different contexts in which these other decisions have been and will be taken.

3 First Act: The Portuguese Judges' Case[48]

In contrast to *LM*, the 'Portuguese judges' case was far less anticipated and much more surprising. Rather than a rule of law case, it seemed to fall in the Court's line of 'austerity cases':[49] a group of Portuguese judges complained that austerity measures reducing their salaries, adopted in order to comply with the demands of the Memoranda of Understanding signed in the context of ESM financial assistance programmes, violated the principle of judicial independence guaranteed by Article 19 TEU and 47 of the Charter. It is only from this austerity perspective that interest in the case was growing,[50] especially after the Opinion of the Advocate General, who argued for the applicability of the Charter to ESM-related measures.[51]

The Court followed however a different path. It remained silent on the applicability of the Charter to ESM-related austerity measures and transformed the austerity case into a 'constitutional backsliding' or rule of law one. It did so by relying on Article 19 TEU, significantly bolstering both its scope of application and its substantive content. First, the Court read in a broad manner the expression 'the fields covered by Union law' that is used in Article 19 TEU (second sentence: 'Member

[48]This section draws on Bonelli and Claes (2018).

[49]See for example the other Portuguese cases CJEU, Order in Case C-128/12, *Sindicato dos Bancários do Norte and Others v. BPN—Banco Português de Negócios SA*, ECLI:EU:C:2013:149; Order in Case C-264/12 *Sindicato Nacional dos Profissionais de Seguros e Afins v. Fidelidade Mundial—Companhia de Seguros SA*, ECLI:EU:C:2014:2036; Order in Case C-665/13 *Sindicato Nacional dos Profissionais de Seguros e Afins v. Via Directa—Companhia de Seguros SA*, ECLI:EU:C:2014:2327.

[50]After a long period in which the Court showed reluctance to engage in judicial review of national austerity measures, the orientation of the Court partially shifted in the *Ledra* (CJEU, C-8/15 P *Ledra Advertising*, ECLI:EU:C:2016:701) and *Florescu* (CJEU, C-258/14 *Florescu*, ECLI:EU:C:2017:448), and some expected Luxembourg to extend the *Florescu* reasoning on the applicability of the Charter to national austerity measures implementing EU-related Memoranda of Understanding to the ESM context: see Markakis and Dermine (2018).

[51]See CJEU, Opinion of Advocate General Øe in C-64/16 *ASJP*, ECLI:EU:C:2017:395.

States shall provide remedies sufficient to ensure effective legal protection *in the fields covered by Union law'*) and created a new 'sphere' of Union law. According to the Luxembourg Court, Article 19 TEU has a broader scope of application than the rest of Union law including the Charter. It brings under the purview of the Court situations that would otherwise fall outside the scope of Union law, because they are not linked to any EU substantive competence.[52] Second, the Court read Article 19 TEU as containing an obligation to ensure the judicial independence of national courts acting in the fields covered by EU law, despite the absence of any textual reference to the concept of judicial independence in the provision. By doing so, the Court *de facto* aligned the substantive content of Article 19 TEU with that of Article 47 of the Charter, which includes the right to an independent court. This broad reasoning allows the Court of Justice to assess against EU standards *any* national measure that affects the judicial independence of courts or tribunals acting in the fields covered by Union law, that is, the vast majority of the national judiciary.

While formally being about Portuguese judges and austerity measures, much in the ruling suggests that the Court had actually in mind the Polish situation. The Court wanted to get a say in the judiciary reforms pushed forward by Law and Justice. Yet, on a traditional reading, these reforms could be considered as falling outside the scope of EU law. In order to bring the reforms under its purview, the Court needed therefore to significantly stretch the reach of EU law and of the principle of judicial independence, and did so by reading Article 19 TEU in the expansive manner just described.

The setting of *ASJP* was thus the following: a preliminary reference challenging the compatibility with EU law, and more precisely with the principle of judicial independence guaranteed by Article 19 TEU, of *specific* domestic measures, namely the salary cuts adopted to implement the Memorandum of Understanding between the EU and Portugal. The Court was not truly concerned with the Portuguese measures under discussion, though, and quickly dismissed the arguments brought by the group of Portuguese judges.[53] Rather, the Court took the opportunity to prepare the ground for a more direct intervention in the Polish crisis. The 'Portuguese judges' case, delivered in February 2018, served as an invitation for the Commission to pursue infringement actions based on Article 19 TEU on controversial aspects of the Polish judicial reforms. The Commission accepted the invitation a few months later, in July, opening an action against the Supreme Court reform[54] and quickly bringing it to Luxembourg. On the other hand, there was no clear connection between *ASJP* and the *LM* situation, which originated in a completely different context (mutual trust obligations), focused on the interpretation of provisions other than Article 19 TEU, and ultimately asked the Court of Justice to conduct another

[52]See Bonelli and Claes (2018), p. 631. The new sphere is thus a 'functional' one: the key factor for falling under the jurisdiction of the Court is not whether the circumstances of the case touch upon matters regulated by Union law, but the function of national courts as part of the European judiciary.

[53]CJEU, *ASJP, supra* note 9, paras. 46–51.

[54]European Commission, Press Release: Rule of Law: Commission launches infringement procedure to protect the independence of the Polish Supreme Court, Brussels, 2 July 2018, Doc. IP/18/4341.

type of assessment. The true next step in the rule of law line of cases, thus, was not *LM*, but the infringement action on the Polish Supreme Court's reform, as will be pointed out in the next section.

4 Second Act(s): The Infringement Action on the Polish Supreme Court and the Other Cases on the Polish Judiciary

As noted in the previous section, the Commission almost immediately followed the 'invitation' of the Court to tackle the controversial Polish reforms through Article 19 TEU and opened an infringement procedure on the Law on the Supreme Court. After two crucial interim orders delivered in the last months of 2018, the Court of Justice decided the case in June 2019, ultimately finding a violation of the second subparagraph of Article 19(1) TEU. Before explaining how the Court approached the case, it seems however appropriate to briefly recall how the Commission had been tackling the Polish crisis up until the *ASJP* decision.

At first, the Commission reacted to the controversies surrounding the composition and functioning of the Polish Constitutional Tribunal by activating the 'Rule of Law Framework'. The instrument, which is a base for political dialogue between the Commission and Polish authorities, did not produce adequate results; on the contrary, after completing the capture of the Constitutional Tribunal, the 'Law and Justice' majority began to reform the other institutions of the judiciary: ordinary courts, the Supreme Court, and the National Council of the Judiciary. After three unsuccessful Rule of Law Recommendations issued under the Framework, the Commission finally decided to move to the next step in December 2017, activating for the first time in EU history Article 7(1) TEU.[55]

Furthermore, already in July 2017, the Commission had launched a first infringement action on the Law on Ordinary Courts, questioning the compatibility with EU law of the reform under two profiles in particular. First, the Commission alleged that the new norms on the judges' retirement age were not compatible with EU gender equality law, as they provided different retirement ages for male and female judges. This first point of contention bore clear similarities with an earlier infringement action on the Hungarian judiciary reforms, which, despite the Commission's victory in Luxembourg,[56] had however not prevented Fidesz's takeover of the judiciary.[57] The Commission, aware that a purely technical, 'indirect'[58] infringement action

[55]European Commission, Reasoned Proposal in Accordance with Article 7(1) of the Treaty on European Union Regarding the Rule of Law in Poland, Brussels, 20 December 2017, Doc. COM (2017) 835 final.

[56]See CJEU, Case C-286/12 *Commission v. Hungary*, ECLI:EU:C:2012:687.

[57]See e.g. Belavusau (2013) and Halmai (2017).

[58]Dawson and Muir (2013).

could not work, raised also a second point: it argued that the discretionary powers assigned to the Ministry of Justice on the prolongation of the judges' mandates and on the appointment and dismissal of courts' presidents undermined the independence of the Polish judiciary under Article 19(1) TEU and Article 47 of the Charter. This second argument added thus an important layer to the Commission's action under Article 258 TFEU and it was one of the first times in which Article 19(1) TEU was mentioned as a possible source of rule of law obligations. The infringement action was then referred to the Court in December 2017 and was still pending at the time of writing.

This is the context in which the 'Portuguese judges' decision arrived. The decision supported the Commission's reliance, in the infringement action on the Ordinary Courts, on Article 19 TEU as a tool to protect judicial independence. The Court agreed that Article 19 TEU is a 'concrete expression'[59] of the value of the rule of law and contains a principle of judicial independence. But in *ASJP* the Court of Justice went even a step further, extending the scope of Article 19 to all national courts acting in the fields covered by Union law. If the infringement action on the ordinary court could still be re-conducted to the ordinary scope of EU law, as the reform was allegedly in conflict with EU anti-discrimination law, the broad reading of Article 19 TEU in *ASJP* liberated the Commission from the need of finding a hook in an infringement of EU substantive law, which could bring with it the application of the Charter and of its Article 47. In plain words, after the *ASJP* decision, the Commission may start a new infringement action for an alleged violation of the principle of judicial independence purely on the basis of Article 19 TEU.

This is precisely what the Commission did in July 2018, starting an Article 258 procedure on the reform of the Supreme Court, after the entry into force of the Polish law imposing the anticipated retirement of the Supreme Court's judges and following the growing controversies on the mandate of the President of the Court.[60] In this new procedure, the Commission did not refer to any alleged breach of substantive EU law. It only relied on Article 19 TEU and, more surprisingly, on Article 47 of the Charter, which however did not seem applicable to the situation at stake as it did not constitute an implementation of EU law.[61] The Commission then referred the case to the Court in September 2018, asking for interim measures and the application of the urgent procedure.[62]

---

[59]CJEU, *ASJP*, *supra* note 9, para. 32.

[60]European Commission, Press Release: Rule of Law: Commission launches infringement procedure to protect the independence of the Polish Supreme Court, Brussels, 2 July 2018, Doc. IP/18/4341.

[61]As will be explained in the next paragraphs, the Court of Justice—as also suggested by Advocate General Tanchev—ultimately assessed the contested norms only on the basis of Article 19 TEU, though it did not explicitly state that Art. 47 of the Charter was not applicable in the case.

[62]European Commission, Press Release—European Commission refers Poland to the European Court of Justice to protect the independence of the Polish Supreme Court, Brussels, 24 September 2018, IP/18/5830.

The infringement actions launched by the Commission—both the Supreme Court one and the earlier action on the Law on Ordinary Courts—follow the Court's approach in *ASJP* much more evidently than *LM*. First, the key provision in both actions is Article 19 TEU, as it was in *ASJP*. Second, while of course the concrete situations are radically different—austerity measures reducing judges' salaries, in *ASJP*, and a full-scale reform of the judiciary in the Polish cases—the Court is asked to conduct a similar exercise, namely to assess whether the national laws in question conflict with the EU principle of judicial independence. In the infringement actions, the Court can do so explicitly and can reach a final decision on whether or not Poland has failed to fulfill its obligations under the Treaties; in the *ASJP* case, a preliminary reference, the Luxembourg Court did not have the competence to assess the measures directly, but still it made clear that EU law does not preclude measures such as those at issue in the proceedings. The similarities between the two settings suggest that what the Court had in mind when it delivered the *ASJP* decision was precisely an action framed like the Supreme Court's infringement procedure.

The Court of Justice's willingness to forcefully intervene in the Polish crisis was confirmed in its two interim orders as well as in the final ruling.[63] In the first order, delivered by the Vice President of the Court *inaudita altera parte* on the basis of Article 160(7) of the Court of Justice Rules of Procedure, the Commission's requests were all satisfied. The Vice President asked Polish authorities to suspend the application of judges' retirement measures, allow the judges to carry out their duties in the same position, and refrain from nominating new judges to the Supreme Court. Remarkably, the interim order was meant to be retroactive and self-implementing: the request to Polish authorities was not to reinstate the judges, but to suspend the application of the law *ex tunc* and thus to consider that the retirement measures had never applied to them. In the second interim order, the Court confirmed, after hearing the Polish authorities, the same requests. Polish authorities were asked to restore the situation as it stood before the approval of the reform and to refrain from adopting any measure that could have interfered with the final decision of the Court of Justice.

As was to be expected after the interim orders, the final decision of June 2019 found a violation of EU law obligations by Poland. In its ruling, the Court of Justice first reaffirmed its jurisdiction to assess the national measures in question, stating that, while the organisation of justice is a competence of the Member States, 'when exercising that competence, the Member States are required to comply with their obligations deriving from EU law',[64] and thus crucially with the obligation to guarantee judicial independence under Article 19 TEU.[65] In substance, the Court accepted both complaints presented by the Commission, the first related to the principle of irremovability of the judges, which was violated by the measures lowering retirement age;[66] and the second concerning the 'external' independence

---

[63]See *supra*.

[64]Para. 52.

[65]Paras. 55 and 57.

[66]See paras. 71–97.

of the judges of the Supreme Court, breached by the decision to assign to the President of the Republic the power to decide on the extension of the judges' mandate.[67]

Compared to the earlier infringement action against Hungary mentioned earlier, the action of the Commission and the ruling of the Court have sharper effects. In the Hungarian case, national authorities were simply asked to offer to the judges concerned an alternative between compensation and reinstatement, with no guarantee that they could return to the same position. Fidesz was thus still able to remove the undesired judges and replace them with more loyal personnel.[68] In the Polish action, on the other hand, the Court of Justice put more far-reaching obligations on national authorities, already in the two interim orders. In simple words, the reform of the Supreme Court had to be reversed, and the judges of the Supreme Court allowed to continue their mandates. The Polish authorities well understood that they had little alternatives, if they wanted to avoid a full-scale confrontation with the Court of Justice and the EU institutions, as well as a possible penalty payment under Article 260 TFEU, had they refused to implement the orders[69] and the final judgement. Even before the final judgment of the Court, the Polish Parliament passed a new law in November 2018, repealing the previous reforms, and the law was then promulgated by the President of the Republic in December, just after the second order of the Court of Justice.

Infringement procedures based on a violation of Article 19 TEU seem therefore to be an excellent framework for the Court's intervention in rule of law crises. Both in its order and in the final ruling, the Court of Justice has demonstrated a certain readiness and willingness to intervene forcefully and to read its powers in a broad manner: in substance, the extensive reading of the scope of Article 19 TEU has been confirmed; procedurally, the Court delivered a rather exceptional order, even before the formal hearing, and requested far-reaching interim measures. What is more, the Supreme Court infringement action is not an isolated decision, and the Court of Justice will have other chances to continue developing its jurisprudence on Article 19 TEU and judicial independence. One opportunity was the other infringement action pursued by the Commission on the Law on Ordinary Courts, although Polish authorities had already modified the regime of appointment and dismissal of courts' presidents. Then, there are the several preliminary references sent by Polish courts themselves questioning the compatibility of parts of the Polish reforms with EU law.[70] But of course the new approach to Article 19 TEU can become relevant also

[67]See paras. 108–124.

[68]The action was considered an instance of 'symbolic' compliance: see Batory (2016).

[69]The possibility to impose penalty payments in case of non-compliance with an order of the Court was affirmed in another case concerning Poland, but unrelated to the judiciary reforms: CJEU, C-441/17 *Commission v. Poland*, ECLI:EU:C:2018:255.

[70]For an analysis, see Biernat and Kawczyńska (2018).

for other cases including the new Hungarian reform of administrative justice[71] and possibly the Romanian reforms of the judiciary.[72]

5 The *LM* Decision As an *Intermezzo* in the Court's Rule of Law Play

The next paragraphs return to *LM* and explain why it should be considered as an *intermezzo* in the Court's rule of law play, rather than a key constitutional moment for the Union. Most importantly, the framing of the case was ultimately not a suitable platform for a strong intervention in the Polish crisis by the Court. Nonetheless, the *intermezzo* was not unrelated to the previous and following acts: the Court still sent a few important messages, showing its concerns with the rule of law situation in Poland and in the continent at large. Finally, the *LM*'s *intermezzo* served also to restate the need for parallel political procedures that can give further bite to the red lines of European constitutionalism.

5.1 The Different Frame of LM

In the first place, it is crucial to recall the perspective through which the *LM* case reached the Court. The gist of the case was the protection of a specific fundamental right (Article 47 of the Charter) of a specific individual (Artur Celmer) and the interpretation of the EAW Framework Decision. On the other hand, the case did not concern—at least directly—the legislative changes operated by the Polish Parliament and generally the *rule of law* situation in Poland.[73] Of course, there were crucial connections between these two facets, but the fact remains that the applicant and the referring court asked to the Court of Justice precisely to reflect on how the general rule of law situation in Poland reflected on the individual position of the applicant and on his right to a fair trial. The Irish Court was only interested in the question of Mr. Celmer's possible surrender. Thus, the substantive situation, i.e. the reforms undertook by the Polish government, while certainly crucial as context and background of the decision, were not the core concern of the Court of Justice. On the other hand, in the infringement procedure on the Supreme Court and the other cases

[71]See Uitz (2019).

[72]See e.g. the preliminary reference sent by a Romanian Court in January 2019 on the obligations deriving from the Commission's Recommendations under the Cooperation and Verification Mechanism and from Art. 19 TEU: www.hotnews.ro/stiri-esential-22941400-decizia-fara-precedent-unei-instante-din-romania-curtea-justitie-uniunii-europene-solicitata-spuna-daca-autoritatile-bucuresti-sunt-obligate-respecte-recomandarile-din-mcv.htm.

[73]See also Konstadinides (2019), p. 751.

mentioned above, the key concern of the Court is whether the Polish legislation complies with Article 19 TEU and the requirement of judicial independence. In other words, the Court in these cases concentrates on the value of the rule of law as 'specified' by Article 19 TEU. Furthermore, in this second set of cases there are no conflicting interests to be safeguarded, such as protecting mutual trust, the smooth functioning of the EAW and generally the effectiveness of EU law.

The differences between the two settings can also be outlined with reference to the consequences and effects of the rulings. A good exercise is imagining what would have happened, if the Court had reached a bolder conclusion in *LM*, perhaps generally suspending the application of the EAW system vis-à-vis Poland. First, the decision would have created a high risk of impunity in the Union's Area of Freedom, Security and Justice: individuals accused or even convicted by a Polish court could have simply crossed the border between Poland and another EU Member State in order to avoid prosecution or detention, as other Member States would have been forced to refuse judicial cooperation with Poland.

The EAW works indeed in a fundamentally different way compared to the Dublin asylum system. In the latter context, the Court of Justice concluded in the *N.S.* case that it is possible to suspend Dublin transfers once systemic problems in a Member State are identified.[74] There is no need for an additional individual assessment of the specific situation of the applicant, i.e. the second prong of the *Aranyosi* test. The reason for this is that, under the Dublin system, the Member State that does not transfer an asylum seeker in view of systemic deficiencies in the other Member State simply takes direct responsibility for the assessment of the asylum claim. Under the EAW, on the other hand, Member States in most cases will not be competent to prosecute or detain the individual subject to the warrant: extraterritorial application of substantive national criminal laws remains confined to exceptional cases. EU criminal cooperation based on mutual trust has not changed the dogma of territoriality of criminal law.[75] This difference between the Dublin and EAW systems was outlined by Advocate General Bot in the Opinion in *Aranyosi*[76] and explains why the individual test was added in the context of the EAW: it plays an important role in preventing cases of impunity in the AFSJ.

Furthermore, taking a strict stance in *LM* would have meant for the Court to assess in abstract the independence of *all* Polish courts, with the possible result of excluding the Member State and its courts from the European legal space.[77] Yet, it is evident that some domestic courts, including the Supreme Court itself, are still playing on the side of the Court of Justice and of the rule of law, by challenging domestic laws on the basis of EU law and sending preliminary references to the

[74]CJEU, *N.S.*, *supra* note 45.

[75]Rizcallah (2019).

[76]CJEU, Case C-404/15 *Aranyosi*, Opinion of Advocate General Bot, ECLI:EU:C:2016:140, in particular paras. 59 and 60.

[77]Biernat (2018), arguing that such a result would be a 'vote of no confidence' against all Polish courts, despite the fact that many are still fighting for the rule of law and judicial independence.

CJEU.[78] Excluding them from the European judiciary *tout court* would have thus prevented this 'bottom up' resistance.[79] Furthermore, it is at least not so clear that *all* Polish courts will not be independent in *all* cases even after the reforms.[80] There is no doubt that the Polish reforms undermine, threaten, reduce judicial independence; but is it so evident that, after the reforms, all Polish civil and criminal proceedings would not comply with EU or ECHR standards? Finally, the reaction at the political level to a strong intervention of the Court expelling Poland from the European judiciary would have most likely been extremely harsh. Further attacks to the Court of Justice's legitimacy and authority could have been easily expected.

On the other hand, the ruling in *Commission v. Poland* was much more targeted and precise. The assessment concerned a specific piece of adopted legislation and its negative effects on judicial independence, and not the abstract independence of all domestic courts.[81] Despite the finding of a breach of Article 19 TEU, there has been no exclusion of Polish courts, including the Supreme Court, from the 'European judiciary' and quite on the contrary, domestic courts—again including the Supreme Court—can still play on the side of the Court of Justice, as they are already trying to do with the preliminary references on the judiciary reforms.

5.2 *The Messages of the Intermezzo*

The *LM* case was therefore not the most suitable platform for a strong intervention of the Court in the Polish crisis. Yet, the Court still sent a few important messages on the rule of law developments in the country and generally on the EU values' oversight scheme. The first message, as already noted in the previous pages, is the space that is dedicated, and the role that is given, to the Commission's reasoned proposal under Article 7(1) TEU. In the opening paragraphs of the ruling, the Court offered a fairly long summary of the document. The CJEU was not in a position to explicitly endorse those findings, but later it made clear that the reasoned proposal is 'particularly relevant' for the first, 'systemic' prong of the assessment to be

[78]See also Spieker (2018), p. 22 on the advantages of keeping Polish courts in the EU legal order and EU law as the 'relevant standard' for cooperation between Member States.

[79]On the role of national courts in fighting 'bottom up' systemic rule of law and fundamental rights deficiencies, see also von Bogdandy et al. (2012).

[80]See also Kosar (2018).

[81]This still has challenges: while it is true that the Court has often been called to adjudicate on the 'independence' of national courts, it did so in a very different context, namely that of Article 267 TFEU, where the Court examines the independence of specific bodies that sent a preliminary reference to Luxembourg. The Court is therefore called upon to develop clearer and perhaps more stringent criteria, something that is not easy to do in view of the differences between Member States in understanding and realizing judicial independence: see Kosar (2018).

conducted by domestic courts.[82] In doing so, it gave some legal bite to what would otherwise be only a political document.

Secondly, the Court underlined the relevance of the principle of judicial independence for the Union's legal order. It held that judicial independence is 'part of the essence of the fundamental right to a fair trial', a fundamental right that is in turn of 'cardinal importance' as it contributes to guaranteeing all other rights deriving from EU law as well as safeguarding the values of Article 2 TEU.[83] Having summarized its approach to judicial independence as having an internal and external aspect, the Court developed in particular a few aspects relating to rules on dismissal of members[84] and on disciplinary regimes, where the Court held that rules must 'display the necessary guarantees in order to prevent any risk of its being used as a system of political control of the content of judicial decisions'.[85] By doing so, the Court clarified its standards for the following cases, and then punctually applied them in the following ruling on the Supreme Court.[86]

There is then a final aspect of the *LM* decision worth highlighting, namely the Court's attention to the political mechanisms available to safeguard EU values. The Court seems to well understand that ensuring democracy or the rule of law is not a task of judicial actors only.[87] In the first place, as already noted several times, the Court gave crucial relevance to the Commission's reasoned proposal under Article 7 TEU. Second, in confirming the second prong of the *Aranyosi* test, the Court held that the competence to generally suspend the application of the EAW in a Member State belongs only to the Council and the European Council. The Court reached this conclusion on the basis of recital 10 of the EAW Framework Decision, which affirms that the implementation of the EAW system 'may be suspended only in the event of a serious and persistent breach by one of the Member States of the principles set out in Article 6(1) EU, determined by the Council pursuant to Article 7(1) EU with the consequences set out in Article 7(2) thereof'. The recital was adopted before the Nice Treaty amendments to the Article 7 system and has never been modified since then, thus it does not mention the preventive mechanism now contained in Article 7 (1) and still refers to 'Article 6' (now Article 2) and to the 'Council' (now the 'European Council'). In *LM*, the Court decided to judicially update the references contained in the recital and read it as requiring first a determination of the European Council under what is now Article 7(2) TEU, and then a decision of the Council on the suspension of the EAW.[88] Once this second decision is taken, judicial authorities 'would be required to refuse automatically to execute any European arrest warrant

---

[82]See CJEU, *LM*, *supra* note 1, para. 61.

[83]See CJEU, *LM*, *supra* note 1, para. 48.

[84]CJEU, *LM*, *supra* note 1, para. 66.

[85]CJEU, *LM*, *supra* note 1, para. 67.

[86]CJEU, *Commission v. Poland*, *supra* note 69, paras. 73–77, which include several references to the *LM* case.

[87]See also Avbelj (2018).

[88]CJEU, *LM*, *supra* note 1, paras. 70–71.

issued by the Member State concerned, without the need to conduct an individual assessment'.[89]

The Court is thus respectful of the political procedures created by the Treaties and of the Council's decision to make a general suspension of the EAW possible only after a decision of the European Council. The system, as it stands, might be disappointing: it is now evident how difficult it is to reach a decision under Article 7(1) TEU, let alone a unanimous decision under Article 7(2) TEU. But the Court could have hardly reconciled a different reading with the explicit text of recital 10 of the EAW Framework Decision.[90] It would rather be for the legislator to modify the preamble of the EAW and more broadly for the political institutions to rethink and reform EU oversight mechanisms. A centralized monitoring scheme seems in fact needed to prevent fragmentation,[91] i.e. the risk that different courts of different Member States reach conflicting decisions on the very existence of systemic threats, and consequently on EAW or Dublin transfers.[92] Yet, it is not the task of the Court to create such a scheme.

Ultimately, the Court's approach to the political mechanisms is not only textually, but also systematically convincing. First, the solution to the constitutional crises of Poland and Hungary is not in the hands of the Court of Justice alone. Problems originating in the political sphere simply cannot be addressed only with legal decisions and ruling;[93] they require a political reaction.[94] Second, it should not be forgotten that the EU Treaties themselves leave space for the 'political game' when it comes to the protection of EU values. Most importantly, they do so when they exclude the Court from substantive deliberations under Article 7 TEU.[95] Hence, while it is true that the Court cannot simply leave all responsibilities to political authorities, it should not completely replace them, nor the procedures created by the Treaties.

---

[89]CJEU, *LM*, *supra* note 1, para. 72.

[90]For a different view, see Bard and van Ballegooij (2018), arguing that the Court should have re-interpreted the preamble of EAW and concluded that the system could be suspended even after a decision under Article 7(1) or perhaps the mere activation of it.

[91]See Lazowski (2018) on how the *Aranyosi* approach might threaten the uniform application of EU law.

[92]On the need for a more centralized assessment, see Wendel (2019) and Bard and van Ballegooij (2018).

[93]And the same is true if we conceive the rule of law crisis as a crisis of trust, see von Bogdandy (2018), pp. 689–690: 'It is inconsistent to diagnose a crisis in trust, but to expect the relevant legal instruments to overcome it, as do some legal analyses of the Commission's "rule of law framework" . . . A crisis in trust cannot be "resolved" by legal instruments, it can only be hedged and gradually allowed to subside over time.'

[94]See e.g. Besselink (2017); see also Kosar (2018), pointing out that ultimately the Polish elections might be more important than any Court of Justice's intervention for safeguarding judicial independence in the country.

[95]See Article 269 TFEU.

6 Conclusion

When read in the broader context described in this chapter, the *LM* case can hardly be understood as a general signal of the Court's reluctance to engage with the Polish rule of law crisis. On the contrary, the Court has shown a proactive approach by re-directing the *ASJP* case from austerity to the rule of law, interpreting Article 19 TEU in an exceptionally broad manner, and thus creating a new tool to enforce judicial independence across the Union. The Commission and the Court immediately exploited the new tool in the infringement action on the Supreme Court. These were the two key acts of the Court's rule of law play and, measured against them, the *LM* decision loses the centrality it was expected to have.

Although there are some not entirely convincing steps in the Court's reasoning and outcome,[96] the approach of the Court was ultimately a balanced one: it maintained the need for the individual prong of the *Aranyosi* test, but left the national court a fairly wide opportunity to refuse referral were it to consider that, in the specific case, the individual suffered a real risk of unfair trial;[97] furthermore, in reaching its decision, the Court also signaled its broad concerns with the rule of law in Poland. The framing of the case, however, did not offer the best opportunity to take a strong stance on the Polish crisis and a broad reformulation of the questions referred could have easily led to accusations of judicial activism, especially after the already creative and groundbreaking decision of *ASJP*.[98] The lesson *LM* seems to teach is that infringement procedures seem to be better suited than 'horizontal' attempts to protect EU values,[99] also considering that mutual trust creates complex problems of a federal and constitutional nature that the Court always needs to take into account.[100] Questions of judicial independence and rule of law are in fact to be addressed in a systemic manner, as it can be done in Commission's infringement actions against violations of Article 19 TEU; on the other hand, it is harder for horizontal preliminary references, based on the protection of individual fundamental rights, to frame the case in the most appropriate manner.[101] The positive impact that well-conducted infringement procedures may have has been further shown by the decisions of the Court in the first *Commission v. Poland* case on the reform of the Supreme Court. This was arguably the first true victory of the EU institutions after several unsuccessful attempts to fight against Polish constitutional backsliding. The forthcoming decisions on the second infringement actions, as well as on the preliminary references raised by Polish courts, offer now further opportunities to safeguard

[96]See Sect. 2 above.

[97]As noted above, however, the national court ultimately rejected the appeal of Mr. Celmer: see Irish High Court, *supra* note 31.

[98]For a different view, see Krajewski (2018) and Wendel (2019).

[99]On 'horizontal' enforcement, see Canor (2013).

[100]Wendel (2019).

[101]Sonnevend (2018).

judicial independence. After the *LM* intermezzo, we are therefore in the truly decisive act of the rule of law play between the EU and Poland.

References

Avbelj M (2018) We still haven't found what we're looking for. Verfassungsblog, www.verfassungsblog.de/we-still-havent-found-what-were-looking-for/

Bard P, van Ballegooij W (2018) Judicial independence as a precondition for mutual trust? The CJEU in Minister for Justice and Equality v. LM. New J Eur Crim Law 9:3

Batory A (2016) Defying the commission: creative compliance and respect for the rule of law in the EU. Public Adm 94:3

Belavusau U (2013) On age discrimination and beating dead dogs: Commission v. Hungary. Common Market Law Rev 50:4

Besselink L (2017) The Bite, the Bark and the Howl: Article 7 TEU and the rule of law initiatives. In: Jakab A, Kochenv N (eds) The enforcement of EU law and values. Oxford University Press, Oxford, pp 128–144

Biernat S (2018) How to assess the independence of Member State Courts? Verfassungsblog, www.verfassungsblog.de/how-to-assess-the-independence-of-member-state-courts/

Biernat S, Kawczyńska M (2018) Though this be madness, yet there's method in't: pitting the Polish constitutional tribunal against the Luxembourg Court. Verfassungsblog, www.verfassungsblog.de/though-this-be-madness-yet-theres-method-int-the-application-of-the-prosecutor-general-to-the-polish-constitutional-tribunal-to-declare-the-preliminary-ruling-procedure-unconstitut/

Bonelli M, Claes M (2018) Judicial serendipity: how Portuguese judges came to the rescue of the Polish judiciary. Eur Const Law Rev 14:3

Broberg M, Fenger N (2014) Preliminary references to the European Court of Justice. Oxford University Press, Oxford

Canor I (2013) *My Brother's Keeper?* horizontal *Solange*: 'An Ever Closer *Distrust* among the Peoples of Europe'. Common Market Law Rev 50:2

Dawson M, Muir E (2013) Hungary and the *Indirect* protection of EU fundamental rights and the rule of law. German Law J 14:10

Halmai G (2017) The early retirement age of the Hungarian Judges. In: Nicola F, Davies B (eds) EU law stories – contextual and critical histories of European jurisprudence. Cambridge University Press, Cambridge, pp 471–488

Konstadinides T (2019) Judicial independence and the rule of law in the context of non-execution of a European Arrest Warrant: *LM*. Common Market Law Rev 56:3

Kosar D (2018) The CJEU has spoken out, But the show must go on. Verfassungsblog, www.verfassungsblog.de/the-cjeu-has-spoken-out-but-the-show-must-go-on/

Krajewski M (2018) Who is afraid of the European Council? The Court of Justice's cautious approach to the independence of domestic judges. Eur Const Law Rev 14:4

Lazowski A (2018) The sky is not the limit: mutual trust and mutual recognition aprés Aranyosi and Căldăraru. Croat Yearb Eur Law Policy 14:1–30

Markakis M, Dermine P (2018) Bailouts, the legal status of memoranda of understanding, and the scope of application of the EU Charter: Florescu. Common Market Law Rev 55:2

Pech L, Scheppele KL (2017) Illiberalism within: rule of law backsliding in the EU. Camb Yearb Eur Legal Stud 19:3–47

Pech L, Wachowiec P (2018) 1095 days later: from bad to worse regarding the rule of law in Poland (Part II). Verfassungsblog, www.verfassungsblog.de/1095-days-later-from-bad-to-worse-regarding-the-rule-of-law-in-poland-part-ii/

Rizcallah C (2019) The challenges to trust-based governance in the European Union: assessing the use of mutual trust as a driver of EU integration. Eur Law J 25:1

Sadurski W (2019) Poland's constitutional backsliding. Oxford University Press, Oxford

Scheppele KL (2018) Rule of law retail and rule of law wholesale: the ECJ's (Alarming) 'Celmer' decision. Verfassungsblog, www.verfassungsblog.de/rule-of-law-retail-and-rule-of-law-wholesale-the-ecjs-alarming-celmer-decision/

Sonnevend P (2018) A clever compromise or a tectonic shift? The LM judgment of the CJEU. Verfassungsblog, www.verfassungsblog.de/a-clever-compromise-or-a-tectonic-shift-the-lm-jugment-of-the-cjeu/

Spieker LD (2018) From moral values to legal obligations – on how to activate the Union's common values in the EU rule of law crisis. MPIL Research Paper Series No. 2018-24

Uitz R (2019) The perils of defending the rule of law through dialogue. Eur Const Law Rev 15:1

von Bogdandy A (2018) Ways to frame the European rule of law: Rechtsgemeinschaft, trust, revolution, and Kantian Peace. Eur Const Law Rev 14:4

von Bogdandy A, Kottmann M, Antpöhler C, Dickschen J, Hentrei S, Smrkolj M (2012) Reverse Solange – protecting the essence of fundamental rights against EU Member States. Common Market Law Rev 49:2

von Bogdandy A, Bogdanowicz P, Canor I, Taborowski M, Schmidt M (2018) Guest editorial: a potential constitutional moment for the European rule of law – the importance of red lines. Common Market Law Rev 55:4

Wendel M (2019) Mutual trust, essence and federalism – between consolidating and fragmenting the area of freedom, security and justice after *LM*. Eur Const Law Rev 15:1

Matteo Bonelli is an assistant professor in European law at the Faculty of Law of Maastricht University, the Netherlands.

Max-Planck-Institut für ausländisches öffentliches Recht und Völkerrecht

Beiträge zum ausländischen öffentlichen Recht und Völkerrecht

Hrsg.: A. von Bogdandy, A. Peters

Bde. 27–59 erschienen im Carl Heymanns Verlag KG Köln, Berlin (Bestellung an: Max-Planck-Institut für Völkerrecht, Im Neuenheimer Feld 535, 69120 Heidelberg); ab Band 60 im Springer-Verlag GmbH

298 Armin *von Bogdandy*, Piotr *Bogdanowicz*, Iris *Canor*, Christoph *Grabenwarter*, Maciej *Taborowski*, Matthias *Schmidt* (eds.): **Defending Checks and Balances in EU Member States**. 2021. X, 474 Seiten. Geb. € 49,99 zzgl. landesüblicher MwSt. Open Access

297 Valentina *Volpe*, Anne *Peters*, Stefano *Battini* (eds.): **Remedies against Immunity?**. 2021. X, 390 Seiten. Geb. € 49,99 zzgl. landesüblicher MwSt. Open Access

296 Björnstjern *Baade*, Dana *Burchardt*, Prisca *Feihle*, Alicia *Köppen*, Linus *Mührel*, Lena *Riemer*, Raphael *Schäfer* (eds.): **Cynical International Law?**. 2021. XVI, 369 Seiten. Geb. € 139,99 zzgl. landesüblicher MwSt.

295 Layla Kristina *Jaber*, Stefanie *Lüer*, Anne-Marie *Thévenot-Werner* (Hrsg.): **Rechtsweggarantie im vergleichenden Verwaltungsrecht**. 2020. X, 220 Seiten. Geb. € 99,99

294 Desirée C. *Schmitt*: **Familienzusammenführung und Rechtsschutz in Deutschland und den USA**. 2020. XXIII, 719 Seiten. Geb. € 129,99

293 Andrej *Lang*: **Die Verfassungsgerichtsbarkeit in der vernetzten Weltordnung**. 2020. XXVII, 646 Seiten. Geb. € 119,99

A. von Bogdandy et al. (eds.), *Defending Checks and Balances in EU Member States*, Beiträge zum ausländischen öffentlichen Recht und Völkerrecht 298,
https://doi.org/10.1007/978-3-662-62317-6

292 Raffaela *Kunz*: **Richter über internationale Gerichte?**. 2020. XIV, 275 Seiten. Geb. € 53,49. Open Access

291 Adele *Kirschner*: **Grenzüberschreitende Implikationen eines Menschenrechts auf Wasser?**. 2020. XVIII, 257 Seiten. Geb. € 89,99

290 Anne *Peters* (ed.): **Studies in Global Animal Law**. 2020. VIII, 183 Seiten. Geb. € 49,99 zzgl. landesüblicher MwSt. Open Access

289 Oliver *Strank*: **Common Concern of Humankind im Völkerrecht**. 2019. XXVIII, 666 Seiten. Geb. € 119,99

288 Alix *Schlüter*: **Beweisfragen in der Rechtsprechung des Europäischen Gerichtshof für Menschenrechte**. 2019. XVIII, 500 Seiten. Geb. € 119,99

287 Martin Philipp *Sommerfeld*: **Staatensouveränität und ius cogens**. 2019. XVI, 424 Seiten. Geb. € 99,99

286 Laura *Hering*: **Fehlerfolgen im europäischen Eigenverwaltungsrecht**. 2019. XXI, 385 Seiten. Geb. € 99,99

285 Marten *Breuer* (ed.): **Principled Resistance to ECtHR Judgments - A New Paradigm?**. 2019. XVIII, 350 Seiten. Geb. € 109,99 zzgl. landesüblicher MwSt.

284 Stephan G. *Hinghofer-Szalkay*: **Verfassungsrechtsentwicklung aus rechtstatsächlicher Perspektive**. 2019. XVII, 383 Seiten. Geb. € 109,99

283 Arthur *Brunner*: **Subsidiaritätsgrundsatz und Tatsachenfeststellung unter der Europäischen Menschenrechtskonvention**. 2019. XVI, 188 Seiten. Geb. € 53,49. Open Access

282 María Pía *Carazo Ortiz*: **Das Länderberichtsverfahren der Interamerikanischen Kommission für Menschenrechte**. 2019. XX, 475 Seiten. Geb. € 109,99.

281 Romy *Klimke*: **Schädliche traditionelle und kulturelle Praktiken im internationalen und regionalen Menschenrechtsschutz**. 2019. XVIII, 530 Seiten. Geb. € 99,99

280 Elisabeth Veronika *Henn*: **International Human Rights Law and Structural Discrimination**. 2019. XVI, 237 Seiten, € 89,99 zzgl. landesüblicher MwSt.

279 Eike *Blitza*: **Auswirkungen des Meeresspiegelanstiegs auf maritime Grenzen**. 2019. XIII, 294 Seiten. Geb. € 89,99

278 Anna Katharina *Struth*: **Hassrede und Freiheit der Meinungsäußerung**. 2019. XV, 472 Seiten. Geb. € 109,99

277 Franziska *Sucker*: **Der Schutz und die Förderung kultureller Vielfalt im Welthandelsrecht**. 2018. XXIV, 635 Seiten. Geb. € 109,99

276 Clemens *Mattheis*: **Die Konstitutionalisierung des Völkerrechts aus systemtheoretischer Sichtweise**. 2018. XXIV, 557 Seiten. Geb. € 109,99

275 Aydin *Atilgan*: **Global Constitutionalism**. 2018. X, 312 Seiten. Geb. € 114,99 zzgl. landesüblicher MwSt.

274 Andreas *Kolb*: **The UN Security Council Members' Responsibility to Protect**. 2018. XXI 624 Seiten. Geb. € 199,99 zzgl. landesüblicher MwSt.

273 Matthias *Goldmann*, Silvia *Steininger* (eds.): **Democracy and Financial Order: Legal Perspectives**. 2018. V, 230 Seiten. Geb. € 114,99 zzgl. landesüblicher MwSt.

272 Jochen *Rauber*: **Strukturwandel als Prinzipienwandel**. 2018. XXXIV, 970 Seiten. Geb. € 159,99

271 Anja *Höfelmeier*: **Die Vollstreckungsimmunität der Staaten im Wandel des Völkerrechts**. 2018. XX, 356 Seiten. Geb. € 89,99

270 Rudolf *Bernhardt*, Karin *Oellers-Frahm*: **Das Max-Planck-Institut für ausländisches öffentliches Recht und Völkerrecht**. 2018. XII, 344 Seiten. Geb. € 89,99

269 Philine *Wehling*: **Wasserrechte am Nil**. 2018. XVI, 351 Seiten. Geb. € 84,99

268 Katharina *Berner*: **Subsequent Agreements and Subsequent Practice in Domestic Courts**. 2018. XLV, 298 Seiten. Geb. € 114,99 zzgl. landesüblicher MwSt.

267 Josephine *Asche*: **Die Margin of Appreciation**. 2018. XII, 255 Seiten. Geb. € 84,99

266 Nele *Yang*: **Die Leitentscheidung**. 2018. XI, 362 Seiten. Geb. € 84,99

265 Roya *Sangi*: **Die auswärtige Gewalt des Europäischen Parlaments**. 2018. XV, 179 Seiten. Geb. € 69,99

264 Anna *Krueger*: **Die Bindung der Dritten Welt an das postkoloniale Völkerrecht**. 2018. XII, 434 Seiten. Geb. € 89,99

263 Björnstjern *Baade*: **Der Europäische Gerichtshof für Menschenrechte als Diskurswächter**. 2017. XVIII, 543 Seiten. Geb. € 99,99

262 Felix *Lange*: **Praxisorientierung und Gemeinschaftskonzeption**. 2017. XIV, 403 Seiten. Geb. € 94,99

261 Johanna Elisabeth *Dickschen*: **Empfehlungen und Leitlinien als Handlungsform der Europäischen Finanzaufsichtsbehörden**. 2017. XIX, 277 Seiten. Geb. € 84,99

260 Mohamed *Assakkali*: **Europäische Union und Internationaler Währungsfonds**. 2017. XV, 516 Seiten. Geb. € 99,99

259 Franziska *Paefgen*: **Der von Art. 8 EMRK gewährleistete Schutz vor staatlichen Eingriffen in die Persönlichkeitsrechte im Internet**. 2017. XV, 220 Seiten. Geb. € 69,99

258 Tim René *Salomon*: **Die internationale Strafverfolgungsstrategie gegenüber somalischen Piraten**. 2017. XXXII, 743 Seiten. Geb. € 129,99

257 Jelena *Bäumler*: **Das Schädigungsverbot im Völkerrecht**. 2017. XIX, 379 Seiten. Geb. € 89,99

256 Christopher *Peters*: **Praxis Internationaler Organisationen - Vertragswandel und völkerrechtlicher Ordnungsrahmen**. 2016. XXVIII, 498 Seiten. Geb. € 99,99

255 Nicole *Appel*: **Das internationale Kooperationsrecht der Europäischen Union**. 2016. XVIII, 608 Seiten. Geb. € 109,99

254 Christian *Wohlfahrt*: **Die Vermutung unmittelbarer Wirkung des Unionsrechts**. 2016. XIX, 300 Seiten. Geb. € 84,99

253 Katja *Göcke*: **Indigene Landrechte im internationalen Vergleich**. 2016. XVII, 818 Seiten. Geb. € 139,99

252 Julia *Heesen*: **Interne Abkommen**. 2015. XXI, 473 Seiten. Geb. € 94,99

251 Matthias *Goldmann*: **Internationale öffentliche Gewalt**. 2015. XXIX, 636 Seiten. Geb. € 109,99

250 Isabelle *Ley*: **Opposition im Völkerrecht**. 2014. XXIII, 452 Seiten. Geb. € 94,99

249 Matthias *Kottmann*: **Introvertierte Rechtsgemeinschaft**. 2014. XII, 352 Seiten. Geb. € 84,99

248 Jelena *von Achenbach*: **Demokratische Gesetzgebung in der Europäischen Union**. 2014. XVI, 522 Seiten. Geb. € 94,99

247 Jürgen *Friedrich*: **International Environmental "soft law"**. 2014. XXI, 503 Seiten. Geb. € 94,99 zzgl. landesüblicher MwSt.

246 Anuscheh *Farahat*: **Progressive Inklusion**. 2014. XXIV, 429 Seiten. Geb. € 94,99

245 Christina *Binder*: **Die Grenzen der Vertragstreue im Völkerrecht**. 2013. XL, 770 Seiten. Geb. € 119,99

244 Cornelia *Hagedorn*: **Legitime Strategien der Dissensbewältigung in demokratischen Staaten**. 2013. XX, 551 Seiten. Geb. € 99,99

243 Marianne *Klumpp*: **Schiedsgerichtsbarkeit und Ständiges Revisionsgericht des Mercosur**. 2013. XX, 512 Seiten. Geb. € 94,99

242 Karen *Kaiser* (Hrsg.): **Der Vertrag von Lissabon vor dem Bundesverfassungsgericht**. 2013. XX, 1635 Seiten. Geb. € 199,99

241 Dominik *Steiger*: **Das völkerrechtliche Folterverbot und der "Krieg gegen den Terror"**. 2013. XXX, 821 Seiten. Geb. € 139,99

240 Silja *Vöneky,* Britta *Beylage-Haarmann,* Anja *Höfelmeier,* Anna-Katharina *Hübler* (Hrsg.): **Ethik und Recht - Die Ethisierung des Rechts/Ethics and Law - The Ethicalization of Law**. 2013. XVIII, 456 Seiten. Geb. € 94,99

239 Rüdiger *Wolfrum,* Ina *Gätzschmann* (eds.): **International Dispute Settlement: Room for Innovations?** 2013. XIV, 445 Seiten. Geb. € 94,95 zzgl. landesüblicher MwSt.

238 Isabel *Röcker*: **Die Pflicht zur rahmenbeschlusskonformen Auslegung nationalen Rechts**. 2013. XXIII, 410 Seiten. Geb. € 89,95

237 Maike *Kuhn*: **Die Europäische Sicherheits- und Verteidigungspolitik im Mehrebenensystem**. 2012. XIII, 325 Seiten. Geb. € 79,95

236 Armin *von Bogdandy,* Ingo *Venzke* (eds.): **International Judicial Lawmaking**. 2012. XVII, 509 Seiten. Geb. € 94,95 zzgl. landesüblicher MwSt.

235 Susanne *Wasum-Rainer,* Ingo *Winkelmann,* Katrin *Tiroch* (eds.): **Arctic Science, International Law and Climate Change**. 2012. XIX, 374 Seiten. Geb. € 84,95 zzgl. landesüblicher MwSt.

234 Mirja A. *Trilsch*: **Die Justiziabilität wirtschaftlicher, sozialer und kultureller Rechte im innerstaatlichen Recht**. 2012. XIX, 559 Seiten. Geb. € 99,95